Advance Praise for *On Xi Jinping*

"Public servant, prime minister, diplomat, scholar—Kevin Rudd's résumé is also a stellar CV for the elite caste of scholar-bureaucrats that managed the Chinese empire for over a millennium. *On Xi Jinping* focusses the experience of a political practitioner engaged with China since his teenage years to analyse Xi Jinping's Party Empire and its global ambitions. Rudd also attempts the seemingly impossible by offering words of guidance and hope in this darkling age."

—**Geremie R. Barmé**, editor of the *China Heritage*

"In this book, Kevin Rudd provides all who care about peace a huge service. Drawing on his extraordinary knowledge of China and the Chinese system, Rudd reveals a side of Xi Jinping only comprehensible through his extensive ideological writings—giving us all unique insights into a man upon whom much of the future depends and helping scholars and policymakers alike better understand Xi's motives and anticipate his actions. A remarkable read!"

—**Meghan L. O'Sullivan**, Director of the Belfer Center for Science and International Affairs and Jeane Kirkpatrick Professor of the Practice of International Affairs, Harvard University's Kennedy School of Government

"Understanding Xi Jinping's worldview and what it means for China and us is more crucial now than ever. Rudd's superb analysis provides the reader with a comprehensive guide to Xi's thinking on domestic policy and global affairs. Rudd takes Xi's words seriously and teases out the consequences: a politics and economics that has moved to the left and a foreign policy that has turned to a form of rightist nationalism. Rudd encapsulates these processes with the phrase 'Marxist-Leninist Nationalism.' This work is essential reading for anyone interested in understanding where China has come from, where it is heading and the consequences for all of us."

—**Anthony J. Saich**, Daewoo Professor of International Affairs, Harvard Kennedy School

"Understanding Xi Jinping, his plans for China, and how they will affect the world is the central challenge for the United States and policymakers everywhere. As a foreign policy practitioner, a scholar, a Chinese language speaker, and a former world leader himself, Kevin Rudd is uniquely well placed to answer the question of what Xi Jinping actually believes. He does so brilliantly by drawing on Chinese primary sources, in-depth research, and a lifetime of experience dealing with China's leadership."

—**Stephen J. Hadley,** National Security Advisor to President George W. Bush

ON XI JINPING

HOW XI'S MARXIST NATIONALISM IS SHAPING CHINA AND THE WORLD

KEVIN RUDD

OXFORD
UNIVERSITY PRESS

Oxford University Press is a department of the University of Oxford. It furthers the University's objective of excellence in research, scholarship, and education by publishing worldwide. Oxford is a registered trade mark of Oxford University Press in the UK and certain other countries.

Published in the United States of America by Oxford University Press
198 Madison Avenue, New York, NY 10016, United States of America.

CIP data is on file at the Library of Congress
ISBN 978–0–19–776603–3

DOI: 10.1093/oso/9780197766033.001.0001

Printed by Sheridan Books, Inc., United States of America

Dedicated to the memory of Pierre Ryckmans, also known as Simon Leys (1935–2014), who made his academic home the Australian National University where he inspired a generation of young China scholars. A brilliant sinologist, man of letters, and soulmate of Saint Thomas More, Pierre inspired in me a love of China over many years, including as my teacher in Chinese language, literature, and aesthetics and supervisor of my undergraduate thesis on the concept of 'rights' in the Chinese classical and modern traditions. A truly great mind driven by a searing and scholarly conscience.

Contents

Preface

My reason for writing this book is to try to answer the questions that many people around the world routinely ask me about China. What does Xi Jinping actually believe? And what are his plans for China's and the world's future? These questions are hard to answer, but not impossible. That is because much of Xi's belief system is outlined in the complex contours of his writings on Chinese Communist Party (CCP) ideology. The party's ideology contains within it an underlying body of meaning that explains how the party actually sees the world and what they intend to do about it. The CCP has always taken ideology seriously, and Xi is no different. It's time, therefore, that we did the same. This book seeks to understand how the party communicates within itself by decrypting the complex code language of its internal Marxist-Leninist discourse.

The book is different in scope and style to my previous effort, *The Avoidable War*. Published in 2022, *The Avoidable War* outlines what I see as Xi Jinping's ten concentric circles of domestic and foreign policy interest, their impact on the future of US-China relations, and how the risk of crisis, conflict, and war between them could be reduced through what I describe as 'managed strategic competition'. It was written for the general, intelligent reader who wanted to understand more about China's rise and what could be done to reduce the risk of conflict, without having to wade through a dense academic text. Indeed, *The Avoidable War* was criticized by some for not having footnotes! Despite that omission (or more likely because of it) the book has proved remarkably popular. To my great surprise, it has now been translated into Chinese, Japanese, Korean, French, German, Spanish, Italian, and Swedish. And I have now been asked to write an updated version for 2025.

By contrast, this book is a harder read. It seeks to define Xi Jinping's underlying ideology, how it is different from that of his post-Mao predecessors, and how it is reflected in the overall direction of China's domestic and foreign policy during his first decade in power. It also explores how an understanding of Xi's ideology may help us see where he wants to take China and the world in the years ahead. The book is designed to be readily digestible for the intelligent reader but is also intended to contribute to the wider body of academic literature focusing on Xi Jinping's China. In seeking to straddle both constituencies, there is always a danger that the book will fall between two stools: too turgid for those wanting a quick primer on Xi Jinping Thought while, at the same time, not sufficiently engaged in the vast, existing literature and academic debate on Xi that has been generated by world-class China scholars across Sinology, sociology, political science, political economy, and international relations theory. My hope is that the book achieves a reasonable compromise between the two. (Incidentally, in deference to my critics, this volume now boasts nearly a thousand footnotes and an extensive bibliography of sources in both Chinese and English!)

Some readers, however, may be less than enthusiastic about wading through the detailed textual analysis of the Chinese official sources that make up the bulk of the book's middle chapters. For these good folks, having taken five years to research the book, I can only sympathize. I therefore suggest they read chapters 1, 3, and 4, followed by chapters 14, 15, and 16 as a sort of 'cheats' guide'. Chapter 1 summarizes the book's main arguments and concludes with shorter summaries of each of the chapters that follow. Chapter 3 provides a short historical survey of China's evolving ideological worldviews in both the classical and Communist periods. Chapter 4 outlines the basic tenets of Xi's ideological framework based on an examination of five major texts that bear his name and which occupy a prominent place in the party's theoretical literature. Chapters 14 and 15 fast-forward to the time of publication (2024) and look at how Xi has responded to recent challenges—the outbreak of COVID-19, the slowing of the economy, and the rolling crises in US-China relations—and whether these have prompted any deeper ideological and political reappraisal of China's future course. Chapter 16 looks to the longer-term future and asks what Xi's ideological framework can tell us about China's likely political, economic, and foreign policy trajectory for the decade ahead, and what a post-Xi China might look like. For those who, by contrast, actually enjoy wrapping themselves in the detail of the ideological argument and its evidentiary basis, please get your hair-shirts ready and hop into the whole text.

The book's underlying research is based on my Oxford University doctoral dissertation titled 'China's New Marxist Nationalism—Defining Xi Jinping's Ideological Worldview', which I successfully defended in late 2022. In preparing for the book, I have also sought to update, correct, and improve on my original work, particularly given the pace and complexity of unfolding developments in Chinese domestic politics and foreign policy since then. My reason for undertaking an Oxford DPhil program in the first place was to force myself to read systematically Xi's written works to understand the ideological message he was sending his party and country about the changes he intended to bring about. The book, therefore, is primarily a textual analysis of ideological change, relying on an at-times-excruciating examination of the primary documents. The book also, from time to time, includes long extracts from Xi's speeches and articles to familiarize the reader with how China's paramount leader actually communicates change, however stilted and sometimes-unreadable for a Western audience Xi's prose may appear to be. This is something we are all going to have to get used to. It is different from having Western scholars simply interpreting the text for the benefit of the reader. Instead, I have chosen to provide both: distilled analyses of what Xi is saying, reinforced, where necessary, with selections from the raw, primary text. And in doing so, I have generally avoided the sort of poetic revisions that sometimes attend official translations from the Chinese originals for the benefit of English-language readers.

In analysing Xi's ideological oeuvre, I have also avoided a rolling commentary on the facts underpinning his analysis. The objective facts of Chinese and world history are actually far less relevant to understanding Xi's worldview than his own subjective analysis and the official histories of the CCP that he relies on. For this reason, I caution readers against concluding that Xi's assertions of historical or philosophical fact, as described and reported in this book, are somehow beyond scrutiny. They are not. But my principal objective here is to understand what Xi actually believes and why, rather than to debate whether he happens to be right or not. The beginning of wisdom in politics and international relations is to understand what the other party thinks and to describe it accurately and effectively. And that can readily be done without compromising one's own values and views.

The arguments outlined in this book will inevitably attract criticism from various parts of the Western academy. The book's thesis is that Xi has embarked on an integrated ideological campaign of what I call 'Marxist Nationalism'—taking Chinese politics to the Leninist left, Chinese economics to the Marxist left, and Chinese foreign policy to the nationalist right. For some, this will seem controversial because, at first blush, it is intuitively impossible for a Communist Party to move simultaneously both to the left and the right. My response is that I have simply gone where the evidence has taken me, however much this may offend more traditional academic taxonomies. And I have judged it important for China scholars to present their evidence in a manner that is usable for policymakers trying to make sense of the Xi Jinping phenomenon, rather than burying it in an unintelligible avalanche of 'China-speak'.

There is likely to be much greater criticism of the book from the Communist Party itself. Many elements of my analysis may make uncomfortable reading, including for personal friends within the CCP. At the risk of burning some of those bridges, the burden of academic inquiry is to call a spade a spade. I am a lifelong student of China, its people, and its civilization. I am an admirer of China's many national achievements, both in classical and modern times, including since 1949. But these facts cannot, and have never, prevented me from challenging CCP political orthodoxy. The party is unlikely to approve of any analysis that finds Xi having taken the party and the economy to 'the left' because, they would infer, it means that Xi is repeating the errors of Mao. Nor will they welcome any conclusion that Xi's foreign policy changes reflect a move to the nationalist and revisionist right in his wider ideological discourse because they would normally reserve such terms for the far right. Indeed, any criticism of Xi moving either to the left or the right is likely to be contested by Beijing, not least because it implies the re-emergence of factional lines of division, if not debate, within the party itself. Nonetheless, I am not new to being criticized by the Chinese system. It happened many times while serving as Prime Minister and Foreign Minister of Australia, and later as the President of an American think tank, the Asia Society, in New York. I believe the role of academics in public life should never be to please any particular government. In fact, the responsibility of scholars is to call it as best we see it. And where the CCP is concerned, open and well-reasoned criticism is far better than calculated appeasement.

Both the book and the dissertation have benefited greatly from my two academic supervisors. Professor Rana Mitter, formerly Director of the

Oxford University China Centre and now the ST Lee Chair of US-Asia Relations at the Harvard Kennedy School, has been a source of continuing encouragement and academic admonition, for which I am deeply grateful. On the complex business of structuring a dissertation and complying with the arcane academic rules of a mediaeval institution, I would also thank Professor Paul Irwin-Crookes of the China Centre for his rock-solid support. Similarly, I am indebted to my two examiners, Professor Tony Saich of the Ash Centre at Harvard University, one of the world's foremost historians of the CCP, and Professor Todd Hall, a specialist in Chinese foreign policy and international relations theory, also from the Oxford China Centre. My friends and colleagues, Professors Graham Alison and Joe Nye of the Harvard Kennedy School, have also been important supporters of my belated efforts in life to convert a practitioner's knowledge of China into something approaching academic rigour. I thank all these university colleagues for their steadfast professional counsel and unstinting personal support.

After leaving the prime ministership of Australia, I spent eight years of my life as President of the Asia Society Policy Institute (ASPI) in New York (2015–2023), and the last two of those years as President and CEO of the Asia Society as a whole. I would like to thank Asia Society colleagues for all their support and encouragement as I worked my way through the writing of *The Avoidable War* and then finalizing my Oxford dissertation. In completing both tasks, I was able to draw in part from my previous writings and research for ASPI and its Centre for China Analysis. It took me nearly five years to complete my DPhil, with the vast bulk of it done while running the Asia Society. I also used much of my spare time during the COVID-19 lockdowns of 2020–2021 writing *The Avoidable War* on the side. Part of my reasoning was that, early in the life of the Biden administration, I thought it more useful to have a book published on the immediate, real-world challenges of the US-China relationship than trying to incorporate it into a longer-term analysis of CCP ideology. Ideology could wait for a while. This made for many sleepless nights trying to juggle all three worlds at once. But it was well worth it.

In particular, I would like to thank my friends and colleagues at the Asia Society. Thom Woodroofe, who worked as my chief-of-staff at Asia Society for many years and who, in a previous life as an Oxford scholar, helped me find my way around the university during my residential tenure, has been of enormous assistance throughout this project. Similarly, Jared Owens and Melanie Arnost from my former prime ministerial staff in Brisbane have been invaluable in casting a critical eye over the proofs of this book.

Of course, none of this would have been possible without the enduring support of my long-suffering family. Thérèse, my wife of over forty years, has been steadfast through all this. Many conversations have been had walking along Queensland's Sunshine Beach during the pandemic, discussing together the core arguments of the thesis. Our children Jessica, Nicholas, and Marcus and grandchildren Josephine, McLean, and Scarlett have also endured their father and grandfather tapping away quietly long into the night, often neglecting his family responsibilities. I thank them all for their love, patience, and understanding, and the countless conversations we have shared about China's future. All our children have lived, worked, or studied in China, at various stages of their lives, over many, many years. Our family has a deep affection for China. It has touched all our lives.

Finally, whatever help I have received from others on the way through, this book in the end is entirely my own work. None of the views contained in its pages represents those of the Australian Government for which I now work as Ambassador in Washington. Indeed, the dissertation on which the book is based was completed well before my being asked to serve in my current assignment. Therefore, all responsibility for the views expressed in this book is mine personally—and mine alone.

Kevin Rudd
Easter Day, 2024
Brisbane, Australia

I

Hiding in Plain Sight

Xi's Ideological Framework for China's Future

This book began as a doctoral dissertation at the University of Oxford China Centre, completed between 2017 and 2022. Starting a doctorate at the tender age of fifty-nine is not for the faint-hearted. The last time I had undertaken formal academic research was in 1981 when I graduated from the Australian National University in Chinese language and Chinese history. My research thesis back then focussed on political dissent in the People's Republic of China (PRC) following Deng Xiaoping's re-emergence as its paramount leader in 1978. But across the decades, China's rise has been a continuing focus of my personal and professional life—whether as a scholar, a professional diplomat (including at Australia's embassy in what, back then, we still quaintly called 'Peking'), a state government official, a businessman, a member of parliament, as foreign minister, as prime minister, as president of an American think tank, and more recently as Ambassador to the United States. China, for me, has been a lifelong vocation.

The reason I wrote a dissertation on this particular subject, however, was not simple intellectual curiosity. It was to try to make sense of *why* China's current paramount leader, Xi Jinping, has embarked on such a radical change in political and policy direction, both at home and abroad, compared with his post-Mao predecessors. I wanted to see what patterns there were in the changes he had wrought already in order to understand where China is most likely to go in the future. These were also the questions I have most often been asked by political, corporate, and opinion leaders around the world, including in the Middle Kingdom itself, as well as by ordinary citizens trying to make sense of the often bewildering reporting they read on Xi Jinping's China.

In order to answer these questions, my Oxford research programme required me to examine the primary documents of Xi's internal political and theoretical discourse within the ranks of the Chinese Communist Party (CCP). This was necessary to decipher the underlying ideological dialect of intra-party communication. These contain the core change messages that Xi has been conveying to the party at large since coming to power. I have also sought to match these with parallel changes in China's formal domestic and foreign policy discourse, as well as, where possible, with observable changes in official Chinese actions and behaviours on the ground. Some might describe this as some form of rigorous triangulation—by cross-referencing, sequencing, and interpolating ideological, policy, and behavioural change. I am more cautious in making any such bold claim. But I do argue that this approach is the best available, that it sheds real light on what is unfolding before us in real time, although often it is still as if we are 'but peering through a glass dimly' as we seek to penetrate the inbuilt opacity of the CCP's decision-making apparatus.

For these reasons, I respectfully ignored the wise counsel of academic supervisors to define a doctoral research topic as narrowly as possible, so as to demonstrate the argument being advanced as rigorously as possible. By contrast, there could be no broader, and potentially inaccessible, subject as 'What does Xi Jinping really think and what impact does it have on China and the world?' It poses a range of empirical and methodological problems, including how we equate Xi's ideology, on the one hand, with what he actually thinks, on the other. It also encounters the parallel problem of determining how much recent ideological change in China is the product of Xi the individual leader, as opposed to the CCP as a system. Nonetheless, while the inner decision-making world of the CCP remains largely opaque to the rest of the world, there is still a minimum requirement for the party leadership to publicly communicate macro-ideological change across the entire political system. Moreover, these broad, and at first glance often unintelligible, ideological communications have influence well beyond the detailed, classified party circulars that foreigners generally do not get to see. Indeed, this is the type of ideological messaging that sets the parameters within which a more granular, internal political and policy discourse can proceed.

This brings me to my final reason for researching this dissertation and now converting it into what I hope is a more readable form. The problem with much of contemporary Western Sinology is that, while there is an abundance of *analysis* of where different parts of Xi's enterprise might now be headed, there is a paucity of *synthesis* that tries to makes sense of it all—by asking 'why' is it headed that way, where it is likely to go next, and what, therefore, can usefully be done about it. Synthesis is hard. We are all conscious of the exceptions that may contradict the rule, reinforcing the general academic retreat to the safer terrain of narrow specialization and analytical detail. But the absence of intelligent synthesis on Xi's China, for which granular analysis is the cornerstone, is not useful to policymakers, corporate leaders, and senior military strategists working in the real world, who are all time-poor. Indeed, in the absence of specialists seeking to produce time-relevant, intellectually digestible syntheses of where China is headed under Xi, the ground is then yielded to grand cultural generalizations often generated by those who have never studied a word of Chinese in their lives.

Therefore, it is time for those of us who have spent a lifetime studying, observing, and sometimes living in the Middle Kingdom to try to join the dots, to paint a wider and more intelligible canvas, rather than simply responding to each new phenomenon in Xi's universe as if it is somehow a freestanding and unique development detached from its wider context. It is in this spirit of inquiry that the core argument of this book is that Xi's ideological worldview offers us a unifying 'red thread', providing a useful, albeit incomplete, illumination of the unfolding contours of Xi's plans for China and the world. In this sense, the book does not set out to be a biography of Xi Jinping.[1] That would entail a much wider undertaking, separating out fact from hagiography, and perhaps bringing us no closer to the subject of 'who Xi Jinping really is'. Instead, the book is a form of intellectual biography, assuming of course we can comfortably equate the terms 'intellectual' and 'ideological'. Does that then get us any closer to 'what Xi Jinping really thinks'? To that my answer is an unequivocal 'somewhat closer', albeit still through the opacity of the regime's official filter. That is because it reflects the worldview he has promulgated across multiple forums for more than a decade, and within it the type of political, economic, and international order that he seeks for the party's and the country's future. The core point remains: Xi's ideological blueprint for the future is out there on the Chinese public record for all to see—assuming, of course, we have the eyes to see it, read it, and understand it within its own terms. Indeed, the outline of Xi's brave new world is now hiding in plain sight for us all.

How Xi Jinping's China Is Changing the World

China's dramatic transformation over the half-century since the death of Mao, and most spectacularly in the decade since Xi Jinping's rise, has become the single greatest disruptive change now confronting the post-war political, economic, and security order. Xi's China now openly challenges the political values underpinning the preexisting international order and offers instead an alternative authoritarian development model for the world.

This is made possible, in the first place, by the sheer scale of the Chinese economy. China's global economic footprint—notwithstanding slower growth brought about by self-inflicted ideological, demographic, and debt-related drags on growth—remains second only to that of the United States. It has been the world's largest trading power since 2015, the third-largest source of foreign direct investment for the world since 2020, and is now locked in a death struggle with the United States to secure the commanding heights across all critical domains of technology, most crucially artificial intelligence. Most important, it is unprecedented in modern economic history that a single massive national economy of China's scale can now fundamentally disrupt the regular operations of global markets by intervening as a single, integrated economic actor in the form of the Chinese party-state. Such interventions are driven not by the normal competitive dynamics of supply and demand determining price in accordance with standard liberal economic theory, but by the actions of a unified corporate state deploying a multidimensional and integrated trade and industrial policy at a scale we have not seen before. Not only are the normal operations of global markets being upended by these unprecedented powers of monopoly and monopsony, their disruptive impact is compounded by the ever-present threat of trade bans driven by political, not market, considerations. We now see the full impact of these forces at work across global markets ranging from critical minerals, batteries, renewable energy systems, and electric vehicles through to the entire spectrum of finished industrial products. Because of the scale involved, this model therefore represents the deepest assault on liberal economic theory that the world has seen, giving rise to the growing bifurcation of the global economic order through de-risking and de-coupling, and the rise of a new wave of protectionist and industrial policy across the West and parts of the rest.

Geo-politically, Xi's China is intent on not merely adjusting its land and maritime borders in its immediate neighbourhood. Beijing is also determined to become the preeminent power in the rest of East Asia economically and militarily and, at the same time, is actively redesigning the norms, rules, and institutions of the international system writ large. Put simply, China, under Xi Jinping, is no longer a status-quo power. Xi's intention is not just to change China. It is also to change the international order itself, underpinned by an increasingly powerful China as the emerging geo-political and geo-economic fulcrum of that order. And all this is made doubly possible by what Xi sees as the inexorable decline of the United States and the West. During an earlier period in post-war history, the collapse of the Soviet Union in 1991 was arguably of comparable strategic significance. The Soviet Union also saw itself as the harbinger of an alternative development model, the centre of a rival international system, although never effectively competing with the United States for global economic superpower status. But the events of 1989–1991 saw Washington's triumph over Moscow after decades of foreign policy containment and near-lethal nuclear confrontation, culminating in the largely peaceful end of a Cold War that had dominated global geo-politics for more than forty years. It resulted in the redrawing of the strategic map of Western, Eastern, and Central Europe, the Caucasus, and Central Asia. The implosion of the Soviet Union also removed the strategic rationale that had underpinned two decades of Sino-American political normalization and military collaboration against their common Soviet foe. This, in turn, paved the way for Beijing's rapprochement with Moscow during the 1990s and their later realignment against the United States during the 2000s, culminating in Xi's and Putin's dramatic declaration of a 'strategic partnership without limits' on the eve of the Russian invasion of Ukraine in 2022.

No less significant has been a third great systemic disruption of our age: a rolling digital revolution over the last forty years that has swept aside the languid pace of an earlier analogue world. This has been turbocharged by the explosive impact of artificial intelligence (AI) now challenging all domains of politics, economics, and security, as well as creating the new challenge of retaining human control over the very machines we have created. Within the AI revolution, the political and policy debate has not yet settled as to whether it generates greater threats or opportunities for the domestic governance of democratic or authoritarian states. For example, will generative AI enhance or undermine the capabilities of the surveillance state in systems like China, Russia, North Korea, Iran, and would-be authoritarians in other parts of the world? Will AI finally resolve the long-standing dilemmas of planned economies to navigate the billions of random decisions that have hitherto represented the allocative efficiency advantage of market economies—both in managing scarce resources and in benefiting from the broader disciplines of price theory? Will AI therefore suspend the classical rhythms of long-standing development theory which has held that rising living standards always result in irresistible demands for economic, social, and eventually political freedoms that challenge the underlying legitimacy of repressive regimes? And will the current race between China and the United States across AI, quantum computing, semiconductors, and the full spectrum of other paradigm-shifting technologies result in one leap-frogging the other as the classical competitiveness of nations is turned on its head?

Beyond AI's political and economic impact within individual nation-states, what will its disruptive impact be on the already tinder-dry world of geo-politics? How will it affect militaries competing for tactical and strategic advantage in the speed and accuracy of the real-time surveillance, targeting, and deployment of next-generation autonomous weapons systems? And on top of all the above, what of the ultimate AI dilemma concerning continuing human autonomy over weapons systems themselves? Does this finally become a unifying concern and platform for agreed policy action across the human family as it confronts its collective 'Frankenstein' moment? Or does it cause the United States and China to double down in an 'AI' race to the bottom in the ultimate manifestation of 'strategic competition' without guardrails and without limits? China, once again, lies at the fulcrum of all these technological mega-disruptions, particularly given Xi's prescient declaration in 2018 that "artificial intelligence is an important driving force of the new round of the scientific and technological revolution and industrial change" and that "accelerating the development of a new generation of AI is a strategic issue concerning China's ability to seize these opportunities".[2]

China too lies at the centre of a fourth great global disruption: climate change. While climate has no respect for national boundaries, the carbon intensity of China's economic modernization over the last four decades has, since 2015, made it the largest single contributor to global greenhouse gases. Based on current trajectories, by 2030, China will account for a quarter of annual global emissions (with the United States coming a distant second at just under 10%). At their present course, by 2040, China's combined current and historical emissions will produce a cumulative carbon footprint larger than that of the United States over the preceding 190 years of industrial development.[3] In other words, the planet's future will increasingly rest on what Beijing does to decarbonize its economy to keep average global temperature increases by century's end within 1.5 degrees centigrade to avoid catastrophic climate change. Notwithstanding Xi's 2020 declarations that China was now committed to a 'double zero' target of achieving carbon peaking by 2030 and carbon neutrality by 2060, more recent decisions to slow decarbonization to offset an overall slowdown in economic growth has sounded global alarm bells. Indeed, against China's emissions trajectory, the United Nations has warned that instead of remaining within the safer limits of 1.5 degree temperature increases by 2100, the world is now on course to hit nearly 3 degrees, with catastrophic consequences for all.

And then there is demography—the fifth of the great global change-drivers confronting our world—where China is also key. China's population growth has slowed markedly, exacerbated by Deng's one-child policy for roughly forty years from the 1970s. The result is that, in 2023, India for the first time in history surpassed China as the world's most populous nation. And despite desperate attempts under Xi Jinping to reverse population decline since 2017, China's overall population peaked in 2023 after its working-age population had already begun to shrink as early as 2014. This has presented China and the world with a new set of deeply disruptive challenges. China's own date with demographic destiny is accelerating. It is already generating budgetary pressures as revenues and expenditures adjust to a shrinking income tax base, while expenditures on health, ageing, and retirement incomes compete with the military for public resources. Then there is the impact of demography on China's capacity to drive global economic growth as it has done for the last quarter of a century, as well as its effect on Beijing's historical ambition to overtake the United States as the world's largest economy. This has long been seen, both in China and around the world, as the bulwark of Beijing's future claim to global geo-political leadership. Finally, the one-child policy has produced an unprecedented gender imbalance within the country of more than 30 million after decades of male preference, sex-selective abortion and female infanticide. This has resulted in an unofficial policy of sending large numbers of unmarried men to the developing world to find partners, build businesses, and strengthen familial ties with the motherland. Indeed, this appears to complement China's grand strategy, articulated in part by the Belt and Road Initiative (BRI), that its long-term economic interests lie in cultivating markets, supply chains, and other political and social ties with Africa, Latin America, and the Islamic world. This is where population growth will add over 3 billion to the human family by mid-century, while China contracts by 120 million.

China is central to all five of these major, global change-drivers as they ricochet around the world—from core geo-politics and geo-economics, through disruptive technology, demography, and accelerating climate change. Its centrifugal force is now being felt in most countries, across most geographies, and in all domains of public policy. We are still unclear where each of these might land given that the Chinese economic policy juggernaut has encountered heavy weather at home and is now encountering growing levels of political resistance abroad. Nor do we understand fully what lasting impact China will have on the global rules-based order. Nonetheless, the sheer quantitative impact of the Chinese policy footprint is already big enough to warrant the world paying the closest attention to what Beijing does next.

Critically, for our purposes here, China's impact across these mega-changes and the ripples of effect they are generating across the world are not policy accidents. Nor are they random events. They are fully intended. Indeed, they are the direct consequences of considered policy choices by the Chinese leadership over time. This has particularly been the case under China's paramount leader, Xi Jinping, when the pace, scope, and trajectory of policy change within China has been breathtaking. Indeed, in all five of the global policy domains outlined above, China's strategy is now vastly different to what it was when Xi took over China's leadership in 2012–13, just as we see equally profound changes in China's politics, economy, social control, foreign policy, and military posture over the same decade. In short, given its sheer scale, changes in Chinese policy settings at home now reverberate across the world at large.

Understanding China was once a boutique concern for salons of academic specialists. It now matters for the world at large as we scramble to comprehend what China will do next. China, therefore, not only represents a profound global, geo-political and geo-economic disruption in its own right, it is also central to the other great global disruptions that the international community are confronting at the same time.

The Purpose of This Book

The question, therefore, being asked around the world is not only *what* are we seeing by way of changes in Chinese political and policy posture, but *why*? The world wants to understand the conceptual logic underlying the profound changes in policy direction we have seen so far so as to make better sense of our times. It may also help us better understand their likely trajectories for the future. For these reasons, this book asks the following questions:

- Are policy changes under Xi Jinping simply the inevitable consequence of China's changing power relativities with the United States, the West, and the rest, and driven by an historical desire, pre-dating CCP rule, for the Middle Kingdom to reassert itself in the world? In other words, now that China has finally achieved its 150-year long aspiration for national 'wealth and power', is Beijing's principal motivation to protect itself from the future predations of great powers circling its periphery? And beyond that, is it also driven by its own historiography to restore its self-perception of global centrality, political primacy, and national unity?
- Could these changes in China's policy posture instead be driven by pragmatic national responses, consistent with long-standing CCP strategy, to China's changing external circumstances, including the different international responses Beijing has observed towards China's rise, depending on whether these have been combative, accommodating or noncommittal?
- Are they simply being driven by their own internal analytical logic and the advice of Chinese technocratic professionals in each individual economic and security policy domain, but without any particular 'grand plan'?

- Or is there something particular to Xi Jinping's individual leadership that has fundamentally altered the velocity, intensity, and trajectory of previous policy settings under his three post-Mao predecessors—Deng Xiaoping, Jiang Zemin, and Hu Jintao—to the extent that what we are seeing today represents much more discontinuity than continuity from China's recent past?
- And if so, is there a common 'red thread' to Xi Jinping's ideological worldview that provides an underlying, ideational drive to China's new strategic direction?

Or is it more likely that what we are seeing is a complex combination of all of the above?

The purpose of this book is therefore not to document how Xi Jinping is changing China and the world. There are already many authors who have done so over the last decade, some more optimistically than others, although the degree of enthusiasm for Xi's great project has waned greatly as this grim third decade of the twenty-first century continues to grind on.[4] Instead, my purpose here is to understand why exactly Xi has decided to turn much of Chinese politics, economics, and foreign policy on its head from the decades of Communist Party rule that preceded him. In particular, I want to explore what it is about Xi's ideological worldview that has shaped his vision for China's future, together with the statecraft he has relentlessly deployed over the last decade in translating this vision into reality. In doing so, I will analyse how Xi's new ideological canon is vastly different from the thirty-five years of economic and foreign policy pragmatism that preceded him under Deng Xiaoping, Jiang Zemin, and Hu Jintao. I will also explore how Xi went about signalling this to the party and the country through his systematic deployment of the party's theoretical publications and propaganda apparatus to convey a clear message that under him, ideology was no longer a matter of expedient formalism. Indeed, ideology was now a real barometer of much deeper change.

I also examine whether this new ideological orthodoxy of 'Xi-ism', or what the party and state constitutions now torturously describe as 'Xi Jinping Thought on Socialism with Chinese Characteristics for the New Era', is a form of post-facto rationalization for policy actions already taken by Xi's regime for other reasons. Or whether there is a significant, new element of ideological causation in Xi's ideation which of itself is pushing the party in an increasingly hard-line policy direction.

In examining this question of causation, I will not argue that ideology is the only driving force that animates Xi's political and policy program. But I do argue that it represents a new and significant driving force, which we ignore at our peril.

A related question is whether ideological change has become a necessary precursor for policy change in Xi's China in addition to more pragmatic factors. In other words, is understanding Xi's ideational world a useful guide to understanding the 'real world' of politics and public policy that he inhabits in the day-to-day work of the central leadership in Zhongnanhai? For example, a major speech early in Xi's presidency on the centrality of ideology to the Central Ideological and Propaganda Work Conference of July 2013 turned out to be deeply predictive of where he would take the party in the anti-corruption campaign and rectification movement in the decade that followed. Similarly, Xi's formal redefinition of the party's 'principal contradiction' at the 19th Party Congress in 2017 to underscore the problems of the 'reform and opening' period was an ideological precursor of his moves against the private sector between 2017 and 2022. On the international front, his unceremonial junking in November 2014 at the party's Central Foreign Policy Work Conference of Deng's long-standing theory of diplomacy (summarized as 'hide your strength, bide your time, never take the lead') heralded a decade of unprecedented foreign policy activism and assertiveness. Of course, there have been other causative factors at play in this decade-long process of political and policy change. But we would be naive to ignore the predictive role that ideology can play in the world of Xi Jinping.

Importantly, the book does not simply provide an ideological interpretation of the decade that has just passed—the first decade of Xi's rule between the 18th Party Congress in 2012 and the 20th Congress in 2022. It also seeks to offer a level of ideological insight into the critical period that lies ahead, one I have long called the 'decade of living dangerously' between 2022 and 2032. This is when Xi hopes China will surpass the US economy as the world's largest and become the predominant military power in the region. In particular, in the conclusion to the book, I look at the possible intersection between Xi's ideological framework and if, and when, Xi may be led to take fateful decisions to return Taiwan to Chinese sovereignty by armed force. On this critical point, while hard-headed military and strategic considerations will remain paramount in Xi's calculus, his strident ideological statements on where China's 'struggle' is now located within an intellectual framework of dialectical materialism, historical materialism, and a Chinese nationalist equivalent of 'manifest destiny' is also relevant.

This goes to a further reason for writing a book on *why* Xi's actions are taking a particular course, rather than simply focussing on *what* specific actions we may be observing, or *how* his policy decisions are being implemented. For the world, it is necessary to understand the extent to which Xi views reality through a different historical, cultural, and ideational lens to that which we might assume to be logical, normal, or even 'self-evident' in the West. International relations history and theory are replete with examples of 'projectionism'—or the unconscious imposition of our own perceptual lens on the political cultures of others who may not share the same conceptual, analytical, or even empirical assumptions as 'us'.[5] My hope is that understanding Xi's ideological worldview may give us additional insight into where Xi might want to take China and the world in the future, irrespective of whether we think it is in his rational self-interest or not.

All this assumes, of course, that Xi continues to navigate successfully his own domestic politics with the same type of Machiavellian agility we have seen so far, without falling foul of what Susan Shirk has elegantly described as 'overreach'.[6] This too will be examined in the conclusion, where I explore how politically durable Xi's ideological revolution is likely to be, given the cumulative levels of opposition and resistance it is generating across the party and the country. Not all in the party have welcomed Xi's return to Leninist control, particularly those who have become victim to his rolling political purges in the name of anti-corruption and the broader return to ideological rectitude that he has championed. This includes the families, colleagues, patronage networks, and institutional affiliations of the millions who have now felt the party's disciplinary 'blade'.[7] Many are also counting the cost of declining growth, rising unemployment, and relatively stagnant living standards in the aftermath of Xi's turn to the Marxist left on the economy. Similarly, national security and foreign policy elites are quietly questioning the cost of Xi's unapologetically assertive posture in the region and the world—including his personal relationship with Vladimir Putin and the damage delivered to China's international brand by so fully supporting Putin's Ukraine crusade. These costs impose a cumulative political price for Xi's leadership. But Xi, the master politician, further empowered by the force multiplier of an increasingly formidable surveillance state, has so far proven to be several steps ahead of the political and policy play. While internal opposition may be growing to Xi's overall political, policy, and ideological direction, it would be a brave call indeed to predict that he will be unable to prevail.

One final question for the world is where these forces of discontent may take China after Xi has likely left the stage at some point in the 2030s, or perhaps even beyond. By then he would be aged in his eighties, or even early nineties, assuming his familial longevity genes have not skipped a generation. Xi has demonstrated a proven capacity so far for navigating unexpected crises (e.g. COVID-19). As with Mao in the years following his death in 1976, the forces in Chinese politics that might seek to take the party back to the safer ground of the ideological and policy centre would be more likely to prevail once Xi has left the scene, rather than while he was still in office.[8] Therefore, barring unanticipated internal or external crises, at this stage the possibility of any fundamental course correction while Xi remains in power seems remote. For these reasons, it is prudent to assume that Xi will still be the one directing traffic for the 'decade of living dangerously' that lies ahead.

This matters for us all. Xi Jinping's China has already become a core change-driver for the world across multiple geo-political, economic, technological, environmental, and ideational domains. The size of China's global footprint, the extent of its policy dissonance from the United States, the West, and parts of the rest, and Xi's new culture of political assertiveness command our attention. Now more than ever, we are required to understand, to the extent that we can, the underpinning ideational engine room of China's leadership. The stakes are high indeed—for Xi's China, for America, and for the rest of the world.

The Core Argument

The core argument of this book goes to the central role of ideology in Xi Jinping's China as a precursor for change in the real world of Chinese domestic and international policy. Specifically, I argue that:

- Xi has reified the role of ideology in general in the Communist Party as a means of enhancing personal and party control, CCP political legitimacy, and as a mechanism for foreshadowing broad policy change across the Chinese system;
- Xi has also changed the CCP's ideological footings by developing what I call a new form of 'Marxist-Leninist Nationalism' (shortened henceforth to 'Marxist Nationalism') within the unfolding framework of what the party now calls 'Xi Jinping Thought for the New Era';
- In doing so, Xi since 2012 has taken Chinese politics to the 'Leninist left', by which I mean reasserting the leader's power over the party's collective leadership, redeploying a Mao-like party rectification movement to restore party discipline, and reinforcing the dominant role of the party over the professional technocratic machinery of the Chinese state;
- Since 2017, Xi has also moved the centre of gravity of Chinese economic policy to the 'Marxist left' by asserting the primacy of state planning over market forces, the state-owned enterprise sector over private firms, and greater income equality over rampant inequality;
- Internationally, Xi has moved Chinese foreign and security policy to the 'nationalist right' as reflected in increasing, top-down, nationalist campaigns about Chinese civilizational centrality, an enhanced grievance culture about the West's past occupation and continued containment of China, the prospect now for the 'great rejuvenation of the Chinese nation', articulated by a new 'wolf warrior' diplomacy legitimizing a more assertive and aggressive posture towards the world, all harnessed by a new, ideological assertion that China's time has now come with 'the rise of the East, and the decline of the West';
- Taken together, these different elements of Xi's new 'Marxist Nationalism', rather than remaining an ideological abstraction, have been accompanied by measurable new directions in Chinese real-world politics and in China's economic and foreign policy;
- For these reasons, Xi's evolving ideological worldview also offers some predictive value on the likely contours of Chinese policy in the future, including CCP views on the shape of an alternative international order with significantly different norms, values and institutional arrangements to the US-led order that has, by and large, prevailed since 1945.

This is a complex set of arguments to advance from the available evidence, particularly as we are dealing with contemporary developments as they have unfolded over little more than a decade. It is like writing a history when at best only the first few chapters are known, and even then only partly. The book seeks to peer into the immediate future by interpreting the recent past through the lens of Xi Jinping's changing ideological worldview.

Something new is happening with Xi's China. It is also being worked out on a grand scale. More fundamentally, there are big ideas behind all this which we must equally understand. Otherwise, we are merely dealing with the tip of the Chinese iceberg—the manifestation of change rather than its causation and construction. Because the stakes for China and the world are now so high and the possibility of large-scale geo-political conflict so great, it is more urgent than ever to deploy every intellectual effort to get to the truth of what is unfolding before us, why it is happening, and, for policymakers, what can intelligently be done in response to it. And if that requires breaking some traditional academic crockery on the way through, it is a price worth paying. We no longer have the luxury of perfectly conclusive scholarship. We could, of course, wait until all the data points are in. But by then, in another decade's time, it is likely to be too late in the real world of politics and geo-politics, given emerging timelines over Taiwan, to make any credible difference. Besides, this book finds there is already sufficient, if not absolute, clarity on the shape of Xi's ideational universe and its deep inter-relationship with China's changing policy posture. I argue that we ignore Xi's clarity of ideological purpose at our peril.

Some have argued that the changes we have seen in China over the last decade reflect the underlying and continuing nature of the party itself, rather than the impact of any particular leader.[9] This, of course, is part of a much broader, long-standing debate between 'agency' and 'structure' in political science, international relations, and across the social sciences in general. Applied to the circumstances of contemporary China, this would mean that it didn't really matter who happened to become CCP General Secretary after Hu Jintao in 2012 in shaping the changes that then emerged. Instead, it was the underlying 'structure' of the inherent political nature and authority of the party, together with China's emerging national wealth and power relative to its neighbours and the United States, that meant that China would inevitably become more assertive in its dealings with the world. By the same logic, it would also mean that the dramatic changes that have emerged in the shape of Chinese politics and the economy after 2012 were driven by the underlying structural forces of the party rather than the individual impact of Xi Jinping's leadership. This book does not accept that thesis. By contrast, it argues that there is something unique to the individual 'agency' of Xi's particular form of political statecraft that has been a major force in changing China's national direction. It also argues that these changes have not simply been the result of the successful application of Xi's remarkable Machiavellian *political* craft, it is also because he has brought to bear a different *ideological* worldview to his post-Mao predecessors which has shaped the policy direction in which he has deployed his hard-won political power. In other words, it has been both the power of Xi's ideology and the force of his individual political leadership that together have formed the integral, operating elements of Xi's 'agency' in effecting a great number of the changes we have seen unfold. There is little about the inherent 'structure' of the CCP that mysteriously made it inevitable that under Xi, there would be a decisive turn to a more Leninist party, a more Marxist economy, or a more nationalist and assertive international policy. Indeed, the core argument of the book is that these changes, together with those in foreign policy and national security policy, have been driven from the top. Or as Xi himself has often proclaimed, through the agency of 'top-level design'.

For these reasons, the central argument of this book remains that we need to understand the nature of Xi's ideational worldview as a means of unlocking where he has taken China so far, as well as where he may take it next. The book is therefore not an abstract exercise in political theory, however interesting that may be. Rather it goes to the core, practical questions of what shapes Chinese public policy in the real world. It also goes to the critical, longer-term question of what happens in a post–Xi Jinping China? If, for example, we were to accept the argument that all is being shaped by the underlying 'structure' of Chinese politics and the CCP, then we are left with the conclusion that so long as the CCP is in power, it doesn't really matter who leads the party in the future, because the die has already been cast. If, however, we conclude that is has been the individual 'agency' of Xi's leadership that has shaped much of the change we are seeing, then it follows that this *may* well change once he has left the scene and when other political possibilities emerge. Whereas the bulk of this book seeks to explain what we have seen during the first decade of Xi's rule, and to validate the argument that the decisive factor driving political and policy change has in fact been the leader himself, the last two chapters begin to prize open the question of what a China after Xi Jinping might look like—whenever that might occur.

Structure of the Book

The book's introductory chapters seek to define basic concepts and terms before locating Xi's contemporary worldview within the wider ideational and ideological inheritance from Chinese history. It then turns to Xi's core ideological texts and looks at how these are reflected through changes in Chinese politics, the economy and foreign policy since 2012. The book next examines Xi's efforts to consolidate his Marxist-Nationalist ideology within the new framework of Xi Jinping Thought, before looking at more recent events and the likely implications of Xi's apparent determination to double-down on his hardline ideological direction into the 2030s. It then concludes with a chapter on 'China after Xi'.

Chapter 2 defines the critical terminology used throughout the text and examines the assumptions underpinning these core concepts and terms. These include the vexed debate on the meanings of 'ideology' and 'ideological worldview', both in the general social science literature as well as their particular application to the ideational world of the CCP. The chapter presents working definitions of other terms such as 'Marxism', 'Leninism', and 'nationalism', each of which has generated its own formidable and deeply contested literature. It also examines and defines the concepts of 'left', 'right', and 'national assertiveness', both in their general usage and also in their particular usages within the CCP.

Chapter 3 locates Xi's ideological framework within the wider spectrum of Chinese worldviews across time. The chapter analyses changing Chinese understandings of the world during both the classical and Communist periods. This includes Chinese traditions of 'all under heaven', 'tributary states', classical realism, and Mao's 'Three Worlds

Theory', through to the period of 'reform and opening' after 1978. The chapter argues that Xi Jinping has inherited three worldviews from the past: a classical worldview of Sino-centric nationalism; a Marxist framework anchored in activist struggle, albeit within a determinist view of history; all tempered by an abiding strategic realism that still cautions against political and military risk.

Chapter 4 examines five major articles and speeches by Xi Jinping on the centrality of ideology to his regime, his definition of the ideological struggle in which he believes he is engaged both domestically and internationally, and the centrality of a Marxist-Leninist worldview to make sense of this struggle. Most critically, it probes his redefinition of the CCP's 'central contradiction' for the 'new era' over which he now presides. These documents are: Xi's 2013 address to the Central Propaganda Work Conference (consolidated in a communiqué circulated within the party by its General Office known as Document Number 9); his two dedicated Politburo study sessions in 2013 and 2015 on dialectical materialism and historical materialism respectively; his 2017 address to the 19th Party Congress; and his remarkable 2018 address on the 200th anniversary of Karl Marx's birth. These form the basis of the book's subsequent analysis of ideological changes in Xi's approach to Chinese politics, economic policy, and foreign policy during his period in office.

Chapter 5 analyses Xi's shifting of the centre of gravity in Chinese politics towards the Leninist left. It argues that his rehabilitation of a classically Leninist party has occurred in ten critical areas: a new demand for political loyalty to the party centre beyond all other loyalties; a parallel demand for absolute loyalty to Xi personally as "the core leader"; a radically reduced space for political and policy dissent within the party; the purging of any perceived personal or political opposition; the increased policymaking power of the party centre at the expense of the State Council, particularly in executing economic policy; the internal 'cleansing' of Xi's Leninist party through a comprehensive anti-corruption campaign after 2013; the wider political cleansing of the party through a 'rectification campaign' launched in 2020 across the party's entire political and legal affairs apparatus; the party's new agenda on the 'securitization' of everything, including the reassertion of party control over the People's Liberation Army (PLA) and the relocation of the People's Armed Police (PAP) under the party's organizational umbrella as opposed to the State

Council, including major changes in the control and direction of cybersecurity and party surveillance systems; the renewed centrality of the party to all domains of public policy and private life, including its institutional relationship with the media, universities, non-governmental organizations, arts and culture, as well as the institutions of religious governance; and, finally, the paramount importance of ideological discipline for party members as reflected in a new series of party regulations and party education campaigns, all aimed at resuscitating the CCP's Marxist-Leninist core and enlivening a new community of secular faith around it.

Chapter 6 traces the beginning of the gradual migration of Chinese economic policy to the Marxist left under Xi. It examines the general role of ideology in shaping China's overall economic policy discourse by examining the evolution of a number of critical 'banner terms' signifying change in China's macro-policy direction. The chapter explores how this process has been uneven over time. It starts with a more accepting approach to the role of the market during Xi's first term as reflected in the 'Decision' of 2013, his concept of the 'New Normal', and the initial phase of 'Supply-Side Structural Reform'. The chapter also analyses a significant speech by Xi from April of 2021 which sought retrospectively to explain his economic decisions between 2012 and 2017, including re-examining the basis of Deng's core ideological proposition from 1982 that China was still in the 'primary stage of socialism'. This had been the ideological foundation of Deng's era of 'reform and opening' in the first place, including the party's preparedness to tolerate high degrees of economic inequality while it unleashed the factors of production, while relegating the 'relations of production' on sensitive issues of class equality and inequality.

Chapter 7 looks at the deeper changes in economic ideology that emerged at the 19th Party Congress in 2017 with the proclamation of Xi's 'new era' and, most critically, the definition of the party's new contradiction of 'unbalanced and unequal development'. The chapter emphasizes how these significant ideological changes have impacted the real world of economic policy. This is reflected in Xi's new overarching framework of the 'New Development Concept' which has increasingly replaced 'reform and opening' as the central organizing principle of economic policy. It is also reflected in new statist concepts of 'national self-sufficiency', the 'dual circulation economy', 'common prosperity', 'security in development', and now a battery of 'new productive forces' to drive growth. The chapter concludes that these changes have required a significantly more interventionist role by the party and the Chinese state than was previously the case during the Deng-Jiang-Hu period. Taken over the span of Xi's first full decade in office, these measures also represent a significant shift to the Marxist left in China's macro-policy settings on the economy.

Chapter 8 traces a parallel process of moving China's micro-economic policy settings to the left, as reflected in China's 14th Five-Year Plan. It explores Xi's discourse on the difference between the 'real economy' and 'building a modern economic system', on the one hand, as opposed to a 'fictitious economy' based on a finance-fuelled property sector, on the other. This is followed by an examination of the reinvigoration of state industrial policy under Xi. The chapter then analyses the hardening of policy in relation to state-owned enterprises (SOEs) and the new restrictive requirements imposed by Xi on the private sector, including personnel recruitment disciplines. Finally, the chapter outlines Xi's significant redefinition of China's traditional policy of opening to the outside world by inserting the term a 'new pattern of opening' into the ideological vernacular, which incorporates a range of new self-sufficiency, mercantilist, and nationalist arguments. This last section of the chapter also deals with the apparent contradiction between this overall statist trend in China's general economic policy settings and the continued liberalization of China's financial sector.

Chapter 9 examines the interconnection between China's rising 'nationalism' under Xi and the party's new culture of foreign policy 'assertiveness'. It also outlines the relationship between Marxism-Leninism and nationalism in Xi's overall ideological worldview. This is followed by a short examination of potential factors that shape a more assertive Chinese foreign policy apart from nationalism, rather than assuming that nationalism is the sole driving force of foreign policy change. The chapter then analyses the importance of several key nationalist 'banner terms' and 'signature phrases' that have been deployed in the party's official foreign policy discourse under Xi. Specifically, it looks at the ideological significance of four such banner terms: 'the great rejuvenation of the Chinese nation', 'China's outstanding traditional culture', China's growing 'comprehensive national power', and China's role in 'changes in the world not seen in a hundred years'.

Chapter 10 analyses a second set of terms, developed in tandem with those in the previous chapter, designed to give more direct ideological guidance on what this new nationalist self-confidence means for the future direction of China's foreign policy. These are: Xi's formal ending of the Deng era of 'hiding and biding' (*taoguang yanghui*) and moving instead towards a new era of actively 'striving for achievement' (*fenfa youwei*); China's new neighbouring-states diplomacy (*zhoubian guojia waijiao*); China's changed posture towards the United States as part of its 'new type of great power relations' (*xinxing daguo guanxi*); and China's new activism to reform the global order (*guoji zhixu tiaozheng*). Taken together, the chapter argues that these represent a new and consistent nationalist narrative of foreign policy assertiveness, as Xi explicitly authorizes his diplomats and the PLA to go out and change the international status quo.

Chapter 11 tests this proposition of growing foreign policy assertiveness by examining China's record at the UN Security Council. This is done by collating the accounts of a number of UNSC permanent representatives and other senior UN officials who served alongside Chinese officials after 2012. All ambassadors interviewed for this project reported major changes in China's multilateral diplomacy over the period under review. This was observed in: China's changing activism on the UNSC; China's newfound aggression after 2013 on the Human Rights Council; a more subtle set of desired changes to UN peacekeeping operations in defence of the principle of state sovereignty; a preparedness to use new levels of budgetary largesse for the UN; and the use of economic leverage against smaller UN member states to secure Chinese leadership of UN agencies, obtain new UN staff positions, or reduce opposition to preferred Chinese policy positions. These ambassadors also reported an unfolding, longer-term campaign to change the normative language of UN resolutions in a direction more supportive of Chinese foreign policy concepts and institutions, and much less accommodating of the universalist claims of the West. Taken together, these represent major changes in China's UN policy and evidence a new strategy of multilateral assertiveness under Xi Jinping.

Chapter 12 investigates how the various individual strands of Xi's overall ideological worldview—Leninism, Marxism, and nationalism—have been increasingly brought together within the unifying framework of 'Xi Jinping Thought for the New Era'. The chapter examines how this is rendered plainly through the party's 2021 historical resolution celebrating the CCP's centenary. It looks at Xi Jinping Thought's core ideological self-confidence that China's rise is unstoppable, delivered through the application of the 'scientific laws' of historical materialism and dialectical materialism. It also looks at how this is reinforced by an intensifying nationalist agenda anchored in the rejuvenation of Chinese national power, a new form of cultural nationalism, and an increasingly binary outlook of political and ideological struggle with the United States and the West. This emerging worldview within the framework of Xi Jinping Thought has been accentuated by an officially sanctioned campaign against mounting external threats to the Chinese nation, including fears of foreign disruption, subversion and encirclement. This, in turn, gives rise to Xi's all-encompassing 'national security concept'. The chapter argues that there is no official narrative on China's overall ideological framework produced during the Deng-Jiang-Hu period that compares with the party's 2021 historical resolution. Indeed, Xi Jinping Thought embraces a Chinese corollary to the American concept of 'manifest destiny': an all-powerful Leninist party and leader; a people committed to relentless struggle against contradictions both at home and abroad; a nation besieged by threats from all sides; and all reinforced by the invocation of national pride, national power, and national ambition. The chapter concludes that, in post-Mao China, much of this is new.

Chapter 13 focusses on the role of the 20th Party Congress in October 2022 in consolidating Xi's political and ideological strategy after his first decade in power. This goes to core questions of ideological fundamentals, political control, the further subjugation of the economy to the dictates of national security, and an increasingly nationalist foreign policy. It argues that Xi presented the most ideological Congress report of any since the end of the Cultural Revolution, with a record number of references to the centrality of Marxism. It states that Xi's 'winner take all' approach to Politburo appointments, combined with the constitutional entrenchment of Xi's 'core leadership' status in the party constitution, has turned a Leninist CCP into Xi's CCP. On the economy, the chapter examines the relative relegation of the party's overall economic development agenda as it became increasingly overwhelmed by national security priorities as part of Xi's new 'security in development' concept. As for foreign policy, Xi's nationalist message to the party at the 20th Congress was that China's long-term assumptions that the country would continue to enjoy a benign strategic environment were over. References to the 'period of strategic opportunity', cited at successive congresses since 2002, were deleted. The chapter concludes that Xi is preparing for an increasingly binary international order.

Chapter 14 deals with the political and policy impact of the complex developments that unfolded following Xi's sudden abolition of the 'zero-COVID' strategy in December 2022, and China's collapsing economic growth between 2021 and 2023. It probes whether these challenging developments have prompted any ideological reappraisal of Xi's Marxist-Nationalist agenda. It examines China's interests in moderating its tactical message to re-embrace the private sector at home and abroad, and to stabilize geo-political tensions with the United States, both with the object of rebuilding economic growth. The chapter concludes, however, that none of these measures reflects a fundamental strategic change of direction on Xi's part. They appear to be primarily tactical in nature. Xi's underlying ideological mission on the power of the party and economic control remains intact.

Chapter 15 looks specifically at whether changes in China's foreign policy direction arising from the 2023 summit between President Biden and Xi Jinping are likely to be tactical or strategic. It examines the continued role of Marxist Nationalism in shaping foreign policy in an increasingly binary direction over time. The chapter concludes that the party's December 2023 Central Foreign Affairs Work Conference makes plain that Xi's long-term direction towards the United States and the reforming of the international system in a manner more compatible with Chinese interests is likely to continue unabated.

The book's final chapter looks at where Xi's ideological agenda may be headed in the decade of 2023–2032, and the implications of this agenda in building a new 'Marxism for the twenty-first century'—not just for China, but for the world. It analyses Xi's new directives on incorporating classical Chinese culture into the language and concepts of a modern 'Sinified' Marxism, in what he has called the 'second integration'. The chapter examines how Xi adapts core and compatible parts of the Chinese classical tradition into Marxism to try to future-proof the latter against the inevitable challenges of modernity. It speculates on whether this could lead to a future 'third integration' by then incorporating aspects of world cultures into the Marxist linguistic and conceptual lexicon. Both exercises would be designed to preserve Marxism as a robust ideological worldview for the long-term future, rather than succumbing to the rise and fall of individual civilizations, states, and belief systems. The chapter concludes with a description of the costs to China of Xi's sustained ideological enterprise—both economically and in its international standing—and argues that, despite internal disquiet about these costs, Xi will likely remain in power for the long term because of the formidable powers of the new surveillance state. It also examines the potential for the party, post-Xi, to eventually self-correct towards a more pragmatic and sustainable political equilibrium. In the meantime, navigating the Xi Jinping era through effective deterrence and diplomacy will remain the most critical and complex foreign and security policy challenge for the United States and its allies since the end of the Cold War.

Conclusion

The book's overall conclusion is that so long as Xi's ideological worldview holds fast, and his individual political authority remains unchallenged, the overall direction in the domestic and foreign policy changes we have seen during Xi's first decade in office are likely to be sustained during his second decade. This means that under Xi, it is highly unlikely that we will see further fundamental changes in China's overall policy direction. When policy changes do occur, they are more likely to be tactical rather than strategic—that is, short-term changes to navigate unanticipated obstacles lying in Beijing's path, rather than any deeper ideological reappraisal of the path itself. Indeed, Xi Jinping's 2023 formulation on the need for the party to undertake 'extreme scenario thinking' (*jixian siwei*), together with his long-standing injunction to the party to engage in 'struggle' for the party's and the country's future, indicates that Xi sees multiple obstacles ahead. But these formulations do not contemplate any change to Xi's fundamental ideological line: to re-entrench the power of the party within China, to check the growing power of the private sector, and to project Chinese national power in its region and the wider world to create an international order more compatible with the CCP's interests, values, and worldview. In short, under Xi Jinping at least, the ideological die appears to be well-and-truly cast.

2

Defining Core Concepts

In defining Xi Jinping's ideological worldview, as noted in the introductory chapter, I argue that he has moved Chinese politics to the Leninist left, taken the Chinese economy to the Marxist left, and also shifted China to the nationalist right through a more assertive foreign and national security policy. This raises a number of questions concerning core definitions, including critical terms such as 'ideology', 'worldview', 'Leninism', 'Marxism', 'nationalism', 'left', and 'right'. These definitions are important in order to be as clear as possible in our discussion on the actual content, direction, and significance of ideological change.

Defining 'Ideology'

A central assumption of this book is that ideological worldviews still matter for the CCP—not just as theoretical abstractions for the delectation of party intellectuals, but as a practical guide for officials in shaping or reflecting changes in policy direction in the real world. Indeed, this has been the case throughout CCP history both as a revolutionary party and national liberation movement prior to 1949 and subsequently as a political party in power defining its blueprints for 'national construction'. For example, Mao's ideological worldview on the role of permanent class struggle at home, permanent revolution abroad, and his theory of primary and secondary 'contradictions' were reflected in profound changes in real-world Chinese policy during the Great Leap Forward, the Cultural Revolution, his opposition to Soviet revisionism, and ultimately his strategic embrace of the United States. Similarly, Deng's repudiation of permanent class struggle and his formal embrace of the theory of the 'primary stage of socialism' provided the ideological underpinnings of nearly forty years of 'reform and opening' between 1978 and 2017. In similar vein, Xi's decision to revise Deng's redefinition of the party's 'major contradiction' at the 19th Party Congress in 2017 (away from unbridled reform to one which prioritized the 'imbalances' of reform) foreshadowed much of the change in the party's economic policy line since then—including the return of the state, the partial repudiation of the private sector, and the embrace of the 'common prosperity' agenda. In other words, deep shifts in formal ideological statements by the party and its leader have been used throughout the party's long history both to signal impending changes in policy direction on the ground and to reflect policy changes that have already occurred in order to afford them a level of theoretical legitimacy. Either way, ideological change is an important signalling device for changes in the political and policy world—be it ante-facto, post-facto, or both.[1]

This brings us to the question of how we define the term 'ideology' itself. There is a vast literature on the subject, to the point that political scientists and sociologists disagree on whether there can be any real definitional consensus on the core meaning of the term.[2] Indeed, as John Gerring noted caustically in his seminal 1997 study: "It has become customary to begin any discussion of ideology with some observation concerning its semantic promiscuity", adding that despite being "condemned time and again for its semantic excesses, for its bulbous unclarity, the concept of ideology remains, against all odds, a central term of social science discourse".[3] 'Ideology', as a term in its own right, first appears as *idéologie* during the French Revolution when it was introduced by A. L. C. Destutt de Tracy broadly to refer to the 'science of ideas'.[4] Its conceptual evolution during the nineteenth century, however, meant much more than simply being a passive analysis of the world as it was. It was, in addition, a systematic program for changing (or, by reverse logic, preserving) the world through political and social action, for good or for ill, as seen through the lens of a particular group or class. From one end of the spectrum, Napoleon in post-revolutionary France despised 'ideology', asserting that "states do not prosper by ideology",[5] arguing instead that the task of leadership lay in uniting all classes across a nation in a singular cause transcending ideological division. From a radically different tradition, Marx and Engels, in *The German Ideology*, used the term to refer to the distorted and delusional beliefs that capitalists and intellectuals held about society, rather than the 'objective' truth of its underlying injustice (a concept later Marxists would describe as 'false consciousness' and extend to the exploited classes' acceptance of their supposedly natural place in society).[6] While usages of the term continued to range from pejorative to more neutral representations of political belief systems, Max Weber and Karl Mannheim sustained and developed the Marxian argument that ideology represented systems of ideas that embodied class interests; that these interests were largely concealed; and that the task of sociology was to make clear what Mannheim called the actual "life conditions which produce ideologies".[7]

In contemporary social science, however, it is useful to return to Gerring's magisterial survey of the existing literature on ideology and his identification of seven core meaning-bearing elements of what can be meant by the term. These begin with what he identifies as an ideology's **location**: whether it is primarily 'located' in thought, language, or behaviour; and, despite the universal nexus between discourse and behaviour, whether thought nonetheless "remains ideology's central desideratum".[8] Second, it includes **the scope of its subject matter**: whether it is focussed narrowly on politics, which Gerring calls "the 'home turf' of ideology", or whether it refers to power more broadly as argued by Marx and his observation that "the distinction should always be made between the material transformation of the economic conditions of production . . . and the legal, political, religious, aesthetic, or philosophic—in short, ideological forms in which men become conscious of this conflict and fight it out".[9] Third, Gerring underlines the **subject** of an ideology and whether that is limited to a class, a group, or any groups or individuals combined. Gerring also emphasizes the dominant or subordinate **position** of that subject, and then the interest-based or non-interest-based **motivation** of the subject, in undertaking any given ideological enterprise. Gerring then outlines what he calls the **multifunctionality** of ideology, including its integrating, explanatory, motivational, and legitimizing functions, as well as what he describes as its 'repressing' function in preventing certain phenomena from being addressed because they lie outside the normative universe that ideology creates. Finally, Gerring deals at length with the **cognitive and affective structure** of ideology across multiple variants. These include logical hierarchy, internal coherence, and external contrast; abstraction, specificity, and sophistication; simplicity, facticity, and distortion; conviction, insincerity, and dogmatism; as well as the complex realms of consciousness and unconsciousness.[10] Gerring's stark and surprising conclusion from this exhaustive survey of the field is that the only universal, defining characteristics that can be discerned from the literature for the concept of ideology are internal coherence, external contrast, and consistency over time: "Ideology, at the very least, refers to a set of idea-elements that are bound together, that belong to one another in a non-random fashion . . . implying coherence vis-à-vis competing ideologies and . . . coherence through time."[11] Beyond this, Gerring argues that every other definition must be "context-specific . . . situated in a particular problem, region, time-period, and methodology". To this Gerring adds that, while "different definitions of ideology will be useful for different purposes", his seven-part framework nonetheless "establishes a uniform grid upon which one can identify, and hence compare, definitional choices".[12]

How then do we understand the concept of ideology within the particular epistemology, geography, history, and culture of contemporary China and the specific problems the CCP has sought to confront in its century-long organizational existence? Once again, there is significant literature on this subject,[13] although much of it is concentrated on the Mao and pre-Mao periods in the long decades before Deng Xiaoping's famous aphorism from 1979 that the time had come for the party to 'stop debating theory' (*bu zhenglun*).[14] The most comprehensive textual treatment, however, on the continuing significance of ideology and its meaning within the ideational and institutional universe of the CCP remains Franz Schurmann's defining work *Ideology and Organization in Communist China*.[15] Although written in 1968 at the height of the Cultural Revolution (some thirty years before Gerring's general survey), Schurmann's work remains the classic in the field of CCP theory, ideology, and political organization. If we apply Gerring's framework to Schurmann's general definition of ideology, we discover that Schurmann prioritizes three major aspects of Gerring's matrix: the interconnection between thought, language, and behaviour; the importance of motivational functionality; as well as the critical characteristics of internal and external coherence at the core of Gerring's definition. Accordingly, Schurmann states:

> We regard ideology as a manner of thinking characteristic of an organization. If organization is 'a rational instrument engineered to do a job', then the human beings who create and use it must do so on the basis of a set of ideas. **However abstract these may be, they must have action**

> **consequences, for the purpose of organization is action**. The more systematic organization becomes, the greater is the need for a systematic set of ideas to govern it. . . . Thus, ideologies which serve to create organization require a conscious conception of unity; they cannot rely on an underlying spiritual matrix to give unity to their ideas. Such ideologies achieve unity through systematization of their ideas. In fact, since real organization can rarely be fully systematized, it is often only in the realm of ideology that systematization is achieved.[16] (My emphasis)

Schurmann goes on to elaborate the processes by which an idea is translated into reality through what he describes as 'pure' and 'practical' ideology:

> Though such ideas ultimately give rise to action, the link between idea and action may be direct or indirect. Thus, the leaders of an organization may propound an idea, for example a policy, which they expect their followers to implement. Such an idea may be said to have 'one-to-one' action consequences. However, these same leaders may propound an idea which aims mainly at shaping the thinking of people, rather than producing immediate action. The former type of idea we may regard as 'practical', and the latter type of idea we may regard as 'pure'.[17]

I will return to Schurmann's definition of CCP ideology below, where we will see how he applied almost the full spectrum of Gerring's matrix of meaning in his rendering of Chinese Marxism-Leninism. But for our purposes here in settling on a useful general definition of the term 'ideology', I draw on Schurmann's elegant definition above. I argue, therefore, that ideology should be understood to be a systematic body of ideas that provides an organization with a defined unity of purpose, giving rise to a program of action, irrespective of whether those actions arise as a direct or indirect consequence of that body of ideas.

Defining 'Worldview'

In the West, the term 'worldview' comes from the German *Weltanschauung*, which was first used by Immanuel Kant in 1790 before undertaking its long conceptual evolution through G. W. F. Hegel, Søren Kierkegaard, Martin Heidegger, Marx and Engels, and Sigmund Freud.[18] For Kant, *Weltanschauung* meant simply our perception of the world as mediated by the senses.[19] Hegel took Kant's concept further by incorporating it into his idealist understanding of human progress through the dialectical processes of thesis, antithesis, and synthesis—all before progressing towards a common 'absolute good'. Hegel also conceived of different individual and national worldviews. Indeed, Hegelian concepts of worldview would later cause Richard Rorty to note that "the notion of alternative conceptual frameworks has been a commonplace in our culture since Hegel".[20] In other words, universal realities could be perceived through different individual or collective 'worldviews'—although in Hegel's idealist schema, these ultimately found common purpose through the 'dialectics' of historical and human progress.

It was the specific imprint of Hegel's concept of 'dialectics', as developed further by Marx and Engels in their theories of dialectical and historical materialism, that would eventually bring us to current Chinese Communist usages of the term 'worldview' (*shijieguan*). Major differences would emerge over the course of the nineteenth century between classically Kantian and Hegelian worldviews on the one hand, and those of Marx and Engels on the other. Both Kant and Hegel are generally categorized as 'idealist' in that their conceptualization of consciousness, reasoning, and ideation were considered 'a priori' to the material world. By contrast, Marx and Engels were decisively 'materialist', whereby matter not only preceded consciousness but also determined it. Furthermore, through Marx and Engels, the nature of dialectical thinking had also evolved from Hegel's earlier understandings. 'Dialectical materialism', given its absolute focus on human knowledge arising from human interaction with the physical world alone, replaced Hegel's much broader concept of 'dialectics', which embraced both idealist and materialist aspects of reality. 'Dialectical materialism', as a form of worldview in itself, became both a method of reasoning about the mechanisms of historical change and a means by which progressive material change could be accelerated through conscious political action.

Marx and Engels applied 'dialectical materialism' to real-world processes through a parallel concept of 'historical materialism'—the temporal framework through which the dynamics of dialectical materialism would play out. It was only through the dialectical dynamics of class struggle over the course of human history that progress would be achieved. For Marxists, 'dialectical materialism' became the 'scientific' machinery for all human progress, both in the physical sciences (including Darwinian evolution) and in the social sciences (including politics, sociology, and economics). In other words, dialectical and historical materialism combined became a comprehensive worldview embracing all domains of knowledge. It offered a scientific method of analysis to understand the causal relationships that existed within and between these different domains of knowledge. It also offered an understanding of how humans could act in order to advance historical processes, not simply to observe them. Furthermore, because of dialectical and historical materialism's claims to scientific universality and objectivity, its adherents rejected the possibility of alternative worldviews as inherently 'un-scientific' and therefore irrelevant to any legitimate debate on political consciousness, ideation, or action. As Marx himself famously observed: "The philosophers have only interpreted the world in various ways; whereas the point is to change it."[21] For Marx, the 'end-state' of this dialectical process of change, through the mechanism of class struggle, was a communist society in which all material human needs would be met sufficiently, equally, and without class exploitation.[22] And, to Marx and Engels, this was objectively true.

There are, therefore, several possible meanings that could be included in a working definition of 'worldview'. One approach is to see it primarily as a Marxist analytical methodology, drawing on the foundational disciplines of historical and dialectical materialism, the theory of opposites, and the use of struggle to achieve progress in the face of irreconcilable contradictions. Another approach is to focus instead on the actual analytical conclusions reached by the party on the nature of China's circumstances at a given time in history. A third approach is to focus on the party's optimal response to changing circumstances that the party concluded was analytically appropriate at a given time in history.

The definition of ideological 'worldview' I propose to adopt in this book seeks to embrace all three. Despite the sometimes impenetrable formalisms of Marxist epistemology and its Chinese ideological variants, how the CCP formally ideates its view of the world, and how the party communicates its political response to the world it so observes, actually matter. It provides us with insights into the inner world of ideological constraints and opportunities that confront a party that continues to describe itself as Marxist-Leninist. Furthermore, it offers insight into the party's changing ideological, political, and policy priorities over time. Where new conceptual language is deployed, particularly in a political and institutional culture that is notoriously conservative in its approach to politico-linguistic innovation, it invites us to examine what new realities it is seeking to describe.

Schurmann's study once again adds to our understanding of the necessary connection between ideas and action in his own explanation of the idea of 'worldview' and its relationship with the wider concept of ideology. According to Schurmann:

> A world view may give the individual a certain outlook, but it does not indicate to him how he should act. But principles of revolution and organization have action consequences. We shall therefore suggest that the two major components of Chinese Communist ideology are . . . pure ideology and practical ideology. Since this distinction also applies to ideologies of organization other than that of the Chinese Communists, we shall offer a general definition. Pure ideology is a set of ideas designed to give the individual a unified and conscious world view; practical ideology is a set of ideas designed to give the individual rational instruments for action. Let us illustrate this distinction by the example of an organization governed by Marxist ideology. The members of that organization will accept the view that all political and social conflict is basically class struggle. This view gives them a certain outlook through which they can put the complex phenomena of history and actuality into perspective; it does not, however, indicate to them how they should act. If that organization now adds the Leninist principle of the vanguard party to its ideology, it has acquired an instrument for organizational action. . . . Without pure ideology, the ideas of practical ideology have no legitimation. But without practical ideology, an organization cannot transform its *Weltanschauung* into consistent action.[23]

For our purposes here, China's ideological worldview should therefore be defined as the CCP's analytical methodology for understanding the world both at home and abroad and its conclusions about the changing nature of the world they face, including the range of strategic threats and opportunities they identify as a result of this analysis. It also includes their view on how the Chinese party and state should respond to these changing circumstances through political and policy action.

Defining 'Marxism', 'Leninism', and 'Moving to the Left'

The preceding discussion on the definitions of 'ideology' and 'worldviews' has already bled into the wider debates about useful definitions of Marxism and Leninism and the connection between ideation and action in Xi Jinping's China. Once again, there is extensive literature on both Chinese Marxism and Leninism offering a range of definitions for each.[24] Schurmann's early navigation of this complex definitional terrain has once again proven itself invaluable, particularly given the ideological divergences between Soviet and Chinese communism in the eighty years since the dissolution of the Communist International (Comintern) in 1943. Even leaving the Sino-Soviet split after 1959 to one side, there have been multiple Marxism-Leninisms in modern Chinese history, each coloured by the CCP's leadership configurations and party congresses over the last hundred years: Chen Duxiu in 1921; Qu Qiubai in 1932; Mao Zedong in 1942; the 7th Party Congress in 1945; the 8th Congress in 1956; the Anti-Rightist Movement, Great Leap Forward, and Cultural Revolution, which together spanned the tumultuous years between 1957 and 1976; Deng Xiaoping and the seminal ideological debates and resolutions between 1978 and 1982; and now Xi Jinping in the years since the 19th Congress in 2017. The complex question, therefore, is whether there are certain irreducible definitions of Marxism-Leninism that hold across the entire period, thereby offering a framework for understanding the nature of ideological change within it.

This task is made harder not just because of disruptive and sometimes violent changes in the party's political leadership that have resulted in dramatic lurches in the party's line. It is also because the CCP has seen itself as the conscious inheritors of a dynamic, rather than static, ideological tradition—one that is constantly seeking to adapt the enduring principles of Marxist-Leninist theory to the practical circumstances of the Chinese revolution and national construction. This deliberately dynamic approach to Marxism-Leninism is reflected in Mao's speech to the Yan'an Party School as early as 1942 when he stated that:

> Marxism-Leninism is the theory that Marx, Engels, Lenin, and Stalin created on the basis of actual fact, and it consists of general conclusions derived from historical and revolutionary experience. If we have only read this theory and have not used it as a basis for research in historical and revolutionary actuality, have not created a theory in accordance with China's real necessities, a theory that is our own and of a specific nature, then it would be irresponsible to call ourselves Marxist theoreticians.[25]

Eighty years later, in 2022, Xi Jinping made similar remarks at a Politburo Study Session on 'Adapting Marxism'. Xi stated:

> Marxism points the way for advancing human society. It is a powerful theoretical weapon for us to understand the world and its underlying trends, seek the truth, and change the world. Marxism is not a set of rigid dogmas, but a guide to action that must evolve as the situation changes. Whether Marxism can serve its guiding role depends on whether its basic tenets are adapted to the conditions in China and the features of the times. In a fast-changing world and a fast-growing country, we cannot be fettered to old conventions and rigid thinking, and we must be bold enough to update our theory. If we cannot answer questions concerning the present and future of China and its people and the wider world, we will lose momentum in advancing the cause of the Party and the country, Marxism will wither, and people will lose faith in it.[26]

Therefore, given the positive value the CCP has attached to ideological innovation for much of its history, we return to the question of defining the *irreducible elements* of Chinese Marxism that make up its essential, ideational canon and which have survived tumultuous political change. Based on the detailed studies of Schurmann and others[27] and drawing on the conclusions outlined in the earlier sections of this chapter, I argue that there are seven. First, Chinese Marxism represents a definitively materialist rather than idealist view of history, meaning that knowledge proceeds from human interaction with the material universe rather than any form of metaphysics. Second, this knowledge forms part of a consistent set of irresistible, scientific laws of development which apply across both the physical and social sciences. Third, one such set of universal laws is the theory of historical determinism of Marx and Engels, which ultimately sees a communist society emerge through immutable dialectical processes from the injustices of slave, feudal, capitalist, and even socialist societies. Fourth, the machinery of change in this process is dialectical materialism, based on the concept of the unity of opposites, the inter-permeation of phenomena, and the theory of contradiction. Fifth, within this framework of dialectical materialism, the law of contradictions operates when opposites (i.e. progressive and reactionary forces) collide, requiring resolution through either violent or non-violent struggle, depending on whether those contradictions are with 'the enemy' or among 'the people'. Sixth, these universal laws apply as much to contradictions between classes within a society as they do to contradictions between states of the capitalist and imperialist world, and between these states and the socialist world. Struggle is, therefore, universally applicable, both within states and between them. Finally, the various laws described above are both determinist and voluntarist—that is, although the irresistible forces of world history are propelling the world in this direction, the pace at which the world advances is also determined by the active political agency of individual and collective actors. As Schurmann noted of the CCP: "The essence of their theory or *Weltanschauung* is that, at all times, a manifest or latent polarization exists between progressive and reactionary social forces in the world."[28] To this he adds that the "central value of the pure ideology of the Chinese Communists is the notion of struggle" and "from this value has emerged the central idea of the thought of Mao Tse-tung", concluding that "this notion of struggle, however, has its roots in the basic *Weltanschauung* of the pure ideology of Marxism Leninism".[29]

This, of course, is where Leninism enters the ideological equation as the second major pillar of CCP ideology. Vladimir Lenin emphasized the role of a centralized, disciplined vanguard party to prevent the dictatorship of the proletariat being undermined or diluted by 'opportunists' taking advantage of diffuse power structures. As the Bolshevik leader wrote in 1917:

> We are not utopians, we do not indulge in 'dreams' of dispensing at once with all administration, with all subordination. . . . But the subordination must be to the armed vanguard of the exploited. . . . We shall establish strict, iron discipline supported by the state power of the armed workers, we shall reduce the role of state officials to that of simply carrying out our instructions.[30]

Chinese Leninism also holds that it is only through the agency of a vanguard party leading proletarian, peasant, and other progressive forces through the processes of struggle that human progress can be accelerated. A Leninist party is therefore defined as a political organization that applies the disciplines of historical and dialectical materialism, the theory of contradiction, and the targeting of political struggle, on the one hand, to the praxis of current, real-world circumstances, on the other. It therefore analyses where contradictions exist, whether they are major or minor, whether they are violent or non-violent, and what form of struggle is required in order to achieve resolution and progress. The Leninist party is also responsible for maintaining both ideological and organizational discipline within the party so that revolution at home and abroad can be achieved without internal political dissolution, or through deviation from the agreed ideological line. These form the core tenets of Chinese Leninism. As Schurmann has noted:

> Lenin created a practical ideology for the revolutionary movements leading to the creation of the world's Communist parties by propounding principles of organization derived from the application of Marxist theory to the problems of contemporary reality. The Chinese Communists have gone further by developing a practical ideology based on Leninism but enriched by their long experiences in revolutionary struggle.[31]

Schurmann was also absorbed, unlike any other specialist in Chinese elite politics, with defining further the actual processes of transmutation of Marxist ideation into the actions of a Leninist party. This is particularly relevant to this study of Xi Jinping and the relationships between ideological direction and political and policy action. As noted above, Schurmann had observed that "without pure ideology [i.e. elucidated through Marxism], the ideas of practical ideology [i.e. delivered through Leninism] have no legitimation. But without practical ideology, an organisation cannot transform its *Weltanschauung* into consistent action".[32] This transmission process is achieved not only through the general functions of language, cognition, and a form of inner conversion of the party adherent, but also through the particular intellectual discipline of dialectical analysis. It is this discipline (dialectics, contradiction, and struggle) that Schurmann identifies as the essential intellectual machinery linking cognition, emotion, morality, language, and finally action. For the purposes of this study of Xi's ideology as a guide to action in the real world, it is worth quoting Schurmann at some length:

> Ideas are formulated thoughts expressed in a particular language. The ideas set forth in the Party rules are formulated in the language of Marxism-Leninism. They are like the differently shaped parts of a machine. Each idea is different, but is shaped by a uniform language. Together, these ideas constitute the structure of the ideology. Some students of the Chinese Communists often speak of their 'ideology' as being the cause of a particular policy. In such a case, they implicitly regard ideology as a whole machine, seen only from the outside, and performing some task. How the machine works in the inside is not taken into consideration. Other students of the Chinese Communists go deeper, focus on the formal ideas, and describe their shapes; they look at the parts of the machine. Such an approach may be described as exegesis. . . . Yet, neither of these approaches tells us how the different parts function with each other, how they move within the ideology to produce a particular effect. In short, these approaches do not reveal the manner of thinking to which the ideology gives rise. . . .

> Only by seeing how these abstract ideas are transformed into concrete action can one begin to perceive the manner of thinking. In a machine, a few parts have central significance. So in ideology: there are ideas which give a certain energy to all the other ideas with which they come in contact. . . .
> The moving threads that go through all these writings can be said to constitute the central ideas of the ideology.[33]

According to Schurmann, central to this is the "dialectical conception of Chinese society" which describes "the manner of ideological thinking most characteristic of the Chinese Communists, that is to say how formal ideas are combined with central ideas to produce an analysis of concrete reality with action consequences".[34]

Based on these definitions of Chinese Marxism and Leninism, it is also important to define what I mean by 'moving to the left' as a way of describing the nature of ideological change under Xi. As with the terms 'ideology' and 'worldview', 'left' and 'right' have also been defining features of Western political discourse since the French Revolution. 'Left' and 'right' originally referred to seating positions in the National Constituent Assembly of 1789 in relation to the president—those to the right being in defence of the monarchy, the aristocracy, the church, and the political status quo; the left being advocates of reform, revolution, and 'movement'.[35] While the fault lines between left and right within modern political systems have evolved significantly over the last two centuries, Andrew Nathan and Tianjian Shi in their studies of Western (and separately Chinese) understandings of these terms argue that "two issues have dominated the ideological space of the West: the role of the state and the conflicting norms of equality and achievement in the distribution of goods",[36] and that while the "Left generally favors more government intervention in the economy and more-egalitarian income distribution; the Right typically stands for relative freedom of private enterprise from state intervention and toleration of higher levels of income inequality".[37] Nathan and Shi acknowledge that these differences have even deeper historical origins, citing earlier analysis by Lipset and Rokkan that "the political cleavages embodied in modern European party systems crystallized the results of four major historical struggles: between center and periphery, church and state, town and country, and owners and workers".[38]

Importantly, Nathan and Shi also go to the underlying class interests of the political constituencies of the left and right:

> Members of different social groups have different economic and other interests, which partly determine their positions on the ideological spectrum. Attitudes on the left tend to be preferred by the working class, urban residents, young people, and members of minority ethnic and religious groups, because they are dissatisfied with their share of benefits in society and think they would be better off if the state intervened to redistribute resources. People who are more satisfied (or less dissatisfied) with the status quo tend to take a more conservative stance toward government activism, social change, and redistribution. In Western societies these groups usually include white-collar workers, suburbanites, middle-aged people and members of dominant ethnic and religious groups.[39]

The importation of concepts of 'left' and 'right' into China's political vocabulary came through the ideas of democracy, social democracy, Marxism-Leninism, and later fascism during the first three decades of the twentieth century.[40] In imperial times, 'left' and 'right' had no particular political significance, as Li Honglin, a former leading theoretician from the CCP Central Propaganda Department, has observed of earlier usages:

> Unlike its definition in contemporary Chinese politics, 'left' in ancient times was despised, whereas 'right' was respected. 'Right' was superior and 'left' was inferior. To say a person was intelligent, one would use the phrase 'no one is more to the right than he'. 'Being moved to the left' meant a downward move for an official.[41]

Li also observes that these traditional uses were turned on their head during the Communist period as cadres, focussing on the art of CCP political survival, reflected the "famous dictum [that] says 'left' is *always* better than 'right' ".[42] Indeed, within the political universe of the CCP, Mao's ideological position on left and right was clear. His definition of 'left' extended to those who stood on the side of revolutionary progress, as opposed to conservative reactionaries of the right who defended the status quo. Class struggle would always be fought against the right, either capitalists at home, or capitalist imperialists abroad. Mao's concept of permanent revolution also meant that those designated as 'right' would evolve over time—from landlords and bureaucratic capitalists outside the party, to capitalist roaders within the party, to right-wing deviationists in the Soviet Union. Meanwhile, within the left, those who got too far out ahead of historical trends could be designated as 'ultra-left', 'left dogmatists', or even 'left opportunists'. Of course, Mao sat permanently in the middle.

Party history became, therefore, an immensely complex process. Different periods of the revolution and post-1949 construction were designated by successive party congresses as belonging to different points across the left-right spectrum. Mao, for example, conducted a twenty-year campaign from the 8th Party Congress in 1956 to the end of the Cultural Revolution championing the left and attacking the right (including Liu Shaoqi, Chen Yun, and Deng Xiaoping) while also authorizing a national propaganda campaign against his onetime designated successor Lin Biao as a 'left opportunist'.[43] Following Deng's rehabilitation, the 6th Plenum of the 11th Central Committee in 1981 concluded through 'A Resolution on Certain Questions in Party History' that this entire twenty-year period from 1957 to 1976 instead represented a disaster for both party and people because Mao had committed a series of 'extreme left errors'.[44] Importantly, as we will see in chapter 12, Xi Jinping's revisitation of the 1981 resolution in his own 2021 historical resolution sought to strike something of a balance between Mao and Deng. He declined in 2021 to explicitly repeat the attacks on Mao made in the 1981 resolution, while at the same time barely mentioning Deng's achievements throughout the decades of reform and opening in between. In fact, Xi studiously avoids the terms 'left' and 'right', implying, like Mao in an earlier period, that Xi Jinping Thought now constitutes the new ideological *Zhong Yong*, or 'Golden Mean', between left and right—or perhaps even transcending them.[45]

This history of use and abuse of the terms 'left' and 'right' throughout decades of internal party debates could lead to the conclusion that they are simply terms of factional convenience used to denigrate vanquished political opponents. But this overlooks the fact that there is also a body of meaning that lies beneath each of these terms, which has been moulded through the party's internal ideological discourse over the decades. In CCP history, 'left' and 'right' as political labels have been shaped around several recurring, core issues within the party's debates over more than a century. Principal among these are: the scope of the dictatorship of the proletariat; the dangers of bourgeois liberalism and democracy; the primacy and permanency of class struggle; the centrality of the relations of production over the factors of production; the importance of equality and inequality; deep questions of the periodization of party history, including the primary stage of socialism; the socialist law of value; the socialist market economy; the relative roles of the party, the government, and the state; and the legitimacy of supporting world-wide revolution beyond China's borders. In other words, the ideological epithets of 'left' and 'right' are therefore not simply hollow phrases designed for prosecutorial purposes and devoid of substantive meaning. Indeed, throughout party history, they have been both tools of intra-party politics as well as means of expressing real-world ideational, political, and policy divergence.

These high debates among party elites on political ideology have, over many decades, also translated into more widely held positions across Chinese society. Notions of 'left' and 'right', often re-rendered as 'conservative' and 'liberal', have, as a result, developed broader societal meanings as well. These are reflected in the remarkable survey work undertaken by Nathan and Shi in 1990 which tested underlying social attitudes on questions such as democracy, reform, and equality.[46] Although this study demonstrates significant variations between Western and Chinese definitions of ideational cleavages within contemporary societies, there were also significant convergences on questions concerning calls for greater government intervention to overcome socio-economic inequality. For example, as Nathan and Shi observe:

> . . . the [Chinese] Economic Welfare Agenda resembled the agenda of the Western Left. It was also 'left' in the Chinese context—or 'conservative' according to the label reversal common in postsocialist and reforming socialist countries—in the sense that it ran counter to the reform effort to reduce direct government participation in the economy and to create more autonomous enterprises operating under market conditions.[47]

Similar findings are evident in later Chinese social attitudes surveys analysed by Jennifer Pan and Yiqing Xu in 2015. Once again, attitudinal cleavages within society fell along similar fault lines as they did back in 1990. Of broader relevance to this book, the later surveys—taken in the early years of Xi's rule—also indicated that nationalism was beginning to produce similar deep resonances within overall Chinese political sentiment. As the authors note:

> The configuration of preferences across different issues reflects known debates and falls along the following dimensions: (i) preference for authoritarian institutions and conservative political values versus preference for democratic institutions and liberal political values, (ii) preference for pro-market economic policies and non-traditional social values versus preference for state intervention in the economy and traditional social values, and (iii) preference for nationalism. We find that respondents' estimated latent traits

> in the three dimensions are highly correlated with one another, and we refer to these highly correlated latent traits as 'China's ideological spectrum'.[48]

For these reasons, I argue that concepts of 'left' and 'right' still have broadly defined sets of meanings that continue to offer useful definitions of basic dividing lines in Chinese politics, political economy, and even nationalism. In politics, I define Xi's move to the Leninist left as the reassertion of the centrality of the party over everything, the concentration of Xi's personal political control within the party, and the reification of ideology itself as a disciplinary mechanism to reinforce party control. I also argue that this movement to the left has been evidenced across numerous specific, albeit inter-related, political domains. The main organizing principle across all these has been Xi's unapologetic reinvention of a disciplined, Leninist party as the irreplaceable political machinery lying at the heart of the Chinese military, state, and nation. For Xi, the party has become indispensable in the realization of his overriding ideological and national mission. And the core of this renewed party mission has become the creation of a more equitable Marxist society at home and a more powerful Chinese state to advance the party's interests abroad.

As for China's political economy, where I argue there has also been a move towards the Marxist left, I define 'left' as meaning:

- greater ideological justification to intervene in the economy to correct 'imbalances' delivered by the era of reform and opening;
- greater powers of economic policy direction being relocated to the party over the technical apparatus of the Chinese state;
- a greater role for state industrial policy in the allocation of resources as opposed to the market;
- an expanded role for SOEs and a diminished autonomy for the private sector; and
- a large-scale, unfolding agenda on income redistribution to deal with inequality.

Furthermore, this trend towards the Marxist left in overall economic policy settings parallels the adjustment in the party's overall political ideology to the Leninist left as described above. Indeed, both these ideological shifts are brought together in Xi's decision at the 19th Party Congress to launch a 'new era' in both politics and the economy and the general reassertion of the power of the party overall. In all this, Xi's party is now the unassailable, ideological centre of all significant public policy, including the domestic machinery of political control, the overall direction of economic policy, and the future course of foreign policy. And in all three domains, we also see the deep preferencing of ideological and political loyalty over technical policy expertise in the appointment of critical personnel. In Mao's China, it was essential to be 'red' rather than 'expert'. In Deng's China, it was important to be 'expert' above being 'red'. In Xi's China, it is once again important to be 'red' at least as much as being 'expert', if not more-so. These are significant changes.

Defining 'Nationalism', 'Moving to the Right', and 'National Assertiveness'

The third dimension of Xi Jinping's overall ideological revolution identified in this book is that he has deliberately moved Chinese nationalism to the right—and that this has been reflected through a much more assertive foreign and national security policy. Each of these three core concepts ('nationalism', 'moving to the right', and 'assertiveness') therefore requires definition. While political science and international relations theory once again offer a vast literature on each of these subjects, there is some degree of consensus on the critical meanings associated with each.

As Andrew Chubb noted in his examination of the relationship between Chinese nationalism and the country's changing policy and posture in the South China Sea, "the word nationalism describes an unwieldy array of social phenomena; for political scientists, the range of usages within academic works on the subject can be 'annoyingly wide' ".[49] Despite this unwieldiness, Jessica Chen Weiss, in her analysis of contemporary Chinese nationalism, accepts Ernst Haas's general definition of nationalism as an ideology that makes "assertions about the nation's claim to historical uniqueness, to the territory that the nation-state ought to occupy, and to the kinds of relations that should prevail between one's nation and others".[50] I agree with Alistair Iain Johnston's general definition that "nationalism is a complex, multidimensional set of sentiments" that "includes basic favorable attitudes toward the national in-group, but it also includes a more nativist element that is strongly attached to country and territory and that denigrates outsiders" and is further "associated with worldviews that are sensitive to relative gains over out-groups".[51]

In China's case, nationalism has taken multiple forms since the collapse of the Qing in 1911. As Weiss again observes: "There is no single Chinese nationalism, with distinct and competing visions articulated by state propaganda, liberal and conservative intellectuals, and grassroots activists, making it all the more difficult for the Chinese Communist Party to harness nationalism in support of its rule."[52]

Indeed, the literature on Chinese nationalism, both in the Communist and pre-Communist periods, generally divides into two schools of analysis—one focussing on 'populist', 'bottom-up', or 'genuine' nationalist sentiment; the second on 'elite', 'top-down' nationalist narratives manufactured by the leadership itself. Populist nationalism is defined by Chubb as "public actions or sentiments favouring more assertive foreign policy actions".[53] Such nationalism has been measured in the past using various opinion polls, such as the Beijing Area Study cited by Iain Johnston. Johnston's findings, over eleven separate surveys using a constant set of questions on different aspects of nationalist sentiment between 1998 and 2015, were "that there has not been a continuously rising level of nationalism among the survey respondents" and, "indeed, most indicators show a decline in levels of nationalism since around 2009".[54] Johnston emphasizes, however, that this survey data did not set out to test the levels of 'elite nationalism' over the same period—that is, the efforts of the Communist leadership to instil nationalist sentiment, the purposes for which the leadership sought to do this, or the effectiveness of those efforts. Johnston also concedes that this survey series "does not represent the final word on rising Chinese nationalism" and only represents "a starting point for the more systematic analysis of Chinese nationalism across time".[55]

My principal concern in examining China's changing official worldview under Xi Jinping is what the Communist Party leadership has sought to do at the elite level through nationalist ideology, propaganda, and political messaging. It is, however, much more difficult to assess the effect these elite-driven nationalist campaigns are having in shaping the views of China's citizenry. Presumably, this is because of the party's overall tighter political control and reduced academic freedom, particularly in sensitive areas of collaboration with foreign universities such as domestic opinion polling. What we do know, however, is that the party invests considerable time, resources, and high-level political attention to these campaigns and the ideological language used within them. This is because they are judged to be useful in consolidating popular support for the regime and its overall policy direction. If they were not considered effective, it is unlikely they would be continued. Indeed, Yan Xuetong, a leading Chinese international relations scholar at Tsinghua University, has reported with some alarm the increasingly nationalist worldview of young people attending Chinese elite universities today. Although Yan does not directly attribute these attitudes to the impact of elite campaigns, he does lay responsibility at the feet of officially sanctioned social media influencers for shaping the international views of the first generation of students who have come to adulthood under Xi:

> According to Yan, post-00s college students tend to have a strong sense of superiority and self-confidence, often view other countries with a 'condescending' mentality and view international affairs with a 'wish mentality', believing that China can easily achieve its foreign policy goals. They often look at the world in a dichotomy between China and foreign countries, regard other countries except China as the same kind of countries, regard universal human values such as peace, morality, fairness and justice as unique traditions of China, and think that only China is just and innocent, other countries, especially western countries, are 'evil', and westerners have a natural hatred for China.[56]

As noted above, however, the focus of this book is the ideological content of China's elite nationalist discourse during the Xi Jinping period. This is to determine whether there has been a change in the content, intensity, and relative significance of the party's band of nationalist meaning when compared with Xi's post-Mao predecessors. The CCP argues, of course, that embracing a positive 'patriotism' (*aiguozhuyi*) about China's future cannot be equated with narrower and negative forms of 'nationalism' (*guojiazhuyi*) focussed on China's perceived superiority in relation to others. Or as Zhou Enlai put in the earliest years of the People's Republic, "socialist patriotism is not narrow nationalism; rather it is patriotism that inspires national confidence but is enlightened by internationalism".[57] Nonetheless, the sustained negative references to America, Japan and 'the West' in more recent Chinese mass nationalist campaigns tend to suggest otherwise.

In this book, I argue that Chinese nationalism has 'moved to the right'. By this, I mean that Xi Jinping has used the language and imagery of China's growing power, prestige, and perceived cultural preeminence to validate new forms of international action in pursuit of specifically defined national interests and values. Under this definition, 'moving to the right' does not necessarily mean any nationalist intention to acquire foreign territory in the tradition of European imperialism, German fascism, or Russo-Soviet claims to Eurasian hegemony. It does, however, include the possibility of a revisionist approach to the return of disputed territories to Chinese sovereignty, the reassertion of Chinese power after 'a century of foreign humiliation', and, more broadly, the rejection of various elements of the existing international order perceived to be hostile to Chinese national interests, values, and identity.

This definition also stands in contrast to the Chinese nationalism of the 1950s and 1960s which Mao had taken 'to the left'. In that period, Mao advanced an interventionist agenda abroad in pursuit of a worldwide Marxist-Leninist revolution, while doing so proudly in the name of China's own national revolution. By contrast, Xi's nationalism is sui generis—it differs significantly from the forms of defensive nationalism often found in the Deng-Jiang-Hu era, but neither is it a simple reprise of Mao-type revolutionary nationalism. Although the nationalist component of Xi's overall ideological worldview is clearly driven by a number of revisionist ambitions from 'the right', there is also evidence of a number of residual Marxist-Leninist concepts. These are further reinforced by certain classical Chinese ideations of the 'Middle Kingdom', all combined in an eclectic vision of a form of future Chinese-led international order. In other words, Chinese nationalism under Xi is emerging as a composite of three inter-connected traditions. It evidences: a nationalist-revisionist core; a Marxist, historically determinist rationale concerning the inevitable collapse of the international capitalist order led by the United States; while also wrapping itself in the classical garmentry of universal Confucian values, *Tianxia*, and other forms of more ancient Sino-centrism.[58]

One further concept requiring definition for the purposes of chapters 9, 10, and 11 is the idea of 'assertiveness'. If, as I argue, the ideological content of party-driven elite nationalism under Xi Jinping has moved to the right, then the next question is whether this new nationalist posture has been reflected in the real world of Chinese foreign and security policy. In other words, have Beijing's declaratory language and foreign policy actions in the outside world become more 'assertive' in response to Xi's new nationalist narrative at home? Here I support Nien-Chung Chang Liao's endorsement of Narizny's definition of 'assertiveness' as "a level of activism in a state's foreign policy that involves a state's 'willingness to pay the costs, whatever they may be, for a particular strategy'".[59] On the substantive question of whether Xi's external policy has in fact been more activist, risk-taking, and therefore 'assertive' than his post-Mao predecessors, I agree with Swaine, Womack, Christensen, Liao, and Doshi that China's level of international assertiveness increased after 2009 compared with the previous norm.[60] Where I disagree with this '2009 assertiveness consensus' argument, however, is that I believe the evidence points to China's having become significantly more activist and assertive in its international behaviours across the board under Xi after 2013. In other words, there has been a radical sharpening in the trajectory of China's real-world international assertiveness under Xi, and this has mirrored the intensification of Xi's domestic ideological narrative on Chinese nationalism.

Conclusion

Beyond these definitions of critical ideas, concepts, and terms, one further question that remains for the rest of this book to deal with is: what core function does Xi's Marxist-Nationalist ideology actually perform within the overall political ecosystem of the CCP? I have argued that throughout its history, the party has always taken ideology seriously. But this does not answer the more fundamental question of why this is so.

One possibility, of course, is that Marxist-Leninist ideology is little more than an intellectual parlour game played among party elites, completely detached from political and policy reality. Under this view, the principal objective is simply to preserve the CCP's moral legitimacy as a movement aimed at changing China and the world for the benefit of ordinary people everywhere. But this would render Marxism-Leninism as relevant to the real world today as the medieval Scholastics were to early Christian Europe. In other words, the mysterious, anonymous, and immutable forces of historical change, as deciphered through the secret (but somehow scientific) codes of Hegelian dialectics, take us in the same metaphysical direction as Thomas Aquinas calculating the numbers of angels dancing on the end of a pin.[61] Alternatively, is the underlying utilitarian purpose of CCP ideology simply to maintain a level of intellectual, and therefore organizational, coherence for the party, militating against the inevitability of institutional entropy and decline? Or is ideology instead, as indicated earlier in this chapter, primarily a rhetorical device for dealing with political opponents on the right or left? Or is it really an analytical framework and conceptual methodology for interpreting the world 'as it objectively is', as Marxist-Leninists formally claim it to be? And, if so, what does that world really look like and what real-world measures should be embraced to change it?

This book rests unapologetically on this latter proposition, namely that Xi's Marxist-Leninist Nationalism is actually believed. It is not just cynically seen as a convenient intellectual fiction to hold the party together and to define its enemies both within and without. Indeed, it is this level of apparent belief that makes Xi such a potent challenge to the United States and the rest of the West. I will seek to substantiate this argument on the core role of ideology in the three major sections of the book that follow—dealing respectively with Xi's changes to Chinese Leninism, Marxism, and nationalism and their interconnection with the real world of Chinese policy. As noted in the previous chapter, it is not argued that ideology is the exclusive driver of political and policy change under Xi. Suffice it to say here, however, that the sheer volume of time, energy, and effort expended by Xi and those around him on their monumental ideological project of Marxist Nationalism—particularly when compared with the combined ideological efforts of his three post-Mao predecessors—suggests that ideology under Xi means considerably more than a simple exercise in theoretical formalism. Indeed, the intensity of this effort alone tells us that ideology does have real-world political and policy resonance in Xi Jinping's China. Otherwise, Xi could reasonably have been expected to use his limited time and political resources elsewhere, given the competing, practical demands he faces in his day-to-day statecraft in these most challenging of times.

3

Continuity and Change in Chinese Worldviews

An Historical Survey

This chapter provides a brief survey of various Chinese ideational or ideological worldviews that have prevailed at different times in the country's history. Xi Jinping does not live, work, and think in an historical or conceptual vacuum. His own views of domestic and international reality are shaped by the ideational world he has inherited. Therefore, understanding previous worldviews, from both the pre-Communist and Communist periods of Chinese history, is important in interpreting what has changed under Xi Jinping and what has remained constant. In fact, in crafting his own ideological worldview, Xi draws on two principal sources: first, China's classical traditions of political philosophy and practical statecraft that developed over many centuries to deal with the ever-recurring challenges of Chinese governance; and second, arriving in China only a century ago, the complex intellectual universe of Marxism-Leninism, including its application to the practical needs of the CCP's revolution. Xi's worldview incorporates an eclectic mix of both traditions. From the classical tradition, we see the conceptual resonances of the ancient Chinese 'realism' of the Legalist school, an increasingly nationalistic, Sino-centric worldview derived from *Tianxia* ('All under Heaven'), together with a neo-tributary state framework on China's historical expectations of its economic and political relationships with its neighbours.[1] From Marxism-Leninism—as we began to explore in the previous chapter—we see the ideological imprint of the party's central role in bringing about profound domestic revolution across Chinese politics, society, and the economy, and creating a wealthy and powerful state capable of asserting China's influence in the world. For Xi's Communist Party, both ideological inheritances—ancient and modern—are relevant to how the party interprets its domestic and foreign policy circumstances, and how the party should best respond.

The Impact of the Classical Tradition on Contemporary Chinese Worldviews

'*Tianxia*' or 'All under Heaven'

The impact of different classical traditions of Chinese strategic and military thought on the worldviews of subsequent generations of Chinese political leaders has been profound. One of the earliest understandings of a Chinese worldview is embodied in the universalist idea of '*Tianxia*', or literally 'All under Heaven'. This emerged from the mythical, literary, and philosophical traditions associated with China's earliest dynasties, the Xia, Shang, and Western Zhou, which governed between 2070 BC and 722 BC. The Chinese emperor, or 'Son of Heaven' (*Tianzi*), presided over 'all that was under Heaven', given that he was uniquely equipped to maintain the cosmological balance necessary between earth below and Heaven above, thus ensuring political and social harmony among men. As John King Fairbank observed in his account, *The Chinese World Order*, the Son of Heaven "became in theory omnicompetent, functioning as military leader, administrator, judge, high priest, philosophical sage, arbiter of taste, patron of arts and letters, all in one".[2] The Son of Heaven also possessed 'the Mandate of Heaven' (*Tianming*) to discharge these functions, although Heaven's mandate might be withdrawn if the emperor failed to execute his responsibilities properly, at least as defined in the classical Confucian texts of Chinese governance. Even worse, a failure to satisfy Heaven would result in a collapse of order, the manifestation of 'chaos', or '*luan*', the fall of the emperor, and even the collapse of the dynasty itself. These principles would become deeply embedded across Chinese political elites for millennia, often expressed as 'domestic chaos and foreign disaster' (*neiluan waihuan*)—a fate to be avoided at all costs. Internal disorder was seen in the classical tradition as opening the door to external threat, a potent and recurring combination throughout Chinese history, sometimes culminating in the extinguishment of the Han state altogether and its temporary replacement by a barbarian dynasty.[3] Or as Fairbank pithily observed: "China's external order was so closely related to her internal order that one could not long survive without the other."[4]

This brings us to the critical question of the intended geographical scope of 'all under Heaven' and its implications for what was understood to be the 'Middle Kingdom', or the 'central kingdoms' (*zhongguo*). The term 'central kingdoms' first appeared in the Western Zhou dynasty (c. 1046–771 BC), referring to political entities and ethnic groups along the Yellow River Valley who would later be classified as 'Han'. The 'central kingdoms' were therefore narrower in scope than the all-encompassing '*Tianxia*' which, by definition, knew no boundaries. Beyond these central kingdoms, however, lay the lands of the 'barbarians'. One of the wonders of classical China is its remarkable capacity for a taxonomy for almost everything, matched by an equal capacity for enumerating the permutations and combinations of each category so defined. This also applied to the conceptualization of the various ranks of 'barbarians', or '*yi*'. From as early as the Western Zhou, there are records of the distinction between the civilized lands of the central kingdoms, and the lands of the 'four barbarians'—eastern, southern, western, and northern. By the Han, these had expanded to become the 'nine barbarians', with the names of individual tribes used to specify groups well beyond simply the cardinal points of the compass. Yet in China's always-complex schemata of the world, some barbarians were deemed more barbarian than others. During the first millennium BC, the ever-creative Chinese bureaucratic mind began marking out areas or zones radiating out from the central kingdoms—at first five, later nine, but broadly categorized as either 'inner' or 'outer' barbarian areas.[5] Fairbank's distillation of the complexity of this emerging Sino-centric world is that it developed as a series of broadly concentric circles, beginning with the Han cultural core at the centre; then the 'Sinic' cultures of latter-day Korea, Vietnam, the Ryukyus (and, episodically, Japan); followed by the 'inner' barbarians made up of Tibetans to the west and Mongols, Manchus, and Uyghurs to the north; before finally reaching the 'outer' barbarians beyond the seas with whom the centre had much less contact.[6]

This may seem esoteric, but these classical categorizations have a continuing resonance in modern Chinese worldviews, most particularly as they relate to China's political and cultural expectations of its nearer neighbours. In classical times, these expectations and the assumptions on which they were based were relatively clear. First, the Son of Heaven saw his temporal domain as like the never-ending ripple of a pebble in a pond, unconstrained by the boundaries of anything approximating a modern state. Second, the Middle Kingdom was culturally superior to both the Sinic and barbarian worlds beyond the centre. Third, others could approach the centre and be enhanced, even *transformed*, by their exposure to Chinese culture through a process of *laihua*, literally 'coming to China'. Fourth, most of these groups would be welcomed to bring tribute to the emperor and then perhaps to regularize trade, having first paid appropriate obeisance (the 'tributary state system' as it operated in the middle-to-late imperial period is outlined in greater detail below). For any who violated the protocols of engagement with the centre, the official commentaries are clear on what was expected of the Son of Heaven: "When any of the wild tribes, south, east, west, or north, do not obey the king's commands, and by their dissoluteness and drunkenness are violating all the duties of society, the king gives command to attack them."[7] Most important, the Chinese emperor saw his external political relationships with the world beyond the Middle Kingdom as a logical, hierarchical extension of the internal social hierarchies within China itself. Therefore, in the perfect ideational worldview of the imperial Chinese court, if you were the 'Son of Heaven' and your domain was 'all under Heaven', by definition the throne lay at the apex of both these worlds—foreign and domestic. Indeed, one social and political order folded almost seamlessly into the other. Although the real world would turn out differently—particularly at times of dynastic weakness, failure, and collapse—the Sino-centrism inherent to this worldview would continue to reverberate well into modern times.

One classical aphorism that is consistent with *Tianxia*—and one that Xi Jinping has repeatedly cited when addressing foreign audiences[8]—is: "Where there is a common aspiration, no distance, whether of mountains or seas, is too far" (*zhihezhe, buyi shanhai weiyuan*). This sentence is borrowed from Ge Hong, a fourth-century scholar of the Jin Dynasty. It conveys the idea that, within the framework of 'all under Heaven', the central kingdoms would be willing to cooperate with parts of the world that shared a similar worldview. It was the Son of Heaven, however, who remained at the apex of this system.

Strategic Realism in the Classical Chinese Worldview

China as a unified, centralized state presented problems for its rulers that were measurably different to those of their political predecessors prior to

Chinese unification under the Qin Dynasty in 221 BC. Before unification, China, for five hundred years during the 'Spring and Autumn' and 'Warring States' periods (722–221 BC), had been divided into multiple independent kingdoms spread across much of what we now call northern China. This period saw an explosion in philosophical discourse including the emergence of China's three major indigenous schools of thought: Confucianism, Daoism, and Legalism. In significant part, these dealt with the practical demands of domestic statecraft, as well as complex codes of morality for individuals navigating their relationships with their families, their communities, and the state. At the same time, there also emerged a body of tactical and strategic literature to help monarchs and their officials prevail in the essential business of state survival.[9] This great literary and philosophical outpouring occurred in a period of rolling military campaigns between the kingdoms, culminating in all-out warfare among the seven remaining states of the 'Warring States' period, eventually resulting in the triumph of the Qin.

China's first emperor, Qin Shihuang, drew on the realist strategic tradition espoused in the seven military classics, many of which were already available by the time of unification. Qin Shihuang's achievement in unifying the nation would become an abiding narrative across two millennia of official history: that emperors who united the country were good, whereas those who let it fall apart were to be despised. Importantly, in the Communist period, Mao Zedong would laud the Qin emperor on his achievements, both in national unification, as well as his relentless, authoritarian approach to domestic administration.[10] Reflecting on Qin Shihuang's infamous decision to bury alive hundreds of dissenting Confucian scholars, Mao boasted in 1958, "we surpass him 100 times"![11] As early as the 1930s, Mao candidly stated that he intended to rule China as "Marx plus Qin Shihuang".[12] He came to lament that his own party had split between those who valued the emperor's authoritarian achievements in uniting and strengthening the country, and those weaklings who shunned his legacy.[13]

These classical texts on Chinese strategic and military realism, and the Legalist philosophical school of which they were part, have had a profound impact on the worldviews of subsequent generations of Chinese political leaders. They have regularly been referenced when addressing the core thematics of state power, state survival, and the prevention and conduct of war. They form part of what Alistair Iain Johnston aptly described as

"China's strategic culture" in his seminal work, *Cultural Realism*.[14] While some may contest whether a country's 'strategic culture' can strictly be equated with its 'worldview', as Rod MacFarquhar pointedly observed: "the Chinese are no less concerned with the use of military power than any other civilization—a point that scholars have traditionally disputed because . . . they misread the Chinese classics."[15] The same applies to the modern era. Indeed, as early as the Yan'an period (1935–1947), when the Communist Party was still fighting for its long-term survival, Mao instructed his lieutenants to investigate how the principles of Marxist dialectics could be applied to the Chinese military classics and the disciplines of modern military science.[16] Chinese leaders across the centuries have accepted an axiomatic link between China's classical worldview and the enduring business of state power and state survival. This applied as much to the tributary state system of the later imperial period as to the tumultuous politics of the first half of the twentieth century and beyond.

A related aphorism used repeatedly by Xi Jinping in his public remarks[17] is: "The one who stands alone finds it difficult to rise, while those who move together find it easy to advance" (*gujuzhe nanqi, zhongxingzhe yiqu*). Appropriated from Wei Yuan, a nineteenth-century scholar of the Qing Dynasty, this sentence carries a dual meaning. The first is that a great leader should perform his duties properly to lead smaller countries (including 'barbarians' in the 'Tributary States system') from all over the world to 'move together' with the responsibilities expected of the 'Son of Heaven'. And, second, that these countries in moving together, should also engage in cooperative frameworks; that only by doing so can nations have a better future, otherwise a positive future may be unattainable if you 'stand alone'.

The Tributary States System

The tribute system represented one concrete expression of the Sino-centric, hierarchical worldview that lay at the heart of the classical concept of '*Tianxia*'. Fairbank's scholarship on the tributary system of the Qing Dynasty (1644–1911) and its significance as a model for Chinese concepts of 'world order' is formidable, albeit not uncontested.[18] In Fairbank's schemata, non-Chinese polities engaged the Chinese world using the prescribed ceremonials (*li*) of the imperial court. This involved:

an elaborate process of investitures of foreign princes as members of the Qing nobility; the provision of royal seals for correspondence with the capital; the presentation of tributary gifts and laudatory memorials during heavily regulated official visits; physical prostration before the emperor and his court; the receipt of imperial gifts in return; and the granting of specified trade privileges with the Middle Kingdom, both in the capital and at the border. By the middle Qing, regular tributary missions were listed in the official records from Korea, the Ryukyus, Annam, Laos, Siam, Sulu, Burma, the Netherlands, and the 'Western Ocean' (meaning Britain, Portugal, and the Papacy).[19] While Fairbank's work focussed almost exclusively on the Qing, the documentary evidence suggests the tribute system in the preceding Ming Dynasty was even more extensive in its reach. This included a 125-year period in the middle Ming (from 1425 to 1550) when the imperial court insisted that all its engagements with the outside world be conducted through this complex machinery.[20] For Ming and Qing China, the tribute system represented an unabashed expression of cultural superiority that continually reaffirmed Han political legitimacy within the empire, as well as a practical mechanism to regulate and control China's overall contact with barbarians of different hues.

Fairbank's analysis of the tribute system as a model for understanding imperial China's foreign relations has been taken further by David Kang.[21] In Kang's view, for the half millennium before the Opium Wars, the tribute system represented a universal, unipolar, hierarchical system across wider East Asia, based on an accepted inequality of political actors. Kang's argument reflects some of Johnston's earlier scholarship that, within the overarching scheme of the tributary state system, there were in fact two different ecosystems at work: one for the 'Sinic' world of Korea, Vietnam, Japan, and the Ryukyus, who shared what Kang called China's 'Confucian worldviews'; and another for the barbarian tribes of the Mongols, the Manchus, the Uyghurs, and the Tibetans, whom Johnston described as being in a continuous state of 'para bellum' with the celestial throne. In Kang's view, it was their shared worldview that mostly explained the virtual peace among the major powers of the Sinic world for 500 years (while admittedly citing two major historical exceptions with Japan), whereas with the northern and western barbarians, violence, invasion, and counter-invasion were the near-continuous norm.[22]

Kang's hypothesis is both descriptive and normative. He argues, controversially, that the "centuries of stability" under this hierarchical Sino-centric worldview compared favourably with the Westphalian order of politically equal sovereign states that emerged as the organizing principle for Western international relations after 1648.[23] In the West, inter-state war was 'incessant'. To minimize the risk of war, or to maximize a state's prospects of success if war came about, the balance of power, including 'balancing against the "hegemon"', became an almost universal strategic logic in the West. Not so, in Kang's argument, in Asia. In fact, in maritime East Asia, the near-universal recognition of China as the central, dominant power led to a set of tributary arrangements between the centre and the periphery that were mutually beneficial among the participants, while still according the peripheral polities "substantial latitude in their actual behaviour".[24]

Taken to its logical conclusion, Kang challenges the assumption that a Sino-centric world is by definition worse than the brutally realist alternative of the Westphalian West. This includes challenging the Waltzian assumption that, across all geographies and cultures and "through all of the centuries we can contemplate"[25], and however regrettable it may be, that tragically was what 'the real world' was like. Kang's historical survey of what he defines as the benefits of the tribute system therefore leads him to explicitly challenge Aaron Friedberg's conclusion that "for better or for worse, Europe's past could be Asia's future".[26]

By the time modern reformers began confronting China's existential challenges during the late Qing, dynastic history had therefore bequeathed its political successors a long and deep intellectual tradition of how to view the world. But none of these worldviews, or the policies that sprang from them, was effective in responding to the powerful new enemies arriving on China's shores from the 'outer barbarian' lands beyond the seas. European colonial powers presented Beijing with a newly lethal variation of China's ancient fear: internal division and external threat. The magnitude of this threat exceeded anything that China's classical tradition had faced before. 'All under Heaven' had, in fact, collapsed. The 'Son of Heaven' was no more. The tribute system had already been a dead letter for decades. Cultural superiority had been exposed as a myth, as had the natural hierarchy of states centred on the Middle Kingdom and the centralized trade restrictions that followed. What remained was the continuing thread of ancient 'strategic realism', on which emerging generations of reformers and revolutionaries would draw as they sought to 'save the nation' or '*jiu-guo*'. Whatever the warm afterglow of centuries of self-affirming Sino-centrism, with the empire now gone and foreign barbarians now within the gates of the city, all that really mattered was an abiding realism about the existential dangers of systemic collapse and national dismemberment that China now faced, and how materially to respond to it. These were the intellectual and political preoccupations of the generation of Nationalists, Communists, and other patriotic reformers who would dominate Chinese politics over the decades that followed the Xinghai Revolution of 1911.

Marxist-Leninist Worldviews, Mao Zedong, and the CCP

Marxism-Leninism, as introduced to China, represented a complete philosophical system and comprehensive worldview. As noted in the previous chapter, it contained its own ontology, epistemology, and logic. These in turn gave rise to what Marxists called 'objective laws' of natural science, social development, and individual consciousness, which drove and determined the long-term course of history. These determinist 'laws' underpinned a comprehensive explanatory framework that integrated economic, social, and political theory. The overriding purpose of this ideational system was to enable a revolutionary party both to interpret the world in which it operated and to equip itself with the knowledge to act in ways that accelerated the underlying historical processes of progressive change.

Marxism therefore offered its Chinese adherents a complete worldview that was radically different in content and scope from anything in the classical period. First, it offered a universal methodology for interpreting and understanding all reality. Second, it provided its followers with what they believed was an 'objective' diagnosis of China's national predicament, its causes, and how to respond in conformity with the 'scientific laws' of Chinese historical development. Third, it provided a parallel analysis of the world beyond China's shores, including China's 'internationalist' responsibilities towards a worldwide revolution. This was a worldview writ large and, over time, Mao became the party's Marxist ideologist-in-chief as well as its political and military leader in the field. In doing so, Mao modelled himself on Lenin in providing both intellectual and operational leadership for China's nascent Communist movement, thereby further entrenching his personal power. As Nick Knight has argued of Mao: "While philosophy was only one of the themes on which he wrote (military strategy was another), he recognised that an acceptable level of competence in Marxist theory and philosophy was essential to those who aspired to leadership of a Marxist Party."[27] As I will argue, this model of leadership would reappear under Xi Jinping.

Mao's Interpretation of Dialectical and Historical Materialism

One of Mao's major philosophical works, 'On Contradiction', published in 1937, repeats the general Marxist proposition on the opposing worlds of 'materialist dialectics' and metaphysics. Mao emphasized the abuse of metaphysics by the bourgeoisie to retard human progress, including, in China's case, various forms of Confucian thinking such as "Heaven changeth not, likewise the Dao changeth not."[28] By contrast, Mao cites Lenin as his authority on the universality of dialectical materialism's law of 'contradictory' opposites being "present in all things"—and that "the struggle between these aspects determine the life of all things and push their development forward". Mao goes on to list the universal applications of this law across the mathematical, mechanical, physical, chemical, military, and social sciences. Within this schema, 'struggle' becomes not just a voluntary political act, but the articulation of a universal law as relevant to the practice of politics as to the laws of physics. This deep conclusion that dialectical laws are applicable to all natural and human phenomena underpins much of the ensuing century's ideological certainty on the part of orthodox CCP ideologues: when the party reached a considered position about itself or its place in the world, this was not mere opinion; rather, it was 'objective', 'scientific', and therefore 'correct.' As we shall see, this too continues to resonate with the current worldview of Xi Jinping.

'On Contradiction' adopts Lenin's core schema of dialectical materialism in its totality. This was reinforced by the translated works of Mitin and Shirokov that had been delivered to Mao's north-western redoubt in 1935.[29] Indeed, it was there that Mao referred to Marx, Engels, Lenin, and Stalin as "the great creators and continuers of Marxism".[30] According to Mao:

> The world outlook of materialist dialectics holds that in order to understand the development of a thing we should study it internally and in its relations with other things; in other words, the development of things should be seen as their internal and necessary self-movement, while each thing in its movement is interrelated and interacts with the things around it. The fundamental cause of the development of a thing is not external but internal; it lies in contradictariness within the thing. There is internal contradiction in every single thing, hence its motion and development. Contradictariness within a thing is the fundamental cause of its development, while its interrelations and interactions with other things are secondary causes.[31]

From this central conclusion, Mao, like his Marxist-Leninist predecessors, argued that these irreconcilable contradictions could be found: between society and nature; between society's 'productive forces' and the 'relations of production'; between the 'economic base' and the social 'superstructure' (including politics and ideology); between the great masses and feudal society; between the bourgeoisie and the proletariat; between peasants and the working class; between imperialists and their exploited colonies; and even between contradictory forces within the Communist Party itself. Not only were these contradictions part of 'the essence of things', so too were the processes to resolve these contradictions. Central to these was the continuing 'struggle' between progressive and reactionary forces. This struggle was rendered inevitable through the operation of the permanent laws of motion, which caused one thing to react against the other. Then, through the inter-permeation of things, struggle would result in a temporary equilibrium through a unity of opposites, before a fresh set of contradictions emerged that set the entire process in motion once more. Hence, in this worldview, history was ultimately determinist in its progressive trajectory, as societies moved inevitably through various feudal, capitalist, imperialist, socialist and finally communist stages.[32]

Contradiction, Struggle, and the CCP

Mao, however, was not simply interested in dialectical and historical materialism as an analytical tool to elegantly describe the party's and the country's current dilemmas. As Mao wrote in 'On Practice', his other major theoretical work of 1937, "Marxist philosophy holds that the most important problem does not lie in understanding the laws of the objective world and thus being able to explain it, but in applying these laws actively to change the world."[33] Here Mao lifts directly from Lenin in settling for the Chinese party the central dilemma of Marxism itself: the tension between individual political agency on the one hand and an ideological worldview that embraced a determinist view of history on the other. At one level, historical determinists believed that, because the law of contradictions was already at work, there was little that human intervention could achieve to either advance or resist these great tides of history. But, at a different level, as Knight has argued, as "a revolutionary, Mao had to discover the formula that revealed the possibilities for purposive historical change inherent in human consciousness and activity." Otherwise, Mao's political mission was without meaning.[34] This dilemma within Marxism was as old as Marx's original observation that "men make their own history, but not of their own free will; not under circumstances they themselves have chosen, but under the given and inherited circumstances with which they are directly confronted."[35]

Mao's response to this universal Marxist dilemma was to examine Chinese history for contradictions in the relationship between the economic base (the domain that 'determined' social reality) and its social superstructure (the repository of ideas, ideology, and political action). As Mao wrote in 1937:

> In the contradiction between the economic base and the superstructure, the economic base is the principal aspect. . . . It should be realized that under normal conditions, and viewed from a materialist point of view, they really are unchanging and absolute things; however, there are historically many particular situations in which they do change. . . . The creation and advocacy of revolutionary theory plays the principal and decisive role in those times of which Lenin said, "Without revolutionary theory, there can be no revolutionary movement." . . . When the superstructure (politics, culture etc.) obstructs the development of the economic base, political and cultural changes become principal and decisive. . . . This does not go against materialism; on the contrary it avoids mechanical materialism and firmly upholds dialectical materialism.[36]

In other words, Mao concluded that, while the determinist forces of history were ultimately decisive in producing socialism, the role of the party was to accelerate this dynamic process. The party did so by participating actively, dialectically, and decisively in the real world, thereby helping to remove political obstacles to progress. Mao also divided 'principal' contradictions from 'secondary' ones to prioritize the revolutionary tasks of the party at any moment in history—a conceptual discipline that Chinese Marxists continue today. For example, Mao argued that, during the age of imperialism, when colonial powers collaborated with Chinese capitalists using the "milder means" of political, economic, and cultural oppression, the principal contradiction was between the Chinese working class and this capitalist coalition, thus warranting civil war.[37] Then, during the 1930s, when the major contradiction lay with resisting and defeating the Japanese invasion, the party needed a different course of action; all other 'contradictions' and their associated struggles needed to take a "secondary and subordinate" position.[38] But with the defeat of Japan in 1945, the theoretical elasticity inherent in Mao's rendition of dialectical materialism's primary and secondary contradictions enabled the CCP to rapidly redefine their political and strategic circumstances: defeating the capitalist forces represented by the Nationalists (soon to be supported by a new force of imperialism, the United States) would now become the party's central contradiction. As a result, combatting these new forms of imperialism would become the organizing principle of all party activism for the new period (both in terms of ideology, as well as political and military effort). This principle of defining the party's primary and secondary contradictions, as applied to China's evolving national circumstances, remains deeply relevant to Xi Jinping's ideological worldview today.

Some will ask: do these complex ideological contortions really matter? After all, the reasons for changes in China's domestic and foreign policy strategy under Mao, Deng, and Xi seem relatively self-evident responses to changing facts on the ground. Did these facts need to be interpreted through an ideological prism to produce these policy conclusions? Would a hypothetical non-Marxist-Leninist Chinese state have responded in a similar way? This brings us back to the central question, discussed in the previous chapter, of whether we are witnessing ideological causation or ideological post-facto rationalization of political and policy changes initiated as a result of other factors. Suffice it to say here that, within the worldview of Xi's CCP, ideological and empirical analyses are neither separate nor mutually exclusive endeavours. Indeed, they are seen as mutually reinforcing, to the point that once deep conclusions are reached through rational or empirical analysis, ideology then has a 'doubling down' effect on the subsequent direction of policy. Put differently, because Marxism-Leninism is perceived as being 'scientific', policy responses to changing facts can become grounded in the verities of ideological faith and, as a result, assume the qualities of longer-term strategic direction.

The Impact of Ideology on the Real World of Domestic Politics and Foreign Policy

Understanding Mao's articulation of an orthodox Marxist worldview is one thing. Relating that worldview to what the CCP actually did in the period before the establishment of the People's Republic in 1949 is another. This task continues to be difficult given the relative paucity of primary sources that enable us to attribute ideological causalities, on the one hand, to real-world policy decisions, on the other. Nonetheless, several recurring thematics emerged as a deeply ideological party encountered the brutal realities of Chinese politics, many of which presented life-or-death consequences for the nascent Communist movement. While ideation was always important, the compromises necessary for national, political, or even personal survival were vital. As the preeminent historian of CCP foreign policy Michael Hunt has noted, Marxist-Leninist ideology "has been one source for policy and that, as a source, it can sustain not one policy but a wide variety of them".[39] Ideology nonetheless remained important as an organizing principle for the fledgling party. During the pre-1949 period, it became a flexible political instrument for Mao to manage growing internal and external challenges including how to deal with the various forms of Western and later Japanese imperialism, how to manage the party's complex relations with great powers like the Soviet Union and the United States, how to respond to the immediate threats from the Nationalists, and how the party should manage its role within an internationalist movement informed by a global communist worldview.

From the beginning, the Communist Party's program to defeat imperialism was inextricably linked with the transformation of the country from within. In the party's mind, they were one mission, driven by the same patriotic impulse for national salvation as earlier generations of Chinese reformers had had since the second half of the nineteenth century. Indeed, as Hunt has argued, "the late Qing constituted the matrix out of which the CCP's approach to world affairs would emerge" as "calls to restore the state . . . soon turned into a search for ways to remake China from top to bottom", inspiring in turn the "revolutionary impulses that brought the CCP to life, and informed its thinking in foreign relations".[40] This deep sense of patriotism in response to state collapse dominated the earliest writings of CCP leaders in the 1920s, rather than a definitive ideological view about the capitalist construct of global imperialism. This crisis of the late Qing and the early republican state became "the intellectual crucible for the founding fathers of the Chinese Communist Party, as well as their political sons and heirs".[41]

Just as Marxist worldviews did not provide a complete explanation for the CCP's response to Japanese imperialism between 1936 and 1945, similar complexities arise in explaining the party's dealings with other great powers—most particularly the Soviet Union and the United States. For a Chinese Marxist party, a seamless relationship with Moscow should perhaps have been the natural product of their common worldview. But Marxism was not the sole motivational force at work in CCP domestic and foreign policy behaviour in the pre-1949 period. Nationalism was, and would remain, a significant factor driving party behaviour, with a reach well beyond the ideological dictates of dialectical and historical materialism. Similarly, cold, hard, classical realism remained alive in the party's existential calculus for navigating the shoals of internal threat and external challenge during these long decades of foreign invasion and civil war. China's own national exigencies similarly tempered the party's ideological predilection for communist internationalism. Indeed, all four factors (Marxism, nationalism, classical realism, and wariness about the cost of any form of full-blown internationalism) are evident in the CCP's worldview well before the proclamation of New China in 1949, just as they would remain constant themes in the unfolding debates about the People's Republic's international outlook.

Changing Ideological Frameworks in the People's Republic

Although Western historians of modern Chinese domestic and foreign policy[42] use different conceptual frameworks and taxonomies to interpret changes in the PRC's policy language and behaviour, there is a level of agreement that both the classical and Marxist worldviews described earlier in this chapter continued to contend for political and policy space after 1949. Steven Levine elegantly summarizes the academic contest over how best to evaluate the relative impact of Marxism-Leninism on PRC foreign policy as follows:

> Perspectives on the subject range from older notions that Chinese foreign policy was the practical expression of the Marxist-Leninist *Weltanschauung* to newer views that ideology is a minor factor in foreign policy, invoked by leaders to rationalize decisions that are reached on other grounds.[43]

In reality, Marxist-Leninist orthodoxy waxes and wanes as an effective explanatory framework for interpreting changing Chinese policy behaviours, including during the 1949–1976 period when Mao himself was both the party's ideologist-in-chief and the central figure in the real-world political and policy process. But Marxism-Leninism would never completely disappear from the stage, nor degenerate into mere theoretical formalism, even after Mao. The Marxist bass note could be heard throughout, even when drowned out by the more familiar sounds of policy pragmatism.

Levine argues that Marxism-Leninism produced a basic set of five 'ideological predicates' that shaped the CCP's worldview as they interpreted and responded to international reality from October 1949 forward:[44]

- The world was divided into two inherently hostile, warring camps that mirrored the basic class division of contemporary society.
- The socialist camp and its allies (including the proletariat and other so-called progressive forces in imperialist states) were engaged in a worldwide, historic struggle against imperialism that would eventually lead to the victory of socialism.
- Beneficial relations between socialist states and members of the imperialist camp, while desirable, would always be limited by their instrumental and transitory character. Genuine, long-term co-operation with imperialist states was impossible given the historic conflict between the two opposing systems.
- Relations between socialist states were based on common identity rather than transitory interests. Socialist international relations were relations of a new type, characterized by peace, long-term mutual interest, genuine cooperation, and fraternal solidarity.

- Socialist states could forge coalitions with nationalist states and political movements, even when these were non-socialist in character, on the basis of their shared opposition to imperialism.

Levine also notes Mao's responses to the formidable array of practical domestic and foreign policy challenges faced in the post-1949 period:

> There was no reason to expect that the inconsistencies between ideological predicates and political realities would lead Chinese Communist leaders to question their *Weltanschauung*. Instead, what happened is that the function of ideology in Chinese foreign policy began to undergo a metamorphosis. While its identity-defining dimension remained, formal ideology gradually ceased functioning as a guide to action in the foreign policy arena and was increasingly transformed into a set of abstract principles and behavioural norms used to criticize the conduct of other states.[45]

While I might disagree with Levine on the degree of 'abstraction' in the relationship between theory and practice, particularly in the conduct of Chinese foreign policy during the first half of the Cultural Revolution, I nonetheless agree with his general argument that the relevance of ideology as a guide to policy has fluctuated over time since 1949.

Despite the pragmatic challenges of managing the Chinese state, Mao's formal ideological worldview remained deeply binary. His November 1957 address to the representatives of sixty-four communist and workers' parties gathered in Moscow for the fortieth anniversary of the 1917 Revolution left no doubts about his profoundly Marxist framework for analysing international challenges. Mao's tour d'horizon of growing Soviet and Chinese power, American retreat, and collapsing Western colonialism across Asia and Africa represented a classical case study of dialectical analysis in motion. It also contained a number of remarkable resonances with Xi Jinping's worldview more than sixty years later. As Mao candidly observed:

> I believe that the east wind is prevailing over the west wind. That is to say, the forces of socialism are overwhelmingly superior to the forces of imperialism. . . . In my view, all imperialists are like the sun at six o'clock in the afternoon and we are like the sun at six o'clock in the morning. Hence a turning-point has been reached, that is to say the Western countries have been left behind and we now clearly have the upper hand. . . . In the final analysis, this [dialectical materialism] is also true of the imperialist and capitalist systems, which are bound to be replaced in the end by the socialist system. The same applies to ideology, idealism will be replaced by

> materialism, and theism by atheism. Here we are speaking of the strategic objective. But the case is different with tactical stages, where compromises may be made. Didn't we compromise with the Americans on the 38th Parallel in Korea?[46]

When the Sino-Soviet split erupted in full public view at the Moscow and Bucharest conferences of communist and workers' parties in 1960, it shattered the global image (and whatever remained of the political reality) of a unified socialist worldview. While the schism was multidimensional in nature, Mao's writings make clear that nationalist factors also helped drive the split. With an eye to the future leadership of international communism himself, Mao in 1961–1962 wrote that the "centre of the revolution has been shifting from the West to the East", moving from the French Revolution, to the German revolution (presumably of 1848) in Marx's time, to the Russian Revolution leading the first half of the twentieth century, to the Chinese Revolution in the second half.[47] Furthermore, basic nationalist resentments and aspirations, once directed against Western imperialists, would now begin to be trained with equal willingness against Moscow.

Considerable ideological efforts were made to reframe the threat of 'Soviet social-imperialism' as the new external 'primary contradiction' that demanded maximum 'struggle'. The United States would remain a contradiction but, importantly, only a secondary one, at least for the foreseeable future. Ironically, it would fall to China's leading 'capitalist roader', Deng Xiaoping (himself only recently rehabilitated from being purged during the Cultural Revolution), to expound on this new version of China's official worldview to the United Nations in 1974.[48] Building on previous formulations—notably the CCP's 'three zones' of 1922, and Mao's 'intermediate zones' of 1946 and 1963[49]—Deng now articulated Mao's theory of the 'three worlds': the first comprising the two superpowers, whose struggle for global hegemony meant exploiting the rest of the world; the second world comprising the developed countries, who were fracturing under the oppression of their larger 'allies'; and the third world comprising the developing countries united in their struggle against hegemony, colonialism, and imperialism. This formulation liberated China on a number of ideological fronts: first, it kept the Soviet Union as its principal foreign policy contradiction until its collapse in 1991; second, it was able to ignore a more distant America as an ideological, strategic, or political threat until the bloodshed on Tiananmen Square in 1989 and the beginnings of rapprochement with Moscow during the 1990s; and third, it enabled China to inhabit an ideological intermediate zone, hazily pledging to "warmly endorse and firmly support all just propositions made by third world countries"[50] in order to realize a 'new international economic order' at some ill-defined point in the future.

Indeed there were a wide set of influences on the CCP's evolving domestic and international worldview in the pre-1976 period. Mao's interpretation of Marxist-Leninist ideological imperatives was clearly evident in his domestic decision-making framework in the anti-landlord movement, the Great Leap Forward, and the Cultural Revolution. In all three, class struggle remained dominant. Externally, Mao's Marxist-Leninist worldview informed his decision to "lean to one side"[51] with the Sino-Soviet Friendship Treaty, his decisions to support both North Korea and Vietnam against US imperialism, and his assertion of Chinese ideological leadership of the international socialist movement after the Sino-Soviet split. Mao's Marxist-Leninist ideological predilections, however, were never divorced from classical strategic realism. This was evidenced in his approach to armistice talks in Korea, refraining from a territorial assault on Taiwan, and ultimately his decision to lean to the other side when he became convinced that a hostile Soviet Union was in the ascendancy over the United States. At the same time, Mao's obsession with 'catching up' with the West,[52] his ideological and political rivalry with the Soviet Union, and his championing of a new Chinese form of 'Marxist internationalism'[53] during the Cultural Revolution, indicated that nationalism too remained an active element in shaping China's overall worldview.

Deng Xiaoping, China's Revised Worldview, and the Centrality of Economic Development

Deng's emergence as China's dominant leader in 1977–1978, combined with the political forces he represented within the CCP, fundamentally impacted China's official ideological worldview at multiple levels. First, the ideational content of party ideology changed from the paramountcy of political struggle (as expressed through the continuing priority of the 'relations of production' and the processes of permanent revolution) to a new imperative of unleashing economic development through the 'forces of production'.

Second, the principal party resolutions of the Deng period that set 'the line' for China's policy direction for the next thirty-five years were overwhelmingly domestic in focus. These included the November 1978 Central Party Work Conference held prior to the much-celebrated Third Plenum of the 11th Central Committee in December. It also included Deng's 'Four Cardinal Principles' speech of March 1979[54] to safeguard the future political control of a Leninist party. And, most important, it incorporated the 1981 'Resolution on Certain Questions on the History of Our Party since the Founding of the PRC'.[55] While these documents dealt only peripherally with the world beyond China's shores, their ideological redefinition of the acceptable parameters for domestic economic development would in fact determine much of China's subsequent engagement with the Western capitalist world. China's realist concerns about the Soviet Union would continue, becoming even sharper under Deng amidst fear of Soviet strategic encirclement through Vietnam, Cambodia, Laos, and eventually Afghanistan. The CCP's new form of united front with the United States against Soviet 'social-imperialism' was reinforced, although its critique of 'Soviet revisionism' unsurprisingly began slipping from the CCP's formal political lexicon as Deng advanced his own program of pro-market economic reform. Nonetheless, this combination of China's existing definition of the Soviet strategic threat, coupled with its new definition of the United States as a potential major economic partner, would drive China's approach to international relations and its wider worldview for the next forty years. This included Deng's critical decision to relegate, at least temporarily, the question of Taiwan.[56]

Central to this book is the argument that these profound changes in the party's worldview under Deng nonetheless retained the ideological framework of Marxism-Leninism and its twin disciplines of dialectical and historical materialism. The major changes in politics and policy of this period were not simply the product of haphazard decisions driven by an immediate need to explain the Maoist excesses of the Great Leap Forward, and the Cultural Revolution, the military coup against the Gang of Four, and the removal of Hua Guofeng. Nor were they simply a politically expedient exercise to rescue a financially bankrupt Chinese state.[57] It was essential, both to justify Deng's personal rise and to reassert the party's political legitimacy, that these fundamental changes in the party line be explained in terms of Marxist ideological orthodoxy. Marxism remained the ultimate language of legitimacy within party decision-making—both on the composition of its leadership, and how new national policy directions would be explained to China's wider political ecosystem.[58] In this sense, the Third Plenum of the 11th Central Committee in 1978 was not just like a papal conclave selecting a new pope; it was more like the Second Vatican Council, which redefined orthodoxy itself, albeit within a continuing framework of Marxist belief.

In Deng Xiaoping's revised worldview, Mao had erred in his interpretation of dialectical and historical materialism by insisting that class struggle remained China's major contradiction after 1956. In the Dengist interpretation of CCP history, the transition to basic socialism had already been completed that year through the full transition from private to public ownership. Indeed, this had been formally confirmed in 1956 by the Eighth Party Congress, which determined 'socialist construction' as the party's new central task.[59] As Deng noted in September 1978: "From the viewpoint of historical materialism, correct political leadership in the end should manifest itself in the growth of the productive forces of society and the improvement of the growing material and cultural needs of the people."[60] Deng was even clearer a year later, stating the principal contradiction then facing the country was "socialist modernization".[61] Similarly, the 1981 'Resolution on Party History' concluded that "the objective of our party's struggle in the new historical period is to turn China step by step into a powerful socialist country with modern agriculture, industry, national defence and science and technology".[62]

Deng, and those party leaders and theoreticians who supported him, sought to entrench this ideological redefinition of the party's central mission by locating 'socialist modernization' within the wider framework of historical materialism. Party theoreticians Xue Muqiao, Su Shaozhi, and Feng Langrui, drawing on Marx's much earlier distinction between lower and higher levels of communism, argued there were three stages in the evolution of socialism: a primary stage involving the transition from a capitalist mode of production to a socialist one, achieved by transferring private property to collective ownership; a second stage involving the fullest development of the forces of production; and finally the third phase of a fully socialist society.[63] China, they argued, had not yet emerged from the basic stage and if the party was serious about fully realizing socialism, then it had to prioritize economic development by fully harnessing the 'forces of production'. This meant relegating the ideological significance of the 'relations of production' or class. Critically, this also meant accepting the reality that during this 'primary stage of socialism', China's productive forces could only be effectively developed by applying the 'objective laws' of economics. Most important, this required the party to accept market pricing and the unequal distribution of income. This was followed in 1981 by the formal redefinition of the party's 'principal contradiction' within this primary stage of socialism as "the contradiction between the people's growing material and cultural needs, and the backward state of social production".[64] This definition would remain the essential ideological orthodoxy underpinning the priority the CCP attached to economic development, reform, and opening during the primary stage of socialism—until Xi Jinping formally amended it thirty-six years later at the 19th Congress in 2017.

The import of Deng's ideological redefinition of the party's worldview would be felt across China and around the world. The 1981 'Resolution on Party History' underlined its significance in both political and ideological terms: "These momentous changes in the work of the leadership signified that the party had re-established the correct line of Marxism ideologically, politically and organizationally."[65] Yan Sun, in her monumental documentary analysis of the Marxist theoretical literature of this period, argued that these changes could not be explained away as simply post-facto ideological camouflage, nor as a new mechanistic prescription for a form of post-socialist modernization.[66] Instead, Sun highlights the meaning, nature and scale of the post-Mao reformers' "break with the past". It was a break that had to be explained within the ideological confines of the Marxist system they were operating within, rather than by ignoring, let alone repudiating, that system. In Sun's view, "in a long-established socialist regime, Marxism-Leninism alone furnishes leaders with a conceptual framework for organizing their understanding of the world."[67] In other words, it was Marxism-Leninism itself that became the ideological vehicle through which Deng repudiated Maoist orthodoxy on class struggle, economic equality, and the totalizing control of the party, and allowed a new political and policy paradigm to prevail that supported the pursuit of individual and national economic prosperity.

Deng's ideological change in China's overall political economy also fundamentally changed Chinese foreign policy. As Deng told the UN secretary-general in 1982:

> The primary task we have set as the initial goal for the realization of modernization is to create comparative prosperity by the end of this century...

> Within the ensuing 30 to 50 years, we shall approach the level of developed countries... Therefore, we cherish the hope for a peaceful international environment. Should war break out, our plan would be thwarted... At present, our domestic situation is fairly good. The Chinese people are wholeheartedly concentrating on economic development. Our foreign policy coincides with this magnificent goal.[68]

Deng's message to the country and the world was that China's global engagement would be driven by its domestic economic vision of achieving middle-income status by 2000 and developed economic status sometime between 2030 and 2050. Moreover, achieving these economic goals would require continued international strategic stability. Deng also made plain that a core part of this new worldview would depend on China's relationship with the United States as an essential partner in its economic development.

These, then, were the dominant themes that formed the foreign policy component of Deng's econo-centric worldview: domestic economic development, accommodated by efforts to enhance international peace and expanding economic engagement with world markets, all made possible through a realist balance of power against the Soviet Union (also justified in Marxist terms as the CCP's principal external contradiction) in partnership with the United States. Deng did not formally abandon the party's internationalist solidarity with the 'Third World'. But any continuing material support for international revolutionary movements was effectively abandoned as an impediment to China's new, pragmatic economic development agenda, which needed politically uncomplicated access to foreign markets across both the developed and the developing worlds.[69] Deng continued his rhetorical support for what he had already called a 'new international political and economic order' that would one day be free from great power competition, while ruling out any possibility of China leading such a movement because of Beijing's still limited national resources.[70] This, like much of Deng's basic ideological program, would change dramatically under Xi Jinping.

It was this logic that gave rise to Deng's famous twenty-four-character foreign policy aphorism in 1992, following the imposition of Western economic sanctions after the violent suppression of students in Tiananmen Square in 1989 and the dissolution of the USSR in 1991. Deng stated that China should "observe calmly; secure our position; cope with affairs calmly; hide our capacities and bide our time; be good at maintaining a low profile;

and never claim leadership".[71] Deng's strategy was precisely that: a tactical means to a strategic end that he had already articulated in his revised worldview of 1979, namely to build a strong state on the back of a strong economy without generating any unnecessary outside opposition by contesting the United States for regional or global leadership. Deng's strategic patience would be rewarded by the gradual lifting of sanctions over the following decade. Deng's strategic resolve would be further reflected in his doubling down on China's pro-market development model during his 'Southern Expedition' in 1992. Deng deliberately used this tour to proclaim the need to further intensify economic reform. This came after a sharp, internal political reaction against his overall reform program following Tiananmen's direct challenge to party power, the subsequent imposition of Western sanctions and, most spectacularly, the collapse of the Soviet Communist party-state in 1991. All three developments underlined the potential political vulnerability of Deng's reform program to conservative ideological attack. Yet Deng, still operating within the parameters of Marxist-Leninist orthodoxy, continued to defend his version of 'socialism with Chinese characteristics'[72] as the best encapsulation of the balance between market and state during the primary stage of socialism. Deng further entrenched his redefinition of ideological orthodoxy at the 14th Party Congress in 1992, when it formally adopted the concept of a 'socialist market economy' as official party dogma.[73] For Deng, protecting his new economic development model remained fundamental to the preservation of his overall worldview: a strong China, built on the foundation of a strong economy, underpinned by a long-term program of market reform and opening that would fully unleash China's underdeveloped 'productive forces'.

Jiang Zemin, the Rise of 'Market Economics', the Constitutional Entrenchment of Deng Xiaoping Thought, and Jiang's Theory of the 'Three Represents'

Following a degree of political and policy uncertainty between 1989 and 1992, new CCP General Secretary Jiang Zemin not only preserved Deng's redefined ideological worldview but accelerated its reformist trajectory. Deng's preoccupation with market-driven economic development was sustained as per-capita income increased rapidly despite income inequality increasing even more so.[74] While rising inequality would normally generate ideological tensions within a Marxist-Leninist party and challenge its worldview, during Jiang's term, inequality was justified as the necessary price to be paid for unleashing the underdeveloped 'factors of production' during the primary stage of socialism. It was deemed necessary to increase overall national wealth and build a powerful socialist state.

Jiang would deal with the political complexities arising from a newly emerging Chinese capitalist class by welcoming them formally into the ranks of the party. In effect, Jiang introduced institutional measures designed to complement (and, in part, compensate for) the ideological adjustments under Deng that had brought China's burgeoning private sector into existence in the first place. Jiang also began encouraging, developing, and harnessing the forces of nationalism once the official measures of Chinese national wealth and power began pointing in a significantly positive direction. Beijing protested repeated US provocations against its national sovereignty in this period—over Tiananmen and Taiwan, reconnaissance flights along its coastline, and the bombing of China's embassy in Yugoslavia—but an abiding strategic realism continued to temper Chinese responses given the limitations of its military and economic power. Jiang also called for the development of China's 'national spirit' through a 'patriotic education campaign' not rooted in Marxist ideology, but in new forms of nationalism specifically targeted at China's first post-reform generation.[75] Jiang's worldview, therefore, reflected all three continuing traditions from China's classical and communist past: a redefined Marxist ideology that accommodated growing individual and national prosperity; an enduring sense of Chinese nationalism; and an underlying realism about China's overall national strategic circumstances, notwithstanding the removal of the Soviet threat from its borders after 1991.

Jiang continued to entrench the ideological worldview of reform and opening that he had inherited from Deng across the 14th, 15th, and 16th party congresses in 1992, 1997, and 2002, respectively. At the 14th Congress, Jiang explicitly stated that "if reform and economic development are to proceed smoothly, they must have powerful ideological and political guarantees."[76] Jiang reaffirmed historical and dialectical materialism as providing the only 'scientific approach' for determining the party's future ideological direction.[77] Deng, in Jiang's schema, had pioneered the second major revolution in Chinese Marxist theory: Mao, as a revolutionary theorist, had brought about national liberation in 1949, while Deng had pioneered the ideological breakthrough necessary to construct a modern socialist state. Jiang's major theoretical innovation at the congress in 1992 was to evolve his earlier formulation of a 'planned commodity economy' into the more robust terminology of a 'socialist market economy' as a critical "component part of the basic system of socialism".[78] This new formulation included emphasizing diverse forms of economic ownership in which the state sector would remain dominant, although the private sector would play an increasingly significant role. Jiang, during this period, was purposefully advancing broader ideological cover for the expansion of a widening reformist project.

Five years later, at the 15th Party Congress in November 1997, Jiang managed the reality of Deng's physical passing nine months before by entrenching his ideology within the party constitution. Jiang formally elevated Deng Xiaoping's Theory of 'socialism with Chinese characteristics' to co-equal status with Mao Zedong Thought, forming a new trinitarian CCP orthodoxy of 'Marxism-Leninism, Mao Zedong Thought and Deng Xiaoping Theory.'[79] Jiang's congress report reaffirmed economic development as the party's 'central contradiction', arguing that China continued to languish in the primary stage of socialism. On the party's international worldview, Jiang's report reflected greater confidence than at the previous congress held in the aftermath of Tiananmen. In the execution of foreign policy, however, Jiang reminded his party to continue adhering to "the ideas of Deng Xiaoping about diplomatic work", which cautioned the country against taking global leadership positions given the continued centrality of China's economic development task.

At Jiang's last congress as general secretary in 2002, he added two major elements to previous formulations on Deng Xiaoping Theory. The first was a full articulation of Jiang's own theory on 'the Three Represents' — a theoretical innovation to further legitimize the 'liberation and development of the productive forces' within the primary stage of socialism:

> Our Party must always represent the development trend of China's advanced productive forces, the orientation of China's advanced culture and the fundamental interests of the overwhelming majority of the Chinese people. They are the inexorable requirements for maintaining and developing socialism.[80]

This concept was expressly designed to deal with the emergence of China's new entrepreneurial and professional classes by bringing them into the ranks of the party despite their ownership of substantial private property. Jiang was mindful of the need to harness broad-based, nationalist political sentiment from these new emerging social forces to support the party's overall ideological and economic endeavour. Importantly, Jiang also began the process of ideologically softening some of the jarring edges of the party's overall market economic reform program. For the first time since 1982, the party general secretary began pointing to new secondary contradictions including ecological sustainability, regional inequality and "pressure from developing countries".[81] In other words, as with Deng, Jiang's worldview was a composite of: a redefined, reformist Marxist orthodoxy; continuing classical strategic realism about China's actual power in the world; and new and emerging forms of Chinese proto-nationalism. And within this emerging ideological framework, Jiang remained sufficiently conservative to recognize there were "increasingly conspicuous" although lesser contradictions in Chinese society that the party would soon need to address.

Another ideational innovation of the 16th Congress, consistent with the party's now near-total preoccupation with economic development, was Jiang identifying the next two decades (through to 2020) as a new 'period of strategic opportunity.'[82] According to Jiang, China had to "seize tightly" these opportunities to advance the first two stages of a three-stage program of comprehensive development: the doubling of per-capita GDP between 2000 and 2010; quadrupling total GDP by 2020; and a new 2049 mission for 'national rejuvenation' by which time China will have modernized into a "a strong, prosperous, democratic and culturally advanced socialist country".[83] Importantly, the latter two of these tasks preceded the 'two centenary goals' of Xi's 2012 'China Dream' by a full decade.[84] Critically, Jiang couched this 'period of strategic opportunity' as a prerequisite for China's domestic development needs, its changing international circumstances and the necessity of maintaining strategic stability to achieve China's national economic ends. The report's analysis that peace, development, and multipolarity were the 'irresistible trend' of the time strengthened previous formulations from the 14th and 15th congresses. Jiang argued that China must "promote a harmonious coexistence of diverse forces and maintain stability in the international community".[85] This foreshadowed Hu Jintao's later call for 'a harmonious world',[86] to help consolidate China's optimal strategic environment for the full development of its economy.

As Jiang stated clearly: "The purpose of China's foreign policy is to maintain world peace and promote common development."[87] Jiang also, for the first time, bluntly acknowledged a long-term strategic rationale for the entire Dengist project—"reform and opening up are ways to make China powerful".[88] He also became more bullish on China's 'overall national strength' where the party had now made great strides. Consistent with China's growing power, for the first time, there was also evidence of a broader embrace of specific international policy initiatives where China might begin to deploy its newfound national power. To match China's long-standing call for 'a new international economic order', the 16th Congress issued a parallel call for a 'new security concept', apparently foreshadowing the earliest manifestations of emerging Chinese foreign policy activism around the Shanghai Cooperation Organization. Jiang's 'new security concept' also resonated ideologically with Beijing's emerging proposals for a new strategic architecture in Central Asia that was capable of accommodating China's long-standing geo-political interests along its continental periphery.[89] This nascent foreign policy activism, however, would remain greatly constrained in accordance with Deng's diplomatic guidance that China should keep a low profile. This would continue to be the case until Xi formally jettisoned Deng's guidance in 2014.

Hu Jintao, the 'Theory of Scientific Development', the Beginnings of a New Activism in Chinese International Policy, and a New Military Strategy

Hu Jintao, like Jiang Zemin, would sustain Deng's general ideological worldview on the centrality of economic growth, albeit calibrated by his own concept of 'scientific development'.[90] This was designed to deal with rising inequality and the environmental consequences of unrestrained growth. Chinese nationalist campaigns, already fostered under Jiang, would develop further in the decade of the Beijing Olympics, although still within defined constraints. Nonetheless, classical Chinese realism, including the perceived relative decline of the United States, would cause Hu Jintao's China to begin embracing a more assertive approach in China's near abroad, particularly in relation to historical territorial claims in the East and South China Seas. Under Hu Jintao, we therefore saw an evolving worldview where the economic imperative remained dominant, albeit with greater reservations about unconstrained markets; the continued, steady development of Chinese official nationalism; and the beginnings of a new level of regional foreign and security policy activism, driven by a realist analysis of strategic opportunities that had been created by a more powerful China and a distracted and diminished America, then preoccupied with its decade-long 'War on Terror'.[91]

The changing ideological formulations deployed by Hu Jintao in his reports to the 17th and 18th Party Congresses in 2007 and 2012 also reflected changing domestic and international developments in the real world of Chinese policy. As Josef Gregory Mahoney and Xiuling Li have observed in relation to this period:

> Politics in Beijing takes place on two levels. One level is the frequently obscured calculus of elite politicians formulating policy. The other level is that of theory. While there is a dialectical relationship between the two, parsing their similitudes and contradictions at any given moment is very difficult.[92]

These policy debates included the implications of World Trade Organization membership in 2002, the Global Financial Crisis in 2008–2009 and rising income inequality, coupled with America's strategic preoccupation with its various wars in the wider Middle East, the election and re-election of the pro-independence Democratic Progressive Party in Taiwan, and Japan's nationalization of three of the disputed Diaoyudao/Senkaku islands in 2012. Although Hu's 2007 congress address reaffirmed Deng's redefinition of the party's central contradiction within the primary stage of socialism, he went one step further by defining Deng Xiaoping Theory, Jiang's 'Three Represents', and his own 'Scientific Outlook on Development' as belonging to an integrated "system of theories of socialism with Chinese characteristics"—a system that was dynamic, not static.[93] Hu defined his contribution as having multiple reformist components, including: a deeper "understanding of the laws governing the socialist market economy"; introducing "institutions to give better play to the basic role of market forces in allocating resources"; and accelerating the "transformation of the mode of economic development". But Hu also called on the congress to promote 'social harmony' (*shehui hexie*), social equity, and social justice as tempering disciplines for the market by introducing national free education, pensions, and basic health care systems, as well as putting new emphasis on environmentally sustainable development.

Similarly, Hu's language on 'deepening political restructuring' addressed more extensively than any of his predecessors the development of grass-roots democracy, the possibility of non-party candidates being selected for high office, and an enhanced role for the National People's Congress (NPC) in supervising the state.[94] These not insignificant political and ideological reforms would be effectively repudiated by Xi barely a decade later.

In Hu's analysis, China's international circumstances remained positive because: peace, development and cooperation were "irresistible"; the trend towards multipolarity was "irreversible"; and economic globalization was "developing in depth". As a result, Hu concluded the international balance of power was changing in the direction of 'world peace' (i.e. not continued American unipolarity). Based on this analysis, Hu repeated Jiang's argument that China still enjoyed a 'period of strategic opportunity' which it had to grasp. This meant China should: implement a 'go global' strategy for its corporations (a new expression); expand its 'all-directional diplomacy'; encourage 'win-win' economic relationships with foreigners, including gradually opening the Chinese economy to further foreign penetration; and engage in a new global approach aimed at environmental and ecological balance.[95] Hu's 2007 report also called for the development of an 'harmonious world' as part of China's international strategy, consistent with his vision for a 'harmonious society' at home. Hu developed his nascent concept of a 'harmonious world' in his 2005 address to the UN General Assembly, which was followed by government white papers in 2005 and 2011.[96] Keyuan Zou, citing state news agency Xinhua, describes Hu's four-point proposal for 'an harmonious word' in the following terms:

> (1) multilateralism should be upheld to realize common security; (2) mutually beneficial cooperation should be upheld to achieve common prosperity; (3) the spirit of inclusiveness must be upheld to build a world where all civilizations coexist harmoniously and accommodate each other; and (4) the UN needs rational and necessary reform to maintain its authority, improve its efficacy and give a better scope to its role in meeting new threats and new challenges.[97]

Hu's concept of an 'harmonious world' was arguably the first comprehensive strategic proposal the Chinese government had initiated for the future international order since Mao.[98] As such, it sought to add detail to Deng's and Jiang's earlier yet still elusive concepts of a 'new international order' and a 'new security concept.' In the concrete world of Chinese foreign and security policy, the concept of an 'harmonious world' would nonetheless remain abstract. At a theoretical level, the idea was anchored in ancient Daoist traditions of harmony and balance, while also incorporating implied Confucian principles of hierarchical coordination and concepts of mutual reciprocity. At a more realist level, it represented China's first effort to answer a question increasingly posed by foreign governments: how does China propose to deploy its national 'wealth and power' once fully realized? And, from Beijing's perspective: how to counter the early emergence of what Chinese literature had begun referring to as 'the China threat thesis'?[99] Operationally, it also foreshadowed the emergence of a more activist Chinese policy, at least within the constraints of the UN multilateral system, than in the past.

The most important new development in Hu's 2012 party congress report concerned the Chinese military.[100] As with China's tentative steps towards a more proactive foreign policy, Hu brought in new language on the future role of the People's Liberation Army. Noting that China had risen from being the world's sixth-largest economy to the second-largest over his ten-year term, Hu announced: "building a strong national defence and powerful armed forces that are commensurate with China's international standing and meet the needs of its security and development interests is a strategic task of China's modernization drive".[101] Similarly, Hu deployed entirely new language on the purpose of this military modernization:

> We must, responding to China's core security needs and following the three-step development strategy for modernizing national defence and the armed forces, ensure both economic development and the development of defence capabilities, intensify efforts to accomplish the dual historic tasks of military mechanization and full IT application . . . [and] implement the military strategy of active defense for the new period. . . . We should attach great importance to maritime, space, and cyberspace security. We should make active planning for the use of military forces in peacetime, expand and intensify military preparedness, and enhance the capability to accomplish a wide range of military tasks, the most important of which is to win local wars in an information age.[102]

This was the first congress report to explicitly refer to a new doctrine of 'active military defense' with the objective of China fighting and prevailing in high-tech warfare. It was an implicit reference to China's unfolding military strategy for the South and East China Seas, the Taiwan Straits, and against the United States and its regional allies. In some respects, Hu's language foreshadowed changes in China's military doctrine and posture that would receive greater focus, intensity, and resources under his successor, Xi Jinping.

Conclusion

Several conclusions emerge from this review of the evolving official worldviews throughout China's classical history and the history of the People's Republic. First, the evidence demonstrates that Marxist-Leninist ideology mattered, both before and after 1978, in terms of the party's ongoing claims to national political legitimacy in the eyes of its membership and the people. It mattered as a central medium for both internal party discourse and as a guide to substantive policy action by the Chinese state. This was clear under Mao and continued under Deng—even when Deng deliberately sought to de-ideologize the party in furtherance of the economic pragmatism needed to achieve his political, policy, and development objectives. Deng's pragmatism nonetheless still had to be justified within the complex ideological frameworks of a Marxist-Leninist party—including dialectical materialism (by redefining the party's 'principal contradiction') and historical materialism (the 'primary stage of socialism'). Mao and Deng, however much they disagreed on policy and strategy, were nonetheless united by a common Marxist-Leninist ideological objective of lifting the Chinese people out of poverty and building a powerful socialist state.

Second, beyond Marxism, nationalism played a continuing role in constructing the CCP's overall worldview and its search for long-term, sustainable political legitimacy. In doing so, the party drew on classical concepts of Sino-centrism, the nineteenth- and twentieth-century narrative of Chinese victimhood at the hands of foreign powers, and national pride in China's more recent re-emergence as a global power. Nationalism as a force in Chinese politics ebbed and flowed but, by the time of Hu Jintao, it began re-emerging from the long shadows of the Cultural Revolution as an important prism through which the party and the country viewed their future role in the world at large. Indeed, as popular belief in Marxism-Leninism as a guiding ideology collapsed amidst Maoist political excess, nationalism gradually grew under Deng, Jiang, and Hu as China's national wealth and power increased. Nationalism, in this sense, began to emerge not just as a supplement, but also as an alternative to Marxism-Leninism in the party's ongoing search for legitimacy. And this, in turn, would be developed much further by Xi Jinping in the decade that would follow within a new ideological framework of what I have called Xi's Marxist Nationalism.

Third, strategic realism, derived in significant part from China's classical tradition—including the dynamics of the balance of power—played a continuing, central role in practical statecraft under Mao, Deng, Jiang, and Hu. Realism tempered Mao's ideological impulses over the United States and the Soviet Union, including his interventions in the Korean and Vietnam wars. It shaped Deng's view of the strategic triangle between Beijing, Moscow, and Washington, as well as his deep analysis of national economic development as a necessary precursor to any form of national strategic power, just as realism caused Jiang and Hu to conclude that changes in the balance of power during their twenty-year 'period of strategic opportunity' would afford China greater freedom of strategic manoeuvre in relation to other great powers. Deng, Jiang, and Hu, however, remained ideologically disciplined in their respective levels of policy activism because of their underlying recognition of the continuing preponderance of American strategic power. This tempering view of strategic reality, however, would no longer prove to be as persuasive and constraining a discipline in Xi Jinping's new era.

Finally, it is clear that in all three domains—Marxism-Leninism, Chinese nationalism, and strategic realism—the party's international worldview was inseparable from its domestic worldview. In a political system where the party in power holds a totalizing view of reality, we cannot fully understand one without the other. Under Mao, the ideology of China's domestic revolution was inseparable from his views on the Soviet Union, the United States, global revolution, and the revolutionary logic of his "Three Worlds Theory". Similarly, under Deng, Jiang, and Hu, the party's core domestic mission was to overcome mass poverty and build a powerful Chinese state, but without sacrificing the party's Leninist grip on political control. This domestic worldview produced a deeply instrumentalist rationale for China's patterns of international engagement after 1978. Under Deng, China recognized that it could only concentrate on economic development if it were free from external strategic threat from the USSR; hence China's temporary strategic alliance with the United States. Beijing also saw the United States, Japan, and the collective West as essential sources of technology, investment, and markets to drive up Chinese living standards, modernize its economy, and build a powerful Chinese state: hence the sublimation of other Chinese strategic and political interests to this overriding domestic economic objective. The same logic applied to China's relationships within the developing world, which were seen as important sources of raw materials and emerging export markets for Chinese goods; hence China's so-called good-neighbour approach, its multidirectional foreign policy to minimize differences, and the relegation of the revolutionary demands of international socialist solidarity. For these reasons, China's permissible areas of foreign policy friction with other states were limited to core threats to its political system domestically (e.g. Tiananmen) or to reunification with Hong Kong and Taiwan externally. Beyond these, China sought to minimize any differences with the world at large, fully recognizing its own relative weakness in the international system and the underlying imperative of economic development, at least until its national power relativities significantly improved.

All this would change, however, in the brave new world of Comrade Xi Jinping.

4

Changes to China's Ideological Worldview under Xi Jinping (2012–2017)

Dialectical materialism is the worldview and methodology of Chinese Communists.

—Xi Jinping, *Qiushi*, 2019

Xi Jinping's report to the 19th Party Congress in 2017 represents the most significant shift in the CCP's official worldview since 1982. It reflects Xi's interpretation of Marxist-Leninist ideology, its application to contemporary Chinese history and the centrality of the party's 'struggle' with opponents of his prescribed course for the country's future. A core element of this change has been Xi's official redefinition, within the formal analytical paradigms of Chinese Marxism-Leninism, of the 'major contradiction' (or, in non-Marxist language, central challenge) that the party now faces. This redefinition, and the processes that led to it over the preceding five years, form the ideological headwaters for the changes that have moved Chinese domestic politics and economic policy overall to the left. We see this in the newfound primacy of political ideology over pragmatic accommodation, the reassertion of the party's centrality over everything, and the concentration of political control in Xi personally. We see the same in the Chinese economy's parallel move to the left with the reassertion of state planning over private markets, state industrial policy and state-owned enterprises over the private sector, and a new doctrine of 'common prosperity'. By analysing Xi's report to the 19th Congress, and contrasting its content with the writings of Deng, Jiang, and Hu, it becomes clear that these pointed to a major ideological shift. As Xi himself claims, his period in office represents a substantive, rather than merely rhetorical, 'new era' in China's politics and political economy. Xi's ideological reformulations go well beyond the more predictable ebbs and flows of CCP political language that have accompanied previous changes in the party's post-Deng leadership. Indeed, they have become harbingers of radical policy change in the real world.

One further reason to emphasize the significance of the 19th Party Congress in defining changes to the party's worldview is the renewed importance of ideology itself under Xi. As argued in the previous chapter, ideological discourse has remained the prime mechanism for signalling political and policy change throughout the party's history. This was the case even for avowed non-ideologues like Deng, who still deployed Marxist ideological paradigms to legitimize his de-ideologization of the CCP to advance pro-market policies between 1978 and 1982. These post-1982 ideological parameters continued to be acknowledged in the official political discourse of Deng's two immediate successors, Jiang and Hu, albeit with subtle variations in the overall thematic of market-oriented economic development. In other words, even after nearly forty years of 'reform and opening', the Communist Party system still placed an internal political premium on its definition of Marxist-Leninist orthodoxy. This was reflected in both the particular developmental stage that the party believed it had reached in its relentless march forward through history, as well as its considered, dialectical definition of the 'central contradiction' of the present time. Taken together, these validated the party's overall political line and policy direction.

In Xi's case, the sheer scale and increasingly prescriptive content of his ideological oeuvre underscore the importance he attaches to using ideology in his wider political messaging to the party when compared to his post-Mao predecessors.[1] Xi's 19th Congress report is explicit that, under his leadership, the "importance of Marxism as a guiding ideology" was being "better appreciated".[2] He spoke forcefully of "the scientific truth of Marxism-Leninism"; the need to "ensure our theory evolves with the times, deepening our appreciation of the objective laws" of Marxism; and the importance of the CCP's Leninist character as "the vanguard of the times, the backbone of the nation, and a Marxist governing party".[3] Expounding on the features of "socialism with Chinese characteristics for a new era", Xi reminded his audience that: the party "has continued to uphold dialectical and historical materialism"; that "Chinese socialism's entrance into the new era is . . . of tremendous importance . . . in the history of the development of international socialism and . . . of human society"; and that "the Marxism of twenty-first-century China will, without a doubt, emanate a more mighty, more compelling power of truth".[4] And lest there be any doubt on the centrality of ideology and theory to the party's entire enterprise, Xi concluded this marathon address with the exhortation: "Theory is fundamental to Party building. Our revolutionary ideals soar beyond the skies. The noble ideal of Communism and the shared ideal of socialism with Chinese characteristics are our source of strength and political soul as Chinese Communists; they also form the theoretical foundation of Party solidarity and unity."[5] Previous reports by Deng, Jiang, and Hu, while all adhering to certain irreducible ideological fundamentals demanded by the high occasion of a party congress, cannot compare with Xi's full-throated gusto in embracing the centrality of his Marxist worldview to the party's and the country's future.[6]

Xi's more fundamental commitment to Marxism-Leninism had been underlined in a series of other party addresses delivered well before the 19th Party Congress in 2017. These include Xi's remarkable address to a Politburo study session in January 2015 on dialectical materialism, published nearly four years later in the party's theoretical journal *Qiushi* under the title 'Dialectical Materialism Is the Worldview and Methodology of Chinese Communists'.[7] Taken together with three other major party documents—a further Politburo study session conducted by Xi on historical materialism; his 2013 address to the National Ideology and Propaganda Work Conference; and his 2018 speech marking the 200th anniversary of Marx's birth[8]—these five addresses represent an early substantive ideological exposition of Xi's Marxist-Leninist worldview. They do not lead to a systematic definition of 'Xi-ism' or Xi Jinping Thought. They do, however, point to a different set of ideological priorities that differentiate Xi from all three of his post-Mao predecessors.

Xi on the Importance of Ideology and Propaganda

The most graphic example of Marxism-Leninism's centrality to Xi Jinping's ideological worldview lies in his reported remarks to the National

Conference on Ideology and Propaganda barely nine months into his general-secretaryship on 19 August 2013.[9] This address was framed in classical Marxist terms: the primary stage of socialism; the "hard rationale" of a "strategic ideology of development"; and the need to persevere in this mission unless "fundamental change occurs in great domestic or foreign trends".[10] Xi was candid that while "economic construction is central work, we do not say that . . . one pretty thing can conceal a hundred ugly things". He continued, just ensuring "that the masses' material lives are good" is an "incomplete" understanding because the Communist Party's "mass basis and governance basis includes both material *and* spiritual aspects".[11] In Xi's view, this meant the party must "resolutely overcome the phenomenon of vulgarization brought about by going all the way to meet the market."[12] In other words, Xi was already foreshadowing the need to adjust the party's ideological response to the political, social, and environmental impacts of unrestrained economic development after thirty-five years of reform and opening.

Equally remarkable from this August 2013 speech is Xi's stark rendition of the ideological divide between China and the West, the priority he attached to waging this 'struggle' effectively both at home and abroad, and his determination to roll back what he sees as China's excessively defensive ideological posture towards its critics. While Chinese political leaders have perennially reflected on how Western values impact the party's efforts to sustain Marxist orthodoxy, Xi's ideological offensive against the West, combined with his activist defence of Marxist-Leninist orthodoxy in general, is unique in the post-Tiananmen period. While Deng, Jiang, and Hu made episodic references to China's ideational divide with the West, and launched periodic campaigns against 'bourgeois liberalism',[13] Xi made clear that this would now become core, continuing business for the CCP. Xi warned the party that "the struggle in the international, ideological and cultural area is profound and complex"; that "Western countries see our country's development and expansion as a challenge to their values, systems and models"; that they are intensifying their "ideological and cultural infiltration of our country"; and that the "struggles and tests that we face in the ideological area are long-term and complex".[14] Although the term 'struggle' (*douzheng*) had remained in the party's official political discourse after 1976, leaders used it infrequently, forever mindful of Maoist excesses in the Cultural Revolution, including the Chairman's destructive exhortation to 'continuous' class struggle.[15] However, Xi's multiple references to struggle in this and subsequent speeches greatly exceed those of his post-Mao predecessors.[16] Indeed, Xi's deliberate invocation of ideological, revolutionary, and political consciousness, articulated through the medium of 'struggle', has become increasingly characteristic of his speechmaking as general secretary.

Xi was also candid in this speech on the importance of ideological struggle to sustaining party legitimacy: "The disintegration of a regime often starts from the ideological area, political unrest and regime change may perhaps occur in a night, but ideological evolution is a long-term process; if the ideological defences are breached, other defences become very difficult to hold."[17] Xi's preoccupation here with the preservation of political legitimacy, against the historical spectre of Soviet collapse, is a recurring theme across many of his speeches. Indeed, it has become a central rationale for the re-engineering of party ideology and the intensification of 'ideological work' that Xi would now require of the party overall. He argued here that the party must lift its ideological efforts given that it was up against a formidable, systematic, and professional ideological challenge from Western 'propaganda'.

While Xi's diagnosis of the ideological challenges facing the party focused on the defensive (i.e. protecting the party's domestic legitimacy), his prescription for action was decidedly offensive. He called on the party to "use scientific theory to arm our minds and incessantly foster our spiritual garden . . . by systematically grasping the basis of Marxist theory." He called on the party to believe that it had "justice on our side" and not be "evasive, bashful or mince our words" in dealing with the "ideological baselines" of Western countries and the interests their political parties represent. Xi added: "If the question is asked which party, which country and which nation can be self-confident, then the Chinese Communist Party, the People's Republic of China and the Chinese nation have reason for self-confidence, and on this point, truth is on our side." He contrasted this confidence with those in his own ranks who had "an inferiority complex and always believe that nothing in China is good, that everything foreign is good, and have the illusion of using Western systems to transform China". Xi argued that the party should instead synthesize the inherent strengths of Chinese culture with the scientific insights of Marxism-Leninism, "making clear that China's excellent traditional culture reflects the superiority of the Chinese nation, an important spiritual pillar for the Chinese nation . . . and our most profound cultural soft power".

Xi attacked the weaknesses of the West as demonstrated by the US-originated global financial and debt crises as "abuses" wrought by the "Western capitalist system". He attacked continued systemic inequality in the West. He railed against large-scale Western aggression in the wider Middle East, posing the rhetorical question: "While Western countries are exporting their values system and institutional models everywhere, in which country has this met with true success?" Xi then called on leading cadres to "stand in the teeth of the storm and conduct struggle" and "dare to bare the sword . . . contending for the absolute majority, launching a struggle for public opinion in a rational, beneficial and proper manner". Xi premised this trenchant ideological call to arms against the West on a withering assessment of his own party's ideological disrepair as inherited from his predecessors:

> Among our party members and cadre teams, lack of belief is a problem that needs to attract high attention. Among a few people, some have made criticism and mockery of Marxism into a 'fashion' or a comedy. Some are spiritually vapid and believe that Communism is a purely illusory fantasy. They 'don't pay attention to common people but to ghosts and spirits'. They hanker after fortune-telling and physiognomy, they pray to Buddha for help and fetishize 'qigong masters'. Some waver in their faith, migrate their spouses, sons and daughters abroad, store money abroad, and 'leave a back passage' for themselves, preparing to 'jump ship' at any time. Some are slaves of material things, believe in the supremacy of money, the supremacy of fame and the supremacy of enjoyment. They don't have any reverence in their hearts and their acts don't have any baseline at all.

Xi's prescription for the party's propaganda apparatus marked a new approach to countering the West's ideological offensive both at home and abroad. He cited the need to struggle against the doctrine of universal values, through which the West wanted "to vie with us for the battlefields of people's hearts and for the masses, and in the end to overthrow the leadership of the Chinese Communist Party and China's Socialist system". This meant cracking down on intellectuals, including those "harbouring dissent and discord against the party". It also meant a new focus on China's burgeoning cyberspace where, according to Xi, "Western anti-China forces continue to vainly attempt to 'topple China' . . . and infuse (it) with Western ambitions". For Xi, the China Dream was the ideological antidote. It was the key to unlocking a positive, alternative narrative, both within China and around the world. He argued the China Dream has not only helped mobilize Chinese domestic public opinion, but "also triggered a vigorous response abroad". He claimed that "international society is paying further attention to the glorious prospects and great opportunities for our country's development", with the result that in "Asia, Africa, Latin America and many other countries, leaders are all openly saying to us that they wish that the Chinese Dream becomes a reality". This meant that China needed to lift its ideological game globally to sell China's positive international message more effectively.

Xi Jinping's new campaign on ideology was turbocharged by a leaked internal party circular from the Central Committee General Office, also produced in 2013, which would become known as Document Number 9.[18] Officially titled 'A Communiqué on the Current State of the Ideological Sphere', it is likely to have followed Xi's August speech to the Central Propaganda Work Conference. The circular warns the party to be prepared for "intense" ideological struggle focusing on a number of "false ideological trends" that were aimed at destroying the party. It then lists seven of them:

- The use of Western "capitalist class concepts" of constitutional democracy and the separation of powers "to undermine the leadership of the Communist Party" and "bring about a change of allegiance by bringing Western political systems to China";
- The danger of Western concepts of universal values being used by the advocates of "reform and opening" to "supplant the core values of socialism", exploiting confusion within China as to whether Western values were the ultimate foundation of "long-standing Western dominance in economics, military affairs, science and technology";
- The use of civil society by "Western anti-China forces" to "squeeze the party out of its leadership of the masses", "even setting the masses and the party against each other" and creating "a serious form of political opposition";
- The promotion of "freedom of the media" to "attack the Marxist view of news", promote the "free flow of information on the internet", "oppose the party's leadership of the media and gouge an opening through which to infiltrate our ideology";
- The "nihilist" challenge to the party's "accepted conclusions on historical events and figures" to deny the "scientific and guiding

value of Mao Zedong Thought" and "cleave apart the period that preceded reform and opening from the period that followed"—all with a view to "denying the legitimacy of the CCP's long-term political dominance";

- The problem, created by some supporters of "reform and opening", that the reform of the political system had lagged well behind (and now impeded) economic reform, "banging on about how we should use Western standards to achieve so-called thorough reform"; and
- The problem of Western "neo-liberalism" and neo-liberal globalization pressuring China to embrace "complete marketization" with the "aim of changing our country's basic economic infrastructure and weakening the government's control of the national economy".[19]

The common thread with all the above is Xi Jinping's fundamental concern with the seriousness of the ideological threat to the party's Marxist worldview—both from the West, and from those within China supporting Western values. Document Number 9 went on to claim that "Western anti-China forces and internal dissidents are still actively trying to infiltrate China's ideological sphere and challenge our mainstream ideology". It concluded its general analysis of the ideological difficulties facing the party, stating: "This clearly indicates that the contest between infiltration and anti-infiltration efforts in the ideological sphere is as severe as ever and so long as we continue with the leadership of the Chinese Communist Party and socialism with Chinese characteristics . . . will not change."[20] The communiqué also outlined a series of measures to be implemented by the party under the general heading of 'Pay Close Attention to Ideological Work'. These include the supreme priority now attached to ideological struggle, "distinguishing between true and false theory", ensuring full Marxist control of the media, and managing "the ideological battlefield" thoroughly to "allow absolutely no opportunity or outlets for incorrect thinking or viewpoints to spread".

In short, Document Number 9 offers the single most candid exposition of the real level of central political concern with the party's ideological vulnerability. It offers an even more graphic account of Xi's anxieties in the ideological domain than his own address in July that year. Moreover, a central committee communique from the General Office on this subject could only have been issued with Xi's personal authorization. Xi's 2013 speech, reinforced by Document Number 9, therefore provides a remarkable, early enunciation of Xi's ideological worldview. First, he underlined the centrality of ideology to CCP survival when compared with the fall of the Soviet Union where, in his view, the rot had set in first with ideological decline. Second, Xi declared China's material progress was inadequate unless accompanied by progress in the spiritual (meaning ideological) domain, otherwise China would become victim to the 'vulgarization' of the market. Third, Xi saw China engaged in a Manichaean ideological struggle with the West for its very 'soul'. Fourth, he saw the contemporary CCP, after a long period of reform and opening, as being in a state of ideological disrepair, suffering a crisis of faith and needing to wage ideological struggle within its own ranks. And fifth, it was time to go on the ideological offensive against Western failures, to rekindle a fundamental belief in the Marxist-Leninist cause, and reinforce this ideological revival with Xi's new nationalist narrative of the 'China Dream'. These themes would resonate over the next decade of Xi's leadership.

Xi on Dialectical Materialism

Following the Marxist-Leninist revivalism of Xi's address to the Ideology and Propaganda Work Conference in 2013, his 2015 address on dialectical materialism was a paean of ideological praise for Mao's "shining example for our Party in grasping and applying" this core theoretical concept in the CCP's work.[21] Deng, by contrast, was relegated by Xi to secondary or even tertiary significance in his speech, while his references to Jiang and Hu were almost perfunctory. Xi's praise of Mao's two seminal ideological works, 'On Practice' and 'On Contradiction', was particularly significant. As noted in the previous chapter, these works were both written in 1937, just after Mao's political ascendancy in the party's leadership following the Zunyi Conference in 1935. Invoking Mao's ideological spirit was not just about restoring the party's theoretical rigour; it was also about entrenching the leader's power within the party.

For Xi, the intellectual engine room of Marxism is dialectical materialism, proclaiming it in his very first sentence as "the worldview and methodology of Chinese Communists". He stated that in "realizing the party's Two Centenary Goals and the Chinese dream of national rejuvenation, our Party must continue to draw on the wisdom of Marxist philosophy, and *more* consciously uphold and apply the worldview and methodology of dialectical materialism".[22] The insertion of the word 'more' during the careful process of drafting articles for the party's leading theoretical journal would not be accidental. Indeed, with this and other statements, Xi appears to be deliberately contrasting himself with his immediate predecessors' comparative neglect of the centrality of Marxist-Leninist ideology.

Xi then proceeds to expound on a number of core areas for further focussed party study on dialectical materialism, including its analytical methodology, across the full spectrum of the party's theoretical work. This included the "material unity of the world", the "universality and objectivity of contradictions", the "movement of opposites", the role of political "consciousness", the centrality of ideology in directing consciousness, the inter-relationship between knowledge and practice, and the dynamic application of these core principles of dialectical materialism to contemporary problems. In a relatively short work, Xi nonetheless sought to be comprehensive in executing his newfound responsibility as the party's ideologist-in-chief. He draws extensively on the ideological legacies of Mao and other political precursors in the CCP. But, adding his own claim to philosophical originality, Xi pointed also to many elements of the Chinese classical tradition which, he argued, reinforced the universality of dialectical materialist precepts. These included Xi's rendition of '*Yin*', '*Yang*', and the '*Dao*' as underscoring the universal truth of the unity of opposites, the laws of motion and the reconciliation of contradictions within an overall Marxist trajectory of progress. In other words, in exercising his powers as China's new philosopher-king, Xi's worldview now proclaimed that critical elements of Chinese tradition both pre-dated and separately validated Marxism's central ideological claims to objective, progressive truth.

Most important, Xi placed particular emphasis on the 'objective laws' of contradiction to correctly identify trends and challenges at work within contemporary China. Of equal importance, Xi made plain that contemporary China confronted much more than the single principal contradiction of economic under-development that Deng had identified in 1982—a point he would formalize in his report to the 19th Party Congress in 2017. He emphasized that these rising 'secondary' contradictions could not be ignored because of their unfolding relevance to Chinese society. Xi, in a much more deliberate swipe at his predecessors, also argued that China could no longer sustain the "long-term accumulation of problems" particularly when newer ones were "generated during the process of solving old ones". To continue amassing these contradictions or underlying challenges, in Xi's argument, would risk them coalescing into a critical mass and becoming a "disruptive force." He was vague about the nature of these current and emerging contradictions, but listed: the need for a new economic development model, rather than focusing purely on GDP growth as in the past; rising ecological damage; and a nascent equality agenda "so that all people can benefit more thoroughly and more fairly from the fruits of reform".

Xi's presentation on 'dialectical materialism' did not simply reassert Marxist ideological orthodoxy for Chinese politics, economics, and society on the home front; it included language relevant to China's international worldview as well. Although less explicit than in its domestic formulations, this article significantly adds to our analysis of Xi's ideological framework for understanding and responding to the world beyond China's shores. First, Xi argued that the analytical paradigm of dialectical materialism was important for China's 'strategic thinking' across the board; it is a framework "to better balance the relationships between phenomenon and essence, form and content, cause and effect, contingency and necessity, possibility and reality, internal cause and external cause, and generality and specificity". Furthermore, by using this framework, Xi claimed that "we will be able to enhance our capacity for dialectical thinking and strategic thinking and perform more effectively in *all* areas of our work". In other words, dialectical materialism was as relevant to international relations as it was to managing the emerging domestic challenges of China's political economy. Second, Xi declared that the analytical methodology of dialectical materialism applied to the party's conclusions on China's own enhanced national power, as well as those international forces now working against it: "China's productive forces [and] national strength (*zonghe guoli*) . . . have made historic leaps forward, and as the substance of China's basic national conditions shifts constantly, important changes have also emerged in the domestic and international risks and complex issues that we face." Xi added that "some problems that haunted us in the past no longer exist, but new ones are constantly surfacing, many of which have not been encountered or handled before". Third, dialectics also recognized that China's rise would inevitably give rise to international reaction. Although Xi's language appears deliberately guarded at this point (there is, for example, no explicit reference to the United States), the implications are relatively clear: "Most of [our] problems, however, are newly emerging alongside changes in China's overall circumstances and environment. The surfacing of many of them is inevitable in the current stage of development, and they cannot be avoided or sidestepped." Here the term "environment" refers to China's external strategic circumstances.

Finally, and arguably the most significant insight into Xi Jinping's general predisposition to tackle major domestic and international contradictions head-on through dialectical analysis and political struggle rather than simply deferring them, there was his lengthy presentation on the importance of preemptive action: "If we turn a blind eye to challenges, or even dodge or disguise them; if we fear to advance in the face of challenges and sit by and watch the unfolding calamity, then they will grow beyond our control and cause irreparable damage." This latter formulation—advocating a decisive, proactive approach to dealing with the vast array of contradictions that China now faced—was not explicitly directed at *either* China's domestic *or* its international agenda. It was, however, explicit throughout the *Qiushi* article that Xi's Marxist framework for analysing and dealing with contradictions applied to the *full* spectrum of the party's work. What was not made explicit, however, was whether the party's methods for struggling against these contradictions were to be—using Mao's original schemata[23]—'antagonistic' (i.e. violent) or 'non-antagonistic' (i.e. peaceful).

Xi on Historical Materialism

To remove any doubt about Xi Jinping's fundamental reaffirmation of the importance of orthodox Marxist-Leninist analytical frameworks to contemporary China, Xi expanded his ideological canon to include a separate address to the Politburo explicitly dedicated to dialectical materialism's twin discipline: historical materialism. Delivered first in January 2013, but not published until 2020 in *Qiushi*, the article was titled 'Maintaining the Importance of Historical Materialism in Unceasingly Pioneering New Boundaries for Contemporary Chinese Marxism'.[24] In it, Xi reminded the party that, during his five years as head of the Central Party School, his core message was that Marxist philosophy was *the* principal subject (*zhuyao timu*) for all party cadres. Xi recalled his earlier address to the school where he cited approvingly the view of Chen Yun, a former leading party conservative and one of Deng's principal internal opponents in the 1980s and 1990s.[25] Chen Yun had said that "in studying theory, the most important challenge is to deploy the correct ideological method; it is therefore essential to study philosophy to understand the correct ideological methodology for observing things; and if you do not understand dialectical materialism, you will always make mistakes".[26] As with Xi's speech on dialectical materialism, Xi in this article draws extensively on Mao's 'On Contradiction' and 'On Practice', as well as Mao's earlier 'Notes on Dialectical Materialism' (*bianzheng weiwulun jiangshou tigang*) on which those two works were based.[27]

Xi, however, also made more expansive use of Mao's 1942 speech entitled 'Rectify the Party's Style of Work' (*zhengdun dangde zuofeng*), delivered at the height of a campaign criticizing Mao's internal party opponents, many of whom would later be purged.[28] This appears to be a deliberate reminder to Xi's tremulous party colleagues of his own zeal for party building and anti-corruption, as emphasized in his earliest remarks as general secretary.[29] Indeed, the publication of this address in 2020, seven years after it was delivered, immediately preceded Xi's launch of his own rectification movement proper (along Yan'an lines) in August that year. In this speech, Xi approvingly quoted Mao as "calling on comrades to learn how to: use the standpoint, position and methodology of Marxism-Leninism in the analysis of China's history, economics, politics, military and culture; to use detailed material in deepening our analysis on every subject being dealt with; and then integrate this analysis with theory".[30] This lengthy tribute to Mao's ideological rigour in applying Marxism-Leninism across the totality of the party's practical challenges concludes with Xi calling on the contemporary party "to adopt the same correct attitude to our study of historical materialism today".

Xi also used this 2013 address on historical materialism to begin foreshadowing the ideological grounds for formally redefining the party's 'major contradiction' in 2017. Xi asserted that all the correct decisions in CCP history were taken through the analytical lens of historical materialism. This included 'reform and opening' which followed the party's recognition of China's undeveloped factors of production in its present stage of historical development—namely the primary stage of socialism. Therefore, Xi said, this meant understanding the complex "mutual interaction, mutual restrictions and mutual control" exerted between "the factors of production and the relations of production", as well as between the "economic base and the social superstructure". This meant the party had to engage in continuing "adjustment" (*tiaozheng*) of the interaction between the relations of production and the social superstructure on the one hand, and their accommodation of the dynamism being unleashed by the factors of production and the economic base (through the operation of a socialist market economy) on the other. However, Xi goes on to caution that these relationships were "extremely complex" and they could sometimes generate a "counter-reaction from the social superstructure towards the economic base". This meant the party could not afford to "set aside its concerns about the state of the relations of production". Xi reminded the party that it has had a long tradition of "grasping two things simultaneously" (*liangshouzhua*)—including balancing "material and spiritual civilization", "development and stability", and "reform and opening together with evil and corruption"—and this same approach would be needed again. This would require what Xi called "a new top-down design, a new total plan, which understood the interrelationship of all the aspects of reform" and one that was "capable of solving the problems emerging within the relations of production and the social superstructure".

These tortured theoretical formulations provide an ideological justification for reining in the political, social, and environmental excesses that were generated over decades of unrestrained, pro-market economic development. While Xi does not explicitly mention economic inequality, his extensive references to 'the relations of production' underscore his concerns about emerging class divisions. They also point to the new 'contradictions' that Xi refers to elsewhere in his written works that needed to be addressed. By Xi's logic, these now had to be dealt with, rather than the party continuing to ignore them by simply pushing on with its decades-long exclusive focus on economic development. This conclusion would finally lead Xi's party to redefine formally its major "contradiction" four years later at the 19th Party Congress.

Report to the 19th Party Congress

Xi Jinping's report to the 19th Party Congress in 2017 returned to the theme of the absolute centrality of ideology to the CCP's political legitimacy. Touting "significant advances on the theoretical and cultural fronts", Xi told the Congress he had "*strengthened* Party leadership over ideological work and explored *new* ground in advancing Party-related theories"; and now "the importance of Marxism as a guiding ideology is *better* appreciated" (my emphasis).[31] According to Xi, the "scientific truth of Marxism-Leninism" had saved China from its culture of national "passivity", resulting in a nation now "taking the initiative". This had happened through the agency of a "Marxist governing party" that needed to "remain the vanguard of the times [and] the backbone of the nation". In short, Xi's language conveys and reinforces the imperative of ideological renewal following a period of ideological decline.

Xi's core argument was that, given China's changing conditions in the 'new era', the full application of orthodox Marxist methodology demanded a new body of thought to guide the party's future. Warming to his theme about the party's and the country's future, Xi frames this for his colleagues as "the question of an era (*shidai de wenti*) to which our answer must be a systematic combination of theory and practice that addresses what kind of socialism with Chinese characteristics the new era requires us to uphold and develop, and how we should go about doing it". Answering his own question, Xi emphasizes his recourse to classical Marxist analytical methodologies. And the unsurprising result of this process of deep ideological analysis over the previous five years was now the 'Thought on Socialism with Chinese Characteristics for a New Era'—or, in its now customarily shortened form, 'Xi Jinping Thought':

> In answering this question, our Party has continued to uphold dialectical and historical materialism; has considered carefully the new conditions of the era and the new requirements of practice; **and has adopted an entirely new perspective to deepen its understanding of the laws that underlie governance by a Communist party**, the development of socialism, and the evolution of human society. It has . . . achieved major theoretical innovations, ultimately giving shape to the Thought on Socialism with Chinese Characteristics for a New Era. (my emphasis)

This is a critical paragraph in Xi's overall exegesis of the need for theoretical and, therefore, ideological change. It explicitly states that, by applying the core Marxist disciplines of historical and dialectical materialism to Chinese realities after thirty-five years of reform and opening, "an entirely new perspective" was now needed to conform to the scientific laws of

Marxist development. This was necessary to correct the ideological indolence of the past, including its excessive emphasis on material rather than spiritual development. And it was also needed so that the party could go on the ideological offensive internationally, consistent with Xi's injunction at the party's propaganda work conference in 2013. Indeed, these were now the essential epistemological determinants of Xi's 'new era'—a phrase which of itself signifies a deliberate break from the ideological past, rather than a more gradual shift in practical policy direction that was still within the previous theoretical framework inherited from Deng, Jiang, and Hu.

The bulk of Xi's report in 2017 emphasized the importance of the brand-new ideological world the party was now embracing. This ideological change was not only significant to China but, in an almost messianic way, it also now held global significance well beyond the few remaining outposts of the socialist world:

> Chinese socialism's entrance into a new era, in the history of the development of the People's Republic of China and the history of the development of the Chinese nation, is of tremendous importance. In the history of the development of international socialism and the history of the development of human society it is of tremendous importance.

And, in case Congress delegates still failed to grasp that Xi Jinping Thought was now central to the future of Marxism globally, the general secretary observed that "if we respond to the call of our times and have the courage to uphold truth and correct errors, the Marxism of twenty-first-century China will, without a doubt, emanate a more mighty, more compelling power of truth". In this phrase, Xi was invoking language used by none of his predecessors since the end of the Mao era.

To a Chinese political audience, this language was particularly sharp in light of the seminal debates of the late 1970s and early 1980s on "practice as the sole criterion for testing truth".[32] These were debates that Deng had resolved resolutely on the side of practice and against theory (*buzhenglun*). In Deng's China, the leader had argued there had been too much theory and too much politics—and not enough practice and not enough economics. In Xi's China, by contrast, there was not enough theory and not enough politics. Forty years after Deng's ascension, Xi starkly reifies thought, theory, and ideology in this 'new era' as political ends in themselves, rather than as pragmatic means to maximize economic and national praxis:

> Theory is fundamental to Party building. . . . Our top priority in building the Party through theory . . . is to make all Party members keep firmly in mind the Party's purpose, have unwavering convictions as Communists, resolve the fundamental issue of the worldview (*shijieguan*), outlook on life, and values we should embrace, and maintain deep belief in and faithfully practice Communism and socialism with Chinese characteristics.[33]

The theoretical crux of Xi Jinping's transformation of party ideology, however, lies in his redefinition of the 'principal contradiction' faced by Chinese society in this new era: "the contradiction between unbalanced and inadequate development and the people's ever-growing needs for a better life".[34] Xi did not elaborate in his 2017 address on the precise meaning of 'unbalanced and inadequate development'; but, within the Chinese ideological system, these terms represent a critique of past approaches to economic reform and opening that kept market principles consistently at the centre.[35] This new reference to 'unbalanced and inadequate development' provided ideological and political support for the return of a greater role for the party in relation to the market, greater state involvement in the private economy, and greater party and state intervention against social inequality and unsustainable environmental practices. To be sure, Xi's continuing reference to 'the primary stage of socialism'—and the implied need for the long-term development of the factors of production—provided some support for further market reform and opening, and for China's growing entrepreneurial class. Nonetheless, the official redefinition of the party's principal contradiction explicitly changed the balance between these two sets of policy imperatives. Moreover, on the economy, this shift was reinforced by a new reference in Xi's report to China's need for future economic 'self-reliance' (*ziligengsheng*), rather than greater exposure to international sources of supply through continued, largely untrammelled globalization. Once again, the political significance of this formal rewriting of the party's ideological direction, including its potential impact on all areas of public policy, is explicitly underlined by Xi himself:

> We must recognize that the evolution of the principal contradiction facing Chinese society represents a historic shift that affects the whole landscape and that creates many new demands for the work of the Party and the country. Building on continued efforts to sustain development, we must devote great energy to addressing development's imbalances and inadequacies. . . . With this, we will be better placed to meet the ever-growing economic, political, cultural, social, and ecological needs of our people.[36]

Thus China's ideologist-in-chief made plain his theoretical justification for returning the party and state to the centre stage of China's development—at the expense of the primacy of markets and private enterprise as it had been over the previous thirty-five years.

Xi on the National and Global Significance of Marxism

Six months after the party congress, in May 2018, these changing thematics within China's overall ideological discourse were enunciated with even greater clarity in his national address commemorating the 200th anniversary of Marx's birth.[37] Once again, there is nothing comparable in the collected works of Deng, Jiang, or Hu. Running to 15,000 characters, the speech was an unprecedented exhortation of the historical, contemporary, and future significance of Marxism to China's national and international destiny. Xi praised Marx as "the greatest thinker in human history", and declared *Das Kapital* "the bible of the working class" with theories that continued "to emanate their brilliant rays of truth". Xi lauded the ethical value of Marxism because of its core mission: "the emancipation of humankind" by providing "a powerful source of inspiration for people to understand and remould the world". Indeed, in a calculated rebuke to non-revolutionary political traditions, Xi notes: "the basic difference between a Marxist political party and other political parties is that the former always stands with the people and fights for their interests". Marx was also recognized for scientifically identifying the patterns of human development, including "the laws governing capitalist operations", proclaiming afresh China's continuing "firm belief in the scientific truth of Marxism".

Remarkably, Xi Jinping also attributed China's economic success during the period of reform and opening to Marxism rather than the market. According to Xi, it was Marx's critical insight into the centrality of the proper relationship between the factors of production and the relations of production that enabled the party to "complete a process of development that had taken the West several centuries to complete, thus propelling our country's high-speed rise to become the world's second-largest economy". For China's current leaders, Marxism therefore remained "a formidable theoretical tool which we use to understand the world, grasp its underlying patterns, search for its truth, and effect change." For these reasons, the party needed "to have a complete mastery of the worldviews and methodologies of dialectical and historical materialism, and fully understand that realizing Communism is a historical process involving the step-by-step achievement of milestones along the way". This was particularly important in China's current circumstances because "at present, the importance of reform, development, stability, the number of contradictions, risks, and challenges, and the tests of our capacity to govern are all at an unprecedented level". This meant it was "essential that we continually improve our ability to utilize Marxism to analyse and resolve practical problems, and continually improve our ability to utilize scientific theories to guide us in responding to major challenges and addressing major contradictions".

While Xi Jinping was adamant that there was no "doctrinal" or "immutable version of socialism" on offer, Marx provided a universal methodology for investigating and responding to the world which remained essential. To discard the principles of 'scientific socialism' derived from Marxist methodology would be to discard socialism itself given that "it was with the victory of the 1917 October Revolution [in Russia] that socialism transformed from theory to reality and thus broke the global capitalist order which had dominated the world".[38] And in a bold declaration of ideological bravura, Xi added that, despite international socialism encountering "complications in its development [i.e. the Soviet Union's collapse] the overall trend in human development had not changed, nor would it change." Indeed, Xi argued that Marxism continued "to advance the progress of human civilization, to provide theoretical and discursive systems of major international influence such that Marx to this day continues to be acknowledged as the 'number one thinker of the millennium' ".

This brought Xi directly to the question of 'world history'—particularly his approach to the applicability of Marxist historical determinism to the future of the international order. Xi argued that Marxist theory remained universally applicable, not just to China, because the global modes of capitalist production that emerged through economic globalization would inevitably generate their own internal contradictions. These would, in turn, drive the world to change:

> Studying Marx requires us to study and practice Marxist thought on world history. Marx and Engels once said that, "The more the original isolation of separate nationalities is destroyed by the developed mode of production,

> commerce, and the division of labour between various nations naturally brought forth by these, the more does history become world history." Marx and Engels's prediction of those years has since become a reality; history and reality increasingly prove the scientific value of this prediction. . . . We need to look from the perspective of world history and examine the development trends and the problems we face in the world today.[39]

Xi Jinping's ideological observations on the relevance of Marxism beyond China's shores are significant to his overall worldview. In this speech, there is evidence that Chinese Marxism as an intellectual system itself was beginning to shape the CCP's international worldview in a way we had not seen since before 1978. Xi, for the first time, publicly invoked the inexorable forces of 'world history' now at work unravelling global liberal capitalist hegemony. In other words, China's emerging international worldview is driven not just by rising Chinese nationalism (which will be addressed later in this book) or by the search for strategic advantage in the classical balance of power. It is also driven, at least in part, by a Chinese Marxist view that the inherent contradictions of the capitalist world are speeding its inevitable decline and putting fresh wind in the sails of China's inevitable rise.

Conclusion

These five addresses on ideology, each dealing with different aspects of Xi's Marxist narrative, point to a number of critical changes in the party's official worldview. First, Xi is the first party leader since Mao to deliver speeches explicitly dedicated to Marxist analytical methodology. While not adding to the conceptual content of Marxist methodology, Xi consciously parted company from Deng, Jiang, and Hu by restating its importance at length, and early in his period in office. And he emphasized that Marxist frameworks needed to be applied in analysing *all* China's current policy challenges, not just on the domestic front. Second, Xi levelled a remarkably sharp ideological critique of his predecessors for having failed to deal with the "new contradictions" generated by decades of market economic reform. Xi raised alarm about "disruptions" to the system because so many challenges had been "left undone",[40] even forecasting "unfolding calamity" unless the party tackled them head-on. Third, on the substantive definition of these new contradictions, Xi was explicit that the party needed to adjust its economic development model to deal with rising inequality, rejecting the 'marketization' of everything. Ideologically, Xi made plain that this shift on income distribution was part of a wider ideological 'readjustment' (*tiaozheng*)[41] in the relationship between the economic base and the social superstructure, or between the factors of production and the relations of production. In other words, Xi was concerned that China's market economic reforms were not only potentially producing a new class of capitalists, but that this class could undermine the politics of the superstructure, where ideological consciousness remained fundamental. This longer-term danger was posed by those demanding liberal-democratic political reforms, or by the corruption of the party's revolutionary culture, or both. Indeed, Xi's articulation of this new set of contradictions represented an implicit repudiation of Jiang Zemin's doctrine of the 'Three Represents' which sought to deal with the problem of a rising capitalist class by welcoming them into the ranks of the Communist Party itself, rather than remaining ideologically vigilant against their material excesses. Fourth, Xi saw this definition of the party's new principal contradiction as heralding a 'new era' in the party's history, following the thirty-five-year period of reform and opening which had followed the principal contradiction that was determined back in 1981. This new contradiction and new era, therefore, required a new body of thought to navigate the party's future course—namely Xi Jinping Thought.

Furthermore, in all this, Xi saw himself as engaged in an existential ideological struggle with the West—not just for China's political soul, but also in the world at large. This can be inferred from the first four texts examined in this chapter, but it is clarified beyond any real doubt in Xi's extraordinary 2018 address on the 200th anniversary of Marx's birth. Xi's discourse thus represents what I call a new form of 'Marxist Nationalism' as a core part of his new, unfolding ideological worldview. Xi's identification of the West as China's principal ideological opponent is radically different from the recent past, as is his determination to engage in a full-frontal political assault on those attacking China's own ideological model. Deng, Jiang, and Hu at different times warned the party of the dangers of bourgeois liberalism, while routinely being clear that China's most dangerous ideological challenges still came from 'left'[42] critiques of the country's pro-market economic development model. Under Xi, although the terms 'left' and 'right' were no longer used, he clearly identified the major threat as now lying on the ideological right. Xi also, for the first time, called for an ideological offensive against the West, including its domestic sympathizers within China, because both the country and the party were now powerful enough to do so. And he argued that the party should also have confidence in the righteousness of its Marxist-Leninist cause in exposing the abject failures of the capitalist system—both at home and abroad.

Finally, Xi Jinping's various speeches fully rehabilitated the terminology of 'struggle' in both the domestic *and* international discourse of the CCP. For Xi, struggle had become the principal verb across the full range of the party's endeavours. For example, Xi mentioned the term 'struggle' a total of forty-five times in his reports to the 19th and 20th National Congresses, compared with twenty-five references by his predecessors in all five previous congresses combined. This is not just a rhetorical device; a careful analysis of its use in these critical texts indicates its intrinsic real-world significance—referring as Mao once did to the active process by which change is secured through conscious dialectical conflict between progressive and reactionary forces. Moreover, there is nothing to suggest from Xi's discourse that this rehabilitated concept of active struggle is limited to the party's domestic challenges. Indeed, in Xi's worldview, 'struggle' is a universal concept, incorporating China's struggle for the future of the international system as well.[43] And it remains unclear from the discourse whether these various forms of struggle, foreign and domestic, are to remain permanently peaceful.

5

Ideological Change under Xi and the Transformation of Chinese Domestic Politics

Given the dramatic ideological changes introduced by Xi Jinping during his first term (2012–2017), the question arises as to their impact in the real world of Chinese politics and public policy. This brings us back to a core question underlying this book: is ideology a precursor to policy change, a post-facto rationalization for changes already taken for more pragmatic reasons, or, as I argue, an untidy combination of both? Wherever the balance lies, it would be foolish for Western analysts to ignore the rarefied world of CCP theoretical discourse, not least because the party under Xi, despite its multiple challenges, dedicates extraordinary attention and resources to the ideological domain. Whether ideological shifts in the party's official discourse precede or follow changes in the real world, they are pored over by Chinese political elites to interpret the context, content, and significance of new directions in the hard-edged domains of politics and public policy. Our task as foreign analysts of the Chinese system is to try to do the same, while recognizing that we are looking into a rarefied world where our level of illumination remains incomplete.

There are a range of scholarly opinions on the nexus between ideology, politics, and policy in Xi Jinping's China. Elizabeth Perry, for example, argues that Xi has elevated the overall political significance of ideology itself within the Chinese party system, reclaiming for the ideological domain "an explicit primacy and global ambition that scholars can no longer ignore."[1] Other scholars of the Xi period, most particularly Kerry Brown, contend that ideology has always played a significant role in the life of the CCP. Brown and his coauthor, Una Aleksandra Bērziņa-Čerenkova, recognize that while ideology has become more 'nuanced' in the post-Mao period, it nonetheless remains "a body of practices, beliefs, and language which have been bequeathed to them by previous leaders, and which show that they are part of the same historical movement that runs from 1921 to 1949, and through 1978 until today".[2] Indeed, ideology provides the CCP what has been elegantly described as an accepted 'band of meaning' within which high-level political communication occurs across party elites.[3] In fact, few if any scholars argue that ideology can simply be ignored, or else dismissed as mere formalism in which the CCP no longer has any level of actual belief.

The following four chapters analyse the relationship between, on the one hand, Xi Jinping's changing ideological worldview, and, on the other, a number of major real-world shifts in Chinese politics and its political economy. This chapter does so in relation to Xi's power within the party, in particular as its new ideologist-in-chief; the role of the party and its relationship to the institutions of the Chinese state; and a new preference for ideological over professional competence in cadre selection and elevation. Chapters 6, 7, and 8 deal with the changing direction of economic ideology under Xi as the Chinese economy becomes increasingly statist and less supportive of the market; more embracing of the state-owned sector and less supportive of the aspirations of the private sector; and more inclined to 'common prosperity' rather than tolerating income inequality. I argue across all four chapters that, for the party elite, ideology, and the band of meaning it represents, remains essential. It provides a basis for policy direction, organizational coherence, institutional discipline, and as a sense of higher moral purpose—quite apart from the party's continuing search for enduring political legitimacy. In fact, ideology pervades all the above. As argued in a previous chapter, it represents, in reality, a continuing 'red thread' across all that the party seeks to do.

I do not contend, however, that ideology provides the total explanation of *all* policy change under Xi Jinping, or that ideology is some sort of perfect CCP transmission system from theory into practice. I argue instead that ideology represents a significant signalling device for unfolding change in the hard and often brutal world of Chinese politics and public policy. This remains the case irrespective of whether it can be established that ideological change has *caused* a given policy shift, or whether ideology has been adjusted post-facto to legitimize a change that may have originated elsewhere, as, for example, Michael Oakeshott and Benjamin

Schwartz argued in the 1950s and 1960s.[4] This book argues that the concept of ideology providing a band of meaning within the established patterns of CCP discourse offers the most useful framework for analysing the practical policy impact of Xi's evolving worldview. And as argued above, if ideology was not recognized as an important mechanism for high-level intra-party political communication, it would beg the question as to why Xi personally has dedicated so much time, effort, and attention to the content and direction of CCP theory (as does the system around him). For Xi, the question of ideological worldview remains fundamental to all, at least as measured by the importance attached to his writings and actions to date. And if Xi takes ideology seriously, then so should those seeking to make sense of Chinese politics and public policy in his so-proclaimed 'new era'.

Ideology, Internal Politics, and the Shift to the Left

A central argument of this book is that the reification of Marxism-Leninism under Xi Jinping, and its instrumentalization across multiple party and policy domains since 2013, has been accompanied by a decisive shift to the left across Chinese domestic politics. The central organizational factor across all these changes has been Xi's unapologetic reinvention of a disciplined Leninist party as the irreplaceable political machinery at the heart of the state. For Xi, the party has become indispensable to the realization of his overriding ideological mission, the core of which is to create a more equitable Marxist society at home and a strong Chinese state whose power and influence can be projected abroad. These new ideological priorities have been reflected in:

- a new expectation of political loyalty towards the party centre (most particularly, absolute loyalty to Xi himself), radically reducing the space for internal political and policy dissent, and purging any perceived political opponents;
- empowerment of the party centre to deliberate on and execute policy (particularly economic policy), thereby diminishing the role of the more technocratic State Council;
- the internal 'cleansing' of Xi's Leninist party through a comprehensive anti-corruption campaign after 2013;

- a wider political cleansing of the party through a 'rectification campaign' launched in 2020 across the party's entire political and legal affairs apparatus;
- a new agenda on the 'securitization' of everything, including reasserting party control over the PLA, relocating the People's Armed Police from the organizational umbrella of the State Council to the party itself, and in the control and direction of cyber security and party surveillance systems;
- the renewed centrality of the party to all domains of public policy and private life, including its institutional relationships with the media, universities, non-governmental organizations, arts and culture, as well as the institutions of religious governance;
- and finally, instilling the paramount importance of ideological discipline for party members, as reflected in a new series of regulations and education campaigns aimed at resuscitating the CCP's Marxist-Leninist core and enlivening a new community of secular faith around it.

The Centralization of Power

The concentration of political power in the person of Xi Jinping since 2012 is reflected in several specific changes in the party's internal institutional arrangements and in the nomenclature used to describe Xi's evolving status within the party hierarchy. The most obvious of these changes has been Xi's chairmanship of a growing number of CCP Central Committee 'Leading Groups' to coordinate policy, rather than the administrative agencies of the Chinese state. While Hu Jintao headed four of these groups between 2002 and 2012, by 2021 Xi was chairing at least eight, spanning the breadth of all policy development across the Chinese system.[5] Xi has also formally enhanced the institutional status of these leading groups; by 2018, the National People's Congress had elevated five of them into 'Central Policy Commissions' as well as creating another three additional commissions from scratch.[6] Most spectacularly, principal policy responsibility for finance, the economy, and the future direction of 'comprehensive reform' has been effectively transferred from the State Council to the central party bureaucracy.[7]

Moreover, at the Fifth Plenum of the 18th Central Committee in October 2016, Xi was bestowed the title 'core leader', with all party members instructed to "closely unite around the CCP Central Committee with Comrade Xi Jinping as the core."[8] As Miller and others have noted, the notion of a core leader was not of itself new; Deng Xiaoping had stated as early as June 1989 that "a collective leadership must have a core" and designated Jiang Zemin as 'core leader' to reconsolidate the central leadership following the purge of Zhao Ziyang.[9] By contrast, the 2016 decision on Xi's core leadership status represented, in effect, a self-coronation, rather than reflecting the consensus position of party elders. Importantly, Hu Jintao was never accorded the honorific title of 'core'.

Xi's core leadership status was codified in the party's 'Regulations on the Work of the Central Committee' for the first time in September 2020.[10] Previously the stated institutional practice was that all Politburo members enjoyed equal status in internal debates. By contrast, Xinhua reported that Xi's new status represented "an inevitable requirement for strongly safeguarding the authority and centralized leadership of the Central Committee" while also being of "great and far-reaching significance in advancing socialism with Chinese characteristics in the new era".[11] Before this, as early as October 2017, the Politburo had approved 'Regulations on Safeguarding and Enhancing Centralized, Unified Leadership' requiring them to "firmly safeguard Xi's position at the core of the CCP Central Committee and the whole party".[12] This provision, among a set of centralizing measures to "fully implement" the requirements of the 19th Party Congress, had never been used for his predecessors. According to the 2020 regulations, all members of the Politburo and Central Committee would report annually on their efforts to "earnestly implement democratic centralist principles and procedures" within the party.[13] In other words, other central leaders were now required to respect, safeguard, and report to the party's 'core leader'. Xi was no longer first among equals; he had become China's unqualified paramount leader.

As these new powers were entrenched within the Politburo and Central Committee, a parallel change enjoined the PLA that "in staunchly safeguarding the core, the most important thing is resolutely safeguarding and implementing the Central Military Commission chairman (Xi Jinping)'s responsibility system".[14] Following the 19th Congress, the PLA leadership defined this mandate as "accomplishing all the important items that

Chairman Xi has determined, and doing all the work that Chairman Xi has put them in charge of, and in all their actions obeying Chairman Xi's commands".[15] CMC Vice-Chairman Xu Qiliang lauded Xi as the "core of the party Central Committee, the core of the entire party, and commander (*tongshuai*) of the military".[16] Meanwhile, General Fan Changlong took these honorifics to a new level altogether by referring to Xi as a 'great leader' (*lingxiu*)—a title previously reserved for Mao alone.[17]

Amidst this intense season of power consolidation, the constitutional change that underscored Xi's entrenchment of long-term personal authority came with the National People's Congress's decision in March 2018 to abolish the two-term limit for the presidency of the PRC. While China's official commentary was quick to point out that the abolition of term limits did "not signify life tenure for offices of leading cadres",[18] it conceded the decision was nonetheless "necessary to provide surety for the nation's progress".[19] This singular treatment of Xi was underlined by the maintenance of two-term limits for all other state positions, including the premier, vice-premier, and chairman of the National People's Congress. Xi's two other party positions—general secretary of the CCP and chairman of the Central Military Commission—have never had formal term limits.

Consistent with this extraordinary concentration of political power in office, Xi Jinping has also wielded his power with considerable effect in the purge, trial, and incarceration of those deemed to be his opponents for "serious violations of discipline and law". These have included: former Politburo Standing Committee member Zhou Yongkang; former Politburo members Bo Xilai, Guo Boxiong, and Xu Caihou; and serving Politburo members Sun Zhengcai and Ling Jihua.[20] Pre-2017 leaders of the Central Military Commission were also removed[21] along with outspoken non-party critics such as Ren Zhiqiang.[22] While all were dealt with on the pretext of 'anti-corruption', other official statements have pointed explicitly to resistance to Xi's political and policy direction and the formation of anti-party 'cliques' operating against the central leadership.[23]

Just three years after Xi had been hailed within the CCP with the new status of '*tongshuai*' and '*lingxiu*', the Fifth Plenum of the 19th Central Committee in November 2020 added a further honorific which deliberately paralleled Mao Zedong's status as the party's 'Great Helmsman' (*weida duoshou*) which the PRC's founder had used during the Cultural Revolution. In Xi's case, the Plenum bulletin praised him as "the pilot at the helm" (*linghang zhangduo*): "With Comrade Xi Jinping as the core of the Central Committee of the CCP, and the pilot at the helm at the core, with the whole Party and full unity of people of all ethnic groups in the country, tenaciously struggling, we will surely be able to overcome the various difficulties and obstacles that appear on the road forward, and we will surely be able to energetically advance the forward progress of socialism with Chinese characteristics in the new era."[24] In the space of four years, Xi had become 'the core', the 'marshal', the 'great leader', and now 'pilot at the helm' of his increasingly Leninist party. This is particularly important given the historical significance attached to each of these terms by the Chinese political class and the perceived authority that would therefore be attached to each of Xi's individual ideological pronouncements. With the single exception of the title 'core leader', which had been used for Jiang Zemin, none of these titles had been used by any of Xi's post-Mao predecessors.[25]

In only five years, a cascading set of actions and announcements had therefore built Xi Jinping's new Mao-like status, reinforced by an almost Mao-like cult of personality. But beyond all these accolades, Xi's ultimate power as China's ideologist-in-chief was underscored by the critical decisions of the 19th Party Congress in 2017 and the 13th National People's Congress in 2018 to entrench 'Xi Jinping Thought on Socialism with Chinese Characteristics for the New Era' into the party and state constitutions.[26] This constitutional elevation of Xi Jinping Thought has occurred remarkably early in Xi's tenure, relative to the theoretical contributions of his recent predecessors, underlining further the speed with which his personal political power had become entrenched. Moreover, like Mao and Deng, Xi Jinping Thought now attached his personal name to the body of philosophy for which he was responsible (unlike Jiang's and Hu's ideological contributions). Furthermore, Xi Jinping has the singular distinction of joining Mao Zedong alone in carrying the loftiest title of all—'*sixiang*', meaning 'thought'—to describe the overall content of his ideological contribution. The 'theories' and 'outlooks' of Deng, Jiang, and Hu do not carry this title.

Each of these developments since 2012 represented a significant change in Xi Jinping's political status relative to his post-Mao predecessors. Taken together, they reflect a major transformation in the distribution of political power—between party and state in general and, most specifically, between the party leader and the rest of the central leadership. Some have disagreed with the characterization of these power consolidation measures representing a broad shift to the 'left' in Chinese politics.[27] Nonetheless, in Xi's ideological worldview, it was only through strengthening the party's leadership in all policy domains, and entrenching his personal power within the party, that there was any real prospect of realizing China's overarching socialist and nationalist ambitions. Furthermore, through the CCP's long historical, political, and ideational lens, the concentration of power in the hands of a leader at the expense of the party's collective leadership was almost universally seen as a move to the left—bearing in mind the deeply entrenched post-1981 critique of Mao's abandonment of the principles of collective leadership during the Cultural Revolution as an extreme leftist error.

Finally, the practical consequences of moving the locus of power in the Chinese political system to the party institutionally, and to Xi Jinping personally, was also clear. Policy debate among party and professional elites (in the civil service, diplomatic service, military, academy, and media) had become less contestable as policy technocrats gradually yielded more power and space to the professional political class. Indeed, Xi himself made this new direction clear in his 2017 address to the 19th Party Congress Party when he conspicuously rehabilitated a slogan of the Cultural Revolution: "In government, in the military, in civilian administration and in the academy—across east, west, south, north, and the centre—the party leads in everything".[28] For Xi, the restoration of the full powers of a Leninist party, together with the reassertion of the paramount powers of the leader within it, was axiomatic in the execution of the ideological vision he had already outlined in his address to the ideology and propaganda work conference in 2013.

Party Institutions Replacing the State Council in Policy Leadership

This leftward movement of Chinese politics under Xi Jinping is also seen in a series of specific new institutional arrangements governing the party's relationship with the State Council. This extends beyond the establishment of the eight central leading groups and policy commissions led by Xi under the Politburo referred to above. It is also evidenced in a broader transformation across the entire fabric of domestic governance, upending a four-decade trend in public administration reform. In Deng's 'On the Reform of the System of Party and State Leadership', based on an internal speech in 1980, Xi's predecessor argued that the party should not "direct and decide everything".[29] He specifically warned against 'over-concentration of power' (*quanli guofen jizhong*), 'life tenure' (*zhongshenzhi*), and the absence of a technical elite, professionally trained in the disciplines of public administration. While the subsequent trajectory of Chinese public sector reform under Zhao Ziyang, Jiang Zemin, and Hu Jintao had been uneven,[30] Deng's original principles of separating the institutions of party and state (*dangzheng fenkai*) and separating those of politics and enterprise (*zhengqi fenkai*) have now been put into reverse under Xi.

Rather than maintaining some level of separation between ideological or political functions, on the one hand, and administrative or commercial functions, on the other, Xi's alternative concept of leadership has been one of 'top-level design' (*dingceng sheji*). This concept has been adapted by Xi, an engineer by training,[31] into the policy world. It prioritizes the party's centralized ideological, political, and policy direction as a guide for all other institutions. 'Top-level design' is not limited to economic or industrial policy settings in high technology. It would now apply across the full gamut of China's public policy and administrative arrangements, where the ultimate locus of power would rest within the party centre, with Xi's policy commissions acting as the 'über-cabinets' of his regime.

This process of political and policy re-centralization, anchored in the institutions of the party, began early in Xi's first term. It accelerated following the amendment of the Chinese state constitution in March 2018 to introduce the overriding power of the CCP into its first operational clause.[32] Prior to this, the only reference to the party's paramount power was contained in the state constitution's preamble. Xi's change at the 13th National People's Congress put beyond any doubt the legal and practical reality of where substantive political power actually lies in contemporary China—namely, with the party and the party alone. More important, it cleared the constitutional path for a series of legal and regulatory changes to further entrench the party's formal powers in relation to the state's administrative and policy machinery.[33] This constitutional amendment preceded a detailed Central Committee policy document entitled 'Plan on Deepening the Reform of Party and State Organs' (*shenhua dang he guojia jigou gaige fang'an*), which became a blueprint for absorbing multiple state agencies into preexisting party institutions.[34] This, in turn, formed what Grünberg and Drinhausen have described as "an unprecedented degree of codification in the laws and regulations" of the CCP's "rule and ideology" with a view to "cementing the party's hold on power".[35]

This consolidation, codification, and constitutional entrenchment of party power has also been reflected in major changes to China's sprawling personnel system, including its public service recruitment, training, and staff deployment regulations. The biggest institutional manifestation of these changes has been the absorption of the preexisting 'National Academy of Governance' into the Central Party School with the explicit objective of enhancing the political and ideological rigour of all senior party, state, and SOE cadres.[36] The preexisting 'bi-directional entrance' and 'cross-appointment system', which had enabled the movement of staff between party and state institutions as well as state-owned enterprises, has also been enhanced. Among other regulatory changes, there is a proliferation of ideological guidance documents on educating cadres in the party's spirit (*dangxing jiaoyu*).[37]

To remove any doubt about the political *and* ideological rationale underpinning these various constitutional, legal, regulatory, and personnel recruitment changes, the official reporting of Xi's statements at a 'Party Building Work Conference for Central and State Organs' in July 2019 made this crystal clear:

> Under the new situation, the central and state agencies should take the party's political construction as the command, focus on deepening theoretical arms . . . and comprehensively improve the quality of party building among the central and state agencies. In-depth study and the implementation of the party's ideology and theory sets an example in maintaining a high degree of consistency with the Party Central Committee. It also sets an example in the resolute implementation of the Party Central Committee's various decisions.[38]

On this reading, the core rationale for reasserting party power across the entire fabric of the state administrative apparatus was to "deepen" the penetration of the CCP's theoretical aims and enhance the "implementation of the party's ideology and theory". Here we find a clear causal link between Xi's ideological worldview on the centrality of the Leninist party and his transformational agenda for the administrative agencies of the Chinese state. Xi's critique of administrative reform under Deng, Jiang, and Hu had been that, by loosening the party's reins, they had taken the political system dangerously to the reformist right by creating independent power centres staffed by technocratic elites who were beyond CCP control. It was this concern that underpinned the draconian content of Document Number 9 outlined in the previous chapter. Indeed, administrative reform was now seen as a slippery slope leading towards what party ideologues feared would become the more formal separation of party and state under the banner of 'constitutionalism'—the cause championed by a dwindling reformist band who dreamed that China's policy and administrative apparatus would become free-standing centres of technical excellence, increasingly independent of day-to-day party control. Under this alternative worldview, the party's role would be restricted to setting broad national priorities and providing general theoretical and conceptual guidance for the technical engine room of the professional Chinese state. But this type of macro-guidance and macro-priority setting would be delivered through the general resolutions of the CCP's major plenums, congresses, and periodic Politburo meetings—not through party ideologues and political loyalists micro-managing the professional machinery of the State Council. Xi's moves to 'correct' these long-established trends in political and administrative reform represent a significant move to the ideological left to prevent the once-powerful apparatus of the Chinese state from becoming a long-term challenger to the political *and* operational primacy of a Leninist party.[39]

Enhancing Political Control through the Party's Anti-Corruption Campaign

Xi Jinping's decisions to launch an anti-corruption campaign within three months of being appointed general secretary, continue it over his first two terms in office and now beyond, and expand its scope to include administrative efficiency, policy compliance, and political loyalty are consistent with his overall approach to absolute party control. But it has also been part of the political machinery that gives institutional effect to Xi's ideological vision. Unlike previous anti-corruption drives during the post-Mao period, which were short in duration and limited in focus, the current campaign has intensified over the last decade and expanded its political remit. In fact, it has become the single-longest internal political campaign in the party's 100-year history.

The anti-corruption campaign was institutionalized further after the 13th National Party Congress in March 2018 with the merging of several preexisting state anti-corruption bodies into a single National Supervision Commission.[40] This commission, together with the Party's Central Commission for Discipline Inspection (CCDI), which spearheaded the anti-corruption campaign during Xi's first term, would become 'one team with two names' operating with overlapping staff and a common physical office in Beijing.[41] This effective merger placed both party *and* state employees under the disciplinary control of a single party structure. Right across the country, 'central inspection teams' comprising the National Supervision Commission, CCDI, the Central Committee's Organization Department, and the National Audit Office, among others, have been systematically dispatched to party and state institutions. Indeed, for the first time in CCP history, the party has boasted "full inspection coverage of provinces and municipalities, central state agencies, key state-owned enterprises, central financial units, and centrally managed universities" within a single five-year term.[42] Implementation reports from each 'inspected' agency are produced, typically within six months of an inspection having concluded, with the prospect that agencies will be inspected again in the next cycle. And this rolling system of party inspection, audit, and control has been further institutionalized by a raft of new central regulations.[43] In other words, through a combination of central political direction, dedicated institutional muscle, and enhanced regulatory powers, the compliance machinery now available to Xi under the party structure had become near complete.

It is not just the existence and execution of the anti-corruption campaign that was significant to Xi Jinping's overall party-centric worldview. It was also its multidimensional utility. First, in executing the most basic anti-corruption agenda, Xi had made plain that the party must be 'clean' for its long-term political legitimacy.[44] This had been reinforced by party directions that disciplinary work should be focussed in areas where "the public has a strong reaction" or where "political and economic problems were intertwined".[45] Second, the widening scope of the campaign underlined its relevance to the efficiency and effectiveness of governing institutions in implementing the party's critical policy agenda—including poverty alleviation, environmental pollution, and reducing financial risk (the so-called three great battles, or *sanda zhanyi*) as well as the Belt and Road Initiative.[46] Third, the campaign has also targeted Xi's political opponents and assisted in his power consolidation process. Frequent, unannounced, and wide-ranging inspections targeting individuals and agencies have produced a rolling reign of terror across the Chinese political class, further entrenching the actual and perceived power of the leader.[47] Fourth, the campaign has officially embraced loyalty to the party centre and the leadership core as part of its formal remit. Christopher Carothers, for example, noted in his assessment of the CCDI's 2018 work reports across thirty provinces that 17% of remedial measures demanded by inspectors involved perceived problems of party loyalty. Among the most common prescriptions was more intensive study of Xi Jinping Thought, further underlying the importance of political and ideological loyalty as a core feature of the campaign. Indeed, in response to criticisms of insufficient party loyalty in Fujian, provincial authorities created a television propaganda series to stimulate 'deep gratitude' for Xi and 'emotional identification' with the leader. Only 28% of CCDI's remedial measures were targeted at conventional forms of corruption (such as fraud, nepotism, and racketeering) while 44% were focussed on improving organizational capacity (through, among other things, grassroots party-building).[48]

For these reasons, I agree with Carothers' conclusion that this campaign has become a much wider mechanism for enhancing centralized political and party control over the state than was evident in its originally stated anti-corruption mandate.[49] But beyond political control, in the post-2017 period, the anti-corruption campaign has also become an institutional vehicle for much more fundamental ideological control across the party through the expanding role of Xi Jinping Thought. This merging of material crime with political and ideological crime is redolent with reminders of the authorized campaigns of the Cultural Revolution. There are, of course, different debates and contending perspectives on the significance of individual aspects of the anti-corruption campaign.[50] But Xi's ideological transformation of the party (including the power of the leader within it) has been translated into real-world political change through a new system of punishment and purges through the now universal agency of the anti-corruption campaign.[51] And within the overall prism of modern Chinese politics, and the relatively recent memory of previous Maoist campaigns, they also represent a clear-cut shift to the ideological left.

Power Consolidation through Xi's Party Rectification Campaign

Between 2013 and 2017, as Xi Jinping's anti-corruption campaign was unfolding across China, his propaganda apparatus launched a parallel series of 'party education campaigns' (*dangde zhuanti jiaoyu huodong*). These campaigns went by several different names: the 'mass line' (*qunzhong luxian*), the 'three stricts and three earnests' (*sanyan sanshi*), and the even more abstruse 'two studies, one action' (*liangxue yizuo*). To put this in context, in his first five-year term alone, Xi launched the same number of party education campaigns as Jiang and Hu had over the previous twenty-three years.[52] Xi's campaigns have combined ideological indoctrination and self-criticism, as well as criticism and reporting on the activities of others, blurring the lines between political disloyalty, professional non-performance, personal rivalries, and simple corruption. Li Ling has noted that mandatory reporting processes have also enhanced the powers of the CCDI in the anti-corruption campaign. It has done this by removing the limited legal protections that previously existed in the criminal justice system, such as protection against any self-incrimination that might arise during mandatory self-criticism sessions.[53] Apart from the implications for individuals under investigation, Li's extensive research concluded that these cascading campaigns between 2013 and 2017 have had a profound political impact:

> First, the power-consolidation process is two-pronged, driven by the ideological and disciplinary campaigns. The two campaigns are not only synchronized but also feed into one another: the ideological campaign defines the political outlook of the disciplinary campaign and the disciplinary campaign provides potency to the ideological campaign. Second, a shift of emphasis from anticorruption to policing political conduct was gradually introduced . . . around the midterm and became intensified afterwards.[54]

Against this background, Chen Yixin, the secretary-general of the party's newly established Central Political and Legal Affairs Commission, announced in July 2020 a full-blown 'rectification campaign' (*zhengdun dangfeng*) explicitly to "scrape the poison off the bones of our political and legal systems".[55] This included the entire public security, judicial, procuratorial, and legal apparatus. This campaign went beyond the scope of Xi's previous party education and anti-corruption campaigns. It was to be run by staff drawn from the CCDI, National Supervision Commission, and the party's General Office, many of whom now had extensive field experience from the previous campaigns.[56] Its focus, however, when compared with the earlier campaigns, was decisively political. The significance of Chen's July 2020 statement is clear; despite there having been approximately fifty smaller party rectification campaigns since 1949, it was the first time since 1953[57] that the country's legal and security apparatus was the formal and explicit target. Moreover, Chen directly invoked the party's original rectification campaign in Yan'an in 1942–1945, reminding his audience (as Xi had done on earlier occasions) that Mao Zedong had used violence, incarceration, and, in some cases, execution as he consolidated political and ideological control.[58] Further, to make the disciplinary intent of the campaign even plainer for his party audience, Chen stated his goal was "pointing the blade inward, to completely remove the cancerous tumor, to remove the evil members of the group, and ensure that the political and legal team was absolutely loyal".[59] These were chilling messages for party elites. Between 2013 and 2021, four vice-ministers of the Ministry of Public Security had been removed from office, together with several senior provincial and local public security officials.[60] These were in addition to the purge in 2014 of Zhou Yongkang, a factional rival of Xi who had been the Politburo Standing Committee member responsible for the entire political and security system (*zhengfa xitong*).[61]

Xi's party rectification campaign has deliberately deployed numerous political tactics closely identified with Mao. In addition to the invocation of Yan'an, the emphasis on political loyalty to the party leader was pivotal to the entire campaign, reinforced by the emergence of a new totalizing ideology (Xi Jinping Thought) as the campaign's ideational focus. As Wu Guoguang has observed, "such continuous purges have been altering the dynamics of Chinese elite politics, marked by certain significant features, such as the decline of post-Mao norms".[62] Although Wu and others have noted differences between Mao's and Xi's political tactics and strategy—for example, the avoidance so far of mass campaigns as occurred during the Cultural Revolution—the commonalities are nonetheless clear. Li Ling has similarly concluded, following her examination of Xi's post-2013 party education and rectification campaigns, there had been a "paradigm-change" in Chinese politics which had seen "the reversal of the de-politicization process of the Party's disciplinary regime"[63] that started in the 1990s. In doing so, Xi has been consistent with the formal guidance he himself gave the Central Political and Legal Work Conference in January 2015. There Xi called for "a political-legal team that was loyal to the party, the country, the people, and the law" in order to "ensure that the knife is firmly in the hands of the party and the people".[64] Xi's reference to the party holding this blade clearly accords with his determination to do whatever it takes to reassert the absolute power of a Leninist party.

Xi Jinping has also adapted ideological and political methods from the Mao period by reinvigorating regular party 'democratic life meetings' (*minzhu shenghuohui*). These were historically used to focus party members on the correct ideological line, criticism, and self-criticism. Democratic life meetings have most been associated with periods of political crisis in the party leadership. Prior to Xi's appointment in 2013, the last protracted democratic life meeting conducted by the central leadership was in 1987 when then General Secretary Hu Yaobang was purged. Xi, however, changed that practice when extended meetings of the Politburo started to be dedicated exclusively to ideological questions. These were regularized after 2015 as official annual, two-day Politburo democratic life meetings on a chosen ideological theme. This was reinforced in 2016 by overhauled party regulations refocussing these meetings on "establishing correct political consciousness, carrying out criticism, and maintaining loyalty and responsibility".[65] Over the following years, democratic life meetings conducted at the Politburo level focussed on such topics as Xi Jinping Thought and 'Setting an Example on Upholding General Secretary Xi Jinping as the Core of the Party'.[66] Indeed, after one particular meeting in 2017, the Politburo's statement glowingly noted that "under the leadership of the CCP Central Committee with Xi at the core, China has made historic achievements and witnessed profound changes" since 2012; and, furthermore, that "Xi has shown firm faith and will, clear commitment to the people, extraordinary political wisdom and tactics, and a strong sense of responsibility in leading the CCP and China in the great struggle with many new contemporary features."[67] In modern Chinese politics, the cult of personality had come back to life, and done so with a vengeance.

The rebirth of democratic life meetings, alongside ongoing party rectification and anti-corruption campaigns, have given rise to deep institutional memories of Chinese political norms pre-dating the 'reform and opening' period that had been introduced by Deng. These measures were designed in part to deal with the 'imbalances' that have arisen in party life through decades of reform, and which Xi addressed through his redefinition of the party's central contradiction in 2017. But more generally they also sought to roll back the ideological rot that Xi referred to in his August 2013 address on ideology and propaganda.[68] Although not always addressed in such explicit terms, these various measures have sought to correct Xi's long-term sense of a party that had drifted towards the political and ideological right. And Xi was determined to change that.

The 'Securitization' of Everything

This movement of Chinese politics to the Leninist left—renewing the centrality of the party, the paramount leadership of Xi Jinping within it, together with rolling enforcement campaigns—has also been reflected in the national security domain. By emphasizing the significance of new internal and external challenges to China's security, and the need for harsh new measures to guard against them, Xi has underscored the case for an even more powerful vanguard party. Xi set the scene for this 'securitization' or '*anquanhua*' of Chinese politics as early as January 2014 in internal speeches warning of a "treacherous international situation" and "an intensifying contest of two ideologies", with the United States desperate to Westernize and split China just as the global balance of power was shifting in Beijing's favour.[69] Two months later, Xi described Chinese security and development as "two sides of the same issue, two wheels in the same driving mechanism; security guarantees development just as development is the goal of security".[70] By January 2019, this concept of security was further extended from economic security to the political security of the entire regime. The Central Committee's new Political-Legal Work Directive stipulated the "absolute leadership of the CCP over all political-legal affairs"; that such work was now to be directly "supervised" by the party centre and General Secretary Xi; and that safeguarding "political security" was now a major task of the party.[71] This ever-widening concept of security reached its totalizing extreme two years later when, in November 2020, Xi launched yet another 'leading group' to craft new national security directives, stressing the necessity of achieving security in practically every facet of China's existence "including national security, scientific and technological innovation, public health, bio-safety and ecological civilization".[72] Although these had first been raised in 2017, Xi's all-pervasive national security focus acquired a new political and institutional status from 2020.

Xi Jinping's call for the securitization of everything was given practical effect by a vast array of legal, regulatory, and institutional measures. This began in November 2013 at the Third Plenum of the 18th Central Committee at which Xi announced that "establishing a national security commission (NSC) to strengthen the unified leadership of state security work was an urgent need".[73] In July 2015, the party adopted a new National Security Law (NSL) underpinning that commission, explicitly linking economic development to national security.[74] The NSL also gave security agencies a stronger legal footing to curb perceived threats from government critics, while designating an annual 'National Security Education Day' focussed on the school curriculum. This was followed in June 2017 by China's first National Intelligence Law (NIL) requiring all individuals, organizations, and institutions to assist public security and state security officials in carrying out a wide array of 'intelligence' work.[75] The NIL paralleled Xi's earlier Counter-Espionage Law (CEL) of January 2014, which empowered authorities to act against organizations or individuals over any behaviours regarded as damaging to China's interests, while leaving those behaviours and interests largely undefined.[76] Under the CEL, new 'counter-espionage regulations' were promulgated in April 2021 allowing national security authorities "to draw up lists of companies and organizations that are susceptible to foreign infiltration and require listed [institutions] to adopt security measures to prevent" it.[77] This heightened perception of external and internal security threats was underlined by state media reporting that "foreign espionage activities were everywhere, not something far away from our lives".[78]

Central to the party's institutional response to these increased threat perceptions has been its new approach to internet governance. As early as August 2013, Xi was warning that the internet was the "major battlefield of public opinion", and it was therefore important to "construct a powerful internet army" to gain control of it, adding that social media would be "managed" and used to promote the party's views.[79] China subsequently adopted a sweeping new Cybersecurity Law in November 2016, which toughened obligations for companies to gather information on Chinese users, to store sensitive data on servers on the Chinese mainland,

and cooperate with security authorities.[80] The regime developed a raft of other regulations seeking to give effect to Xi's internet dictum, and these were consolidated in December 2019 into new 'Provisions on the Governance of the Online Information Content Ecosystem' defining prohibited political content.[81] These new powers were anchored explicitly in the omnibus provisions of China's 2015 National Security Law.

These multiple new institutions, laws, and regulations on internet governance came together in China's 'social credit system' (*shehui xinyong tixi*) overseen by the CCP's Central Commission on Comprehensively Deepening Reform. This program was designed to aggregate positive and negative points for every individual Chinese citizen based on their level of compliance with party expectations. While the system was first piloted in 2009, preceding Xi's elevation to general secretary, it has since been strengthened, extended across the country, and connected to a vast national network of physical and electronic surveillance. According to a 2020 report by the Supreme People's Court, its net effect was to blacklist some 15 million 'dishonest' people, barring them from such 'luxuries' as air travel, high-speed trains, and holidays until they discharged their obligation to society.[82]

The centrality of Xi Jinping's new security framework, coupled with its integration within the party's wider political and economic agenda, was underscored further by the inclusion of an entire section on national security in the country's Five-Year Plan.[83] In the terms of the 2020 plenum statement, under the plan the party "will improve its centralized, unified, efficient and authoritative national security leadership system, improve national security legislation . . . and strengthen national security law enforcement".[84] Citizens were warned once again that "security is the premise of development and development is the guarantee of security."[85] According to Chen Yixin of the party's Central Political and Legal Affairs Commission, the underlying political intent of Xi's new national security framework was to build an 'iron wall' around the country's 'political security', and the role of the party and Xi's leadership within it:

> Focussing on political security, we will build an iron wall to prevent infiltration, subversion and sabotage by hostile forces outside the country, eradicate the soil that affects political security. With regard to social stability, it will accelerate the modernization of social governance, build a 'front-line headquarters' for social governance in cities and ensure that major conflicts and risks are resolved.[86]

This combination of hardened official language, harsher institutional powers, and stronger coercive measures gives effect to an increasingly restrictive security regime under Xi Jinping. These are not just about national security; they are in large part also about the perceived heightened security needs of the regime, the party, and even Xi himself. They are also part of a clear ideological throughline along with Xi's earlier warning to the party of foreign and domestic threats in his 2013 address on ideology, and Document Number 9. Within the wider framework of post–Cultural Revolution Chinese politics, these ideological and institutional changes evidence a significant move in the overall direction of Chinese politics. This was in line with an overarching ideological worldview that values the power of an increasingly Leninist party (in this case, through the national security apparatus) against the already-limited political freedoms afforded to individual Chinese citizens—freedoms in themselves that had only gradually evolved over the long decades of reform and opening.

The Reassertion of Party Leadership across All Domains

This picture of Xi Jinping's and the party's growing political, institutional, and security reach across the country becomes more complete when we also examine Xi's actions in tightening control over the media, universities, arts and culture, religion, non-governmental organizations, and, most fundamentally, the legal system. The release of Document Number 9 in 2013 by the General Office of the CCP, together with Xi's address to the Ideology and Propaganda Work Conference in 2013, made clear the future direction of press censorship and the wider role of the media as an absolute instrument of political control by the party. Document Number 9 specifically attacked any "promotion of the West's idea of journalism which challenges China's principle that the media and the publishing system should be subject to Party discipline".[87] This was followed in September 2013 by a joint legal opinion, issued by the Supreme People's Court and the Supreme People's Procuratorate, on the criminalization of online 'rumours' and 'libellous' posts, stating that offenders could face three years' prison.[88] By February 2016, this tightening of media control was underscored by Xi's much-reported visit to major state media centres where he stated that the party required 'absolute loyalty' from journalists.[89] The precise nature of this 'absolute loyalty' was underlined at a practical level by the growing number of journalists incarcerated—and the number of independent and semi-independent publications closed down as a result of legal and disciplinary breaches.[90] Requirements for journalists to pass courses in Marxism in order to have their press cards reissued, first introduced in 2014, were sharpened in 2019 to test loyalty to Xi personally:[91]

> One question in the test asks, "What is the first priority when it comes to news and public opinion work?" The correct answer is "The leadership of the CCP." Another asks for Xi's policy for the news media, with the expected answer: "Unity, stability, and positive propaganda." A third asks what the internet is for. The correct answer is "a new space in which the party can build consensus."[92]

Further, from 2023, candidates were required to "conscientiously study, publicize and implement" Xi Jinping Thought, "resolutely implement the party's theory, line, principles, and policies", and follow "the correct political direction and public opinion guidance".[93] Anyone with a record of "unhealthy newsgathering and editing practices" is barred from sitting the test.

Similar political and ideological control over the Chinese media has also been seen across the arts, culture, and higher education. Xi's October 2014 address on the need for stronger political leadership in arts and culture invoked Mao's 'Yan'an Talks' of 1942 on this subject.[94] Indeed, Xi's position on arts and culture echoed his wider reference to the Yan'an Party Rectification Movement as a continuing model for political and ideological discipline. In his 2014 address, Xi emphasized the need for all creative endeavour to serve the needs of the party and, through it, the realization of 'the China Dream'. This formed the basis for the Central Committee's release twelve months later of formal 'Opinions on the Prosperity and Development of Socialist Arts and Culture' (*zhonggong zhongyang guanyu fanrong fazhan shehuizhuyi wenyi de yijian*) instructing that these be guided by the 'core values of socialism', the repudiation of 'historical nihilism' (*lishi xuwuzhuyi*), as well as opposition to the "undermining of national unity, the distortion of the history of the party or the country, or any slandering of the image of the state."[95] This 'Opinions' document also called for tighter party leadership across arts and culture; elevating the excellence of 'traditional Chinese culture' together with Marxism as a 'guiding principle for arts and culture'; and greater support for Chinese patriotism while avoiding excessive promotion of 'foreign' cultural products.[96] While similar principles had been reasserted episodically in the post-Mao period as part of the ebb and flow of national censorship guidelines, Xi's campaign to enforce political conformity has been longer, more intense, and has seen more sustained political and legal enforcement than before.[97]

These developments in arts and culture have paralleled those across higher education since the ascension of Xi Jinping. Within months of becoming general secretary, Xi released new rules by which universities would compile files on 'faculty virtue', organize young faculty members to study the CCP's "foundational theories, policies, guidelines, experience and requirements", and promote academics based on socialist virtue ahead of professional accomplishment.[98] This was followed by the general offices of the Central Committee and the State Council issuing joint 'Opinions Concerning Further Strengthening and Improving Propaganda and Ideological Work in Higher Education under New Circumstances' which emphasized the need to: enhance political training for faculty; standardize textbooks used within university disciplines; and apply more focus to moulding the social sciences—journalism, law, economics, political science, sociology, and ethnic studies—to enhance political orthodoxy.[99] In case this message was lost on the country's university leadership, Xi used a March 2019 symposium to personally remind them that their mission was to "deliver the country's mainstream ideology and directly respond to false ideas and thoughts".[100] A national propaganda campaign also attacked university teachers challenging Marxist orthodoxy, including those who "are wont to share their superficial 'impressions from overseas study', praising the Western 'separation of powers' and believing that China should take the Western path" to the point of openly questioning "the major policy decisions of the CCP's Central Committee, or even speak[ing] directly against them".[101] This return to a more rigorous ideological orthodoxy has also been reflected in university research programs, as demonstrated in Carl Minzner's analysis of the changing profile of China's National Social Science Foundation list of approved research projects between 2011 and 2019.[102] Projects focussing on socialism, Marxism, party history, and party building had "doubled or tripled in number", with new projects examining the application of 'Xi Jinping Thought' to a vast new range of academic disciplines. Political and ideological background checks have also now become mandatory for the engagement, promotion, and even retention of academic staff. Approval processes for international academic contact have also been significantly tightened. As Minzner concluded: "The party's tightening grip over the intelligentsia . . . [is] tied to a fundamental political decision: to turn China away from reform-era norms and back in the direction of its pre-1978 Maoist past. . . . The current tightening—over culture, religion, and education—now reflects a decision to revive party sinews in more private fields of human endeavour."[103]

Xi Jinping's dual emphasis on traditional Chinese culture and Marxist ideological orthodoxy in higher education policy has also been applied to religion, ethnic minorities, and the regulation of foreign non-governmental organizations (NGOs). Xi's keynote speech at the Communist Party National Conference on Religious Work in April 2016 stressed the urgency of the 'Sinicization' of religion, upholding the principle that religions in China must be Chinese in orientation, and the need to "actively guide the adaptation of religions to socialist society".[104] Importantly, this occurred in the same month as the National People's Congress adopted a new law requiring foreign NGOs to register with an authority under the Ministry of Public Security and submit all aspects of their operations, including finances, to scrutiny by Chinese security agencies at any time—causing thousands of NGOs to cease operating in China altogether.[105] Subsequently, in March 2017, the party released a new 'De-Extremification Regulation' (*xinjiang weiwuer zizhiqu quqiduanhua tiaoli*) for Xinjiang, including a call for 'transformation through education', thus initiating a large-scale campaign of involuntary detention of ethnic Uyghurs.[106] This was followed in June 2017 by new 'Regulations on Religious Affairs', stipulating oversight of faith organizations to "put core socialist values into practice, and safeguard national unity, ethnic unity, religious harmony and social stability".[107] Parallel actions by Chinese authorities in tearing down unauthorized religious structures have particularly focussed on 'foreign' religious traditions (notably Christianity and Islam), accompanied by the incarceration of religious leaders deemed to be operating outside the formal control structures established by the party.[108]

This reassertion of party power and control across the media, education, arts and culture, ethnic minorities, religion, and NGOs has been underpinned by profound changes to the country's legal system under the rubric of 'law-based governance' (*yifa zhizheng*). This is a systematic effort on the part of Xi's administration to formally insert the ultimate prerogative of the party across the entire fabric of criminal and civil law. The political and ideological foundations of this recentralization of party control has once again been underscored by Chen Yixin: "With the profound insight and theoretical creativity of a Marxist statesman, theoretician and strategist, Xi Jinping adhered to the Marxist position, point of view and method, and enriched and developed the Marxist theory of the rule of law in response to a series of major problems in the construction of the socialist rule of law in China."[109] Signalling the nature of these 'major problems', Chen was equally forthright that the party needed to remain supreme and that China "will not copy the models and practices of other countries, nor adopt so-called 'constitutional government', 'separation of powers', or the 'independent judiciary' of the West", as had been debated in the past.[110] Instead, China had to "grasp the political direction indicated by Xi Jinping Thought on the Rule of Law . . . promote the institutionalization of Party leadership and the rule of law, and ensure the effective implementation of the Party's line, principles and policies through the rule of law".[111]

Chen's totalizing concept of party rule through the legal system is reflected further in his clarion-clear statement that the overall objective of Xi's campaign for "law-based governance" was the "acceleration of the formation of a *complete* system of legal norms", "an efficient system of rule of law implementation", and a "strict system of rule of law supervision", which collectively constituted "the party's basic strategy for governing the country".[112] To this end, Chen once again provides absolute clarity that there should be no distinction between the party leadership and the rule of law:

> In developing the socialist rule of law with Chinese characteristics, General Secretary Xi Jinping has profoundly clarified several important relationships and cleared up relevant ideological confusion, providing us with scientific, methodological guidance—correctly handling the relationship between politics and the rule of law, deeply understanding that . . . the party's leadership and the rule of law are highly unified and that the socialist rule of law must adhere to the party's leadership.[113]

At its most practical level, this has meant that previous notions of defence lawyers somehow evolving into independent officers of the court—or that the courts themselves could, in time, acquire their own institutional independence—were no longer to be tolerated.[114] Or, as Chen reminded his audience, it was a "basic requirement" for legal service personnel to "uphold the leadership of the Communist Party".[115] This radical correction from ideological 'confusion' under previous leaders was already evident earlier in Xi's administration with the mass arrest of Chinese human rights activists and lawyers in July 2015.[116] Chen's 2020 remarks to his CCP audience conveyed a further determination to prosecute the party's Leninist claim to absolute authority over the criminal justice system: "With a firm grasp of this focus, the party will dare to gnaw hard bones, wade through dangerous shoals and cut through the chronic diseases that have accumulated for many years, continuing to push forward reform in the field of the rule of law to solve outstanding problems."[117]

Under Xi Jinping, there is, therefore a new and totalizing role for ideological and political control across all domains. In the media, the academy, arts and culture, education, religion, ethnic minorities, NGOs and the law, the common thematic is the reassertion of political control by a fully empowered Leninist party as the essential vehicle for realizing China's socialist and nationalist mission. This reflects, in turn, a parallel reification of the centrality of the Chinese tradition of resisting foreign culture, concepts, and beliefs, particularly those that would challenge the idea of an omnipotent party. Consistent with Xi's comprehensive ideational worldview and the organizational role of the party across nearly every dimension of life and work, there would be no exceptions. The contraction of the private sphere and expansion of the public sphere controlled by the party represent a further profound shift in the centre of gravity of Chinese politics under Xi.

Party Building, the Systematization of Ideological Education, and a Return to 'Belief', 'Faith' and a New 'Baptism' in Marxism-Leninism

Another measure of these profound movements in Chinese politics under Xi is that, as ideology has returned to virtually every aspect of party and personal life, the level of ideological fervour now demanded of party members in order to prosper has also heightened. This is reflected in new forms of almost quasi-religious language deployed by Xi on the high virtues of Marxism-Leninism. He speaks of 'faith' in the efficacy of the party's vision and, seeking to buttress 'belief' in this founding mission, he seeks to build a party of members 'baptized' afresh in party ideology. This language once again evokes the Cultural Revolution and reflects Xi's early decision to codify the party's twelve 'core socialist values'[118] as he sought to revive the CCP's original ideological and moral purpose. This eclectic cocktail of Marxist and selected traditional Chinese beliefs stood in stark contrast with the party's pragmatic preoccupations with business, finance, and economic development over the previous decades of reform and opening. While work on core socialist values had been underway through the central propaganda apparatus since 2006, it was Xi who concluded and executed it in 2013 before personally directing the launch of a mass campaign aimed at entrenching them into wider public consciousness.[119] Xi reinforced the campaign with new institutional and educational measures that made political and professional advancement within the party impossible without demonstrable levels of personal compliance.[120] And, for the first time since the end of the Cultural Revolution, there has been renewed public discussion on the proper balance between being 'red' and 'expert'. As noted in previous chapters, while Deng had resolved firmly in favour of being 'expert' in the critical debates of 1977–1978, Xi concludes that being 'red' is at least as important as being 'expert', and possibly more so.

The importance of 'belief' (*xinyang*) in Xi Jinping's ideological worldview is also evident across his writings. As early as 2013, Xi had reminded the party that "when the people have faith, the nation has hope, and the country has power".[121] Because of this, it was critical that the party "resolutely prevent the replacement of faith in Marxism-Leninism with faith in ghosts and gods—and the replacement of faith in truth with faith in money" (*jianjue fangzhi buxin malie xin guishen, buxin zhenli xin jinqian*).[122] This was underlined in January 2019 when the party released 'The CCP Centre Opinions on Strengthening the Political Construction of the Party' (*zhonggong zhongyang guanyu jiaqiang dang de zhengzhi jianshe de yijian*) and its invocation that "in implementing this effort, the party is to promote revolutionary culture, pass on red genes, and guide party cadres and members to lead lives as firm believers in the core values of socialism".[123]

Xi added to the debate on ideological education, formation, and belief in March 2019 in an address to lecturers in political theory at the Central Party School, where he stated it was "necessary to constantly enhance the ideological and theoretical affinity and relevance" of courses so that the link between theory and practice was always clear.[124] Xi would, in later years, enjoin the party to understand and preach to the world "why Marxism works and why socialism with Chinese characteristics is good", while also gaining "a profound understanding of the historical inevitability of upholding the party's leadership".[125] In other words, for Xi, questions of belief, faith, and systematic ideological education were now essential to both the continued political legitimacy and institutional survival of the CCP. It was also now a core component of party building *(dang jianshe)* and party education.

Xi's overriding thematic on the need for ideological belief was consummated in May 2019 with a new party-wide education campaign launched by the central leadership on the theme 'Don't Forget the Party's Original Intention, Keep the Mission in Mind'. In his speech officially launching this campaign, the leader issued a call to "study and implement" Xi Jinping Thought in depth with "the specific goals of gaining theoretical learning and being baptized in ideology and politics".[126] The campaign's stated goal was to "recharge the party's ideological awareness, reinstate its moral status and legitimacy as a ruling party, and deepen its social reach".[127] In doing so, the campaign would target all CCP cadres "from the top level down to the local community".[128] By January 2020, Xi was reviewing the progress of the first phase of the campaign in glowing terms. He re-emphasized the importance of the foundational texts of Xi Jinping Thought, Marxism, and Leninism in making cadres "more aware of the importance of connecting knowledge and beliefs with action".[129] Furthermore, he argued that the ensuing campaign of criticism and self-criticism had strengthened leading cadres' "faith in Marxism and their conviction in socialism with Chinese characteristics".[130] This was necessary because "the advanced and wholesome nature of a Marxist Party will not be naturally preserved as time goes by, nor will members' Party consciousness automatically strengthen with their length of service or job advancement".[131] Invoking Mao as his authority, Xi reminded the party that "ideological education is the key link to be grasped in uniting the whole Party for great political struggles" and that it was only through party members' "pursuit of the truth" using "the scientific theory of Marxism" that they could improve their "ideological and theoretical understanding" and "stay true to our original aspiration".[132]

Xi, as noted above, has also sought to "systematize" the ideological education, institutional discipline, and organizational rules necessary to sustain the Marxist faith. In doing so, Xi creatively deploys the language of the great anti-ideologist Deng Xiaoping himself by citing Deng's admonition that "if systems are sound, they can place restraints on the actions of bad people, and if they are unsound, they may hamper the efforts of good people or indeed, in certain cases, may push them in the wrong direction".[133] Borrowing Deng's framework, Xi then expresses a determination to strengthen the CCP's ideological 'system' to achieve the party's overall disciplinary purpose by making yet another thinly veiled attack on the ideological laxness of his predecessors. He argued that a renewed party campaign "based on its systems and regulations" was now essential to sustain the CCP on its proper ideological course for the future.[134] In other words, within Xi's worldview, ideological rigour was about a totalizing system of beliefs whose 'red genes' could only be passed on through a systematic approach to ideological education and training.

These various strands of Xi's ideological worldview—the quasi-religious language of faith, belief, and mission; an appeal to Marxist ideals; and the deployment of dialectical analytical methodologies—were drawn together in a remarkable address to the Central Party School in March 2021.[135] As noted previously, the Central Party School had subsumed China's National Academy of Governance in 2018, thus merging the hard ideological focus of the former with a twenty-four-year-old professional training academy established at the beginning of the reform period and tasked with the technical formation of China's public service elite. Xi stated: "Whether young cadres were standing in the world or working in politics, they must first resolve the questions of 'who am I, for whom do I work, and on whom do I rely?' He enjoined them to "pursue the spiritual realm" in which "I have no self and I live only for the people". Sustaining this spiritual analogy, while also linking it with his earlier rehabilitation of Mao's mass line, Xi then proclaimed that "we must worship the people as our teachers". He called on young cadres "to learn to fight in the struggle, grow and improve in the struggle, and strive to become warriors who dare to fight and are good at fighting", to be "firm in our will to fight, be unyielding and indomitable, and never shrinking from a setback or retreating whenever difficulties were encountered". Xi concluded his address by returning to his ever-present dialectical methodology, applied now to the challenges of the new era and with even greater political urgency:

> It is necessary . . . to improve our ability to see the subtle and understand the true, to see the essence through the phenomenon, accurately recognize changes, scientifically adapt to changes, take the initiative to bring about changes, gain insights, seek advantages and avoid disadvantages . . . to strengthen strategic

> planning, grasp the overall situation, grasp the main contradictions, identify the main aspects of the contradictions, distinguish priorities, scientifically arrange our forces, and to firmly grasp the initiative in the struggle."[136]

This worldview is, in its most elemental ideological form, both Marxist in its theoretical construction and Maoist in its invocation of recent political memory. It embodies an approach to Chinese politics that preferences ideological awareness, dialectical analysis, and, in the real world, political struggle. And despite Xi's rhetorical device of incorporating his ideological opponent Deng within his own worldview, Xi's worldview stands in radical contrast to the most basic Dengist axioms of relegating the discussion of theory, attending to the pragmatic demands of Chinese statecraft, and developing the economy rather than engaging in sustained political struggle.

Conclusion

Changes in the real world of Chinese politics since 2012 have not been accidental. There is a pattern. What unites this vast array of political initiatives, policy changes, and regulatory measures under Xi is an underlying ideological view of the paramount importance of the power of a Leninist party and a determination to roll back previous measures that might threaten that power. This view was evident as early as 2013 from Xi's first ideological pronouncements on the role of the party, well before the slew of political and policy measures that followed. For these reasons, it is entirely reasonable to attribute some level of ideological causation to the actions Xi then took in the real world of Chinese power politics—and politics more generally.

This process of ideological and political change can be traced through the growing constitutional and institutional powers of the party apparatus, which grew after 2013, while the powers of the traditional machinery of the Chinese state receded. We see it in the radical enhancement of the powers of Xi Jinping himself as paramount leader at the expense of the institutions and practices of collective party leadership that had been crafted in the decades following the Cultural Revolution. We can also see it in the raft of new security arrangements, anchored in the party's institutional authority, which increasingly circumscribe the freedom of individuals. These are matched by the vigorous extension of the party's political and ideological reach into the media, education, arts and culture, religion, and the rule of law. Furthermore, this rapid strengthening of the real powers of the party has been underpinned by an almost fundamentalist ideological zeal on Xi's part and the imperative to implant this in the souls and systems of the wider party membership. Indeed, this was the core component of his relentless campaign to restore the CCP's faith in its Marxist-Leninist origins and, as later chapters will describe, its nationalist origins as well.

Of course, an alternative explanation is that many of these changes in Chinese politics can simply be explained by Xi's basic interest in power consolidation. According to this view, such actions do not require any elaborate political theorization, other than to justify a universal Machiavellian impulse for power by disguising it with a higher ideological purpose. However, this assumes that personal power consolidation, and an ideological mission to re-entrench the power of the party, are conceptually and practically irreconcilable. They are not. In fact, the reality of Chinese politics under Mao was that the accumulation of the power of the leader and the entrenchment of the institutional powers of the party were often, although not always, mutually reinforcing. The same applies under Xi, whose determination to become the paramount leader within the CCP is reinforced, rather than undermined, by his program of rebuilding the power, ideological legitimacy and political integrity of the party itself.

While it may be impossible for academic researchers to conclusively answer the ultimate question of 'what does Xi himself actually believe', it defies logic to dismiss the entire ideological edifice erected by him as little more than an exercise in calculated political cynicism. Xi's elaborate ideological architecture is designed to entrench the party's essential role as the vanguard for realizing a Marxist vision for China's future, as well as his own essential role as its 'leadership core'. Even in the absence of definitive proof of the genuineness, or otherwise, of Xi's stated belief system, what can be measured is the clear correlation between his published ideological worldview, on the one hand, and, on the other, the clear direction of political change and real-world policy behaviours that have followed in its wake. For these reasons, it is clear that Xi, like Mao before him, albeit with significant differences between them, has deliberately advanced an ideological framework that has taken Chinese politics decisively back towards the Leninist left.

6

The Impact of Ideology on Xi's Economic Policy

For Xi Jinping, Marxist-Leninist ideology offers both a comprehensive theoretical worldview as well as practical guidance in the real world of public policy. For the multiple changes in Chinese politics and economics that have unfolded during his first decade in office, it is Xi's ideological framework that provides the organizing principle, ideational momentum, and connective tissue—or, as argued in previous chapters, the continuing 'red thread'—for his overall policy program. But unlike the immediate movements to the Leninist left in domestic politics that were observed soon after Xi's address to the Central Work Conference on Ideology and Propaganda in 2013, the movement to the Marxist left in China's political economy has been more gradual. While there was some evidence of an emerging economic policy shift on several fronts before the 19th Party Congress in 2017, it was Xi's formal ideological redefinition of the party's 'principal contradiction' in that year's congress report (from unbridled growth to a more 'balanced' development model capable of addressing economic inequality) that marked the turning point. As discussed at some length in chapter 5, it was this redefinition of the central contradiction that formed the ideological headwaters for the cascading set of political and policy changes that followed soon after.

These shifts in China's macro-policy settings have been profound. During Xi's early years in office, the party emphasized the 'decisive role' of the market in allocating resources, as outlined clearly in the 'Decision' of the Third Plenum of the 18th Central Committee in 2013.[1] But, seven years later, Xi's address to the Central Economic Work Conference in late 2020[2] signalled a full and resolute return to the state directing economic policy, where even the word 'reform' barely rated a mention. Indeed, these two documents (from 2013 and 2020) represent the reformist and statist bookends of China's changing economic ideology during Xi's rule. While the evolution of China's macro-policy settings over Xi's first two terms is uneven, overlapping, and from time to time contradictory, the overall trend line has remained relatively clear: it runs from an early consensus around pro-market reform towards increasing levels of party and state control of the economy.[3]

Under Xi Jinping, Marxist-Leninist ideology continues to have agency, meaning, and influence for the CCP in both analysing and responding to substantive economic policy challenges. As in politics, ideology may never be the exclusive factor in determining Xi's economic policy choices; but the evidence increasingly suggests it has become a significant factor. This is clear in the content and direction of individual policy decisions. But it is also reflected in Xi's re-engineering of China's overarching Marxist-Leninist ideological narrative from above—a narrative that pushes the Chinese economy back into the hands of the party-state and away from the disciplines of the market and the dynamism of private-sector decision-making. In doing so, Xi has deliberately and progressively moved the overall centre of gravity in Chinese economic policy to the Marxist left.

Xi's Unfolding Economic Ideology

Whereas Xi's ideological views on the absolute centrality of the party in Chinese politics were stated clearly from 2013, it would take another seven years for similar clarity to emerge on the future course of Chinese economic policy. For this, we must turn to Xi's major speech to provincial and ministerial-level officials on 'Implementing the Guiding Principles of the Fifth Plenary Session of the 19th CCP Central Committee' in January 2021.[4] While this speech did not appear publicly until six months later, when it was published in the party's official theoretical journal, *Qiushi*, the fact that it was promulgated through such an authoritative political platform underlines its ideological importance in the eyes of the party leadership. In it, Xi makes his most comprehensive ideological case for the statist economic policy changes he had explicitly championed since the 19th Party Congress. In interpreting such a speech, as with other ideological orations from the leadership, there is always a danger that it may partly represent a retrospective effort to impose Marxist theoretical order on a series of sometimes disconnected economic policy events. Nonetheless, whatever its ante-facto or post-facto character, we should not discount the speech's value in explaining the prevailing ideological environment in which these decisions were taken, nor what it also says about the likely future direction of Chinese economic policy under Xi.

The scope of the January 2021 speech was vast. Consistent with Xi Jinping's renewed emphasis on Marxist analysis, it included a new periodization of recent Chinese economic history based on his fresh application of the principles historical and dialectical materialism. Xi argued that the redefinition of the party's 'principal contradiction' at the 19th Party Congress around the problem of unbalanced development had not only given rise to 'a new era' in Chinese politics after 2017, but it had also created the ideological need for 'a new stage of development' for the economy. Since it was normal in Marxist economic history for 'the principles of development' to change in response to changes in the real world, he argued the party now needed to embrace a 'new development philosophy' and 'new development dynamic' to deal with these dynamics. On the critical question of what substantive economic policy changes would result from this new ideological framework, Xi pointed to several specific shifts in policy direction that had already been announced since 2012. But of all these changes, Xi insists the "most important" has been the change in philosophical approach, which, in his argument, offered the party a new 'theoretical system' for future development. Xi's elaboration of this new theoretical system, which is examined below, makes clear that almost all the measures he recommended would require greater state control, intervention, and ownership in the economy than before.

In many respects, Xi's 2020 speech, as published in 2021, represents the formal ideological conclusion of the previous forty-year period of 'reform and opening' for the Chinese economy. While Xi is careful not to be so blunt as that (there are still obligatory references to further round of 'high-standard openings' of the economy, particularly in financial markets), the speech is remarkable for the virtual disappearance of the terms 'reform' and 'opening' from the CCP's approved ideological lexicon. This is a highly significant development. In an 11,745-character-long hallmark speech on the economy, there are only twelve appearances of the word 'reform', or *gaige*—the party's decades-long leitmotif for increasing market orientation across all forms of economic activity. By contrast, *gaige* appeared 137 times in the party's 21,548-character 'Decision' document of 2013. Given the importance of banner terms like 'reform and opening' in communicating and interpreting the party's overall ideological, political, and, therefore policy direction, this represents a major change.

The Transition from the 'Primary Stage of Socialism' to a 'Higher Stage of Socialism'

As noted in chapter 4, periodization is a core concept in the overall framework of historical materialism, and it has generated a considerable body of literature throughout Chinese Communist history.[5] In the *Qiushi* article, Xi began his treatment of the periodization question by recapping the three major phases of the party's revolutionary history: the period of 'New Democracy' between 1921 and 1949, based on multi-class collaboration with the dual objective of overthrowing feudalism and imperialism; the socialist revolution from 1949 with the transition to state ownership; and the subsequent era of 'socialist development' after 1956. Having glossed over the gross failures in 'socialist development' between 1956 and 1978—from the 'anti-rightist movement', through Mao's Great Leap Forward and the Cultural Revolution—Xi then further divided the post-1978 period into two periods: the era of 'reform and opening'; and then a new period when "socialism with Chinese characteristics crossed the threshold into a new era".[6] Consistent with previous theoretical justifications going back to 1982,[7] Xi argued the period of 'reform and opening' was validated by the party's conclusion that China remained in a 'primary stage of socialism'. The designation of this period as the primary stage of socialism was entirely compatible, Xi argued, with Mao's view that there were at least two stages of socialism: an 'underdeveloped' stage; followed by a 'comparatively developed' stage; followed, in turn, by a period of "most ample . . . material production and spiritual prosperity"[8] that would finally represent the first stage of communism.

The underlying ideological logic of this official periodization of China's development trajectory is that it determined the level of class inequality to be tolerated at each stage in order to raise the people's overall living standards.

But, in Xi's logic, the ideological purpose of generating greater wealth was not to permit higher levels of inequality forever; it was to accelerate the overall economic development process towards higher levels of socialism. In the primary stage of socialism, higher levels of class inequality have been permitted in order to generate more rapid economic growth. However, as the party moved towards more advanced levels of socialism, that inequality must be moderated before being eliminated altogether under communism. Again, citing Mao as his authority, Xi's speech made plain that Marxist theory dictates that every stage of development has a 'boundary' that must be overcome before China can go through to the next stage.

Having reprised these relatively conventional arguments on Marxist historical periodization, Xi then began to amend the official ideological periodization of his predecessors by pointing to a transition beyond the initial *phase* of the primary stage of socialism to a more advanced *phase*, albeit still located within the same primary *stage*. According to Xi:

> The primary stage of socialism is not a static, cast-iron, or stagnant period, nor is it a spontaneous and passive stage that can easily and naturally be passed through. Rather, it is a stage of dynamism, action, and promise, one that should always brim with vitality. It develops gradually but ceaselessly, moving from quantitative increases to qualitative leaps. Fully building a modern socialist China and basically socialist modernization are essential for China's development in the primary stage of socialism, and essential for China to advance from the primary stage to a higher stage of socialism.[9]

This is a new ideological formulation on the primary stage of socialism compared with Deng, Jiang, and Hu. For the first time, it points to different phases within this primary stage. This is important because, as a matter of ideological logic, as China advances through the various *phases* of the primary stage of socialism, the next *stage* of a higher level of socialism begins to approach. In other words, the second stage of socialism moves from the distant future—"several dozen" generations away, Deng reckoned in 1992[10]—to a more proximate time in the nearer term. In other words, in Xi's complex Marxist framework of historical materialism and the detailed questions of periodization that lie within it, the end of the primary stage of socialism was now moving from ahistorical time to historical time. This is critical because Deng, Jiang, Hu, and even Zhao Ziyang (who pioneered the term in 1987) had repeatedly declared that the primary stage of socialism was very long in duration indeed. Moreover, the central contradiction for that primary stage remained the need to develop the factors of production, on which basis the pro-market economic mantra of 'reform and opening' was legitimized.[11] There was no foreseeable end to the primary stage of socialism under these previous ideological formulations. So long as this primary stage persisted, the party's central contradiction mandating the primacy of market-driven economic development, including a high degree of political toleration for the inequality and imbalances that flowed from it, would continue. However, the implication arising from Xi's new ideological formulation of 2021 was twofold: he was indicating that the conclusion of the primary stage of socialism was now much closer than previously assumed; and that this, in turn, provided the ideological rationale for changing the party's central contradiction at the 19th Congress in 2017 to authorize new levels of state intervention in the market. Indeed, these two declaratory changes in 2017 and 2021, taken together, prepared the ideological ground for major new policy changes across China's Marxist political-economy.

This brings us to a second significant addition to Xi's formulation on the periodization of China's current stage of socialism: that "fully building a modern socialist China and basically realizing socialist modernization were essential for China's development in the primary stage of socialism and were essential for China to advance from the primary stage to a higher stage of socialism". This phraseology is remarkably similar to the second of Xi's 'centenary goals'—that is, to "build a modern and socialist country that is prosperous, strong, democratic, culturally advanced, and harmonious" by 2049.[12] By inserting this new ideological logic, Xi was beginning to firmly define the realization of this mid-century goal as the official benchmark for formally ending the primary stage of socialism—while stopping short of saying so in so direct and bald a fashion. By extension, that meant that from 2049, China could move to a much higher level of socialism. In other words, Xi was not only indicating a timetable for concluding the primary stage of socialism that distinctly differed from the multiple generations described by Deng; he was also indicating that, in his estimation, China could be now less than twenty-five years away from this critical transition to a more advanced form of socialism.

Most important, this further change in ideological periodization has significant implications for economic policy in the lead-up to 2049 as the imperative of income equality began to loom larger for the first time since 1978. Xi had already indicated at the 19th Party Congress in 2017 that the remaining period until 2049 would be divided into two distinct phases: a period of "socialist modernization", which would be "basically realized" by the approximate midpoint, 2035; followed by China becoming "a great modern socialist country that is prosperous, strong, democratic, culturally advanced, harmonious, and beautiful" by mid-century. This sub-periodization between 2020–2035 and 2035–2049 was also reflected in the Outline of the 14th Five-Year Plan for National Economic and Social Development and the Long-Range Objectives through the Year 2035, released in March 2021.[13] Against this background, Xi's 2021 speech therefore signaled a possible conclusion of the primary stage of socialism at some point after 2035 but before 2049.

At this point of his analysis, however, Xi appeared to realize he had a political problem on his hands. For the first time, a paramount leader had inferred an explicit conclusion date for the primary stage of socialism, whereas Xi's predecessors had conspicuously refused to do so. This potentially put him in the position of committing a 'nihilist error' by explicitly repudiating the accuracy of the party's historical decisions on such a crucial matter as the 'primary stage of socialism'. Intriguingly, Xi deals with the problem by audaciously redefining the preexisting ideological orthodoxy of his predecessors:

> In 1992, Deng Xiaoping stated: "We have been building socialism for only a few decades and are still in the primary stage. It will take a very long historical period to consolidate and develop the socialist system, and it will require persistent struggle by several generations, a dozen or even several dozens. We can never rest on our oars." In my opinion, Deng made this remark from a political perspective. He was pointing out that it would take a fairly long period of hard work to turn China into a modern country based on the weak economic foundations of the time. But he was also saying that we must persevere with China's socialist system from one generation to the next, even after modernization is achieved.[14]

In other words, Xi is implying that the sheer, unanticipated success of China's recent economic development meant that Deng's virtually unlimited timeframe for continuing the primary stage of socialism had largely been superseded—and that Deng's earlier, more open-ended timeframe had only been his personal opinion. Or put more starkly, because of China's rapidly accumulating national wealth and power, Deng's economic modernization timeline had been proven wrong and, by inference, reaching a higher level of socialism was now within reach of the present generation. Indeed, Deng's position that multiple generations would live under the primary stage of socialism (equalling, in effect, hundreds of years) had only, in Xi's rendering of it, been Deng's "political" perspective. According to Xi, writing in 2020, this did not exactly amount to sacred writ.

So what does all of this really mean in terms of real-world economic policy? As noted above, the political and policy significance of this arcane ideological debate about historical periodization is that it determines the permissible limits of inequality at any given stage of development. Under Deng, large-scale inequality between people and between regions was deemed permissible under the primary stage of socialism because the central challenge was to eliminate poverty, lift overall living standards, and build national power by unleashing the underdeveloped productive forces within China's economy—and, as a consequence, temporarily relegate the ideological significance of the 'relations of production' or class inequality. However, the ideological justification for large-scale inequality begins to collapse as the end of the primary stage of socialism begins to approach. At one level, this could be interpreted as meaning that inequality would need to be fully addressed after 2049 once the formal transition to a more advanced form of socialism occurs. But, on a different reading, it meant that because Xi had now decreed that China had entered a 'new development stage', albeit still within the twenty-five or so remaining years of the 'primary stage of socialism', it was important that the party *begin* addressing inequality in the lead-up to 2049. In other words, Xi's 2020 speech had the effect of relocating the economy's current stage of economic development (within the overall framework of historical materialism), bringing it fully into line with his additional ideological breakthrough (within the framework of dialectical materialism) at the 2017 Congress that redefined the party's central contradiction. Because the primary stage of socialism was drawing to a close, economic inequality had, as a matter of ideological logic, emerged as the party's primary domestic challenge, and this could only be addressed through vigorous intervention in the market economy by the Chinese party-state. And this is precisely what Xi Jinping had set about doing.

In Marxist terms, this relocation of the economy within the periodization framework of historical materialism, combined with the redefinition of the party's central contradiction, required a rebalancing of the 'relations of production' (i.e. class) with the changing nature of the 'forces of production'. This also meant readjusting the social superstructure and its relationship to the economic base—including the vexed question of the future roles of the public, private, and mixed ownership of the factors of production. Indeed, it might also mean revisiting the question of 'class' itself in the context of Xi's 'common prosperity agenda'. Given the party's challenge in maintaining ideological consistency over time, it is worthwhile noting the party's position at the time of the 13th Party Congress back in 1987 when the primary stage of socialism debate was in its earliest days. Then general secretary Zhao Ziyang had said:

> A correct understanding of the present historical stage of Chinese society is of prime importance for building socialism with Chinese characteristics, and it is the essential basis on which to formulate and implement a correct line and correct policies. Our Party has already made a clear and definite statement on this question: China is now in the primary stage of socialism. There are two aspects to this thesis. First, the Chinese society is already a socialist society. We must persevere in socialism and never deviate from it. Second, China's socialist society is still in its primary stage. We must proceed from this reality and not jump over this stage. . . . Under the specific historical conditions of contemporary China, to believe that the Chinese people cannot take the socialist road without going through the stage of fully developed capitalism is to take a mechanistic position on the question of the development of revolution, and that is the major cognitive root of rightist mistakes. On the other hand, to believe that it is possible to jump over the primary stage of socialism, in which the productive forces are to be highly developed, is to take a utopian position on this question, and that is the major cognitive root of leftist errors.[15]

It seems that nearly thirty-five years before Xi's *Qiushi* article appeared, Zhao may have been anticipating the possibility of a future 'leftist error' in prematurely bringing the primary stage of socialism to a close, without first having fully developed the factors of production. Indeed, under Xi, mainland per-capita income as of 2022 had not grown beyond middle income status and economic productivity has been growing at its lowest rate since the 1980s when Zhao was still in office.[16] Yet for Xi, the end of the primary stage of socialism now seemed to be in sight. Zhao, who expected this transition to occur in the very distant future,[17] might have called Xi's intervention a new 'utopian' age of economic equality brought about by a premature wave of party-state intrusion in the market. But then again, Zhao had long since been purged and was, by 2021, well and truly dead and buried.

The Changing Use of 'Banner Terms' in Economic Ideology

Changes in Xi's underlying economic ideology, as reflected in these complex debates about 'the primary stage of socialism', can also be seen in the changing use of 'banner terms' (*qizhiyu*) in major Chinese political statements when compared with those of his predecessors. This form of analysis has a long pedigree in charting the shifts in the official political and policy lines of the CCP. The disciplines of language, frequency of use of particular words, the use of certain formulations (*tifa*) by senior leaders, and the discontinuation of old *tifa* in favour of new ones are all barometers of changing sentiment in Chinese high politics and policy.[18] Indeed, Chinese political elites themselves find these tools as important as foreign analysts in trying to make sense of the CCP's internal political discourse. As Mao himself remarked in 1963: "One single [correct] formulation, and the whole nation will flourish; one single [incorrect] formulation and the whole nation will decline—this is what is referred to here as the transformation of the spiritual into the material."[19]

The declining ideological significance of market reform within the framework of Xi Jinping's 'new development philosophy' is reflected in significant changes in his use of a number of key terms frequently deployed by his predecessors. These include 'reform and opening'; 'socialist market economy', or its near-equivalent 'market economics'; and even references to 'Deng Xiaoping' himself, given that Deng remained synonymous with the period of reform and opening as its foremost political and policy architect. This can be seen in the language used by Jiang, Hu, and Xi in their formal reports to Party Congresses from 1992 (Jiang's first as general secretary) through to the 20th Congress in 2022 (Xi's second) as detailed in table 6.1.[20] The findings of this simple analysis are instructive. At the 2017 Party Congress, in what was the longest congress speech on record,[21] Xi made only 9 references to 'reform and opening', compared with 56 by Jiang in 1992 and 34 by Hu in 2007. Similarly, Xi's references to Deng Xiaoping by name show a similar pattern: only 2 in 2017, compared with 13 in 1992 and 11 in 2007.

This pattern is even starker in the official summaries of the party's annual Central Economic Work Conferences (CEWCs) published in state media since 1994.[22] Deng had been named a total of 41 occasions between 1994 and 2011 but, under Xi, he has not been named at all since 2015. As for the core reformist concepts of 'market economics' and a 'socialist market economy', the contrast is also clear: when Jiang led the conference, these terms appeared 20 times; they appeared 23 times under Hu; but only 11 times under Xi's leadership—and, in half of those years, not at all. An informed Chinese reader looking at the changing patterns of use for these three sets of emblematic banner terms would conclude that Xi's ideological commitment to Deng's era of market-based reform and opening had rapidly diminished.

By contrast, a similar examination of other banner terms that convey a greater partyist or statist significance—such as 'ideology', 'patriotism', and 'struggle'—reveals the reverse trend. For example, the term 'ideology' was mentioned only 13 times by Jiang and Hu over five party congresses spread across twenty-five years, whereas Xi used it 8 times at his first congress alone. For 'patriotism', the divide is less clear-cut: Xi narrowly holds the record over Hu at party congresses, despite Hu having hosted China's greatest patriotic event in its modern history with the 2008 Summer Olympic Games. Meanwhile, Xi's references to 'patriotism' were, on average, 1.5 times those of Jiang Zemin across the latter's three congresses.[23] Perhaps the single clearest contrast, however, lies in Xi's extensive use of the core ideological concept of 'struggle'. Here Xi used the term a total of 45 times at the 2017 and 2022 Congresses, compared with 34 references by his predecessors at the previous five congresses combined over a twenty-five-year period. Once again, a clear pattern emerges of a strong ideological preference for the agency of the party and state, and for the ideologically transformative processes of struggle, compared with the disciplines of the market, to bring about change.

Qian Gang, in a much broader textual analysis of leaders' reports in a total of eight congresses spanning thirty-five years, starting in 1982, found more discontinuity in political language between Hu's last congress report in 2012 and Xi's first in 2017 than between any previous pair of adjacent congresses. The only exception was the transition from the 12th to the 13th congresses in the 1980s, when the period of reform and opening was newly launched against the backdrop of significant political and ideological opposition from party conservatives. Across this broad historical sweep, Qian concluded that quantitatively "there is significant difference in political vocabulary between the 19th and 18th Congresses".[24] Indeed, Qian makes the broader point that, in his analysis of the life cycle of banner terms more generally over the twenty-five years between the 14th and 19th Party Congresses (1992–2017), "the relative frequencies of specialized banner terms in the political reports . . . tell us that prior banner terms have now become history with the 19th Congress."[25]

In other words, in Qian's analysis, the broad ideological 'band of meaning' shared across party congresses from 1992 to 2012 under Jiang's and Hu's leadership had receded into the distant past, and a new ideological lexicon was replacing it. Of course, previous conceptual frameworks could not be formally repudiated because the party rarely, if ever, admits it was wrong. To concede such fallibility would be to undermine the CCP's claim to ideological consistency and continuing political legitimacy. Instead, the framework is simply reinterpreted through the insertion of new language and the gradual removal of older, less convenient phrases. Importantly, Qian

Table 6.1a Key Dengist Terms in Party Congress Reports (14th–20th)

	Jiang Zemin			**Hu Jintao**		**Xi Jinping**		**Median**
	14th	**15th**	**16th**	**17th**	**18th**	**19th**	**20th**	**14th–20th**
Key term	**(1992)**	**(1997)**	**(2002)**	**(2007)**	**(2012)**	**(2017)**	**(2022)**	**(1992–2022)**
Reform and opening	56	27	14	34	19	9	11	19
Market economy	21	22	22	13	6	3	5	13
Deng Xiaoping	13	62	16	11	6	2	1	11
Total	**90**	**111**	**52**	**58**	**31**	**14**	**17**	**52**
Deviation from median	**+38**	**+59**	**—**	**6**	**−21**	**−38**	**−35**	**—**

Occurrences of '改革开放', '社会主义市场经济'/'市场经济'; and '邓小平'.

Table 6.1b 'Ideology', 'Patriotism', and 'Struggle' in Party Congress Reports (14th–20th)

	Jiang Zemin			Hu Jintao		Xi Jinping		Median
	14th	15th	16th	17th	18th	19th	20th	14th–20th
Key term	(1992)	(1997)	(2002)	(2007)	(2012)	(2017)	(2022)	(1992–2022)
Ideology	3	4	2	3	1	8	10	3
Patriotism	4	4	8	8	9	10	13	8
Struggle	9	9	7	4	5	23	22	9
Total	**16**	**17**	**17**	**15**	**15**	**41**	**45**	**17**
Deviation from median	**-1**	**—**	**—**	**-2**	**-2**	**+24**	**+28**	**—**

Occurrences of '意识形态', '爱国主义'/'爱国', and '斗争'.

points out that the term 'party leadership' (*dang de lingdao*) attained its highest frequency of usage at the congress in 2017, compared with all previous congresses going right back to the 8th in 1956, just as the term 'authority' (*quanwei*) was also found to be at record highs in 2017 compared with the past.[26] In short, the analytical picture to emerge from the 19th Congress under Xi was of a leader determined to draw an ideological dividing line with the past when compared with his post-Mao predecessors.

Conclusion

From this initial analysis, it is clear that Xi's overall ideological settings concerning the economy had changed from those of his predecessors. By altering the established parameters of the 'primary stage of socialism', Xi had fundamentally shifted the deep terms of the economic policy debate. The long history of this concept of the primary stage of socialism in Chinese Marxist economics had provided the party with its overall rationalization for the policies of reform and opening, as well as the social and economic inequalities to which they gave rise. But by adjusting the basic terms of this apparently abstract theoretical debate, Xi was creating the ideological conditions to adjust the party's 'principal contradiction', which would then flow through to the real world of economic policy. In other words, having turned the economic debate around at its most fundamental ideological level, Xi could then justify significant shifts in the political line in support of larger-scale, direct party intervention in economic policy, and not just for income redistribution purposes. This change has also been reflected in significant shifts in the use of economic 'banner terms' signalling the decline of the previous era of 'reform and opening' and 'market economics'—and the beginning of a 'new era' of politics, ideology, and 'struggle'. And over time, this underlying ideological change would come to be reflected in other, much more specific 'banner terms' on the economy that would underscore the practical extent of the unfolding changes in the substantive world of public policy.

7

Changes in China's Macro-Policy Direction on the Economy

Xi Jinping's ideological dividing lines on the economy are also reflected in accelerated changes to China's overall macro-policy settings over Xi's first two terms in office. Here, 'macro-policy settings' does not refer to monetary and fiscal policy as the classical tools of macroeconomic policy; rather, it refers to the party's overarching political and policy guidance for the economy as a whole, as expressed primarily through the changing language of the party's annual Central Economic Work Conferences (CEWCs) and other major economic conclaves. The evolution from more 'reformist' to more 'statist' language can be seen in six major macro-policy transitions over the decade from 2012 to 2022:

- the apparently pro-market 'Decision' (*jueding*) of the Third Plenum of the 18th Central Committee in 2013;[1]
- the proclamation of the 'New Normal' (*xin changtai*) at the 2014 CEWC;[2]
- its associated concept of 'Supply-Side Structural Reform' (*gongjice jiegou gaige*), which emerged from the 2015 Central Finance Leading Group meeting of the Politburo;[3]
- the 'New Development Concept' (*xinfazhan linian*) as Xi's new overarching economic framework for party and state interventionism in 'the new era' (while this first appeared in late 2015, it stayed largely dormant until after the 19th Congress in 2017);[4]

- the 'dual circulation economy' model (*shuangxunhuanjingji*) and its underlying logic of greater national economic self-reliance, released by the Politburo Standing Committee in May 2020;[5] and finally
- a macro doctrine of 'common prosperity' (*gongtong fuyu*) on the redistribution of wealth—a major thematic from late 2020.[6]

Making sense of macro-policy change through this cascading set of 'banner terms' is complex. Prior to 2013, the unifying rubric of 'reform and opening' provided a simple ideological framework indicating an overall preference for greater market disciplines in the domestic economy, together with greater market-driven integration with the global economy. While 'reform and opening' had been relegated in the Chinese public discourse after 2017, there were still obligatory references to it at party ceremonials acknowledging its ideological correctness in the past, but much less so for Xi's new era of interventionism for the future. However, it was after the emergence of the 'New Development Concept' as the recognized banner term for this newly interventionist era, and the full breadth of the statist and partyist 'band of meaning' contained under its umbrella, that it became the general ideological framework replacing Deng's age of 'reform and opening'. Meanwhile, the banner terms 'common prosperity', 'the dual circulation economy', and a redefined 'Supply-Side Structural Reform' became the phalanx of economic concepts that operationalized this new statist approach to income redistribution, industrial policy, and self-reliance.

These changes in macro-policy direction reflect a significant move to the Marxist left in the party's overall economic framework following the 19th Party Congress. However, this changing economic rubric has not been applied evenly across all elements of policy. Nor has it been systematic, with one new macro-policy concept neatly folding into the next, as the party leadership would have international observers believe. Indeed, some older concepts have been retained in parallel to a replacement concept. Others have been reinterpreted as explanatory mechanisms for later additions to the ideological canon. Meanwhile, a number of older, reformist formulations have been eliminated altogether. Nonetheless, this analytical complexity cannot conceal the overall trend line towards the Marxist left.[7] Nor should it disguise how this trend parallels the overall adjustment in political ideology to the Leninist left and the general reassertion of the power of the party going back to 2013. Xi's party had now become the unassailable, ideological centre of all significant public policy, including economic policy.

The 2013 'Decision'

In ideological terms, the 'Decision on Several Major Questions about Deepening Reform' by the Third Plenum of the 18th Central Committee in November 2013—often referred to simply as 'the Decision'—was an ambitious document.[8] It comprised 60 major recommendations and a total of 336 individual policy initiatives.[9] It combined both pro-market and pro-state recommendations. Its reformist recommendations spanned the Chinese economy including land, labour, enterprise, finance, innovation, investment, competition, trade, fiscal, and environmental reform. The core organizing principle of this reform programme was its declaration that the party would "let the market play the decisive role in allocating resources".[10] As Nicholas Lardy noted, this bold ideological declaration "had never appeared in an official document of the Chinese Communist Party" before then.[11] The adjective 'decisive' (*juedingxing*), describing the role of market forces in allocating resources, contrasted sharply with the party's previous, more conservative language on the role of the market, which simply referred to the market's 'basic' (*jichude*) role in the economy.[12] Under these earlier formulations, the market was still not the ultimate arbitral mechanism, thus leaving considerable administrative discretion for intervention by the state. However, 'the Decision' outlined a different, more reformist worldview where the core responsibilities of government would henceforth be "redirected to five basic functions: macroeconomic management, market regulation, public service delivery, supervision of society, and environmental protection".[13] On its surface, and in an authoritative commentary published in the *People's Daily*, 'the Decision' was heralded as a "breakthrough" for a third wave of market reforms comparable to the second wave initiated by Deng following his Southern Tour in 1992.[14] In practice, however, this would prove to be short-lived.

Against these pro-market breakthroughs, 'the Decision' also included decidedly non-reformist language concerning the expanded significance of state-owned enterprises. To use the political vernacular of the party communiqué, the CCP would still "unswervingly consolidate and develop the public economy, persist in the dominant position of public ownership, give full play to the leading role of the state-owned sector, and continuously increase its vitality, controlling force and influence".[15] While this appears to be as 'statist' as other parts of 'the Decision' appear reformist, the *People's Daily* stressed that the Plenum recognized the 'equal importance' of both state and non-state ownership.[16] According to 'the Decision', SOEs would shift from "managing enterprises to managing capital", enabling them to invest more widely in the rest of the economy, including in "mutual fusion" with other market participants, such as private firms.[17] This would be done through the creation of "state-owned capital investment companies" which would "serve the strategic goals of the state, invest more in key industries and areas that are vital to national security and are the lifeblood of the economy".[18]

The stated policy objective of this recommendation was to drive efficiency through greater competitive neutrality—both among SOEs, and between SOEs and the private sector—through an effective national competition policy. Theoretically, this was consistent with the market being the decisive allocator of scarce economic resources, although any dislocation arising from this reform would still need to be tempered against the need for stability. Indeed, barely a month after the Third Plenum had released the 'Decision', the 2013 CEWC used the classical Marxist analytical framework of dialectical materialism to explain the symbiotic relationship between advancing reform and preserving stability. The meeting emphasized that the party would be "seeking progress in a stable manner" since "steady development and reform are dialectically united and mutually conditional. To seek steady growth, we need to stay focussed; to seek reform, we need to maintain order."[19] While the relationship between reform (which is inherently disruptive) and stability had long been a practical preoccupation of the party, this may be the first time that the leadership publicly resorted to Marxist dialectics to explain this specific creative tension.

Notwithstanding the intellectual symmetry of Xi's dialectical architecture, the net effect of the new policy direction outlined in 'the Decision' on the future of state-owned enterprises was to re-empower them to resume their previous role as the leviathans of the Chinese economy. This time, however, they were to draw on their newfound investment arms to invest energetically across both the domestic and international economy, and in both the public and private sectors. SOEs were also unleashed in pursuit of industrial policy objectives without regard to market disciplines at all. Indeed, the vigorous implementation of 'the Decision' in relation to SOEs, in addition to the less-than-vigorous implementation of its more reformist recommendations for the rest of the economy, prompted a growing analytical consensus by 2017 that the market reform agenda outlined in 'the Decision' of 2013 had effectively ground to a halt.[20]

Importantly, the same Third Plenum in 2013 had also decided to create a new 'Leading Group on Comprehensively Deepening Reform' within the party centre. It would be charged with implementing 'the Decision', rather than leaving that responsibility to the battery of professional economists working in the State Council under the Premier, as had occurred with major economic policy changes in the past. This new institutional arrangement would further diminish the overall political importance of market reform. Whereas the reform agenda had previously been driven by economic technocrats within the state apparatus, as of 2013 these powers were once again being vested in the institutions of the CCP as the party returned to the commanding heights of Chinese economic management. This Leading Group became the central intersection point between party ideology and long-term public policy across the board—and not just on the economy. It became the new institutional nerve centre of the entire Chinese policy system with Xi himself as director, and his chief ideologist and non-economist Wang Huning as deputy director and director of its general office, rather than the Premier or a relevant vice-premier with direct responsibility for the economy.[21] These institutional arrangements further accentuated the drift of the economic policy agenda to the partyist left as, increasingly, major decisions were no longer effectively contested by robust technocratic advice from the sophisticated policy apparatus of the State Council.[22] In other words, the implementation of 'the Decision' had been handed to the party centre—an institution that not only failed to understand its policy significance but, in all probability, culturally and instinctively did not believe in it.

It is also significant that the term 'the Decision' would itself drift from regular public use, rarely mentioned in official communications after 2015. Nor did 'the Decision' generate its own 'banner term' capable of taking forward the 'reform and opening' mission into the 'new era' of Xi Jinping. Instead, the party's market reform agenda, like 'the Decision' itself, withered on the vine. Its principal recommendation on the reinvigoration of SOEs, however, would become a precursor for what Nick Lardy and Jude Blanchett would respectively call 'the State Strikes Back' and 'CCP Inc'.[23] Scheduled for full implementation by 2020, 'the Decision' as an integrated policy reform blueprint effectively died without political fanfare. But because in the Chinese political system the party can never be wrong, Xi decreed in the official record of the party's major achievements for its centenary celebrations in June 2021 that "2,485 reforms" had been introduced since 'the Decision', resulting in its goals having been fully completed on schedule![24] And that, it seems, was that. At a formalistic level, the reformist dimensions of 'the Decision' and the central role of market forces had therefore been preserved. More than that, it was deemed to have been an outstanding success. But at a macro-policy level, let alone an operational level, it was effectively dead and buried less than five years after it was first brought into being.

The 'New Normal' of 2014–2015

At the December 2014 CEWC, Xi Jinping's party vowed to "understand the new normal, adjust to the new normal and develop under the new normal".[25] This particular "banner term" first emerged that May during Xi's inspection tour of Henan[26] and would remain in official circulation for the next three years before being marginalized after the 2017 CEWC. The 'New Normal' referred to a fundamental adjustment to China's overall economic development model, concentrating on three essential elements: first, the transition from 'high-speed' growth to stable, sustainable, 'medium-speed' growth; second, a transformation of China's major growth drivers from basic exports and public infrastructure investment to domestic consumption and innovation; and third, a transformation from quantitative growth through bigger-scale production, to qualitative growth based on efficiency, productivity, and environmental sustainability throughout the production process.[27] Of these, the third was defined as the most important, or in Xi's language: "When looking at China's economy, one should not focus on the growth rate only. . . . We will focus on improving quality and efficiency, and give even greater priority to shifting the growth model and adjusting the structure of development."[28] These would become the core elements of 'the New Normal', which the party now described as "the term that had become the governing logic of China's economic development".[29]

The question, however, was where to locate this broad concept of the 'New Normal' within the overarching ideological debate between the re-assertion of the party-state's economic powers, on the one hand, and the continuation of market reform, on the other. Like 'the Decision', the 'New Normal' in its initial enunciation appeared to be decidedly reformist, emphasizing cuts to state investment and improving the productivity of firms. This was reinforced at the time by reformist academic literature from such institutions as the Chinese Academy of Social Sciences from senior Chinese public economists. In one such article, 'China's Economic New Normal—Growth, Structure and Momentum',[30] Cai Fang, argued that the 'New Normal' formed part of a domestic and international market reform framework and that "having an appropriate understanding of the new normal is conducive to sustaining China's economic growth through reform". Cai further argued that "reform must be regarded as integral to China's new normal".[31] Indeed, contributors to Cai's volume dedicated to the "New Normal" describe supply-side market reform—an economic "rebirth" to "completely do away with the old system" of state subsidy and broader market intervention—as the only means to secure reasonable growth of between 5% and 6% in the 2020s.[32] This was partly because of the large-scale structural inefficiencies that were built into state corporations, financial institutions, and the wider economy, including the consequences of unprecedented stimulus measures during the Global Financial Crisis of 2008–2009.[33] Importantly, it was argued, the 'New Normal' would be "conducive to rationalizing the relationship between the government and the market" and required China "to strengthen the principal status of enterprises and their dominant role in resource allocation and maximize resource allocation according to the rules, prices, and competitions already extant in the market".[34]

It is reasonable to conclude that the initial purpose and policy content of the 'New Normal' campaign on the economy from late 2014 was the furtherance of the broad-based market reform agenda articulated in 'the Decision' of late 2013. It is significant, therefore, that the 'New Normal' did not much survive as a 'banner term' beyond 2017, the year that Xi Jinping's 'new era' and his 'New Development Concept' were launched at the 19th Party Congress. Nor did it survive the Congress' redefinition of the party's new, interventionist, and left-leaning 'principal contradiction' that same year. Indeed, 2017 would become the ideological tipping point in the subsequent direction of Chinese economic policy.

'Supply-Side Structural Reform'

The agreed policy framework for giving operational effect to the 'New Normal' was entitled 'Supply-Side Structural Reform', or SSSR (*gongjice jiegou gaige*). This policy aimed to enhance reform on the supply side of the economy, rather than compensating for weaker growth by simply resorting to episodic, counter-cyclical responses on the demand side. The need for supply-side reform had already been underscored in the 2014 CEWC report, which argued that "insufficient supply was the major contradiction that had plagued China for a long time".[35] But it was the 2015 CEWC that underlined the explicit linkage between SSSR and the 'New Normal'. As the party's June 2021 resolution on the 'Centennial Achievements of the CCP' would later record, it was at the 2015 Central Economic Work Conference that Xi "emphasized that advancing Supply-Side Structural Reform was a major innovation to adapt to and lead a New Normal in economic development".[36] Or, in the words of the CEWC itself: "Firming up stable economic growth will require greater focus on structural Supply-Side Structural Reform."[37]

To give effect to SSSR, the CEWC also resolved that the party's five major economic tasks for 2016 would be: resolving overcapacity; helping companies reduce costs; resolving property inventory; expanding effective supply and deleveraging; and preventing and resolving financial risk.[38] And as if to underline the overall reformist direction of SSSR, the 2015 CEWC report concluded in language more clear-cut on the state-market divide than anything since:

> The meeting emphasized that we must adhere to the major principles of socialist political economy with Chinese characteristics, adhere to the liberation and development of social productive forces, and adhere to the direction of socialist market economic reform, so that the market can play a decisive role in the allocation of resources, which is the main line of deepening economic system reform. The task for the government is to adopt a different role and allow the market to make independent decisions and bear its own risks. The government should not take the place of market players in making decisions and should not rush to lead innovation activities on the front line but should strive to build an external environment that is willing to innovate and take risks for all types of innovation entities.[39]

However, this full-throated commitment to a further wave of market reforms embedded in 'the Decision', the 'New Normal', and SSSR was then forced to confront China's major share market implosions of 2015–2016 when shareholders' wealth was slashed by 30% in the space of a month.[40] Xi Jinping may have been assured back in 2012–2013 that the reformist direction for the economy that he had partly embraced in 'the Decision' was necessary to continue to grow the economy, notwithstanding his Leninist resolve to reassert the party's control over Chinese politics. But the 2015 stock market crash, and the widespread social and political instability it threatened to unleash, appear to have destroyed whatever confidence Xi had in the utility of unfettered markets. Large-scale losses by ordinary Chinese citizens, followed by the sheer scale of the failed interventions undertaken by the Chinese state as Xi tried to stabilize markets, seem to have had a traumatizing effect on the party leadership. In Xi's view, China's econocrats plainly did not know what they were doing, with the result that the entire Chinese financial and economic system then went into what Barry Naughton has described as "full-on 'stability' mode".[41] This included a large-scale expansion in state credit and investment delivered through SOEs (and some private firms) acting at the direction of the party centre and funded by a new tranche of local government debt. It also included a new regime of capital controls to stem the outflow of foreign currency holdings. These emergency interventions clearly ran counter to the reformist thrust of SSSR, the 'New Normal', and 'the Decision'. Indeed, there was real concern that the remedy now being imposed to deal with major stock market instability would compound the underlying statist policy legacy left over from the interventions during the Global Financial Crisis.[42] The New Normal-SSSR policy regime was intended to rectify these statist excesses, not exacerbate them. But the post-2015 retreat to stability would end up collapsing any remaining political momentum for continued economic reform. The tables, it seemed, had turned through a combination of Xi's underlying ideological conservatism and the full political and economic ramifications of the 2015 financial market collapse.

SSSR's market reformist orthodoxy managed to survive the 2016 CEWC, the last before the 19th Party Congress in 2017. The 2016 Conference still stated its clear-cut "belief that the root cause of China's economic contradictions and problems resulted from a major structural imbalance, thus making structural supply-side reforms necessary in order to improve the quality and efficiency of supply".[43] Indeed, the CEWC continued that "the fundamental way of doing that was to deepen reform, which was to improve the system and mechanism under which the market played a decisive role in the allocation of resources".[44] This doubling down on SSSR was underlined further in the 'major tasks' adopted by the CEWC for the year ahead, which included yet another, characteristically cryptic policy *tifa* of 'Three Cuts, One Lowering, One Strengthening' (*sanqu, yijiang, yibu*)—a reference to the previous year's CEWC priorities of "cutting overcapacity, destocking, deleveraging, reducing corporate costs and shoring up weak links in the economy".[45] This gave rise to the understandable impression that the party's commitment to the market-reformist direction of SSSR, as reflected in the strengthened language of the CEWC reports over the 2014–2016 period, was once again becoming more resolute in its pursuit of the 'New Normal' and the broader ideological remit of 'the Decision' itself.

Much of this, however, would disappear after the 2017 Party Congress. This was reflected in: the changing official language of the Congress Report itself on Xi's 'new era'; the party's new 'central contradiction' on market intervention; and in the rapidly changing content of annual CEWC reports between late 2017 and 2020. For example, the principal objective identified by the 2017 CEWC for the year ahead was neither the New Normal nor SSSR. Instead, the party's central economic mission was to respond to the demands of 'the new era'.[46] This meant the policy implications that flowed from Xi's newly redefined 'central contradiction' concerning 'unbalanced and inadequate development'. Second, while SSSR was retained in name as the first of the party's 'eight major' tasks for 2018, its significance was diluted by the other seven tasks, most of which had little if anything to do with reform. Third, the second of these eight major tasks for 2018 concerned the renewed future of SOEs, effectively repudiating the overall reformist logic of SSSR and 'the Decision'. Here the conference called for "stimulating the vitality of various market entities, in particular promoting the strengthening the role of state-owned capital . . . and strengthening the party's leadership and party-building in SOEs".[47] Fourth, by the 2018 CEWC, SSSR policy priorities had effectively been removed from the list of the party's seven major tasks for 2019. In fact, five of those seven tasks arguably required more, rather than less, state intervention in the economy, including the accelerated expansion of investment by the state-owned sector and pressing ahead with mixed-ownership.[48] Fifth, the diminution of SSSR and most of its active component parts would continue in both the 2019 and 2020 CEWCs, consistent with the expanding role of the party and state across an ever-widening range of economic policy interventions.[49] And finally, as noted above, the reformist term 'New Normal' itself largely disappeared from the party lexicon after 2017, replaced by other banner terms such as the largely mercantilist concept of a 'dual circulation economy', the equalitarian appeal of 'common prosperity', and Xi's all-encompassing 'New Development Concept'. While the term SSSR is retained throughout these reports, it is explicitly redefined as a means of executing long-term SOE reform in order to prepare them for the larger role they would now play in the Chinese economy. But this was radically different from the reformist set of policy missions outlined in the original, pre-2017 'New Normal' objectives for SSSR. Therefore, notwithstanding the tortuous political journey that China's economic reform agenda had undertaken prior to 2017, after the 19th Party Congress held that year there emerged a new, more Marxist economic orthodoxy that increasingly preferenced the party and state ahead of the market and private firms.

The 'New Development Concept' as Xi Jinping Thought for the New Era

The movement to the Marxist left in the party's overall economic ideology intensified after 2017. But it would take another three years until the Fifth Plenum in October 2020 (and Xi's later commentary on that plenum in July 2021[50]) for the full dimensions of this ideological shift to become plain to the wider policy community.[51] The new 'banner term' to signify this fundamental ideological and policy change became the 'New Development Concept' (hereinafter the NDC). Although launched as early as 2015, the NDC struggled for real definition until 2020–2021, by which time it had become an umbrella term incorporating a number of subsidiary concepts including: the 'dual circulation economy'; 'common prosperity'; 'security in development'; and the centrality of Xi's so-called real economy that would be driven by industrial policy, as opposed to the 'fictitious economy' of finance and property speculation. These terms were imbued with a range of overlapping meanings, but their common ideological denominator was the legitimization of new forms of party and state intervention in the market. And their overarching purpose was to address the new 'contradiction' identified by the 19th Party Congress in 2017, which now formed the central ideological nervous system of Xi's 'new era'.

The NDC's first appearance came as early as the Fifth Plenum of the 18th Central Committee in October 2015. This was when Xi put forward a five-pronged development concept comprising "innovation, coordination, sustainability, openness and sharing" in response to China's "new historical conditions" and the "many grave challenges of increasing contradictions and growing numbers of risks and dangers".[52] Then, in early 2016, Xi explained this amorphous new concept with the curious new metaphor that the NDC served "as both the baton and the traffic lights" of the overall economic system.[53] And by December 2016, Xi had told the CEWC of that year that one of the main tasks for the following year was to concentrate the party's efforts to firmly establish and implement the 'New Development Concept'.[54] Indeed, by the eve of the 19th Party Congress, in July 2017, Xi was emphasizing the need to implement this still-amorphous NDC in response to China having reached a "new historical starting point".[55] In short, for the two years leading up to the 2017 Congress, starting just after China's 2015 domestic financial crisis, the party's propaganda apparatus had been advancing this soon-to-be-all-important, but still ill-defined, new banner term. Nonetheless, the full ideological significance of Xi's latest ideological catch-cry would become clear in the wake of the 2017 Congress itself. This was when the NDC would become the stark dividing line between the market interventionism of the future, and the era of reform and opening that was now the past. Indeed, it would become the new economic framework through which Xi's 'new era' policy priorities would be delivered.

The ideological significance of the NDC representing the economic dimension of Xi Jinping's 'new era' was impressed across the full range of Xi's party audiences. It was underlined in bold by the title given to the fifth section of Xi's 2017 Congress Report, 'Applying the New Development Concept and Developing a Modern Economic System'.[56] In the 2017 CEWC held the following month, Xi delivered to the party the surprising news that during his first five years in office, the CCP had "formed the New Development Concept as the principal content of Xi Jinping economic thought on socialism with Chinese characteristics for the new era".[57]

He pointed to the centrality of the NDC as not only the recognized economic framework for the 'new era' but, more specifically, as the policy vehicle for realizing his overall economic ideology as outlined in 'Xi Jinping Thought.' Put simply, Xi had made plain that on the economy, the NDC was to become Xi Jinping Thought in action. This relationship between ideology and policy became even clearer by the time of the 2019 CEWC. This conference identified the first of the party's six important tasks for 2020 as "unswervingly implementing the New Development Concept".

Most critically, Xi used the conference to explicitly tie the NDC directly to the party's redefined principal contradiction by stating that "party committees and governments at all levels had to adapt to the inevitable requirements of our country entering a new stage of development and changes in the major social contradiction". Xi added that this had to be done "by firmly grasping the New Development Concept . . . and focussing on solving various problems of imbalanced and inadequate development". Xi also underscored the importance of the NDC within a Marxist-Leninist framework of historical and dialectical materialism by asserting that the translation of economic ideology into policy represented "a comprehensive and holistic concept that follows the laws of economic and social development".[58] Twelve months later, at a seminar at the Central Party School in early 2021, Xi would expand further on the ideological significance of the NDC, describing it as "a systematic theoretical system that answered a series of theoretical and practical questions about the purpose, motivation, method and path of development, clarifying our party's political stance, value orientation, development model, and development path".[59] By 2021, therefore, the ideological hand of the Marxist-Leninist party-state was beginning to rest heavily on the shoulders of the New Development Concept.

On the substantive content of the NDC, its practical implementation and its importance for national rejuvenation, Xi at the 2019 CEWC emphasized the direct relevance of the NDC in five specific areas: innovation, coordination, greenness, openness, and shared development.[60] Furthermore, implementing the NDC had become "an important yardstick for testing leading cadres at all levels".[61] By the 2020 CEWC, Xi was stating that implementing the NDC and building the 'new development pattern' (a new term[62]) were now necessary for the economy's 'new stage of development' that had come with the new era that China had now entered. And by the Politburo Study Session of January 2021, Xi was calling on the party to promote "innovative development, coordinated development, green development, open development, and shared development . . .working together as a joint force, without being too light, or too heavy, or by simply adopting a generalized approach to everything".[63]

Importantly, there would be "complete, accurate and comprehensive implementation" of this new policy direction through China's national planning machinery, the 14th Five-Year Plan.[64] In other words, it would not simply rely on a series of market signals to the private sector. This thorough process of central planning and implementation was necessary because "seeking happiness for the people and rejuvenation for the nation is not only the starting point and goal of our party's leadership in the modernization drive, but also the 'root' and 'soul' of the New Development Concept".[65] In other words, Xi saw the NDC not just as an abstract ideological idea, but as the basis for a new direction in substantive economic policy in state-coordinated development, innovation, sustainability, and 'shared' economic outcomes. The NDC was, therefore, rapidly becoming a macro-political concept incorporating new forms of party and state intervention in the economy to produce a range of real-world public policy outcomes. The precise nature of these proposed interventions would become clearer during the course of 2021.

A fuller definition of the NDC would finally come with Xi Jinping's article in *Qiushi* of July 2021 entitled 'Understanding the New Development Stage, Applying the New Development Philosophy, and Creating a New Development Dynamic', based on a January 2021 speech.[66] As of the end of 2023, this had been the single most definitive statement on what Xi meant by his new banner term. It is not, however, a systematic exposition of an integrated intellectual proposition. Instead, it is an eclectic collection of disparate ideas connected by an underlying thematic of greater party and state intervention in the market to overcome the problems of 'unbalanced and inadequate development'. Indeed, in some respects, Xi's *Qiushi* article reads as an attempt retrospectively to explain in ideological terms all that he had done on the economy since 2012. As argued earlier in this chapter, Xi's evolution from supposed market reformer to unabashed state interventionist had been an uneven process. Nonetheless, the centre of economic policy gravity had clearly changed from Xi's first term, which had been dominated by the broadly reformist orientation of 'the Decision', the New Normal, and Supply-Side Structural Reform. In his second term, these reformist frameworks had been increasingly supplanted by the explicitly statist concepts of common prosperity, the dual circulation economy, and national self-reliance. This drift to the interventionist left can be seen in the relative weighting of thirteen defining 'characteristics' of the new economic strategy listed in Xi's authoritative *Qiushi* article. Eight of these are interventionist, including the centrality of the new contradiction itself; people-centred development; policies to realize an eco-civilization; the dual circulation economy; the securitization of development; and the promotion of shared growth. Four are reformist: the 2013 Decision; the New Normal; SSSR; and arguably 'structural adjustment' in response to the overreach of official stimulus. One of the thirteen could be described as technically neutral—the development of a 'modern economic system'—although there is further textual evidence to suggest that this phrase is more oriented to the new, more activist role of the state through industrial policy, than to any continued reliance on the market.

This public balancing act between different schools of thought on the economy, and the various banner terms held aloft by each of them, is relatively normal in Chinese official commentary as the system strives for an acceptable level of collective consensus. Nonetheless, it is equally clear that the new ideological 'band of meaning' now represented by Xi's new conceptual umbrella on the economy—the NDC—had shifted. By any measure, the NDC was more directly interventionist in the operations of the market than was the case during earlier periods of reform and opening. As Xi himself wrote in his 2021 *Qiushi* article: "the introduction of the new development philosophy [in 2015] marked a fundamental change for the entire development context of our country". He went on to say:

> In reviewing this course of events, I wish to underscore the theories and concepts on economic and social development that we have put forward since our Party's 18th National Congress in 2012. Of these theories and concepts, the new development philosophy is the most important.

In summary, on the economy, Xi's New Development Concept represents his overarching ideological alternative to Deng's concept of 'reform and opening'. It is designed for the 'new era' that had been heralded by the 'higher phase' of the primary stage of socialism that Xi believed China had now reached, as the country proceeded along its pre-ordained path—one that had been determined long ago by the ineluctable forces of historical materialism. It was within this new era that Xi also saw the NDC as the innovative, statist model necessary to address the 'central contradiction' of significantly unbalanced development that the party's leadership now confronted. And this conclusion on the need to deal now with these new challenges of unbalanced development was based, in turn, on what Xi had divined through the processes of dialectical materialism, the ideological twin of historical materialism, within the overall intellectual armoury of Marxism-Leninism.

The Dual Circulation Economy

There are three major elements to this overall shift to the ideological left on the Chinese economy encapsulated within Xi Jinping's New Development Concept: the 'dual circulation economy', including the revitalization of the concept of national self-reliance; Xi's new approach to 'security in development', as part of his 'securitization of everything' agenda discussed in chapter 5; and, most important, his new doctrine of 'common prosperity'.

Xi dedicated an entire section of his 2021 *Qiushi* article to the concept of a 'dual circulation economy' (*shuangxunhuan jingji*), which he calls the 'new development dynamic' (*xinfazhan dongneng*). The purpose of this new 'dual circulation economy' concept was to animate the entire NDC over the next fifteen years, he wrote. Xi stated that national 'self-reliance' was a core part of this agenda. He emphasized that the 14th Five-Year Plan (2020–2025), together with China's 'Long-Range Objectives through the Year 2035', had "defined the creation of a new development dynamic that focuses on domestic flow and features positive interplay between domestic flow and international engagement as a major strategic task that concerned China's overall development interests". As will become clear, Xi's repeated references to the 'domestic flow' component of the dual circulation economy concept is a new indicator of internal demand becoming the core driver of China's long-term economic growth. By contrast, a smaller 'international flow' (i.e. exports and imports) was to become less critical to long-term growth over time. The 'dual circulation economy' was also, therefore, a call for greater national self-reliance against the risk of future international trade restrictions in critical areas of strategic risk. In the meantime, it advocated the leveraging of other countries' continued trade dependency on China's domestic market to expand Beijing's influence in global economic rule-setting and wider foreign policy leverage. For all these reasons, under the 'dual circulation' concept, China was to become less economically dependent on the world, while making the world more economically dependent on China. In that sense, 'dual circulation' represented a neo-mercantilist, economically nationalist and increasingly non-market approach to Chinese economic policy.

In justifying this change in policy direction, Xi's article emphasized China's changed external strategic and economic circumstances. He cites a "backlash against economic globalization" and the fact that "the COVID-19 pandemic exacerbated the trend of deglobalization and many countries have now become more inward-looking." Reflecting on what all this meant for China's overall economic strategy, Xi stated that by April 2020 he himself had "realized just how much things had changed; the environment and conditions that had facilitated large-scale imports and exports were no longer in place" and "given these new circumstances, we needed to come up with new thinking to steer development". In Xi's retelling of it, these external changes caused him to conclude by the Fifth Plenum of the 19th Central Committee in October 2020 that China should establish a new development dynamic as "a strategic and proactive step for taking the initiative in development, a major historic mission that must be fulfilled in the new development stage, and an important measure for applying the new development philosophy". In other words, China's change of economic strategy towards a more interventionist, nationalist and mercantilist position had been driven in large part by Xi's analysis of the country's changing international circumstances, not just by his views on the need to adjust the domestic growth model to deal with the problem of inequality. The Chinese economy of the future therefore needed to be 'steered' more vigorously by the Chinese state than had been previously the case. And, of equal importance, in Xi's view, the economy now needed to be much less dependent on unfettered access to the global economy for its future growth.

Xi Jinping, having attributed the principal cause of the NDC to changing external forces, then uses his *Qiushi* article to launch a full-throated call for national economic self-reliance, the dual circulation economy and the importance of 'domestic flow', by citing Mao himself:

> In 1936, Mao Zedong made a remark that still holds true for us even today. He said, "No matter how complicated, grave, and harsh the circumstances, what a military leader needs most of all is the ability to function independently in organizing and employing the forces under his command. . . . Failure to do so spells defeat. The initiative is not something imaginary but is concrete and material." If we can, by dint of our own efforts, ensure unimpeded domestic flow to effectively shield ourselves from harm, we will have the vigour and vitality to not only survive but thrive amid volatile international situations, making it impossible for anyone to keep us down or to back us into a corner.

Xi's description of himself as a Mao-like general now marshalling the nation's economic resources to respond to new international security threats is remarkable in its heroic reliance on the leader's unique skill in plotting the way forward. There was not even fleeting reference to the objective laws of economics in this discussion. Rather it was an essential case of the party's leader responding in classically Leninist fashion to what was increasingly seen as an existential economic security threat.

Xi, however, was also aware that his rallying cry in support of a new era of Chinese economic nationalism and national self-reliance would be liable to extreme interpretation across the Chinese bureaucratic system. This would be particularly so for those already predisposed to more radical forms of statist behaviour. That is why Xi also used his *Qiushi* article to press for balance between extreme forms of self-reliance, on the one hand, and the continuation of reasonable levels of export-driven growth for the immediate future, on the other. In doing so, Xi offered a remarkably frank insight into the internal fault lines of the Chinese economic policy debate being conducted under the 'dual circulation economy' banner. According to Xi, when speaking of the dual circulation economy:

> In practice, there are some misunderstandings that we need to guard against. First, some people tend to only speak about the first half, or the domestic flow element as the main factor, of the new development dynamic, and call for China to sharply reverse its opening to the outside world. Second, some others speak only of the latter half, or the positive interplay between domestic flow and international engagement, and still subscribe to the old development dynamic of large-scale imports and exports with two ends of the economic process—markets and resources—being located abroad, despite the changes to the international landscape. . . . All of these understandings are incomplete or even erroneous."

Nonetheless, despite these efforts to balance the message to the party, in other renditions of the 'dual circulation economy' formulation in China's official media, Xi has routinely prioritized 'domestic flow' over 'international engagement'. Indeed, Xi made his predominant message crystal clear elsewhere in the same *Qiushi* article, writing that "the essence of the new development dynamic is realizing a high level of self-reliance" (*zili gengsheng*). Furthermore, the policy vehicle to achieve this independence in 'scientific and technological innovation' would be the 14th Five-Year Plan itself.[67] In other words, under the banner of the 'dual circulation economy' and the NDC of which it is part, Xi made it plain to party elites that a major ideological shift had occurred: the 'old development dynamic' of rampant reform, opening, and globalization was dead and buried; and Xi's brave new economic world of national self-reliance had arrived.

One further rationale offered by Xi for swinging the economic pendulum towards statism, nationalism, and mercantilism through the extraordinary ideological pastiche of the NDC, the 'dual circulation economy', and national self-reliance is the leverage it offered China in dealing with the rest of the world. In his *Qiushi* article, Xi went so far as to explicitly describe China creating "a strong gravitational pull for global production factors and resources, a strong ability to hold our own amid intense international competition, and powerful momentum for the allocation of global resources". Xi added that Beijing should be in the business of seeing "that China's domestic circulation plays a stronger guiding role in dual-flow dynamics and foster new advantages for China's participation in international economic cooperation and competition". Properly decoded, Xi in reality was arguing that a more mercantilist China would use its vast import power—presumably in minerals, energy, and agriculture—to its advantage by dominating global markets. Second, as the world's largest exporter, China could also leverage its position as the "world's factory"[68] to control global industrial supply. And third, although less clear from Xi's language, China's global economic dominance would help it to shape the future rules, standards, and institutional arrangements for international economic engagement in a manner more consistent with its interests and values. These are not only statist perspectives; at the same time they represent mercantilist, monopsonistic, and monopolistic worldviews. They are certainly not market-driven or market-sensitive.

We should, therefore, not underestimate the long-term ideological and policy significance of the 'dual circulation economy' thrust within the NDC. In its policy substance, it is about the new era rather than the old; the New Development Concept rather than the old; a new statist approach to domestic economic management rather than a reliance on markets to distribute resources rationally; a new commitment to state-driven national self-reliance rather than relying on global markets; and now the conscious leveraging by the state of China's newfound national economic power to challenge and change the prevailing market-based rules of the global economy. Its policy endpoint, as noted above, is a world that is increasingly economically dependent on China, while decreasing the country's economic dependence on the rest of the world.

For these reasons, the ideological reframing of Chinese economic policy and strategy to the left represents a profound change, one involving a combination of domestic and international factors. At its most fundamental level, these policy changes are a product of Xi's ideological redefinition of the party's domestic central contradiction, reasserting the power of the party to rectify imbalances in development that had arisen during reform and opening. But, by 2021, as reflected in Xi's article in *Qiushi*, he was adding a foreign ideological rationalization that the NDC and the 'dual circulation economy' were also needed to deal with adverse international developments. Here Xi was referring to the US-China trade war which commenced in 2018, the broader trend of economic re-risking and de-coupling between China and the United States (and its allies) after the outbreak of COVID-19 in 2020, and the general intensification of geo-political competition between Washington and Beijing writ large.

This, however, raises the question of whether we can legitimately describe these underlying geo-economic and geo-political factors as being in any way 'ideological'. Surely these are all questions of strategic logic that would be equally applicable in any political system, Marxist or non-Marxist? This, of course, is true. But we should also recall that the central claim of this book is that Marxist-Leninist ideological change represents *one* cause of political and policy change, not the *only* cause. We should also recognize that what we might call 'strategic' factors—that is, factors that exist independently of any underlying ideational claims of individual political systems—may nonetheless be interpreted differently through the particular ideological lens of a Marxist-Leninist worldview. Indeed, as noted in earlier chapters of this book, the language of 'contradictions' in CCP usage has never been exclusively applied to domestic developments in China's political economy alone. It has also been applied to the interpretation of international factors throughout party history. Within the party's new ideological framework of the 'dual circulation economy' and the NDC, we can see that both these sets of internal and external contradictions (i.e. imbalances in development and external economic threat) therefore come together. Both underpin Xi's new, state-driven economic strategy, including a conscious and calculated departure from market disciplines both at home and abroad. And this represents deep change when compared with Xi's post-Mao predecessors.

Common Prosperity, People-Centred Development, and the Mixed-Ownership Model

Within the overall ideological framework of Xi's New Development Concept, both the 'dual circulation economy' and Xi's doctrine of 'common prosperity' represent significant new political interventions in the pre-existing dynamics of the market. The 'dual circulation economy' has focussed on the reassertion of party and state control over the macroeconomy, the re-emergence of industrial policy to drive national self-reliance, and the role of state-owned enterprises in 'steering' the economy in this new direction. But Xi's doctrine of 'common prosperity' is qualitatively different, focussing on greater party and state intervention to deliver a more equitable redistribution of income. In this respect, the 'dual circulation economy' is in part about Chinese economic nationalism, while 'common prosperity' is about a redefinition of Chinese socialism. Together they represent concrete reflections of the type of 'Marxist Nationalism' that lies at the centre of Xi Jinping's overall ideological worldview.

To elevate the ideological significance of 'common prosperity' within the framework of the NDC, Xi argued in his 2021 *Qiushi* article that if the "dual circulation economy" represented the NDC's "new development dynamic", then "common prosperity" was its "new development philosophy" (*xinde fazhan zhexue*).[69] The conceptual relationship between these two terms had already been underscored by Xi at the December 2020 CEWC, which stated that the "foundation for expanding domestic demand lay in the promotion of employment, improving social security, optimizing the income distribution structure, expanding middle-income groups and steadily promoting common prosperity".[70] In other words, 'common prosperity' was not only desirable ideologically because it contributed to greater equality; it was also now deemed essential economically in increasing aggregate domestic consumer demand. This in turn would make China less dependent on net exports as the major driver of economic growth for the future. Once again, this was where Marxism met economic nationalism: consumers with greater spending power would boost economic equality while, at the same time, also boosting China's national economic power and reducing its international economic dependency.

The ideological importance that Xi attaches to 'common prosperity' was rendered even more explicitly in the official readout of the Central Finance and Economic Affairs Committee (CFEAC) in August 2021.[71] In this document alone, the term 'common prosperity' is used sixteen times. In the frequency-of-use indices for Chinese banner terms, 'common prosperity' has been near the top. Xi also used the 2021 CFEAC to reinforce the ideological orthodoxy of 'common prosperity' within the framework of China's new national economic development policy, as well as the party's centennial plan for national rejuvenation:

> China is moving towards its second centenary goal, adapting to the changes in the principal contradiction in our society, and working to better meet the ever-growing needs of the people for a better life; we must make the promotion of common prosperity for all people the focus of our efforts.[72]

Indeed, in his speech to the CFEAC, Xi described "common prosperity" as "the essential requirement of socialism"[73], reinforcing his message in *Qiushi* that "realizing common prosperity is more than an economic goal. It is a major political issue that bears on our Party's governance foundation."[74] In this way, the deep ideological bearings of the common prosperity agenda are underscored by Xi's recourse, once again, to the fundamental conceptual framework of 'contradictions', the centrality of equality and the basic tenets of socialism.

Ideologically, Xi readily acknowledges that this doctrine of common prosperity represents a significant adjustment to Deng Xiaoping's earlier formulations on individual prosperity which permitted (or even encouraged) significant inequality in the interest of unleashing the forces of production. In his 2021 CFEAC presentation, Xi conspicuously alluded to Deng's comment in 1986 that "some people and some regions should be allowed to prosper before others".[75] But Xi here inserts his own analysis that, while Deng had indeed favoured letting some Chinese "get rich first", it was often forgotten that this was only a shortcut to "speed up" development and attain "common prosperity".[76] In Xi's analysis, China had reached the "stage of history" to begin "solidly promoting" common prosperity.[77] In other words, Xi was claiming that, in the 'new era' of Chinese socialism heralded at the 19th Party Congress in what now may well be the last phase of the 'primary stage of socialism', the purpose of the NDC was to begin dealing with the many inequalities that had arisen from the past.

Beyond Xi's efforts to claim a consistent ideological lineage from Deng, he was also at pains to point out that his move towards 'common prosperity' was not an ad-hoc, latter-day thought-bubble, but was a core part of his long-term ideological plan for the party. Xi anchors this claim to theoretical continuity in his having "put forward the vision of people-centred development" (*yi renmin wei zhongxin de fazhanguan*) sometime before, while happily ignoring the fact that this idea had been at the heart of his predecessor, Hu Jintao's 'scientific development concept' between 2002 and 2012.[78] Without reference to Hu, Xi dated his own advocacy of 'people-centred development' back to 2012 and 2015:

> First, we have committed to a people-centred philosophy of development. In my address to the domestic and foreign press during the debut of the Standing Committee of the 18th Central Committee Political Bureau on November 15, 2012, I stressed that "The people yearn for a better life, our goal is to help them achieve it, and we must unswervingly follow the path of common prosperity." At the Fifth Plenary Session of the 18th CCP Central Committee on October 29, 2015, I put forward the vision of people-centred development. At the Fifth Plenary Session of the 19th CCP Central Committee on October 29, 2020, I further underscored the need to strive for substantive progress in promoting common prosperity for all our people. . . . We have [also] introduced the new development philosophy. I proposed the idea of innovative, coordinated, green, open, and shared development at the Fifth Plenary Session of the 18th CCP Central Committee in October 2015. I noted that innovative development was focussed on addressing the issue of growth drivers, coordinated development on redressing imbalances, green development on creating harmony between humanity and nature, open development on coordinating internal and external development, and shared development on ensuring social equity and justice.[79]

In substantive terms, the basic definition of 'common prosperity' offered by Xi at the Fifth Plenum in 2020 was that "all people shall make more tangible progress in substance" in accordance with the party's goals in the new Five-Year Plan.[80] However, it was in his 2021 *Qiushi* article that Xi became most explicit about inequality and income redistribution when he wrote: "We cannot allow the gap between the rich and the poor to continue growing—for the poor to keep getting poorer while the rich continue growing richer. We cannot permit the wealth gap to become an unbridgeable gulf."[81] This message was reinforced at the CFEAC, which declared that "common prosperity does not mean the prosperity of a few, but nor is it neat and tidy egalitarianism. . . . We must open up channels of upward mobility, create opportunities for more people to become rich, and form a development environment with participation from everyone."[82] This mirrored Xi's call for "adjusting excessively high income", "cracking down on illegal income", and "encouraging high-income groups and enterprises to give back more to society".[83] It was a significant addition to the debate, as it pointed for the first time to taxation, wages, and a form of compulsory philanthropy as new areas for reform.

Xi's address to the CFEAC in 2021 was especially explicit on income redistribution, arguing redistribution was to be accomplished in part through the "tertiary distribution of wealth". This called on the rich to participate in charitable causes and assume more social responsibility by giving more wealth back to the community.[84] This tertiary phase of income distribution would come after the primary distribution among businesses, workers, and governments through the taxation system, and the secondary distribution facilitated by government social safety nets.[85] These formulations represent a major ideological repositioning by the party on national income policy, with potentially major implications for the profitability of Chinese private firms. On income distribution, Xi's future model for national income was "an olive-shaped distribution, where the middle is large and the two ends are small".[86] Or, as underlined in the statement of the 2022 CEWC: "To realize common prosperity, the nation should first 'make a bigger and better cake' through joint efforts of the people, and then divide and distribute the cake properly through rational institutional arrangements."[87] The significance of Xi's 'common prosperity' agenda in relation to income redistribution was clear. And he was signalling that things were about to change.

However, it was not just taxation, social security, income, profits, and philanthropy that were now under ideological scrutiny within the framework of 'common prosperity'. There was also a more fundamental question about the future of private and public ownership within what Xi describes elsewhere as 'a modern economic system'.[88] Xi for some years had been experimenting with what he had earlier called a 'mixed ownership model' whereby state-owned enterprises would be encouraged to take equity stakes in private firms—just as private firms would be encouraged to buy into certain defined (and usually ailing) state-owned enterprises.[89] Xi had already emphasized the ideological significance of his mixed ownership model by elevating it to the pages of the party's theoretical journal in a piece excerpting his speech to the CFEAC.[90] Taking the concept well beyond its previous place in the party's technocratic policy discourse, Xi was now formally incorporating the 'mixed ownership' model within his wider 'common prosperity' agenda, thereby reinforcing the critical role of the state sector within his wider ideological construct of the NDC. As Xi noted explicitly in *Qiushi*: "We must maintain the public ownership system as the mainstay and simultaneously develop the economics of a variety of ownership systems. . . . We should allow some people to get rich first, while emphasizing that those who get rich first should bring along others and help them get rich."[91]

Finally, as already noted above, Xi's ideological exposition of his 'common prosperity' agenda is also seen as fundamental to the party's long-term political legitimacy. He argues that the concept of 'people-centred development' is not only core to socialism. He also contends, consistent with his earlier arguments about the need to augment domestic consumption through wider income redistribution, that 'common prosperity' is critical for the success of China's 'national rejuvenation'. And he argues forcefully that failure to keep economic policy anchored in the people would be a recipe for CCP's political collapse, as happened with its Soviet counterpart. As Xi wrote in *Qiushi*:

> The Soviet Union was the world's first socialist country and once enjoyed spectacular success. Ultimately however, it collapsed, mainly because the Communist Party of the Soviet Union became detached from the people and turned into a group of privileged bureaucrats concerned only with protecting their own interests. Even in a modernized country, if a governing party turns its back on the people, it will imperil the fruits of modernization.[92]

There is, therefore, a profound Marxist ideological imperative behind Xi's common prosperity, people-centred development, and mixed ownership agendas. These were now seen as axiomatic in realizing the party's most basic socialist values. These agendas also represent a significant assault on the equality-inequality nexus of the Deng-Jiang-Hu period, when the primary stage of socialism had been ideologically moulded to tolerate much higher levels of inequality. Xi's redefinition of the party's central contradiction away from the factors of production towards the relations of production was fundamental to this ideological change, as was his decision to begin signalling that China's primary stage of socialism may well be coming to a close sooner rather than later.

Of course, both these decisions would become deeply controversial in the years after 2017 as the Chinese private sector began to take fright, the level of private fixed capital investment declined, and productivity growth continued to stall—all alongside falling economic growth, private business formation, and overall employment.[93] Political ideology was about to have a rough encounter with the economics of the real world that Deng and his successors had carefully created over thirty-five years. Within their collective worldview, the future of growth rested very much in the hands of China's once-burgeoning private sector. But with the single stroke of a pen in 2017, Xi's ideology on income redistribution and the mixed economy model had unleashed a political assault on private investor confidence.

Security in Development

Beyond the 'dual circulation economy' and 'common prosperity', a third aspect of Xi's New Development Concept outlined in *Qiushi* is his concept of 'security in development'. As noted in the previous chapter, Xi had already introduced his idea of all-encompassing security after 2015—including economic, financial, and technological security. As with other elements of the NDC, Xi is adamant that his views on security in development have been consistent throughout his period in office. But in his 2021 *Qiushi* article, Xi expanded this concept further than before by defining the broad spectrum of internal and external economic 'risks' the party now faced. These extended right across the development spectrum, he wrote, and it was the party's responsibility to protect both the people and the state from them. Importantly, Xi explicitly listed security in development as one of the essential components of his 'new development philosophy'.

This emphasis is reflected in the frequency and intensity of Xi's mentions of 'security' (*anquan*) within the economic policy debate. For example, 'security' appeared 146 times in the 13th Five-Year Plan (the first under Xi)—exactly double the 73 mentions found in the preceding 12th Plan—before soaring to a record 177 instances in the most recent 14th

Plan. By contrast, the latest Plan contains fewer references to 'innovation' than in previous iterations, but calls on the party to "closely guard against and crack down on infiltration, sabotage, subversion, and separatist activities of hostile forces".[94] The Plan also outlines a raft of measures that seek to enhance China's national economic self-reliance including food, energy, and resource security; security from financial risk (both from home and abroad); enhanced bio-security; national emergency management; and a new approach to managing domestic social instability. These all form part of Xi's comprehensive security agenda as elaborated in the Plan.

Seen in the wider context of the shift in China's overall ideological parameters to the left, the most important, real-world impact of Xi's new 'security in development' agenda is to further empower the institutions of China's party-state to do whatever they believed to be necessary to "protect the people's fundamental interests".[95] In other words, the new security agenda further entrenches the tendency towards greater and greater state intervention already evident in other elements of the NDC. It reinforces the mercantilism of the dual circulation economy, Xi's growing demand for national self-reliance, growing distrust towards markets both at home and abroad, and the new redistributionist thrust of Xi's common prosperity agenda targeted against the other locus of economic power in the Chinese system—the private sector. All three major components of the NDC agenda therefore represent a return of the ideological power and position of the Chinese party-state across the full spectrum of China's economic policy agenda. However, all three have also coincided with a significant decline in Chinese domestic and international investor confidence and, as a result, overall economic growth. The rebirth of ideology, it seems, had come at considerable economic cost.

Conclusion

Xi Jinping's ideological move towards a more prominent political and policy role for the party has been reflected right across China's macro-policy settings for the economy. But this has not been an even process. There was a more tolerant approach to the role of market reform during Xi's first term as reflected in 'the Decision' of 2013, the 'New Normal' and the initial phase of 'Supply-Side Structural Reform'. But this began to change after the 19th Party Congress in 2017 with the proclamation of

Xi's new era, a new periodization of the party's economic development suggesting an end to the primary stage of socialism by 2049, and the redefinition of the party's new contradiction on unbalanced and unequal development. These fundamental ideological changes impacted the real world of economic policy as reflected in the new, overarching framework of the 'New Development Concept' which has increasingly replaced the era of 'reform and opening' associated with Deng. It is also reflected in new statist concepts of national self-sufficiency, the dual circulation economy, common prosperity, and security in development. All these required a more interventionist role on the part of China's party-state than was previously the case during the Deng-Jiang-Hu period. And taken over the full span of Xi's first decade in office, they collectively represent a significant shift to the Marxist-Leninist left in China's macro-policy settings on the economy.

This raises the fundamental question of why Xi was willing to bring about such a major ideological shift. If Xi himself was unaware of the likely real-world economic consequences that would flow from this radical change in policy direction, then experienced economic advisors and practitioners such as then premier Li Keqiang, then vice-premier Liu He, and then vice-president Wang Qishan, all of whom were part of Xi's leadership team, would have been. But this line of reasoning ignores a core element in Xi Jinping's ideological logic. The consistent tenor of his writings from the beginning of his period in office has reflected Xi's deep fear of two factors: an increasingly corrupt relationship between the party and the private sector, and a rapidly expanding private sector writ large that increasingly exceeded the party's capacity to control it politically. Xi feared these forces much more than any decline in business and consumer confidence, or a slowdown in economic growth that might result from any reassertion of ideological and political control. In Xi's personal variation of Maslow's 'hierarchy of needs',[96] his primal concern has long been the survival of the CCP itself, and his own position within it. This had been reinforced by his deep study of the Soviet Communist Party's demise and his belief that this was brought about by the political and economic softening that occurred with *glasnost* and *perestroika* under Mikhail Gorbachev.[97] To secure Xi's overriding political objective of long-term survival for the party, between 2017 and 2022 he appears to have judged that the potential price of weaker economic growth arising from tighter political control over the private sector was therefore one well worth paying.

In other words, Xi saw clearly the country's future under a continuation of the Deng, Jiang, and Hu political and economic policy programme and he did not like what he saw. Xi could foresee an increasingly marginalized party as the price to be paid for continuing high levels of growth under Deng's reform and opening strategy. And, rather than see that future continue to unfold under his own leadership, Xi chose to intervene with a different and more statist growth model, knowing full well that this would produce significant economic dislocation. But in this, Xi's eyes were wide open; he did not make a mistake. In Xi's view, this was an economic price worth paying in exchange for the political objective of long-term party control he was seeking to secure. While it may be debated whether this underlying calculus has undergone further review given the extent of China's economic malaise in the post-2022 period, it seems clear that Xi was implicitly aware of the political and policy trade-offs he was making after 2017. What is less clear is whether he was equally aware of the scale of the ideologically driven economic slowdown that would ensue as business and consumer confidence began to unravel as the country re-emerged from COVID. This will be analysed further in chapter 14.

One further question that arises is why Xi's major shift in economic ideology to the Marxist left occurred, in the main, some five years after an earlier shift to the Leninist left in Chinese politics. There are a number of possible explanations for this. The first is that this was Xi's ideological intention all along. There is some support for this view in that even the original 2013 'Decision' on the "decisive role of the market in the allocation of resources" was, on close inspection, a highly qualified document. Its emphasis on the expanding role of state-owned enterprises and the future of the mixed economy model suggests that Xi's statist impulses were already embedded in the original document alongside its market reform agenda. Furthermore, the slow pace with which these market reforms were implemented during 2013–2015 indicates that the party's Leading Group on Comprehensively Deepening Reform under Xi's chairmanship was at best lukewarm about this part of the original 2013 programme. A second explanation, referred to earlier in his chapter, is the political impact of the 2015–2016 stock market implosion and Xi's subsequent intervention in the market to try to restore social and political stability. It is possible that this was a truly catalytic event in Chinese politics, representing the last straw in Xi's already thin commitment to further market reform, and causing him to accelerate the reassertion of much tighter macro-control over the economy by the central apparatus of the party-state. A third possibility, also referred to above, is the combined impact of the US-China trade war, the pandemic, and the emerging risk of economic decoupling. Certainly, this has been a key element of Xi's later public narrative concerning his changes in economic policy direction. But the changes in ideological banner terms discussed in this chapter largely predate the full impact of these various external factors. Nonetheless, it is clear from the chronology that China's changing international economic circumstances reinforced Xi's preexisting ideological predisposition, driven by domestic political and economic factors, that the time for the party to resume effective control of the commanding heights of the Chinese economy had well and truly come.

8

Ideology, the 14th Five-Year Plan, and the Direction of Micro-Economic Policy

The previous chapter examined the ideological migration of China's general economic policy to the Marxist left following the political ascension of Xi Jinping. This chapter describes parallel movements in a number of micro-economic policy settings towards the left, away from the market, and towards the state. This is particularly evident in China's 14th Five-Year Plan (2021–2025), the reinvigoration of industrial policy under Xi, and a new ideological discourse on the 'real economy' as opposed to what Xi describes as a 'fictitious economy', chiefly characterized by finance and property. This shift is also reflected in the hardening of state-owned enterprise policy and new requirements imposed by Xi on the private sector, including the party's growing role in personnel recruitment for firms. Moreover, this new approach to industrial policy, SOEs, and a more circumscribed role for the private sector has been accompanied by a revised policy on openness to the outside world. Xi's ideological discourse now refers to a 'new pattern' of opening, rather than the simple catch-cry of 'reform and opening' without any qualifying phrase. Indeed, this 'new pattern' of opening incorporates a number of new nationalist, mercantilist, and protectionist arguments that were not part of China's previous globalization narrative. And this, in turn, is taking 'reform and opening' in a new, more restrictive direction, albeit with some notable carve-outs, such as continued access to international financial markets and the role of foreign financial firms within China itself.

The interrelationship between the ideological imperatives of Xi Jinping's more doctrinaire approach to Marxism-Leninism, on the one hand, and the broad directions of economic policy, on the other, is made plain in the initial chapters of 14th Five-Year Plan released in March 2021.[1] This can be seen in the plan's overarching 'Guidelines' and 'Principles', where the centrality of Xi's New Development Concept, described in the previous chapter, is put beyond doubt. For example, the party is enjoined to "ensure the *new development philosophy* is applied fully, in both letter and spirit, and in every stage and aspect of development". Moreover, the party "must build a *new development paradigm, effectively change the development model*, work hard for better quality, higher efficiency, and more robust drivers of economic growth through reform, and strive to achieve higher-quality development that is more efficient, equitable, sustainable and secure". The centrality of Xi's NDC mantra is further underscored by a series of arguments that, while circular in their logic, are nonetheless clear in their political and policy intent. For example, Xi reminds cadres that over the next five years: "we must ground our efforts in the *new stage of development*, apply the *new development philosophy* and create a *new development paradigm*". He adds that "understanding the *new development stage* is the realistic basis for implementing the *new development philosophy* and creating the *new development paradigm*". And that "implementing the *new development philosophy* provides a guide for understanding the *new development stage* and fostering the *new development paradigm*".[2] The document adds to this repetitive absurdity (a practice by no means unique to Xi Jinping's administration among Chinese leaders) by stating that "the *new development paradigm* is a strategic choice in response to the opportunities and challenges in the *new development stage* and for implementing the *new development philosophy*" (all italics are my emphases).[3] Despite the overwrought repetition of this triptych of ideological novelties—the new development stage, new development concept/philosophy, and new development paradigm—the language of the Five-Year Plan is designed to underline the overriding significance of the ideological shift in economic policy direction under Xi. The broad policy content of this shift is then outlined in the body of the plan itself, as reflected in its treatment of the dual circulation economy, common prosperity, and security in development, as well as new forms of industrial policy, SOE policy, and private-sector management.

In stark contrast to the blunt exposition of the NDC's new statist direction in the 14th Plan, its language on 'reform and opening' is sparse and weak. Indeed, reformist language is generally thin across the entire document when compared with its treatment of the NDC and the battery of new banner terms used to signify Xi's changed approach to economic management. Even when reformist language is deployed, there is a new conditionality attached to it that jars with previous Five-Year Plans. For example, the 14th Plan states that "we must strengthen major reform and opening-up measures *that are conducive to improving the efficiency of resource allocation and mobilizing the enthusiasm of the whole society*" (my emphasis). In other words, reform is now only possible if it both enhances economic efficiency *and* has popular support.

We can see a similar strategy at work in the 14th Plan's efforts to redefine the purposes of Supply-Side Structural Reform. As noted in the previous chapter, SSSR had been largely a pro-market concept aimed at increasing the efficiency of resource allocation across the economy. This was to be done through the pursuit of a judicious deleveraging strategy and related reforms to enable both state and private firms to become more robust market participants. By contrast, the 14th Plan presents SSSR as a means of advancing the national self-sufficiency aspect of the 'dual circulation' economy. The purpose of SSSR is now to lift domestic demand, reduce the exposure of China's supply chains to critical imports, and make the country less dependent on net exports as a future driver of economic growth. This conservative redefinition of SSSR is made explicit in the document itself, which defines the precise supply-side structures that must be remedied for China to realize a more 'virtuous economic cycle' within Xi's new 'dual circulation model'. In other words, the concept of SSSR had been ideologically repurposed as part of an increasingly mercantilist set of measures to improve the balance of trade, reduce international trade dependency, and enhance national economic self-sufficiency. This is a radically different SSSR compared to its original formulation as part of an integrated reformist project to enhance overall productivity growth, as it had been first conceived in the years prior to the 19th Party Congress in 2017.

Industrial Policy

It is beyond the scope of this book to examine comprehensively the evolution of Chinese industrial policy, how it developed during the 'reform and opening' period from 1978, or its effectiveness in driving Chinese economic growth. My purposes here are much narrower: first, to explain China's turn to a more expansive industrial policy in the 14th Five-Year Plan; and second, to identify the extent to which it reflects deeper ideological debates on the role of the Chinese party-state in setting the overall direction of economic policy. In doing so, I accept Naughton's definition that 'industrial policy' refers to "any type of selective, targeted government intervention that attempts to alter the sectoral structure of production toward sectors that are expected to offer better growth than would occur in the (non-interventionist) market equilibrium".[4] I also accept Naughton's analysis of the historical development of Chinese industrial policy since 2006, which so far has covered three distinct phases: a modestly funded 'Medium and Long Term Program for Science and Technology', including sixteen mega-projects for the period to 2020; a significantly expanded 'Strategic Emerging Industries' program from 2010, incorporated in the 12th Five-Year Plan and intended to be more market-oriented than the previous plan; and the current phase of industrial policy developed since 2015, incorporating such plans as 'Made in China 2025', the 'Internet Plus Program', and the post-2016 'Innovation-Driven Development Strategy' (IDDS) financed by large-scale, state-controlled 'Industrial Guidance Funds'.[5] It is accepted, therefore, that industrial policy interventions in the Chinese economy pre-dated Xi's ascension, although the evidence indicates that these have expanded significantly in their policy ambition, financial scale, and state-centric orientation throughout Xi's rule.[6]

As noted in the earlier discussion of Xi's ideological foundations for the 'dual circulation economy' and its implied doctrine of national economic self-reliance, industrial policy is the critical mechanism identified by Xi Jinping as giving practical effect to his new strategic direction for the economy. The ideological significance of industrial policy to Xi is in reinforcing the central role of the party-state in directing investment in the Chinese economy under the NDC. Its policy significance is that Xi's new industrial policy is not simply confined to planning documents, indicative targets, or the moral exhortation of economic actors. By contrast, it is given effect through active political direction, actionable state targets, and Industrial Guidance Funds of unprecedented scale, directed in large part through the state-owned sector and explicitly targeting innovation and technology. This new statist ideological and policy direction under the 14th Plan was underlined in Xi's 2021 article in the party's theoretical journal, *Qiushi*:

> I have previously mentioned that the essence of the new development dynamic is realizing a high level of self-reliance. . . . As a result, the Recommendations for Formulating the 14th Five-Year Plan for Economic and Social Development and Long-Range Objectives through the Year 2035 put forward two major measures of promoting scientific and technological innovation and removing bottlenecks in industry. We must understand these issues as being vital to the survival and development of our nation. We should comprehensively strengthen planning for scientific and technological innovation to bring together superior resources, and implement the mechanism to competitively award research projects in order to promote strong and steady progress in innovation. We must better align the chains of innovation and industry, and draw up roadmaps, timetables, and systems of responsibility.

Naughton's analysis is that the intensification of industrial policy under Xi Jinping is driven by a range of practical imperatives well beyond the dictates of a hardening ideology. As evidence, Naughton points to the changing mission statements of various industry programs over time: from merely 'catching up' with the West to 'surpassing' it by embracing future technologies in telecommunications, data, and artificial intelligence; from sector-specific technology plans to economy-wide, innovation-driven transformation; from indicative industry-wide goals to harder, measurable targets to be delivered by the state; and from modest aggregate investments to eye-watering Industry Guidance Funds equivalent to 11% of GDP as of the end of 2018.[7] However, these accelerating changes in industrial policy also occur within the wider ideological context of Xi's emerging Marxist Nationalism: his reification of the Chinese party-state across the board; his new emphasis on 'top-level design' as a theoretical precursor for more prescriptive forms of central planning; and his authorizing a whole new wave of market scepticism under the New Development Concept. In other words, a sector-specific rationalization for a particular industrial policy initiative on the one hand is entirely compatible with a broader ideological predisposition to preference the state over the market on the other.

This underlying ideological direction is also reflected in the overall language, conceptual content, and policy structure of the 14th Plan. The formal structure of the 14th Plan is largely consistent with Xi's 13th Plan of 2015–2020. The inclusion of prescriptive industrial policy chapters on 'Innovation-Driven Development', 'Industrial Modernization to Strengthen the Real Economy', and 'Building a Digital China' substantially accords with the preceding plan. However, the addition of an entire chapter on the centrality of national security in all forms of development underscores the new statist imperative of the document as a whole. The 14th Plan also uses language that enhances the prescriptive nature of planning, compared with the 13th Plan. For example, on science and technology, it states:

> We will accelerate the transformation of government functions in science and technology management, enhance the guiding role of planning and policies and the creation of an innovative environment, and reduce direct interventions in financial and physical resources and in projects. The government funding system for research will be consolidated, with an increased focus on strategic and key sectors, and the problems of compartmentalization and small and scattered funding will be effectively addressed.[8]

While the 14th Plan does not explicitly refer to military-civil 'fusion', its conceptual content is entrenched in the 14th Plan as a further arm of Xi's new industrial policy to "boost military-civilian collaborative innovation in science and technology".[9] This builds on Xi's formal 2017 amendment to the party constitution stating it was "necessary to implement a strategy of rejuvenating the country through science and education . . . a strategy of innovation-driven development . . . a strategy of regional coordinated development . . . and a strategy of development through military-civil fusion".[10] Also anticipated was the passage of a proposed 'Military-Civil Fusion Development Law' designed to maximize civilian industry, innovation, and technology collaboration with the military sector.[11]

Taken together, these changes in Chinese industrial policy settings under Xi Jinping are consistent with his changing ideological framework. They underline the resurgent role of the Chinese party-state in the economy, as well as a profound paradigm shift to a new form of state-driven economic governance. Naughton, the leading international authority on Chinese industrial policy, has described this as "government steerage" of the economy:

> Specific instruments for carrying out industrial policy are part of a broader effort to increase the amount of government steerage of a market economy. Whether or not it is in practice possible to impose so much government control on the economy without damaging market institutions remains to be seen, but Chinese policymakers certainly believe that they are pioneering a new system of a government-guided market economy. Indeed,

this seems to have become the most recent definition of the long-standing model of "a socialist market economy with Chinese characteristics".[12]

Beyond Naughton's analysis, there is a broader consensus across the literature that Chinese industrial policy has changed significantly under Xi Jinping. For example, Fischer, Gohli, and Habich-Sobiegalla have argued that industrial policy under Xi has been driven by a combination of 'hard' and 'soft' steering, both aimed at delivering sector-wide and sometimes enterprise-specific national industrial outcomes.[13] On the particular question of Xi's Made in China 2025 (MIC25) strategy—which is designed to increase the domestic market share for Chinese suppliers in "basic core components and important basic materials" in critical technology areas to 70%—Wübbeke, Meissner, Zenglein, Ives, and Conrad argued in 2016 that the program's "significant weaknesses" included being "limited by the mismatch between political priorities and industrial needs".[14] MIC25 was likely to foster a small vanguard of efficient, advanced manufacturers but would "probably fail" to upgrade the Chinese economy at large, they wrote. Meanwhile, Huang Tianlei warned that while over 1,600 government-guided investment funds had now "emerged as engaged investors in China's equity investment market . . . with hundreds of billions of dollars in capital", most of them "do not even have their own websites, and their investments are barely known to the public".[15] Huang continued: "Except in the high-priority semiconductors area, it is not clear whether there is much central control over investments by local government-guided funds."[16]

Zenglein and Holzmann, by contrast, concluded in 2019 that MIC25 has been less derivative of Chinese communist traditions than it has been rooted in the 'East Asian Development Model', characterized by "industrial policies that target strategic sectors, and a strong government that effectively aligns business interests (state-owned as well as private) with national targets".[17] Despite MIC25's explicit intention to support the strategy of national self-sufficiency, Zenglein and Holzmann found that "trigger words such as 'self-sufficiency rate', considered indicative of China's efforts to replace foreign products and tech, were largely dropped from policy papers" in response to international criticism. They nonetheless conclude that dumping this rhetoric was "a tactical move" and China has not remotely "abandoned its economic—and strategic—goal of catching up with Western industrialized countries and gaining a competitive edge in high-tech and emerging technologies". The MIC25 program was "here to stay", representing "the CCP's official marching orders for an ambitious industrial upgrading," they wrote. MIC25 and other industrial policies remained "in the eyes of China's leadership . . . part of an effort to optimize China's hybrid state capitalist system".

What is clear from these analyses of China's industrial policy architecture under Xi, and the extent to which it deviates from his predecessors' policies, is its intensified status, scale, and scope since 2013. There is still latitude to engage China's private sector firms under Xi's new industrial policies, but SOEs are now the dominant vehicle for their execution. Indeed, as Lo and Wu have argued, direct intervention in the Chinese economy through industrial policy has shown a specific preference for SOEs in the development of 'frontier technology'—new high-speed railway technologies being a prominent example.[18] It is clear from these various analyses that, notwithstanding critiques of the funds wasted and resources misallocated through the blunt instrument of Chinese industrial policy, Xi has demonstrated a high level of confidence in the state's ability to provide direct 'steerage' of SOEs to achieve his overall policy objectives. And he has exhibited a similar confidence in indirectly manipulating politically compliant private firms through the potential to access Xi's gargantuan Industry Guidance Funds. In Xi's economic-nationalist logic, both are designed to secure China's national industrial and technological dominance for the future.

Manufacturing, the 'Real Economy', and Building a 'Modern Economic System'

Beyond industrial policy, Xi Jinping has deployed several second-tier 'banner terms' impacting micro-economic policy that further point to an overall shift to the interventionist left. The most important of these is Xi's exhortation to build the 'real economy' (*shiti jingji*) based on manufacturing, as opposed to a 'fictitious economy' (*xuni jingji*) based on real estate, financial services, and speculative activity. Xi argues that these sectors misallocate resources and contribute to systemic financial risk. Importantly, although not stated explicitly, the manufacturing sector was also expected to retain a major SOE component. This contrasts with the services sector in general, and the expansion of China's property sector in particular, which are driven primarily by private firms.[19] Xi's references to the 'real economy' have also increased significantly over time: from a single reference in Volume 1 of his *The Governance of China*, to 15 references in Volume 2, then climbing to 19 in Volume 3 released in August 2020.[20] Xi first used the term as early as the 2012 CEWC and, since then, has used it more frequently and broadened its meaning.[21]

Following China's domestic financial crisis of August 2015, Xi told that year's December CEWC that the declining profit margins of the real economy were resulting in "a large amount of finance flowing to the virtual economy" and this "causes expanding asset bubbles [and] emerging financial risks".[22] Twelve months later, at the 2016 CEWC, Xi's critique had become even sharper: there he stated that "real estate returns had further induced funds to turn from the real [economy] to the fictitious [economy], causing economic growth, fiscal revenue and bank profits to become increasingly dependent on 'real estate prosperity', thereby pushing up costs for the real economy and worsening its rates of return".[23] At the Leading Group on Finance and Economic Affairs in February 2017, Xi's attack was starker still, stating baldly that "houses are for living in, not for speculation"—a message he repeated at the 19th Party Congress later that year.[24] Xi's references to real and fictitious economies are not accidental, nor was his ideological assault on the property sector. These were intended to move the dial. And they did.

The notion of a 'fictitious economy' has a long Marxist, ideological pedigree. Indeed, the research literature on Chinese finance theory traces the term 'fictitious economy' to the Marxist term 'fictitious capital', which, in turn, finds its origins in *Das Kapital*'s third volume and its chapter titled 'Credit and Fictitious Capital'.[25] 'Fictitious capital' contrasts with what Marx called 'real capital'—the 'productive and commodity capital' that is actually invested in production.[26] Whereas, Marx warned, assets such as securities and stocks represented "mere claims on revenue and no capital". Furthermore, the "money-value of the capital represented by this paper in the safes of the banker is itself fictitious".[27] In other words, Xi's choice of terms has a deliberate ideological origin, content, and implied critique. Indeed, this critique was likely to have been sharpened by the implosions in the market value of this 'fictitious capital' on Chinese stock markets during 2015. Not only was financial investment in property assets seen as unproductive when compared with the capital needs of the real economy, including manufacturing, it was also seen as dangerous because it compounded systemic financial risk. And Xi had long identified financial risk as one of the party's 'three major economic challenges' for the future.[28]

Following the 19th Party Congress, Xi's new ideological orthodoxy on the 'real economy' in general, and manufacturing in particular, became the foundation stone of what he increasingly called the 'modern economic system' that China needed to build:

> The real economy is the foundation of a country's economy and source of wealth. Advanced manufacturing is one key area of the real economy and . . . economic development cannot be separated from the real economy [to benefit the fictitious economy] at any time.[29]

Xi's ideological position on finance servicing 'real' producers as opposed to 'fake' speculation had hardened considerably since the 2015 crisis, just as it would harden further in 2020–2021 as Chinese regulators began their legal and regulatory assault on property and financial firms associated with the real estate conglomerate Evergrande.[30]

In summary, Xi's recourse to Marxist language on the real and fictitious economies, together with his increasingly vocal attacks on the private sector-dominated property sector as a source of systemic financial risk, reflects a significantly more statist economic worldview compared to those of his recent predecessors. As Xi made clear to a 2018 Politburo Study Session on the 'Modern Economic System', building this system required several measures, the first of which was for the party to "vigorously develop the real economy as the solid foundation of a modern economic system". This was because "the real economy was the foundation of a country's economy, the fundamental source of wealth creation and an important pillar of a country's prosperity." As for the specific meanings that Xi was now attaching to his 'real economy concept', he used the same 2018 study session to marry it to other nationalist and statist themes including SSSR, industrial policy and manufacturing:

> We will deepen supply-side structural reform, accelerate the development of advanced manufacturing industry, and promote the deep integration of the internet, big data and artificial intelligence with the real economy. We will promote the concentration of resources to the real economy, orient policies and measures to the real economy, and strengthen our workforce for the real economy.[31]

State-Owned Enterprises

The evolution of SOE policy parallels that of Chinese industrial policy over the last two decades of the inter-relationship between state planning and the party-state, on the one hand, and the market and its private sector participants, on the other. State planning, industrial policy, and SOEs were the three handmaidens of the Soviet economic model introduced into China during the 1950s. They dominated China's economic structure until the reform and opening period started in 1978. During the pre-Xi period, the thrust of SOE reform was a combination of consolidation, corporatization, and privatization under the 1999 rubric of "grasp the big and let go of the small" (*zhuada fangxiao*).[32] Under this, SOEs were retained in defined strategic industries and their number was reduced in their thousands through mergers, privatizations, or dissolution.[33] The ideological rationale for this approach was reflected in a determination to retain state ownership as the "leading force of the national economy", as legally required under the terms of the Chinese state constitution.[34] But the economic rationale for introducing greater diversity of ownership, management, and market disciplines within the sector was to secure better productivity growth, reduce debt in the banking sector, and produce better returns on investment for the Chinese state as the ultimate shareholder.

However, from the early Xi period, this broadly market-driven approach to SOE reform began to change. First, as noted above, the Third Plenum of the 18th Central Committee in 2013 resolved the state should focus on 'managing capital' rather than 'managing enterprises' themselves.[35] According to 'the Decision', managers of state-owned capital had to "serve the strategic goals of the state, invest more in key industries and areas that are vital to national security and are the lifeblood of the economy".[36] This would be done through a new breed of state-owned capital investment companies with the State Asset Supervision and Administration Commission (SASAC) providing strategic direction, resource allocation, and the expected rate of return. This was different to the direct administrative direction of SOEs as in the past.[37] Second, in December 2015, the party issued an SOE reform blueprint outlining their role in Xi's new mixed-ownership strategy and encouraging private capital to invest with SOEs in state projects.[38] Third, the party advanced the process of consolidating existing SOEs into a smaller number of even larger behemoths by formally dividing SOEs into 'commercial' and 'public interest' categories.[39] This would see a further reduction in the number of central SOEs from 189 in 2003, to 96 in 2020, and, subsequently, to 80.[40] Then, in July 2016, the party promulgated further guidelines for the purpose of aligning each category of SOE with China's overall national economic strategy.[41] Thus SOE reform was aligned with the role of the newly established 'state-owned capital investment companies'. It also underscored the role of China's new Industrial Guidance Funds as large-scale state investment vehicles to help realize Xi's new industrial policy objectives in innovation, science, technology, and advanced manufacturing.[42]

Well before the 19th Party Congress in 2017, these changes had established a clear pattern of greater party and state direction of the strategic investment, industrial policy, and mixed economy functions of SOEs. Xi also moved to enhance the direct power of the party's own leadership cells within SOE structures through a slew of additional regulatory 'reforms'. This began in October 2016 when Xi chaired a meeting on party building in SOEs, directing party organizations to serve as a 'leadership core' as well as a 'political core' within the enterprises.[43] This built on a September 2015 document[44] and was followed by a State-Owned Assets Supervision and Administration Commission instruction in January 2017 requiring all central SOEs to revise their articles of association to incorporate party-building.[45] All this was reinforced by a formal State Council directive in April of that year paralleling Xi's previous instruction that SOE party committees must henceforth play 'core leadership' and 'core political' roles in overall corporate governance.[46] This entire process was finally consummated at the 19th Party Congress when the Party Constitution itself was revised to entrench the principle that party committees should "play a leadership role" in all SOE decision-making.[47]

This plethora of changes to SOE structure, mission, and party direction represents a deep reversal in the market-driven approach to SOE reform prior to 2012. This shift to the left on SOEs is concisely summarized in Xi Jinping's clarion-clear statement at the 19th Party Congress that state capital should become "stronger, better, and larger".[48] Ideologically, this is consistent with Xi's Marxist-Nationalist worldview on the centrality of the party in driving the Chinese economy in new strategic directions through a combined SOE and mixed-ownership model. Importantly, it also provided a vehicle for the Chinese party-state to expand its investment reach into the private sector and served Xi's broad industrial policy objective of enhancing national self-sufficiency. SOEs, therefore, were joining Xi's new front line in securing China's national economic interests in what he saw as an increasingly adversarial global economy where neither domestic nor international markets could any longer be fully relied on. For these reasons, leading analysts of the trajectory of SOE reform such as Lardy and Blanchette agree that, taken together, these represent a paradigm shift from the past. Indeed, as noted above, Lardy's seminal text on the subject is titled *The State Strikes Back*. Blanchette, mindful of the enhanced role of the party in SOE strategy, now refers to the rise of 'CCP Inc' (as opposed to 'China Inc'), the emergence of the Chinese 'investor-state', and the evolution of what he describes as a new hybrid form of state capitalism:

> This recent shift also seems to mark the CCP's full embrace of its hybrid political market economy, wherein overall political guidance and control is nested within a complex system of industrial planning/guidance and market mechanisms. Rather than seeing "markets" and "planning" as standing on opposite sides of a spectrum, the Xi administration has forged a system that seeks to render obsolete the previous conceptual taxonomy.[49]

Xi and the Private Sector

Xi Jinping's approach to the private sector is the logical corollary to his Marxist-Leninist worldview on the central role of the party, his ideological view of equality, and his reification of state planning, industrial policy, and the critical role of state-owned enterprises. Indeed, Xi's overall shift to the ideological left on the economy is seen most directly in the new constraints he has imposed on private firms. In Marxist theory, private ownership goes to the heart of the contradiction between the ownership of the factors of production (land, labour, and capital) and the relations of production (class). As discussed at some length in chapter 6, this contradiction was temporarily suspended by earlier CCP leaders through the ideological expediency of the theory of the 'primary stage of socialism'. But with the proclamation of a 'new era' from 2017, the evolution of the NDC, and the enunciation of the common prosperity agenda, Xi was arguing that this stage in China's economic development history may well be coming to a gradual close. And if that was the case, so too perhaps was the party's long and expansive embrace of the Chinese private sector that had characterized the primary stage of socialism since 1982.

As a matter of political and policy practice, the real-world tensions between changing patterns of economic ownership, on the one hand, and the reality of new and emerging economic classes, on the other, had long been clear in contemporary China. These tensions were anchored in China's continuing ideological and constitutional requirement that the economy remain predominantly in public ownership. But while this overriding political constraint on the expansion of China's entrepreneurial class had been clear, these underlying tensions had become accentuated by a rapidly growing private sector and the sharpening class divisions it had been producing. Indeed, the party itself had recognized this unfolding economic contradiction at the Third Plenum of the 18th Central Committee in November 2013—the same plenum that birthed large-scale, state-owned capital investment companies—when it stated that private businesses were a "key component of the socialist market economy that provides significant bases for social and economic development".[50] This real-world economic reality was underlined further by Vice-Premier Liu He in October 2018:

> There must be no irresolution about working to consolidate and develop the public sector; and there must be no irresolution about working to encourage, support and guide the development of the non-public sector. . . . The private sector plays an important role in the economic system, contributing more than 50% of tax revenue, 60% of GDP, 70% of technological innovation, 80% of urban employment, and 90% of new jobs and new firms.[51]

This, however, was the last resolute, clear-cut defence of the importance of the private sector by a senior Chinese leader. Conflicting social, economic, and political realities between private wealth and growing inequality were becoming increasingly problematic for China's leadership. Either the private sector's profit motive or the party's social equality imperative would eventually have to be constrained. Under Xi, the rise of the common prosperity agenda indicated that new economic restrictions would be placed around the former in order to ease the emerging political contradictions associated with the latter.

China's Communist and entrepreneurial elites remained acutely conscious of how these contradictions between the public and private sectors—or between the factors of production and the relations of production—had been resolved in the early decades of the People's Republic. This included the Anti-Landlord and Land Reform Movements of 1946–1953; followed by the Socialist Transformation Campaign of 1954–1956 when China's emerging party-state fully nationalized agriculture, industry, and commerce; and open class warfare against 'capitalist roaders' during the Cultural Revolution between 1966 and 1976.[52] All of these were resolved through violent struggle. For these reasons, there is growing uncertainty among China's private entrepreneurial class as to how these current contradictions between ownership, inequality and class will now be resolved within the framework of Xi's 'new stage of development'. These concerns have been heightened by the populist dynamics of Xi's 'common prosperity agenda'. Xi's complex navigation of this ideological shift to the left on the future of China's private sector is therefore one of great political, economic, and historical sensitivity.

Party control of the private sector has been a political challenge since the initiation of reform and opening in the 1980s. This began with foreign-owned businesses and continued from the 1990s with the rapid development of China's own private sector. In March 2012, Xi presided over a national meeting on 'Document Number 11' produced by the CCP Central Organization Department which formalized the party's intention to establish party committees in all private sector firms—large and small—right across the country.[53] This was followed in November 2018 by new CCP regulations empowering party branches to "guide and supervise" private firms in their "strict compliance with national laws and regulations".[54] By the end of 2019, the party was boasting that, based on these new regulations, China had "around 4.6 million party cells embedded in party and state organs, private firms, associations, and social enterprises", including "some 61% of all social organizations, 73% of non-state-owned enterprises, and 95% of public institutions."[55]

This, however, was just the beginning. In September 2020, Xi moved to further tighten the party's control of the private sector when the Central Committee General Office published a new document titled 'Opinions Concerning Strengthening the New Era of United Front Work in the Private Economy'.[56] In this document, Xi asserts that "United Front work in the private sector is now a major effort for the entire party", with CCP members advised to "strengthen" their efforts as "an important means of achieving the party's leadership over the private economy". On the future of public and private ownership, it outlined three basic directives: maintaining "the two unwavering principles" (of consolidating the public-sector economy while encouraging and guiding the private sector); bringing private economic actors and organizations into the party's orbit; and "more effectively promoting the healthy development of the private economy". On ideology, it called on the party to "build the foundations of ideological and political work for private economy practitioners . . . by arming their minds and guiding their practice with Xi Jinping Thought on Socialism with Chinese Characteristics for a New Era".[57] Organizationally, it called for the "*further strengthening of party-building work for private enterprises by giving full play to the role of party organizations as battle fortresses*, by being the vanguard and the exemplary role of party members. . . . The United Front departments and party committees at all levels must implement responsibility systems for ideological work in the private economy sector in order to guard our land with responsibility, accountability, and diligence"[58] (my emphasis). On recruitment, this would now mean "standardizing political arrangements by adhering to selection and employment standards with high ideological and political requirements, strong industry representation, and high requirements for participation in politics".[59] All these measures represent a significant tightening of party control over private entrepreneurs and a substantial change from the recent past.

Although the formal ideological and regulatory approach to private firms has hardened considerably under Xi Jinping's rule, his political messaging to the sector has waxed and waned depending on the country's economic circumstances. In 2018, as the trade war with the United States intensified, Xi adopted a more conciliatory mode, assuring entrepreneurs that "the non-public sector's status and functions in the country's economic and social development have not changed".[60] Xi said "the principle and policies to unswervingly encourage, support and guide the development of the non-public sector have not changed, and the principle and policies to provide a sound environment and more opportunities to the sector have not changed either". Xi also acknowledged that "over the past forty years, the private sector of the economy has become an indispensable force behind China's development", stressing that "private enterprises and private entrepreneurs belong to our own [national] family". And, mindful of the immediate danger of faltering growth amidst the trade war, Xi extended the conciliatory hand of China's party-state to private companies who had "recently encountered some difficulties and problems in their development in terms of [the] market, financing and transformation". Indeed, he said new policies must create a "more caring" and "better environment for the development of private enterprises" in tax, finance, competitive neutrality, policy implementation, and the protection of personal and property rights.[61]

In the same spirit, in October 2018, Vice-Premier Liu He explicitly attacked criticism emerging on social media that Xi's administration had presided over a period of the "state advancing with private firms retreating" (*guojin mintui*). Liu complained that this criticism was "both one-sided and inaccurate" and that while some private enterprises had expanded rapidly through high debt and had encountered liquidity difficulties, the truth was that "state-owned banks and state-owned enterprises have helped and even reorganized various private enterprises to deal with these difficulties".[62] Indeed, Liu argued that, in this new period, state and private firms had entered new forms of mutual assistance to help navigate each other's difficulties.

However, by the middle of 2020, having survived the worst economic consequences of the trade war, the onset of COVID-19, and a collapse in economic growth in the first half of the year, Xi returned to the offensive. He called once again for all entrepreneurs to "enhance their patriotic feelings", to "have a high sense of mission and a strong sense of responsibility for the country and the nation . . . and the happiness of the people", and to "take the initiative to shoulder responsibility and share the worries of the nation".[63] Xi also called for the development of a "large cadre of patriotic entrepreneurs," which the United Front Work Department called "a backbone team of private businesspeople that was dependable and usable in key moments".[64] These statements represented the clearest indication so far of the party's new expectations of how a state capitalist system should work in practice, where private firms would always remain politically compliant with (and responsive to) the party's directions, including when and where to deploy their capital. Therefore, while Xi's public political language concerning the private sector may have changed depending on the evolving economic circumstances, the underlying trajectory of political and regulatory tightening towards the private sector since 2012 had become increasingly clear. By 2020, it was apparent to all that the independence of the Chinese private sector was now in significant ideological, political, policy, and operational retreat.

Xi's 'New Pattern' of Opening Up to the Outside World

The most significant ideological signpost of a change in China's official rationale for continued global economic engagement is the 14th Five-Year Plan's statement that "a *new pattern* of opening up to the outside (*duiwai kaifang de xingeju*) would be formed".[65] The important point to note here is Xi's departure from the traditional use of the term 'reform and opening' and the insertion of the qualification, "a new pattern (*xingeju*) of opening up". This expression directly parallels the overarching concept of a '*new pattern* of development' that defines Xi's ideological differentiation from past definitions of reform and opening. In other words, 'opening' is no longer being advanced as the continuation of the Deng-Jiang-Hu era market reform agenda when applied to China's global economic engagement. Instead, it is being presented in new ideological language with the objective of securing 'new advantages' for China from this 'new pattern' of international economic engagement. This is also part of what Xi routinely refers to as 'high-quality opening' (*gao shuiping kaifang*) for the future, as opposed to that which had been realized from the unbalanced 'reform and opening' policies of the past.[66]

Xi is clear that this new form of 'opening' is not just part of the 'new development pattern'; it is also an explicit part of the new national self-reliance doctrine incorporated within the 'dual circulation economy' concept. His 2021 *Qiushi* article stated that, for the future, this 'new pattern of opening' must be about exploiting China's growing power in international markets to leverage advantageous access for the nation to global capital, product, and resources markets. Xi wrote: "In today's world, markets are the scarcest resource. China's market is thus a huge advantage of our country. We must make full use of this factor and continuously consolidate it to make it a strong pillar for creating a new development dynamic."[67] And according to the 14th Plan:

> Based on the great internal circulation, we will coordinate and promote the construction of a strong domestic market and the construction of a trade powerhouse, form a powerful gravitational field to attract global resources and factors of production, promote the coordinated development of domestic and foreign demand, imports and exports, and the introduction

> of foreign capital and foreign investment, and accelerate the cultivation of new advantages to be used in international cooperation and competition.[68]

This was reinforced by Xi's statement that China's 'opening' to the outside world was now to serve China's interest in maximizing its international leverage to help change the international regulatory and standards regime to China's national economic advantage. This stood in contrast to previous rationalizations for reform and opening, which aimed instead to improve the allocative efficiency of the Chinese economy by exposing it to international competition. Instead, Xi now wrote:

> We should continue to deepen opening up based on the flow of production factors such as goods, services, capital, and personnel, and steadily expand institution-based opening up with regard to rules, regulations, management, and standards. We should see that China's domestic circulation plays a stronger guiding role in dual-flow dynamics and foster new advantages for China's participation in international economic cooperation and competition.[69]

This shift in the ideological rationale for the opening of the Chinese economy based on the concept of the 'great internal circulation' (*danei-xunhuan*) also carries with it a new rationale for the specific role of a more liberal foreign direct and portfolio investment regime under Xi Jinping. Under the 14th Five-Year Plan, the future financing needs of both Chinese public and private firms would start to change from a long-term dependency on domestic bank credit backed by local government bonds, to other forms of direct financing, including from foreign bond and equity markets.[70] Furthermore, China would also begin diversifying its sources of direct finance to include a greater role for foreign investors in Chinese domestic financial markets, thereby reducing the overall financial risk to the Chinese state.[71] Moreover, by gradually increasing the quantum of foreign capital in all categories within the Chinese financial system (across both portfolio and direct investment), China would reduce pressure on its own domestic financing requirement. Foreign stock and bondholders would, however, still be kept to a limited position within China's overall financial market, whatever their holding in an individual Chinese institution might be. But because Chinese debt and equity markets had become the second-largest in the world, Xi's overarching logic is that Chinese markets would progressively become more important to foreign financial institutions, while foreigners would still only hold a relatively small proportion of the

Chinese market itself.[72] Over time, this would also increase China's political and policy leverage over foreign financial institutions, mirroring the more general experience of foreign corporations' dependency on China's goods and services markets on an already massive scale.[73] Over time, in the party's calculus, this would also likely enhance Beijing's influence over the foreign governments where these same foreign financial institutions were domiciled. These increasingly mercantilist approaches to international economic and financial engagement explain the type of measures announced in the 14th Five-Year Plan to lift the equity limits on foreign direct investment in Chinese financial institutions. As Xiao Gang, the former chairman of the China Securities Regulatory Commission, stated openly on 9 July 2020:

> The Central Committee of the Chinese Communist Party has never placed such emphasis on the capital market as it does now. . . . The competition between China and the US is intensifying as China has deeply integrated into the global economy. In fact, the core of the competition is the wrestling between them in the technology and financial sectors.[74]

Therefore, there is little that is ideologically inconsistent between this series of financial liberalization measures, on the one hand, and Xi Jinping's overall move to a more statist and mercantilist approach to economic ideology, on the other. What is important for our purposes here is that the explicitly stated rationale for Xi's 'new pattern of opening' is not to better integrate the Chinese and global economies under international market principles as stated by previous Chinese leaders.[75] Instead, the new rationale is one of exploiting the sheer scale of Chinese markets to influence foreign corporations and governments for a range of other political, foreign policy, and economic policy purposes. As foreign exporters became increasingly chronically dependent on the scale of the Chinese market, China had already selectively applied political pressure to leverage its wider international policy objectives. And at a much deeper level, Xi's approach to the selective opening of its financial system to international investors has, at least in part, been intended to do the same.

Conclusion

In summary, Xi's ideological worldview on the centrality of the party to the direction of the economy has been reflected in his re-engineering of state industrial policy, his new approach to SOE reform, and the new constraints imposed on the private sector. It has also been evident in Xi's redefinition of China's 'new pattern' of opening to the international economy in which mercantilism has increasingly replaced a commitment to the market. Indeed, there are few economic policy domains that have remained immune to the political and ideological changes that have unfolded since Xi's rise. On the economy, as with politics, Xi's shift to the left has been a whole-of-system phenomenon, incorporating China's macro-policy direction as well as its practical articulation in individual economic sectors. In large part, that is because Marxist-Leninist ideology itself is a whole-of-system worldview that leaves little outside its political and policy purview. And the central organizing principle of that worldview is the return of the Leninist party-state to the absolute centre of Marxist economic decision-making. The key question, which we will return to in the concluding chapters of this book, is: what damage is this deep ideological and policy shift doing to domestic and international business confidence, to innovation and productivity, and, as a result, to the long-term growth of the Chinese economy and the living standards and employment prospects of the Chinese people? And, if the damage is great, will Xi change course?

9

Nationalism in Xi Jinping's Worldview

> We must coordinate the overall strategy of the great rejuvenation of the Chinese nation and the world's unprecedented changes in a century, and deeply understand the changes brought about by the major contradictions in our society. We must understand the new characteristics and new requirements of the country, and the new contradictions and challenges brought about by the complex international environment, daring to fight, being good at fighting . . . and having the courage to overcome all risks and challenges.[1]
>
> *Xi Jinping, Address on the Centenary of the CCP, 1 July 2021.*

Another significant change in China's ideological worldview under Xi Jinping has been the new form of Chinese nationalism he has used to move the party's overall nationalist discourse towards the right. As discussed in chapter 2, 'right' is defined as the deliberate exploitation of the language and imagery of China's growing power, prestige, and cultural preeminence to validate an increasingly assertive posture in Chinese foreign policy and, at the same time, to build regime legitimacy in the eyes of the people. Xi's new nationalist formulations have grown in scope and intensity in the party's official discourse during his first decade in office. They have also been reflected in a new culture and practice of foreign policy assertiveness over that period as observed, documented, and analysed by a growing number of foreign interlocutors.

Nationalism (as '*jiuguo*', or 'saving the nation' from foreign predation) has played a prominent role in the overall ideological fabric of Chinese Marxism-Leninism since the party's founding in 1921. But while the relationship between Chinese nationalism and socialism has changed over the last century, nationalism has become more prominent under Xi than under any of his post-Mao predecessors. As Xi himself said in his 2014 address to a symposium on arts and literature: "Among the core values of socialism with Chinese characteristics, the deepest, most basic, and most enduring is patriotism. . . . Our modern art and literature need to take patriotism as its muse, guiding the people to establish and adhere to correct views of history, the nation, the country and culture."[2] This is an important, clear-cut statement on the centrality of the nationalist narrative to Xi's overall ideological worldview. It also underscores the core argument of this book that Xi's worldview is as much Marxist-Leninist as it is nationalist, and that a composite concept of Marxist Nationalism offers the most accurate and appropriate description of his overall belief system. Whereas this type of ideological amalgam will inevitably be challenged by those arguing that an ideology cannot rationally move both to the 'left' and 'right' at the same time (i.e. left on politics and the economy and right on foreign policy), the empirical evidence supporting this more eclectic approach is clear.

As with Xi's move to the Marxist left on the economy, Xi's unfolding nationalist narrative can be traced through a number of 'banner terms' and 'signature phrases' deployed in the party's official narrative. Four major sets of nationalist expressions are directly relevant to China's increasingly forward-leaning foreign policy: 'the great rejuvenation of the Chinese nation'; 'China's outstanding traditional culture'; China's growing 'comprehensive national power'; and China's role in 'changes in the world not seen in a hundred years'. Each of these terms evokes growing Chinese national power and pride, reinforced by the party's depiction of Chinese culture's purported superiority relative to the United States and the West. A further set of banner terms (analysed in the next section) translates the party's conclusions about China's enhanced national power into a series of axioms endorsing the active use of this newfound power to change the international status quo. In all this, the explicitly stated nationalist purpose is to bring about substantive change in China's real-world strategic circumstances, thereby ideologically upending decades of adherence to Deng Xiaoping's "diplomatic guidance" that China should "hide its strength, bide its time, and never take the lead".[3] Xi's unapologetic embrace of nationalist rhetorical constructs as part of his overall ideological vision for China's future has made this long-held doctrine of foreign policy restraint redundant. And his principal vehicle for doing so, as with the changes he has wrought across Chinese politics and the economy, has been the sturdy redoubt of his increasingly Leninist party—the common ideological and institutional denominator of Xi Jinping's wider revolution.

Xi's Deployment of a New Set of Nationalist 'Banner Terms'

The centrality of Chinese nationalism to Xi Jinping's overall ideological framework, and as a guide to China's changing foreign policy behaviour, has been clear from Xi's public language and political discourse since 2012. This is explicit in Xi's statements on the positive role of patriotism within the framework of China's official Marxist-Leninist ideology and the negative threat posed by foreigners to China's national interests and values. This is also made clear in the ideological 'banner terms' used by Xi and his propaganda apparatus to convey specific nationalist meanings to China's wider policy establishment and to shape public opinion at large.

The single most elucidating document describing Xi's approach to the party's nationalist discourse remains Document Number 9 of 2013. As noted in chapter 4, this leaked, confidential report represents an unvarnished version of Xi's ideological worldview intended for the internal consumption of the party's central propaganda apparatus. This was the apparatus charged with conveying a new, nationalist message across the country's entire political and policy elite and, appropriately distilled, to the wider Chinese public. Document Number 9 dealt at length with the need to rekindle the party's Marxist-Leninist ideological zeal. But it was also clear in its articulation of an underlying Manichaean and nationalist worldview which pitted China against the liberal democracies of the West. Xi defined clearly the virtues and values of the Chinese nation and delineated them from the political, ideological, and historical posture of the United States and the collective West. Indeed, this was not just a case of technical delineation of China from the West; it was equally a case of ideological cleavage, hostility, and unvarnished enmity. Drawing once again on the discursive tools of dialectical materialism, contradiction, and struggle, it will be recalled that Xi had stated in 2013 that "the exchange, blending and clashing between all sorts of ideologies and cultures on a global scale is increasing in frequency and the struggle in the international ideological and cultural area is profound and complex".[4]

This was reinforced by the fact that "Western countries see our country's development and expansion as a challenge to their own values, systems and models."[5] And this, in turn, intensified the "ideological and cultural infiltration of our country so that the struggle and testing that we will face in the ideological area will be long-term and complex".[6] All this amounted to an ideological declaration that, whatever the public diplomacy, Xi Jinping's China was now engaged in a full-blooded ideational and nationalist struggle against the Western world.

In this spirit, Xi called on the national propaganda apparatus to understand four critical aspects of China's national culture that formed the wellspring of Chinese nationalism:

> Propaganda must . . . make clear that the Chinese nation has, in its civilizational development process of 5000 years, created a wide-ranging and profound Chinese culture. China's culture has accumulated the profound spiritual pursuits of the Chinese nation, contains the most basic spiritual genome of the Chinese nation, represents the unique spiritual symbols of the Chinese nation and the rich nourishments for the Chinese nation to multiply endlessly, develop, and expand; to make clear that China's excellent traditional culture is significantly superior . . . and represents an important spiritual pillar through which the Chinese nation can constantly strive to renew itself, unite, and struggle . . . and make clear that socialism with Chinese characteristics is rooted in the soil of Chinese culture . . . and the Chinese nation will therefore be able to create new glories from China's traditional culture.[7]

Xi explicitly contrasted this great national cultural achievement with the depredations China had suffered at the hands of the West, underscoring that this part of the CCP's historical grievance culture should never be diminished in the telling of China's national story:

> In comparison with the China from before the establishment of the New China, or in comparison with the China from after the Opium War, the present-day China is poles apart! In the present world, if it is asked which party, which country and which nation can be self-confident, then the Chinese Communist Party, the People's Republic of China, and the Chinese nation have reason for self-confidence. On this point, truth is on our side. In the West, there are people who say that China should change the angle of its historical propaganda, that it should no longer make propaganda about its history of humiliation. . . . As I see it, we cannot heed this. Forgetting history means betrayal. History objectively exists. History is the best textbook. A nation without historical memory does not have a future.[8]

Xi then draws sharp political and ideological battle lines with the West, both at home and abroad, enjoining his ideology and propaganda apparatus to respond to Western slights by seeking to "mould the nation's spirits and the nation's souls through history, understand and grasp the development laws of Chinese society, and encourage the people's confidence and courage to continue to advance". These remarks formed the ideological headwaters of the 'wolf warrior' era of diplomacy as Chinese officials, diplomats, and the official media launched an offensive against China's critics around the world for much of the following decade.

The burden of putting political flesh on the ideological bones of Xi Jinping's deeply nationalist resolve as outlined in 2013 was borne by a series of banner terms and associated mass campaigns over the following years. These would convey to China's domestic and international audiences the regime's growing nationalist determination to respond robustly to what Beijing saw as a series of mounting internal threats, external challenges, and expanding opportunities. In analysing these banner terms, I will draw on Xi's principal political and foreign policy statements over the period, including: his 2012 Address at the National Historical Museum on 'The Road to Rejuvenation'; the Conference on Peripheral Diplomacy in 2013; the Central Foreign Affairs Work Conferences of 2014 and 2018; China's annual ambassadorial conferences since 2013; China's Central National Security Committee meeting of 2014; the 19th Party Congress in 2017; and the 2021 Resolution on the 'Major Achievements and Historical Experiences of the Party's Centennial Struggle'.[9] I have also taken from Xi's separate addresses launching: the Asian Infrastructure Investment Bank (AIIB); the Belt and Road Initiative (BRI); and the community of common destiny for all humankind (CCD). I have, in addition, drawn from Xi's address on China's role in the Conference on Interaction and Confidence-Building Measures in Asia (CICA), as well as his remarks on globalization at the World Economic Forum at Davos in 2017.[10] Where necessary, these will be supplemented by major interpretative speeches by State Councillor (and later Politburo member) Yang Jiechi, Foreign Minister (and later State Councillor) Wang Yi, and other articles drawn from the Chinese official media. A rising nationalist narrative emerges across all these statements—one which both invited and authorized an increasingly assertive foreign and security policy as Xi Jinping set out to challenge the international status quo.

Xi's Nationalist Meta-Narrative: The Great Rejuvenation of the Chinese Nation

The centrepiece of Xi Jinping's nationalist discourse is his call for the 'great rejuvenation of the Chinese nation'. This banner phrase was formally embraced by Xi in November 2012, immediately after being installed as CCP general secretary, when he led the newly appointed Politburo Standing Committee to the National Historical Museum. There they inspected an exhibition titled 'The Road to Rejuvenation' which focussed on the party's response to China's 'hundred years of national humiliation'. Xi stated:

> Through 170 years of continuous struggle since the Opium Wars, the prospects for realizing the great rejuvenation of the Chinese nation are great. We are now closer to realizing this great national rejuvenation than at any previous period in history. We are more confident than in any previous period that we have the ability to achieve this ambition. . . . I believe the great rejuvenation of the Chinese nation has now become the greatest dream of the Chinese race in modern times. . . . I firmly believe that, by the time of the party's centenary (in 2021), China will have become a moderately prosperous society, and that by the centenary of the People's Republic (in 2049) we will have become a modern, socialist state that is wealthy, powerful, democratic, civilized, and harmonious, thereby realizing the dream of the great rejuvenation of the Chinese nation.[11]

Considerable ideological meaning was packed into this stark statement. Indeed, Wang Jiayu has described Xi's national rejuvenation concept as a political "metadiscourse" in pursuit of a "hybrid type of nationalism".[12] Meanwhile, Maria Adele Carrai interprets it through the prism of Maurice Halbwachs's idea of 'collective memory', turning the past into the servant of the present and future, manipulating the historical discourse into a set of selectively chosen past traumas, glories, and amnesias.[13] Indeed, in Xi's statement, he is advancing a number of separate nationalist concepts within a single formulation. All these are anchored, however, in the overarching nationalist imperative of restoring China's former historical greatness. Moreover, Xi's point of historical reference—the Opium Wars in the middle Qing Dynasty, when China had the largest economy in the world[14]—makes plain that surpassing the United States was now necessary for true national restoration and rejuvenation to be achieved. Furthermore, China's restoration was now a natural and inevitable consequence of the national humiliation imposed on China by the West. And all of the above are now to be embraced in Xi's overriding national mission to be called the 'China Dream'.

As Rush Doshi reminds us, however, much, although not all, of this language was drawn from Xi's predecessors. The underpinning concept of national 'wealth and power' has an ancient pedigree, revived by the late Qing reformers, through Sun Yat-sen, Kang Youwei, and Liang Qichao in the Republican period, to Mao Zedong, Chen Duxiu, Zhou Enlai, and Deng Xiaoping under the Communists.[15] Similarly, the phrase 'national rejuvenation', as the necessary antidote to 'national humiliation', was used by Jiang Zemin in his reports to the 15th and 16th Party Congresses when he stated that the party had "shouldered the great and solemn mission of national rejuvenation since the day it was founded".[16] This line was sustained by Hu Jintao in both the 17th and 18th Congresses when he said the party was "striving for the great rejuvenation of the Chinese nation for which countless patriots and revolutionary martyrs yearned".[17] Even the two centenary goals contained within Xi's national rejuvenation formula had their earliest formalizations under previous leaders. As noted in previous chapters, the more modest social and economic goal for 2021 had its origins with Deng,[18] whereas the more ambitious national wealth and power goal for 2049 was first outlined in 2001 by Jiang on the party's eightieth anniversary:

> In the 100 years from the middle of the 20th century to the middle of the 21st century, all the struggles of the Chinese people have been to achieve wealth and power for the homeland . . . and the great rejuvenation of the nation. In this historic cause, our party has led the people of the country for 50 years and made tremendous progress; after another 50 years of hard work, it will be successfully completed.[19]

Despite this political pedigree, Xi Jinping has nonetheless elevated the centrality of China's national rejuvenation project in several critical respects. First, he has encapsulated the rejuvenation mission into the new and more populist political language of the 'China Dream', which in turn formed the centrepiece of a large-scale national propaganda campaign. Second, national rejuvenation became Xi's first nationalist policy announcement, alongside the launch of his first ideological campaign against party corruption. Third, he then entrenched this nationalist mission into both the party and state constitutions in 2017 and 2018.[20] Fourth, at the 19th Party Congress, he sharpened the quantitative goals for the party's great rejuvenation project by introducing new national achievement benchmarks for 2035 as a mid-point between 2021 and 2049.[21] Fifth, Xi also, for the first time, made clear the specific benchmarks for 2021, 2035, and 2049 that his predecessors had only referred to in the most general of terms—stating that by mid-century "China would become a global leader in terms of composite national strength and international influence", construct a "world-class" army, be actively involved in "global governance", and foster "a new type of international relations" by building "a community with a shared future for mankind".[22] Sixth, Xi injected a new sense of urgency into the national rejuvenation mission when, at the 2014 Foreign Affairs Work Conference, he stated that China was now at a "crucial stage of achieving the great renewal of the Chinese nation".[23] And lastly, Xi in Document Number 9, unlike his predecessors, underlined the direct threat posed to China's national rejuvenation mission by 'the West'.[24] In other words, Xi had moved the 'rejuvenation of the Chinese nation' from the margins to the absolute centre of China's nationalist ideological discourse. In doing so, he was unapologetically wrapping both himself and the Leninist party he led in the flag of Chinese nationalist exceptionalism. This deliberate fusion of broad nationalist rhetoric and specific revisionist call to reclaim China's lost territories, together with an underlying sense of historical destiny associated with the CCP's Marxist-Leninist mission, would become a hallmark of Xi's ideological leadership.[25]

One simple measure of a changing ideological emphasis over time is the number of references to banner terms such as 'great rejuvenation' (*weidafuxing*), or even the 'Chinese nation' (*zhonghuaminzu*). For example, if we use common bases of comparison across the selected works of Jiang, Hu, and Xi (up to 2022), a clear-cut pattern emerges. Across the three leaders' selected works, the banner term 'great rejuvenation' was used 51 times by Jiang over 13 years in office, 159 times over 10 years under Hu, and 347 times after only 8 years in office by Xi. As for references to the 'Chinese nation', it was used 315 times by Jiang, 419 times by Hu, and 709 times by Xi across the same time span (see table 9.1). A similar pattern emerges across the three leaders' National Congress addresses over this period. CCP Congress reports represent the most important statements of the party's ideological orthodoxy. Jiang used the term 'great rejuvenation' 10 times across his three congresses, compared with Hu's 15 times across two congresses. Meanwhile, Xi has already used it 43 times over his first two congresses. As for the term 'Chinese

Table 9.1a Key Nationalist Terms in Party Congress Reports (14th–20th)

	Jiang Zemin			Hu Jintao		Xi Jinping		Median
	14th	**15th**	**16th**	**17th**	**18th**	**19th**	**20th**	**14th–20th**
Key term	**(1992)**	**(1997)**	**(2002)**	**(2007)**	**(2012)**	**(2017)**	**(2022)**	**(1992–2022)**
Chinese nation	4	12	17	15	18	43	26	17
Great rejuvenation	0	1	9	7	8	27	16	8
Total	**4**	**13**	**26**	**22**	**26**	**70**	**42**	**26**
Deviation from median	**−22**	**−13**	**0**	**−4**	**0**	**+44**	**+16**	**—**

Table 9.1b Key Nationalist Terms in Selected Works (Jiang Zemin, Hu Jintao, and Xi Jinping)

	Selected Works of Jiang Zemin			***Selected Works of Hu Jintao***			***Xi Jinping: The Governance of China***				
Volume	**I**	**II**	**III**	**I**	**II**	**III**	**I**	**II**	**III**	**IV**	**Median**
Chinese nation	103	114	98	65	158	196	229	117	363	220	138
Great rejuvenation	1	12	38	15	57	87	108	56	183	105	57
Total	**104**	**126**	**136**	**80**	**215**	**283**	**337**	**173**	**546**	**325**	**187**
Deviation from median	**−90**	**−68**	**−58**	**−114**	**+21**	**+89**	**+143**	**−21**	**+352**	**+131**	**—**

Occurrences of '中华民族' and '伟大复兴' respectively.

nation', it was used 33 times by Jiang, 33 by Hu, and 69 by Xi. This is consistent with Carrai's statistical analysis of the growing use of the term over the period 1997–2019 across *all* Chinese official media, when compared through three different administrations.[26]

Cultural Nationalism: 'China's Outstanding Traditional Culture'

Chinese cultural nationalism has been promoted by the CCP in various forms since the launch of Jiang Zemin's Patriotic Education Campaign in

1991. But under Xi Jinping, this campaign has extended in intensity and scope beyond educational institutions to become a much wider ideological campaign around the new banner term of 'China's outstanding traditional culture' (*zhonghua youxiu chuantong wenhua*). While James Townsend argues that "the history of modern China is one in which nationalism replaces Culturalism/Tianxiaism as the dominant Chinese view of their identity and place in the world", the CCP propaganda apparatus has nonetheless seen great utility in exploiting traditional cultural sentiment to augment its overall nationalist project.[27] Once again this is clear from Xi's exposition of the ideological utility of Chinese traditional culture back in his 2013 address to the Propaganda Work Conference. Indeed, Ning Jiang, in her analysis of 'Fostered Idols and Chinese Identity', argues that the ideology and propaganda apparatus expanded this approach to include the active co-option of the symbols of *contemporary* popular culture as well into defined political and ideological messaging.[28] We can therefore see new modes of Chinese cultural nationalism, in both its traditional and modern forms, unfolding on a grand scale under Xi. This is reflected not only in his elevation of 'China's outstanding traditional culture', but also through his broader campaign on the need for 'cultural self-confidence' (*wenhua zixin*). As Xi put it explicitly: "Our path, theory, and system have our own clear characteristics and clear superiorities. We cannot indiscriminately copy Western methods. Bringing them over would only result in them failing to acclimatize in the new environment; they would be doomed to fail. . . . Some [comrades] have an inferiority complex and always believe that nothing in China is good, and everything foreign is good; they have the illusion of using Western systems to transform China."[29]

As with most major elements of Xi Jinping's nationalist narrative, this is not simply an assertion of China's positive national virtues. It is simultaneously a critique of Western political, economic, and cultural vices as proof of the 'superiority' of Chinese culture, systems, and ideology. The elevation of 'China's outstanding traditional culture' also forms a core part of Xi's doctrine of the 'Four Self-Confidences', or '*sige zixin*', launched in 2016 as a direct response to the array of spiritual maladies he diagnosed so bluntly—both in his 2013 speech on propaganda and in Document Number 9. These 'Four Self-Confidences' are outlined in Xi's address on the ninety-fifth anniversary of the party's founding in July 2016.[30] Building on Hu Jintao's call in 2012 for "self-confidence in the 'road', 'theory', and 'system' of socialism with Chinese characteristics", Xi in 2016 added a fourth: 'self-confidence in our culture'.[31] These 'Four

Self-Confidences' were a core feature of his address to the 19th Party Congress in 2017, where he warned that "cultural self-confidence is the most basic, profound, and sustainable foundation of a state and a nation's development" and that the party should "promote the creative evolution and development of China's outstanding traditional culture" while, importantly in terms of the ultimate political control of the party, ensuring "we have our say in the realm of ideology".[32] He continued: "Culture is the soul of a state and a nation. Culture rejuvenates a state, and it strengthens a nation. Without a high level of cultural self-confidence . . . it will not be possible to achieve the great rejuvenation of the Chinese nation."[33] It was in this address that Xi Jinping made clear the absolute centrality of cultural nationalism to his overall ideological project. For Xi, cultural nationalism, cultural exceptionalism, and a number of elements of cultural xenophobia made up the core nationalist components of his overall ideology. And within his composite Marxist-Nationalist ideological construct, "self-confidence in socialist theory, the socialist system, and the socialist road" make up its Marxist-Leninist component. In Xi's view, nationalism and Marxism make for a potent combination, bringing together millennia of cultural cohesion, continuity, and pride with the revolutionary mission of Marxist theory—all effected through the political agency of a newly disciplined Leninist party.

There are, nonetheless, clear differences between Xi's exhortation of China's 'outstanding traditional culture', on the one hand, and his simultaneous call for self-confidence in 'the culture of socialism with Chinese characteristics', on the other. The former is identified as the 'fertile soil' for the Sinification of Marxism-Leninism, while the latter represents the final result of this blending of traditional culture with socialist theory and practice.[34] China's traditional culture would, therefore, continue to be drawn upon for the purposes of the party's ongoing process of Sinifying socialism. In Xi's view, while Chinese traditional culture should be a source of great national pride, it would remain the party's prerogative to define which elements of the classical canon would be embraced and incorporated into its overall ideological orthodoxy—and, importantly, which would not. Therefore, while China's 'outstanding traditional culture' would remain a major part of Xi's new doctrine of 'cultural self-confidence', the Leninist party would retain the utilitarian prerogative to filter out the unacceptable. For instance, traditional Chinese religious beliefs and practices, both Daoist and Buddhist, would still be reined in by an all-pervasive party.[35] There were many aspects of this rich cultural heritage, it seems, that were still decidedly unhelpful.

This potent combination of diagnoses and exhortations on Chinese national culture *could* perhaps be read as a defensive, rather than as an assertive, form of CCP nationalism. Certainly, Document Number 9 was clear that Xi was most concerned with the domestic political threat of ideological and cultural infiltration from the West, rather than Beijing necessarily asserting China's newfound cultural self-confidence abroad. There are, however, several factors militating against this interpretation. On careful reading, the 'Four Self-Confidences' campaign is designed *both* defensively *and* offensively. They form the foundation stone of the propaganda apparatus' efforts to forcefully reject international criticism of China's authoritarian model in its own media *and* in the foreign media. Further, as noted previously, they form part of the permission slip authorizing the party's 'wolf warrior' diplomats to go on the offensive in a direct attack on Western development models, ideology, and culture, irrespective of whether China was attacked first. Moreover, Xi refers to Chinese culture as not only 'outstanding' (*youxiu*), but also 'superior' (*youshi*), in a clear reference to the inferior cultures of the West.[36] And finally, in other speeches delivered in 2013 and 2017 on Xi's approach to foreign policy, Politburo member and Director of the Foreign Affairs Office Yang Jiechi also outlines various traditional Chinese cultural concepts such as *yi* (justice) and *li* (benefit) as now forming the philosophical basis of China's approach to the reform of global governance. So rather than China continuing to accept prevailing intellectual and cultural paradigms from the West, it would now advance its own Confucian-Communist ideational framework in the world.[37] Indeed, a state television production first aired in 2023 entitled 'When Marx Met Confucius' seeks to take this new ideological synthesis into Chinese popular culture.[38] These are important changes, marking the first time that the CCP has sought to use Chinese cultural norms, appropriately 'Marxified', as global norms—and now applicable well beyond China's national borders.

As with Xi's advocacy of the 'great rejuvenation of the Chinese nation', his use of terms loaded with cultural nationalism has significantly increased since 2012. If we compare the usage intensity of the terms 'Chinese civilization' (*zhonghuawenming*), 'Chinese culture' (*zhonghuawenhua*), 'traditional culture' (*chuantongwenhua*), 'cultural self-confidence' (*wenhuazixin*), and China's 'fine traditional culture' (*youxiuchuantongwenhua*) across the published selected works of Jiang, Hu, and Xi, a clear pattern emerges: 32 references in Jiang's three volumes, 74 in Hu's, and 217 in Xi's. Similarly, in their respective party congress reports: only one reference in Jiang's three congresses, 12 in Hu's two congresses, and 39 in Xi's two congresses so far. Given Xi coined the formal expression 'cultural self-confidence', it is perhaps understandable that the record across the three leaders' selected works on this particular expression reflects a strong weighting towards him: there are zero references in Jiang's, two in Hu's, and 34 in Xi's. Indeed, Xi delivered at least six speeches on this theme of 'cultural self-confidence' between 2014 and 2017, delivering guidance on further ideological work to be done in this area, including the incorporation of its core concepts into his 'Global Civilization Initiative'.[39] These general trends on Xi's predilection to deploy the language and emotion of Chinese cultural nationalism are consistent across party congress reports when compared with the Jiang and Hu periods. These results are detailed in table 9.2.

Table 9.2a Key Cultural Terms in Selected Works (Jiang Zemin, Hu Jintao, and Xi Jinping)

	Selected Works of Jiang Zemin			*Selected Works of Hu Jintao*			*Xi Jinping: The Governance of China*				
Volume	**I**	**II**	**III**	**I**	**II**	**III**	**I**	**II**	**III**	**IV**	**Median**
Chinese civilization	2	6	9	0	12	3	12	10	29	9	**9**
Chinese culture	1	4	1	0	21	21	24	12	27	26	**10**
Traditional culture	4	1	0	3	3	3	20	18	29	19	**8**
Cultural confidence	0	0	0	0	0	2	1	21	36	18	**3**
Fine traditional culture	3	1	0	2	1	3	15	12	26	18	**2**
Total	**10**	**12**	**10**	**5**	**37**	**32**	**72**	**73**	**147**	**90**	**12**
Deviation from median	**−2**	**0**	**−2**	**−7**	**+25**	**+20**	**+60**	**+61**	**+135**	**+78**	**—**

Table 9.2b Key Cultural Terms in Party Congress Reports (14th–20th)

	Jiang Zemin			Hu Jintao		Xi Jinping		Median
	14th	15th	16th	17th	18th	19th	20th	14th–20th
Key term	(1994)	(1998)	(2002)	(2007)	(2012)	(2017)	(2022)	(1992–2022)
Chinese civilization	0	0	1	0	0	1	4	0
Chinese culture	0	0	1	4	2	6	5	2
Traditional culture	0	0	0	1	2	5	6	1
Cultural confidence	0	0	0	0	1	6	5	0
Fine traditional culture	0	0	0	0	2	5	6	0
Total	**0**	**0**	**2**	**5**	**7**	**23**	**26**	**5**
Deviation from median	**−1**	**−1**	**+1**	**+4**	**+6**	**+22**	**+25**	**—**

Occurrences of '中华文明', '中华文化', '传统文化', '文化自信', and '优秀传统文化' respectively.

The Nationalism of State Power: The Concept of 'Comprehensive National Power'

There is no more elemental term in Xi Jinping's expression of Chinese nationalism than 'comprehensive national power' (CNP). It lies at the fulcrum of multiple ideological, strategic, and foreign policy purposes including: a strategic calculus of the changing balance of power derived from the traditional realism of the Chinese military classics; a Marxist-Leninist dialectical analysis of the power of contending revolutionary and reactionary forces; a practical guide to the effective operational scope of modern Chinese statecraft; a source of the party's public claim to continued domestic political legitimacy; as well as a powerful appeal to national pride in responding to the 'century of national humiliation' narrative which had depicted China as 'the sick man of Asia'.[40] In this sense, changes in CNP became an objective yardstick that measured Xi's progress in the realization of his grand, nationalist meta-narrative of 'the great rejuvenation of the Chinese nation.'

As with many others, 'comprehensive national power' was an existing banner term within the CCP vernacular into which Xi has breathed fresh life and vitality. It was first used during the Deng period, based on his observation that "in measuring a country's national power, one must look at it comprehensively and from all sides".[41] Here Deng draws from both Soviet analytical theory (such as the 'correlation of forces' between capitalist and socialist countries) and China's Seven Military Classics (including the 'Wuzi', which cites 'six scenarios' in which, if an opponent holds superiority, retreat is advised: population, domestic power, the legal system, the wisdom and meritocracy of the military, quantity and quality of troops, and international aid[42]). Studies show that Chinese scholars as early as 1984 were conducting analyses of China's national power as part of a study of its national defence strategy out to the year 2000.[43] They drew on what they described as a Marxist-Leninist 'foundation' while also attempting to be more quantitative in their analysis than the Soviet 'correlation of forces' model. They also rejected Western definitions of 'power politics' because of their failure to take account of science and technology among other factors. This study generated a further series of efforts to calculate the CNP of China, the United States, and other major powers by: Tsinghua University;[44] the PLA Academy of Military Science;[45] the Ministry of State Security's China Institutes of Contemporary International Relations;[46] and the Chinese Academy of Social Sciences.[47] However, the publication of these detailed league tables suddenly ceased after 2010.[48] There has been no public explanation for why this stopped, but it seems the Chinese leadership became concerned about how foreigners might perceive China's official estimation of its own overall national power as it rapidly rose up the international rankings.

Chinese leaders have nonetheless continued to use the term 'comprehensive national power' (minus the tables themselves) to give broad indications to the party and populace of China's increased international standing. Xi Jinping has sharpened this public commentary compared to his predecessors, supplemented by other terms pointing to a tilting in the overall balance of national power in China's favour. These include the 'international balance of forces' (*guoji liliang duibi*)—a wider concept than CNP alone because it refers to a rolling comparison between China, on the one hand, and the United

States and its allies, on the other.[49] They also include references to increasing 'multipolarity' (*duojihua*) in the international system—code language for the trend away from American unipolar power and, according to one party document, one of the "basic judgements on the international situation in the new century" made by the "central party and state".[50] Xi's party also increasingly refers to the "irreversibility" (*bukenizhuanxing*) of the historical trend towards multipolarity, including the 'irreversible' movement towards the great rejuvenation of the Chinese nation, indicating that these changes in the distribution of global power away from the United States are now permanent.[51] This, in turn, forms the analytical basis for the increased use of the expressions the 'rise of the East' and the 'decline of the West' (*dongsheng xijiang*) as euphemisms for China surpassing the United States. This has been reinforced by a new phrase, first used by Xi in 2017, that what we are now witnessing are 'changes to the world not seen in a century' (*shijie bainian weiyouzhida bianju*).[52] In the eyes of a CCP audience, this made the historical significance of this new, deep shift in global geo-politics comparable to the Russian Revolution of 1917. Further, as if this were not enough to convey his meaning, Xi began regularly referring to 'China now moving toward the centre of the global stage' (*bijiang riyi zoujin shijie wutai zhongyang*)—a self-explanatory reference to China's role at the core of the new global system now emerging.[53] The overall nationalist thematic painted by these terms is one of rising Chinese power, declining American and Western power, and a new global order with China at its centre.

Xi Jinping's public articulation of China's national power has been sharper, more self-confident, and more expansive in his political language and policy scope than under either of his predecessors. Xi spoke of 'profound changes in the international balance of forces'.[54] For the first time, a Chinese leader also began publicly predicting 'deep adjustment' in the 'international system and international order', signalling Xi's conclusion that the post-1945 order constructed by the United States could no longer be sustained unilaterally by US national power.[55] By the 19th Party Congress in 2017, almost a year into Donald Trump's iconoclastic presidency, Xi's language on the relative decline of American power hardened further when he stated that "relative international forces are becoming more balanced" and that associated "changes in the global governance system and the international order are speeding up".[56] Xi also used the 19th Party Congress Report to describe how China was promoting its "economic, scientific, technological, military, and comprehensive national power" to the extent it was being propelled into "a leading position" in the world, resulting in an "unprecedented increase in China's international standing" and "unprecedented transformation in the standing of our party, our state, our people, our military, and our nation", all with the result that "the Chinese nation, with an entirely new posture, now stood tall and firm in the East". These were all new formulations by Xi. And all exhibited a new, decisively nationalist tone on China's rising national greatness.[57]

Xi used the same 2017 Congress report to cast ahead three decades to 2049, by which time "China will have become a leading (*lingxian*) nation in the world in terms of its comprehensive national power and the level of its international influence." This too was a new formulation, directly linking Xi's projection of Chinese CNP by 2049 (comprising both economic *and* military power) to China's leading status among global powers. This is strikingly overt in its nationalist tone compared with all of Xi's predecessors, perhaps with the exception of Mao's grand claims about the Chinese economy during the Great Leap Forward and his repeated references to US 'paper tigers'.[58] Both Jiang and Hu may have used the term 'comprehensive national power' more frequently than Xi across their respective selected works. But what changed dramatically under Xi was the qualitative use of 'CNP' (and the related terms described above) to convey the clear, nationalist message that China was now on track to surpass the United States militarily and economically. Previous Chinese leaders had been clear that this calculus of relative CNP was a useful mechanism for China's leadership to calibrate how assertively they could prosecute their national interests. Hu Jintao perhaps expressed this with the most refreshing candour of all when he told diplomats in 2003 that "the more multipolarity develops, the greater our freedom of manoeuvre".[59] But this almost utilitarian reflection on China's level of policy autonomy is significantly different to Xi's use of CNP as a cornerstone of his grand, nationalist claims about China's emerging global dominance.

The importance of Xi's new language on Chinese CNP is that it provides the underlying military and economic rationale for Xi's abandonment of Deng's historical guidance on diplomatic caution when Chinese national power was weaker. This would be replaced by a new era of foreign policy activism, given that China was now strong enough to manage the risk of external sanction (this will be discussed at greater length in chapter 10). Xi's new language on Chinese national power also foreshadowed a potential shift from Jiang's diplomatic guidance after 2002 that China could look forward to a twenty-year 'period of strategic opportunity' (*zhanlue jiyuqi*) during which China, in the absence of any major risk of armed conflict, would focus on economic development in order to further enhance its CNP.[60] Xi too had initially sustained this language of a 'period of strategic opportunity'.[61] But as noted in previous chapters, it was summarily deleted in the 20th Party Congress report in 2022. The overall point, however, is that, at a practical level, because Xi's CNP calculus had changed significantly, the level of tolerable risk associated with this new period of Chinese foreign policy activism has also been recalibrated. The bottom line was that more risks could be taken than before and China could now weather the inevitable reaction from a progressively weakening America. And the fact that Xi's language on China's changing CNP calculus was public, rather than internal, itself provided a new level of ideological permission for Chinese officials to prosecute more assertively Chinese foreign and national security policy aims. Most important, it also signalled that China's growing national power should be seen as an expanding and legitimate source of nationalist pride.

Xi's Nationalism Abroad: 'World Changes Not Seen in a Century'

At the Chinese Ambassadorial Conference that immediately followed the 19th Party Congress in 2017, Xi Jinping introduced a banner term that built on the nationalist narrative of his first five years in office: "In today's world, *we are facing great changes unseen in a century* . . . the multi-polarization of the world has accelerated, the international pattern has become increasingly balanced, and this international trend is now irreversible."[62] The following June, Xi expanded on this new 'hundred years' formulation at the party's 2018 Central Foreign Affairs Work Conference, calling for a new level of policy activism based on these changing power relativities:

> Our country is now in its best period of development since the advent of modern times; and the world is undergoing momentous changes unseen in a century. . . . These developments are conducive to conducting our foreign affairs for now and in the years to come.[63]

Two months later, he added that China "must have a strategic vision, establish a global vision, have a sense of both risks and urgency, as well as having a sense of historical opportunities, and strive to grasp the course ahead in these great changes unseen in a century".[64]

These three interventions convey the essence of Xi's conclusions about China's rapidly changing power relativities with the United States: that this change was permanent and the time had come for China to accelerate the pace of its global policy agenda. And given Xi's Marxist-Leninist ideological pedigree, the fact that the 'hundred years' mantra was adopted in late 2017—within two months of the centenary of the Russian Revolution—is also of significance: just as the Bolshevik Revolution and its reverberations around the world had dominated much of history in the twentieth century, China would now do the same in the twenty-first. Over the next three years, Xi reinforced this 'hundred years' thematic in at least forty separate speeches incorporating his new, nationalist banner term, including in his last meeting with Henry Kissinger in Beijing in July 2023.[65]

Importantly, at an ideological level, Xi Jinping has been at pains to point out that these major changes in world politics were consistent with, and driven by, forces that are uniquely comprehensible through a Marxist-Leninist analytical framework. In April 2019, Xi confronted a presumably bemused UN secretary-general with the unerringly Marxist-Leninist analytical logic that "the world today is undergoing profound changes unseen in a century, and we must see the essence from within all kinds of chaos and *grasp the laws* [at work] from the historical dimension".[66] This is the unmistakable language of dialectical and historical materialism and 'scientific socialism'. Several days later, Xi reflected further on the impact of these universal, scientific laws on the wider cause of global Marxism by predicting that "the world is experiencing profound changes unseen in a century and the world socialist cause is facing new opportunities for development".[67] Two years later, Xi expounded again on the deep dialectical forces driving these 'once-in-a-hundred-year changes', urging the party at a conference on 'Party History Learning and Education Mobilization' to enhance its understanding of them, thereby improving the party's capacity to predict future changes, as well as China's optimal strategic response:

> "A man may have wisdom, but that is not as good as seizing a favorable opportunity." One must know history to see far, and one must understand history to go far. All Party members need to be educated and guided so that they can

> do the following: carry in their hearts the overall strategy of the great rejuvenation of the Chinese people and the great changes in the world unseen in a century, establish a macro-historical outlook, analyze and investigate the long river of history, the tide of the times, and global storms to discover the evolutionary mechanisms and historical patterns therein, put forward response strategies, and make work more systematic, forward-looking, and creative.[68]

The ideological and historical significance of this 'hundred years' formulation was underscored by the party's theoretical journal. *Qiushi*, in an August 2021 analysis that coincided with the CCP's centennial celebrations, somewhat breathlessly proclaimed that this new banner term had provided "enlightenment to the benighted" as well as a new "rousing of the deaf" (*zhenlong fakui*). Drawing on the party's Marxist-Leninist claim to objective scientific truth, *Qiushi* went on to declare that this particular formulation "constituted a major judgement made by our party based on the overall strategic situation of the great rejuvenation of the Chinese nation, *scientifically understanding the general trend of global development*, and having a profound insight into the changes in the patterns of the world" (my emphasis).[69] Little cause for doubt or further reflection there! Xi's profound ideological self-confidence, as reflected in these writings, laid out a powerful analytical, ideational, and political foundation for the new forms of national assertiveness that would follow. Not only had China saved Marxism-Leninism after the collapse of the Soviet Union, but the Chinese nation under the leadership of Xi's CCP had now become the historical vehicle for a new Marxist international mission driven by the unerring laws of scientific socialism. Indeed, these same laws were now propelling the Chinese nation in this direction, accelerated by Xi's bold ideological and political leadership. This born-again Marxist Nationalism and internationalism had also been on full display in Xi's 2018 address on Marx's bicentenary, described in chapter 4.

Moreover, Xi's 'hundred years' thematic also provided an ideological foundation for greater levels of Chinese foreign policy action in both the region and the world. Indeed, the core logic of Xi's evolving nationalist narrative under this 'hundred years' rubric was that, as a result of the changes in China's and America's CNP, international power relativities now made it possible for China to seize this historical opportunity to advance its own national vision through a new program of foreign policy activism. As Xi himself noted explicitly in a 2018 address to the joint

Chinese academies of engineering and sciences: "We are now in a historic period that brings us both rare opportunities and severe challenges."[70] The following year, Xi indicated at a Politburo Study Session that seizing this opportunity would involve sharper competition with the United States, although China still held the advantage:

> The world today is facing profound changes unseen in a century. The competition between countries is becoming increasingly fierce. In the final analysis, it is the competition of national systems. . . . Our country's national system and our legal system have significant advantages and strong vitality, and this is the basis of our firm 'Four Self-Confidences'.[71]

As Xi noted in late 2019, greater Chinese national power and more foreign policy activism would mean making 'historic changes' in China's bilateral relationships with many countries.[72] It would also mean changing the current system of global governance as American power began to slide: "The global governance system and the changes in the international situation are unsuitable and asymmetrical."[73] Moreover in Xi's view, "injustice and inequality in international relations" were "still prominent".[74] This, therefore, warranted profound changes in the multilateral system based on a recognition of changing underlying power realities (i.e. changing US-China CNP relativities) and the need to build a new system shaped by Xi's overarching, Sinocentric concept of a "community of common destiny for all humankind". As Xi stated:

> The world is undergoing changes unseen in a century, and now is the time for major development and major transformation. To uphold multilateralism in the twenty-first century, we should promote its fine tradition, take on new perspectives, and look to the future. We need to stand by the core values and basic principles of multilateralism. We also need to adapt to changes to the world structure and respond to global challenges as they arise. We need to reform and improve the global governance system on the basis of extensive consultation and consensus-building.[75]

This reference to 'changes to the world structure' is critical. It refers to China's emerging global power dominance within this 'structure'. It signals that, from China's perspective, the future will not be some free-floating, self-propelled, spontaneously cooperative multilateral system, but rather it would be anchored in new international power realities. And in this new reality, China's growing national power would be the fulcrum of the emerging international system; it would not be an international structure still underpinned by historical American power—or by some loose, power-sharing arrangement with others. This reference to 'changes to the world structure' is not accidental; it is a clear signpost of a future international order anchored in the reality of Chinese national power, not simply the common multilateral interests of the international community.

From 2020, Xi's 'hundred years' thematic, however, had to embrace the uncomfortable reality of the COVID-19 pandemic and its impact on the changing international power relativities he had proclaimed with such confidence at the Party Congress in 2017. This was clear as early as April 2020 when he stated with some alarm to the Central Financial and Economic Affairs Commission: "The world today is undergoing profound changes unseen in a century. This epidemic is also a once-in-a-lifetime situation. It is both a crisis and a big test."[76] By July, Xi also began explicitly acknowledging COVID-19's increasingly disruptive potential both at home *and* abroad: "At present, the profound changes in the world unseen in a century are accelerating. The COVID-19 epidemic has had a profound impact on the international landscape and our country's security situation has become more uncertain and unstable."[77] But by August 2020, with the full impact of COVID-19 on the United States also becoming apparent, Xi began to refer to the pandemic as the latest factor accelerating the changing power relativities between the two countries, thereby helping to build yet another nationalist narrative that China had now become the world's only guarantor of globalization, free trade, and multilateralism:

> Since the 19th Party Congress, I have mentioned multiple times that the world as we know is facing significant changes never seen before in the past century. These changes are being accelerated by the raging pandemic of COVID-19. Protectionism and unilateralism are on the rise, while the world economy dives low. Production chains worldwide are challenged by non-economic factors. The international economy, technology, culture, security, and politics are undergoing fundamental shifts in many ways. The world is entering into a time of turbulence and transformation. For a while, we will face an external environment with more adverse forces. Therefore, we must be prepared for a series of new risks and challenges.[78]

Xi emphasized both these thematics (accelerating international structural change and China as a potential multilateral guarantor) during his 2020 UN General Assembly address: "At present, the world is battling the COVID-19 pandemic as it goes through profound changes never seen in a century. Yet, peace and development remain the underlying trend of the times, and people everywhere crave even more strongly for peace, development and win-win cooperation."[79] Xi doubled down again in November 2020 when he implied that not only was the United States now leading the global forces of 'unilateralism and protectionism', but that, as a result, the United States was also losing its standing in the international structure more rapidly than before: "At present, the world is undergoing profound changes unseen in a century. The global pandemic of the novel coronavirus has accelerated the evolution of this great change. Unilateralism and protectionism have risen, the international structure has been profoundly adjusted, and unstable and uncertain factors have increased significantly. In the future, we will face a more complex and changeable external environment."[80] And just in case Xi's increasingly Manichaean analysis of this global COVID-19 international morality play had been missed by his global audience, he returned to it in his APEC address at year's end:

> This is an unusual time in history for humanity. The COVID-19 pandemic has accelerated changes unseen in a century in the world. The global economy finds itself in deep recession . . . and governance, trust, development, and peace deficits continue to grow. Mounting unilateralism, protectionism, and bullying as well as backlash against economic globalization have added to risks and uncertainties in the world economy.[81]

Meanwhile, on the domestic front, Xi claimed that the pandemic's first year had not only accelerated the growing structural shift in the distribution of power between the United States and China, but that China had now moved to the 'centre stage' of global affairs. In other words, if there were domestic concerns that the Chinese origins of COVID-19 might have undermined Xi's core proposition that China was now moving to surpass the United States more rapidly than before, he was now claiming exactly the reverse: that, in fact, the United States had been so weakened by the pandemic and by its failure to provide global pandemic leadership, that China had become the new driving force in global governance. Indeed, a new banner term—'China moving toward the centre of the global stage' (*bijiang riyi zoujin shijie wutai zhongyang*)—would become a dominant theme for 2021. As Xi said in late 2020:

> At present, the world is undergoing profound changes unseen in a century. Peace and development are still the themes of the times. However, the instability and uncertainty of the international environment have risen markedly. The impact of the COVID-19 pandemic has been far-reaching

> and wide-ranging. Our country continues to grow and develop and is increasingly approaching the centre of the world stage.[82]

Further, in 2020 and 2021, Xi further integrated his two great nationalist thematics: 'the great rejuvenation of the Chinese nation' and 'world changes not seen in a century'. From 2019, Xi had highlighted these as the two great organizing principles of his overall policy enterprise—one foreign, the other domestic, and both serving the same nationalist mission. As Xi remarked: "I have often said that leading officials should have two factors in mind: one is the strategic goal of achieving national rejuvenation, the other is the world experiencing a level of change unseen in a century. This is the prerequisite to preparing our planning work."[83] Then at a January 2021 Politburo Study Session, he sought to explain the mutually reinforcing logic of these two national missions when he stated that "it is necessary to coordinate the overall strategic situation of the great rejuvenation of the Chinese nation and the great changes in the world unseen in a century" because by "actively participating in global governance it creates a favourable environment for domestic development".[84] Critically, Xi then elevated this new, integrated, nationalist narrative to an ideological level in his landmark address on the 110th anniversary of China's 1911 revolution in October 2021. He did this by presenting China's domestic and international challenges within a single analytical framework of 'contradiction' and 'struggle'. As Xi said:

> We must coordinate the overall strategy of the great rejuvenation of the Chinese nation and the world's unprecedented changes in a century, and deeply understand the changes brought about by the major contradictions in our society. We must understand the new characteristics and new requirements of the country, and the new contradictions and challenges brought about by the complex international environment, daring to fight, being good at fighting . . . and having the courage to overcome all risks and challenges.[85]

This was the first time in a single major speech that Xi ideologically fused the Marxist-Leninist concepts of 'contradiction' and armed struggle to his analysis of *both* China's domestic *and* foreign policy. This is Xi's Marxist Nationalism writ large: a dialectical analysis of 'contradictions' between opposite forces both at home and abroad, together with an exhortation to the party and the nation to 'struggle' to deal with each. There is no language like this in the writings of Deng, Jiang, or Hu.

This series of statements underlines the nationalist significance of Xi Jinping's new 'not seen in a hundred years' formulation within his overall ideological worldview. First, his 'hundred years' narrative is a public exposition to both domestic and foreign audiences that Chinese national power is on track to surpass American power, both economically and militarily. Second, because of external events, this transition was now happening more rapidly than even China itself had anticipated. Third, beyond diagnostic analysis, this 'hundred years' formulation is a nationalist call to action to both expand China's geopolitical footprint and reform the global order. Fourth, rather than simply remaining silent (or at least elliptical) about these conclusions, Xi instead chose to publicly declare China's newfound national power to the world. It was, therefore, a nationalist appeal to both the party and the country to craft a new Chinese-led order. But it also put the international community on notice that profound international 'structural change' was now underway, driven by a combination of Chinese policy activism and the active deployment of its national power. Fifth, to remove any doubt concerning the relevance of Xi's 'unseen in a hundred years' narrative, his decision to deliberately link it with his overarching nationalist discourse around the 'great rejuvenation of the Chinese nation' makes its purpose clear. Both the analytical and policy significance of this 'unseen in a hundred years' concept served to reinforce Xi's overall nationalist message of a China once again acting as the most powerful nation on earth—just as China had before, during the glories of its imperial past. Overcoming the legacy of foreign humiliation, asserting Chinese strategic primacy over the United States, bringing about the 'rise of the East' and the 'decline of the West', and 'China entering the centre stage of world affairs' are all central to this narrative.

Finally, and arguably most important, Xi for the first time began expounding his combined national and global vision within a unified Marxist-Nationalist ideological framework, including his own rendition of dialectical and historical materialism, national and international contradictions, and continuing political struggle. Taken together, these formulations do not represent some vague, patriotic fondness for the virtues of traditional Chinese culture and the wider Chinese nation. Instead, they reflect an activist nationalism that explicitly contrasts China with the United States and the West, and accepts the inevitability of struggle to determine which of these competing ideologies, political systems, and nation states will prevail as the preeminent global power for the twenty-first century.

Conclusion

All four of the banner terms discussed above point to a more direct and decisive expression of public nationalist sentiment than was the case under Xi Jinping's post-Mao predecessors. Furthermore, this has occurred within a wider ideological framework of Xi's Marxist-Nationalist amalgam. The 'not in a hundred years' formulation in particular moves the Chinese nationalist discourse further to the right by arguing for a new, more assertive foreign policy agenda to bring about substantive change in China's international strategic circumstances. Xi Jinping is signalling loudly and clearly through his expanding nationalist narrative that the time has come to take active measures to change the international status quo in a direction that is more compatible with Chinese national interests, values, and power. This includes consciously and actively reshaping the international rules-based order. It also means resolving outstanding challenges to China's perception of its territorial integrity. The following chapter examines an additional set of banner terms that take this new nationalist narrative further by describing how Chinese power should be deployed in specific policy domains, including China's neighbouring state diplomacy, its bilateral relationship with the United States, and its reform agenda for the global order as a whole.

10

Nationalism and the Narrative of Foreign Policy Assertiveness

The 'banner terms' discussed in the previous chapter dealt with different elements of Xi Jinping's increasingly nationalist mission during his first decade in office and their place within his overall ideological discourse. In addition to these new signature phrases, further concepts were developed to give more specific ideological guidance to China's foreign policy establishment. These were intended to interpret what these new levels of nationalist self-confidence would mean for foreign policy practitioners. Principal among these were:

- a new era of: 'striving for achievement' (*fengfa youwei*), bringing to a formal conclusion the period of 'hiding and biding' (*taoguang yanghui*);
- a new 'neighbouring states diplomacy' (*zhoubianguojia waijiao*);
- China's changed relationship with the United States as part of its 'new type of great power relations' (*xinxing daguo guanxi*); and
- China's activist approach to 'reforming the global order' (*quanqiu zhili tixi gaige*).

Taken together, these represented a new nationalist narrative of foreign policy activism and assertiveness. It gave rise, in part, to what the world would come to describe as 'wolf warrior' diplomacy, in which Chinese representatives unleashed against foreign governments in response to political or policy disagreements with levels of invective not seen since the Cultural Revolution. Governments around the world reeled in response to Chinese assertiveness, aggression, and economic coercion. Some buckled. Most did not. But what they all experienced was a different face of China.

By the end of 2023, however, as Xi began his third term in office, there were some signs of course correction as Beijing questioned whether the purported foreign policy and reputational dividends of wolf warrior diplomacy had aided or impeded the prosecution of real-world Chinese national interests. It is still too early to tell whether this correction will remain tactical in nature, but this should become clearer as Xi approaches the 21st Party Congress due in 2027 when he is likely to seek reappointment for a record fourth term. This is also the deadline Xi has given the PLA to complete the reform and modernization of China's military.[1] It therefore looms as the earliest stage of a possible medium-term timeframe during which Xi might consider unilateral military action against Taiwan to secure his grand national objective of reunification. For these factors, and in the absence of telling evidence to the contrary, it is reasonable to assume that the nationalist ideological line laid down during Xi's first decade in office will continue for the foreseeable future. This is the best underlying indicator of the likely course of China's substantive foreign policy direction for the future, whatever diplomatic language may be chosen to stabilise its various foreign policy relationships at a given time.

The End of 'Hide and Bide' and the Beginning of Xi's Doctrine of 'Striving for Achievement'

The most fundamental change in China's foreign policy guidance under Xi Jinping has been his decision in 2013 to abandon Deng's long-standing 'diplomatic guidance' on China's overall foreign policy direction which had been applied during the period of reform and opening. As noted previously, Deng prescribed that China should "observe calmly, secure our position, cope with affairs calmly, hide our capabilities and bide our time, keep a low profile, never claim leadership, and accomplish something where possible" (*lengjingguancha, zhanwenjiaogen, chenzuoyingdui, taoguangyanghui, shanyushouzuo, juebudangtou, yousuozuowei*), hereafter abbreviated as 'keeping a low profile' or KLP.[2] Doshi, in his detailed study of the evolution of this phrase, notes that this "conscious strategy of non-assertiveness" was first articulated by Deng to the CCP Central Committee in 1989 as China's strategic circumstances were fundamentally changed amid the searing international isolation and sanctions that came after Tiananmen.[3] This also broadly coincided with the unravelling of the CPSU, the disintegration of the Soviet Union, and the end of the Cold War. The collapse of the USSR was ideologically and politically traumatic for the CCP. In a series of speeches developing the concept, Deng reportedly stated that only by following KLP "for some years can we truly become a relatively major political power, and then when China speaks on the international stage it will make a difference. Once we have the capability, then we will build sophisticated high-tech weapons."[4] Jiang Zemin reinforced this logic in 1998 when he emphasized that "at this important historical period at the turn of the century, we must unswervingly implement Deng Xiaoping's diplomatic thinking. . . . We should hide our capabilities and bide our time, draw in our claws, preserve ourselves, and consciously plan our development. . . . The contrast between our country's conditions and international conditions determines that we must do this."[5] Meanwhile, Hu Jintao, as late as 2006 at a Central Foreign Affairs Work Conference, underscored that China needed to "adhere to the strategic guideline" of keeping a low profile and "getting something done", warning explicitly that while "some countries are optimistic about us and hope that we can play a greater role and bear more responsibilities . . . we must [nonetheless] keep a clear head, we cannot let our minds get heated because we are living a little better. We must insist on not speaking too much and not doing too much, and even if our country develops further, we must insist on this point."[6] Indeed, this conscious policy of non-assertiveness was consistent with China's perception of its relatively modest national power. And it would more or less remain Chinese strategic orthodoxy until the ascension of Xi Jinping.

All this would change with Xi's first major foreign policy address to the party's Conference on Diplomacy with Neighbouring States in 2013 when KLP disappeared from the official public discourse. It was replaced by a new expression of 'striving for achievement' (*fenfa youwei*, hereafter SFA).[7] Doshi has sought to establish that this change had, in fact, occurred during the last years of Hu Jintao rather than under Xi. As evidence, he offers Hu's remarks to the 11th Ambassadorial Conference in 2009 when China's then-leader added the adverbial prefix 'actively' (*jiji*) to 'accomplish something' (*yousuo zuowei*) as the final limb of Deng's guidance. Doshi argues that this signalled a more active Chinese effort to bring about real change in Beijing's foreign policy environment, consistent with China's changing comprehensive national power.[8] Doshi's analysis is well-founded—up to a point. His claim that this change came after China had concluded that American power had been significantly impaired by the Global Financial

Crisis is certainly true. However, in Hu's amended formulation, the addition of 'actively' was finely balanced by the parallel insertion of 'persevere with' (*jianchi*) in Deng's previous phrase of 'keeping a low profile'. This meant that, while Hu was encouraging his foreign policy audience to '*actively* achieve something', he was also reminding them that they were expected 'to *persevere* with [the principle of] keeping a low profile'.[9] Doshi correctly points to the intentional dialectical relationship between these two poles in Hu's amended formulation—namely, caution at one end of the spectrum and assertion at the other. Indeed, Hu, in the same 2009 speech, stated bluntly that these two positions were part of a 'dialectical unity' with each other rather than being diametrically opposed principles, with one urging continuing restraint while the other urged greater ambition.[10] Doshi goes on to argue that 'restraint' was Hu's dominant watchword before the Global Financial Crisis, but it was gradually overtaken by 'ambition' during the last three years of his administration. This causes Doshi to conclude that Hu's changes were, therefore, far from 'trivial declarations' and that this in fact constituted the real political precursor for the more assertive foreign policy posture that is now associated with Xi Jinping.[11]

Doshi raises an important argument. It is clear that the 2009 Diplomatic Conference produced an internal debate on China's future foreign policy direction. But Hu's modification of the Deng formula was relatively modest, bearing all the hallmarks of a political and foreign policy compromise. It did not fundamentally disrupt, let alone abandon, Deng's underlying twenty-eight-character formal diplomatic guidance laid out in 1989. It added a single adverb to the last clause, and then counterbalanced that by inserting another neutralizing adverb to Deng's signature caution to never claim leadership. While other elements of Hu's post-2009 language pointed to unfolding changes in the balance of power with the United States, within the constraints of the party's overall ideological discourse, these were largely diagnostic rather than prescriptive. They did not formally recommend a major change of course for Chinese foreign policy.

All this stands in stark contrast with two core changes after 2012. In Xi's first major foreign policy address to the party as general secretary, Xi eschewed *all* reference to Deng's diplomatic guidance, including 'keeping a low profile'; and, second, he replaced it with a new doctrine of 'striving for achievement'.[12] Indeed, by the Ambassadorial Conference of December 2017, Xi incorporated SFA into the formal, new responsibilities for

Chinese diplomats in the 'new era' that he proclaimed at that year's Party Congress. Xi demanded that diplomats should "strive for new achievement" and "compose a colourful new movement [for the symphony] of Chinese diplomatic work".[13] Since Xi had never referred to KLP in any speech or article during his entire period in office, official commentary by 2017 was stating explicitly that it was time to leave Deng's doctrine behind altogether.[14] Reinforcing this change in the CCP's strategic and ideological position, the 2014 Central Foreign Affairs Work Conference (the year following the announcement of his new SFA doctrine) outlined a slew of new foreign policy concepts which left Xi's audience in no doubt about the new and more activist line now being advanced by the party.[15]

Within the framework of China's overall nationalist discourse, SFA formed the connective tissue between Xi's ideological narrative of China's growing national power, on the one hand, and a newly assertive foreign policy, on the other. It is notable that the term 'SFA' has not been used extensively over recent years; since 2017, its meaning appears to have been subsumed under the banner of 'changes never seen in the world in a hundred years' discussed in the previous chapter. In fact, this 'hundred years' formulation had come to signify *both* rapid changes in the balance of power *and* the 'historical opportunity' for China to now act more assertively in the world than ever before in its modern history by using that power to change the status quo. Indeed, this new approach also complemented Xi's 'new era' for China's domestic political economy in which the world would need China more than China would necessarily need the world.[16] The overall significance of this shift in Xi's worldview is underlined in other commentaries from the time. As Yan Xuetong, dean of the Institute of International Relations at the prestigious Tsinghua University, put it starkly in late 2013:

> In the past, we had to keep a low profile because we were weak while other states were strong. . . . Now, with 'striving for achievement', we are indicating to neighbouring countries that we are strong, and you are weak. This is a change at a very fundamental level.[17]

SFA's role in linking Xi's nationalist ideological narrative to a new practice of policy assertiveness is reflected in a number of specific domains, including China's neighbouring state diplomacy; its great power diplomacy (primarily vis-à-vis the United States); and its broader global diplomacy that would increasingly focus on China's proposals for a new international order. These initiatives all unfolded at considerable speed after 2013. And while Xi's nationalist discourse is not the only explanation for understanding China's increasingly assertive foreign policy behaviour in this period, it has nonetheless been a significant factor.

China's New Neighbouring Country Diplomacy

Under this new doctrine of 'striving for achievement', one major change in China's foreign policy priorities during Xi Jinping's first term in office was the centrality now attached to Beijing's so-called 'neighbouring state diplomacy'. After making it plain that he was maintaining KLP as China's official foreign policy doctrine, Jiang Zemin had summarized China's top three external priorities as: first, the United States—memorably defined by Jiang as the 'most important of the important' (*zhongzhong zhi zhong*)[18]; second, China's neighbouring states; and third, the developing world.[19] However, Xi's address to the 2013 Conference on Neighbouring States Diplomacy (hereinafter NSD) effectively turned all this on its head. In addition to replacing 'hide and bide' with 'striving for achievement', this speech elevated the significance of China's near abroad and relegated the strategic importance of the United States. China historically had viewed preserving stability between Beijing and Washington as its core external priority, sitting well above all the rest. But under Xi, the United States was now seen primarily as a factor constraining China's realization of its other foreign policy priorities. The NSD forum therefore provided the first opportunity to extend Xi's newly formed, assertive, SFA narrative into a practical foreign policy domain. The stated tasks of this conference were "to determine the strategic goals, fundamental policies and general arrangements of China's diplomatic work for neighbouring countries in the coming five to ten years; and clarify the thinking and execution plans for major issues facing China's diplomacy with neighbouring countries".[20] A subsequent *People's Daily* commentary underscored the forum's significance, describing its new approach to peripheral states diplomacy as China's new 'grand strategy'.[21] It seems that, following his first US-China presidential summit at California's Sunnylands with President Barack Obama in June 2013, Xi concluded China could increasingly move to become the undisputed centre of its own East Asian hemisphere—rather than being permanently constrained by the overriding imperative of maintaining the strategic stability of its relationship with the United States. In other words, under Xi Jinping, the United States, distracted by its rolling wars in the wider Middle East, had become a less decisive factor in shaping China's overall strategic calculus.

Xi's new directions for NSD represented a deviation from the normal, instrumental evolution of Chinese foreign policy practice. Instead, Xi elevated NSD to the ideological level, linking it directly to his nationalist grand narrative. As Xi put it starkly: "The strategic goal of China's diplomacy with neighbouring countries is to serve the cause of national rejuvenation, for which China must consolidate its friendly relations with neighbouring countries and make the best use of the strategic opportunities China now has."[22] Xi went further by stating that China should now help its neighbouring states "interpret" the idea of "Chinese national rejuvenation" from the perspective of their own development aspirations.[23] Indeed, the expansive scope of this proposed new political endeavour is reflected in the strategic breadth of Xi's national foreign policy frame of 'striving for achievement':

> We must strive to make our neighbours more friendly in politics, economically more closely tied to us, and we must have deeper security cooperation and closer people-to-people ties. . . . Cooperation with neighbors should be based on . . . a close network of common interests. . . . [These should] become the shared beliefs and norms of conduct for the whole region.[24]

In other words, the essential operating principle for these enhanced regional relationships was to induce behaviours on the part of neighbouring states that were more compliant with Chinese national interests and values. This was explained more explicitly by Chinese foreign minister Wang Yi, who wrote that China would "consider more favourably the interests of those neighbouring and developing countries that have long been friendly to China".[25]

Xi's nationalist narrative at the 2013 NSD Conference also put greater emphasis on the security dimensions of regional engagement than had been the case under his predecessors. Xi said "efforts shall be made to promote regional security cooperation", noting that "security cooperation was the common need of all" and urging adherence to "a *new* outlook on security, featuring mutual trust, reciprocity, equality and coordination".[26] These contributed to a concept of "comprehensive, common and cooperative security" under which China would "advance security cooperation with neighbouring countries, actively participate in regional and subregional security cooperation, and enhance cooperation mechanisms and strategic mutual trust".[27] Before this, China's overall posture in Southeast Asia had been driven primarily by economic engagement, reinforced by a general, but by no means total, reluctance to confront regional states over their conflicting territorial claims in the South China Sea.[28] All that would change from 2013–2014 as Xi's 'new outlook on security' was re-prioritized and recalibrated in relation to the continued expansion of China's regional trade and investment footprint. The centrepiece of this change would be China's more assertive prosecution of its regional territorial claims, demonstrated most dramatically by the PLA's extraordinary engineering feat of building (and then militarizing) seven separate island redoubts in the disputed Spratly Islands.[29] These actions put to rest analysts' lingering doubts as to the seriousness of Xi's newly assertive, recidivist, and, in this case, aggressively nationalist foreign policy agenda. From Xi's strategic perspective, the region's role would simply be to accept the reality of China's dominant security presence, not to challenge it. And for this, there would be either economic reward—or economic punishment.

These doctrinal changes were taken to a new level altogether in the new 'Asian Security Concept' dramatically announced in Xi's 2014 address to the Conference on Interaction and Confidence Building-Measures in Asia (CICA). In this address, Xi directly attacked the continued legitimacy of the United States' long-standing strategic role in Asia by declaring that "in the final analysis, it is for the people of Asia to run the affairs of Asia, solve the problems of Asia, and uphold the security of Asia".[30] Xi's simple message to Asia writ large was clear: no Western power any longer had a legitimate security role in the region. In Xi's view, it did not matter whether the United States had been invited to do so through treaty or sub-treaty arrangements, willingly entered into by independent, sovereign regional states. This was a big, new doctrinal shift. Xi's choice of CICA as the forum for his 'Asian Security Concept' declaration was no accident, given that CICA was the only pan-regional security forum that excluded the United States (other than the Shanghai Cooperation Organization). However, lest neighbouring states view Xi's appeal to Asian security policy regionalism as a sign of China softening its territorial and maritime claims against neighbouring states, his later address to the National People's Congress in 2018 reminded regional governments that 'not one inch' of territory could ever be separated from China.[31] In other words, Xi's 'Asian Security Concept' would be implemented on China's terms, nobody else's.

Beyond the region, Xi used his 2013 NSD address to explicitly link his new approach for the region to his grander global narrative of a 'community of common destiny for all humankind' (*renlei mingyun gongtongti*), henceforth abbreviated as CCD. Xi argued that this form of global political consciousness, anchored in both Confucian and Marxist concepts, should be encouraged to "take root" among China's neighbouring states.[32] Within this global strategic narrative, CCD reflected China's newly assertive posture on territorial disputes, the inherent illegitimacy of US treaty arrangements in Asia, and the ideational structure of a possible future international order. CCD itself will be discussed in greater detail below. But for our current purposes, Xi was making plain that the region should not merely take account of China's core national *interests*, but also those Chinese *values* that underpinned Xi's global vision for the future. This normative construct includes some ancient Chinese values such as 'justice' and 'righteousness' (*yi*). These, however, were amorphous concepts that the CCP alone would have the authority to define and interpret within the overall ideational architecture of Xi's increasingly Sino-centric order. Xi was therefore messaging that Chinese interests, values, and worldviews, rather than Western ones, would shape *both* the global *and* the regional orders of the future. Once again, these represent major changes from the recent past.

In summary, Xi's overall nationalist narrative permeates almost every aspect of China's new discourse on neighbouring state diplomacy. China's elevated 'comprehensive national power' meant that it would no longer be content as a status-quo power; that its interests must be taken into account by the region; and that the United States would no longer be relevant to the region's future. Furthermore, Chinese values (rather than Western values) should underpin the future regional and global orders. These are not only 'realist' propositions based on China's increasing national power. They are equally ideological propositions, as they also go to an underlying CCP worldview and the Marxist-Leninist values on which it is based. Indeed, Xi made this plain in his concluding remarks to the NSD that his foreign policy vision was inseparable from his domestic political worldview, reminding his audience that policy and strategy remained "the lifeline of the party" together with its diplomatic work.[33] In Xi's worldview, these formed a seamless ideological whole—not separate, free-standing policy endeavours conducted in isolation from each other and entrusted only to professionally trained foreign policy elites.

By contrast, Doshi has argued that much of Xi Jinping's ideological and policy line on China's neighbouring states diplomacy is attributable to shifts in analytical conclusions under Xi's predecessor Hu Jintao. He bases this on Hu's statements that "from a comprehensive perspective, we need to strengthen our strategic planning for the periphery"; that China "must more actively promote the resolution of international and regional hot-spots related to China's core interests and . . . strengthen our strategic planning"; and that China should "make more offensive moves and actively guide the situation to develop in a favorable direction".[34] Once again, there is logic to Doshi's position that some change in policy course did occur under Hu. But, by any quantitative and qualitative measure, the most fundamental changes in China's neighbouring state diplomacy have occurred under Xi, including: his dramatic actions in the South China Sea; the assertion of a new Sino-centric regional security agenda linked to future regional and global orders under the 'community of common destiny' concept; and, most important, the anchoring of Xi's new neighbouring state diplomacy in an overarching nationalist narrative of 'national rejuvenation'. In comparison with Hu, the change in China's nationalist discourse under Xi on neighbouring states diplomacy has not simply been additive. It has been transformative. The dimensions of this transformation are also reflected in a much-publicized research note from the Chinese Academy of Social Sciences on the 2013 NSD Forum:

> The importance that China places on its relations with its neighbours will surpass that accorded China-US ties. The Working Conference illustrated that neighbouring states will become the priority focus of Chinese diplomacy. . . . The Chinese government realizes that for a state to rise, it must first rise in the region to which it belongs. If it cannot establish a favourable regional order, building good relations with a distant country will be of limited use. . . . The so-called great rejuvenation of the Chinese nation is actually the equivalent of becoming a superpower. The term is by no means a new one, but China has been quiet about the extent to which it will accomplish such rejuvenation.[35]

A New Type of Great Power Relations with the United States

Another expression of China's more nationalist foreign policy narrative and more assertive foreign policy behaviour is the banner term 'a new type of great power relations'. As with other emblematic foreign policy *tifa* under Xi Jinping, this phrase also has its origins in the late Hu Jintao period. It appeared in China's official discourse in July 2009 when Dai Bingguo, then a state councillor, told the US-China Strategic and Economic Dialogue that both sides should "build a new type of relationship between major countries . . . rooted in mutual respect, harmonious coexistence, and win-win cooperation in an age of globalization" in which "countries of different social systems, ideologies, cultural traditions, and development stages come together to meet new challenges".[36] However, the standalone phrase 'a new type of great power relationship' was not used by Hu himself until the last few months of his term:

> People believe that US-China cooperation provides the world with a great opportunity, whereas US-China confrontation would deliver to the world great harm. Irrespective of constant international change and however domestic developments may unfold in the two countries, both sides should persist with being co-operative partners and promoting a new type of great power relationship that puts our own people and the peoples of the world at ease. . . . Right now both sides face an opportunity to further develop . . . a new pathway towards this new type of great power relations based on mutual respect and mutual benefit.[37]

According to Hu, this 'new type of great power relationship' would require creative thinking, mutual trust, a spirit of equality and mutual understanding, positive steps, and a deepening friendship. However, these remarks in May 2012 were delivered to a foreign audience. It was not until the 18th Party Congress that November, just as he was relinquishing the general secretaryship to Xi, that Hu actually used the formulation at a formal CCP gathering. Even then, Hu only made passing reference to it as part of a broader framework for future relations with advanced countries in general, rather than as a specific mechanism for managing the relationship with the United States. Hu simply said: "We need to improve our relations with advanced countries, broaden the areas of cooperation, handle differences well, and develop a long-term, stable, and healthy new type of great power relations."[38]

It is significant that Xi had begun using this new banner term for the US relationship *before* he replaced Hu Jintao as general secretary and *before* Hu himself first used it publicly. When Xi visited the United States as Chinese vice-president in February 2012, he called for "constant new progress in China-US cooperative partnership and to strive to shape such a partnership into a new type of relations between major powers in the 21st century".[39] Then, during the course of Xi's first year in office in 2013, China's leading foreign policy duo (then state councillor Yang Jiechi and foreign minister Wang Yi) began to expound on the strategic assumptions and conceptual content of a 'new type of great power relationship'. Importantly, when explaining the logic of this new framework for US-China relations in June 2013, Wang noted that "the international balance of power is moving toward greater equilibrium"[40]. This, once again, hints at Beijing's assessment that China's 'comprehensive national power' was beginning to rival that of the United States. Wang added that "China would actively build a new model of major-country relationship" because "historically, it seemed inevitable for major countries, especially emerging powers and established powers, to engage in competition and end up in confrontation or even conflict".[41] Wang repeated this in Washington in September 2013, warning of the dangers of 'Thucydides' Trap' (whereby rising powers and established powers were likely to resort to armed conflict in their quest for supremacy) and arguing that 'the new type of great power relations concept' was important as a regional and global framework for the peaceful future of US-China relations. According to Wang:

> China and the United States have more converging interests and frequent interactions in the Asia-Pacific than anywhere else. Therefore, it is both possible and imperative that our two countries start the building of this new model of relationship from the Asia-Pacific. Just think: if China and the United States can avoid conflict and confrontation in the Asia-Pacific, there is no reason we cannot co-exist in peace in other parts of the world.[42]

Meanwhile, Yang Jiechi, in a definitive *Qiushi* article on the future course of foreign policy under Xi Jinping, asserted that Xi and Obama's first meeting at Sunnylands in 2013 had "agreed to work together to build a new model of major-country relationship . . . thus charting the course and drawing the blueprint for growing China-US relations in the future".[43] The US-China Strategic and Economic Dialogue's fifth round had achieved "good progress in implementing the agreement of the two presidents in advancing the building of a new model of major-country relationship", Yang added.[44] As for the operating principles of this new concept, Yang said that Xi had advanced three core 'insights' at Sunnylands:

> First, non-conflict and non-confrontation. That requires the two sides to view each other's strategic intention in an objective and sensible way, stay as partners instead of adversaries, and properly handle their differences and disputes through dialogue and cooperation instead of taking a confrontational approach. Second, mutual respect. That requires the two sides to respect each other's choice of social system and development path, respect each other's core interests and major concerns, seek common ground while shelving differences, uphold inclusiveness and mutual learning, and make progress side by side. Third, win-win cooperation. That requires the two sides to abandon the zero-sum mentality, accommodate the other's interests while seeking one's own, promote common development while developing oneself, and continue to deepen the pattern of shared interests.[45]

According to Yang, Xi believed that while the development of a new type of great power relations between the two countries would be "an unprecedented endeavor", if pursued it would promote the healthy and stable evolution of the relationship. Indeed, it was "the inherent requirement" of China achieving its two centenary goals (as part the great rejuvenation of the Chinese nation) and the "inevitable demand for our overall strategy of peaceful development".[46] In its essential logic, the Chinese concept of a 'new type of great power relations' was a kind of mutual non-aggression pact with the United States, anchored in the mutual acknowledgement of each side's core national interests including, in Beijing's case, its unresolved territorial and maritime disputes. It was also based on the United States and others formally recognizing the legitimacy of the Chinese political system. It was, therefore, an ambitious Chinese plan for advancing Xi's core ideological and strategic agenda: first, by securing international political legitimacy for the Chinese Marxist-Leninist state against long-standing internal and external liberal-democratic critique; and second, by providing a strategic mechanism to reduce the risk of American military action or retaliation as China advanced its territorial and maritime agenda as part of Xi's more assertive neighbouring states diplomacy. In other words, for Xi, it was a means of managing America into a more accommodating posture towards China's rise, and its prosecution of core Chinese national interests, as Beijing sought to change the regional and global status quo. Most critically, Xi did so by treating the United States and China as two superpowers of co-equal status, deviating from his predecessors' practice of approaching Washington as the unchallenged, dominant power in the world. This was Xi's new, assertive form of Chinese nationalism—hard at work, and now on a grand scale.

Xi publicly embraced the phrase 'new type of great power relations', together with a parallel concept of a 'new type of international relations', at the Fourth Central Foreign Affairs Work Conference in November 2014.[47] This major conference—only the fourth since 1971, but the first of three within a decade under Xi[48]—had stated that its purpose was to gain "a full understanding of the changing international developments and China's external environment, lay down the guidelines, basic principles, strategic goals, and major mission of China's diplomacy in the new era, and endeavor to make new advances in China's foreign relations".[49] Xi anchored this need for Chinese foreign policy activism around his nationalist meta-narrative of national rejuvenation, pointing out China had already entered "a crucial stage" in the realization of the great rejuvenation of the Chinese nation.[50]

Important for our understanding of ideology's influence on the direction of Chinese international policy, Xi's remarks to the party's foreign and security establishment reverted to his preferred Marxist frame of analysis. He warned the party that "in observing the world, we should not allow our views to be blocked by intricate developments. Instead, we should observe the world through the prism of historical laws". Further, given his analysis of changing power relativities and long-term geo-political trends, Xi claimed China now confronted "a world in which new opportunities and new challenges keep emerging, a world in which the international system and international order are going through deep adjustment, and a world in which the relative [balance of] international forces are profoundly shifting in favor of peace and development"—that is, towards China. Xi argued that "China is still in an important period of strategic opportunity for its [economic] development endeavor in which much can be accomplished" and where "our biggest opportunity lies in China's steady development and growth" of its national power.[51] Because these deep trends were working to China's advantage, Xi concluded that the party had "new tasks that should be carried out under new conditions" requiring "creative" foreign policy theory and practice. This made it necessary to "highlight the global significance" of Chinese national rejuvenation and continue advocating "a new type of international relations underpinned by win-win cooperation". Drawing these varied threads together, Xi's assessment was that, because of China's strengthening comprehensive national power relative to the United States, the time had come to advance a different framework for the US-China relationship. Previously, China had regarded itself as too weak to carve out a relationship of strategic equals. But, because of China's growing power and associated national prestige, all that was about to change. Indeed, as noted above, if the idea of 'a new type of great power relations' was to achieve nothing else, it was to bring about a new nationalist narrative both at home and abroad: for the first time, China would enjoy equal geo-political status with the United States as a fellow great power on the world stage, and no longer as a supplicant.

In explaining China's perceptions of what needed to change in both US-China relations and the broader global order, Xi also used his 2014 Work Conference address to draw on classical concepts to differentiate between national self-interest, on the one hand, and the interests of all states and the international system, on the other. Xi stated that China must follow "a policy of upholding *justice* (*yi*) and pursuing shared *interest* (*li*)" and champion "a new vision featuring common, comprehensive, cooperative and sustainable security" and "build a new model of major-country relations".[52] To this, Xi added that China "should manage well relations with other major countries [and] build a *sound and stable framework of major-country relations*" (my emphasis).[53] But in all this—including the pursuit of neighbouring states diplomacy, "reform of the international system", and this new "framework" for great power relations—Xi adds his own sobering and deeply realist conclusion: that in the balancing between '*yi*' and '*li*', or between 'justice' and 'interests', the latter must always prevail. Properly decoded, this meant that, whatever China's aspirations for a just or righteous international system might be, these would always come second to its pragmatic calculus of the country's core national interests. Or, as Xi himself put it plainly: "While we pursue peaceful development, we will never relinquish our legitimate rights and interests, or allow China's core interests to be undermined."[54]

So how do we interpret the relationship between this complex discourse on a new type of great power relations in general, the management of the US-China relationship in particular, and Xi's wider ideological narrative on Marxist Nationalism? First, as noted above, the concept of 'a new type of great power relations' is ideologically located within Xi's nationalist meta-narrative of 'the great rejuvenation of the Chinese nation'. This is consistent with his new, more nationalist discourse on neighbouring state diplomacy and with Xi's abandonment of Deng's doctrine of 'keeping a low profile' in favour of 'striving for achievement'. Second, Xi's 'new great power relations' narrative is made possible by explicit changes in Chinese national power relative to the United States, as with Xi's rationale for changes in China's regional diplomacy and his general doctrine of renewed Chinese foreign policy assertiveness. Third, both Xi's and Wang Yi's exposition of great power relations are based on an underpinning nationalist-realist logic of rising powers (China) and established powers (the United States), and managing the risk of conflict between them. Fourth, both Xi and Yang Jiechi justify a new type of great power relations within an explicitly Marxist analytical framework: Xi refers to 'historical laws', whereas Yang has claimed that 'Xi Jinping Thought on Diplomacy' outlines an entirely new 'philosophy' of foreign relations which "spells out the historical mission" and "profoundly reveals the essential requirements, inherent laws, and future direction of major-country diplomacy with Chinese characteristics in the new era".[55] In other words, both the Xi and Yang formulations clearly invoke universal Marxist 'laws' of historical and dialectical materialism as ultimately underpinning China's national rise under the leadership of the CCP. China's rise to now become a great power of co-equal status with the United States was not just the product of effective Chinese statecraft, nor was it simply the result of random external developments. Xi's claim is that China's future emergence as the dominant global power was because, in Marxist terms, it was an irreversible 'trend of human development'[56] determined by 'the inherent laws' of scientific socialism. In this worldview at least, history was now on China's side.

Also crucial to the 'new type of great power relations' concept is the role of the United States as the CCP's principal external propaganda foil in service of its domestic political legitimacy requirements. From a combined Marxist-Nationalist perspective, Xi's 'great power' construct reinforced both the party's official nationalism campaign for the country at large, and also the CCP's long-standing Marxist ideological fervour among the professional apparatchik class. Consistent with the party's domestic propaganda narrative that the United States was using every possible means to frustrate China's national rise and its long-awaited return to national greatness, Xi's great power relations narrative therefore became a useful mechanism for the domestic political management of the 'American problem'.[57] The official position was that China had now formally arrived as a global great power—the global equal of the United States. Therefore any doubts about the political legitimacy of the CCP and the long-term durability of China's return to its proper place on the global stage could now be officially dismissed. As Yan Xuetong has noted: "the term 'major country' [i.e. great power] no longer refers to foreign powers, but to China itself".[58] At a conceptual level, in the overall evolution of the US-China relationship, the 'new type of great power relations' framework therefore became the ideational midwife for the emergence of US-China great power parity in China's official nationalist and ideological discourse.

At a more practical level, Xi's new great power relations narrative was not simply a crude exhortation for China to assert itself against Washington. In fact, its strategic logic was to attempt to engage the United States in a longer-term, negotiated accommodationism that, from Beijing's instrumentalist perspective, would free the rising China from the risk of premature armed conflict. Instead, China hoped it would now have the strategic space to plant its geo-political footprint in its immediate neighbourhood and beyond, without generating an unmanageable US political or strategic reaction. In fact, when Xi, Yang, or Wang referred to the non-negotiable nature of China's 'core national interests' and ceding 'not one inch' of Chinese territory, the objective of the 'new great power' framework was to neutralize or reduce US freedom of policy action. In other words, if China could convince the United States to accept its new great power status, it followed that the United States, as a fellow great power, would then also be able to accept Chinese 'core interests'. Indeed, this was central to the proposed great power deal. If China succeeded in bringing the United States into this framework, it would also free Beijing's hand to prosecute even more assertively the harder edges of its regional diplomacy in the East and South China Seas, and across the Taiwan Strait. In the real world of foreign policy, this is precisely what Xi then set out to do with China's program of island reclamation in the South China Sea between 2013 and 2015. While Xi, Yang, and Wang were engaged in this broad-ranging policy debate with US officials on the grand narrative of a non-conflictual framework for the management of great power relations, China was simultaneously engaged in changing strategic realities on the ground in the islands and seas around the country's immediate periphery.

The reasons for America's eventual rejection of Xi's framework for a 'new type of great power relationship' are beyond the scope of this book.

Nonetheless, the impact of this rejection on Beijing's domestic discourse on the overall US relationship is important. China, as a result, intensified its nationalist narrative, rather than retreating from it. The redefinition of China's great power relations discourse after 2017 was left largely to Yang Jiechi, who then reframed the original proposal in robustly nationalist terms. This is clear, for example, in Yang's 2018 remarks on 'Xi Jinping Thought on Diplomacy':

> Persistent efforts should be made to promote China's major-country diplomacy, which is tasked with realizing the rejuvenation of the Chinese nation. This is the historic mission bestowed upon China's diplomatic work in the new era. The success of diplomatic efforts in the new era will . . . create a favorable external environment and gain more understanding and support in order to realize the Two Centenary Goals and the Chinese dream of national rejuvenation.[59]

This was reinforced by Yang's major article in the party's theoretical journal *Qiushi* entitled 'Xi Jinping Thought on Diplomacy Guides Our Efforts in Promoting Chinese-Style Major-Country Diplomacy'. Here Yang widened the definition of a 'new type of great power relations' to also include Russia and Europe as great powers and so minimize the relative significance of the United States within the overall frame.[60] Yang also expounded on China's approach to "building partnership networks across the world" as its answer to the US system of global and regional alliances. China was "developing relations with [all] great powers", deepening its "comprehensive strategic relationship" with Russia, "stabilizing the relationship" with the United States, building China-Europe partnerships, and "promoting the construction of an overall framework for the stable and balanced development of China's great power relations".[61] While technically both Russia and Europe were both mentioned in China's earlier formulations on great power relations,[62] this more expansive 2017 formulation was a world away from Beijing's initial, almost exclusive, strategic focus on the single great power that was the United States.

The denouement of the 'new type of great power relations' concept also fell to Yang Jiechi during a lengthy, live-to-air nationalist peroration in Anchorage, Alaska, opposite US secretary of state Antony Blinken, in late 2021. In remarks that elicited an enormous, spontaneous nationalist response across Chinese social media, Yang publicly detailed the views of Chinese senior officials on what they saw as American political hypocrisy.[63] Such views are normally not placed on the public record during bilateral exchanges. Yang, however, launched a full-court press on: America's human rights record; its history of using force to settle international disputes; its support for the "so-called rules-based international order", as opposed to the United Nations–based international legal system; and US standing in the international community more widely.[64] Returning to his nationalist thematic, Yang said continuing American attacks on China "only lead the Chinese people to rally more closely around the Communist Party of China and work steadily towards the national goals that we have set for ourselves". Yang then concluded his public broadside against the United States by drawing Blinken back to the fundamentals of the original 'new type of great power relations' concept:

> So the way we see the relationship with the United States is as President Xi Jinping has said—that is, we hope to see no confrontation, no conflict, mutual respect and win-win cooperation with the United States. And, during the phone call between the presidents, President Biden himself also talked about the importance of having no conflict or confrontation between our two countries. So, at our level, I think it's vital that we do everything we can to fully and faithfully follow up and implement the understandings reached between [them].[65]

Although the banner term 'a new type of great power relationship' failed as a real-world framework for US-China relations because it was rejected by Washington, it elucidated Xi Jinping's nationalist narrative on Chinese foreign policy at multiple levels. At its core, it was China's first formal assertion of its own aspiration for national great power status. It did so through its unilateral assertion of a new and equal power status with the United States, based in part on its own deep calculus of the changing balance of national power in China's favour. It also reflected a new level of national self-confidence on China's part to advance a new framework to the United States for the management of the bilateral relationship, rather than simply waiting for the United States to take the initiative. For the first time, China sought to become a *price-setter* rather than simply being a *price-taker* in framing the overall terms of the relationship. Furthermore, this nationalist self confidence in China's rise was anchored in an underlying ideological confidence in the immutable Marxist laws that were working in its favour against those whom it was struggling against. Finally, the failure of Xi's great power relations formula as a diplomatic mechanism to constrain

American power gave rise to newer, sharper, and even more public forms of official Chinese nationalism directed against the United States than before.[66] And this we saw most dramatically on display with Yang's public broadside in Anchorage and its nationalist reverberations across China.

Nationalism and the Global Order: A Community of Common Destiny

Xi's concept of a 'community of common destiny for all humankind' (CCD) takes China's new, self-confident culture of nationalist assertiveness into the realm of global governance. Like Xi's approaches to 'neighbouring state diplomacy' and a 'new type of great power relations', this amorphous concept exhibits several different nationalist meanings and directions within China's overall foreign policy discourse. But unlike Xi's approach to China's neighbours and its bilateral relationship with the United States, this *mega-concept* spans the entire fabric of China's wider global engagement in the 'new era' proclaimed in 2017. It has come to embrace, and in some cases subsume, several related sub-themes including: 'China contributing its wisdom and solutions to the world' (*weishijie gongxian zhongguo zhihui zhongguo fangan*); 'the reform of the global governance' (*wanshan quanqiu zhili*); 'China upholding the global order' (*weihu guoji zhixu*); and, as previously discussed, 'China moving to the centre stage of the world' (*zhongguo zouxiang shijie wutai de zhongxin*). A common nationalist thematic across all these formulations is that China's time has arrived to deploy its newfound national power to restructure the international system to better suit Chinese interests and values. Xi foreshadowed this to the 2014 Central Foreign Affairs Work Conference as he described a 'new type of international relations' that would offer a multilateral complement to his 'new type of great power relations'.

In a single, stark, and ideological phrase at the 2014 Foreign Affairs Work Conference, Xi called on the party "to be ready to plan for a long-term struggle for the international order" (*yao chongfen guji guoji zhixu zhizheng de changqixing*).[67] Xi's deliberate use of the deeply ideologically laden term 'struggle' within the framework of international relations as early as 2014 may seem logical in retrospect, but it was jarring at the time.[68] While Xi had already referred to 'struggle' in his leaked 2013 address to the Ideology and Propaganda Work Conference, this was primarily in connection with restoring ideological and political rigour to the party itself. The application of this core Marxist-Leninist concept of 'struggle' to underlying international contradictions—not just domestic ones—represented an extension of the ideological contest well beyond China's shores. Indeed, some three years before the United States in 2017 declared a new age of 'strategic competition' with China,[69] Xi Jinping had already effectively declared a new age of ideological competition for the future structure of the international system. This is the enduring significance of Xi's 2014 address: 'struggle' had been rehabilitated, re-legitimized and re-authorized as a tool of Chinese international policy some forty years after Deng had consigned it to history.[70]

Like Xi's new approach to neighbouring states diplomacy and great power relations, the 'community of common destiny for all humankind' concept also has its origins in the late Hu Jintao era. It made a notable appearance in China's 2011 Foreign Policy White Paper.[71] Hu had already called in 2009 for 'more actively developing multilateral diplomacy' and greater Chinese activism in international institution building.[72] But, as with great power relations, Hu would not personally embrace the overarching concept of CCD until the 18th Party Congress in 2012 via a short, single reference secreted deep within the text of the long foreign policy section of his report:

> In promoting win-win cooperation, we should raise awareness about a community of common destiny for humankind. It means accommodating the legitimate concerns of others when pursuing one's own interests; and it means promoting common development of all countries when advancing one's own development. Countries should establish a new, more balanced and equal type of global development partnership, sticking together in times of difficulty, sharing rights and responsibilities, and promoting the common interests of humankind.[73]

On a strict reading of the text, these are all definitions of the term 'win-win cooperation', of which CCD was rendered as one sub-definition, rather than an expansive elaboration of the 'common community' concept in its own right. So while CCD technically has its origins in the Hu Jintao period, the documentary record demonstrates it was used little and late and its scope was narrow. Whereas under Xi, particularly after the 19th Congress in 2017, it would become an almost universal mantra for Xi's vision for the world. Indeed, as a national mission statement,

CCD would become the foreign policy equivalent of what 'the great rejuvenation of the Chinese nation' meant domestically—so much so that, in 2017, Foreign Minister Wang Yi would describe CCD as one of the "overarching goals of China's foreign policy in the years ahead".[74]

Xi Jinping first referred to CCD in Beijing in December 2012, and then in Moscow in March 2013 during his inaugural visit abroad as Chinese president.[75] Following the enunciation of Xi's new neighbouring state diplomacy that year, CCD was first fully articulated, albeit in a regional context, in his 2015 Boao address titled 'Towards a Community of Common Destiny and a New Future for Asia'.[76] It was expanded to become a global proposition in Xi's UN General Assembly address that September,[77] although its most comprehensive conceptual definition would come in January 2017 at the UN in Geneva.[78] Domestically, Xi made CCD the conceptual chapeau for his entire foreign policy program at the 19th Party Congress in November 2017.[79] The formal elevation of CCD as the overarching banner term of Xi's international policy project was then formally cemented into the CCP and PRC constitutions in 2017 and 2018 as a central mission for both the party and the state.[80] CCD has also featured consistently in almost every major foreign policy address by Xi Jinping since 2015, including at summits of the G20, BRICS, Shanghai Cooperation Organization, Belt and Road Initiative, and UN Framework Convention on Climate Change, as well as the launch of the Asian Infrastructure Investment Bank. It has also been used extensively during his most significant bilateral meetings and visits abroad. With dozens of substantive references across Xi's remarks every year, CCD has increasingly permeated the entire Chinese foreign policy narrative.[81] Indeed, it became the foreign policy meta-narrative for practically everything that Xi now sought to do in the international arena—and not just in the multilateral arena. Almost all significant external initiatives were now grouped under its moral and conceptual umbrella.

The CCD concept contains a number of significant nationalist thematics within its overall ideological frame of Marxist Nationalism. First, CCD, like Xi's other foreign policy banner terms, is grounded in the overall ideological narrative of national rejuvenation. This is clearer in Xi's domestic expositions of CCD than in those speeches designed for foreign audiences, where Xi is keener to convey a sense of Chinese policy altruism, as opposed to the simple prosecution of core Chinese national interests and power. For example, the foreign policy section of

Xi's 19th Party Congress Report is entitled 'Promoting the Building of a Community of Common Destiny for All Humankind' and emphasizes the party's efforts to enhance China's comprehensive national power.[82] And as noted previously, to underscore CCD's nationalist origins, the party's theoretical journal *Qiushi* published a commentary just after the 2017 congress stating the China Dream and CCD were basically one and the same: "To realize the China Dream [of national rejuvenation], the party must promote the establishment of a human community with a shared future, facilitate changes in the global governance system, and make new and greater contributions to the cause of peaceful human development."[83]

CCD is therefore explicitly based on changing CCP assumptions concerning Chinese national power and China's national capacity to now bring about international change. As Xi Jinping himself noted in his 2015 presentation on CCD at Boao: "The international situation continues to experience profound and complex changes with significant development in multipolarization" and in "facing the fast-changing international and regional landscape, we must see the whole picture, follow the trend of our times and jointly build a regional order that is more favourable to Asia and the world".[84] Yang Jiechi added to Xi's formulation in more explicit terms when he said that "multilateralism remains the call of the people and the trend of our times" but despite this there were "certain countries, driven by misguided unilateral and protectionist policies" to the extent that the international community now demanded "a new international political and economic order that is just and reasonable".[85] For these reasons, Yang argued that CCD embodied "the call of our times" and that the CCP not only "seeks happiness for the Chinese people; it is also a political party that strives for the cause of human progress".[86] China's development and that of the wider world were hence part of the same enterprise. In 2019, yet another official commentary noted:

> As long as countries around the world uphold the concept of a community of shared future for mankind, adhere to multilateralism, and follow the path of unity and cooperation, they will surely be able to jointly address various global issues. . . . China will . . . always regard making new and greater contributions to humanity as its mission. As General Secretary Xi Jinping emphasized: "On the new journey, we must . . . promote the building of a new type of international relations, promote the construction of a community of shared future for mankind . . . opposing hegemonism

and power politics." . . . When the world is good, China can be good; when China is good, the world will be better.[87]

Together, these reflect a clearly stated nationalist demand for a new regional and global order, that China should lead the building of this order, and that it should draw on its own reservoir of national wisdom in doing so. As such, these propositions represent a major departure from Deng's underlying argument that Beijing should work within the framework and structures of the existing international order as a continued precondition for maximizing China's national economic development. And once again, we see that the central ideological construct of 'struggle' unifies both Xi's domestic and international missions. Xi also refers to Marxist understandings of the 'underlying trends' that warrant this new exercise in international institutional reform or 'struggle', as an old, American-led order passes away and a new Chinese-led order comes into being. These same 'underlying trends' have presumably been divined by applying the inerrant laws and analytical tools of scientific socialism to changes unfolding in the real world. Moreover, it is asserted this new Chinese-led order will be clothed in a new moral purpose that "will be more rational and just", sticking with the world "through thick and thin", rather than simply being seen as a naked extension of Chinese realist power.[88] Most important, this search for global justice now unites the CCP's project on behalf of the Chinese nation with an international mission on behalf of all peoples around the world. Indeed, this makes Xi's newly stated ambition for the world today not radically dissimilar to Mao's earlier formulations in support of proletarian internationalism. We should remember that the banners adorning the Gate of Heavenly Peace today still proclaim the universalist symmetry of China's overriding revolutionary mission: 'Long Live the People's Republic of China. Long Live the Great Unity of the Peoples of the World' (*zhonghua renmin gongheguo wansui. Shijie renmin datuanjie wansui*).

Xi Jinping's 'community of common destiny' narrative is also consistently presented as an alternative to the failings of the current US-led international order. Xi's language routinely offers a binary view: in one corner, US and Western decline and growing global dysfunctionality; in the other, the natural alternative of China's rational, orderly, and more inclusive CCD. As Xi put it in 2022: "The contrast between Chinese order and Western chaos has become even sharper."[89] Although usually without naming the

United States, Chinese official commentary routinely presents CCD, both in its domestic and its international discourse, as a series of binaries: first, China's support for globalization versus American isolationism and protectionism; second, Chinese recognition of the multipolar reality versus the continuing American fantasy of a unipolar world; third, Chinese embrace of multilateralism versus multiple examples of American unilateralism; fourth, Chinese support for the UN-based multilateral system versus the 'so-called US-led international rules-based order'; and fifth, the wealth of Chinese national wisdom, aided by the wisdoms of other world cultures, to reform global governance and solve the deep-rooted international problems of today, versus the intellectual dominance of the West. As former Chinese vice-foreign minister Fu Ying stated with remarkable candour in the *Financial Times* in 2016: "The western-centred world order dominated by the US . . . is like an adult in children's clothes. It is failing to adjust."[90]

This binary nationalist discourse on China's rise, American (and broader Western) decline, and the consequential need for the urgent reform of the global order is evident across the breadth of Xi Jinping's CCD narrative. Yang Jiechi once again put it bluntly in 2017:

> An international landscape dominated by the West, and a concept of international relations that is mainly oriented towards Western values, is hardly sustainable. Western governance concepts, systems, and models have become increasingly difficult to adapt to the new international structure and the trend of the times . . . and the bigger Western powers are themselves confronted with poor governance and many, many questions . . . therefore demanding a new concept of global governance.[91]

This analysis is reinforced by a series of Xi's own remarks, comparing and contrasting China's national position with the imputed position of the United States. At the same time, Xi prescribes the defining features of a new, more preferable global order. On the sovereign equality of states, Xi states that China "stands for democracy in international relations and the equality of all countries"[92] and that "big countries should treat smaller ones as equals, instead of acting as a hegemon imposing their will on others".[93] On non-interference in other states' internal affairs, Xi once again makes the contrast clear:

> To respect one another and treat each other as equals, countries need, first and foremost, to respect other countries' social systems and development paths of their own choice, respect each other's core interests and major

> concerns and have objective and rational perceptions of other countries' growing strength, policies and visions. . . . All of us must oppose interference in other countries' internal affairs and reject attempts to destabilize the region out of selfish motives.[94]

As for security arrangements, Xi argues these should be based on the principles of common security rather than military alliances: "To build a community of common destiny, we need to pursue common, comprehensive, cooperative, and sustainable security; in today's world, security means much more than before and its implications go well beyond a single region or time frame."[95] This means that a CCD should "resolutely reject a Cold War mentality and power politics, adopt a new approach to developing state-to-state relations with communication, not confrontation, and with partnerships not alliances".[96] Xi's renditions of Chinese and American history on the unilateral use of armed force strike the same chord: "We see great truth in the saying that 'a warlike country, however big it might be, is bound to perish'. Some people are fanning up the so-called China threat.... Let me be clear: China is committed to peaceful development and pursues an independent foreign policy of peace. This is not an expediency. It is a strategic decision made by China as well as the solemn pledge it has made to the world."[97]

These various CCD thematics come together in Xi Jinping's championing of the UN multilateral system, as opposed to an American-led order of which the UN is only one part. According to Xi:

> We should renew our commitment to the purposes and principles of the UN Charter, build a new type of international relations featuring win-win cooperation, and create a community of common destiny for all humankind.... The principle of sovereign equality underpins the UN Charter.... We should be committed to multilateralism and reject unilateralism.[98]

In 2017, when the Trump administration was withdrawing from or defunding significant institutions across the UN system, Xi began referring to China as the "upholder of the international order" while Yang declared Beijing would work to "safeguard international fairness and justice".[99] Yang shone a spotlight on this contrast in his remarkable 2021 exchange with Blinken in Anchorage: "What China and the international community follow or uphold is the United Nations–centred international system and the international order underpinned by international law, not what is advocated by a small number of countries of the US-led 'so-called rules-based international order.' "[100] In other words, China under Xi Jinping has thrown down its national gauntlet as the new defender of the UN multilateral system which, it alleges, the United States has effectively abandoned. It is a binary appeal for the position of global multilateral leadership. Indeed, China now claims to 'uphold' the very system that the United States substantially created in 1945. At the same time, China argues that it also now leads the reform of that very same system—both to create "a more just and equitable world order" for the Global South, and to better reflect the emerging geo-political realities (i.e. China's growing national power).[101]

The CCD narrative articulated by Xi and Yang, reinforced by other official commentary, also seeks to maximize the domestic political legitimacy dividend flowing from the perceived levels of international support for Beijing's efforts to defend and reform the multilateral system. As Xi noted in his 2018 address to the Boao Forum: "I proposed the initiative to build a community with a shared future for mankind and I have since had many in-depth discussions with various parties. I am glad that this proposal has been welcomed and endorsed by a growing number of countries and their peoples. It has also been written into important UN documents."[102] To this Yang has added in his domestic political commentary that CCD has "demonstrated vividly China's confidence", enhancing its international prestige and fully allowing the international community to appreciate China's "trustworthiness and vision."[103] Other commentaries point to the CCD enhancing China's national 'discourse power' in foreign policy and international strategic affairs in a manner previously monopolized by the United States.[104] In other words, the new nationalism that has underpinned the assertion of China's national power to transform the international system has had a dual utility: in addition to shaping the global discourse, common values, and institutional architecture of the system abroad, the CCP regime is also enhancing its legitimacy at home by depicting a positive foreign reception for its newfound international activism.

As part of the ideological framing of CCD within Xi Jinping's overall Marxist-Nationalist construct, Xi, Yang Jiechi, and Wang Yi are all careful to attribute this 'community of common destiny' idea to the evolving canon of Chinese Marxist-Leninist thought. Their vehicle for doing so is 'Xi Jinping Thought on Socialism with Chinese Characteristics for the New Era' as the latest iteration of Chinese Marxism. This includes its foreign policy doctrine, 'Xi Jinping Thought on Diplomacy'. As discussed in previous chapters, in Xi's ideological worldview, Chinese Marxism is the principal analytical framework not just for China's domestic political and economic challenges; it is the framework for understanding and responding to challenges and opportunities in the world beyond as well. As Wang Yi has made plain: "Xi Jinping Thought on Diplomacy is the fundamental guideline for China's diplomatic work and is an epoch-making milestone in the diplomatic theory of New China."[105]

At one level, 'Xi Jinping Thought on Diplomacy' could be seen as a simple exercise in ideological formalism to make more morally presentable, both at home and abroad, the hard-nosed *realpolitik* of a twenty-first-century Leninist party. But at a different level, we would be foolish to disregard it as a framework for analysing and responding to contemporary international relations. And at another level again, Xi Jinping Thought can also be seen as a reflection of the absolute political and ideological authority of Xi himself over all aspects of policy, both domestic and foreign. Indeed, this represents Xi's alternative to simply keeping foreign policy as the exclusive preserve of China's traditional cadre of professional diplomats. That had been the case for decades under Deng, Jiang, and Hu. But that age had now passed. Xi has instead slotted into the Chinese foreign service a new cadre of party ideologues with more limited international experience, to keep the Foreign Ministry mindful of their fundamental political mission, rather than becoming too pragmatically accommodating of the interests of foreigners.[106]

Just as ideology has become foundational to all the party's political and policy endeavours, Xi Jinping Thought on Diplomacy now plays a substantive, rather than just a purely notional, role in the evolution of core foreign policy concepts. This is evident, in part, from the party assuming a new position at the centre of the foreign policy machinery in Beijing. Ideology is also now more prominent in the party's internal discourse on foreign policy than at any time since Mao. The ideological imprint of Marxist-Leninist concepts can be seen in the rehabilitation of core terms such as 'contradiction', 'struggle', and the 'laws of development' in the party's internal discourse on international relations—concepts that naturally imply the inevitability of conflict arising from major contradictions abroad and the need, therefore, to prepare for them. This stands in stark contrast with the recent past, when it was argued that economic integration with the wider world could render war 'avoidable'.[107] Moreover, it is plain from Xi's commentary that he sees Marxism-Leninism as a global, and not just a Chinese, national ideological project.[108] In other words, Marxism-Leninism, Xi Jinping Thought on Diplomacy, and Xi Jinping Thought in general are not just a means of reaffirming the domestic ideological legitimacy of the party and the political primacy of the leader; they also represent the growing ideational influence of Marxism-Leninism on the content, trajectory, and perceived historical inevitability of China's overall foreign policy project.

This Marxist-Leninist framework applies in particular to the grand narratives of Chinese foreign policy under Xi, including CCD. For example, when listing China's foreign policy priorities in his report to the 19th Party Congress, Xi stated: "The Thought on Socialism with Chinese Characteristics for a New Era . . . makes clear that major-country diplomacy with Chinese characteristics aims to foster a new type of international relations and build a community with a shared future for mankind."[109] Yang Jiechi elaborated on the ideological and theoretical significance of CCD as "a scientific theoretical system which is rich, comprehensive and profound".[110] The use of the term 'scientific theoretical system' is, once again, code language for a Marxist-Leninist frame of analysis and the ongoing discovery of the universal laws of political and economic development. Yang, writing for a domestic audience in an article not published in English, also observed:

> Xi has mastered the laws of development arising from human history, starting from the standpoint of China's interests and the world's interests, has advanced the proposal of CCD . . . and has comprehensively made manifest both the sensibility and responsibility of great power leadership towards the world.[111]

Note again the 'laws of development'—a hallmark of Marxist analysis. Yang is also at pains to point out that CCD demonstrates that the Communist Party (as opposed to the Chinese state) not only sought happiness for its own people, but was a party of struggle for the progress of all of humanity. In all these statements, the Marxist-Leninist component of Xi's overall Marxist-Nationalist worldview is loud and proud. It cannot simply be cast aside as if it is irrelevant to China's internal foreign policy discourse. While Xi's new form of Marxist-Nationalist ideology is not the only consideration driving China's changing foreign policy behaviour, it is a significant explanatory factor that cannot be ignored.

It is true that Xi's 'community of common destiny' proposal remains deliberately vague. This too is a conscious feature of Chinese political statecraft. Under Xi, Chinese diplomacy has often sought to maximize initial international support for a new idea by advancing relatively nebulous concepts with vast moral appeal and minimal policy detail. The second stage is to enhance this initial ideational appeal with a plethora of international conferences to build a global political consensus around them. This explains the priority attached by Xi to UN-related legitimacy. For example, Chinese officials have laboured with remarkable success across multiple multilateral agencies to have core Chinese concepts such as CCD incorporated into the normative language of the UN system.[112] The third stage is to then gradually populate the original broad proposal with greater policy detail as specific programs are unfurled to give it effect. This pattern has been evident with such grand-scale initiatives as the Belt and Road Initiative, the Global Civilizational Initiative, the Global Security Initiative, and the Global Development Initiative. All have begun as vague, inoffensive concepts before acquiring more concrete political shape and policy form sometime later. Indeed, it is likely that, in time, these myriad initiatives will be folded into Xi's mega- and meta-concept of a community of common destiny. In the fullness of time, Xi would perhaps see this new emerging Sino-centric structure supplementing, if not replacing, the UN Charter. The latter, while still supported as a core pillar of Chinese foreign policy, is also seen in Beijing as primarily a Western construct, driven by Western interests and values, having been pieced together by the victorious colonial powers after the Second World War. The CCD, by definition, is not.

Conclusion

Taken together, the various 'banner terms' examined above have reinforced Xi Jinping's nationalist narrative within the overall ideological framework of Marxist Nationalism. In the previous chapter, concepts such as China's 'national rejuvenation', its 'outstanding traditional culture', its growing 'comprehensive national power', and its generation of a profound transformation of global geo-politics 'not seen in a hundred years' all sought to *describe* an unfolding power transition between the United States and China. Whereas in this chapter, additional concepts such as 'striving for achievement', a new 'neighbouring state diplomacy', a 'new type of great power relations', and Xi's mega-concept of 'a community of common destiny for all humankind' collectively set out to *prescribe* what Chinese diplomacy should now be doing to accelerate this process of change. In other words, by pointing to deep changes in the underlying balance of power between the United States and China, Xi has created an ideological narrative on the inevitability of China's national ascendancy. At the same time, Xi has constructed a parallel discourse on how China must now prosecute a more assertive foreign policy in relation to the United States, the region, and the world, that seizes the historical opportunity with which it has now been presented. The first set of terms defines the national power that China now has at its disposal, while the second set outlines how China should now go about using that power.

For these reasons, I argue that Xi Jinping has moved China's nationalist narrative to the right. He has used it to construct both the ideological and moral foundation for a new era of Chinese foreign and security policy assertiveness designed to challenge and change the international status quo. Indeed, in terms of China's long-standing territorial claims within the region, he has built an ideological foundation that justifies a Chinese revisionist agenda. Xi has also constructed an ideological discourse in which the forces of both national and revolutionary history have come together. Both have been harnessed through the political agency of a Marxist-Leninist state, and both now render it necessary for China, through a consciously more assertive foreign policy, to bring about major changes to the strategic order.

In this sense, Xi's new nationalism seeks, through a newly assertive foreign policy, to bring about three major changes to existing international structures: first, to create more compliant relationships with its neighbouring states, confident that America's economic power and security relevance are of declining significance; second, to build the norms and institutions of a new, more Sino-centric international system, noting carefully the importance of the new Chinese power realities that will underpin the unfolding global order, and confident that the United States is progressively abandoning the field; and third, on a bilateral basis, to begin treating the United States dismissively as a declining power—at best a temporary equal, and at worst a manageable obstacle to the realization of China's foreign policy ambitions. Importantly, within all three domains, the changes sought through a more assertive Chinese foreign policy are both nationalist in nature and binary in their desired outcome. They also bear all the substantive hallmarks of 'strategic competition', despite Beijing's claim that such language represents an 'outdated Cold War mentality', and its rhetorical insistence that the US-China relationship be based on 'no conflict, no confrontation, mutual respect, and win-win cooperation'.

Finally, underpinning this entire nationalist narrative is the ideological certainty that pervades Xi's overall foreign policy discourse. This is the ideological confidence he derives from the application of underlying, immutable Marxist-Leninist 'laws of development'. These references to universal laws can routinely be found in the textual presentation of most, if not all, of the multiple sets of banner terms examined so far. It is also important to remember that these public explanations of China's new direction are intended for *external* audiences. Therefore, the Marxist-Leninist references to 'laws of development' are likely to be relatively spare in their public rendition. While it cannot yet be proven, it is equally likely that the party's *internal* assessments of China's and America's strategic trajectories would contain a much more expansive rendition of Marxist analytical frameworks, and the ideological and political conclusions the Chinese system derives from them. Xi's ideological worldview represents a hybrid form of Marxist Nationalism in which Chinese nationalism is not simply validated by the prospective redress of China's historical grievances against the United States, Japan, and the West; it is also an internationally righteous cause, validated, animated, and reinvigorated by universal Marxist-Leninist tools of analysis, the conviction that such conclusions are objectively 'correct', and that a powerful China now becomes the international moral vehicle for bringing about a more just global order for all—so long, of course, as Chinese national power becomes its geopolitical fulcrum and Chinese national interests (*li*) are respected.

11

Nationalism, Foreign Policy Assertiveness, and Chinese Policy towards the United Nations

There are several possible ways to test the argument that under Xi Jinping's new ideological framework of Marxist Nationalism, Chinese foreign policy has become more assertive and, in some cases, revisionist. One way is to examine China's principal foreign and national security policy statements, actions, and engagements over the decade 2012–2022. These include China's more recent approaches to its bilateral relationships with the United States and its treaty allies (such as Japan, South Korea, Australia, and Canada), as well as with Southeast Asia and India. It would also include changes to China's regional and global military profile, deployments, and operations. Another approach would be to examine separate Chinese foreign policy initiatives including the Belt and Road Initiative, the Asian Infrastructure Investment Bank, and the increasingly global diplomatic effort attached to the advancement of the community of common destiny for all humankind. These analytical approaches involve assessing China's changing policy declarations and posture across numerous different foreign policy domains against parallel changes in Xi's ideological framework. There is already a considerable literature on each of these.[1] While conclusions differ as to the causes of each of these policy and behavioural changes, there is little analytical disagreement on the basic proposition that Chinese foreign and security policy actions have become objectively become more assertive during the Xi Jinping period.

An alternative approach is to examine quantitatively the number of military and para-military deployments, interceptions, and incursions associated with specific disputed territorial and maritime claims. These would include PLA incursions against Taiwan; incidents in the South China Sea including island reclamations; altercations with US and allied military assets and associated actions against South China Sea claimant states; and other military actions against Japan in the East China Sea, Korea in the Yellow Sea, and India along their shared border. Once again, there is considerable literature on each of these, based on data disclosed by various national governments. Raw incident data provides little insight into the broader military or foreign policy circumstances of each individual event, but paints an overall picture of significantly increased Chinese military and para-military activity in all categories since Xi came to power. For example, Figures 11.1–11.5, taken from official Taiwanese, Japanese, and Korean government agencies, indicate a general pattern of increased military assertiveness over time. These offer one means by which we can attempt to correlate broad changes in Xi's nationalist ideological narrative with real-world behavioural change on the ground. Additionally, in Korea's case, Figures 11.6–11.7 quantify Chinese economic pressure in the form of reduced Korean car sales to China following Seoul's decision to deploy US THAAD missile-defence systems on its soil. This was also reflected in the retail sector, with the most high-profile case being Korea's Lotte Group which announced its withdrawal from China in 2022 amidst a campaign of political pressure.[2] All seven figures demonstrate a dramatic change in Chinese military and economically coercive behaviours since Xi Jinping came to power.

Figure 11.1 PLA Incursions into Taiwan's Air Defense Identification Zone[3]

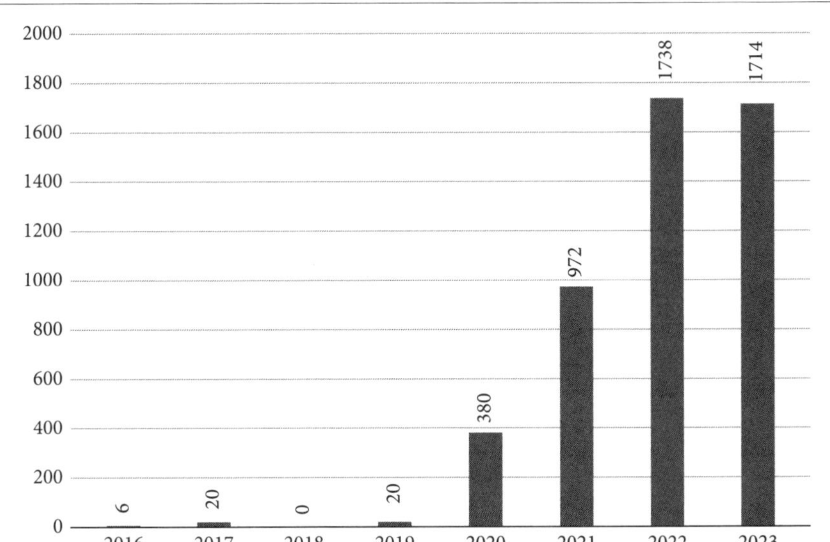

Figure 11.2 Japanese Air Self Defense Force Scrambles against Chinese aircraft[4]

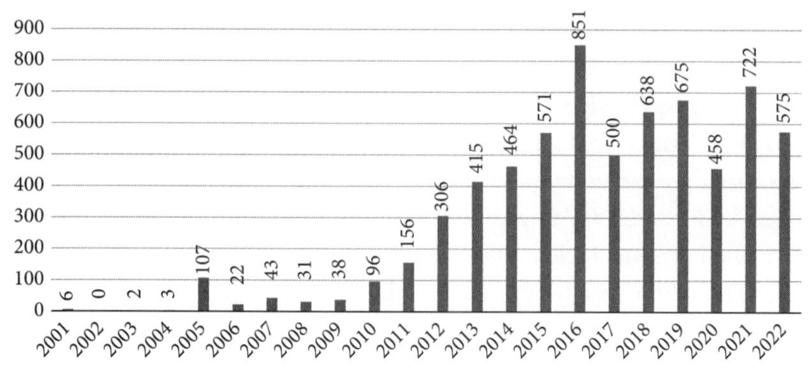

Figure 11.3 PRC Government Vessels Entering the Senkaku Territorial Sea[5]

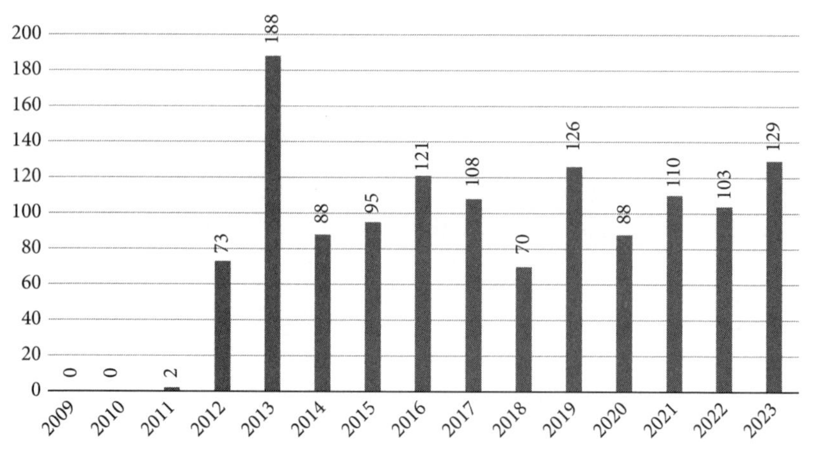

Figure 11.4 PRC Government Vessels Entering the Senkaku Contiguous Zone[6]

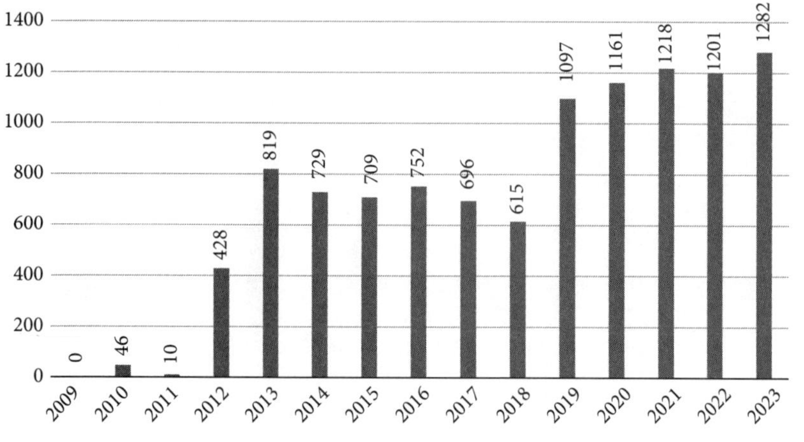

Figure 11.5 Scale of Chinese Military Spending Compared with US Treaty Allies in Asia (2000–2022)[7]

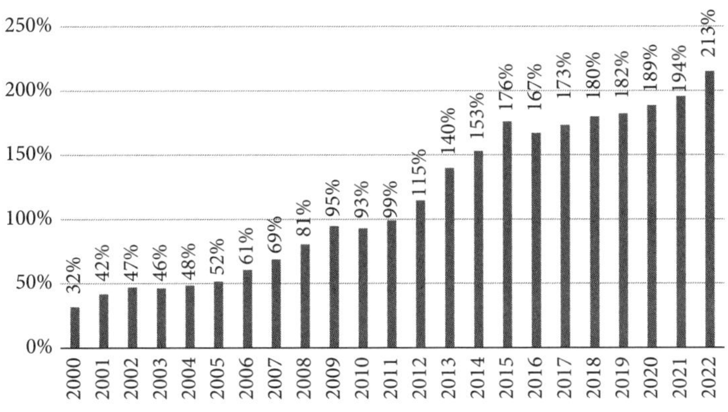

Figure 11.6 Hyundai Annual Vehicle Sales in China[8]

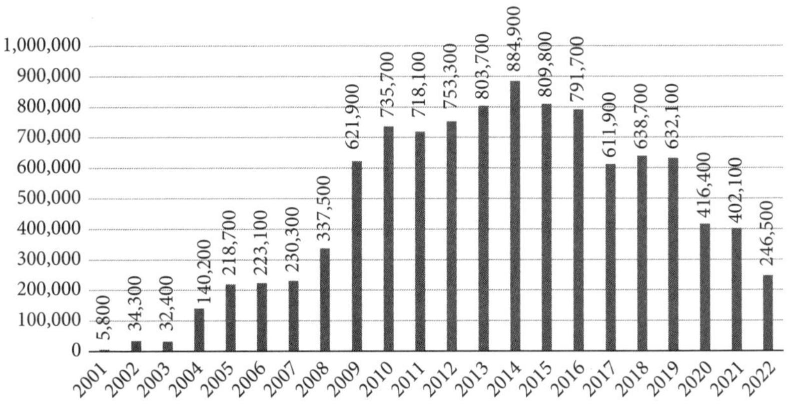

Another approach to measuring foreign policy assertiveness is to examine China's changing patterns of policy activism, innovation, and multilateral assertiveness through Beijing's evolving policy posture at the United Nations. This approach enables us to test the proposition of greater foreign policy assertiveness across different policy areas and international relationships. And it does so in a manner that is readily visible to a large number of foreign governments participating in the same multilateral fourms.

Figure 11.7 Kia Annual Vehicle Sales in China[9]

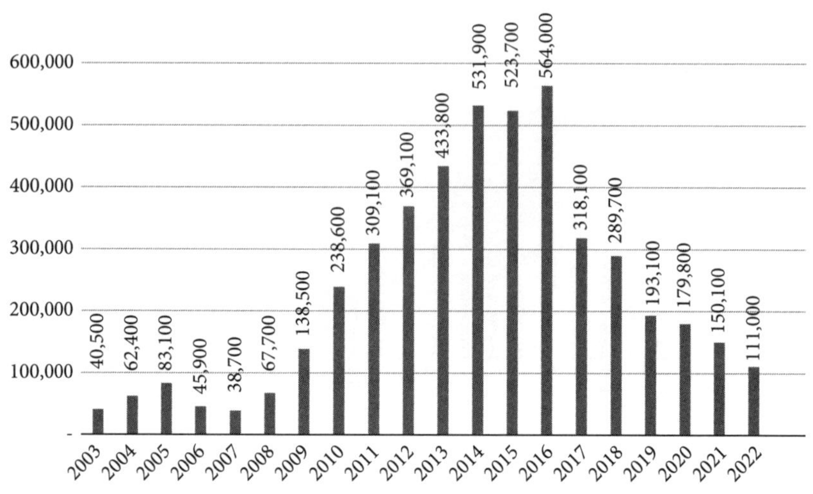

Furthermore, changes in this type of policy behaviour are usually visible to third parties—for example, the UN Secretariat—thereby providing additional and more independent verification of China's changing policy activism. For the purposes of this book, and the research project on which it is based, confidential interviews were therefore conducted with a number of former ambassadors to the UN who served alongside China's representatives on the UN Security Council, covering both the periods before and after Xi Jinping came to power. Former senior UN officials who observed China's changing posture both within and beyond the Security Council were also interviewed. Once transcribed, these interviews with Western and non-Western officials amounted to 150 pages. Each interviewee was assured anonymity given that many were still serving as senior officials. While this interview-based approach does not provide an unbiased account of China's changing policy posture at the UN, the interviews do provide a general (and not always unsympathetic) picture of China's actual multilateral diplomacy from the perspective of first-hand observers.

The overall picture that emerges from these interviews is that China became significantly more forthright in its multilateral diplomacy after 2017, as opposed to this change becoming immediately apparent after Xi's elevation in 2012. This is generally consistent with the analysis in chapter 10 that China's ideological intention of becoming a major new global actor only became clear after the Central Foreign Affairs Work Conference in late 2014, Xi's major speeches on CCD, and his new foreign policy platform delivered at the 19th Party Congress in 2017. While interviewees ranged far and wide in their observations, their conclusions can be grouped into five broad categories:

- China taking a more active role in the drafting and final content of Security Council resolutions in areas beyond its usual core interests;
- China's more aggressive posture in redefining traditional UN human rights norms;
- China's efforts to leverage a greater role in UN peacekeeping operations to reduce their operational scope to 'intervene' in the internal affairs of states;
- China's new approach to UN resourcing, candidatures, and influencing the operations of the UN Secretariat—including influencing the voting patterns of other member states;
- Efforts to insert language into UN resolutions derived from Chinese multilateral concepts and institutions such as the Belt and Road Initiative, the Shanghai Cooperation Organization, and CCD, thereby enhancing their normative status.

China's Role on the UN Security Council

The ambassadors interviewed for this project were asked whether China was an active or passive participant in Security Council negotiations on major resolutions, and whether this pattern changed in the years after 2012. One diplomat, 'Ambassador A', said that until 2017, China almost exclusively took their lead on the Council from Russia:

> China was always looking to their Russian counterpart, just taking their cues from there, not grandstanding. I mean, even to say grandstanding in the context of Chinese diplomacy then would have been nonsensical. They didn't seem at all to have that muscle memory or instinct. So, it was very much a followership role. . . . Basically, what was clear is that there was not a lot of independent action but a very clear sort of tactical orientation, which was that Russia would speak first in meetings and the Chinese representative would echo what Russia would do.[10]

Ambassador A could not recall "a single issue that China had the pen [for] between 2013–16".[11] Even on resolutions regarding North Korean nuclear testing during this period, which would have been of great national security significance to China, the diplomat was surprised that Beijing did not demand to submit the initial draft: "I thought 'oh, they've got to have had the pen on North Korea'. . . . Absolutely not at that time. The US had the pen and would present to them the first version of that resolution."[12] Although China became galvanized on the content of the draft from late 2014 and early 2015, it still ceded responsibility to others to take the lead in the drafting process:

> This was the only issue in which China was a driving force with the Council on an issue of profound consequence for international peace and security . . . the North Korea nuclear issue was the first time I saw China as a determined, knowledgeable powerhouse in the UN Security Council.[13]

Another diplomat, 'Ambassador B', pointed to 2017 as the turning point in China's posture within the Council:

> The period of time that we're talking about, 2013 to 2017, I think was a time of pretty little change in terms of Chinese behaviour in the Security Council, and it really was starting around 2017 that they really took the gloves off and started to be more assertive, at least in their cooperation with Russia. And more vocally defensive on what they viewed as their core interests.[14]

'Ambassador D' broadly agreed but pointed to 2018 as the year when China's approach began to change significantly:

> It was as if their posture had accelerated. Something they had told us they would not do for fifteen years, they had begun to do: taking a much greater role in the drafting of Security Council resolutions; they had a view on resolutions that were not directly applicable to China or the region; they aligned much, much more closely with Russia, and therefore supported Russia purely.[15]

China initially took a gradual approach. According to Ambassador D:

> First of all, they weren't that big on that many issues compared to the UK and France or the US. They would take an interest in certain African peacekeeping missions that seemed to be driven by their economic interests. They would say: "let's do X in such and such country" or "we want to help you hold the pen in such and such country". And that was usually reflecting an economic interest. They liked that they could do what's called 'burden share' . . . or share the pen as it were. . . . When they were drafting, the principles that

would come out would be consent of the host state or the need to persuade the host state gently to do something.[16]

This emerging posture from 2018 did not initially mean automatic opposition to everything the United States sought to do on the Security Council. Indeed, on contentious questions such as securing humanitarian access for civilians in war-torn Syria, China sought to craft compromises between the US and Russian positions, before finally siding with Moscow in the final vote. As Ambassador D recalled:

> They never actually blocked what the Americans wanted to do, it was always watering down. However, over the course of two years [between 2018 and 2020], they started to move further and further towards the Russians and, in the end, voted with the Russians to block humanitarian corridors. Although they had tried to work with the UK and France to sort that out, they put forward a compromise which the UK amended and the Chinese said yes, we agree with the UK, and we'll support the UK. . . . You could see that the rest of the Council thought that this was a new China that was trying to find a diplomatic way through. In the end the Russians voted no, and I said to the Chinese, "Can't you have abstained?" "Why did you have to vote with Russia's veto?", and he said that he agreed but that it was "not within the realm of practical policy to even ask Beijing if he could abstain".[17]

Another interviewee, 'Ambassador E', drew a similar conclusion concerning China's changing posture during 2019–2020:

> My key impression was that the Chinese became . . . more active in the Council . . . also insisting on their positions, making life more difficult. . . . Basically, what they tried to do is not only make their position known, but then play hardball in trying to implement it during our period in the Council.[18]

The same ambassador pointed to a resolution on the UN Assistance Mission in Afghanistan: "Germany were the pen holders for the Afghanistan Resolution, the prolongation of the UNAMA Mandate. And there, they gave the Germans a very hard time, because they didn't want to mention human rights or civil society."[19] This then happened again in 2020 on the Syrian resolutions where Germany and Belgium had taken the lead in drafting the relevant humanitarian access resolution:

> In July of 2020, Germany, together with Belgium, were the pen-holders, on the so-called Cross-Border Resolution which . . . deals with the

crossing points that allow humanitarian goods to enter Idlib, the northwest of Syria. And there, the Russians and Chinese . . . were trying to cut down on these crossing points, because they wanted to put priority on . . . the sovereignty of the Assad regime, and they didn't want to give permission to a crossing point which is not under the sovereignty of Syria. But this remained the only way how humanitarian aid could get into the northwest of Syria. Germany and Belgium went all the way and put their resolutions to a vote on two occasions—resolutions which they believed would serve the NGOs and the humanitarian aid organizations best—and both times they forced Russia and China to cast a veto. And then the German ambassador attacked the Russian and Chinese and asked them: "Well, tell those that are now preventing humanitarian aid to get into the country and preventing 500,000 children from getting proper food and medicine that they are responsible." He asked them to ask those who gave the Russian and Chinese PRs [permanent representatives] their instructions if they were still able to look into the mirror. Then it went . . . viral. The Chinese hated it. And after that, their relationship with the German ambassador was appalling . . . and on his last day on the Council, when he gave a speech . . . in December of 2020, the Chinese ambassador publicly said "good riddance" to his leaving the Council. . . . So, the relationship between the Chinese and Germany really deteriorated in the end.[20]

In summarizing China's changing approach to its position on the Security Council, 'Ambassador C' reported a more subtle set of changes than other interlocutors:

As of 2018, I did see a change, but it was probably less dramatic than some of the colleagues I've spoken to who were on the Security Council. . . . The Chinese also treated the UN Secretariat differently than the other P5 did.[21] The Chinese did not roll up their sleeves and deal with the UN Department of Political Affairs in any way that the other P5 states did, so they had much less engagement with the Chinese than with any of the other P5.[22]

By contrast, Ambassador E, pointing to the 2019–2020 period, observed much sharper changes:

They would speak on all issues and you could see that there was a line, a clear thread going through what they were saying. . . . I think they had instructions to make sure that they were active, participating in all the issues. I think that they have somehow said that, with the perceived decline of the US and the West, that they were now in the business of taking over. And they had to manifest that. . . . I observed them becoming more active. And during my period at least, they also [became] more aggressive.[23]

These interviewees all agree that China did not take the lead in *drafting* any UN Security Council resolution prior to 2018, including the North Korea (DPRK) resolutions which dealt with significant nuclear issues right on its doorstep. Nonetheless, various ambassadors noted that, as of 2015, China became much more assertive about the *content* of the American draft on the DPRK than had previously been the case. Furthermore, while China had long generally followed the Russian lead in the Council, they did so with greater vigour after 2018. Ambassador C observed that China also became more bullish in pursuing their core defensive interests on human rights and state sovereignty: "So, not activist in, as it were, advancing an issue before the Council but, on certain questions concerning their internal affairs, they moved from a more passive position to a more active, opposing position."[24] This was evident across a range of resolutions well beyond China's immediate regional interests in the Asia-Pacific region, including Syria and Africa.

Beijing's Changing Posture on Human Rights at the UNSC and the UN Human Rights Council

China's international posture on universal human rights norms has become increasingly assertive during the Xi Jinping period. Ted Piccone and others have studied this shift since China's return to the Human Rights Council in 2013 under Xi.[25] This shift became evident, Ambassador A noted, in China seeking to "skinny down" the human rights clauses in Security Council resolutions. China also began obstructing briefings to the UNSC by representatives of the UN Human Rights Council (HRC). China supported efforts to defund human rights observer positions and posts through the UN budget and increased institutional and personal pressure on the Office of the High Commissioner for Human Rights (OHCHR). It also applied political pressure on the Commissioner through the UN Secretariat and the Office of the Secretary-General. While China long opposed the further expansion of universal human rights norms through its bilateral and multilateral diplomacy, every ambassador interviewed pointed to a qualitative shift in China's level of assertiveness and aggression under Xi's administration in each of the four areas listed above. To some extent, this new assertiveness pre-dated the generally acknowledged turning point of 2017 in China's overall posture at the UN. But by 2020, assertiveness had become the norm. And in some cases, assertiveness had turned into aggression.

Ambassador A pointed specifically to China's systematic campaign under Xi to strip the Security Council of its traditional capacity to interpret major domestic human rights violations as stepping stones to potential threats to international peace and security. As Ambassador A noted:

> [The UN] had long established that the way you treat your people internally can metastasize into something that creates regional and international havoc. So, they [China] were arguing—anachronistically but probably prophetically, because that's where they were going—to try to skinny down the Security Council jurisdiction across the board.[26]

This notably came to a head with the North Korea resolutions of 2014–2015 when China tried to remove any references to domestic human rights abuses and defend North Korean national sovereignty as inviolable against any UN intervention or intrusion. Ambassador A observed that China, seeking to avoid a long-term generic precedent to intervene in other states, took the extraordinary step of calling a vote to identify the DPRK as a unique case where human rights practices should be examined as a possible threat to security. Ambassador A said:

> This was fascinating because China felt compelled to do what it never did, which is to call a procedural vote, effectively declaring the human rights conditions inside North Korea as a unique threat to international peace and security. . . . It was just on this single issue—not on what you should do about North Korea over human rights, but just whether human rights belonged [at all] in the Security Council.[27]

This analysis was supported by Ambassador B, as China sought to reduce human rights interventions to a bare minimum:

> China was just in lockstep in terms of standing with countries that did not want an assertive UN presence of any kind, kicking the tires on human rights and individual freedoms, or even humanitarian issues. . . . I wouldn't say they were vocal, but they were certainly quite staunch in standing with Russia and on Burundi and their former president, who did not want any, any sort of UN presence. These negotiations took place primarily in 2015 or 2016—mainly 2016, I think—but they definitely viewed the kind of assertive UN Security Council action that we had managed to secure for Libya . . . that we were trying to get done in Burundi . . . as somehow counter to their view of the purposes and principles of the UN Charter and,

in particular, the Article 2 part that talks about interference in the internal affairs of other countries.[28] We can speculate for a long time about why. . . . I personally speculated it was defensive because China didn't want any sort of UN fact-finding missions in Xinjiang or any place like that. But it did become somewhat more pronounced.[29]

Ambassador C had a similar recollection of the period up to 2018:

I don't remember the Chinese ever taking the initiative to bring something [to the Council], but I do remember them getting increasingly vocal in pushing back some of the human rights concerns that the UN Department of Political Affairs (DPA) would raise. . . . They would be increasingly outspoken on the principle of non-interference in the internal affairs of other states. . . . The DPA did not have the ability to put something up on the agenda formally . . . in the chamber, but usually they would ask to brief the Council on any other business behind closed doors as part of the consultation. . . . The Chinese and the Russians would often use the occasion to oppose whatever it was that had been raised. The Maldives would be a good example, where China would say, "How in the world could anything that happens in the Maldives be a threat to the international peace and security? A small state with internal tensions should have nothing to do with the Security Council."[30]

'Ambassador F' recalls that China then began to extend this practice (of rejecting informal briefings) to one of rejecting both formal and informal briefings to the Council on the human rights situations in particular countries. They recalled how the UN High Commissioner for Human Rights himself was formally blocked from attending a Council session in New York on Syria in 2017–2018, despite having travelled specifically from Geneva for that purpose, because of Russian and Chinese objections.[31]

Ambassador C described this increasingly hostile approach to China's overall human rights diplomacy as seeking to narrow the Security Council's mandate:

It was consistent with their concerns about overemphasis on human rights, on internal interference, etc. that they had elsewhere. When the Council was looking at Burundi, China said that we simply shouldn't look at Burundi, because that's an internal matter. . . . So there was a trust factor that the African leaders saw China as protecting them against the scrutiny of the Council in terms of how they were managing internal political tensions. That gave the Chinese automatic allies in the Council on many issues.[32]

The ambassador noted that the Security Council's procedural votes were carried by an affirmative vote of nine of its fifteen members; a de facto coalition of China, Russia, and the Council's three African countries therefore came close to a blocking minority in its own right. However, China's approach could also be counterintuitive:

> China seemed to see the Syria file as being an important symbol of being able to push back against Western ideas about human rights, responsibilities, protections, etc. They also used Yemen as a way to criticize the United States and its allies. I think they saw Yemen as an opportunity to poke the Americans in the eyes for being close partners with Saudi Arabia and others that were waging the war in Yemen.[33]

According to Ambassador D, China began adopting a similar, narrowing strategy on human rights at the UNHRC in Geneva after about 2016. The diplomat also reported similar hostility in the Security Council on China's part towards any independent criticism of human rights practices:

> Previously, I would have said that they had been passive and had never come out [unless] direct Chinese interests were engaged. And those interests were quite narrowly defined as around Taiwan, around 'one country, two systems' in Hong Kong and around certain aspects of human rights. Then, in Geneva, they started to get more assertive on the human rights piece and started to be more allied to Russia and certain other nations, particularly in Africa. So, they would deliberately, instead of standing back in the Human Rights Council, support Syria or they would support the Africans who were pushing back on the HRC.
>
> Sometimes when I was at the Human Rights Council and they were trying to stop NGOs from speaking, they were just overly aggressive. They couldn't work with us to get a compromise. And the Chinese of ten years before wouldn't have done that, wouldn't want to stick their necks too high above the parapet if there wasn't a way forward that could be found. This was really in-your-face stuff.[34]

Once the human rights agenda began to focus on their own policies and practices in Xinjiang, Chinese diplomacy then went into overdrive:

> And then we got the whole Uyghur thing starting up. This is another big difference, I think: in the past, human rights resolutions that were against Chinese policies, the Chinese had either ignored them as irrelevant or they threatened to veto; and I think for the first time around 2018, in Geneva the Chinese started to get people and other countries to make a statement saying how brilliant the Chinese were for looking after the Uyghurs. So they started, again, to come out fighting, not just to be passive, but go on the offensive and get loads of people signing up to their tangential statements.[35]

Ambassador E confirmed this escalation of Chinese diplomatic assertiveness, recalling the annual UN Permanent Forum on Indigenous Issues meeting in 2018, when Uyghur issues were gathering global attention:

> It was Dolkun Isa, the president of the World Uyghur Congress, that represented this German NGO at this committee on Indigenous populations. They [China] tried everything to prevent him from participating in the meeting. And they intervened with the secretary-general and even had the secretary-general call the German ambassador to discuss the issue. . . . The secretary-general told the German ambassador this has repercussions for his relations with China. But, in the end, the secretary-general was re-elected. So it wasn't that bad. But it demonstrated the extent to which China tries to influence the UN.[36]

The same UNSC ambassador observed that Germany led a push with the Americans and British for a resolution on China's Uyghur policy at the UN's Third Committee which deals with social, humanitarian, and cultural issues in 2020. The statement, which had attracted twenty-three countries in 2019, attracted thirty-nine that year. "China hated this," the diplomat said. "Actually, according to reports, the (relevant) director-general was fired in the Chinese Foreign Ministry because he was not able to prevent it."[37]

Ambassador E also recalled a Xinjiang-focussed event in May 2020 featuring Human Rights Watch and Amnesty International, supported by the United States, the UK, and Australia:

> The Germans invited the new UNHRC High Commissioner Ms [Michelle] Bachelet to participate and, you know, just before [the event], she said "no", she could not participate. We tried to get her deputy, Ms [Ilze Brands] Kehris, the Latvian ASG (assistant secretary general), and she also said "no", she couldn't participate either. So, this is maybe only one example, but you could feel that . . . the secretary-general [of the UN] has not been very clear in countering violations of the charter when it came to human rights.[38]

Another example of China's hardening approach to multilateral human rights diplomacy has been Chinese efforts to defund UN programmes and positions, particularly field positions reporting on human rights violations. Three of the ambassadors interviewed had clear recollections of China's tactics in the Fifth Committee, which approves the UN's budget, to leverage its newfound significance as a major funder of the UN system.[39] Ambassador A recalled:

> There's the G77 plus China on one side of the room. There is a like-minded group on the other side of the room with Australia, the US, the Europeans, Japan, and all the richer countries that pay their share. . . . And then there's a moment where . . . the Chinese representative starts moving his chair in between the two groups because China . . . at a certain point it is like 'fuck this'—it's very vivid—so it's totally in their interest that they become a cost-cutting force. This is around either 2014 or 2015. However, that's where the story gets worse. . . . So you have China on your side, but what do they try to do? . . . They start using this leverage through this intermediary role to request cuts in the budget, which is new, but then it's infected by their indifference to the human rights expansion that has occurred at the UN . . . so the budget cuts they seek in the peacekeeping budget are to cut out of the peacekeeping missions these human rights positions, like women's rights, children's rights, prevention of sexual violence, or just straight up human rights positions.[40]

Ambassador C also reflected on this effort:

> On the budget discussions, whether in the UN Advisory Committee on Administrative and Budgetary Questions (ACABQ) or the UN Fifth Committee, they [China] would be much more active in 2016–2018 in trying to strip out things like human rights models. This became a particular problem during the Trump administration because the Trump administration no longer provided the momentum behind maintaining the human rights monitoring [role], so part of the issue behind maintaining the human rights focus stalled under the Trump administration. This meant that the Russians and the Chinese were able to push towards stripping out human rights funding. They very rarely succeeded. There were usually different deals done to maintain the budget for human rights because the budget process in the UN tends to be done by consensus through trade-offs. But they became much more vocal in trying to do it and occasionally would succeed in reducing the budget for things like human rights.[41]

Ambassador F offers a more graphic account of China leveraging its new funding prominence to degrade the UN system's human rights functions after the Office of the High Commissioner for Human Rights in 2017 named various Chinese human rights defenders who had either died in captivity or had been detained on questionable grounds:[42]

> The UN Human Rights Council had sixty-five presences [around the world] and many of the posts are on the peacekeeping account . . . not part of the regular HRC budget . . . as a result of human rights provisions being included in a text adopted by the Security Council. Those posts were being attacked. . . . In the Fifth Committee, they would oppose the funding of

> these posts and, yes, they did so successfully. . . . The Office of the Human Rights Commissioner also had a plan to decentralize, to move several posts out of Geneva into the field. And it was modest—5% of the staff in Geneva were to be moved out—and that was also killed late in the day. . . . They [China] can marshal a lot of countries to do their bidding when it comes to voting on these issues. And so the UNHRC would often succeed [in] getting something through ACABQ. But then when the proposal is sent on and the peacekeeping budgets are presented to the Fifth Committee, that's where they would attack. They started doing that in 2016–2017.[43]

According to Ambassador F, China increased its direct political pressure on both the High Commissioner, Zeid Ra'ad al-Hussein, and UN Secretary-General António Guterres on the human rights agenda:

> The Chinese kept calling the High Commissioner [for Human Rights] an enemy of China in their meetings. They kept saying to him "you will be an enemy of China if you do this". And then he would do it. So therefore, he became an enemy of China. . . . The High Commissioner challenged the Chinese, saying that if he was infringing on their sovereignty by making comments pertinent to their internal situation . . . then they [China] should provide the UN with the legal reasoning as to how it was that criticism of this sort amounted to an infringement. This is what the High Commissioner would throw back at China. He said that the General Assembly had already made it clear . . . that verbal criticism doesn't amount to a usurpation of sovereign decision-making. . . . He wasn't sending in the commandos.[44]

According to Ambassador F, UN Secretary-General Guterres also came under pressure from the Chinese upon taking office in 2016. They recalled the Deputy High Commissioner, an Australian, being approached by the UN Secretariat to change course. According to the ambassador, the Secretariat said:

> "We would like you in OHCHR to do more on economic, social and cultural rights and focus more on that." So she responded acidly, saying: "look, we will do that, we're happy to do that, but who's going to do the civil and political rights in the UN? You tell us who will do the civil and political rights and we will do the economic, social, and cultural." Of course, no one else will do it. And so, in that sense, they were trying to sort of get [it toned down by] the OHCHR.[45]

Finally, Ambassador F reflected on comments by the secretary-general on the changing geo-political environment that the UN was facing with China's rise and its implications for the overall human rights agenda:

> Guterres said something along the lines that he didn't believe that there was a universal rights agenda, that the rights agenda was fundamentally

> Western, and he gave the impression that . . . the UN was already tacking to a China-dominant twenty-first century. This was being given some flavour by the secretary-general's thinking. He was bending in that direction.[46]

At a more general level, Ambassador C reflected on the differing importance attached to the overall human rights mission of the UN under two successive secretaries-general—Ban Ki-moon (2006–2016) and Guterres (from 2017)—as China's change agenda became clearer:

> Ban would show up for all this stuff [convened by China] but I did get the sense that it was more ceremonial pandering than substantive pandering, whereas I think Guterres would try much harder to think about what the Chinese were after substantively and try to address it. Where Ban would say, "okay, I'm showing up for this meeting; that means I'm checking this Chinese box" . . . his instincts were not to reflect politically on what the Chinese were after. . . . [Ban] was more vocal on human rights . . . as one of the pillars of the UN and [he considered] that it was his duty to speak out on human rights when there were problems. Whereas I think Guterres was trying to figure out how to maintain his close relationship with all the member states. And human rights was not a winning portfolio, particularly when the Trump administration wasn't being an engine behind human rights. So I think it was a different relationship that Ban and Guterres had with the Chinese, although both recognized the importance of maintaining a close relationship with Beijing.[47]

Xi Jinping's position on 'universal human rights' had already been made crystal-clear in Document Number 9 in 2013. It is therefore unsurprising that this was translated into a changing Chinese posture at the UNSC on human rights as early as the 2014–2015 debates on North Korea. Nor is it surprising that this further intensified following the release of China's new approach to multilateral reform and its broader 'community of common destiny' agenda in 2015. More significant is China's preparedness to leverage its newfound financial and political muscle to defund UN human rights positions and pressure the High Commissioner, UN Secretariat, and secretary-general to show more sensitivity to its political concerns. Pressure was also applied to UN activities in relation to China's domestic and international political sensitivities on Xinjiang after 2018. For these reasons, all ambassadors observed a growing Chinese effort to roll back the UN's traditional human rights pillar. As Ambassador C concluded:

> There was the quip that the US undervalues the multilateral system, Europe overvalues the multilateral system, and China wants to change the

multilateral system; and you could find evidence to support that case. But things like trying to strip out [rights], or add rights between states rather than individual rights, were the sorts of games the Chinese would play with language. You could draw the conclusion they were trying to change the basic operating system of the UN and the underlying principles of the UN.[48]

A New Approach to UN Peacekeeping Operations

Several ambassadors also observed China's approach to UN peacekeeping operations change after 2015, when it became the second biggest contributor to the peacekeeping budget.[49] Ambassador A said they would have welcomed Chinese support to fill pronounced gaps in peacekeeping but its renewed engagement proved to "create very problematic dynamics on the Security Council":[50]

> Protecting civilians is written into all of our resolutions and expectations that the peacekeepers are going to be very mobile, out and about, protecting people. That evolution has occurred and, at just the time this evolution is happening . . . China's numbers go from 500 to 1,200 to 2,500. . . . But they, in the Security Council, start using this unprecedented leverage . . . and they start seeking to use it to set us back, to bring peacekeeping back to the Middle Ages, basically—to have peacekeepers just kind of stay on their bases and not be out and about . . . . And it's a battle for the soul of peacekeeping.[51]

Ambassador A cautioned that enthusiasm for Chinese commitments, such as Xi's promise in 2016 to develop an 8,000-person standby peacekeeping force,[52] should be tempered by wariness of this 'passive' attitude:

> What they're bringing in is passive peacekeeping. We have a rich empirical dataset from the 1990s of what happens when peacekeepers just stand by whilst civilians are being killed. Because there is so much more conflict and more atrocities happening . . . China is trying to pull peacekeeping in a very dangerous direction. They're also trying to get [control of] the DPKO [Department of Peacekeeping Operations]. They claim to run DPKO . . . so they're trying to bring in non-interference. They're bringing this really interesting, problematic thing. They're trying to bring non-interference to an interference enterprise.[53]

China's changing posture against 'intrusive' peacekeeping operations complements its campaign against alleged human rights–based 'interference' in the domestic autonomy of sovereign states. Rather than human rights criticism, however, China's sovereignty concerns relate to the operational remit of peacekeeping operations to: protect civilian populations from human rights abuses from their own governments; secure access for humanitarian aid to civilians at times of internal armed conflict involving national governments; and/or protect civilians from all parties to a domestic dispute. In other words, the Chinese position is to roll back the post-Srebrenica/post-Rwanda consensus on the level of activism required on the part of UN peacekeeping operations to effectively discharge their mandates and protect the basic human rights of civilian populations. Beijing has sought to leverage China's level of troop contributions and its overall financial contributions to the peacekeeping budget to bring about a substantive change in UNPKO doctrine to make it more compatible with China's national sovereignty agenda. The vigorous, assertive, and nationalist prosecution of the inviolability of Chinese national sovereignty, as a core foreign policy priority for the Chinese government, represents a central part of Xi's clearly articulated ideological worldview. Indeed, as with human rights, Xi was seeking to internationalize a Chinese domestic political norm, thereby reducing the international normative pressure against the legitimacy of the CCP's historical position on universal human rights, its domestic monopoly on political power, and its doctrine of absolute state sovereignty.

Securing UN Candidatures, Leveraging Its Contribution to the UN Budget, and Influencing Other UN Delegations

Those ambassadors interviewed also pointed to significant changes in the size of China's diplomatic establishment at the UN in New York. They noted new levels of Chinese activism to secure the leadership of multiple UN agencies. They also reported evidence of China's preparedness to use its mission's resources and increasing financial support for the UN system to aggressively pursue Chinese foreign policy interests with other diplomatic missions. In some cases, ambassadors pointed to examples of China successfully pressuring smaller foreign governments in their capitals to withdraw from New York troublesome ambassadors who were resisting China's interests. The overall impact, as reported in these accounts, was a much more assertive China than before 2012.

On the size of the Chinese diplomatic establishment and success in securing candidatures for the leadership of various UN specialized agencies, Ambassador A observed:

> They've left everyone in the dust in terms of specialized and independent agencies. . . . The size of China's mission in New York has doubled and tripled. . . . It's like night and day. They're staffing permanently now in a way that they didn't before.[54]

Ambassador B agreed, noting the role of agency heads in 'norm-setting and standard-setting' within the UN system:

> What I think I've noticed, what everyone has noticed, is [the number of] Chinese candidacies for the heads of UN agencies and, in that respect, they have been more assertive. . . . But the other part of it is that, by placing Chinese nationals at the head of agencies, they then have a seat at the table with the secretary-general on his executive board, and can shape the way the UN approaches things that bump up against core interests of China. And I think that's part of the strategy. I also feel that it's partly an influence game. China wants to maximize its influence around the world . . . and one of the ways you do that in the UN system is not only through the prestigious positions that they had in certain specialized agencies, but also through money. . . . I think that they're perfectly happy to be able to use the amount of money that they put into the system as a lever to get their way on certain things.[55]

Ambassador C pointed to China's changing practices in scrutinizing the appointment by the Secretary-General of Special Representatives (SRSGs), who are granted the autonomy to advocate on specified topics. Ambassador C described the evolution of the Chinese position succinctly:

> The Chinese, in the past, always responded immediately upon presentation [of a candidate for SRSG] with "whoever the Secretary-General wishes to appoint has our confidence". So the Chinese did not play this game like the other P5 did. After about 2014 or 2015, it changed. The Chinese played the same game the others did. The Chinese asked for extensive documentation and background if they didn't already know the candidate, so that was a significant change.

The ambassador said it was not until 2018 that China joined the club of P5 countries in thwarting a French candidate proposed as Special Representative of the Secretary-General for South Sudan:

> The Chinese, with the Russians, were hoping to block the candidate from going forward. . . . If you go back and look at the appointments,

> the appointment of a Chinese national as the No.2 in Sudan . . . and the appointment of Deborah Lyons [from Canada] as SRSG in Afghanistan, which took place more or less at the same time [is significant] because of the pressure from the Chinese to have that DSRSG [i.e. the deputy] position in Juba. It's unusual to have the DSRSG in Juba be a non-African national when you also have a non-African as head. You don't often have both the political DSRSG and SRSG not from Africa if it's an African mission. So I suspect that not only did the Chinese put pressure on the SG and use the approval of Deborah Lyons for Afghanistan as leverage, but I also bet they put pressure on the African Union, because the African Union would normally not accept a non-African DSRSG.[56]

While diplomatic manoeuvring over the appointment of a deputy head of the UN mission in Sudan may seem inconsequential in the wider scheme of things, it is an unmistakable change in the pattern of Chinese foreign policy behaviour. Ambassador C observed:

> The Chinese had force commanders in Sudan and elsewhere but, in terms of the head of a peace operation, [the first Chinese SRSG] was the Chinese special envoy for the Great Lakes Region[57] whom Guterres appointed [in 2019] under pressure from Beijing. It was different that Beijing had decided to insist on an SRSG position; that was something new. . . . I don't look at it as being quite unreasonable, but the question is: once the Chinese are appointed, are they truly UN representatives or is it an outpost for the Beijing MFA [Ministry of Foreign Affairs]?[58]

The same ambassador noted that China became more active in securing staffing positions for its nationals at the Department of Political Affairs in New York, which coordinates the SRSGs' field operations. "The DPA in 2015 got its first Chinese JPO (Junior Professional Officer). The Chinese insisted on having a JPO in DPA and it was quickly followed by a second, and I think there's even a third now. So what's consistent with that timeline is to insert JPOs in the system starting around 2015."[59] These appointments become the pool from which the UN Secretariat over time would recruit their long-term UN policy staff.

Ambassador C speculated that Secretary-General Guterres was influenced by China's promise of a new ten-year discretionary fund:[60]

> My impression was that Guterres was very deferential to all the P5. Certainly, the peace and security fund and the development fund that the Chinese announced from Xi Jinping's 2015 General Assembly speech very much became a joint venture between the SG's office and the Chinese. That was a

> unique tool where the SG and the Chinese worked directly on how to use the funds that Xi had announced in 2015. . . . I can't think of anything where the other P5 had such a tool that was an asset for the SG to use. Obviously, the US was the largest donor of voluntary contributions globally in terms of the absolute amount . . . but the Chinese had its own fund in the UN that they could manage with the secretary-general. . . . I think that was unique. The Saudis did a trust fund. It was initially small, but it grew, for counter-terrorism. The Saudis did not co-manage that trust fund; the Saudis turned over the funds to the UN with the clear understanding that the UN was responsible for those funds. There was not a co-management for those funds in the same way as those funds that the Chinese set up.[61]

The ambassador noted the fund was announced during Ban's secretary-generalship, but "the funding didn't really start flowing until 2017, which was when Guterres came in". The Peace and Development Fund's rules ensure Beijing is consulted on proposals before they are endorsed by a steering committee dominated by Chinese officials.[62]

Ambassador D described China's interest in the leadership of UN agencies, and its preparedness to deploy financial leverage to gain them, as transforming over a fifteen-year period:

> China just got more and more powerful. They just bought more and more of the UN and extended their tentacles everywhere. So, in 2006 the Chinese had one of the under-secretary positions [the under-secretary-general for economic and social affairs]. . . . I went to see him and he said that "naturally, I am supposed to do what Beijing wants, but the UN keeps expecting me to do what the secretary-general wants". He was prepared to say this fantastically openly and I found it very strange. That is actually open-source [information] because he said it again in a speech about ten years later[63] and it's been picked up by the press.

Ambassador D pointed to the scale of 'ad hoc money' flowing to UN institutions by 2018:

> By 2018, China was putting a lot of ad hoc money into the UN. Guterres would say: "If you ever needed money in a hurry for a special project, the Chinese would give it, no questions asked."[64]

At the same time, the number of senior Chinese UN officials expanded rapidly:

> They had many more Chinese officials at senior and other levels of the UN system. . . . They got FAO [the Food and Agriculture Organization]. They

were prevented, because the West got its act together, from taking WIPO [the World Intellectual Property Organization]. They got the Board of Auditors. They were really keen to extend their reach, not just on the political side of the UN, but also in the way that it is run. And then the UN decided to open up new field positions to suitably qualified staff from capitals. . . . The Chinese put 400 people directly into that program; the West couldn't manage 400 staff between them . . . and the Chinese have also started extending their reach by taking on SRSG positions. . . . The Africans, Brazilians, and South Africans are very clear-eyed about what the Chinese are doing; they call it blackmail, except for the ones that the Chinese have bought to block consensus on Security Council reform. There are about ten African countries who are probably paid directly by the Chinese in New York.[65]

Ambassador E used Security Council reform as an example of how China wielded its political and financial influence across the wider UN system to secure its objectives:

The interest of China is not to have a reform of the Security Council, because that would automatically lead to a stronger position for its Asian rivals, for Japan and for India . . . and therefore, they work very hard on the issue. You could see that when the inter-governmental negotiations [on Security Council reform (IGN)] were on the agenda of the General Assembly, the Chinese Ambassador attended those sessions . . . and, in particular, they were very aggressive in influencing the most important group in this game, and these are the fifty-four African states. While on the one hand saying that they support the African position, that Africa should be represented strongly on the Security Council, they did everything to prevent these IGN talks, which are basically talks to develop a real text-based negotiation—where you have actually a text to negotiate, with brackets in it, where you narrow down differences. They want to prevent that. And they have been influencing the Africans to a degree that for a normal person is unimaginable.[66]

Ambassador E highlighted how China would undercut African negotiators by going above their heads to their home governments:

During 2020 . . . when the African spokesperson, the ambassador of Sierra Leone, actually said that they wanted to have a single consolidated text as a basis, they [China] intervened in the capital and the ambassador was withdrawn. They did this with Zambia a few years before. They did this with Jamaica, which is not African but . . . they were the facilitator, the co-chair or the chair, and he was making some progress. He was a very good Jamaican ambassador at the time and he had to step down. So, the Chinese work on capitals: they tell capitals if they don't behave, they may not finance some infrastructure. They go through the capital and it's, of course, very embarrassing

> when you get a call from a capital, you know, taking away the rug under your feet. And this is what they do. They're very aggressive on this issue.[67]

The overall picture, therefore, to emerge over this period, as reported through these ambassadorial interviews, was a change in Chinese strategy towards UN staffing, candidatures, and political leverage—both in relation to the UN Secretariat and to UN member states from around 2015. This trend appears to have accelerated after 2016 with the establishment of a Chinese-funded and co-managed UN Peace and Development Trust Fund. Assertiveness, however, blends into aggression with the reported reasons for the withdrawal of certain ambassadors who did not conform with China's wishes when major Chinese policy interests were at stake with the possibility of Security Council reform (Beijing being deeply opposed to any measure that might result in India and Japan becoming permanent Council members).

Changing the Normative Language of the UN

Ambassadors reported that, apart from Chinese efforts to weaken preexisting normative language in UNSC and other UN resolutions on human rights, China also sought to introduce new language into resolutions supportive of Chinese-led multilateral organizations (such as the Shanghai Cooperation Organization and the Belt and Road Initiative) and concepts (such as the 'community of common destiny' agenda). Ambassador B noted that China had long sought to insert some of these into Security Council Resolutions:

> The Russians and the Chinese would constantly try to insert the Shanghai Cooperation Organization. You know, in any resolution there's always the sort of preambular language where you list all the regional organizations that support you and with which you work so well. And it's prestigious, you know, if you're in a Security Council resolution. . . . I do think that they wanted to add the legitimacy that you get from having those organizations named in Council resolutions.[68]

The ambassador speculated these tactics were "more to try to create networks where Beijing was at the centre, that would work in a complementary way with the UN, as opposed to trying to supplant the UN in any way".[69]

Ambassador D noted the language of international political legitimacy was increasingly 'hard fought over' with China:

> [The West] woke up to this sort of thing late. . . . Some language got through. But then more countries became willing to push back. Some of that is because you reach a point in the UN negotiations where everyone just kind of thinks that "this has gone on far too long, here's the compromise, we'll go for the compromise". But I wouldn't say this has necessarily reflected any real-world shift in perceptions.[70]

The ambassador said that, once Western delegations began to recognize the language of Xi Jinping Thought—such as "all this 'win-win' cooperation stuff"—they had to argue "very hard" to excise it from future resolutions: "Western delegations . . . managed it. But you could tell that it was getting chalked up on the ledger as something to be contested [later on] or paid us back."[71] The ambassador concluded that these efforts to change multilateral language were part of a much broader Chinese strategy: "There is this whole other piece with their approach to competition to reset the rules of international affairs. For the Russians, that's all about shafting the West. But for the Chinese they actually have, in their terms, a positive agenda and they see a good way of doing it."[72] Ambassador D also saw deepening collaboration between China and the UN Secretariat on resolution language, institutional arrangements, and the long-standing normative assumptions of the UN system as reflecting the different approach of the new secretary-general: "Ban was prepared to come out with quite a lot of values-based statements. But Guterres is a real politician. He very rarely wastes time on that sort of thing."[73]

Conclusion

This chapter has not sought to present a comprehensive history of China's changing foreign policy behaviour at the UN under Xi Jinping. Its purpose has been much narrower than that. It has been to distil the observations of a number of senior foreign diplomats drawn from the real world of multilateral diplomacy over the period 2007–2022 with a view to identifying changes in China's overall foreign policy posture. Of course, this approach has several limitations. These ambassadors did not represent a 'balanced' sample of the five formal geographical groupings of the UN system—although they did represent Western and non-Western states.[74] Nor were they selected to represent states known to be supportive, hostile, or neutral towards China. Some were national ambassadors. Others were senior UN officials. But most had served for at least a decade across various UN postings and were therefore capable of making assessments about changing patterns of Chinese behaviour over time. Most of these officials were also deeply critical of US policy towards the UN under the Trump administration, and many offered a combination of positive, negative, and neutral comments about China's changing posture under Xi.

These interviews have not been rigorously 'fact-checked' by, for example, putting their remarks to Chinese or UN officials for comment as to their accuracy. Their purpose has rather been to report accurately these ambassadors' perceptions and conclusions as to what they observed during their various postings and assignments. Nor have China's changing policy positions been contextualized in terms of any wider analysis of the relevant foreign policy debates of the time (such as on Syria, the DPRK, or the Maldives). Nor have we sought here to assess the merits of system-wide positions on the norms, values, structures, or funding of the UN. Rather, our purpose here has been to report on senior diplomatic observations of the *fact* of change itself; whether that change is reflected in new levels of foreign policy assertiveness since Xi's ascension in 2012; and how these changes may correlate with changes in China's domestic nationalist discourse as outlined in chapters 9 and 10.

Every ambassador who was interviewed reported major changes in China's multilateral diplomacy over the period under review as observed in: changing activism on the UNSC; newfound aggression after 2013 on the Human Rights Council; more subtle changes to UN peacekeeping operations; leveraging new levels of budgetary largesse and economic influence on smaller UN member states to secure influential positions at UN institutions or remove opposition to Chinese policy positions; and an unfolding, longer-term campaign to change the normative language of UN resolutions in a direction more accommodating of Chinese foreign policy concepts, organizations, and values (and less accommodating of the historically universalist claims of the West). Taken together, these represent significant changes in China's UN policy. Furthermore, the prosecution of each of these changes, as observed by the ambassadors, has reflected new levels of foreign policy assertiveness and—in the case of the human rights agenda—outright political aggression. Indeed, this change in posture (from passive to assertive) has been evident across the breadth of China's engagement with the UN multilateral agenda. New policy positions have not simply been announced in New York, Geneva, and national capitals and left at that. Rather, China has vigorously advanced a campaign of multilateral 'revisionism', seeking to achieve concrete change by undoing consensus positions that other states had long regarded as settled international norms. This newfound diplomatic activism, assertiveness, and aggression has been observed by all the ambassadors interviewed.

There is a strong degree of correlation between these foreign policy developments, on the one hand (including the vigour of their prosecution), and China's unfolding domestic Marxist-Nationalist narrative, on the other. The domestic discourse about China's increasing national power relative to the United States is clearly reflected in China's new national self-confidence in advancing its own multilateral agenda. It is also important to recall that Xi's nationalist rallying cry on the 'the great rejuvenation of the Chinese nation' is grounded in the language of the 2014 and 2018 Central Foreign Affairs Work Conferences, as are Xi's 'new type of international relations', China's struggle for the 'reform of the global order', and 'China moving to the centre of the world stage'. These three phrases go to the future of the UN multilateral system and the broader global order. A more China-centric UN, within the Chinese analytical framework, is also fundamental to a more China-centric international system.

Furthermore, both the Marxist and nationalist language of Document Number 9 in 2013—including on the superiority of the Chinese political system and the ideological danger posed to it by Western claims to universal definitions of human rights, democracy, and associated international norms—directly informs these new levels of Chinese political activism and assertiveness in UN deliberative bodies. This is evident in China's prosecution of a new global agenda to redefine human rights and democracy with Chinese characteristics. It is most clearly seen in the China-Russia Joint Declaration of February 2022 which contains an extensive section formally redefining the critical terms of 'democracy' and 'human rights'.[75] Indeed, the binary nature of the Chinese nationalist narrative against the United States and the collective West is reflected in China's contest for influence right across the UN system, its proposals to redesign it, and—in its own language—its 'struggle' for the wider international system. This also reflects Chen Yixin's explicit claim on behalf of China's national security establishment in 2021 that Xi's new 'comprehensive national security' concept did not only span the foreign and the domestic, but was predicated more broadly on 'the rise of the East and the decline of the West'.[76]

Finally, Xi's global meta-narrative of the 'community of common destiny'—the international equivalent of his domestic narrative on the 'great rejuvenation of the Chinese nation'—has been the subject of intense Chinese diplomacy to incorporate it into the normative language of the UN system. There is an extensive documentary record of efforts to inject CCD into the formal normative declarations of the UN system.[77] Indeed, this battle was had in the UN General Assembly debate on whether to include CCD in the formal declaration recognizing the UN's seventy-fifth anniversary in 2020. As Indian media reported at the time, New Delhi joined the United States, the UK, Canada, Australia, and New Zealand in objecting to the phrase "a community with a shared future for mankind". The final text instead urged a "common future of present and coming generations".[78]

For all these reasons, the level of correlation between China's newly assertive foreign policy posture under Xi Jinping and the changed nature of his domestic nationalist narrative is significant. There is, of course, as discussed in earlier chapters, a difference between correlation and causation. There may well be other causative factors, both internal and external, driving these changes including China's 'rational actor' response to external developments over which Beijing may have had limited, if any, control. Another variable may be greater willingness on the part of the UN secretary-general, the UN Secretariat, and some member states to accommodate Chinese interests. Nonetheless, China's changing nationalist discourse, as part of Xi's overarching Marxist-Nationalist worldview, represents at least one of these causative factors by providing ideological permission to party and state actors, including Chinese diplomats, to embark on a different and more adventurous course. The level of temporal correlation between China's intensified nationalist discourse at home and the unfolding assertiveness of its actions abroad is too great to ignore.

12

Codifying the Marxist and Nationalist Dimensions of Xi Jinping Thought through the Party's 2021 Historical Resolution

> The Party has mandated that leading officials at all levels cultivate a proper worldview, outlook on life, and sense of values, all of which serve as the 'master switch' for their conduct.
>
> —*Resolution of the CCP Central Committee on the Major Achievements and Historical Experience of the Party over the Past Century, 2021*[1]

Between the 19th Party Congress in 2017 and the 20th Congress in 2022, Xi Jinping sought to synthesize the various Leninist, Marxist, and nationalist threads of his overall ideological project into the ever-expanding and increasingly authoritative canon of 'Xi Jinping Thought'. Xi had used the 19th Congress to proclaim 'a new era' in the historical evolution of the party, a new set of 'contradictions' to be dealt with, and a new body of 'thought' to guide the party's efforts in navigating these uncharted waters. Xi Jinping Thought was therefore to have a new ideological significance in shaping China's future across all policy domains, both foreign and domestic. It was to be sufficiently Marxist to provide a continuing red thread across the totality of the system but, at the same time, sufficiently malleable to cope with changing political and policy contingencies as they arose. Xi's ideology was also to have a new institutional role in cementing party discipline and consolidating his own personal hold on power. Moreover, a new ideology, at a more fundamental level, was to symbolize the passing of an earlier generation of epoch-making Chinese revolutionary leaders and the emergence of a new one. Indeed, in the tradition of both the ancient prophets and modern revolutionaries, it seemed that under Xi, all things under Heaven were to be made new.

Xi's efforts at ideological synthesis are therefore important for a number of reasons. To begin with, Xi Jinping Thought (hereinafter XJPT) seeks to ideologically legitimize political and policy change in the eyes of both the party and the people. XJPT has not only been entrenched in both the party and state constitutions. It is also underpinned by a formal resolution of the 19th Party Congress—the CCP's supreme governing body—deeming it to be "the Party's basic theory, line, and policy so as to better steer the development of the Party and people's cause".[2] XJPT's historical significance was further elevated by the November 2021 Central Committee resolution on party history, which accorded it a new ideological status within the long tradition of the Sinification of Chinese Marxism: XJPT was enshrined as 'the' body of Marxist thought to guide China through the new era, just like Deng Xiaoping Theory during the era of 'reform and opening' and Mao Zedong Thought in the earlier decades of revolution and socialist construction before 1976.

Beyond this political legitimation function, XJPT is intended to be all-encompassing in its reach. If Xi's concept of the *institutional* role of the Leninist party is all-embracing, the new *ideational* role of XJPT is similarly comprehensive in its political and policy scope. Within a year of the 2017 Party Congress, twenty-three areas were listed as having a defined limb of XJPT—from the economy through foreign policy through to the Belt and Road Initiative.[3] Media analyst Qian Gang calculated that, as of late 2018, the four most frequently cited were 'Xi Jinping Thought on Military Strength', 'Xi Jinping Foreign Relations Thought', 'Xi Jinping Ecological Civilization Thought', and 'Xi Jinping Economic Thought with Chinese Characteristics'—underlining XJPT as the comprehensive canonical authority across all political and public policy debate.[4] As John Garrick and Yan Chang Bennett have argued, XJPT represents "a totalising discourse" which gives "little room for dissent."[5] This had largely been the case even before XJPT was officially proclaimed as the new orthodoxy at the 19th Party Congress. Indeed, Xi's 'Four Comprehensives' (*sigequanmian*[6]) by late 2014 had already imposed new ideological disciplines on internal party debate.[7] These would be doubly reinforced by XJPT's formal elevation at the 19th Congress.

Defining Xi Jinping Thought

Nonetheless, despite XJPT's almost encyclopaedic remit, it is wrong to assume that it offers an entirely new, self-contained, integrated theoretical system. It does not offer an alternative epistemology or methodology to that of classical Marxism-Leninism as interpreted through Mao Zedong's principal works on historical and dialectical materialism, contradiction, and practice. Indeed, Xi explicitly affirms these previous approaches but is critical of the party for not having rigorously applied classical Marxist methodologies to the contradictions confronting it under his immediate predecessors. As noted previously, where XJPT does differ significantly from the past is in its periodization of recent Chinese history, its redefinition of the party's principal contradiction, and its articulation of the party's more detailed policy challenges arising in this new era. Beyond these three major changes, however, XJPT does not offer the party a new, free-standing ideological system. Rather, XJPT is highly elastic, building on the ideological inheritance of Mao and Deng, albeit with a decidedly stronger preference for the methodological approach and many of the conceptual conclusions of the former. And, as with Mao Zedong Thought, XJPT can be moulded to meet the party's future political needs by legitimizing actions that Xi may need to take in response to as-yet-unknown policy pressures in the years that lie ahead. In summary, XJPT seeks to *legitimize* political and policy action authorized by the leader. It seeks to *totalize* its conceptual and operational scope, albeit still within the framework of orthodox Chinese Marxism-Leninism. But it also seeks to retain sufficient policy *flexibility* to adapt to unfolding political needs.

These core, defining features of XJPT were underscored by the 'Resolution on the Major Achievements and Historical Experience of the Party over the Past Century' adopted in November 2021. This was only the third occasion on which the party has adopted a formal resolution on party history. The first was in 1945 when Mao Zedong Thought was entrenched as the authorized interpretation of Chinese Marxism, while also formalizing Mao's own power within the party by excoriating the 'left dogmatist' Wang Ming and the 'counter-revolutionary' Zhang Guotao following the party rectification movement in Yan'an.[8] The second was in 1981 when Deng condemned Mao's errors in the Anti-Rightist Movement, the Great Leap Forward, and the Cultural Revolution, thereby consolidating Deng's political position in the unfolding period of reform and opening, and developing what would eventually become Deng Xiaoping Theory.[9] The party's 'historical resolutions' are therefore epoch-defining both in ideological substance and in political perception, having previously formalized two seismic power transitions: first to Mao between the 1935 Zunyi Conference and Yan'an in 1942; and then to Deng following the purge of the Gang of Four in 1976 and the marginalization of Hua Guofeng after 1978.

The 2021 resolution formalized the party's third great power transition in its history to Xi Jinping. This process began in 2012 with his appointment as general secretary. It was accelerated in 2017 with the announcement of 'a new era' in party history, and reinforced by the party's redefinition of its principal contradiction. However, it was the formalization of XJPT by the 2021 'historical resolution' as "the Marxism of the new era"—and therefore as the new body of ideological orthodoxy to guide China's future, as Mao Zedong Thought had done before—that underscored the historical significance of this political and ideological transition to the new Xi Jinping era. As the 2021 resolution itself stated: "These documents [of 1945 and 1981] unified the whole Party in thinking and action at key historical junctures, played a vital guiding role in advancing the cause of the Party and the people, and their basic points and conclusions remain valid to this day." By implication, the 2021 resolution is seen to be similarly significant: Xi's "new era" is referred to as a "new historical period"; XJPT will provide a "guiding role" for the whole party to remain "great, glorious and correct"; and its basic truths reflect a "deeper understanding of the underlying laws" not just now but long into the future. In other words, the resolution is of central importance to Xi's enduring political authority by further entrenching the ideological status of his eponymous, ever-expanding, and increasingly authoritative body of thought.

The Elevation of Xi Jinping Thought as 'the' Marxism for Modern China and the 21st Century

An enduring thematic of Xi Jinping's party leadership has been the reification of ideology itself. This has been the case since Xi's earliest pronouncements at the party's Central Ideology and Propaganda Work Conference in 2013 and the unauthorized release of Document Number 9. However, the 2021 'historical resolution' takes the centrality of Xi's Marxist-Nationalist ideology further than any other party document since his political ascension in 2012. Indeed, it is arguably the party's most densely ideological document since 1981. It speaks at length on party ideology as the 'proper' orthodox method of viewing reality; an assertion of 'scientific truth'; an ideational claim to the inevitable 'decisive victory' of Chinese Marxism by repelling the liberal democratic capitalist worldviews of the West; a means of mass psychological 'mobilization'; as well as now offering Xi Jinping Thought as a basis for the party's long-term political and ideological unity, reflecting the 'common will' of the Chinese people. Indeed, it claims:

> Marxism has brought to light the laws governing the development of human society. It is a scientific truth for understanding and shaping the world. . . . In China, Marxism has been fully tested as a scientific truth . . . and its open-ended nature and contemporary relevance have been fully demonstrated.

To this, the resolution adds Chinese Marxism's superiority over Western democratic capitalism, emphasizing that this contest was now of global ideological significance:

> Our continued success in adapting Marxism to the Chinese context and the needs of our times has enabled Marxism to take on a fresh face in the eyes of the world, and significantly shifted the worldwide historical evolution of and contest between the two different ideologies and social systems of socialism and capitalism in a way that favors socialism.

Indeed, the resolution's plain-speaking conclusion is that Xi Jinping's China now sees itself in open ideological conflict with the West:

> The Party has maintained an accurate perspective on the trends of collisions taking place worldwide between different ideas and cultures, as well as of the profound changes in Chinese people's ways of thinking.

It underscores, once again, the Manichaean nature of Xi's worldview of the underlying Marxist contest for China's national soul in the face of the inroads of Western ideological influence:

> Our faith in Marxism, the great ideal of communism, and the common ideal of socialism with Chinese characteristics are our source of strength and the anchor of our political soul as Chinese communists, and they constitute the ideological foundation for maintaining the Party's unity.

And, in an ideological analogy reminiscent of General Jack D. Ripper's obsession in Stanley Kubrick's *Dr. Strangelove* with America needing to preserve its "precious bodily fluids",[10] the resolution "stressed that ideals and convictions are like *essential nutrients*; without them, we would become frail and susceptible to corruption, greed, degeneracy, and decadence" (my emphasis).

While the party's 2021 'Third Historical Resolution' may appear to some as little more than a formalistic reassertion of the general theoretical claims of Chinese Marxism, in reality, it goes much further than that. It not only proclaims afresh core Marxist-Leninist doctrine but also declares, with the full and formal institutional backing of the CCP, the newfound ideological status of Xi Jinping Thought for the future of Marxism itself. Following a long exposition of what it presents as the ten core components of XJPT, the resolution proclaims that "these strategic concepts and innovative ideas are the important outcomes of the Party's theoretical development based on a deeper understanding of the underlying laws of socialism with Chinese characteristics". Of itself, this too may seem unremarkable compared to previous party communiqués extolling each leader's contribution to the Sinification of Chinese Marxism. But the 2021 resolution goes beyond previous orthodoxy by making the definitive claim that XJPT is now "the Marxism of contemporary China and of the 21st century" (*shi dangdai makesizhuyi, ershiyi shiji de makesizhuyi*) and "embodies the best of China's culture and ethos for our times and represents a new breakthrough in adapting Marxism to the Chinese context". Both the Chinese text and the official English translation are equally clear in this definitive rendering of XJPT's new status within the canon of Chinese *and* global Marxism.

Xi's Ideological Reappraisal of Mao in the Historical Resolution

Xi had already made explicit his position on the ideological significance of both Mao and Deng during the earliest years of his leadership. His January 2013 address to the Central Party School, discussed in chapter 4, described the ideological symmetry between these two principal eras of post-1949 Chinese politics. His political message to reformers and conservatives alike was that repudiating either period was tantamount to historical 'nihilism', which would be disastrous for the party's long-term claim to political legitimacy. In doing so, Xi was deeply mindful of the repudiation of Stalin under Khrushchev which, in Xi's view, resulted in the long-term ideological unravelling of the Soviet Union. As Xi himself stated bluntly just after his ascension: "To dismiss the history of the Soviet Union and the Soviet Communist Party, to dismiss Lenin and Stalin, and to dismiss everything else is to engage in historic nihilism, and it confuses our thoughts and undermines the party's organization on all levels."[11] Xi's ideological response to this 'nihilist' threat was to promulgate the concept of 'the two that cannot be denied' (*liangge buneng fouding*)—that the Mao and Deng periods both needed to be embraced to secure the party's legitimacy. As Kerry Brown and Una Aleksandra Bērziņa-Čerenkova have neatly distilled this formulation:

> The post-Reform and Opening up period cannot be used to deny the pre-Reform and Opening up period, and vice versa. It was made clear that correcting mistakes and learning lessons was an acceptable part of the process, but that there could be no refutal of the path chosen by China in 1949.[12]

Within these parameters, however, one of the most important elements of Xi's ideological project has been to adjust the party's critical narrative on Mao's ideological and political errors and excesses. Equally significant, Xi has also begun criticizing Deng by raising questions about ideological and institutional laxity during the reform and opening period. On close inspection, the 2021 resolution adds substantively to both these ideological reappraisals. On the Mao period, the resolution stated that, in January 1935, the party had "laid the groundwork for establishing the leading position within the Central Committee of the correct Marxist line chiefly represented by Comrade Mao Zedong, as well as the formation of the first generation of the central collective leadership with Mao as its core". This formulation frames Mao as the party's principal ideological interpreter of Chinese Marxism (and its effective 'core leader') after the Zunyi Conference. By contrast, the 1981 resolution simply referred to Mao as the 'leader of the Central Committee and the Red Army' after 1935. The significance of this most recent historical amendment is that it underpins Xi's own claim to now be both the party's 'core leader' and its new ideologist-in-chief. By implication, Xi's political and ideological status in 2021 was now analogous to Mao's after the 1935 Zunyi Conference. And, just as Mao had to deal with the Zhang Guotao anti-party clique at Zunyi, the 2021 document declared Xi was justified in dealing with corrupt and undisciplined elements—both in the CCP and in the PLA—to consolidate his own political leadership. It is also important to note that the 2021 resolution's historical treatment of Mao is much briefer in its critique of his leftist errors during the Cultural Revolution than in 1981. In 2021 there are only four references to the Cultural Revolution, compared with more than sixty references back in 1981. This may be seen as a natural result of the effluxion of time, rather than a substantive change in the party's formal conclusions in 1981 on the multiple disasters of 1966–1976. Nonetheless, the different rendition of the Cultural Revolution in the 2021 document compared with the 1981 resolution fits a broader trend under Xi of presenting Mao in a much more benign light than in the past.

More important, the 2021 document also begins to imply the existence of just two genuinely great ideological innovators in the Sinification of Marxism, not three. By careful drafting and documentary design, the resolution infers that Mao and Xi now occupy parallel positions within an emerging CCP canonical diarchy, while Deng's individual ideological significance is diminished. Indeed, if there is an emerging ideological trinity in the latest historical resolution, it is Marx, Mao, and Xi, rather than Mao, Deng, and Xi. The official narrative may still record three major eras in post-1949 party history (those of Mao, Deng, and Xi). But in the body of the text of the 2021 resolution, there is an increased emphasis on Mao and Xi alone as the party's major ideological leaders. Deng, whose most significant ideological statement was explicitly anti-ideological—"let's stop discussing theory (*bu zhenglun*), let's develop the economy"—begins to recede. This relegation of Deng is underscored further by the consistent pattern in Chinese official press coverage during the Xi period whereby Mao receives much more intensive media coverage than Deng.[13]

Xi on the Ideological Errors of the Deng-Jiang-Hu Era

While the 1981 resolution was a direct attack on Mao's ideological errors between 1956 and 1976, and his failure to adhere to the party line adopted by the 8th Party Congress in 1956 prioritizing economic development, the 2021 document is much more oblique in its criticism of Xi's immediate predecessors. It does, however, critique their collective failure to deal with the imbalances arising under Deng's economic development model and the ideological indiscipline to which it gave rise. Neither Jiang nor Hu was criticized by name in the resolution, not least because they were still alive. But the introduction of the section titled 'A New Era of Socialism with Chinese Characteristics' lists numerous ideological and political failures during the period of reform and opening, together with the measures to be taken under Xi to rectify these deficiencies. These included "lax and weak governance" that had "enabled inaction and corruption to spread within the Party"; hence why Xi's CCP "focussed on dealing with cases involving both political and economic corruption, prevented interest groups from arising within the Party, and investigated and punished corrupt officials such as Zhou Yongkang, Bo Xilai, Sun Zhengcai, and Ling Jihua [Hu's chief-of-staff from 2007 to 2012] for their serious violations of party discipline and the law". Moreover, there was the problem of "judicial and law-enforcement personnel who had bent the law for personal gain, or even provided shelter for criminals". Furthermore, there was "misconduct interwoven with political and economic issues, which had led to a startling level of corruption that damaged the Party's image and prestige and severely undermined relations between the Party and the people". These were no small charges.

The resolution further attacked general institutional and ideological indiscipline across the party, including "a certain period in which we failed to supervise party organizations effectively or govern them with the necessary stringency. This resulted in a serious lack of political conviction among some party members and officials [and] misconduct in the selection and appointment of personnel." On top of these, there were the problems of "money worship, hedonism, ultra-individualism, and historical nihilism, online discourse [that] has been rife with disorder, and certain leading officials [who] have demonstrated ambiguity in their political stance and a lack of fighting spirit". Compounding these there were also "many problems within the party with respect to upholding its leadership, including a lack of clear awareness [and] vigorous action, as well as weak, ineffective, diluted, and marginal efforts in implementation". The document also directly targeted weak political loyalty and discipline in the PLA, where "for a period of time, the party's leadership over the military was obviously lacking" and "if this problem had not been completely solved, it would not only have diminished the military's combat capacity, but also undermined the key political principle that the party commands the gun". This had resulted in "grave violations of party discipline and state laws including those involving Guo Boxiong, Xu Caihou, Fang Fenghui, and Zhang Yang who were thoroughly investigated and punished and their negative influence completely eliminated".

Beyond these stark indictments of party corruption, indiscipline, and diminished political control over the PLA during the pre–Xi Jinping era, the 2021 resolution again pointed to failures to address imbalances in economic development under Deng, Jiang, and Hu. This had "led to a stack-up of institutional and structural problems in China's economy" in which "imbalanced, uncoordinated, and unsustainable development hence became a glaring issue". It included the problem of inequality, requiring a reformed "income distribution system that emphasizes efficiency while promoting fairness" by "adjusting excessive income, prohibiting illicit income, increasing the income of low-income groups, and steadily expanding the size of the middle-income group" in order to promote "an olive-shaped pattern of distribution". This, of course, is what Xi had sought to rectify by formally changing the party's central contradiction in 2017 and introducing his 'common prosperity' concept.

Across this catalogue of errors, however, everything in Xi's worldview ultimately returns to the question of ideology: "With a focus on addressing the issue of lax party leadership in the ideological sphere, the party has replaced faulty practices with effective ones in an effort to clear up muddy waters." Against this critique of China's alleged ideological dissolution and near-collapse during the reform and opening period, Xi's

2021 resolution is almost nostalgic for the ideological certitudes of the distant past, as reflected in the adulatory treatment of Marx and the incremental rehabilitation of Mao.

The 2021 Resolution and Xi Jinping's Cult of Personality

An even starker political and ideological contrast between the 1981 and 2021 resolutions can be found in the overall textual treatment of Marx, Mao, Deng, and Xi as political reference points in their own right. In 1981, there were 10 references to Deng by name. By comparison, the 2021 resolution made 25 explicit references to either Xi Jinping or Xi Jinping Thought. There were no references in official party communiqués to 'Deng Xiaoping Theory on Socialism with Chinese Characteristics' until nearly two decades after the tumultuous events of 1978 when, after Deng's death, the 15th Party Congress in 1997 belatedly institutionalized Deng Theory.[14] By contrast, XJPT was elevated to official status only five years into Xi's rule. And, while references to Deng and Deng Xiaoping Theory in party communiqués continued to increase between 1997 and 2012, these subsequently declined, while references to Marx, Mao, and Xi have increased. This trend reached its crescendo in the 2021 Resolution: 40 references to Marxism, 25 to Xi, 18 to Mao, and only 6 to Deng.[15] Finally, while the political circumstances in 2021 were much less stark than those in 1981, it is important to note that, for a resolution that purported to enumerate the party's "major achievements and historical experience over the last 100 years", nearly two-thirds of the entire 2021 text is dedicated to the nine years since Xi's appointment in 2012. These combined metrics point to a concerted effort throughout the 2021 resolution to underscore the centrality of Xi's personal, political, and ideological leadership.

Beyond these quantitative measures, there are also qualitative aspects that set the 2021 resolution apart from the 1945 and 1981 texts. This is particularly clear in the hagiographic language used to describe the party's new paramount leader. For example, the 2021 resolution states:

> Comrade Xi Jinping, through meticulous assessment and deep reflection on a number of major theoretical and practical questions regarding the cause of the party and the country in the new era, has set forth a series

> of original new ideas, thoughts, and strategies on national governance revolving around the major questions of our times: what kind of socialism with Chinese characteristics we should uphold and develop in this new era, what kind of great modern socialist country we should build, and what kind of Marxist party exercising long-term governance we should develop, as well as how we should go about achieving these tasks.

The resolution's naming of Xi as "the principal founder of Xi Jinping Thought on Socialism with Chinese Characteristics for the New Era" may appear self-evident, but this too represents a departure from the past. In the 1981 resolution, Mao Zedong Thought is officially described as representing "the collective wisdom of the party"—the combined product of "many outstanding leaders of our party . . . synthesized in the scientific works of Comrade Mao"—rather than the genius of a single, great man. Yet the political and ideological centrality of Xi the individual is underscored repeatedly in the 2021 resolution, as reflected in the following section on XJPT:

> The party has established Comrade Xi Jinping's core position on the Party Central Committee and in the party as a whole, and defined the guiding role of Xi Jinping Thought on Socialism with Chinese Characteristics for a New Era. This reflects the common will of the party, the armed forces, and Chinese people of all ethnic groups, and is of decisive significance for advancing the cause of the party and the country in the new era and for driving forward the historic process of national rejuvenation.

Importantly, major parts of the 1981 resolution on the dangers of concentrating political power in a single leader were excised from the 2021 resolution. For example, the 1981 resolution declared that "Comrade Mao Zedong's personal leadership, characterized by 'left' errors, took the place of the collective leadership of the Central Committee, and the cult of Comrade Mao Zedong was frenziedly pushed to an extreme." The 1981 resolution lamented how the CCP "failed to institutionalize and legalize inner-party democracy and democracy in the political and social life of the country, or we drew up the relevant laws but they lacked due authority". This enabled "the over-concentration of party power in individuals" and "the development of arbitrary individual rule and the personality cult in the party". As a result, the party "put an end to the virtually lifelong tenure of leading cadres, changed the over-concentration of power and . . . with the reshuffling of the leading personnel of the State Council and the division of labour between party and government organizations, the work of the central and local governments has improved". Moreover, "in the light of the lessons of the 'cultural revolution' and the present situation in the party, it is imperative to build up a sound system of democratic centralism inside the party. We must carry out the Marxist principle of the exercise of collective party leadership . . . and we must prohibit the personality cult in any form."

None of these conclusions is repeated or reflected in the text of the 2021 resolution. In fact, the hagiographic references to Xi Jinping personally, in addition to the new ideological status now accorded to Xi Jinping Thought, runs directly counter to both the spirit and letter of the 1981 resolution. It might be claimed that the 2021 resolution does not explicitly repudiate those elements of the 1981 text. But, given it was released in the lead-up to the 20th Party Congress, where the party's central political question was whether to reappoint Xi for a third presidential term—thereby breaching the post-Mao convention of a two-term limit—their deliberate omission appears deeply significant.

Xi Jinping Thought, Changes in Party Periodization, and the Launch of a New Era

Previous chapters have discussed the new, three-part periodization of China's post-1949 history into the Mao-era of 'socialist construction' (1949–1976), the Deng-initiated era of 'reform and opening' (1978–2017), and Xi's 'new era of socialism with Chinese characteristics' (since 2017). The party now categorizes these three periods into the eras when China respectively 'stood up', then 'became prosperous', and finally 'became powerful'[16]—and continues to become more powerful under Xi. Further, as noted earlier in this chapter, these transformations have accompanied three designated periods in the ideological evolution of Chinese Marxism under Mao Zedong Thought, Deng Xiaoping Theory, and now Xi Jinping Thought, albeit with an emerging discourse diminishing the significance of Deng Theory relative to the other two. However, the 2021 resolution takes this new approach to political periodization further in significant respects, notably by reinterpreting the recent past through the fresh ideological lens of Xi's Marxist and nationalist missions for the party.

To begin with, the 2021 document redefines the ideological mission of the period of 'reform and opening' beyond its previous historical purpose of advancing the development of the productive forces of the Chinese economy. It broadens the purposes of the reform and opening period to include two new post-facto objectives of building the *right* form of Chinese socialism and advancing the cause of 'national rejuvenation'. In the words of the resolution:

> In the new period of reform, opening up, and socialist modernization, the main tasks facing the party were to continue exploring the *right* path for building socialism in China, to unleash and develop the productive forces, to lift the people out of poverty and help them become prosperous in the shortest time possible, and to fuel the push toward national rejuvenation.

The effect of this textual change is to reinterpret the objectives of Deng's reform and opening period through the ideological lens of Xi's new era of national rejuvenation.

While stopping short of saying so explicitly, the 2021 resolution implies that reform and opening—the universally recognized leitmotif of the entire Deng era—had now served its historical purpose; China had caught up and that era had, by and large, concluded. There are, of course, continuing episodic references to a number of ongoing processes of reform and opening under Xi. But, as noted in chapter 8, even the terms 'reform' and 'opening' themselves have been redefined. The relegation of reform and opening to the realm of historical achievement, rather than retaining it as a core principle for China's future development, is important in defining the point that Xi believes the party has now reached in its historical mission. This is underscored by the extensive use of the past tense marker in this part of the Chinese language version of the 2021 text of the 'historical resolution'. For example:

> China has *achieved the historic transformation* from a country with relatively backward productive forces to the world's second-largest economy, and *made the historic strides* of raising the living standards of its people from bare subsistence to moderate prosperity in general, and then toward moderate prosperity in all respects. *All these achievements marked the tremendous advance of the Chinese nation from standing up to growing prosperous.* Through tenacious struggle, the party and the people showed the world that *reform and opening up was a crucial move* in making China what it is today, that socialism with Chinese characteristics is the correct road that has led the

> country toward development and prosperity, and that *China has caught up* with the times in great strides. (My emphasis)

Moreover, the resolution's rendition of the Xi Jinping period's new and defining features further underscores this transition from one ideological era to the next. The phrase 'reform and opening', once again, is conspicuous by its near-absence.[17] Instead, the 'new era of socialism with Chinese characteristics' is now defined in terms of the party's Marxist objective of building "a great modern socialist country" capable of realizing its new goal of "common prosperity". It also emphasizes the party's nationalist objective of "national rejuvenation" when China resumes its historical role of "global leadership in terms of comprehensive national power and international influence". As noted above, this transition from one era to the next is described as a "key historical juncture" beyond which, by implication, circumstances have now fundamentally changed:

> The Party Central Committee with Comrade Xi Jinping at its core has implemented the national rejuvenation strategy within the wider context of once-in-a-century changes taking place in the world. It has stressed that the new era of socialism with Chinese characteristics is an era in which we will build on past successes to further advance our cause and continue to strive for the success of socialism with Chinese characteristics under *new historical conditions*; an era in which we will use the momentum of our decisive victory in building a moderately prosperous society in all respects to fuel all-out efforts to build a great modern socialist country; an era in which Chinese people of all ethnic groups will work together to create a better life for themselves and gradually realize the goal of common prosperity; an era in which all the sons and daughters of the Chinese nation will strive with one heart to realize the Chinese Dream of national rejuvenation; and an era in which China will make even greater contributions to humanity. This *new era is a new historic juncture in China's development.* (My emphasis)

Finally, the significance of this transition between eras is made even plainer in the later parts of the 2021 resolution where it also begins to redefine 'reform' in a more interventionist direction for the Chinese party-state. The 2021 text refers to earlier 'trials' in reform now being transformed under Xi's rule to become 'an integrated drive' that will "ensure that reform stays on the right path". Likewise, the text refers to a 'more proactive opening-up strategy' that will be increasingly state-directed rather than market-driven. This is to be achieved by leveraging

China's global economic power and maximizing the international utility of its new statist mega-projects such as the Belt and Road Initiative. The party would also continue developing major new 'people-centred' metropolitan conurbations at home. This process of formally redefining the ideational content of 'reform and opening' while preserving, in some respects, its formal language, is made clear beyond any doubt in the text of the resolution:

> The third plenary session of the 11th Central Committee [in 1978] was an epoch-making event that ushered in the new period of reform, opening up, and socialist modernization. In the same way, the third plenary session of the 18th Central Committee [which produced the 'Decision' in 2013] was also of epoch-making significance.[18] It enabled the transformation of reform from trials and breakthroughs limited to certain areas into an integrated drive being advanced across the board, and thus marked the beginning of a new stage in China's reform and opening up. *The party has worked to ensure that reform stays on the right path, that it is inspired and guided by the objectives of promoting social fairness and justice and improving people's wellbeing. . . . The party has strengthened top-level design and overall planning, pursued reform in a more systemic, holistic, and coordinated manner,* stimulated people's creativity, and deepened and consolidated reforms in key areas. (My emphasis)

In summary, the 2021 resolution renders the ideological cleavage between the Deng and Xi eras even clearer than before. The terms 'reform and opening' are no longer used as the defining principles of Xi's 'new era of socialism with Chinese characteristics'. Instead, they are replaced by what I have called a new partyist and statist framework of Marxist Nationalism as expressed through the vast array of new ideological narratives detailed in previous chapters of this book. 'Reform' itself has been redefined in a direction more accommodating of the political imperatives of party-state intervention (i.e. 'top-level design') in order to pursue centrally a range of defined socialist and nationalist objectives, rather than continuing market-based reform as a recognized objective in its own right. And finally, 'opening', which previously represented continued open engagement with the global economy as a recognized objective in its own right, has also been redefined in more limited, mercantilist terms. In other words, the 2021 resolution once again makes clear the ideological shift to the left in China's overall political economy that has occurred under Xi Jinping's rule.

The Changing Content of Xi Jinping Thought

These ideological changes outlined within the framework of Xi Jinping Thought have not occurred at once but have unfolded over the course of Xi's first decade in office. It is therefore important to analyse the evolving content and changing priorities of XJPT in the years following the 19th Party Congress to understand the nature of the ideological shifts now underway. One striking change in the 2021 Resolution (even when compared with Xi's 2017 Congress report[19]) was the prominence given to the centrality of the party and Xi's core position within it. Both documents summarized the core content of Xi Jinping Thought with points that 'make clear' (*mingque*) its most important elements. In 2017, there were eight such points. By 2021, these had grown to ten. In 2017, the section dealing with the party's centrality was placed last; whereas in 2021, it was listed first. And, building on Xi's more oblique call on party members in 2017 to 'follow the leadership core', the 2021 resolution added forcefully:

> All party members must strengthen their consciousness of the need to maintain political integrity, think in big-picture terms, follow the leadership core, and keep in alignment with the central party leadership; stay confident in the path, theory, system, and culture of socialism with Chinese characteristics; and *uphold Comrade Xi Jinping's core position on the Party Central Committee and in the party as a whole,* and uphold the Central Committee's authority and its centralized, unified leadership. (My emphasis)

This represents a significant strengthening in the party's official language on Xi's personal power within the party over the four-year period following the 19th Party Congress.

Another change between the 2017 and 2021 official definitions of Xi Jinping Thought appears in its list of policy tasks flowing from the 19th Congress's redefinition of the party's principal contradiction for the new era. The 2021 version added to the 2017 language in two respects. The first was through Xi's new left-leaning concept of 'whole-of-process people's democracy' (*quanguocheng renmin minzhu*)[20] distancing the party even further from previous encouragement of internal party ballots and local elections for NPC delegates (including non-party candidates) as trialled under Jiang and, more intensively, Hu.[21] Under Xi, these have been systematically replaced with what party journals describe as 'whole-of-process democracy' through ill-defined, rolling consultations with the masses, excluding any form of direct or indirect election.[22] This formalized a further significant shift to the political left under Xi Jinping, reflecting a return to a pre-Jiang (and arguably pre-Deng) form of Leninist 'democratic centralism' in which the legitimacy of the revolutionary party was not to be exposed to any gradual challenge through the incremental expansion of the electoral franchise.

Finally, the 2021 resolution underscored not only the priority Xi attached to the *power* of the party, but also to the party's own *capacity* to give practical effect to his new ideological vision for the country's future. In the 2021 text, Xi states that only if the party itself "engages in great self-transformation (*ziwo geming*), can the party steer great social transformation". This is a significant statement. At one level, it may seem like a rhetorical flourish to the already well-rehearsed sections of the document dealing with 'party building' (*dangjian*). But, at a deeper level, it represents Xi's return to an earlier conception of a role for the party that permeated Mao's writings: namely, that the party must once again become a direct revolutionary agent for engineering profound economic and social transformation. And it must do so through its own, continuing processes of 'self-revolution'.[23] This is different to the view of other CCP leaders since 1978, who held that the party was primarily a vehicle for maintaining Leninist political control while allowing economic and social policy reform to be prosecuted through the professional, technocratic apparatus of the Chinese state. Deng, Jiang, and Hu, for example, saw the party much less as a vehicle to bring about direct social and economic change. They saw real transformation as the product of the reform and opening policy processes, initiated by the party, executed by the state, and delivered largely by the private sector—designed primarily to unleash hitherto underdeveloped productive forces and deliver people from poverty. Indeed, they often saw the party as an ideological and institutional impediment to this task through its bureaucratic indifference, hostility, and inertia.[24] By contrast, the 2021 resolution points to a much more fundamentalist view of the party's central position across every policy domain. The party is no longer just a political control mechanism preventing China from capitulating to democratic capitalism, as might have occurred in 1989. Instead, it would embody, nurture, and transmit socialist and communist values that are capable (in the Maoist tradition) of fundamentally reengineering China's national soul through a process of continuing revolution. Beyond simply transmitting certain core beliefs and maintaining macro-political control, the party under Xi has, in its own right, become seen as the institutional core of real economic, social, and foreign policy change for not only China but the world. This transformational agenda for the party represents a further significant ideological shift from the past.

The Overall Impact of Xi Jinping Thought on Politics and the Economy

Taken together, both the 2017 and 2021 definitions of the ideological content of Xi Jinping Thought underline the continuing shift to the left in Chinese politics and its political economy. This is reflected in a number of areas: the ideological defence of Xi's individual leadership over the post–Cultural Revolution disciplines of collective leadership; the party's new and intrinsically 'transformative' role as the ultimate embodiment of belief and praxis; and the overriding impact of the new principal contradiction of the Xi era that demanded new levels of party intervention in politics, the economy, and society for what had become a new era. These have also resulted in a redefinition of both inner-party and public democracy as so-called whole-of-process democracy, which, once again, reinforces the role of the party as the absolute, uncompromising centre of political power. Moreover, it incorporates Xi's notion of the rule of law, which similarly restores the party to the centre of China's constitutional, legal, and administrative system.

As noted above, the formalization of XJPT also saw the further diminution in the totemic significance of 'reform and opening' in economic policy when compared with the Deng-initiated era. 'Reform and opening' have been formally repurposed to serve the party's redefined socialist and nationalist objectives under Xi, rather than being seen as economic and foreign policy ends in themselves. This has been reflected too in the effective redefinition of the terms 'reform' and 'opening' in their own right within a new partyist and statist frame. The ideological weight of 'Xi Jinping Thought on the Economy' on those in the Chinese bureaucratic system charged with the already technically complex challenges of managing the country's economic growth agenda in challenging times is real. And that is before we take into account its real-world impact on the day-to-day business confidence, investment decisions, and wealth accumulation of an increasingly embattled Chinese private sector.

Beyond these specific impacts, the unfolding and potentially limitless canon of XJPT now seeks to be a totalizing ideology covering all political, policy, and previously private domains. It is also a politically flexible and ideologically adaptable body of thought that subjects all areas of policy to a new and higher socialist and nationalist purpose. Most critically, the content of this rolling redefinition of the party's ideological mission now lies within the exclusive political purview of the core leader and the ideological canon that bears his name. It is, therefore, a worldview that legitimizes both party and/or personal intervention by Xi himself, whenever that is deemed to be necessary, in pursuit of the leader's overriding political and ideological objectives.

Xi Jinping Thought and Chinese Nationalism

The question also arises of where to locate Xi's broader ideological narrative on Chinese nationalism within the emerging framework of Xi Jinping Thought. The shift to the right in nationalism, explored in some detail in chapters 9–11, has been reflected in multiple new political, foreign, and security banner terms, policy statements, and foreign policy initiatives that point to a common ethno-nationalist thematic. At the same time, these have been consistently juxtaposed against the United States and the West in an increasingly binary Marxist-Nationalist worldview. But beyond this changing array of nationalist banner terms and the new forms of foreign policy assertiveness described in earlier chapters, XJPT has also become a wider ideological vehicle for advancing China's changing nationalist discourse. This too is reflected in the party's 2021 historical resolution's formal definition of XJPT and its multiple references to Chinese nationalist aspirations ranging well beyond the narrower ideological remit of Marxism-Leninism. As the resolution states:

> The overarching task of upholding and developing socialism with Chinese characteristics is to realize socialist modernization and national rejuvenation . . . to build China into a great modern socialist country.

The resolution also makes plain that XJPT fully embraces China's military aspirations, declaring that "the party's goal for military development in the new era is to build the people's armed forces into world-class forces that obey the party's command". China's new, more muscular approach to projecting its foreign policy influence is presented as a formal part of XJPT, incorporating Xi's newly assertive approach to the world, the United States, the future of the global order, and the new overarching concept of Xi's 'community of common destiny'. In fact, the formal definition of XJPT now includes "major-country diplomacy with Chinese characteristics" which "aims to serve national rejuvenation, promote human progress and facilitate efforts to foster a new type of international relations and build a human community with a shared future". To this end, the party's 2021 resolution overtly blends Marxist-Leninist ideology with Chinese cultural nationalism:

> The party . . . has stressed that ideological work shapes the collective mind of a country and forges the soul of a nation, and that confidence in one's culture, which is a broader, deeper, and more fundamental form of self-confidence, is the most essential, profound, and enduring source of strength for the development of a country and a nation. Without a thriving culture and firm confidence in it, the Chinese nation cannot achieve rejuvenation.

The language of the 'historical resolution' draws together in a single pronouncement the long series of nationalist campaigns launched by Xi since 2012. But beyond that, the fact that a formal CCP resolution summarizes the party's ideological evolution over its hundred-year history by deliberately blending into a single worldview *both* the Marxist-Leninist *and* the nationalist elements of Xi's overall ideological framework is of itself significant. Whereas Deng's 1981 resolution depicted China as 'dignified' yet 'culturally backward', in Xi's view, Marxism and nationalism were now the twin pistons of the party's ideological engine, driving forward both Chinese national rejuvenation and a China-led global order. Indeed, one without the other is incomplete.

Moreover, the 2021 resolution paints a nationalist picture of a new-era China confronted on every side by mounting international challenges and hostile foreign forces, requiring ever-stronger national responses:

> In the new era, China is faced with more acute national security challenges, as evidenced by unprecedented external pressure, intertwined traditional and non-traditional security threats. . . . China's ability to safeguard

national security falls short of what is required of us by the current circumstances and tasks. . . . We must uphold the primacy of our national interests and take the people's security as our ultimate goal, political security as our fundamental task, economic security as our foundation, military, technological, cultural, and social security as means of guarantee, and international security as the support. We must find a balance between development and security, between opening up and security, between traditional and non-traditional security, between China's domestic security and the common security of the world, and between safeguarding national security and creating conditions conducive to it. Comrade Xi Jinping has stressed that our Party should make national security its top priority. He has put forward an holistic approach to national security, which covers political, military, homeland security, economic, cultural, social, technological, cyberspace, ecological, resource, nuclear, overseas interests, outer space, deep sea, polar, and biological security issues, among others. . . . The Central Committee is acutely aware that, confronted with various types of external encirclement, suppression, disruption, and subversion, we must not be misguided or intimidated, and we must fight to the end with any forces that would attempt to subvert the leadership of the Communist Party of China and China's socialist system, or to hinder or obstruct China's advance toward national rejuvenation. Constant concessions will only invite more bullying and humiliation.

Conclusion

The party's 2021 historical resolution provides a clear articulation of both the Marxist and the nationalist components of Xi Jinping Thought. It remains anchored in two sources: first, ideological self-confidence in historical materialism and dialectical materialism as the fundamental pillars of Marxism-Leninism and the conclusions they have provided the party in response to the challenges of Xi's new era; together with a nationalist agenda anchored in the rejuvenation of Chinese national power that is reinforced by officially sanctioned cultural nationalism and an increasingly binary conclusion that heightened political and ideological struggle against the United States and the West is imperative. This worldview is also turbocharged by an officially sanctioned description of mounting external threats to the Chinese nation, including notions of disruption, subversion, and encirclement. And this, in turn, gives rise to Xi's all-encompassing, totalizing national security concept. No comparable official narrative on Chinese Marxist Nationalism can be found during the Deng-Jiang-Hu period. It encompasses a clear-cut, historically determinist mission for a new era, an all-powerful Leninist party and paramount leader to oversee this mission, and a commitment to relentless struggle to overcome the emerging contradictions identified both at home and abroad through the tools of dialectical materialism. And all this is reinforced by the growing drumbeat of national pride, national power, national ambition, and the perception of a China besieged by threats from all sides.

13

The Dawn of Xi Jinping's Second Decade in Power and the CCP's 20th Party Congress

In 2021 and 2022, following the Chinese Communist Party centennial celebrations and the passage of only the third 'historical resolution' since the CCP's founding, Xi Jinping's party believed it had the wind in its sails. The United States and the wider West were still reeling from the social and economic consequences of COVID-19, whereas China believed it had successfully navigated the pandemic and had emerged with its economy relatively unscathed. China also saw its reputation in the Global South enhanced by having provided material help with vaccines—however comparatively ineffective they may have been[1]—when the West was perceived to have provided little.[2] China further believed it had successfully stared down the United States at a meeting of foreign policy principals in Anchorage in late 2021 and that its robust military response to the visit to Taiwan by US House Speaker Nancy Pelosi in August 2022 had changed the operational parameters for future PLA exercises and deployments across the Taiwan Strait.[3] The humiliation of China's sudden, 180-degree reversal of its so-called dynamic zero COVID strategy in December 2022, amidst mounting domestic protests and dramatically slowing economic growth, still lay ahead, as did the national loss of face from the dramatic shooting down of a Chinese reconnaissance balloon over the United States in February 2023.[4] For much of 2021–2022, therefore, most things still seemed to be going well. The East was still rising and the West declining (at least in the eyes of the party) and, from Xi's vantage point, theory and practice seemed to be increasingly well aligned.

This was the context in which the 20th Party Congress would be held in October 2022. Much had happened on the ideological front since 2017. The 19th Congress had redefined the party's central contradiction, announced a new era in party history, and proclaimed Xi Jinping Thought (XJPT) as the new ideological orthodoxy for dealing with the multiple challenges of unbalanced development. The 2021 historical resolution had entrenched XJPT as the second great ideological contribution to the Sinification of Chinese Marxism-Leninism after Mao and proclaimed it as '*the* Marxism of contemporary China', effectively relegating Deng's theoretical contribution in the scales of party history to almost a cameo role.[5] This in turn was followed by the 20th Congress in October 2022, where XJPT was elevated further by entrenching its new status in the party constitution and requiring the party to 'uphold Comrade Xi Jinping's core position' along with the body of thought that bore his name.[6] These were heady days. And in the period leading up to the 20th Congress, there came a series of equally heady new articles by Xi himself on the centrality of his ideological mission. In Xi's worldview, ideology underpinned his entire political enterprise.

Lead-Up to the 20th Party Congress: Revisiting the Centrality of the Ideology of Contradictions

The most remarkable of Xi Jinping's ideological declarations during this period was his January 2022 address to central party cadres titled 'Better Grasping and Applying the Party's Historical Experience of 100 Years of Struggle'.[7] This was, in effect, a Xi-directed study guide to understanding the party's historical resolution of the previous November. Xi began by attributing the success of China's national mission to the correctness of the party's Marxist ideological direction:

> For a nation to lead in the era, theoretical thinking must be continuous and there should be constant correct ideological guidance; the reason why the Communist Party of China succeeds, and why socialism with Chinese characteristics is effective, fundamentally lies in the effectiveness of Marxism.

Xi further claimed that the particular cause for the CCP's success had been its long tradition of the Sinification of Marxism, beginning with Mao after the 6th Party Congress in 1938. Xi then invoked the party's

2021 historical resolution, claiming that he had followed in Mao's tradition by taking a 'new leap' (*xin de feiyue*) in Marxist thought:

> As the party enters a new era, it puts forward a series of original ideas, new thoughts, and new strategies for governance, establishing the Thought on Socialism with Chinese Characteristics for a New Era, and thereby realizing a new leap forward in the Sinification of Marxism.

Xi then proceeded to list in great detail his individual ideological achievements during the 'new era' including new directions in foreign policy and national security policy. This had also provided the CCP with an opportunity to present a new form of Marxism to other countries:

> When discussing the historical significance of the Communist Party of China's century-long struggle, the resolution of the plenary session on party history emphasizes that the continuous success of the Sinification and modernization of Marxism has presented Marxism in a new light to the world.

Xi argued that China's development challenges were best dealt with by "better unifying the adherence to and development of Marxism . . . using the 'arrow' of Marxism to target the 'bullseye' of contemporary China". So confident was Xi of his argument that he went on to claim that the deficiencies in China's domestic leadership were grounded not in a lack of technical capacity, as Deng had argued, but a lack of ideological capacity: "There is a common issue among current leaders known as a 'capability panic', *with the fundamental deficiency being insufficient theoretical literacy*, so undoubtedly we must adhere to the fundamental principles and fundamental viewpoints of the Party's theory" (my emphasis). This formulation would have caused Deng, the author of 'let's stop debating theory',[8] to roll in his grave.

Xi then launched into the most important part of his address, on the doctrinal significance of the Marxist theory of contradictions to properly understand China's major contemporary challenges, and how best to respond to them. It remains, at the time of writing, the most comprehensive treatment of Xi's understanding of the machinery of dialectical materialism and its practical relevance to public policy. It is therefore worth rendering at considerable length:

> The party's history over the past century tells us that for the cause of the party and the people to progress, we must have a thorough understanding of the principal challenge [i.e. contradiction] facing our society and properly

> identify our central task. Only when this is done can the cause of the party and the people progress smoothly. Otherwise our cause will suffer setbacks. The [historical] resolution presents a full analysis of the party's strengths in focussing on China's principal challenge and central task when advancing work on all fronts. It emphasizes that, in modern China, the principal social contradictions have been the conflicts between imperialism and the Chinese nation, between feudalism and the masses. To achieve the great rejuvenation of the Chinese nation, struggles against imperialism and feudalism were necessary. It underscores that, after the basic completion of socialist transformation in China, the main internal contradiction became the conflict between the people's rapidly growing needs for economic and cultural development and the situation where economic and cultural development could meet those needs. The primary task for the people nationwide was to concentrate efforts on developing social productive forces, achieving national industrialization, and gradually meeting the increasing material and cultural needs of the people. It highlighted that, after reform and opening, the principal social contradiction in China was the conflict between the growing material and cultural needs of the people and the backwardness of social production. Resolving this primary contradiction became our central task. It further emphasizes that, in the new era, the principal social contradiction in China is the conflict between growing aspirations for a better life and the imbalances and inadequacies in development. . . . As Comrade Mao Zedong pointed out in 'On Contradiction': "The study of the various states of unevenness in contradictions, of the principal and non-principal contradictions and the principal and non-principal aspects of a contradiction constitutes an essential method by which a revolutionary political party correctly determines its strategic and tactical policies both in political and in military affairs. All communists must give it attention."[9]

This is a succinct but still complex presentation of Xi's understanding and application of the theory of contradictions to the challenges of contemporary China. Conspicuously, at least in this part of Xi's pedagogical text, he omits Mao's cardinal ideological error in 1956 (at least according to the historical resolution of 1981) of redefining 'class struggle' to retain it as the party's central contradiction, instead of embracing the need to rapidly develop China's factors of production.[10] So as not to disturb the flow of his grand narrative on the party's successful application of the theory of contradictions throughout its history, Xi does make a fleeting reference to the problematic period of Mao's leadership between 1956 and 1976, but only much later in his text. Notwithstanding this marginalization of Mao's misapplication of contradictions theory, Xi remained adamant that the most important challenge in politics today was to analyse major and minor contradictions correctly, to understand their interrelationship and define the party's 'central tasks' that proceeded from them. Of course, he claimed to have done so himself by identifying the need to redefine the party's central contradiction at the 19th Congress. In his argument, this was fundamental to the radical changes in policy course he had then set in motion in China's *domestic* political economy. Xi is less frank, however, about his use of this same methodological framework in relation to China's principal *external* contradiction—the United States. Nonetheless, it would be Xi's upcoming report to the 20th Party Congress later that year that would formally redefine China's external strategic environment from benign to adverse. While the explicit language of 'external contradictions' may not have been used, its strategic conclusion about the US challenge was absolutely clear.

Significantly, having dealt at considerable length with the theory and practice of contradictions, the subsequent section of Xi's January 2022 speech elaborated on 'the dialectical relationship' between strategy and tactics. His essential conclusion is that 'strategy' refers to the interconnected policy decisions that effect the party's response to its principal contradictions:

> Strategic thinking . . . requires us to take into consideration the overall situation, long-term interests and underlying trends. . . . A sound strategy is to be executed through proper tactics, which are dictated by the former and serve the former. They are in a dialectical relationship, in which *the strategy stays consistent while the tactics can be flexible*." (My emphasis)

As a result, although ground-level tactics will shift according to the practical exigencies of the day, they must fully, faithfully and unconditionally implement the strategy determined by the party centre.

Xi would return to the interconnection between strategy and tactics in a more expansive article in 2023, which will be analysed in the following chapter. In this piece, however, Xi goes on to offer examples of effective strategy under Mao. While these are primarily domestic, some also deal with China's military circumstances. Indeed, insights about how Xi may view strategy and tactics in China's current circumstances are offered in his examination of Mao's strategic analysis of enemy strength and CCP weakness amidst the changing circumstances of the Civil War, the Sino-Japanese War, and the Soviet occupation of China's northeast after 1945. Xi ultimately attributed the effectiveness of these strategic decisions to the strength of Mao's dialectical analysis:

> Strategy involves making judgements and decisions from a global, long-term, and overarching perspective. Comrade Mao Zedong vividly addressed this issue, stating: "Sitting atop the command platform, if you can't see anything, you can't be called a leader. Sitting atop the command platform, only seeing a large number of common things that have already appeared on the horizon is ordinary; it cannot be considered leadership. Only when a large number of obvious things have not yet appeared, when the top of the mast is just emerged, and you can see that this is going to develop into a large number of common things and be able to grasp it, is it called leadership."[11] That kind of leadership, which Comrade Mao Zedong described, is strategic leadership.

Doubling Down on Ideology

Beyond his January 2022 opus detailing his deep veneration of Mao's theory of contradictions, Xi Jinping authored numerous additional articles on party theory in the lead-up to the 20th Congress in October. Each of these added significantly to the various ideological themes he had already set in motion since the 19th Congress. Fully armed with dialectical rigour, Xi doubled down on anti-corruption, common prosperity, and his comprehensive assault on Western notions of universal human rights.

On political theory, Xi's address to the Central Commission for Discipline Inspection on 18 January 2022 dealt specifically with his long-standing obsession with the rise and fall of civilizations, states, and parties. Here Xi's concern was "the need to transcend historical cycles, a crucial issue that is linked to the party's great long-term cause, its survival, the success or failure of China's socialist system".[12] Xi's question is profound, driven in large part by his preoccupation with the demise of the Soviet Union and its Communist party, although his prescription is unremarkable. Xi's solution involves a solid cocktail of self-revolution (for which read 'anti-corruption') reinforced by an equally solid dose of ideological formation (for which read 'Xi Jinping Thought'). According to Xi, the CCP needed to "insist on taking ideological development as the fundamental building block of the party, forging sharp ideological weapons through self-revolution".[13] In other words, the future success of a Chinese Leninist party in defending the nation against historical decline, as with everything else in Xi's worldview, lay in a return to party discipline and ideological rigour.

On economic policy, Xi returned in May 2022 to his Marxist theme of common prosperity for all and renewed his attack on what he described as the 'disorderly expansion of capital'. In the party's theoretical journal *Qiushi*, Xi stated baldly:

> The wealthy people of a country must care about enriching the common people. . . . Under China's socialist system, it is not only necessary to continuously liberate and develop social productive forces . . . but also to prevent polarization, and to earnestly promote the all-around development of human beings and the common prosperity of all people to achieve more obvious and substantial progress.[14]

This article, based on his address to the Central Economic Work Conference in December 2021, did not elaborate a prescriptive formula beyond his earlier much-vaunted primary, secondary, and tertiary distributions of more tax, more welfare, and more philanthropy. But Xi nonetheless left his audience in no doubt about his ideological determination, writing starkly that "common prosperity is the *essential* requirement of socialism with Chinese characteristics".[15] Xi's concern with the "disorderly expansion of capital" was driven by a similar interest in protecting the interests of poorer Chinese from the volatilities of financial markets and property markets, and their combined impact on macro-financial stability. Xi argued that "in recent years, due to lack of awareness and lack of supervision, capital has expanded in a disorderly way, manipulated arbitrarily, and made huge profits in some areas of our country, and this requires regulating the behaviour of capital".[16] As with the simple redistributional formula offered for 'common prosperity', Xi's prescription is similarly rudimentary, proposing 'traffic lights' for the regulation of capital: " 'Traffic lights' apply to all means of transportation on the road. The same is true for capital. All types of capital cannot run amok. To prevent the savage growth of some capital, we must fight against monopoly, profiteering, sky-high prices, malicious hype, and unfair competition."[17] Leaving Xi's mechanistic policy prescriptions to one side, his ideological predilection is nonetheless clear: a further retreat from the market and greater recourse to state intervention and 'top-level design' to deal with these deeply disruptive 'imbalances in development' (of which the disorderly expansion of capital was key). These lay at the core of the new central contradiction he had identified at the 2017 Congress.

As for foreign policy, Xi during this 2021–2022 period remained firmly on the ideological offensive. This was reflected at a Politburo study session in late February 2022 focussing on Western hypocrisy on human rights, the need for China to win the unfolding international debate within the Global South on an alternative human rights framework, and the more aggressive diplomacy needed to achieve these ends.[18] Returning once again to his Marxist ideological roots, Xi explicitly rejects Western liberal definitions of universal human rights:

> Karl Marx and Friedrich Engels endorsed the historical value of the bourgeois theory of human rights, meanwhile they firmly refuted the theory's denial of the social, historical, and class-based nature of human rights. "The individual," Marx pointed out, "is a social being." He also argued that "[a] right can never be higher than the economic structure of society and its cultural development conditioned thereby".[19]

Xi concluded that China should embark on a new diplomatic offensive to defeat Western propositions of universality:

> We should take the strategic initiative and work hard to tell China's story of advancing human rights, using vivid and concrete examples, present our outlook on human rights in a more engaging way that will influence more people, build international consensus on human rights to the greatest extent possible, and retain the moral high ground.[20]

And should there be any doubt as to the identity of China's ideological adversary in all this, Xi also makes this abundantly clear:

> Just as democracy is not an ornament to be used for decoration, neither are human rights. In recent years, some Western countries have been bogged down by conflict between political parties, government dishonesty, social disorder, and epidemics that have spiralled out of control. Political polarization, wealth disparities, and racial tensions have all intensified, while racism, populism, and xenophobia have become rife, thus bringing human rights issues to the fore. Yet these countries still use slogans like 'universal human rights' and 'human rights over sovereignty' as a pretext for forcing Western conceptions and systems of democracy and human rights on others and for meddling in the internal affairs of other countries. This has only served to cause recurrent military conflict, ongoing unrest, and the displacement of many from their homes in a number of countries.[21]

These increasingly stark examples of the theory of contradictions at work show Xi Jinping, in the lead-up to the 20th Party Congress, digging evermore deeply into the ideological trenches. There is a relentless, logical consistency to each of the propositions he advances. Xi rightly asserts that his is a systemic approach. These are not random, free-standing propositions.

There is a clear 'red thread' running through each. First, there are continued, intensifying, and increasingly detailed statements on the absolute scientific truth of the Marxist belief system (and the analytical methodologies proceeding from it) that he holds to be fundamental for explaining and responding to all aspects of politics and policy. Second, there is a parallel belief that this sort of ideological rectitude and rigour will ultimately solve the problems of decline and decay inherent in any political organization or national culture, including China and the CCP. Third, as Xi's focus turns to income inequality and financial greed, they become greater animating factors in driving him back towards his Marxist ideological roots. Fourth, this same Marxism also informs Xi's increasingly polarized view of the world—his determination to defeat the West ideologically and become the champion of a new international order anchored in the Global South in which Marxian economic rights will prevail over the narrowly defined political rights championed by the liberal capitalist world.

Xi's ideological preparations for the 20th Congress were, therefore, complete.

The 20th Party Congress

If further evidence were still needed that China under Xi Jinping had radically changed since the days of his post-Mao predecessors, the ideological, political, economic, foreign policy, and personnel outcomes of the 20th Party Congress in November 2022 would provide it definitively and in abundance. Even though the 19th Congress in 2017 marked the official beginning of Xi Jinping's 'new era'—a brave new world in which everything was being turned upside down—official media began retrospectively describing it as having started in 2012.[22] It will be recalled that the 'new era' came about on the back of the formal redefinition in 2017 of the party's central contradiction. This 'new' contradiction warranted, in turn, a 'new' era and a 'new' development pattern. But, after 2022, everything was made new from the very beginning of Xi's political term, making clear to the entire party the absolute cleavage in party history that had occurred that year: that is, in 2012, after thirty-five years, the Deng era ended and the Xi era began. No longer was 2012–2017 some sort of bridging period between the old and the new, as had been the case with the party's semi-official interregnum of 1977–1982 following Mao's demise and Deng's return to power. History had now been forged afresh from 2012 on!

Whatever the periodization might be, across the entire length of his leadership of the party, Xi Jinping had maintained two signature thematics. The first was the return of Marxist-Leninist ideology as defined and interpreted by Xi himself, together with a new and assertive form of Chinese nationalism, as the central driving forces of contemporary Chinese politics, economics, and foreign policy. The second was the disciplined deployment of both these ideological narratives through an audacious new political strategy to achieve Xi's overriding party and national objectives: namely, the realization of a strong, powerful, and prosperous China as the fulcrum of a new international order, to be achieved through the agency of an all-powerful Leninist party which, far from fading away, would endure as long as the Chinese nation itself survived. This political strategy included Xi's preparedness to: overturn long-established ideological orthodoxies; destroy core party conventions on collective leadership, term limits, and the relationship between the party and the state; marginalize (and, where necessary, eliminate) real, potential, or imagined political opposition; and smash through what he perceived as the bureaucratic inertia and entropy inherent to the system. For the first time, it was a strategy that also included taking the challenge right up to his principal international adversary by confronting the United States, and to do so right across the ideological, foreign policy, and military spectrum, as opposed to China simply adapting and adjusting to the strategic terrain as defined by the United States. Indeed, Xi himself had become the living embodiment of his own ideological mantra—'the spirit of struggle'.[23]

Ideological Change

The 20th Party Congress report was more ideological in both content and tone than any other over the preceding forty years. It spoke glowingly of the great ideological progress that had been achieved over the previous decade to open "new chapters in adapting Marxism to the Chinese context and the needs of the times".[24] Indeed, Xi enjoined the party to "gain a good command of the worldview and methodology" of XJPT and to apply afresh the analytical tools of dialectical and historical materialism to understand the great challenges of the time. Xi argued this ideological lens should now be applied to "everything we do" and, in so doing, develop "a new form of human advancement".[25] Once again, Xi made plain that Marxist dialectics should be applied to understanding and developing Chinese policy responses to *both* domestic *and* international challenges.

Communist party officials, as noted previously, have always been acutely attuned to changes in the ideological phraseology in core party documents. For example, the term 'Marxism' appeared twenty-six times in the 2022 report—more than the already highly ideologized report of 2017. There were twenty-two references to the Marxist-Leninist concept of 'struggle' in 2022 as the means by which to realize domestic or international progress against the party's stated objectives—the same number as in 2017. The Marxist concept of 'common prosperity' was also emphasized in equal measure compared to the 2017 document. But it was Xi's overriding nationalist objective of building a 'powerful state' (*qiangguo*) that dominated the new text: there were thirty-two references in 2022—a 60% increase from 2017. Taken together, there could be little remaining doubt as to the overriding Marxist-Nationalist ideological thrust of Xi's brand-new era.

In case Chinese officials were unclear about the significance attached by Xi Jinping to this new ideological framework, this was reinforced by a series of formal amendments to the party constitution at the 20th Congress. These new additions to the constitution included the following paragraphs:

- "Xi Jinping Thought on Socialism with Chinese Characteristics for a New Era is the Marxism of contemporary China and of the 21st century and embodies the best Chinese culture and ethos of this era";
- "Comrade Xi Jinping has put forward a series of new ideas, new thinking, and new strategies on national defense, the armed forces, the united front, and foreign affairs" which "it agrees to include in the Party Constitution"; and
- "All party members [should] acquire a deep understanding of the decisive significance of establishing Comrade Xi Jinping's core position on the Party Central Committee and in the party as a whole and establishing the guiding role of Xi Jinping Thought on Socialism with Chinese Characteristics for a New Era and to fully implement this Thought in all areas and stages of the work of the Party and the country."[26]

As a result, party members were left with little room to move; ideology, and the leader who framed it, were now more deeply entrenched as forces in their own right. Marxism-Leninism was to be embraced as the fundamental ideological framework for the values, end goals, and, importantly, analytical methodology of the party. And XJPT was now to be applied across the board as the primary embodiment of contemporary Chinese Marxism. There could be no doubt as to the ultimate source of political power; this had been settled through the new constitutional entrenchment of Xi's position as 'core' leader, and the parallel responsibility of all party members to 'uphold' his core position. Once again, Xi is plain-speaking in his report about the content, scope, and significance of the ideological project on which he was embarked:

> Marxism is the fundamental guiding ideology upon which our party and our country are founded and thrive. Our experience has taught us that, at the fundamental level, we owe the success of our party and socialism with Chinese characteristics to the fact that Marxism works, particularly when it is adapted to the Chinese context and the needs of our times. The sound theoretical guidance of Marxism is the source from which our party draws its firm belief and conviction and which enables our party to seize the historical initiative. . . . With new changes and practical demands emerging both in and outside of China since the 18th National Congress, there was an urgent need for us to provide in-depth theoretical and practical answers to a series of epochal questions on the cause of the party and the country as well as the party's governance of China. With the courage to make theoretical explorations and innovations, our party has, from an entirely new perspective, deepened its understanding of the laws that underlie governance by a communist party, the development of socialism, and the evolution of human society. It has achieved major theoretical innovations, which are encapsulated in the Thought on Socialism with Chinese Characteristics for a New Era.[27]

This full-throated embrace of Marxism as the single, totalizing worldview for the party is new in its scope. There has been nothing like it in any Congress report since the end of the Cultural Revolution. It is even stronger than the already robust language incorporated in the party's 2021 'historical resolution' discussed in the previous chapter. And, in case there was any continuing lack of clarity about the centrality and content of XJPT, the leader concluded his peroration on ideology by stating:

> The main elements of this theory [XJPT] are summarized in the 10 affirmations, the 14 commitments, and the 13 areas of achievement that were

> articulated at the 19th National Congress [in 2017] and the Sixth Plenary Session of the 19th Party Central Committee [through the 2021 historical resolution], all of which we must adhere to over the long term and continue to enrich and develop.[28]

As noted in the previous chapter, Xi Jinping Thought is a dynamic, not a static, body of ideas, capable of being flexibly adapted to new and emerging circumstances. Its new core concepts were therefore immediately capable of galvanizing political and policy action. And there had been nothing comparable to Xi's attempt to define this new 'Marxism of our times' (the 10-14-13 formula above) on the part of any previous leader in the post-Mao period. Indeed, Xi's bold new ideological world was not intended for the faint-hearted.

Political Impact

Apart from ideology, as a matter of pure politics, Xi's report to the 20th Congress represented a further consolidation of his paramount political status and the deeper entrenchment of the powers of his increasingly Leninist party. Xi dedicated a lengthy section of his report to the 'great changes of the first decade of the new era'—the party's achievements under his leadership.[29] The list is a familiar one, ranging across: the consolidation of the party's leadership overall; the confirmation of China's new status as 'moderately prosperous'; the evolution of his New Development Concept as an alternative to the previous era of reform and opening; the 'eradication' of absolute poverty; and the proper handling of COVID-19 through Xi's so-called dynamic zero-COVID strategy (with no indication of the radical volte-face that would engulf the party and the nation less than a month later). Further afield, it included having 'restored order' in Hong Kong by placing the Special Administrative Region's administration in the hands of 'patriots'; international acceptance of the Belt and Road Initiative; and Xi dealing effectively with a rolling series of 'grave' challenges in China's international environment. The net impact of this stellar record of recent achievement was to further elevate Xi's ideological and political status.

Xi's success in changing the entire face of modern Chinese politics was underscored further by the magnitude of both the 19th and the 20th Party Congresses' departure from the established norms laid down by his predecessors. Xi had defied the prevailing political convention limiting China's national leaders to two five-year terms. This convention had been designed to reinforce collective leadership and to prevent anyone returning to Mao's practice of lifelong tenure.[30] Xi was now, potentially at least, leader for life. Xi had also been constitutionally entrenched as the 'core' leader. Furthermore, Xi had delivered his own body of ideological 'thought' for the 'new era' after only five years in office. And, finally, Xi's anti-corruption campaign had become the longest internal party campaign in its hundred-year history and was a key mechanism for entrenching political loyalty and control. The centrality of that campaign, and its achievements to date, were reaffirmed by the 20th Congress. In fact, the Congress made clear that Xi intended to continue the campaign indefinitely as part of what he routinely calls the machinery of party 'self-revolution' that was necessary to preserve the party's 'red genes' (*hongse jiyin*).[31]

In Xi's political worldview, all these measures were entirely justifiable because of the parlous state of the party he had inherited from his predecessors. He reiterated to his audience:

> Great achievements had been secured. . . . At the same time, however, a number of prominent issues and problems—some of which had been building for years and others which were just emerging—demanded urgent action. Inside the party, there were many issues with respect to upholding the party's leadership, including a lack of clear understanding and effective action as well as a slide toward weak, hollow, and watered-down party leadership in practice. Some party members and officials were wavering in their political conviction. Despite repeated warnings, pointless formalities, bureaucratism, hedonism, and extravagance persisted in some localities and departments. Privilege-seeking mindsets and practices posed a serious problem, and some deeply shocking cases of corruption had been uncovered.[32]

Apart from the Congress itself, there had also been growing evidence of an intensification of Xi's cult of personality. The party's sixteen-part propaganda series developed for China Central Television as a backdrop to the Congress on navigating China's future under Xi Jinping is remarkable for its Mao-like content.[33] This came against the background of an official media campaign referring to the importance of 'one position in the highest authority now setting the tone' (*dingyu yizun*).[34] In Chinese classical and modern traditions, this expression has tended to refer pejoratively to the use and abuse of unconstrained political power.[35] However, official commentaries soon began using it as a positive approach to explaining

Xi Jinping Thought.[36] Throughout 2022, this undiluted focus on the absolute centrality of Xi's individual political power occurred against the 'surround-sound' of three mega-propaganda campaigns on: the 'Four Consciousnesses' (*sige jueyi*), 'Four Self-Confidences' (*sige zixin*), and the 'Two Establishes/Two Safeguards' (*liangge quexin/baohu*).[37] The Four Consciousnesses were the need to: uphold political integrity (i.e. zero corruption); think in big-picture terms (i.e. in ideological and strategic terms); uphold the leadership core (i.e. Xi Jinping); and keep in policy alignment with the CCP central leadership (i.e. Xi again).[38] The Four Self-Confidences referred to confidence in: China's chosen path (i.e. socialism); China's chosen ideology (i.e. Marxism-Leninism and Xi Jinping Thought); China's political system (i.e. CCP leadership); and Chinese culture (i.e. the party's campaign surrounding its definition of China's outstanding traditional culture). The Two Establishes/Two Safeguards refer to Xi's core leadership and that of the party centre.[39] Taken together, these three campaigns have regularly been referred to as '4-4-2' (*sisier*), embodying the core principles of political orthodoxy under Xi.[40] These various campaigns, combined with the specific outcomes of the 20th Congress itself, aligned in a single political trajectory—a leader and a party continuing to move Chinese politics towards the Leninist left and with a growing number of ideological and political resonances of Mao himself.

Economic Policy Change

On the economy, a central question at the 20th Congress was whether development remained the central task of the party, or whether it had now been equalled, or even surpassed, by national security. Another was whether, within the economic development debate, the relative emphasis on market forces or state intervention would change further given the redefinition of the central contradiction in 2017. In answering the first question, Xi's overall shift away from the centrality of China's classical economic growth agenda is reflected in the simple but instructive measure of the reduced number of references to the word 'economy' itself.[41] At the 14th Congress of 1992, when Deng relaunched his economic agenda of market reform and opening, 'the economy' appeared 195 times. By the time of Xi's first Congress report in 2017, that number had come down to 70. In the 2022 report, 'the economy' was referenced on only 60 occasions. Similarly, at

Deng's 1982 Congress, the term 'national security' appeared only once; it appeared 4 times at Hu's 18th Congress in 2012; and rose to 18 references at Xi's first Congress in 2017. There were 27 references in his 2022 report. Of itself, this did not mean that national security had replaced economic development as the party's core priority. But it did put these twin imperatives on a much more equal footing, reflecting Xi's ideological effort to redirect the party towards the securitization of everything amidst the multiple risks and threats he now perceived. This relative downgrade from a near-exclusive emphasis on economic development in previous decades was also underlined in the relatively tepid treatment of the party's economic growth objectives for 2022–2027. The CCP now expected only 'reasonable' economic growth, rather than the fixed and ambitious numerical targets of the past, presumably mindful of the vast array of domestic and international headwinds that were already bearing down on the Chinese economy.[42]

The Congress report's rendition of the party's economic policy settings also indicated a continuing drift away from market principles towards the more comfortable and familiar disciplines of state direction and control. While Xi did make a single reference to the party's 2013 mantra—"giving full play to the decisive role of the market in resource application"—this was tempered by references to the state playing 'a better role'.[43] There was, however, counter-balancing language in the report's relative treatment of state-owned enterprises and the private sector: the party was now told to 'consolidate' (*gonggu*) and 'develop' the public economy while simultaneously moving to "guide the development of the non-public sector". The report spoke of the need for 'national self-reliance' in science and technology and the 'strategic' allocation of resources for new innovation, rather than entrusting that role to China's dynamic, privately owned tech sector. The party was also directed to undertake the "strategic distribution of human resources" rather than letting talent be allocated merely according to the competitive opportunities of the market. In addition, there were numerous references to China's new mercantilism, as reflected in Xi's new dogma on the 'dual circulation economy' whereby China's future growth drivers would primarily be domestic and its reliance on global markets marginal. This was reinforced by a call to "increase the security and resilience of industrial and supply chains" in anticipation of the growing list of incoming national security challenges. All these approaches were nonetheless deemed to be compatible with Xi's embrace of a 'new pattern' of 'opening to the outside world'.[44]

Xi's increasingly market-sceptical approach was nonetheless tempered at the 2022 Congress by his inclusion of a limited number of more reformist concepts. For example, there was a new call to increase total factor productivity across the economy, albeit with little indication of how this might be achieved, given the centrality of the private sector to productivity growth over many decades. Similarly, there was a reference to relaxing restrictions on future inbound foreign direct investment, as well as 'promoting the internationalization of the renminbi in an orderly way' (seemingly driven by a strategy of reducing China's future dependency on Western financial markets in general and the US dollar in particular). In doing so, Xi appears to have been deeply mindful of the economic consequences of financial sanctions against Russia following the invasion of Ukraine; Chinese analysis would undoubtedly have been busy identifying the potential implications for any future Chinese military action over Taiwan.[45] Nonetheless, whatever pro-market signals might be embedded within these various measures, they are overshadowed by Xi's new ideological narrative: 'a Chinese style of modernization'—a model emphasizing state economic 'leadership' at home and greater national self-sufficiency in relation to the future scope of Chinese economic engagements abroad.[46] This also dovetailed with the 2022 Congress report's direct critique of Western, neoliberal globalization as Xi overtly embraced what he now referred to as the 'correct direction of economic globalization' for the future.

Xi's 2022 Congress report therefore continued the upending of Deng's long-standing growth model on the ideological grounds he had laid out at the previous Congress in 2017. This was reflected in his ongoing emphasis on the 'New Development Concept', the revitalization of "stronger, bigger, better" state-owned enterprises and the acceleration of large-scale industrial policy. It was also seen in new restrictions on the private sector, and an attack on private 'monopolies', reinforced by fresh political assaults concentrated on the tech, property, and private education industries.[47] And all this was underlined by an increasingly mercantilist approach to international economic policy in response to what Xi concluded to be a US strategy of systematic decoupling.[48] Indeed, there was no evidence in the 20th Party Congress report that Xi was moving away from the statist development model he had first outlined in 2017. Nor was there evidence that he was now pivoting back towards the market, the private sector, or to more open forms of international economic engagement. Rather, Xi was digging in. His move to the Marxist left in economic policy was instead gathering pace:

> China's economy was beset by acute structural and institutional problems. Development was imbalanced, uncoordinated, and unsustainable, and the traditional development model could no longer keep us moving forward. Some deep-seated problems in institutions and barriers built by vested interests were becoming more and more apparent. Some people lacked confidence in the socialist political system with Chinese characteristics, and, all too often, we saw laws being ignored or not being strictly enforced. Misguided patterns of thinking such as money worship, hedonism, egocentricity, and historical nihilism were common, and online discourse was rife with disorder. All this had a grave impact on people's thinking and the public opinion environment.[49]

Chinese Nationalism, Foreign and Security Policy

On foreign and security policy, Xi's 2022 Congress report also doubled down on his abandonment of Deng's cautious advice to 'hide your strength, bide your time, never take the lead'. By underlining the increasing importance of China's national security challenges and the need to more proactively identify and dismantle the rising number of strategic risks the country now faced, Xi was making plain that China now saw the world through an entirely different lens. Indeed, the most disturbing element of the 20th Party Congress report is its formal analysis of China's rapidly evolving external strategic environment. Party Congress reports since 2002 had routinely cited 'a period of strategic opportunity' (*zhanlue jiyuqi*) underpinned by a benign external environment and China's principal focus on economic development.[50] Instead, Xi warned:

> Our country has entered a period of development in which strategic opportunities, risks, and challenges are concurrent and uncertainties and unforeseen factors are rising. Various 'black swan' and 'grey rhino' events may occur at any time. We must therefore be more mindful of potential dangers, be prepared to deal with worst-case scenarios, and be ready to withstand high winds, choppy waters, and even dangerous storms.[51]

This departure from Xi's predecessors reflects the fact that the world in China's eyes had now changed—or, more specifically, that US strategy towards China had fundamentally changed:

> Confronted with drastic changes in the international landscape, especially external attempts to blackmail, contain, blockade, and exert maximum pressure

on China, we have put our national interests first, focussed on internal political concerns, and maintained firm strategic resolve. We have shown a fighting spirit and a firm determination to never yield to coercive power. Throughout these endeavors, we have safeguarded China's dignity and core interests and kept ourselves well-positioned for pursuing development and ensuring security.[52]

The analytical and policy implications of this conclusion are clear. The party was no longer ruling out the possibility of a major war in the future. And, as noted in the earlier analysis of recent Congress reports, the party's national security agenda was now rivalling (and, in some respects, surpassing) the importance of its economic agenda. This conclusion is reinforced by new formulations describing China's rapidly deteriorating external environment: "severe and complex international developments" in which the party must be "ready to protect against potential dangers in peacetime"; "preparing for the storm"; and requiring the party to continue adhering to "the spirit of struggle".[53] In all of this, Xi refers to the following five years (2022–2027) as "critical" for the project of building a powerful Chinese nation, with national security now being the "foundation of national rejuvenation". This too was a new formulation.[54]

Xi also used his 2022 Congress report to entrench earlier statements on the need for 'an holistic security agenda' incorporating political, economic, strategic, technological, social, and international security. The report directs the party to apply this concept of 'holistic security' across the full spectrum of the party's internal processes. As for the military, Xi vowed to ensure that "our people's armed forces can fight and win"; to train "new types of military personnel" with elevated "combat preparedness"; and to "intensify military training under combat conditions". Importantly, the Congress report re-emphasized the party's long-stated preference to resolve the Taiwan issue peacefully but promising "never to renounce the use of force". While this formulation was not new, Xi did warn that harsher measures adopted towards Taiwan were not targeted at the bulk of the populace but instead at the small minority of Taiwan independence supporters and those foreign states (i.e. the United States) that backed them. And, with clear nationalist resolve, he reminded his Taiwanese audience that the "wheels of history" were still grinding towards the "inevitability of reunification":

In response to separatist activities aimed at 'Taiwan independence' and gross provocations of external interference in Taiwan affairs, we have resolutely

> fought against separatism and countered interference, demonstrating our resolve and ability to safeguard China's sovereignty and territorial integrity, and to oppose 'Taiwan independence'. We have strengthened our strategic initiative for China's complete reunification and consolidated commitment to the one-China principle within the international community.[55]

In summary, on national security—across Taiwan, PLA readiness, and the external strategic environment in general—Xi's 20th Congress report signalled to the Chinese political system that more urgent forms of national security preparedness were the order of the day. These were presented within the wider frame of Xi's nationalist vision of "the great rejuvenation of the Chinese nation", reminding the Congress once again that "our party has dedicated itself to achieving lasting greatness for the Chinese nation". This, in turn, was grounded in Xi's expanding narrative on Chinese cultural nationalism:

> We [the CCP] will stay firmly rooted in Chinese culture, collect and refine the defining symbols and best elements of Chinese culture, and showcase them to the world. We will accelerate the development of China's discourse and narrative systems, better tell China's stories, make China's voice heard, and present a China that is credible, appealing, and worthy of respect.[56]

Based on this growing sense of nationalism and China's expanding national power, Xi concluded his report stating that China should expand its global policy impact, influence, and footprint:

> We will strengthen our international communications capabilities, make our communications more effective, and strive to strengthen China's voice in international affairs so it is commensurate with our composite national strength and international status. . . . Today, our world, our times, and history are changing in ways like never before. The historical trends of peace, development, cooperation, and mutual benefit are unstoppable. The will of the people and the general trends of our day will eventually lead to a bright future for humanity. And yet, the hegemonic, high-handed, and bullying acts of using strength to intimidate the weak, taking from others by force and subterfuge, and playing zero-sum games are exerting grave harm. The deficit in peace, development, security, and governance is growing. . . . China is actively involved in setting global security rules, working to promote international security cooperation, and taking an active part in UN peacekeeping operations. China plays a constructive role in safeguarding world peace and regional stability. Building a human community of common destiny is the way forward for all the world's peoples.[57]

Personnel Changes

This book has focussed on ideological change in Xi Jinping's China and its relationship to political and policy change, rather than the detailed ebbs and flows of CCP high politics, including the rise and fall of individual Politburo leaders. But the dramatic personnel changes to the Standing Committee of the Politburo brought about by Xi at the 20th Congress are relevant not only to his hold on power, but also to his ability to continue taking the party down the new ideological path he has imposed since 2012. Indeed, the leadership changes implemented by Xi at the 20th Congress were audacious.

Until 2022, every leader since Deng—Xi included—had hewed closely to an informal convention that the Standing Committee should broadly reflect a balance of factional and policy interests, as well as accommodating the complex web of family and loyalty networks among party elites. The same rule, which was applied to the composition of other senior party organs, was considered an essential ingredient for long-term political stability and party unity, particularly after the implosion of elite politics in the chaos of the Cultural Revolution. In recent times, this had involved balancing the party's economic reform faction with a conservative group of older-style state planners—two factions that had fought over each step of the reform process from the 1980s onwards, until policy compromises were ultimately forged. The reformist group included the so-called Communist Youth League (CYL) of economic technocrats that had emerged under the patronage of then general secretary Hu Yaobang. Its pedigree included Xi's predecessor Hu Jintao, premier Li Keqiang, and vice-premiers Wang Yang and Hu Chunhua. Colouring this complex factional milieu were the personal loyalty networks surrounding a wider set of groupings: the 'Jiang Faction' historically centred on Jiang Zemin and his organizational enforcer Zeng Qinghong; and another anchored in Xi Jinping himself and the so-called Zhejiang, Fujian, Shanghai, and Shaanxi Factions—each comprising political subordinates who had worked under Xi during his extensive provincial careers and are bound to him through a complex web of personal loyalty and fealty.

Leading into the 20th Congress, the CYL group was represented on the Standing Committee by Li Keqiang and Wang Yang (both aged sixty-seven), with Hu Chunhua (a mere fifty-nine) in the wider Politburo and ready for promotion to the party's inner sanctum. What surprised (even stunned) analysts of Chinese elite politics was Xi's winner-takes-all decision to remove all three CYL faction members from the most senior echelons of the party and state. For some decades, the unofficial rule for China's senior leaders could be characterized thus: "if you're sixty-seven or younger at the time of the Congress, you can stay on, but if you're sixty-eight or over at that time, you retire." Xi, then sixty-nine, was naturally unconstrained by this convention because of the earlier abolition of the two-term limit for the presidency. But his removal of all three CYL candidates—all of whom were beneath the age limit and none of them evidencing any particular political disloyalty to the leader—was deeply surprising. This sent a clear message to the entire Chinese political system that *long-standing* personal loyalty to Xi was now the essential criterion for membership of the most elite tiers of the party. Furthermore, Xi demonstrated he was no longer concerned about how senior personnel appointments would be perceived in the international community, domestic business sentiment, or even the wider ranks of the party.

Every vacancy on the new Politburo Standing Committee was filled by a Xi Jinping loyalist. Li Qiang, the new Premier and No. 2 in the Standing Committee hierarchy, had been Xi's deputy from his days as secretary of the Zhejiang Provincial Party Committee (2002–2007). Despite Li's controversial assignment as secretary of the Shanghai Municipal Party Committee during that city's brutal COVID lockdown, Xi seems to have counted that as a further reason to promote him to the top; Li had passed the loyalty test with flying colours.[58] Second, Cai Qi, who would run the party's Central Secretariat (in effect, becoming Xi's chief-of-staff), was a loyalist from even earlier in Fujian (1995–1999). Xi had subsequently promoted Cai to the General Office of the newly formed National Security Commission, and then to become Beijing Municipal Party Committee secretary. Third, Ding Xuexiang, the new First Vice-Premier, had been responsible for the General Office of the Shanghai Municipal Party Committee during Xi's period as Shanghai Party Secretary in 2007 before becoming Xi's de facto chief-of-staff in 2017. Finally, Li Xi—appointed to head the Central Discipline Inspection Commission, the crucial agency responsible for the party's ongoing anti-corruption campaign, had strong personal ties going back to the 1980s (and even earlier through Xi Jinping's father, Xi Zhongxun).[59]

The degradation of the overall principles of collective leadership under Xi meant that senior personnel appointments were now less important than after previous Congresses. By then Xi had effectively become, as coined by Geremie Barmé, the 'Chairman of Everything',[60] with a myriad of policy commissions and leading groups answering to him across the full spectrum of the party and state machinery. Nonetheless, the premium that Xi has now attached, through his 20th Congress decisions, to absolute political loyalty as a precondition for appointment to a senior role in the party was remarkable. This new loyalty premium is likely to impact the quality of internal debate in the five years leading up to the 21st Congress in 2027, particularly on the economy, since the reformist faction no longer has an effective political and policy voice at the table. The centre of gravity of the new Standing Committee now leans significantly in the direction of the party's new ideological, political, and national security agendas, rather than the long-standing economic development imperatives of times past. Indeed, across ideology, politics, policy, and now personnel, the 20th Congress showed Xi Jinping's 'new era' was well and truly upon us. These profound changes—even compared with the relatively recent past—are the product of a formidable politician who has set to work across the domestic political and policy fronts to consolidate his personal power with signature audacity. More likely than not, we will also see the same audacity applied to China's rapidly changing posture, policies, and actions on the international front. And Xi's fundamental ideological nature, as a committed Marxist-Leninist nationalist, will be to continue to challenge the status quo, both at home and abroad.

Conclusion

The world may never know what was on Hu Jintao's mind as the former CCP general secretary was unceremoniously escorted from the presidium of the Great Hall of the People during the closing ceremony of the 20th Party Congress in November 2022.[61] Hu had long been rumoured as suffering from some form of neurological disease, although he had managed to sit through the lengthy opening session of the Party Congress without apparent difficulty just a few days before. It appears it was only on stage at the closing ceremony that Hu became aware of the final senior leadership list to be approved by the customary unanimous show of hands by Congress delegates and that none of his protégés from the CYL faction had survived Xi's culling. This would explain Hu's extreme agitation on stage and Xi's apparent ordering of his removal from the chamber to prevent the unseemly spectacle of a former leader not raising his hand in support of the new leadership slate. Chinese state media subsequently stated that Hu was "not feeling well" and was taken away to rest. Remarkably, the incident did not prevent Hu from attending Jiang Zemin's brief cremation ceremony six weeks later, although not Jiang's official state funeral the following day, when the official media indicated the former president "could not stand up for long, given [his] age".[62]

If you could imagine yourself as Hu Jintao, observing the world that he had only recently presided over being turned upside down before his very eyes, this would have been a deeply unsettling experience. I personally remember Hu well as a confident young Guizhou Provincial Party secretary visiting Australia in the mid-1980s when I was a junior diplomat, and then two decades later as China's president when I was Australian prime minister.[63] It would have been difficult for Hu to see much of the world he had helped create being so radically changed. Xi Jinping's China had now become a country of rapid—no longer gradual—ideological, political, and policy change. Hu's removal from the stage that day became a powerful physical emblem of the end of an era that was, in reality, already long gone. Indeed, Xi's direct attack on his predecessors' ideological laxity, relativism, and confusion at the party's Propaganda and Ideological Work Conference nearly a decade before in 2013 had proven to be deeply predictive of Hu's final and inglorious demise. The last of the reform generation had literally been shuffled off the political stage.

The 20th Congress heralded the beginning of Xi's second decade in China's highest office, having defied party convention by doing so. He had doubled down on his Marxist-Nationalist ideology in the lead-up to the Congress. This had been demonstrated by his radical re-embrace of Mao's theory of contradictions and their application to both China's foreign and domestic challenges. He then took further measures at the Congress itself: ideologically, XJPT had been further entrenched into the party constitution; politically, he had removed all potential opponents from the Politburo of his increasingly Leninist party; economically, he had fully embraced his new Marxist doctrine of common prosperity, defining it as the essence of Chinese socialism; and internationally, he had radically changed the underlying premise of Chinese foreign policy from a benign strategic environment to a hostile one.

These were big changes indeed. But we should not assume that what we have seen over Xi Jinping's first decade, culminating in the 20th Party Congress, necessarily represents the end point of his ideological revolution. Indeed, it may only be the beginning. And for the CCP, changes in ideology generally represent leading, rather than lagging, indicators of broader changes across the Chinese political and policy spectrum. That is why it remains critical to follow closely the CCP's ideological debates as they continue to unfold to see what further patterns of change may yet emerge, particularly following the unexpected crises and challenges in Chinese foreign policy and the economy in 2023, including the unexplained reversal of the regime's 'dynamic zero COVID' policy in December 2022 and the public health emergency that followed. This will be the focus of the concluding chapters of this book as we seek to use ideology as our guide to look into China's future during this second decade of Xi Jinping's reign.

14

What Xi Jinping's Ideology Can Tell Us about China's Future

As of the end of his first full decade in office—despite Hu Jintao's unplanned, inelegant, but brutally effective removal from the stage on 22 October 2022—the conclusion of the 20th Party Congress marked what future historians may come to see as the apogee of Xi Jinping's political power. He had defied post–Cultural Revolution convention by securing reappointment for a third term as China's paramount leader, with nothing to prevent him becoming leader for life. He had wiped the slate clean across the Standing Committee and broader Politburo, elevating a slew of personal loyalists and removing those who were not. Xi's Marxist-Nationalist ideological framework—Xi Jinping Thought—had become his ideational roadmap for the future of the party, the country, and, according to growing numbers of sycophantic political scribes, the world. Indeed, Xi's ideology had become entrenched as China's new official orthodoxy.

The party, both by ideological design and through changes in institutional practice, had become more decisively Leninist in its reach across every aspect of Chinese politics, economics, and society, anchored in loyalty to Xi's leadership and a growing cult of personality. The economy was more Marxist through Xi's clear-cut, ideological 'top-level design' which prioritizes state-owned enterprises over the private sector, industrial policy over market forces, and common prosperity as China's new formula for wealth redistribution against the 'greed' of the billionaire class. As for China's place in the region and the world, Xi's ideological framework incorporated a more strident form of Chinese nationalism, which both justified and animated a more assertive foreign policy through which Beijing would seek to change the international status quo. Across all these changing policy domains, underlying ideological change had been consistently close to the centre of the transformation process. By the end of the 20th Congress, and with the party's Third Historical Resolution also now successfully entrenched and behind him, it seemed that the world now lay at Xi Jinping's feet.[1]

Ideological Overreach and the Politics of Policy Correction during 2023

If a week is a long time in politics, then a month is a very long time, and twelve months an eternity. Indeed, 2023 would prove to be a difficult year for Xi Jinping, his very own *annus horribilis.* On 7 December 2022, just six weeks after the 20th Congress, Xi's new Politburo approved an abrupt volte-face on its 'dynamic zero-COVID'[2] policy, which had been long claimed to be China's secret formula for success when measured against America's chaos during the global pandemic.[3] China's hospital system was insufficiently prepared and understocked with anti-viral medicines to deal with the large-scale influx of cases. Independent analysts concluded that, as a result, China recorded as many as 1.7 million deaths from the virus over five weeks (by contrast, Chinese officials claimed fewer than 60,000 extra deaths).[4] China's much-anticipated economic recovery, which was expected to be driven by rapidly growing domestic consumption, also failed to materialize. While China's official IMF growth projection for the year was raised to 5.2% after the zero-COVID policy was lifted,[5] unofficial analysts expressed deep scepticism about the party's official statistics. These doubts intensified following China's August 2023 decision to suspend indefinitely the publication of the country's ballooning youth unemployment numbers.[6] Declining business and consumer confidence, driven in part by Xi's underlying ideological fundamentalism, constrained growth in private consumption, private fixed capital investment, and the critical residential construction sector.[7] Meanwhile, Xi's continued geo-political confrontation with the United States and its Asian and European allies over Taiwan, the East and South China Seas, the Sino-Indian border, economic coercion, and emerging restrictions on trade, investment, and technology also undermined the traditional economic strength of China's external account.[8] These faltering drivers of China's economic growth model began to generate a global debate about whether, under Xi Jinping, the Chinese economy had, in fact, 'peaked' and, through policies of its own making, fallen into its much-feared 'middle-income trap'.[9] While much of the ensuing 'Peak China' debate around the world was analytically superficial and wildly premature in its conclusions, it had a palpable effect on international investor sentiment and was widely reported within China itself.[10]

Meanwhile, on the international front, Xi's palpable self-confidence at the Bali Summit with Joe Biden in November 2022—when the US president was seeking to stabilize the bilateral relationship after a long period of escalating tensions[11]—was derailed in February 2023 when the United States shot down a Chinese surveillance balloon that had drifted over the American mainland. China's mismanagement of the incident and international surprise at Beijing's clumsy political response (claiming this was an innocent weather balloon that had simply gone off course) added to Xi's foreign policy challenges.[12] These difficulties were reinforced by a growing number of US diplomatic successes: US-Japan-Korea trilateral security cooperation; the Quad with Japan, India, and Australia; the AUKUS agreement with Australia and the United Kingdom on nuclear-powered submarines and advanced defence technologies; the rebuilding of the US defence relationship with the Philippines; and some advances in the Indo-Pacific Economic Framework.[13] Increasingly anxious Chinese officials rapidly re-engaged US counterparts during the middle months of 2023 to reconstitute the original Bali 'stabilization' agenda and reduce tensions. Prodded by a declining economy at home (compounded, as noted above, by US and allied technology sanctions) and a deteriorating foreign policy environment abroad, Xi finally agreed to attempt a second summit with Biden in San Francisco in November 2023. The result was a mutually agreed framework to 'stabilize' the bilateral strategic relationship, the reconstitution of 'high-level military-to-military' communication channels, and a new dialogue on artificial intelligence.[14]

The 'wolf warrior' diplomats, who had been emblematic of Xi's new age of foreign policy nationalism had, it seemed, at least for a season, been put back into their kennels. Xi also launched and reaffirmed a series of measures designed to reboot domestic and international confidence in China's economy, beginning with the Central Economic Work Conference in December 2022, followed by the National People's Congress in March

2023 and December 2023 Central Economic Work Conference, ahead of the long-delayed Third Plenum of the 20th Central Committee in mid-2024.[15] It appeared that Xi may finally have become acquainted with the practical economic and foreign policy costs and consequences of a decade of ideological overreach. Chinese consumers, local entrepreneurs, and foreign investors were voting with their money. At the same time, many states (including some in the Global South) were seeking to consolidate their own security arrangements by moving closer to the US to balance against an increasingly assertive China that was becoming ever closer to Russia, North Korea, and Iran.[16] Therefore 2023 was an important year. As these economic and international challenges mounted, Xi began to change course in a number of policy areas, both to try to improve China's economy and to stabilize its geo-political relationship with Washington.

Ideological Continuity: Xi's Distinction between Strategic and Tactical Change

The question for analysts, however, is whether these changes would prove to be short-term or long-term, tactical or strategic, refreshingly pragmatic or still fundamentally ideological? The thrust of this book is that, in the absence of fundamental ideological change, there is unlikely to be long-term strategic change to the underlying policy direction that Xi has been charting for his party and country since 2012. This is because, under Xi, ideological change has usually been the precursor of, or at least the signalling device for substantive policy change. Moreover, if ever in doubt, Chinese officials were more likely to take their basic guidance from the ideological line rather than the day-to-day ephemera of what passed for policy debate. After all, ideology always bore the imprimatur of the leader, whereas policies came and went. Yet as of early 2024, there had been no evidence of any real change in the fundamental Marxist-Nationalist ideological settings that Xi had painstakingly put in place over the previous decade. In fact, as we will see in the remainder of this chapter, in a number of areas, Xi would double down further in his resolute pursuit of ideological rigour and underlying policy discipline. It would be imprudent, therefore, to see Xi's apparent shifts in some areas of economic and foreign policy during 2023 as representing any underlying change in Chinese strategy.

Xi's distinction between strategy and tactics was made clear in a critical speech delivered amidst a slew of sharp public health, economic, and foreign policy adjustments during the course of 2023. This was a speech to incoming members of the new Central Committee in a study session on the implementation of Xi Jinping Thought on 7 February 2023—just three days after the shooting down of the surveillance balloon over the United States. The speech, however, was not published until 30 September, after the decision had been taken to proceed with the San Francisco summit with President Biden to stabilize the US-China relationship. This speech was a rare occasion in which Xi had sought to explain the theoretical distinction between strategic and tactical change to a party audience. Indeed, the speech's portentous title, 'On the Management of a Number of Major Relationships in Support of the Chinese Form of Modernization', appears to have been drawn from Mao's major work 'On the Ten Major Relationships' from 1956.[17] The speech analysed the full gamut of China's domestic and international challenges through a Marxist conceptual framework, consistent with his earlier expositions of the intellectual machinery of dialectical and historical materialism. Indeed, the six sets of dialectical relationships listed in Xi's 2023 text cover the full spectrum of the party's policy work: between 'strategy and tactics'; 'top-level design and ground-up practical exploration'; 'ideological righteousness and the culture of innovation'; 'economic efficiency and social justice'; 'dynamism and proper process'; and 'national self-reliance and international economic engagement'. In understanding Xi's ideological and deeply dialectical worldview, it is a seminal text.

In the logic of Xi's ideology, 'strategy' should always remain constant over time, consistent with the party's 'scientific' analysis of major long-term issues, trends, and contradictions that affect the entirety of the party and the country. And critically, this must always remain conceptually distinct from 'tactics', which can be adjusted from time to time to meet the immediate circumstances:

> Strategy and tactics are powerful weapons for our party to lead the people to transform the world, change practice, and promote historical development. The correct application of strategy and tactics is the secret of our party's success in creating a glorious history. . . . To promote Chinese-style modernization, we must pass on, apply, and develop this successful secret well. It is necessary to enhance our forward-looking strategy, accurately grasp the inevitable trend of the development of things, keenly understand the opportunities and challenges that may appear on the way forward, and foresee

> and lead the future with a scientific strategy. In order to enhance the overall nature of strategy, plan strategic objectives, formulate strategic measures, and make strategic arrangements, we must focus on solving major issues that have a bearing on the success or failure of the cause of the party and the country and affect the whole body. To enhance the stability of the strategy, once the strategy is formed, it is necessary to adhere to it for a long time, grasp it to the end, do good work, and not change it at will. . . . Strategy provides a scientific approach to tactical implementation (*celue wei zhanlue shishi tigong kexue fangfa*). The environmental conditions for implementing the strategy change at any time, and we will encounter new situations and new problems at any moment, requiring us to organically combine the principles of strategy with the flexibility of tactics—to be flexible, to adapt to changes, to make decisions in the moment, and to grasp the strategic initiative in adapting measures to local conditions, moving according to the situation, and acting according to the trend.[18]

Ideologically, at least in Xi's conceptual universe, the long-term strategic direction of the party and the country could only be determined through a considered, 'scientific' analysis of the underlying political, economic, and international trends as defined by historical materialism. The analysis of these 'scientific' trends could then be translated into strategy by applying the theory of contradictions, consistent with the principles of dialectical materialism. The third step in this tortured logic was to determine the modalities of 'struggle' that would then be necessary to resolve these contradictions, thereby achieving progress. And it was these modalities of struggle that, in turn, determined long-term strategy. Against this complex process, tactics could simply be adjusted from time to time to maximize the prospects of strategic success.

Applied to China's contemporary domestic circumstances, the principles of historical materialism, as interpreted by China's ideologist-in-chief and those around him, had now dictated that the country was moving towards the final phase of the primary stage of socialism. Meanwhile, dialectical materialism and the theory of contradiction had dictated the need to correct the imbalances, inequities, and spiritual impurities brought about by decades of reform, opening, and rapid development launched by Deng. This was the strategic struggle in which the party was now engaged so that a higher form of socialism could now be achieved within China, and in a reasonable timeframe. But, as noted in earlier chapters, these principles of historical materialism, dialectical materialism, and struggle also applied to China's international reality.

It was a matter of 'scientific law' that the world was now witnessing the inexorable rise of the East (i.e. China) and the decline of the West (i.e. the United States). These were, in fact, 'changes not seen in a hundred years'. They were irreversible trends given that they were driven by the underlying, immutable forces of historical materialism. As a result, under the theory of contradictions—although stated implicitly rather than explicitly in the party's literature—the United States and its allies would actively seek to constrict and contain China's expanding international influence. Consistent with this dialectical materialist framework, struggle would therefore ensue on the international front until such time as China prevailed against its adversaries. According to these theoretical schemata, party 'strategy' must always comply with the party's defined central contradictions. Strategy would, therefore, remain constant for the long term, so long as the definition of these central contradictions remained constant. Tactics, however, would vary, depending on the ebbs and flows of the party's day-to-day calculation of risks and opportunities.

This conceptual distinction between strategy and tactics had been underscored in an explanatory article by the party's Institute of Party History and Literature published in the theoretical journal *Qiushi*.[19] Importantly, this article also made clear the ideological linkage between the party's determination of its main contradiction, on the one hand, and the setting of long-term party and national strategy, on the other:

> The party's 100-year history is a history of correctly grasping the main contradictions in society and relentlessly struggling around the central task. . . . Seizing the main contradictions and central tasks to drive the overall work is an inherent requirement of dialectical materialism, as well as a method of thought and work that our party has always advocated and adhered to. . . . The party's century-long history is a history of claiming the historical initiative, overcoming risks and challenges, and moving from victory to victory with correct strategy and tactics. It is necessary to strengthen strategic thinking and strategic determination, and to always have a 'country's greatness' in mind, so as to enhance the conscientiousness and steadfastness in implementing the party's theory, road, guidelines, and policies. . . . General Secretary Xi Jinping has pointed out that: "strategic judgment must be accurate, strategic planning must be scientific, we must strategically take the initiative, and then there will be great hope for the party and the people's cause." . . . Indeed it can be said that the history of the party is a strategic history. It is precisely because we are good at analysing the mechanism of evolution and exploring the historical laws along the long river of history,

> the tide of the times, and the winds and clouds globally, proposing corresponding strategy and tactics, and enhancing the systematic, predictive, and creative nature of our work, that our party has been able to grow from small to large, weak to strong. It has been able to unite and lead the Chinese people in realizing the great leap of the Chinese nation from continuous decline in the modern era, to a fundamental reversal of its destiny, as it continuously progresses towards prosperity and strength.[20]

For these reasons, within the ideological framework that Xi had reinforced over the course of his first decade in power, whatever *policy* changes that might have been embraced by the party leadership in response to immediate challenges (e.g. on COVID-19, the private sector, or even on aspects of US relations), these would most likely be seen by an educated Chinese political audience as short-term and *tactical* in nature. Long-term strategy was a different matter altogether.

In summary: ideology determines dialectics, which determine contradictions, which determine struggle, which, in turn, determines strategy. These are constants. By contrast, policy and tactics are the transient instruments of strategy and, by definition, can readily be varied. Xi's ideological analysis of the prevailing dialectics between 2017 and 2022 had determined the nature of the two principal sets of contradictions the party faced over the long term: inequality and unbalanced development at home, and America and containment abroad. Both, by definition, required struggle if China and the CCP were to prevail. These, therefore, became the ultimate ideological determinants of the party's strategic priorities. And, as a result, Xi's underlying ideological worldview had not changed despite the tumultuous domestic and international events of 2022–2023. In fact, in some respects, it had become even more deeply rooted.

It followed that whatever policy changes might be needed in response to these more immediate political, economic, and foreign policy exigencies, they were to be seen as tactical and short-term in nature. These conclusions would have made sobering reading for Chinese policy elites and the private sector seeking to decipher the complex dialect of the CCP's internal ideological discourse. Chinese entrepreneurs would have hoped for not only a temporary reprieve from Xi's decade-long retreat from the market, but for clear-cut evidence of an enduring change in his underlying ideological line on the economy. But this was not to be. Similarly, those with responsibility for managing China's relationship with the international community, who may have been looking for a more fundamental change in Xi's binary ideological worldview in relation to the United States, the West and the rest would have been equally disappointed. Once again, the real-world distinctions between strategy and tactics, and between ideology and policy, had been made clear. Ultimately, when it comes to both interpreting and shaping the long-term directions of Xi's party and country, ideology tends not to lie, whatever the politics and policy of the day might happen to be.

Ideology as a Precursor for the Future

This brings us to the wider question of what Xi's hardening ideological worldview can tell us about the likely shape of the decade to come, both for China and the world. On this, there are three core variables at play: Xi's likely personal longevity, the longevity of his ideology, and whether and how much this ideology might change further in response to unfolding developments.

Although it is unknowable whether Xi himself will physically survive the decade, he appears to have robust genetics on his side—he turned seventy-one in 2024, his father lived to eighty-eight and, at time of writing, his mother was still alive at ninety-seven. Together with the first-class medical care normally provided to Politburo members, it is reasonable to assume that Xi would be healthy enough to maintain political dominance until at least the 22nd Party Congress due in 2032, when he would be approaching eighty. Xi would probably seek to govern beyond that date, as he would be anxious about what would happen to his family—let alone his legacy and his vision for China's future—if he were to retire from politics altogether. Although not constitutionally necessary, this could also be achieved by rehabilitating the position of 'party chairman', previously used by Mao, which was distinct from the lesser post of 'general secretary'.[21] Xi's success in marginalizing the legacy and impact of both Jiang Zemin and Hu Jintao after 2012, and his systematic removal of their protégés from the Politburo, serve as clear reminders of Xi's Machiavellian instinct for political survival—and his likely predisposition to remain in office so long as he physically can.

The second factor—the long-term impact of Xi's ideological line—flows directly from the first: that is, how long Xi himself manages to remain in power. Xi has sought to institutionalize his deep reset of CCP ideological orthodoxy through multiple campaigns, movements, and rule changes. But in CCP history, while certain irreducible Marxist-Leninist fundamentals have remained in place (e.g. political legitimacy proceeding from armed revolution rather than electoral participation), broader ideological settings have tended to change with major changes in the party leadership. We have, for example, already seen this pattern in the profound ideological shifts from Mao, to Deng, through to Xi. For these reasons, we should not assume that Xi's unique form of Marxist-Leninist Nationalism would automatically survive his eventual departure from office, or if it does, for how long. This will be discussed at greater length in the concluding chapter.

Another influence on the enduring real-world impact of Xi's ideational worldview is what further additions he may still make to his existing ideological corpus. Xi has long said that Chinese Marxism is dynamic rather than static. The fact that he has introduced such major ideological changes during his first decade in power does not mean that he has finished. For example, since the 20th Party Congress, Xi has already begun to explore new thematics in the intersection between Marxist ideology, approved parts of traditional Chinese culture, and even compatible elements of 'world cultures'.[22] This suggests that further adaptations to the existing canon may be intended to extend the reach and appeal of Xi Jinping Thought to the Global South. Ideological and political life in the CCP is rarely linear and will always have the inbuilt opacities of an authoritarian state. Nonetheless, whatever changes may lie ahead of us in the ever-expanding world of Xi Jinping Thought, it is unlikely that any of the core, new directions that have been developed thus far for his Marxist-Leninist-Nationalist framework will be diluted over the decade ahead. Too much time, effort, and deep textual change has occurred to simply walk away from the ideological shifts that have been put in place over the decade, particularly as Xi's personal political legitimacy is now attached to these changes. If anything, the developments of 2023 suggest that Xi was becoming more ideological rather than less. Since the beginning of his tenure, Xi's overriding view has been that ideological control is fundamental to the party remaining in power and preventing systemic collapse as happened in the Soviet Union between 1989 and 1991. Indeed, an ideologically disciplined party is seen as a precondition for avoiding what Xi fears most from both Chinese and Russian history: namely, the recurrent cycles of rise and fall that have dominated both countries' dynastic histories.[23] For all these reasons, while tactical changes to policy are likely to occur in the decade ahead in response to changing circumstances, strategic changes anchored in Xi's deepest ideological settings are not.

Whither the Party? The Future of Leninist Politics

Will Xi Jinping continue to take the CCP further to the Leninist left over the decade ahead? Unlike with Marxism, Xi has rarely written about Leninism (*lieningzhuyi*) or explicitly examined the term in depth. Nonetheless, Xi has littered the party's theoretical journals with a formidable body of work on 'party building' (*dangjian*).[24] The same applies to his contributions on 'party discipline', 'party rectification', 'party history', 'party style', and 'party education'.[25] These are apart from his rolling program of reforming the party's organizational structure and rules, personnel recruitment, and ideological training. In Xi's belief system, the absolute power of a Leninist party remains axiomatic to the survival, strength, and success of both the party and the nation. Moreover, there is nothing in Xi's literature since the 20th Party Congress to suggest any fresh qualification to this approach, notwithstanding clear concerns arising from the impact of an increasingly all-pervasive party on private sector confidence. Nor have there been organizational changes to deal with the impact of increasingly centralized decision-making on the quality of internal debate and professional advice within the party itself. Indeed, as noted above, Xi appears to have doubled down on his previous definitions of ideological orthodoxy.

This can be seen most particularly in Xi's hard-line speech, reported in *Qiushi* in late December 2022, on promoting the 'spirit' of the Yan'an Rectification Movement.[26] This was delivered to new Politburo Standing Committee members during a study tour to Yan'an in the week following their elevation at the 20th Congress. Here Xi reminded these new appointees that Yan'an was home to a decisive phase in party rectification between 1935 and 1948: it was where Mao finally took full political and ideological control of the party (while not mentioning the number of cadres Mao also had killed[27]). Yan'an was also where Xi himself had laboured during the Cultural Revolution.[28] And it was to this 'holy land' of the party where Xi, on three occasions since his promotion to the central leadership in 2002, had returned to remind himself of the party's transformation into the political and ideological force that would sweep all of mainland China by the end of 1949. Indeed, with clear resonances with the party's current strategic circumstances, Xi stated that Mao's party had confronted "military encirclement and economic blockade".[29] Nonetheless, at Yan'an, the CCP had established its fundamental traditions of adhering to the correct political line, advancing 'common prosperity', promoting 'self-reliance', disciplining itself through the people's supervision under 'the mass line', and persevering with hard 'struggle' throughout. That was because they were "courageous enough to carry out continuing self-revolution within the party".[30] Xi's continued invocation of the circumstances, spirit, and (most disturbingly) practices of the Yan'an Rectification Movement offered a chilling reminder to all party members of his vision for the party's uncompromising Leninist future.

Lest there be any lingering doubt about Xi's plans for the future of an all-powerful and well-disciplined party, he added a further level of Leninist clarity to its mission in his January 2023 speech on 'Improving the Comprehensive System of Strictly Governing the Party and Promoting the Deepening of the New Great Project of Party Building in the New Era'.[31] Once again, this was not a speech for the ideologically faint-hearted. Xi underscored the dissolute nature of the party he inherited. He reminded his audience that "since the 18th Party Congress, the strict governance of the party had become our clear-cut central mission", noting the new era had ushered in "a series of new concepts, new practices and new organizational rules".[32] Xi then catalogued his great achievements in party building over the previous decade, including: the centrality of 'self-revolutionary' party management through continuing rectification; the restoration of the party's ideological discipline and its capacity for theoretical innovation; the consolidation of the party's political direction; the strengthening of the party's central leadership (through the double-dictum of upholding the power of the party centre and Xi's centrality within it[33]); rectifying the weak and demoralized standing of the party organization; the uncompromising and continuing campaign against corruption; and the elimination of hidden political dangers (i.e. factional opponents) within the party. Xi went on to make the even more remarkable claim that "around the world, there is no political party that takes such a conscious, serious, systematic, and scientific approach to its own self-revolution".[34] And to eliminate any remaining doubt about Xi's belief in the level of widespread popular support for

Leninist party discipline, he stated that, after ten years of cracking down on corruption, public approval of his efforts had increased by 22.4% to 97.4%. For Xi, an all-powerful, politically loyal, ideologically united, and non-corrupt party remained central to what he described as "the great cause of the nation and the great plan of the party".[35]

Xi also used the opportunity of the ninetieth anniversary of the founding of the Central Party School in 2023 to underscore the centrality of ideology to all that the party does. He reminded the party that the Central School had been "the headquarters of the entire Yan'an Rectification Movement" and that it had "organized the study of rectification documents, summarized historical experiences, enhanced ideological understanding, and promoted unprecedented cohesion throughout the entire party".[36] If anyone had hoped for a resurgence of pragmatism in response to the party's recent external challenges, Xi took precisely the reverse approach by declaring that a better application of scientific Marxism to China's challenges was in fact the best remedy for all. The core challenge was to start systematizing the party's ideological education in Xi Jinping Thought and apply its theories more rigorously to China's current circumstances:

> The cultivation of theory goes to the core of a leading cadre's general quality. Maturity in theory forms the foundation for political maturity. Political steadfastness originates from clarity in theory. For leading cadres, the more securely they grasp the fundamentals of Marxism, the stronger their political footing. They become stronger in their judgement, comprehension, and execution of politics. Their proactive abilities to observe a situation, develop plans, and prevent or resolve risks increase. The Party School plays a crucial role in promoting the learning of Marxist theory among party members and leading cadres, and enhancing their theoretical literacy. . . . Party schools should further strengthen their education and training in Marxist theory, guiding students to delve into the Marxist classics and truly understand the essence of Marxism. The focus should be on effectively applying the basic principles of Marxism to address the issues of contemporary China. . . . At all levels, party schools must consider the ideology of socialism with Chinese characteristics for a new era as their central content, guiding students to comprehensively and systematically study this ideology and deeply understand its worldview and methodology. This includes its positions, viewpoints, methods, concepts, insights, and strategies for governance. A firmly built political stance based on theoretical clarity should go together with conscious thinking, leading to conscious actions. . . . In the research and interpretation of socialism with Chinese characteristics for a new era, strong efforts should be made to systematize and refine its substance. The study should delve into the historical background, scientific framework,

> spiritual essence, practical demands, and original contributions of the party's innovation. . . . This approach ensures that the ideas are presented vividly, that the theory is thoroughly articulated, enabling the party's innovative theories to resonate deeply with the people.[37]

Importantly for the purposes of this book, Xi used this significant anniversary not merely to drill down on the intrinsic importance of Marxist ideology and methodology, including Xi Jinping Thought. He also made plain that the party should take the widest possible remit in implementing his newfound ideological framework in the real world of day-to-day politics and policy. This included not just party-building as an institutional end in itself. It also meant applying his ideology across the breadth of China's domestic political economy and future foreign and national security policy direction. Ideology would not only shape the country's new 'Chinese-style' development model for the nation. It would shape the evolution of China's future approach to global governance too. In other words, Chinese Marxism-Leninism would no longer stop at the continental shelf, as it had done under Deng. Its remit would also be international, as it once was under Mao, although not as yet returning to the Great Helmsman's full-throated call for global revolution:

> These party schools should organize efforts to investigate major strategic topics related to economic development, political construction, cultural development, social construction, ecological civilization, and party-building—topics that are far-reaching, global, and fundamental. In particular, there should be in-depth research on how to: respond to unprecedented global changes; coordinate domestic and international considerations effectively; deepen and expand China's modernization; establish a new development pattern; promote high-quality development; ensure comprehensive people's democracy throughout the development process; solidify efforts towards common prosperity; accelerate scientific and technological self-reliance and strength; creatively transform and innovatively develop China's excellent traditional culture; advance the modernization of the national security system and capabilities; and unwaveringly enforce strict party governance across the board. They should also contribute to the construction of a community with a shared future for all humanity. These research endeavours should yield substantial, influential, and weighty results. They should contribute wisdom and strength to the party's ever-deeper understanding of the laws of Communist Party governance, the laws of socialist construction, and the laws of social development for all humankind. This is essential for composing new chapters, new contributions, wisdom, and power through the Sinification and modernization of Marxism.[38]

Xi also anticipated that his continuing, hardline, ideological *cri de coeur* was likely to generate opposition. But, in his view, such opposition was inevitable, given that ideological and political struggle remained essential for accelerating dialectical progress. This opposition would arise both at home and abroad since the contradictions the party now faced were both domestic and international:

> It is important to emphasize that the current struggle in the ideological field remains sharp and complex. The entire party should proactively engage in the spirit of daring and adeptness in struggle, firmly maintaining the initiative. Party schools serve as important front-line positions in the CCP's ideological work, and both domestic and international attention is highly focused on the messages that emanate from party schools. . . . Party schools should refute such varied fallacies in a targeted way. They should fulfil their roles as active propagators of the party's innovative theories, steadfast defenders of Marxism's guiding position in the ideological field, and be reliable leaders guiding ideological trends in society in a manner compatible with the party's ideology.[39]

The underlying strategic trajectory that emerges for Xi's Leninist party for the decade ahead appears, therefore, to be relatively set. Anyone expecting Xi to reinterpret his ideological approach to the party's totalizing role following the various economic and foreign policy adjustments of 2022 and 2023 would be deeply disappointed. Indeed, by the early 2030s, it is likely that the CCP's traditions of collective leadership will amount to little more than distant political memory. Xi's position will likely have evolved from one of paramount leader to absolute leader, ruling the party through the contemporary equivalent of a continuing reign of terror. This would be achieved through the processes of so-called self-revolution that continued the 'spirit' of the Yan'an Rectification Movement and justified harsh punishments for any internal dissent. The anti-corruption campaign is also likely to be sustained for yet another decade as the most convenient mechanism for dealing with aberrant comrades, while still avoiding the Stalinist spectacle of political show trials for explicitly political purposes. Ideology will therefore become even more critical to sustaining party unity, more determinative in the party's analysis of China's complex policy circumstances, and more influential in shaping Xi's assessment of optimal foreign and domestic policy responses.

Beyond the life and work of what will, by then, be China's 100 million-plus party members, the rest of the Chinese population is also likely to experience new and more intense political and ideological control in their daily lives. Xi's dictum, derived from Mao, that 'the party rules in all' is therefore likely to become more palpable in the lives of average Chinese citizens. Propaganda, both Marxist-Leninist and nationalist, will become more intense and all-pervasive. Information diversity is likely to have shrunk even further with greater control over universities, new assaults on internet access and a fierce crackdown (potentially an effective ban) on generative AI.

Meanwhile, the party as an institution is likely to become more active internationally, both as a political entity in its own right and as an ideological force for challenging Western ideational and institutional hegemony. Ideologically, this would manifest through new approaches to Chinese regional and global governance and engagement, involving new language, new formulae, and new institutional arrangements that are more Marxist and Sino-centric in tone and content. In other words, for the decade ahead, Xi's increasingly Leninist party is likely to become more ideological, more politically active, and more institutionally determinative of future Chinese policy settings both at home and abroad. And the world needs to be ready for it.

Ideology and the Future Direction of the Chinese Economy

What can Xi's underlying ideological line tell us about the likely direction of the Chinese economy for the coming decade? More specifically, will China's economic policy settings continue to drift to the Marxist left, thereby compromising China's long-term growth performance? The vast range of variables at play on complex questions of the economy make this more difficult to analyse than the simple, uncompromising approach that Xi has charted for the pure politics of the party. Both the number of these economic variables, and the inter-relationships between them, are difficult to evaluate within a single analytical matrix. This, in turn, makes it difficult to predict any single sequence of events that will drive China's economic future. For these reasons, it is important to separate out China's underlying ideological constraints from the changes in the country's economic policy discourse and its real-world economic performance.

Underlying Ideological Constraints

On China's economic policy settings, there are multiple, mutually reinforcing ideological currents impacting decision-makers as they prosecute Xi's overarching Marxist-Nationalist project. To begin with, the sheer weight of Leninist drag that an increasingly powerful party has on China's once resilient, econocratic, and technocratic elite cannot be underestimated. At a practical level, the number of hours each week that economic decision-makers must now spend on ideological study and individual political survival detracts from the already complex task of managing the world's second-largest economy. On top of this, despite Xi's injunctions to 'dare to innovate' and 'dare to struggle', there is the persistent fear of committing an ideological or political error. Officials will likely be reluctant to provide independent policy advice to the party centre—particularly if such advice might be construed as serving either the 'greed' of China's billionaire class or the interests of Western corporations. In such circumstances, it will often be safer to provide advice that is qualified, ambiguous or, worse still, sycophantic.

Then there are the specific impacts of Xi's 'Marxism for the twenty-first century' as policymakers seek to navigate the complex ideological shoals brought about by the leader's new 'balance' between the market and the state. This was brought about by the new 'central contradiction' formally defined by the 19th Congress in 2017 which unleashed a torrent of policy retreat from the previous thirty-five-year economic orthodoxy of 'reform and opening'. Xi's Marxist redux has created unprecedented policy dilemmas for economic policy elites around such fundamental questions as the optimal size of the Chinese private sector and how best to resuscitate an already inefficient state-owned enterprise sector. 'Reform' is in decline, both in language and in substance, at least as it was once understood as meaning greater recourse to the market. Meanwhile, 'planning' in all its forms is being re-legitimized. There are also now a number of new, more elastic definitions of 'competitive neutrality' and 'monopoly', often designed to suit the party's pre-determined ideological preferences for large-scale public, rather than private, enterprise.[40] And, most sensitive of all, there is great uncertainty about what the continued centrality of 'common prosperity' means in practical policy terms on the vexed question of income redistribution, including its wider implications for entrepreneurial innovation and incentive.

Finally, as economists struggle to respond to mounting ideological demands from a resurgent Leninist party and its fresh appetite for new forms of Marxist intervention, decision-makers also have to contend with the policy implications of Xi's ideology of economic nationalism. Xi's new orthodoxy of national self-reliance—pre-dating but nonetheless reinforced by US export restrictions on advanced technologies to China—is likely to increase pressure on Chinese economic policymakers to double down on national planning, industrial policy, and economic coercion against hostile countries. New forms of economic mercantilism would begin to replace older forms of economic globalization as part of what Xi now routinely described as a new type of 'high-level reform' and a 'new pattern' of 'high-quality opening'. Taken together across all these domains, the cumulative economic policy imprint of Xi's new ideological direction has been profound. The ideological dial has shifted. China's economic policy settings have responded. The state is back. Private enterprise is now under duress. And, as of 2023, there was no real evidence of any fundamental change in overall ideological direction for the economy.

Changing Economic Policy Settings

China's economic policy settings will be critical to restoring growth to the 5%–6% levels during the 2020s that were originally projected at the beginning of Xi's reign. The question is whether the regime will be able to undertake the deep economic policy adjustments necessary to restore domestic and international market confidence without fundamentally resetting the underlying ideological framework that Xi has painstakingly laid down over the previous decade. Certainly, at the policy level, 2023 saw numerous efforts by the party to re-embrace the private sector in general, and the tech and property sectors in particular. Nonetheless, it is equally important to understand the very low baseline against which these adjustments were made. The uncomfortable truth was that, from the perspective of domestic and international business, the policy settings of the previous several years had been particularly dark.[41]

The first clear signs of policy correction came as early as the Politburo meeting of 6 December 2022—the same meeting that had ratified the decision to abandon 'dynamic zero-COVID'. In the official readout, Xi outlined China's five key economic policy goals for 2023 as: boosting market confidence; expanding domestic demand; stabilizing growth, employment, and prices; preventing and defusing major risks; and, finally, a nebulous formulation on "improving economic operations overall".[42] This was followed nine days later, with a growing sense of political urgency, by the Central Economic Work Conference producing a more comprehensive list of upcoming policy adjustments.[43] Departing from its 2020 and 2021 reports, the CEWC called for "unwaveringly deepening reform", "unswervingly expanding openness", and

> greater stimulation of market vitality and creativity in society, respect for the laws of the market, the streamlining of government, the delegation of power... the deep development of mass entrepreneurship and innovation, maximizing the release of the innovative and creative potential of society as a whole, fully tapping the potential of the domestic market in enhancing the role of domestic demand in driving economic growth.[44]

The CEWC report also emphasized the need for equal treatment of the private and public sectors; excised all references to Xi's 'common prosperity' doctrine; encouraged the future expansion of the 'digital economy'; removed previous language attacking 'tech monopolies' and 'the disorderly expansion of capital'; and, most important given the property industry's economic heft, re-embraced the sector by calling on financial institutions to satisfy the 'reasonable financing needs of the industry'. By any measure, these changes in official language across such a wide spectrum of politically sensitive policy areas represented a significant departure from the recent past as the party scrambled to rebuild growth.

By the time of the CEWC in December 2023, the party was already beginning to proclaim, albeit prematurely, some success in restoring growth as a result of its changes in policy course. In the conference's official readout, it claimed that "on the whole, the favourable conditions facing China's development outweigh the unfavourable factors, the basic trend of economic recovery and long-term improvement has not changed, and it is important to strengthen confidence and resolve".[45] Despite the bravado, however, the emphasis on the need to continue rebuilding confidence was significant. This applied to consumer confidence, where the CEWC focused on the need to "expand domestic demand, stimulate potential consumption, expand effective investment, and form a virtuous cycle in which consumption and investment promote each other". But the conference also recognized the problem of faltering business sentiment, reflected in its call to "promote the development and growth of private enterprises, implement a series of measures in terms of market access, acquiring factors [of production], fair law enforcement, and protection of rights, as well as support the development of specialized and innovative of small and medium-sized enterprises".[46] Continued problems in the external factors of economic growth were recognized too in a call for "accelerating the cultivation of new drivers of foreign trade, consolidating the basic position of foreign trade and foreign investment, and expanding trade in intermediate goods, services, digital trade, and cross-border e-commerce exports".[47] Recognizing the reality of the continuing growth gap, the CEWC conceded the need for "a proactive fiscal policy that should be moderately intensified" and to make "good use of the fiscal policy space" still available to the government.[48] Consistent with the messaging at the previous year's conference, the party demonstrated a determination to continue deploying the full range of policy inducements available in the policy toolkit to re-embrace the private sector and thereby restore economic growth.

Xi's Continuing Ideological Narrative on the New Development Model

However, while the party's economic policy messaging in 2022–2023 indicated a clear change in direction from previous years, the same cannot be said of Xi Jinping's overarching ideological narrative on the economy. This remained thoroughly and consistently Marxist. In February 2023—two months after the Politburo meeting that supposedly changed China's economic policy direction—Xi delivered a staunch doctrinal defence of his new concept of 'Chinese-style modernization'. If comrades had any doubt about whether long-term ideology should prevail over shorter-term policy adjustments, Xi opened his remarks with a reminder that the 20th Party Congress clearly "pointed out that Chinese-style modernization is *the* socialist modernization pursued under the leadership of the Communist Party of China . . . and not any other form"[49] (my emphasis). Indeed, he said, the principles outlined at the congress revealed "the profound scientific connotations of Chinese-style modernization" and constituted both "a theoretical summary and a practical requirement".[50] Further, Xi reiterated that Chinese-style modernization remained anchored in his New

Development Concept—the ideological framework that, since the 19th Congress in 2017, had effectively replaced 'reform and opening' as the organizing principle and banner term for China's overall national economic strategy. It will be recalled that the NDC was designed to respond to the new principal contradiction he had defined at the 19th Congress. It had subsequently become the umbrella framework for a long series of measures that had progressively rolled back the pro-market economic policy orthodoxies of the past. This included, for example, the introduction of Xi's critical new concept of 'common prosperity'. Whereas the 2022 and 2023 Central Economic Work Conferences had either relegated or dispensed with the explicit language of 'common prosperity', in Xi's 2023 address on 'Chinese-style modernization' it returned to centre stage with full ideological gusto:

> Common prosperity . . . is a defining feature of Chinese-style modernization, and what distinguishes it from Western modernization. The biggest problems with Western modernization are that it is capital-centred rather than people-centred, and that it seeks to maximize capital gains rather than serve the interests of the vast majority of the people. This has created a huge gap between the rich and the poor, and led to severe polarization. In their efforts to achieve modernization, some developing countries once approached the developed country threshold only to fall into the 'middle-income trap' and become mired in prolonged stagnation, or even experience severe regression. A major cause for this is that these countries failed to solve the problems of polarization and solidification of social strata. . . . Both material abundance and cultural-ethical enrichment are lofty features of Chinese-style modernization. Material poverty is not socialism, nor is cultural impoverishment. Western countries' early pursuit of modernization only led to the accumulation of wealth, crises of faith, and insatiable material desires. An important cause of Western countries' predicaments today is their failure to check greed, which is the nature of capital, and to resolve their deep-seated problems of rampant materialism and spiritual impoverishment.[51]

Xi also made plain that Chinese-style modernization was radically different from full integration with the international economy as advocated by his predecessors. Notwithstanding the 2023 CEWC's economic recipe of boosting foreign trade and removing barriers to foreign investment, Xi made clear that resurgent growth would primarily occur within the overall mercantilist framework of national self-reliance. Xi's language suggests an almost dialectical relationship between self-reliance and self-strengthening on the one hand, and opening up to the outside world on the other:

> To advance Chinese-style modernization, it is essential to adhere to independence and self-reliance, to base the development and advancement of the country and nation on our own strengths, and to firmly grasp the destiny of China's development and progress in our own hands. We must accelerate the construction of a new development pattern, achieve domestic recirculation [of resources], and rely on the advantage of our country's super-massive market to attract global resources and productive factors, enhancing the linkage between domestic and international markets and domestic and international resources. It is important to safeguard economic security, especially food security, energy security, and industrial and supply-chain security. We need to improve this new national system, strengthen national strategic scientific and technological forces, be oriented towards national strategic needs, concentrate on making original and cutting-edge scientific and technical breakthroughs, and resolutely win the battle for key technologies.[52]

Xi's deep ideological commitment to national self-reliance and Marxist concepts of common prosperity was not the only evidence that his underlying ideological framework for the economy had not fundamentally changed, notwithstanding the magnitude of China's more recent economic growth challenges. National security also continued without interruption as the party's overriding political and ideological imperative, ranking well above the day-to-day tasks of pragmatic economic management. Even the relatively pro-market CEWC report conveyed clearly that nothing would cause China to deviate from Xi's long-standing agenda on the 'securitization of everything':

> We must adhere to the positive interaction between high-quality development and high-level security, use high-quality development to promote high-level security, and ensure high-quality development with high-level security. Development and security must achieve a dynamic balance and mutually enhance each other.[53]

In other words, anyone looking for China to relax its increasingly draconian national security environment and once again tolerate normal forms of international economic collaboration would be disappointed. Indeed, this same formulation on national security and development bore striking similarity to language used by the CEWC back in 2020.[54]

Therefore, as of early 2024, Xi Jinping had effectively engaged in a process of double-messaging on the economy. On the one hand, Xi had authorized a series of policy announcements designed to soothe the concerns of domestic entrepreneurs and foreign investors on the weakness of Chinese economic growth. On the other hand, in parallel, Xi sent a different message to his party apparatus that, despite these tactical policy shifts, there had been no fundamental strategic change in the CCP's ideological bearings on the economy. Common prosperity remained intact. So too did national self-reliance. And the paramount importance of Xi's all-seeing security and surveillance state would remain undisturbed, including its continued intrusions on the normal operation of firms. In other words, Xi was trying to have his cake and eat it too. Indeed, cadres would likely have noted Xi's decision to expound on the difference between strategy and tactics in this same speech that contradicted the CEWC's efforts to restore domestic and international confidence in market principles. In short, Xi's tactical messages to the private sector about economic policy differed significantly from his strategic message to the party on economic ideology. It mirrored, in many respects, what would also become his double messaging on China's wider approach to international policy. The obvious problem for Xi was that this sort of double-messaging was unlikely to be believed by its intended audiences, or at least not to the extent necessary to navigate the shoals that lay immediately ahead. Unfortunately for Xi, both business entrepreneurs and foreign governments were now sufficiently concerned about China's long-term direction (and sufficiently sophisticated in their approach) to read the party's domestic political and ideological literature as well. And their general conclusion about the political world according to Xi Jinping was that, when in doubt, ideology would always trump policy, however attractively any intended policy message might be packaged and presented.

The Problem of Economic Underperformance

As for China's real-world economic performance, once again there have been many variables at play. Policy, of course, remained central, but so too have been other structural and cyclical economic factors. On the structural side, accelerating demographic change, declining productivity growth, deep-seated indebtedness across the property and finance sectors, and contracting global trade because of compounding geo-political complexity and uncertainty all continued to create formidable headwinds against strong, long-term Chinese economic growth. Meanwhile, on the cyclical side, the challenges confronting China in its post-COVID economic recovery have been compounded by variable private consumption, the near-comatose response of private fixed capital investment, and a combination of cyclical and structural problems in the residential construction sector. Compounding both structural and cyclical uncertainties has been the post-2017 trend of heightened geo-political risk in US-China relations, between Russia and Ukraine, and more recently in the Middle East—all of which have undermined business and consumer confidence.

Aggregating the impact of these structural, cyclical, and geo-political factors on actual Chinese growth numbers has been further complicated by growing distrust of China's official statistics across the professional analytical community.[55] The crackdown on private economic research consultancies located within China through a vast new array of national security and foreign espionage laws has had a sobering effect on analytical integrity.[56] Decisions by the Chinese authorities to withhold certain sets of economic data have added to these uncertainties. It has, therefore, been difficult to reach hard conclusions on the depth and likely duration of China's post-COVID economic slowdown. For example, China's official growth numbers for 2022, 2023, and 2024 have been 3%, 5.2%, and a projected 5% respectively.[57] The International Monetary Fund estimates have largely mirrored these Chinese government-sanctioned numbers. But these stand in stark contrast to private consultancy firms such as the Rhodium Group which rely on unofficial indicators beyond those produced by the National Bureau of Statistics (NBS). Rhodium, for example, has calculated China's 2022, 2023, and 2024 growth numbers as 2.5%, 1.5%, and 3.0%-3.5%. Other independent calculations of Chinese growth have generally fallen somewhere within this very wide range, with the NBS and Rhodium resembling the outer bounds of the optimism-pessimism spectrum.[58]

Notwithstanding this analytical uncertainty, it would be foolish to reach premature conclusions that the Chinese economy has already 'peaked'.[59] It is too early to tell. Indeed, even the most negative economic analysts of China conclude that, even if all other growth drivers fail, the untapped potential of Chinese consumer demand is still likely to push the economy forward. Sustained negative growth therefore appears unlikely, if not impossible. In this sense, much of the 'Peak China' commentary smacks of wishful thinking within sections of the Western political community, rather than the product of dispassionate economic analysis based on the raw numbers that can still be gleaned from unofficial sources. More likely is that, whatever the official economic data may say, there is now sufficient evidence to establish that the Chinese economy as of 2023–2024 was prematurely and significantly 'slowing' rather than 'peaking'. While the Chinese official commentariat for the last decade has predicted lower annual growth levels given that China had already reached middle income status, the magnitude of the slowdown as of 2024 had vastly exceeded many of their most negative projections.[60] The implications of significantly slower growth for the decade ahead (e.g. below 3%) would be profound. A major slowdown would also challenge the political sustainability of China's unofficial social contract, which has long been anchored in rising living standards and plentiful employment as the preconditions for stable CCP rule. Equally, it could derail Xi's nationalist crusade for China to surpass the US economy (as measured by GDP at market exchange rates), with forecasting agencies already pushing back the crossover date from the 2020s to the 2030s.[61]

Ideology and the Likely Shape of Economic Policy during the 2020s

So what do the enduring contours of Xi Jinping's ideological framework mean for the likely shape of Chinese economic policy during the second decade of his rule?

- First, Xi's deep and enduring suspicion of the private sector is likely to endure, despite his need of them. His varied attacks—on capitalism, private monopoly, the disorderly development of capital, the 'fictitious economy' of private finance, speculators in the housing market, and simple greed—are too long-standing, widespread, and systematic to permit any fundamental re-embrace of a private sector as untrammelled as in the past. To do so would be for Xi to embrace an alternate ideological universe, surrendering his deep addiction to 'common prosperity' and its potential reforms in income tax, company tax, inheritance tax, capital gains tax, and social welfare. More fundamentally, Xi also fears that a Chinese economy increasingly dominated by the private sector would effectively yield the 'commanding heights' to forces beyond the control of a Leninist vanguard party.

- Second, and the obverse of the first, is the ongoing rebirth of state-owned enterprises as central to the Chinese economy after decades of privatization, corporatization, and consolidation. This will be accentuated by Xi's 'mixed-ownership model', encouraging greater levels of SOE equity in Chinese private firms. It also conforms with an increasingly popular (albeit unofficial) aphorism, deeply contested by the regime, describing Xi as presiding over '*goujin mintui*'—'the advance of the state sector and the retreat of the private sector'.
- Third, it follows that state planning, industrial policy, and what Xi describes as the 'real economy' of manufacturing, rather than the fictitious economy of finance and speculation, will become increasingly dominant within his overall ideological framework for the economy. Whatever the party's technical position may be on the market's role in allocating economic resources, Xi's language remains littered with references to the state driving the future of critical manufacturing, technology, and innovation through a combination of large-scale industrial funds and SOEs themselves. Indeed, this is taken up afresh in the Economic Work Report delivered to the March 2024 National People's Congress and its emphasis on unleashing these 'new productive forces' (*xinzhishengchanli*) to power the next phase of economic growth under the New Development Concept.[62] Collectively, these represent increasingly statist economic policy frameworks. They are also consistent with Xi's adherence to the Maoist dictum of 'top-level design' (*dingceng sheji*). They reflect a deep predisposition for economic solutions driven by macro-engineering, political intervention, and keeping control of the commanding heights of the economy, rather than the flexible allocation of resources by markets.
- Fourth, Xi's international economic model will also become increasingly mercantilist—irrespective of any official rhetoric about China's continued embrace of globalization. This will be expressed through the ideological orthodoxy of Xi's concept of 'the dual circulation economy'; his belief in 'national self-reliance'; and the minimization of economic vulnerability in an increasingly adverse national security environment. Whatever the United States does in the decade ahead, Xi's China has long embarked on its own program of 'de-risking', and what I have described elsewhere as 'decoupling

with Chinese characteristics'.[63] Xi is already well on the way to making Chinese supply chains as resilient as possible (particularly for energy, critical minerals, and advanced technologies) against an expected wave of trade, investment, and financial sanctions if he decides to take unilateral military action over Taiwan. This will include a range of measures seeking to 'sanction-proof' (to the greatest extent possible) the Chinese financial system, its currency, and the county's rapidly expanding global digital commerce network.

- Finally, Xi has identified 2035 as the target date to achieve economic modernization. As Xi moves towards this major economic milestone, we should be prepared for further ideological developments on where China stands within the framework of historical materialism and dialectical materialism. Xi has selected 2035 as a waypoint between the 19th Party Congress in 2017 and the achievement of full national rejuvenation by the PRC's centenary in 2049. Within the logic of this 'Marxism for the new era', Xi may also begin accelerating the timeframe for concluding the 'primary stage of socialism', thereby ushering in a more radically equalitarian agenda for which 'common prosperity' may be merely a modest precursor. This, in turn, may enable Xi to again formally redefine the party's 'principal contradictions' at some point in the decade ahead, thereby identifying the new objects for domestic and international 'struggle'. It is possible, therefore, given Xi's current ideological trajectory, that as China approaches a geo-political crisis point with the United States, Xi also moves to resolve new and sharper contradictions *within* China through a campaign of struggle against any re-emerging Chinese capitalist class. Indeed, it is possible that such a class could be seen as deeply compromised by their own investments in the West.

This may also result in a new era of contradiction and struggle against what Xi has already defined as declining capitalist and neo-colonial states that continue to threaten China's rise. These states are, in Xi's view, seeking desperately to cling to what remains of both their national power and the increasingly moribund international order from which they have so long benefitted. Indeed, in Xi's ideological view, both Western states and the Western order will be increasingly riven with the internal contradictions of capitalism and imperialism that Marx had predicted so long ago. Much of this may seem fanciful when measured against current realities. And ultimately, such a worldview may not transpire as other factors intervene, such as sustained economic downturn and rising unemployment. However, such scenarios are by no means impossible if we take a long view of the party's ideological evolution since Mao's tumultuous forty-year reign began in 1935. Chinese ideology and politics can move quickly and radically in times of duress.

So what can be said about these unfolding ideological, political, and policy factors and what they may mean for China's real-world economic growth scenarios over the decade ahead? The answer is: little with any precision, although the long-term drag on growth appears real. Indeed, each of the ideological directions outlined above is likely of itself to result in slower growth against a business-as-usual approach. Taken together, the impact is likely to be much greater. If economic growth is ultimately driven by a combination of population growth, workforce participation, and total factor productivity, none of the changes identified in the preceding paragraphs will contribute significantly to China's overall growth formula. For example, the impact of Xi's abiding preference for the public sector over the private sector is likely to slow Chinese technological innovation and overall productivity growth.

The one saving grace in all the above remains Xi's commitment to the individual Chinese consumer, where ideological logic (i.e. poverty elimination) and mainstream economic logic (i.e. enhancing private demand) happen to coincide. This should, therefore, contribute to better economic outcomes than would otherwise be the case, assuming that Xi's policy measures serve to reduce the need for consumers to save for critical family needs in education, health, aged care, unemployment and retirement income, thereby encouraging them to spend. However, consumer demand alone is likely to be insufficient to offset the vast economic headwinds of Xi's own ideological making, let alone the impact on savings from declining property prices, and the deep demographic challenges inherited from his predecessors. Double messaging, mixed messaging, plain muddling through, and general reform fatigue are unlikely to repair the fundamental confidence deficit that China now suffers. Deeper ideological, political, and policy change would be fundamental for confidence to be restored although, as of mid-2024, that seemed unlikely. Economic growth, therefore, is likely to be considerably slower for the decade ahead than it was for the decade that has just passed. That is, unless political desperation prompts some much deeper revision of the party's underlying ideological course.

15

Xi's Nationalist Ideology and Future Trends in Chinese Foreign Policy

If ideology provides us with some indication of likely future trends in Chinese politics and the economy, what does Xi's new form of Marxist Nationalism tell us about the likely shape of China's foreign and national security policy over the 2020s and into the 2030s? As noted in chapter 10, this book does not argue that China's international policy decisions are forced by periodic, spontaneous, populist eruptions of Chinese nationalism. Rather, it argues that official nationalism, and the mass campaigns that give it effect, provide useful barometers of approved party sentiment across a wide spectrum of possible foreign policy responses. As noted previously, there is an observable logic to the 'spigot' thesis that officially sponsored nationalist campaigns can be dialled up or down depending on China's evolving internal and external circumstances, and the strategic parameters that define the acceptable range of regime responses. The same spigot also applies to 'bottom-up' nationalist outbursts, which can readily be contained through the state's social media and other more coercive control mechanisms.

What we *can* deduce from the available evidence is that: the overall nationalist spigot has been opened far and wide for much of Xi's first decade in office; and this has coincided with much greater and more consistent foreign policy and military assertiveness than in the past. Most important, there is little evidence to date that Xi's underlying nationalist campaign is abating, however much the tone and content of individual policy responses to specific external policy challenges may vary, and despite efforts to stabilize US-China relations after the 2023 San Francisco summit. In other words, the broad shift to what I have called the 'nationalist right' during Xi's first term is likely to continue. In large part, this rising spectre of official nationalism is an external manifestation of an underlying change in the party's internal ideological analysis of the real state of power in the world today. Indeed, it is within this historical materialist frame of analysis that American power, and that of the collective West, will continue to be seen as being in relative decline. Similarly, a dialectical materialist framework is likely to cause Xi's party to conclude that the underlying 'contradictions' between liberal capitalist America and socialist China will continue to sharpen, making international crises more acute, and potentially more violent, over time. There is, therefore, little evidence to date that Chinese official nationalism will abate in the future. In fact, so far nationalism has proven to be a remarkably resilient tool in Xi Jinping's overall political and economic statecraft.

The analytical and textual cornerstone of this nationalist shift has been Xi's ever-intensifying ideological discourse on China's newfound national power. The 19th Party Congress narrative that 'under Mao, China stood up; under Deng it became prosperous; and under Xi it had become powerful' (*zhanqilai*, *fuqilai*, *qiangqilai*) shows no sign of being erased.[1] In fact, it has become all-pervasive. 'National power' has also grown in importance as a source of domestic political legitimacy for Xi's leadership. This is particularly the case as other pillars (such as rising living standards and a better quality of life) are weakened by the new ideological constraints imposed by Xi across politics and the economy. For all these reasons, however pragmatically Xi's military and foreign policy leadership may wish to respond to Beijing's new domestic and external challenges, there can be no international policy decision that could be allowed if it in any way reflected a weakened China. To some extent, during the Deng era, China's relative national economic and military weakness was regarded as an acceptable basis for making compromises with America because the consensus among CCP elites was never to directly challenge the United States unless and until China had caught up in the national power stakes. But under Xi, that has changed. After a decade of bold proclamations—including an acceleration in the growth of China's 'comprehensive national power', 'the rise of the East and the decline of the West', 'changes not seen in a century', and the country 'now having moved to the centre of the world stage'—the prevailing nationalist narrative has fundamentally shifted. Policy capitulation, or even significant compromise, could no longer be considered to be politically sustainable.

This underlying hardening of China's nationalist narrative, as noted above, is reinforced by its complex inter-relationship with Xi's Marxism-Leninism and the historical-determinist worldview that lies at its core. To restate its essential three-part argument: Marxism-Leninism holds that universal, scientific laws are given effect through a combination of historical determinism, dialectical materialism, and political and armed struggle. The CCP, as a Leninist vanguard party, has been the historical vehicle for this struggle—both to 'save the nation' from foreign and domestic depredation, and to accelerate China's transformation from a weak, feudal society into an increasingly strong, socialist state. Furthermore, this has depended on the CCP correctly divining not only China's position along the path to communism (through the disciplines of historical materialism) but also by navigating the 'principal contradictions' over which the party has needed to prevail (through dialectical materialism). Moreover, in the CCP's official narrative, it is claimed (albeit with some deviations) that the party has accelerated the course of history by successfully struggling to resolve each of these contradictions—so much so that Xi cites the dialectical machinery of Marxism-Leninism as the party's 'weapon of thought'.[2]

This same ideological worldview applies today with the three sets of major contradictions that the party sees for the period ahead. One of these is publicly declared, while the remaining two, so far, are not. All three, however, require focussed struggle. The first will continue to be the domestic contradiction of defending socialism against the capitalist excesses of thirty-five years of reform and opening, thereby ensuring the emergence of a strong, modern *socialist* state. The second is the external imperative of deterring or defeating the United States and its allies that now stand in the road of China's historic mission of reclaiming the territories lost to foreign forces in the past. The third is the wider international imperative of China now becoming the new incubator for the rebirthing of what Xi sees as a new age of global Marxism. This will be achieved by taking Xi's development model to the world at large as a dialectical alternative to the existing liberal-capitalist international order. And so long as the CCP continues to accurately identify and prudently respond to changes in these central contradictions, the party will continue to prevail in these mutually reinforcing national and international missions.

The party's major task was to work within the grain of the 'trends of the times', as determined by the underlying laws of historical determinism; to apply its dialectical analysis to the principal challenges of the day; and then to achieve progress through the unavoidable processes of struggle.

In other words, within Xi's Marxist-Nationalist ideological worldview, his international policy mission will not simply be about the exercise of China's reconstituted national power (although, of course, power will remain fundamental, as the Chinese military classics had taught generations of Chinese national leaders before). The CCP, having already saved China from collapse and having made it prosperous and powerful, would now fulfil its ideological destiny by deploying its new found national power and influence around the world, propelled forward by the determinist forces of history. Indeed, with history on its side, China under the party's leadership was now unstoppable. The party was on track to complete its revolutionary processes at home, and then take to the world at large the new forms of twenty-first-century Marxism that it had been working on for so long. And within the eclectic ethical universe of Xi's modernized and Sinified Marxism, whose values, concepts, and language will increasingly be drawn from a cocktail of Communist, Confucian, and even international sources, the CCP's future mission will not only be a *nationalist* cause driven forward by the forces of historical determinism. In the eyes of the party, it will also be seen as pursuing a righteous, just, and morally empowered *internationalist* cause both at home and abroad.

For some, this may sound somewhat messianic. But on close inspection of Xi's texts over his first decade in office—for example, his address on Marx's bicentennial in 2018—we see an ideological worldview that unites three distinct, albeit mutually reinforcing, dynamics: the pragmatic deployment of national power; a belief in the forces of historical determinism; and a deep sense of national and international moral purpose to liberate the downtrodden from excessive capitalism at home, together with the enduring legacy of neo-colonialism abroad. In this sense, Xi Jinping's overarching Marxist-Nationalist meta-narrative is now likely to be advanced as a form of Chinese counterpoint to George Washington's 'Divine Providence' (which ordained the birth of the American republic), Teddy Roosevelt's 'Great White Fleet' (which projected American power into the world), and John Winthrop's 'city upon a hill' (a moral beacon for the world).[3] Indeed, it is the sheer scale of the CCP's success in bringing a fifth of humanity out of poverty, at least within the worldview of the party's propaganda apparatus, that means that this great national experiment in Chinese political economy now commands unprecedented respect around the world. Absolute poverty had been 'eliminated' within China, and now the party's wider definition and vision of social justice was available to the world at large, delivered through the alternative international system that China was now building.[4] For Xi, this will be China's 'city on a hill'.

For these reasons, it is important to see China's foreign policy ambitions for the decade ahead through all three ideological lenses—nationalist, determinist, *and* moralist. These, in turn, are reinforced by long-standing traditions of classical Chinese realism about the balance of power, just as they are shaped by millennia of Chinese teachings on the natural state of a Sino-centric international order with which enlightened foreigners of all hues would eventually comply if they truly understood what was best for them. By contrast, the United States, the West, and still many in the Global South see China's international aspirations as indisputably revisionist: the recapture of its 'inseparable' territories including Taiwan, the East and South China Seas, and along the Sino-Indian border; the evolution of an Eastern Hemisphere anchored in Chinese, rather than American, strategic and economic power, as broadly existed under the tribute system in previous Chinese dynasties; and the restoration of China's status and standing as the preeminent global military and economic power as it once was, before the Opium Wars so rudely interrupted what China had previously seen as the natural order of things.

Needless to say, through its own ideological prism, Xi Jinping's CCP does not see these as 'revisionist' claims at all, but rather as the product of historical processes that are ultimately irreversible because they are being driven forward by Marx's universal scientific laws of development. Indeed, far from representing a *regressive* disruption of the international status quo, China's objectives are seen instead as embodying the ultimate *progressive* purposes of global Marxism. Based on these deep and radically different ideological perceptions, in the party's view, China and the United States therefore find themselves on a political, economic, and ultimately military collision course—unless, of course, the United States were simply to capitulate peacefully to the irreversible forces of history. Moreover, this deep, historical process of geo-political change would now be driven forward even more rapidly as a result of China's new and increasingly uncontested claim to the leadership of the Global South as part of a much broader, fundamental realignment in the global balance of power.

Foreign Policy Readjustment after 2023 within a Framework of Ideological Constraint

Over the course of 2023, despite efforts at rapprochement with the United States and its allies to 'stabilize' their respective relationships with China, there is little in the Chinese domestic ideological discourse that has suggested any fundamental change. For example, Xi's major address in February 2023 on 'Chinese-Style Modernization as the Great Pathway to Building a Powerful State and National Rejuvenation',[5] came less than three months after Xi's Bali summit with President Biden and his efforts to stabilize the US-China relationship. But in geo-political terms, there was nothing conciliatory from Xi in his modernization speech at all. Instead, it baldly reasserted the ideological binary between Chinese and Western (read American) approaches to global governance. On Xi's list of five core characteristics of China's modernization strategy, one is his view of the wider global order:

> Adhering to peaceful development, China seeks its own development while firmly safeguarding world peace and promoting global development. Simultaneously, China's better development contributes to maintaining world peace and development, working towards the construction of a community with a shared future for humanity. This is a prominent feature of Chinese-style modernization. The modernization path taken by Western countries is marred by bloody atrocities such as wars, slavery, colonization, and plunder, inflicting profound suffering on many developing countries. The Chinese nation, having experienced the tragic history of aggression and humiliation by Western powers, deeply values the importance of peace and unequivocally rejects the repetition of the old path taken by Western countries.[6]

Despite this clear-cut, doctrinal definition of China's strategic development path and its place within the party's binary global worldview, Xi decided to tactically adjust to a more moderate posture in his remarks at the San Francisco Summit of November 2023.[7] This was designed to lower the temperature, assuage global investor confidence, and dull perceptions of imminent geo-political risk. Xi's forensic effort to blunt the sharpest edges of his decade-long ideological assault on the United States and the West, going back to his celebrated Document Number 9 of 2013, was on full display. His central proposition at San Francisco—that the United States and China were in fact partners, not adversaries—stands in complete contrast to his ideological message to the party since 2017. Xi's claim that China did not seek to 'unseat' the United States was at odds with the strategic logic of his long-standing domestic ideological campaigns on the 'decline of the West', 'changes not seen in a century' going back to when the Soviet Union first challenged Western power in 1917, and 'China now entering the centre of the global stage.' Nonetheless, as Xi told his American audience:

> I have found that, although our two countries are different in history, culture, and social system and have embarked on different development paths, our two peoples are both kind, friendly, hardworking, and down-to-earth. . . . It is the reaching out to each other by our peoples that has time and again brought China-US relations from a low ebb back onto the right track. I am convinced that once opened, the door of China-US relations cannot be shut again. Once started, the cause of China-US friendship cannot be derailed halfway. The tree of our peoples' friendship has grown tall and strong; and it can surely withstand the assault of any wind or storm. . . . Friends, we are in an era of challenges and changes. It is also an era of hope. The world needs China and the United States to work together for a better future. We, the largest developing country and the largest developed country, must handle our relations well. In a world of changes and chaos, it is ever more important for us to have the mind, assume the vision, shoulder the responsibility, and play the role that come along with our status as major countries.
>
> I have always had one question on my mind: how to steer the giant ship of China-US relations clear of hidden rocks and shoals, [and] navigate it through storms and waves without getting disoriented, losing speed or even having a collision?
>
> In this respect, the number one question for us is: are we adversaries, or partners? This is the fundamental and overarching issue. The logic is quite simple. If one sees the other side as a primary competitor, the most consequential geo-political challenge and a pacing threat, it will only lead to misinformed policy-making, misguided actions, and unwanted results. . . . It is wrong to view China, which is committed to peaceful development, as a threat and thus play a zero-sum game against it. China never bets against the United States, and never interferes in its internal affairs. China has no intention to challenge the United States or to unseat it.[8]

Ideological Continuity in Xi's Approach to the World: The Significance of the 2023 Foreign Affairs Work Conference

Importantly, Xi's conciliatory message to his international audience in November 2023 was not reflected in his internal message to China's foreign, defence, and security policy establishment the following month when he addressed the party's Central Foreign Affairs Work Conference. This was the third such meeting held under Xi, previous conferences having been in 2014 and 2018. This equalled the total number of such conferences held by Xi's predecessors since 1971, when Mao first began preparing the party for deep strategic change by starting to embrace America against the then Soviet threat.[9] As noted in chapter 10, these conferences have been used to set the party's strategic direction in foreign and security policy for the medium to long term. The sheer number of these conferences since 2012 of itself reflects the degree of change in international policy settings under Xi when compared with his recent predecessors. While the full, unvarnished text of the leader's remarks to these conferences is never released, the official readouts issued through Xinhua are nonetheless instructive when compared to previous years' texts.[10] And in the case of the December 2023 readout, it has been supplemented by Xi's remarks the following day to China's annual ambassadorial conference[11] and by a later speech by Foreign Minister Wang Yi delivered in mid-January 2024.[12]

Indeed it was Wang Yi who launched the Chinese official commentary on the significance of the 2023 Work Conference and its embrace of Xi's 'new era' in Chinese diplomacy, underscoring the extent to which Chinese foreign policy had now fundamentally changed. Wang stated that "General Secretary Xi Jinping had delivered an important speech in which he comprehensively reviewed the historic achievements and valuable experience of great power diplomacy with Chinese characteristics in the new era, gave a profound exposition on the international environment and historical mission of China's foreign affairs work in the new journey we have undertaken, and outlined comprehensive plans for China's foreign affairs work for the present and coming periods." Wang summarized the scope of the conference's conclusions as follows:

> At the Central Conference on Foreign Affairs Work, the historic achievements of China's foreign affairs work in the new era were summarized. They include

> the following ten points: establishing and developing Xi Jinping Thought on Diplomacy; showcasing the distinct Chinese characteristics, style, and ethos in China's diplomacy; advocating the building of a community with a shared future for mankind; a new model of diplomacy under the strategic leadership of head-of-state diplomacy; fostering major-country dynamics characterized by peaceful coexistence, overall stability, and balanced development; building a comprehensive, high-quality global partnership network; promoting high-quality Belt and Road cooperation; effectively safeguarding China's sovereignty, security, and development interests; leading the way in reforming the international system and order; and strengthening the centralized, unified leadership of the Central Committee of the CCP. To fully appreciate the extraordinary historical process of China's diplomacy in the new era, the key is to understand the common thread and underlying logic of these ten achievements in a multidimensional, systemic, and interrelated way.[13]

Consistent with the overriding theme of this book on the underlying political and policy relevance of Xi's ideological worldview, it is not surprising that 'the establishment and development of Xi Jinping Thought on Diplomacy' was now listed as Xi's foremost foreign policy achievement during his first decade in office. As the Xinhua report stated bluntly: "It was made clear at the conference that in the current and upcoming periods, China's external work shall be guided by Xi Jinping Thought on Socialism with Chinese Characteristics for the New Era and Xi Jinping Thought on Diplomacy in particular."[14] Or, as Wang Yi added, Xi Jinping Thought on Diplomacy now provided "profound strategic thinking about changes of the world, of our times and of historical significance"; it was "rooted in the great practice of major-country diplomacy with Chinese characteristics in the new era"; and it offered "a shining example of applying the basic tenets of Marxism to the practice of China's diplomacy and fine traditional Chinese culture."[15] Wang once again underscores the analytical significance of a Marxist worldview and its utility in understanding current international developments:

> In making strategies and policies, it is imperative to apply systems thinking. The CCP, a Marxist party armed with the theories of dialectical and historical materialism, should know how to analyse, study, and evaluate the international situation with the understanding that things are universally connected and constantly evolving. We should be able to see the present from a historical perspective and look beyond the surface to get to the heart of the matter, to accurately recognize and analyse the laws and direction of the profoundly changing world, and make sound foreign policies.[16]

Beyond its methodological utility, however, it was Xi's Marxist worldview that also formed the basis of China's new claim to international moral leadership, which was why "on major issues concerning the future of humanity and the direction of the world, we must take a clear and firm position, hold the international moral high ground, and unite and rally the overwhelming majority in our world".[17] That was also why, according to Wang, "on major issues of right and wrong, it is imperative to uphold principles". And further, it was why China "*as a socialist country under the leadership of the CCP, should take a clear position by standing on the progressive side of history,* on the side of fairness and justice, work actively to meet the common aspirations and legitimate concerns of the peoples of all countries, and demonstrate the people-centredness of the CCP and the commitment to serving the people in China's foreign policy"[18] (my emphasis). This way, Wang claimed, "we will always rally abundant support for the just cause, hold the high ground of justice and take the strategic initiative".[19] When applying this to the Global South, Wang became even more direct in linking a Marxist theory of development to the needs of the world's emerging economies:

> As the largest developing country and a major country, it is incumbent on China to uphold justice in a world undergoing profound changes and turbulence, to shoulder responsibility at critical moments, and thus to be a staunch defender of world peace and a champion of global development. At the same time, through China's modernization, we are willing to support the efforts of other developing countries which want to achieve development while maintaining their independence, so that all countries can take the right path of modernization through peaceful development.[20]

As for Xi's analysis of the actual state of contemporary international relations, together with China's continuing determination to bring about significant change in the existing US-led order, there is a significant difference between Xi's remarks at the Foreign Affairs conference in December and those reflected at the San Francisco summit in November. According to the Xinhua readout:

> It was noted at the conference that great transformation is accelerating across the world. Changes of the world, of our times, and of historical significance are unfolding like never before, and *the world has entered a new period of turbulence and transformation.* Yet the overall direction of human development and progress will not change, the overall dynamics of world history moving

> forward amidst twists and turns will not change, and the overall trend toward a shared future for the international community will not change. We must have full confidence in these trends of historical impact.[21] (My emphasis)

According to the December conference, this meant that China now faced "*new strategic opportunities*" and its diplomacy would enter "*a new stage where much more can be accomplished*".[22] This meant that 'the central task' of the party and the country was to "explore *new frontiers* in China's diplomatic theory and practice, foster *new dynamics* in the relations between China and the world, and raise China's international influence, appeal and *power to shape events to a new level*"[23] (my emphasis). Together this would "create a more favourable international environment and provide more solid strategic support for building China into a great modern socialist country in all respects and advancing the great rejuvenation of the Chinese nation on all fronts through the Chinese path to modernization".[24] And in a clear reference to US policy, the conference noted: "It is important to resolutely oppose the attempt to roll back globalization and abuse the concept of security, oppose all forms of unilateralism and protectionism, firmly promote trade and investment liberalization and facilitation, overcome the structural problems hindering the healthy development of the world economy, and make economic globalization more open, inclusive, balanced and beneficial to all."[25]

To this Wang Yi added that "*these important conclusions are based on an in-depth analysis of the major changes in the international balance of power*, the transformation and reshaping of the international system and order, and the interplay between different concepts and ideas on a global scale, providing important guidance for our understanding of the international situation"[26] (my emphasis). And in a call to arms for the country's diplomatic establishment to rise to the challenges and opportunities of Xi Jinping's proclaimed new era, Wang concluded that "on the new journey, great power diplomacy with Chinese characteristics will enter a new stage where much more can be accomplished; China must not be complacent about its past achievements, nor be intimidated by strong winds and choppy waters in the external environment".[27] This, in turn, would "promote new dynamics in China's relations with the world, and raise China's international influence, attractiveness and ability to shape events to a new level".[28] These were hardly messages designed to encourage the maintenance of the international status quo. Indeed, they reflect a determination to use the current period of strategic instability to bring about rapid and more fundamental changes to the international order. And all this would be accommodated by the underlying determinist forces of history that were driving China forward.

What appears to be new from the 2023 Foreign Affairs Work Conference is the party's formal and emphatic embrace of China's 'great power diplomacy' and the critical role that Xi Jinping as leader now personally played within it through 'head-of-state diplomacy'. This is a substantial step-up from the 2014 and 2018 Foreign Affairs Work Conferences. It stood also in clear contrast to his three most immediate predecessors. After the 2014 Conference, it will be recalled that the concept of 'a new type of great power relations' was first promoted as a framework for US-China relations and then, more loosely, for China's relations with other 'major powers'.[29] Four years later, Xi called on the conference to 'break new ground' in China's great power diplomacy to contribute to China's domestic prosperity.[30] A decade on, it had evolved into a concept of China now being confident in its great power status, together with the new pattern of international relationships that were emerging between Beijing and the rest of the world. This is a significant evolution as China increasingly identified itself less as a fellow traveller with the rest of the developing world and more as a leader. It had now become, in its own estimation, a significant, new geo-political and geo-economic fulcrum of the emerging global order.

Moreover, the beating heart of China's new great power status and its unfolding great power diplomacy had now become Xi Jinping's very own brand of 'head-of-state diplomacy'. As the official read-out starkly states, China follows "the strategic guidance of the head-of-state" enabling it to play "an increasingly important and constructive role in international affairs".[31] Once again, however, it was left to Wang Yi to provide a more definitive rendition of what was now meant by this formal addition to China's official repertoire of diplomatic statecraft:

> General Secretary Xi Jinping is the core of the Central Committee and the entire party, and the top decision-maker and chief architect of our foreign affairs work. As the highest form of China's diplomacy, head-of-state diplomacy has played an important and irreplaceable role in major-country diplomacy with Chinese characteristics in the new era, achieving exemplary and groundbreaking diplomatic results, and fully reflecting China's image as a confident, open, and responsible great power. It is due to the great foresight and statesmanship of General Secretary Xi Jinping that China has been able to pursue its diplomacy against all odds amidst the great

> transformation of the world, and remain calm, confident, and proactive in the context of a changing international landscape.[32]

In other words, notwithstanding Xi's apparent re-embrace at the San Francisco summit of the importance of the US-China bilateral relationship and continuing American leadership of the current international order, Xi himself would now be a driving force for bringing about fundamental global change. And this would be done through a new and potent combination of 'great power' and 'head-of-state' diplomacy. This would become particularly evident in the prosecution of Xi's signature foreign policy enterprise—the community of common destiny for all humankind (CCD). Unsurprisingly, Xi's great meta-concept and mega-project to rewrite the entire international system was the single greatest focus of attention at the 2023 Foreign Affairs conference of the party centre. Indeed, after 'Xi Jinping Thought on Diplomacy,' it is listed second out of Xi's ten major achievements over his first decade in office. And it was driven by a symbiotic relationship with the first:

> It was pointed out at the conference that building a community with a shared future for mankind is the core tenet of Xi Jinping Thought on Diplomacy. It is how China proposes to solve the questions of what kind of world to build and how to build it based on our deepening understanding of the laws governing the development of human society. It reflects the Chinese Communists' worldview, perception of order, and values, accords with the common aspiration of people in all countries, and points the direction for the progress of world civilizations. It is also the noble goal pursued by China in conducting major-country diplomacy with Chinese characteristics for the new era.[33]

Properly deciphered, the Foreign Affairs Work Conference had explicitly acknowledged that the CCD concept had been built on a Marxist, historical-materialist analytical foundation. It reflected a prospective international system that was anchored in a Marxist concept of global order. And it was an order that embodied universal Marxist values. At least in the Communist Party's telling of it, the CCD had now developed into a fully 'scientific system' (in Marxist parlance, an initiative fully consistent with the socialist laws of development). And it had also already secured global political support: "Since the dawn of this new era, building a community with a shared future for mankind has developed from a Chinese initiative to an international consensus, from a promising vision to substantive actions, and from a conceptual proposition to a scientific system. It has served as a glorious banner leading the progress of the times."[34]

The Marxist calibre of the CCD is, for the first time, clearly defined in the December 2023 official readout. It was now part of Xi's ongoing efforts to provide a totalizing ideology that embraced both the foreign and the domestic. The development of CCD was but one part of the three great questions that Xi had now posed to the Communist Party for the future: what sort of party would remain a ruling party for the long-term future, and how would it be built; what sort of China was to be built, and how to build it; and now what sort of world order was to be built, and how to achieve that through a community of common destiny? Beyond ideological abstractions, however, the real-world policy content of the CCD concept continues to be explained in terms of Xi's four existing global mega-initiatives: "the strategic guidance comes from the implementation of the Global Development Initiative, the Global Security Initiative and the Global Civilization Initiative, and the platform for action is high-quality Belt and Road cooperation."[35] Each of these, in turn, was seeing the gradual roll-out of more specific policies over time. However, if there was one clear common denominator across all four, it was the continuing centrality of the Chinese Communist party-state—in delivering 'balanced development'; in advancing common civilizational values against the ravages of Western modernization; and, most critically, serving as the geo-political anchor of a new international order of so-called common security.[36] As noted previously in this book, there is a certain messianic, almost Augustinian,[37] and certainly universalist ambition to Xi's ideological vision of a new form of marxist global order. But it was a Leninist party, rather than the established church, that was now the indispensable vehicle for sustaining ideological orthodoxy, maintaining institutional discipline, and bringing about necessary political change. This totalizing dimension of Xi's concept of order was underscored by Wang Yi in January 2024:

> A country's foreign policy is closely linked to its domestic agenda as its external and internal imperatives correlate and interplay with each other. At a fundamental level, we should handle the relationship between the three well: a community with a shared future for mankind, global transformation, and Chinese modernization. Building a great modern socialist country in all respects and achieving national rejuvenation through Chinese modernization is the top political priority on the new journey of the new era. To accomplish this central task of the party and the country, we must hold high

> the banner of building a community with a shared future for mankind to steer global transformation in the right direction. We must pursue China's development in the context of the overall development of the world and advance the interests of both the Chinese people and people of the world.[38]

However, beyond ideology and the almost mechanical listing of the GCI, the GDI, the GSI, and the BRI, the real-world policy content of a 'community of common destiny' continued to be elusive. Wang Yi's 2024 address, while arguably the most effusive official paean of praise for CCD since its launch, provides some additional insight on where the Chinese system may take this proposal in the future. According to Wang, "the conference made a systematic elaboration on and comprehensive summary of the essential praxis of building a community with a shared future for mankind over the past decade, and established the pillars for building such a community as a scientific system" for the future.[39] In addition to fully deploying the BRI, GSI, GDI, and GCI as CCD platforms, the party would now engage in "comprehensive consultation" around the world "where the guiding principle was to apply the common values of mankind" in order to establish "the basic foundation of building a new type of international relations".[40] In doing so, Xi himself in his 2023 address to Chinese ambassadors enjoined his diplomats to "skillfully utilize the multilateral mechanisms and rules to seek more understanding and support from the international community".[41] The international community should therefore prepare itself for a fresh wave of CCD diplomatic activity as Xi's foreign policy juggernaut in support of a new concept of global order continues to be rolled out from the centre.

All this may still seem to be deliberately vague. That's because, consistent with long-standing Chinese diplomatic statecraft, it is. As noted previously, the established practice is to advance a general and innocuous concept and then gradually populate it with content and meaning once international coalitions are built around the original proposition. Reduced to their essentials, the GDI is a repudiation of the 'Washington Consensus' that favours development via free-market capitalism over other forms of state-capitalism; the GCI is the repudiation of universal human rights as outlined in the 1948 Universal Declaration in favour of culture-specific 'rights'; while the GSI is the repudiation of US alliance structures in favour of so-called 'common security' concepts.[42] What the last decade has made clear is that with CCD, Xi has constructed a comprehensive conceptual, policy, and now diplomatic ecosystem from what began a decade ago as a single phrase. Furthermore, it was now routinely put forward as the alternative to the current US-led international rules-based order. Moreover, Wang Yi made clear that these mega and meta initiatives represent "the top-level design of China's diplomatic strategy for the new journey".[43] Here the architect-in-chief remained Xi Jinping himself. Just as Xi remained the single decisive actor in bringing about changes to the current system through his new type of 'head-of-state diplomacy', anchored in his 'new type of great power diplomacy' and as he builds his 'new type of international relations'. None of this, however, sits comfortably with Xi's assurances to his US audience in November 2023 that China had "no intention to challenge the United States or to unseat it."[44]

Beyond ideological frameworks and future policy content, the Foreign Affairs Work Conference also dedicated considerable attention to the style of Chinese diplomacy to be adopted for Xi's new era. Here there appeared to be subtle changes from the recent past in outlining a more judicious balance between the ideology of 'struggle' and the need, in the tradition of Dale Carnegie, to win friends and influence people.[45] There is clear celebration in the text of China's 'greater strategic autonomy', greater capacity for 'diplomatic initiatives', 'stronger capacity to steer new endeavours', more 'self-confidence and self-reliance', and, intriguingly after many years of 'wolf warrior diplomacy', a claim to 'greater moral appeal'.[46] Xi Jinping, however, in his remarks to the Chinese ambassadorial conference, emphasized that "*it was essential to be adept at making more friends and extending friendship*" and "the work of winning public support should reach not only governments but also ordinary people"(my emphasis). Xi also emphasized that a "globalized way of communication should be used to better tell China's stories, [and] promote understanding between China and the world through linking the country's past with the present, so that the world will know better about China in the new era". This also meant "making good use of the effective instrument of United Front activities".[47]

Sustaining the spirit of 'struggle' in the party's international policy efforts, however, is never far from the surface in Xi's and Wang's authoritative statements in late 2023 and early 2024. As Wang stated: "In dealing with risks and challenges, it is imperative to maintain our fighting spirit. The CCP has never been deterred by intimidation, swayed by deception, or cowed by pressure. Only with the courage and ability to continue our struggle can we overcome various difficulties and obstacles. In the future, we will face an even more difficult international situation and more complex external environment. We must forge ahead with an indomitable spirit and persistent efforts to open new horizons in our foreign affairs work."[48] Indeed, Xi's remarks at the same conference appear to be equally uncompromising: "Envoys must have the courage and ability to carry on our fight and act as defenders of our national interests. It is necessary for them to enhance their confidence and determination, be strategically sober-minded, firmly keep a worst-case scenario mindset, and, with combat preparedness and a firm determination, never yield to coercive power so as to resolutely defend the country's sovereignty, security, and development interests."[49] Once again, notwithstanding the spirit of the San Francisco summit, neither Xi nor Wang appeared to be sending out messages to their foreign and security policy establishment that a new spirit of compromise should govern Chinese diplomacy for the period ahead—least of all with the United States. There was now a world of difference between China's diplomatic orthodoxy of a decade earlier, when Deng's 'diplomatic guidance' of 'never taking the lead' still carried the day.

The last and most important element of the 2023 Foreign Affairs Work Conference, at least from a diplomatic practitioners' perspective, was what the meeting and its surrounding documents said about the absolute centrality of the party now driving Chinese foreign policy forward under Xi Jinping. This was listed as the tenth of Xi's list of ten achievements during his first decade: "We have strengthened the centralized, unified leadership of the CCP Central Committee, and brought about greater coordination in China's external work."[50] This was also necessary to build "a contingent of personnel involved in foreign affairs and continue to make our external work more science-based (i.e. more mindful of Marxist methodologies), forward-looking, proactive and innovative".[51] Wang Yi was even more explicit on the new role of the party in shaping the future of Chinese foreign policy: "The CCP's leadership is our greatest political strength and the defining feature of socialism with Chinese characteristics. It is also the most fundamental principle and greatest source of strength for China's diplomacy. Since the 18th CCP National Congress in 2012, three Central Foreign Affairs Work Conferences and a symposium on neighbourhood diplomacy have been convened; the system and mechanisms for the Party Central Committee's leadership of foreign affairs work have been improved; and the Foreign Relations Law and the Regulations on the Party's

Leadership over Foreign Affairs have been promulgated. All these have ensured better coordination among various departments under the unified stewardship of the CCP central leadership, thus providing strong political and organizational safeguards for China's diplomacy in the new era."[52] The concluding injunctions to the nation's diplomats should, however, be left to Xi Jinping himself, including his telling reminder of their need to remain politically and ideologically loyal to the party—in addition to their responsibility on behalf of the Central Committee towards the 60 million members of the Chinese diaspora around the world:

> It's necessary for them [Chinese diplomats] to enrich their thinking with the party's innovative theories, sharpen their eyes to tell right from wrong, and always keep to the correct political direction. It's essential for them to have a deep understanding of where the supreme interests of the party and the country lie, and understand and implement the foreign policy of the CCP Central Committee well. . . . [They are] urged to take 'diplomacy for the people' as their commitment, and pass on the CCP Central Committee's care and concern to every overseas Chinese.[53]

In summary, the December 2023 Foreign Affairs Work Conference was a sobering reminder of the centre of ideological gravity that continues to underpin China's foreign policy trajectory for the 2020s. Based on precedent, there may not be another such conference before the end of the decade. As Wang Yi has said: "The Conference [in 2023] has drawn up the blueprint for China's foreign affairs work for the present and coming periods, and all of us engaged in foreign-related work must keenly study the important address by General Secretary Xi Jinping and remain guided by its principles in our thinking and actions."[54] Xi's address was deeply Marxist in both its ideological description of current international relations and in prescribing China's optimal policy path for the future. It asserted that the party would now be able to make even greater strides in the international domain despite the great turbulence that lay ahead. It claimed that China's new form of great power diplomacy driven by Xi's head-of-state diplomacy would now be deployed to achieve changes in the international order that would advance China's national interests and values. Furthermore, Xi's 'community of common destiny' proposal was rapidly evolving into an umbrella concept representing an opposing ideological, political, and policy narrative to the US-led liberal international order. Moreover, this significant change agenda would be driven forward by a new diplomatic establishment answerable to the party's ideological discipline rather than an independent and professional foreign service ethos—a discipline that combined a relentless Marxist-Nationalist spirit of struggle with the pragmatic need to expand China's international influence by peaceful means. Importantly, none of these attributes sits well with Xi's assurance to his American audience in November 2023 that China had "no intention to challenge . . . or to unseat" the United States. Tactics may well have changed, but China's strategic intention, it seemed, had not. This was entirely consistent with Xi's earlier expositions (discussed in the previous chapter) of the fundamental ideological difference between the two.

Ideology as a Precursor for Foreign Policy in the 2020s

Based on Xi's new ideology of Marxist Nationalism, what trajectory can we therefore identify for Chinese foreign and strategic policy for the decade ahead? The uncomfortable truth is that whatever Xi may say about the future of US-China relations, and however that may accord with Beijing's recent shifts in tactical diplomacy, his underlying ideology still calls for maximum preparedness for the real-world possibility of confrontation and conflict with America. It is also the product of Xi's related injunction to the party to engage in 'extreme scenario' planning.[55] This deeply held ideological (and therefore strategic) view is therefore likely to be reflected across the full spectrum of China's regional and global foreign policy and military posture for the decade ahead. Therefore, while the future is always unwritten, we can draw some reasonable conclusions about the most likely course of Chinese policy.

First, despite the resumption of US-China military-to-military dialogue in late 2023, China has shown negligible interest in any nuclear talks that would modify its policy of modernizing, diversifying, and expanding its strategic arsenal. A new nuclear arms race between China and the United States is therefore increasingly probable, as is a redefinition of Chinese nuclear doctrine which, until now, has publicly pledged to "never at any time and under any circumstances be the first to use nuclear weapon".[56] It seems that, from Xi's perspective, nuclear forces are no longer seen purely as instruments of strategic deterrence. There is an emerging debate about whether Xi would integrate his nuclear forces into regional war-fighting scenarios given advances in US ballistic missile defence technology and the deployment of Terminal High Altitude Area

Defense (THAAD) systems in the East Asian theatre. While the detail may be unclear, it can be assumed that the nuclear dimension of Chinese defence policy, having remained static for decades, will be re-evaluated during the decade ahead.

Second, by contrast, China will actively seek to engage the United States on the future of artificial intelligence in warfare. Whereas China appears confident of its future nuclear capabilities, it seems anxious about its competitiveness on AI, including its capacity to undermine the conventional military balance that Beijing has striven to achieve over many decades. US-China strategic competition is therefore likely to be dominated in the decade ahead by the military application of rapidly unfolding, exponentially evolving, AI capabilities across manned and unmanned platforms, nuclear and conventional forces, on earth, in the skies, and in cyberspace. Xi, for good or for ill, sees AI as a strategic game-changer.

Third, whatever diplomacy occurs over Taiwan, Xi's worldview is resolute that the island must be returned to Chinese sovereignty. What remains unclear is his timetable (or whether, in fact, he even has a timetable). What we do know is that Xi has shifted focus away from objective red lines (such as Taipei unilaterally declaring independence) to subjective red lines around Taiwan's perceived 'progress' towards national reunification.[57] The outcome of the 2024 Taiwanese national elections have been largely irrelevant to these calculations given that neither side of Taiwanese politics is capable of delivering the type of voluntary reunification that Xi seeks.[58] Driven both by the injunctions of Chinese national history and the imperatives of Marxist historical determinism, Xi will continue preparing militarily to take Taiwan by force, and hardening the Chinese economy to withstand the international sanctions that would inevitably flow. In doing so, he will seek to deter future US administrations from defending Taiwan militarily. Xi will be electric to possible opportunities in relation to Taiwan, if, for example, a future US president were to withdraw military support for Ukraine's defence against his ally, Vladimir Putin of Russia, thereby signalling a new and more isolationist American worldview. If possible, Xi would want to have secured Taiwan's return without a war with the United States by the end of his fourth term in 2032. The only thing that would prevent him would be effective and credible US, Taiwanese, and allied military deterrence—and Xi's belief that there was a real risk of China losing any such engagement.

Fourth, in the South China Sea, China will continue to intensify its military and paramilitary build-up, forward-leaning deployments, and regional economic diplomacy in order to make the region's eventual acceptance of Chinese maritime and territorial claims a foregone conclusion. China will remain alert to the Philippines' claim in particular, given it is the only US treaty ally among the five ASEAN[59] claimant states and it has been the most forward-leaning. China's strategy will be to isolate Vietnam and the Philippines by engineering separate bilateral agreements with the other three—Indonesia, Malaysia, and Brunei—promising new levels of economic engagement as a reward. Having amicably resolved those three by 2032, Xi would hope to leave China's disputes with Vietnam and the Philippines unresolved until it makes a final judgement about US longer-term political and military resolve in East and South-East Asia.

Fifth, in the East China Sea, Xi will be reluctant to push the Sino-Japanese territorial dispute over Senkaku/Diaoyudao to a crisis point given the importance the United States attaches to its defence treaty with Tokyo. Although China will continue applying military pressure to Japan, it remains deeply cautious about Japanese military capabilities, Tokyo's commitment to ramp-up military spending by two-thirds,[60] and the near-automaticity of US military support for Japan given the preponderance of US bases there. Xi could be expected to undertake extreme political and economic efforts to cleave the Republic of Korea away from Japan, to roll back US-Japan-ROK trilateral strategic cooperation, and work the centre-left of South Korean domestic politics towards a posture more accommodating of China's strategic interests. In doing so, Beijing may offer itself as a more believable security guarantor for the South against a nuclear-armed North Korea than the US strategic nuclear umbrella.

Sixth, Xi will try to stabilize the Sino-Indian border without surrendering an inch of territory gained by China during recent border skirmishes. Xi would be disturbed by the growing military relationship between India and the United States, as well as India's increasingly activist membership of the Quad. For these reasons, Xi will likely seek to put a floor under the China-India relationship until such time as America's future military posture in, and long-term political commitment to, the Indo-Pacific is much clearer. As with many other core foreign and strategic policy decisions, Xi will want to know what any future US administration would be likely to change in relation to its global commitments.

Seventh, Xi will continue to leverage China's regional and global economic footprint to China's foreign policy and strategic advantage. He will want China to be the indispensable economic partner of every region of the world except the United States itself, where de-risking and decoupling has already begun. Xi will continue to drive wedges between the United States and Europe where it can, by making Europe more dependent on the China market over time, while trying to induce collective European amnesia over China's support for Russia's invasion of Ukraine. Xi will more aggressively seek to use China's economic presence across East Asia and the Western Pacific (including Pacific Island countries) to undermine the political and strategic rationale for continuing US military alliances and partnerships. In a decade's time, he would want Beijing regarded as the undisputed economic capital of East Asia, which he would view as a strategic precondition for eroding the political underpinnings of US regional military arrangements. And in all this, he sees the current bipartisan sentiment in Washington for trade protectionism and latent isolationism as his best strategic ally, whichever party happens to control the presidency or the Congress.

Finally, Xi will continue seeking to leverage China as the indispensable economic partner of Africa, Latin America, and the rest of Asia, transforming the Global South into the political support base for its new international order. This will be reinforced by a global network of civilian ports, PLA naval bases, and airfields to provide China with global military and logistical reach. Xi will continue his efforts to build support for a reformed international order through the existing UN system. In doing so, China will draw on the power of its budgetary presence and the size of its voting-bloc support to deliver changes to the existing normative and institutional structure of the international system. But it will also seek to do so independently of the UN through the BRICS group, the Conference on Interaction and Confidence-Building Measures in Asia, the Shanghai Cooperation Organization, the Asian Infrastructure Investment Bank, the New Development Bank, the Belt and Road Initiative, the Global Development Initiative, the Global Security Initiative, and—their newest cousin—the Global Civilization Initiative. We should also be ready for Xi to develop a new global narrative for the latter three in particular, based on his concept of a 'community of common destiny for all humankind', and animated by his existing statements on the global impact of the new 'Marxism of the twenty-first century'. Reminiscent of the Third World experience of the last Cold War, we are likely to see the emergence of a new and much sharper ideological cleavage between the Global North and the Global South, this time driven by a combination of Chinese international socialist theory, and the praxis of modern Chinese economic and military statecraft.

Conclusion

There will be many twists and turns in Chinese politics and foreign and domestic policy during Xi's next decade in office. But these are still likely to occur within the overall parameters of the ideological framework of Marxist Nationalism that he has systematically developed during his first decade. By 2032, Chinese politics is likely to become more Leninist rather than less as Xi's requirement for political control becomes more absolute the longer he stays in power—and as the number of his domestic political opponents, both real and imagined, grows larger. The Chinese economy will be a more complex proposition, with Xi unlikely to depart from the Marxist economic framework he has laid down since the 19th Congress in 2017. But the demands for greater policy flexibility will continue, meaning that double-messaging will also continue, with at best mixed consequences for the all-important Chinese private sector. The Chinese economy can be expected to continue growing because of untapped consumer demand, but not at the rate it did before 2017 because of the combined impact of demography, the drag of ideology, and the constraints of national debt which has already doubled to 288% of GDP between 2008 and 2023.[61] Meanwhile, Chinese foreign and strategic policy will continue to be driven forward by the nationalist and determinist imperatives of Xi's ideology of Marxist Nationalism. Xi will continue to push hard to change the status quo to his advantage—whether over outstanding territorial claims, China's claim to regional preeminence, or Chinese diplomacy gradually advancing the norms and structures of an alternative international system. Nonetheless, Xi will be tactically constrained by the continuing reality and presence of American military and financial power. And he will continue to assess the core question of the long-term capacity and credibility of US military and economic deterrence and, most important, evolving US political resolve—as the security guarantor for its allies and strategic partners, and as the geo-strategic anchor of the current international system. And that, in turn, will largely determine the future of Taiwan.

16

China after Xi

A question the world is now beginning to ask is: what happens when Xi Jinping eventually passes from the scene? As noted in the previous chapter, this is unlikely anytime soon. But for a septuagenarian, the possibility is real enough to force us to start seriously thinking this through. Indeed, it goes to the core question of whether the deep ideological changes that Xi has wrought so far, and those he has yet to implement, will endure under the next generation of Chinese leaders. In other words: will Xi have brought about sufficient structural and cultural change in his party and country to ensure that the core tenets of his Marxist-Nationalist ideological framework remain in place? Could his ideology, in fact, become more extreme as a younger generation of Xi political loyalists carry his banner forward, as happened with Mao during the initial years of the Cultural Revolution? Or will Xi Jinping Thought fade, gradually at first, as happened with Mao between 1976 and 1978 before it was finally repudiated by Deng and his successors? Before we examine the factors that will likely shape the ideological, political, and policy contours of a post-Xi Jinping China, it is important to look first at where Xi himself may take his eponymous ideology in the years ahead.

Future Directions in Xi Jinping Thought

There is a temptation to conclude that, after more than a decade of analysing Xi Jinping in power, we now have his ideological measure. Because his oeuvre is so large, his speeches so numerous, and his track record of achievements and setbacks so extensive, we assume that we now understand the core elements of his domestic and international strategy. While it is unlikely that Xi would repudiate any of the core Marxist, Leninist, and nationalist positions he has already incorporated into the party's ideological orthodoxy, he can still add to them. Indeed, Xi has said on multiple occasions that he intends to do so, stating that twenty-first-century Marxism must continue to evolve in a manner that takes into account developing domestic and international realities.[1] Of course, this is not intended as a freewheeling academic debate by party intellectuals, untethered to Leninist disciplines. As Xi reminded the party in April 2023, the business of theoretical innovation needed to "maintain a high degree of ideological and political consistency with the Party Central Committee".[2]

An important document within this politically disciplined framework for the future development of CCP ideology is Xi's October 2023 article in the party's theoretical journal, *Qiushi*, entitled 'Opening Up New Horizons for the Sinification and Modernization of Marxism in China' (*kaipi makesizhuyi zhongguohua shidaihua xinjingjie*).[3] Xi enjoined the party to "continuously deepen our understanding of the fundamental principles underlying the party's theoretical innovation, and achieve more fruitful accomplishments of theoretical innovation on the new journey in the new era".[4] In the text, Xi appeared to be preparing the party for an entirely new wave of ideological activity, this time drawn from selective elements of the classical Chinese tradition. These would be rendered into modern language, incorporated conceptually within the existing ideological canon, and, through that process, effectively *Marxified*. Xi was signalling that his definition of twenty-first-century Marxism would now incorporate various borrowings from classical Chinese language, values, and concepts. Its purpose seemed to be to further 'Sinify' Marxism by anchoring it more explicitly within the 'roots' and 'soil' of Chinese history, culture, and tradition. At the same time, Xi was seeking to *modernize* Marxist ideology and thereby future-proof it against the exigencies of the rise and fall of nations and dynasties—a perennial problem throughout Chinese history, deeply relevant to its future, and a subject of inquiry that has long preoccupied him. In doing so, Xi appeared to be moving gradually towards a new form of Chinese Marxism that was increasingly grounded in borrowings from Chinese (and even world) culture that were both ideologically acceptable to the party, and politically useful in communicating its message to a wider community beyond the party over time. Over the longer term, Xi's project may well be to construct a new global Marxism, still grounded in classical Marxist-Leninist theory, but clothed in more acceptable and internationally appealing language, thereby reaching new target audiences—within China, as well as among the peoples of the Global South.

The purpose of this enterprise appears to be a systematic re-writing of Chinese Marxism through the language of what, according to the party, are the unifying and ideologically acceptable elements of Chinese and non-Chinese cultures. It is to have a bold logic and embrace a grand new vision of world history. By any measure, this would seem to be a large-scale and breathtakingly ambitious ideological undertaking. Since Xi has described this as a great and urgent task for the party, it is important to render sections of this particular article at considerable length:

> Looking back at the century-long history of the party's struggle, the reason why our party has been able to make significant achievements in various historical periods of revolution, construction, and reform, and to lead the people to accomplish the difficult tasks impossible for other political forces in China, lies fundamentally in the mastery of the scientific theory of Marxism and the constant promotion of theoretical innovations tackling new realities. The party has grasped the powerful force of truth. The reason why the CCP is capable, and why socialism with Chinese characteristics is good, in the final analysis, is that Marxism works, that it is sinified and that it is modernized. The fact that Marxism works is the conclusion of history. . . .
>
> For Marxism adapted to the Chinese context and the needs of the times, this major proposition itself determines that we must not abandon our soul—Marxism—nor abandon our roots—excellent Chinese traditional culture. . . . With Marxism as a guide, we must conduct a comprehensive excavation of the treasure house of Chinese civilization of over 5,000 years, and use Marxism to activate the elements in the outstanding Chinese traditional culture that are excellent and full of vitality, and endow them with connotations for the new era. We must inject the great spirit and rich wisdom of the Chinese nation into Marxism at a deeper level, effectively connect the essence of Marxist thought with the essence of Chinese traditional culture, integrate them to form new theoretical advantages, and constantly climb new ideological peaks.
>
> We need to broaden the theoretical horizons, learn from all the best achievements of civilization in human society with an open mind, innovate and develop the party's theory by drawing from the best ideas and cultural resources in the 'sum of human knowledge', and form a theoretical landscape and atmosphere of inclusiveness and learning from all. . . . The leap of theory is not embodied in the novelty of words and phrases, nor in simple self-consistency and self-evidence of logic, but ultimately in answering practical

> questions and leading the development of practice. Marxism is a theory of practice. . . . Our task of promoting the Sinification of Marxism for the times is not lighter, but heavier. We must firmly establish a broad historical perspective, grasp the development of world history and the correct direction with a broader vision and a longer-term perspective, clearly recognize the overall logic and trends of China's social development and human social development, and grasp the historical evolution and practical requirements of the Chinese path to modernization. . . .
>
> Promoting the systematization of theory and its translation into academic knowledge is an inherent requirement and an important pathway for theoretical innovation. The reason Marxism's influence is deep and far-reaching lies in the fact that it reveals the truth of the development of human society with profound academic theories and demonstrates the scientific nature of its theories with a complete system. Marx once said that his writings were an artistic whole, and Lenin also said that Marxist philosophy is cast from a single piece of steel. Engels wrote such treatises as 'Socialism: Utopian and Scientific', which systematically expounded the basic principles of Marxism, scientifically demonstrated the intrinsic unity among the three constituent parts of Marxism, defended and developed the scientific nature of Marxism with profound doctrines, and, with a complete system, avoided and corrected the fragmentation and vulgarization of Marxism. This fully illustrates the importance of systematization and scholasticization in upholding and developing Marxism.[5]

Xi takes this theme of integrating Marxist theory with Chinese culture one step further from what he describes elsewhere as the 'second integration'.[6] Other explanatory texts make clear that, in Xi's argument, the Chinese Communist Party's 'first integration' was achieved through the Sinification of Soviet communism through Mao Zedong's adaptation of international Marxism to China's evolving *contemporary* circumstances.[7] The second integration, however, would now be achieved through the explicit incorporation of concepts from Chinese *classical* history and philosophy. To do this, Xi begins by defining the ten core concepts in Chinese traditional culture that were potentially adaptable for this purpose. China enjoyed "unique advantages" as a culture, he said, and for those reasons, had been "one of the most prosperous and powerful civilizations throughout a long period of history":

> The traditional Chinese culture encompasses a multitude of significant concepts, including social ideals of pursuing the common good for all (*tianxia weigong*, 'the world belongs to all') and achieving universal peace; governance principles of regarding the people as the foundation of the state and governing by virtue; traditions of striving for great unity in the country and

ensuring unity amid diversity (*jiuzhou gongguan*, 'the unity of the nine states'); traditions of striving for great unity in the country and ensuring unity amid diversity; values of dedicating oneself to self-cultivation, family management, state governance, and peace for all and shouldering one's duties to secure the future of the nation; aspirations of embracing the world with virtue and cultivating integrity; economic principles of enriching the people and improving their lives and pursuing the greater good and shared interests; ecological ideas of promoting harmony between humanity and nature and the coexistence of all living things; philosophical thoughts of seeking truth from facts and combining knowledge with action; the mindset of understanding multiple perspectives and seeking harmony through the middle way; and communication approaches of acting in good faith and being friendly to others. These concepts collectively shape the defining characteristics of Chinese civilization.

At this stage, Xi makes the remarkably Sino-centric claim—without apology to his country's ancient neighbours—that China represented the earth's "only great, uninterrupted civilization that continues to this day in a state form":

> Chinese civilization is distinguished by its continuity. Chinese civilization is the only great, uninterrupted civilization that continues to this day in a state form. This unequivocally affirms the cultural identity and robust vitality of Chinese civilization as it has responded to challenges and broken new ground through self-development. Chinese people's deep-rooted sentiments for the motherland and profound sense of history constitute an ideal for upholding great unity and provide spiritual support for guiding the Chinese nation through countless hardships on the path to national rejuvenation. This continuity inherently dictates that the Chinese nation will follow its own path. If not through the prism of its extensive history of continuity, one would not be able to understand ancient China, contemporary China, let alone the China of the future.[8]

Xi goes on to explain how these traditional Chinese concepts could now be integrated into Chinese Marxism. This was not to be a random process; the party would identify 'the best' of traditional culture that could be integrated. Moreover, the party's interpretation of these traditional concepts' true meanings would be absolute, as opposed to the type of textured debates on each that have permeated Chinese intellectual history. This in turn would initiate a "chemical reaction" with classical Marxism to create "a new organically unified cultural entity", thus embodying the "cultural progress" of contemporary China. And this would be the vehicle through which the next chapter in Marxist ideological history could now be written as a new and evolving conceptual synthesis. It would also enable Chinese economic modernization to be achieved without destroying Chinese civilizational continuity, avoiding the sort of cultural 'disruption' that had occurred in the West and elsewhere:

> The fundamental prerequisite for 'integration' is mutual compatibility. The 'two integrations' is not a far-fetched proposition. Despite their distinct origins, Marxism and traditional Chinese culture exhibit remarkable congruence. . . . Marxism sees the essence of man from the angle of social relations, while in Chinese culture, people are defined by their relationships with their family, their country, and the world. Both reject the notion of viewing humans as isolated entities. Genuine integration can only be attained through mutual compatibility. It is in this vein that we say that the Communist Party of China is a steadfast proponent and practitioner of Marxism, while it also works to keep China's traditional culture alive and strong. . . .
>
> 'Integration' is not a mere 'patchwork' or simple 'physical reaction'; instead, it is a profound 'chemical reaction' that creates a new organically unified cultural entity. On the one hand, Marxism brought advanced ideological theories to China, activating the genes of Chinese civilization with the light of truth, guiding China into the modern world, and driving the renewal of Chinese civilization and its modern transformation. . . . On the other hand, outstanding traditional Chinese culture enriched the cultural life of Marxism, propelling it to achieve continuous leaps in Sinification and modernization. This dynamic interaction has given rise to a distinctly Chinese style and demeanour, making Sinified Marxism the essence of Chinese culture and spirit in this era. The 'second integration' makes Chinese Marxism and outstanding traditional Chinese culture modern, allowing the culture newly formed through 'integration' to become the cultural form of Chinese-style modernization. . . .
>
> The integration of the basic tenets of Marxism with the best of China's traditional culture has endowed the path of Chinese socialism with greater historical depth and broadened its cultural underpinnings. Chinese-style modernization is the grand avenue leading to a strong country and national rejuvenation. . . . Chinese modernization seeks to build upon, rather than erase, China's ancient civilization. It sprouts from the land of China, not a mere imitation imported from any other country. It has stemmed from this rejuvenation, it is not a product of civilizational disruption. Chinese-style modernization is the rebirth of the Chinese nation, destined to help restore the glory of Chinese civilization. . . . More important, the 'second integration' is yet another manifestation of our commitment to freeing the mind. It allows us to fully harness the precious resources of traditional Chinese culture within a broader framework, to explore theoretical and institutional innovations for the future.[9]

In summary, the 'first integration' was between classical Marxism and China's contemporary conditions; Xi's 'second integration' will now be between Marxism and traditional Chinese culture. And these could potentially lead to a third integration (a term not used by Xi at this stage) with world cultures, as suggested by Wang Yi reflecting in December 2023 on the Marxist underpinnings of Xi's Global Civilization, Development and Security Initiatives. As Xi goes on to say:

> Through long-term efforts, we are now more capable than ever of resolving the 'debate between ancient and modern, Chinese and Western'. At the same time, we urgently need a set of cultural achievements that integrate ancient and modern, and bridge East and West. We must adhere to the Sinification and modernization of Marxism, inherit and develop excellent traditional Chinese culture, promote the localization of foreign cultures, and continually cultivate and create socialist culture with Chinese characteristics for the new era.[10]

In all this, culture becomes the new plasticity for Xi's unfolding ideological enterprise, both to preserve the party and its long-term political acceptability within China, and also to extend the party's ideological footprint into the world.

There may well be other developments in Xi Jinping Thought and his underlying ideological framework of Marxist-Leninist Nationalism. But what appears to be driving Xi's future ideological agenda is a concern to further indigenize Chinese Marxism by more explicitly incorporating its 'universal truths' within the more recognizable, acceptable, and durable language of Chinese classical culture. Here the objective appears to be to entrench Marxism within the more enduring forms of Chinese cultural identity, thereby widening its popular appeal over time, well beyond the acquired ideological tastes of the party's narrow apparatchik class. Indeed, by reducing the risk of Marxism collapsing in on itself because of its essentially foreign character, Xi is seeking to reduce the risk of the party's own long-term decline and fall. Xi's second objective seems to be to avoid complete cultural discontinuity with the past, which he sees as a universal problem of Western modernity, together with the implanting of contemporary Western cultural forms as the essential ingredients of an emerging global culture. He seems blissfully unaware that communism, despite its relatively short footprint in the long history of the Middle Kingdom, has proved to be a more violently iconoclastic force in destroying traditional Chinese culture than almost any other foreign ideology or external political assault down through the ages. This uncomfortable truth, rendered most vividly by the wanton destruction of the Cultural Revolution itself, is simply pushed to one side.[11] Xi's goal now is not just to develop a form of Marxism-Leninism that can survive for the long term, but also to construct a new form of Chinese civilization that can survive the rolling cultural assaults of international (i.e. Western) modernity as well.

For the world at large, Xi's further ambition is to use culture as a softer means of universalizing Marxist truths for the Global South. As Xi sees it, with the Washington Consensus in a state of collapse, the appeal of universal human rights diminished, and democracy in retreat, there is now an opportunity to fill an emerging vacuum for an acceptable global narrative capable of reaching across the developing world. When fully formed, Xi's international ideational agenda is therefore likely to become his answer to the long-standing, American-championed narrative of universal, individual political and economic freedom. Indeed, in the future, beyond the pages of the party's internal theoretical journals, it is conceivable that such a new body of thought may not even need to be called 'Marxism' or 'international socialism', notwithstanding its intellectual core. It may become a blend of '*tianxia*' ('all under Heaven'), '*datong*' (the 'great unity') and/or '*zhongyong*' (the 'golden mean'), together with a non-problematic selection of classical Confucian virtues. These, in turn, could be combined with carefully selected and curated concepts and values from world cultures, although the significant role of religion and metaphysics in most of the developing world (where communities of religious faith continue to grow rather than decline[12]) will present its own problems for Xi's avowedly atheist and materialist worldview. But whatever its nomenclature, the underpinning ideational structure of Xi's new narrative for the world is unlikely to stray too far from the 'objective scientific truths' of his beloved Marxism-Leninism.

Following in Mao's Steps in the Modernization and Sinification of Chinese Marxism

The sheer scale of Xi Jinping's ideological aspirations for the decade ahead, and how Xi sees this through the lens of party history, is made plain in an extraordinary leading article in the *People's Daily* by China

Reform Forum chairman He Yiting in February 2024.[13] The executive vice-president of the Central Party School between 2013 and 2021, He Yiting is a long-standing, centrally authorized author, exponent, and leading commentator on Xi Jinping Thought, perhaps best seen as the CCP's ideological equivalent of the Catholic Church's Prefect for the Doctrine of the Faith. Building on Xi's long 2023 speech and *Qiushi* article outlined above, He Yiting effectively argues that, in the ongoing challenge of modernizing and Sinifying Marxism-Leninism, there have only been two major contributors in modern Chinese history: Mao Zedong, who was responsible for the first integration of a foreign ideology with Chinese conditions during the long years of revolutionary struggle and national construction; and now Xi Jinping and his exemplary theoretical and practical contributions in what is now called the 'second integration'. In He's account, both Mao and Xi had done so through their skilled application of the Marxist ideological tools of historical and dialectical materialism. Both had analysed how to build a powerful China. Both had theorized new forms of Chinese economic modernization. Both had built a powerful military. Both had a truly global vision for Chinese Marxism. And both had perfected the hard task of continuous 'self-revolution' in order to maintain a disciplined political vanguard, capable of avoiding the historical dilemma of the rise and fall of parties and states by checking internal corruption, decline, and collapse. What is most remarkable, in He's telling, is that Mao had apparently done no wrong, despite earlier official party evaluations of Mao's litany of political and ideological excesses and public policy catastrophes, including the Anti-Rightist Movement, Great Leap Forward, and Cultural Revolution. Deng, Jiang, and Hu, it also seems, were no longer ideologically relevant, as their theoretical contributions are largely ignored. And Xi, at least as an ideological innovator, had in all respects now become a close second to Mao.

He Yiting then proceeds to outline four major areas in which Xi's ideological achievements should be seen in a similar light to Mao's: in economic modernization; in military reform; in the party's global and not just national missions; and in ongoing party reform and self-rectification. On the first of these, He Yiting argues that both Mao and Xi have been seminal contributors to the theory of Chinese-style modernization as the "only correct ideological path to the realization of a powerful state and the rejuvenation of the nation" (*mingquele qiangguo jianshe minzu fuxing de weiyi zhengque daolu*). According to He, Mao had been the founder of China's path to socialist modernization through the 'four modernizations'[14] which he delivered through two distinct stages: an initial phase of building a 'relatively complete socialist industrial system' and 'set of state-owned enterprises'; the second, through the more complete modernization of China's agriculture, industry, military, and science and technology. His commentary then glides over the entire thirty-five-year period of economic achievement under Deng, Jiang, and Hu, before stating that it was on "the basis of the long-term examination of the period of reform and opening" that a series of "new breakthroughs in theory and practice" had been achieved since the 18th Party Congress in 2012 in developing China's new form of modernization (*zhongguoshi xiandaihua*). According to He, this had been advanced through a series of innovative theoretical breakthroughs by Xi based on the scale of China's population, the concept of the 'common prosperity of the Chinese people', the proper role of spiritual and not just material factors in the modernization process (i.e. the role of politics, ideology, and culture as brakes on homogeneous, Western forms of modernization), and care for the natural environment. In doing so, Xi had not only advanced the party's interests in building a "strong state" and a "rejuvenated nation", he had also offered an "alternative modernization model for the world" (*wei renlei shixian xiandaihua tigongle xinde xuanze*). And all this, in turn, had reflected Xi's major theoretical contributions to the party and to international socialism in both "inheriting and further developing Marxist modernization theory".

He Yiting deploys a similar logic in describing the parallels between Mao's and Xi's achievements in the modernization of the Chinese military, particularly in providing the "scientific guidance on building a powerful military through Xi Jinping Thought that had transformed a people's army into a world-class fighting force". Mao, of course, had begun this process with his early leadership of the party's armed struggle and the initial formation of a people's army. Xi had continued this tradition since coming to power at the 18th Congress through his major contribution of Xi Jinping Thought on the Military with such concepts as "an army that follows the party's command"; a "military that is constructed from politics"; a military that "can fight and win wars"; the building of a truly "world-class military that is totally loyal, totally clean and entirely reliable", and a stronger military through "reform, technology and the highest level of talent". Once again, the message of the propaganda apparatus is clear: there were only two great ideological leaders who drove the modernization of the military, thereby creating a Chinese armed force commensurate with China's global standing, and ensuring that China was ready to face the strategic demands of the new era.

In almost identical vein, He Yiting goes on to claim that it was only Mao and Xi who understood that the CCP was not simply dedicated to the great happiness of the Chinese people, but that "it also stood for the progress of all humankind" and "the great harmony of the entire world". Mao had responded to "the external threats of blockade" by adopting an independent foreign policy that promulgated China's 'Three Worlds' theory, tactically deploying "united front" activities as part of foreign policy, and the adoption of the "heroic spirit of daring to struggle and daring to win" internationally. He Yiting extols Mao for "taking a broad view of the global revolution", adopting an "outstanding strategic posture", manifesting "an indomitable spirit of struggle", and implementing "China's great-power diplomacy with Chinese characteristics in the new era". The memory of Mao's achievements, it seemed, contrary to Deng Xiaoping's abandonment of Chinese support for international revolutionary activity, was now being rehabilitated as representing an early harbinger of China's rightful, longer-term contribution to the global progressive cause. In similar fashion, He's *People's Daily* commentary now claimed that it was Xi Jinping who had finally been prepared to tackle the hard questions of "what sort of world do we want?" and "what do we need to do to build such a world?" In answering these questions, Xi had "dissected the major developments and the great trends of our time" and devised new international concepts. These included a 'community of common destiny for all humankind', a new set of common global values, and now a flurry of multilateral initiatives including the BRI, GDI, GSI, and GCI. These had now been inscribed in the party and state constitutions, "had entered into the language of the resolutions and documents of the UN", and "reflected the common feelings of all the peoples of the world and the wider consensus of the international community". This particular claim, published in the official organ of the Central Committee of the Chinese Communist Party, on the level of purported global support for Xi's slew of foreign policy initiatives, might come as a surprise to many around the world. But what is far more important in this commentary is that the party had now begun conceptualizing Xi's international strategy within the same interventionist ideological framework as Mao. And that was new.

As with all else in the propagation of Xi Jinping's ideological revolution, the critical element in its success rests in its ability to build a party committed to the principles of continuing "self-revolution". On this, He Yiting draws a further parallel with Mao's tradition on the ideological construction of the party, the practice of "criticism and self-criticism", "party rectification", and a party style anchored in "arduous struggle" (*jianku douzheng*). Once again, He praises Xi for being sufficiently bold to ask the hard questions of "what type of long-term Marxist party in power do we wish to be?" and "how do we go about building such a party?" In answering the challenge, Xi had put forward "a series of new principles, concepts, strategies and theories" which he had encapsulated in nine basic ideological beliefs. These included "enabling the party to escape the cycles of history, the problems of rise and fall, and the [periodic] manifestation of disorder". As with Mao, Xi's response to this great challenge of history was to sustain an ideologically and ethically disciplined party in a manner "unprecedented in party history". The *People's Daily* article makes no reference to the mass purges of party officials during Mao's reign, nor their subsequent rehabilitation, including Xi Jinping's father, Xi Zhongxun, who was twice purged by Mao. Indeed, the thrust of He Yiting's commentary is that Xi had correctly built on the harsh traditions of internal party control that Mao had pioneered.

The overall significance of this authoritative *People's Daily* commentary on Xi Jinping's ideology in early 2024 is that it was published many months *after* the decisions of the previous year to moderate several of elements of Xi's economic and foreign policy settings. The underlying message from the commentary is: whatever *apparent* policy changes may be occurring, Xi's fundamental ideological course remained steady. Indeed, the commentary's rolling comparisons with Mao's ideological achievements in politics, the economy, foreign policy, and the military imply that Xi had become even more resolute in bringing about deep change across the Chinese system.

According to He Yiting, Xi remained determined to continue developing a new economic modernization model, with common prosperity at its core, in sharp contrast to that of his post-Mao predecessors. And this was despite the moderating policy messages more recently promoted by Premier Li Qiang.[15] Similarly, notwithstanding the November 2023 San Francisco summit between Presidents Xi and Biden aimed at stabilizing the bilateral relationship, three months later He Yiting effectively declared that Xi's global mission to change the international system through continued struggle against those who defended the old world order would persist. For party members, perhaps the most disturbing message of all was the commentary's explicit and uncritical embrace of Mao's approach to party rectification, self-criticism, and struggle. This signalled that Xi would continue to double down in sharpening the blade of the anti-corruption campaign, together with the other tools at his disposal in the disciplinary machinery of the party. In other words, Xi would become more Leninist and even more Maoist in his approach to party management. In summary, therefore, He Yiting's commentary had made clear that the ideological trajectory laid down during Xi's first decade in office was intensifying, rather than moderating, as he embarked on his second.

Counting the Cost to China of Xi's Return to Ideology

Xi's ideological grand strategy appears to be relatively clear. But the question remains: can it work in the real world? Can the unalloyed rebirth of Chinese 'ideological man' continue to prevail in modern China, let alone in a modernizing world, as the real-world political and economic costs continue to mount? Or will the risk of long-term political instability arising from an ideologically constrained economic growth model, and an increasingly problematic international reaction to Xi's new Marxist Nationalism, impose too high a price on China so that it becomes practically unsustainable over time?

The political cost of suppressing individual freedom using the security state will continue to rise. In the early 2020s, around 70% of mainland Chinese had reached adulthood before Xi took control of the party in 2012.[16] Their education was less tightly controlled, having obtained their majority before the forced injection of Xi Jinping Thought into the formal curriculum. Academic freedom, even as it existed within the confines of China's state universities, has now been curtailed even further.[17] Controls on internet and social media access made alternative news and opinion more difficult to access.[18] International study was now harder to secure, and those who had studied abroad were finding it tougher to secure work in Chinese government institutions amidst growing systemic distrust of Western education.[19] Young people's experience of sexual freedom, particularly for China's significant gay population, was now more constrained.[20] Women faced greater political and social pressure to become mothers for the purposes of producing children as part of their patriotic duty to the motherland, responding to China's collapsing birth rate.[21] Feminist groups supporting more radical forms of gender equality have been suppressed.[22] Religious belief, which had grown rapidly in recent decades, was now much more tightly controlled, not just for Christians and Muslims, but also for Buddhists.[23] Among those who still remembered the Cultural Revolution, there remained widespread distaste for the return of life-long tenure, the cult of personality, and the influence of the surveillance state that encouraged self-censorship of day-to-day conversations among family and friends.[24] And within the ranks of the party itself, there was a palpable fear of living under a reign of terror where the full force of the party's anti-corruption machinery could be deployed on the slightest pretext, or on the basis of a single anonymous complaint.[25] It is not hard, therefore, to imagine the fear and frustration that has attended Xi's ideological decision to reimpose the full disciplines of the Leninist state on his party and people. But when do these forces aggregate to the point that something fundamentally cracks? Absent a major external or internal catalytic event (as, for instance, COVID might have become), the answer is that it remains highly unlikely, given the political loyalty that Xi has extracted from those around him and, more broadly, the growing powers of the surveillance state.

Similarly, there are costs attached to Xi's parallel move to the Marxist and mercantilist left in Chinese economic policy. As noted in earlier chapters on the economy, former vice-premier Liu He reminded the public in 2019 that the private sector contributed "more than 50% of tax revenue, 60% of GDP, 70% of technological innovation, 80% of urban employment, and 90% of new jobs and new firms".[26] But industrialists and entrepreneurs now saw more limited future opportunities in Xi's China. Many were declining to invest further. Many were seeking instead either to leave or to invest abroad.[27] There was parallel disquiet among economic reformers within the party elite.[28] These officials, who spent decades of their careers presiding over rapid economic growth during the era of reform and opening, were now seeing investment, innovation, and productivity in decline.[29] Even party conservatives were concerned about the cumulative impact of lost production and declining economic growth because of its impact on China's race against the United States to become the world's largest economy.[30] Provincial and sub-provincial governments were experiencing revenue downgrades as Xi's ideological and financial policy assault on the property sector (which generates much of their revenues) intensified.[31] Declining growth also squeezed central government financial provision in critical areas such as housing, health, education, aged care, and retirement incomes (including military pensions), all of which remain potential sources of social instability.[32] Finally, there was the overall impact of slower growth on living standards and employment levels for the bulk of the working-age population, with the problem of youth unemployment continuing to grow.[33] All these economic costs are real. Further, in the absence of a consumption-driven economic recovery that returns China to annual growth levels between 5% and 6% over the remainder of the decade, these costs will continue to mount. While there will be some level of policy moderation in response to faltering growth numbers, it would take a full-scale financial crisis to generate the catalyst necessary to bring about deep ideological and policy change. This crisis would also need to be indigenous in nature, given the absence of any significant levels of US dollar-denominated debt.[34] That is not in prospect. Therefore, policy settings are unlikely to fundamentally change and economic discontent will likely continue to simmer.

The foreign policy costs of Xi's new Marxist-Nationalist ideology affect a much narrower constituency within China than those arising from changes in broad politics and the economy.[35] Nonetheless, the party's foreign and security policy elites, together with the security and intelligence apparatus and the PLA, represent vast networks of influence across China's political establishment. At a macro level, Beijing's international policy elites see clearly the scale of geo-political realignment against China in response to its more assertive foreign and security policy posture, including: the Quad; trilateral strategic collaboration between the United States, Japan, and, in particular, South Korea; the creation of AUKUS; the rejuvenation of the US-Philippines security alliance; the hardening of NATO and European Union strategy towards China; the agreement of US allies to impose bans on technology exports; and the creation of the Indo-Pacific Economic Framework (IPEF).[36] Viewed from Beijing, these all represent major foreign policy losses. Xi's embrace of Putin in a strategic partnership with 'no limits'[37] on the eve of Russia's invading Ukraine, and in the quantum of economic support to Moscow since the invasion, has decisively affected baseline European sentiment towards China.[38] Furthermore, wolf warrior diplomacy writ large inflicted great damage on China's global political standing with little gain.[39] Economic coercion attempts against Norway, Sweden, Lithuania, Japan, Korea, Australia, and the Philippines have had a similarly negative reputational effect.[40] China's record of pressuring developing country representatives over votes, candidatures, and other actions across the UN system was also having a negative effect on Beijing's otherwise positive diplomacy towards the Global South.[41] Similarly, with the implementation of China's $1 trillion-plus loans program under the Belt and Road Initiative, Beijing's reluctance to renegotiate debt (and instead to confiscate assets) was also becoming a growing foreign policy liability.[42] Even China's global climate change credentials have been hit as Beijing turned back to coal and slowed its renewable energy transformation in response to slower growth and Xi's overall nationalist economic strategy.[43] As noted in the previous chapter, this growing list of foreign policy failures resulted in a number of policy adjustments during 2023, but the political costs endure. China's standing in global opinion polling across the developed world has collapsed, although the data from the developing world is considerably more varied.[44]

Against all these measures, the real-world cost of Xi's ideological onslaught over the last decade has, therefore, been large. The damage has been real and, in many areas, seems unrecoverable. Furthermore, Chinese political, policy, and business elites have long memories. They can recall, even if the official media does not, what has materially changed over the last decade—what freedoms have been forfeited, what trade, investment, and growth opportunities have been missed, and how China's international reputation has been tarnished. It remains, however, unlikely that Xi himself could substantively change ideological and policy course. More important, he is likely to have already factored in these costs as a political downpayment for the harder gains to come: a politically and ideologically disciplined party; a private sector back under control; and, in his view, a China now confident of its position in the world.

In this sense in particular, as in so many areas, Xi is radically different to his post-Mao predecessors. In all essential respects, Deng, Jiang, and Hu focussed their political energies on the immediate challenges of modernizing a backward economy. They knew that, in doing so, they were unleashing long-term forces of economic, social, and possible political change. But by and large—with the great exception of the Tiananmen Square massacre in 1989—they were prepared to leave open the ultimate question of China's long-term political form. This included the possibility that China might eventually evolve into some form of democracy like Singapore (as a Chinese cultural entity), with even the Nordic social democracies viewed as possible models for adaptation in the more distant future.[45] However, no violent or chaotic attempt to overthrow the system, as occurred in 1989, would be tolerated. The only possible democratic future lay in some form of 'peaceful transition' navigated by the party itself—hence multiple experiments in local democracy starting in the mid-1980s under the official rubric of 'the reform of the political system'.[46] Still, even the most reformist of previous Chinese leaders including Hu Yaobang and Zhao Ziyang (both of whom were purged), a long-term democratic or semi-democratic landing point was at best one of a number of future possibilities.[47] The core point, however, was that the question of China's long-term political destination was to be kept open.

By contrast, Xi Jinping saw this potential political future for China and did not like what he saw. He understood what his predecessors were seeking to do by leaving the democratic door open for the next generation and decided instead to slam it tightly shut. Xi, as an intelligent man, also understood the costs of doing so. But he saw these social, economic, and international reputational costs as well worth paying to preserve the powers of the CCP for the long term. In fact, this is where Xi's position is deeply ideological: because he is a convicted Marxist-Leninist, he harbours fundamental ideological objections to anything approximating a liberal-democratic political and economic model for China. Moreover, as a convicted Chinese nationalist, he believes that democratization would potentially undermine national wealth, power, and unity, and that, in turn, would once again render China vulnerable to the predations of foreign powers, as had been the country's lot through much of its modern history. Furthermore, at a much more personal level, Xi simply would not tolerate any attempt to diminish either his or the party's hold on political power, to which any form of electoral democracy represented an elemental and existential threat. In other words, Xi saw this possible democratic (and increasingly capitalist) future—which his predecessors had been leaving deliberately open for nearly a quarter of a century—and moved immediately to close that option down, fully mindful of the costs it would entail. For him, the cost-benefit analysis of preserving China's Marxist-Leninist nationalist model was self-evident.

Therefore, if there is no real prospect of Xi Jinping amending his deep-seated, ideological worldview, the only real alternative to bring about change would be for Xi to fall. That too, is unlikely because Xi's control over the party's security and intelligence apparatus is tight, and because the infrastructure, technology, and algorithms of social and political control have rapidly improved. Nor is there any credible alternative leader or leadership group around whom internal dissent could readily coalesce. All remaining potential candidates were removed from the central leadership at the 20th Party Congress. It would therefore take a calamitous, catalytic, external event such as a new pandemic, a financial or economic collapse with ensuing social instability, or an unforgivably humiliating foreign policy failure or military defeat. These are possible, but again not probable, scenarios for China's near-to-medium-term future. Even if calamity ensued, recalling Mao's capacity to survive catastrophe after catastrophe, Xi's powers of political survival should not be underestimated. Therefore, the odds are that, despite the mounting costs to China by continuing the current policy course, Xi is likely to remain in power until he dies, is incapacitated, or eventually steps back to a less-taxing (but still powerful) position in favour of a chosen successor.

China after Xi

So what will happen to China's long-term ideological direction once Xi eventually leaves the scene? This will be shaped by a number of factors, the most important of which will be timing. Xi will want to stay in office until he is confident that the generation to succeed him in the party's most senior leadership positions will share his ideological direction and zeal. This presents a problem. Xi constantly rails against his own generation and the one immediately below him for having allowed corruption, careerism, and ideological confusion to reign supreme. That's why his party rectification campaigns have been designed to instil personal and political fear and rigour.

But Xi will likely remain cautious about trusting anyone to replace him who entered a significant position of political authority under his predecessors. He would also be dubious as to whether they would have sufficient personal commitment to continue his ideological and political program into the future. His instinct would be to remain in power until a critical mass of younger party officials, who began their university education under him, have reached higher political office. Xi's constant invocation to 'dare to struggle' (*ganyu douzheng*) has been delivered through the country's party school networks and has been particularly focussed on younger cadres.[48] In doing so, Xi has appealed to their youthful idealism, as yet uncorrupted by the rampant materialism and bourgeois influences of the recent past.

However, this effort to purify the future ranks of the party's leadership would mean relying primarily on cadres born after 1995, who were children when Xi first came to power. By the 22nd Party Congress in 2032, however, 'Xi's generation' would be at most thirty-seven, barely old enough in normal circumstances to be appointed as alternate Central Committee members. At the two subsequent congresses in 2037 and 2042, when Xi would be in his eighty-fifth and ninetieth years, they would be in their mid-forties—the optimum age for placing this rising generation of young Chinese nationalists into positions of real authority, even possibly the Politburo. In other words, it would take a long time to appoint large numbers of this post 'reform and opening' generation to the highest positions in the party. While there will be other ideological conservatives and personal loyalists in the senior ranks of the party whom Xi would trust, this younger generation presents his greatest hope and political bulwark against ideological revisionism once he leaves the scene. They would provide the ballast of political support across the central party leadership that his designated successor would need to avoid becoming a latter-day Hua Guofeng. Therefore, the longer Xi remains in power, the more likely his succession plan will be able to deliver long-term ideological continuity.

Chinese politics after Xi Jinping will also be affected by the unfolding geo-politics and geo-economics of the decade ahead. By far, the most important external strategic development will be the future of Taiwan. If US deterrence fails—either through insufficient US, Taiwanese, and allied military capability or a failure of US political will—and Xi swiftly and (relatively) bloodlessly takes Taiwan by force, his position within Chinese domestic politics would become unassailable. Xi would have achieved what Mao had failed to achieve by reuniting the Motherland. Xi would then, most likely, launch what would be framed as a new age of *Pax Sinica* as American geo-political decline set in across Asia and, in time, the world. Taiwan would be seen within China and the wider region as a profound geo-political tipping point. Domestically, this would afford Xi a maximally advantageous set of circumstances to secure both his desired political succession and the long-term continuation of his ideological legacy. If, by contrast, Xi sought to resolve Taiwan by force and was defeated militarily, there is little doubt he would be forced from office. Such a defeat, coming after more than a decade of official propaganda that only Xi had made China powerful, would count as national humiliation of the highest order. It would, therefore, demand the highest political price be paid. Indeed, the legitimacy of the regime itself would come under direct challenge. However, the third—and, at this stage, most likely—scenario is that deterrence continues to hold through the 2020s and war is avoided. In this case, Taiwan would mean little for Xi's longer-term internal succession planning.

Equally important, if the famously assertive and status quo–challenging Xi Jinping ultimately judged that the risks were still too great to take Taiwan by force, it is highly unlikely that his successors would then be prepared to do so. Alternative diplomatic frameworks for long-term national unity may, under these circumstances, become possible in a new generation of negotiations between Beijing and Taipei. For these reasons, given his desire to surpass Mao's achievements on national reunification, and to do so before the PRC's centenary in 2049, Xi's period in office likely represents the period of *peak danger* on the possibility of war over Taiwan. Navigating the Taiwan question through effective deterrence during the Xi period remains the single most critical strategic task for supporters of the status quo. Indeed, that was the primary purpose of my last book, *The Avoidable War*.[49] It outlines a strategic framework of 'Managed Strategic Competition' between China and the United States to preserve peace across the Taiwan Straits: first by reducing the risk of crisis, conflict, and war by accident by building strategic guardrails between the two; and second by reducing the risk of war by design by enhancing integrated deterrence that continues to elevate the cost to Xi of taking unilateral military action against Taiwan to unacceptable levels.

I argue that the dominant internal political dynamic within the CCP after Xi Jinping ultimately leaves the stage will, most likely, be part of the long-standing processes of natural self-correction that lie within the party itself. Throughout its history, the CCP has oscillated between left and right, conservatives and reformers, isolationists and internationalists, control and release (*fangshou*). In the post-1949 period, for example, Mao's leftism dominated with an emphasis on class struggle, the Anti-Landlord Movement, collectivized agriculture, and nationalized industry. This was until the 8th Party Congress in 1956, when pragmatists sought to readjust the party's centre of economic gravity to promote steady economic development, trade, and commerce. Mao retaliated with the Great Leap Forward in 1959, resulting in widespread famine as he sought to accelerate industrialization at the expense of normal agricultural production. The economic pragmatists, then led by Deng, went on the offensive in the early 1960s, and Mao pushed back with the Cultural Revolution, purging his 'rightist' political opponents and doubling down on both agricultural and industrial collectivization. This ended with Mao's death in 1976, the formal repudiation of Mao's leftist errors, and Deng's initiation of what would become a thirty-five-year era of reform and opening, which re-embraced the private sector for the first time in decades.

Xi, as the party's leading dialectician, is likely to have seen this long series of historical debates within the CCP as the inevitable product of internal dialectical confrontation, contradiction, and struggle to establish the 'correct' party line. Hence his efforts since 2012, and particularly after 2017, to correct the economic and social imbalances left over from the Deng era. As noted above, the political and economic momentum already building against Xi's leftist ideological project is formidable. But as with Mao, it is unlikely to be strong enough to force any fundamental political correction until the leader has formally departed the scene. Whatever interim leadership may replace Xi, the floodgates are then more likely to be forced open for these self-correcting forces to seek a new, more moderate political and policy equilibrium. However, Xi would undoubtedly be aware of this danger, fuelling his recruitment of younger, more idealistic and nationalistic cadres into the leadership echelons of the party as early as possible to pre-empt any longer-term ideological revisionism.

Xi's problem, however, is that he may not have enough time. He would probably have to maintain power well into his nineties to appoint enough ideologically reliable younger cadres to enable his long-term political strategy to take root. Pitted against this strategy will be the underlying forces of political inertia, bureaucratic entropy, and a party historically predisposed to return to the political mean. Even for a formidable politician like Xi, prevailing in such a long-term struggle against the political, economic, and social forces arrayed against him will be a tall order indeed. The irony, therefore, is that Xi, the master dialectician, could well be defeated by dialectical forces of his own making—a direct reaction to decades of his own ideological overreach. China after Xi, as has been the case in previous eras in modern Chinese history, is therefore more likely to correct towards the centre. Unless Xi can hold on for another twenty years or more, China, on balance, is less likely to become more ideologically extreme once he goes. It is likely instead that the party and the country would broadly welcome a return to the centre, given how much of Xi's ideological project has grated against so many individual aspirations, societal norms, and deep economic interests in modern China—as well as giving rise to concern, at least among elites, as to how isolated China has become across much of the world. For these reasons, the challenge for the wider world is to effectively navigate the Xi Jinping era through a combination of deterrence and diplomacy, without recourse to crisis, conflict, and war. War, whatever its outcome, would generate death and destruction at an unimaginable scale. It would also redefine Chinese, American, and global politics and geo-politics in deeply unpredictable yet indelible ways. And the world would never be the same again.

Notes

CHAPTER 1

1. Biographies of Xi Jinping include: Agnès Andrésy, *Xi Jinping* (Lanham, MD: University Press of America, 2015); Kerry Brown, *Xi* (London: Icon, 2022); Kerry Brown, *CEO, China* (London: I. B. Tauris, 2016); Elizabeth Economy, *The Third Revolution* (New York: Oxford University Press, 2018); Chun Han Wong, *Party of One* (London: Simon & Schuster, 2023); Ming Wu, *China's Future* (Hong Kong: CNHK Publications, 2012).
2. Xinhua, "'习近平：加强领导做好规划明确任务夯实基础 推动我国新一代人工智能健康发展'", *cpc.people.com.cn* (1 November 2018), accessed 12 December 2023.
3. See: 'World Emissions Clock', World Data Lab, https://worldemissions.io/ (1 December 2023), accessed 12 December 2023. All trajectories are based on projections that people still conduct business as usual.
4. For comprehensive biographies of Xi Jinping and analyses of his influence on China and its global role, see works such as: Steve Tsang and Olivia Cheung, *The Political Thought of Xi Jinping* (New York: Oxford University Press, 2024); Chun Han Wong, *Party of One* (New York: Avid Reader Press, 2023); Alfred L. Chan, *Xi Jinping* (New York: Oxford University Press, 2022); Lance L. P. Gore, 'Leninism for the 21st Century', *China: An International Journal*, *21/2* (May 2023); Wei Shan, Gu Yongxin, and Juan Chen, 'Layering Ideologies from Deng Xiaoping to Xi Jinping', *China: An International Journal*, *21/2* (May 2023); Steve Tsang and Olivia Cheung, 'Has Xi Jinping Made China's Political System More Resilient and Enduring?', *Third World Quarterly*, *43*/1 (2022); Yuen Yuen Ang, 'How Resilient Is the CCP?', *Journal of Democracy*, *33*/3 (2022); Barry Naughton, 'Grand Steerage as the New Paradigm for State-Economy Relations', in Frank N. Pieke and Bert Hofman (eds.), *CPC Futures* (Singapore: NUS Press, 2022); Andrew J. Nathan and Boshu Zhang, 'A Shared Future for Mankind', *Journal of Contemporary China*, *31*/133 (2022); Arthur S. Ding and Jagannath P. Panda (eds.), *Chinese Politics and Foreign Policy under Xi Jinping* (New York: Routledge, 2021); Masafumi Iida, 'Xi Jinping's Diplomacy and the Rise of His Political Authority', *Journal*

of Contemporary East Asia Studies, 9/2 (2020); Alice Miller, 'Xi Jinping and the Evolution of Chinese Leadership Politics', in *Fateful Decisions* (Stanford, CA: Stanford University Press, 2020); Cheng Li, *Chinese Politics in the Xi Jinping Era* (New York: Brookings Institution Press, 2016); Bruce J. Dickson, *The Dictator's Dilemma* (New York: Oxford University Press, 2016); Elizabeth C. Economy, *The Third Revolution* (New York: Oxford University Press, 2019); Jin Keyu, *The New China Playbook* (New York: Viking, 2023); Kerry Brown, *The World According to Xi*. (London: I. B. Tauris, 2018); Willy Lo-Lap Lam, *Xi Jinping* (London: Routledge, 2024); Carl Minzner, *End of an Era* (New York: Oxford University Press, 2018); Nien-chung Chang-Liao, 'China's New Foreign Policy under Xi Jinping', *Asian Security*, 12/2 (2016); Lutgard Lams, 'Examining Strategic Narratives in Chinese Official Discourse under Xi Jinping', *Journal of Chinese Political Science*, 23/3 (2018); Susan L. Shirk, 'China in Xi's "New Era"', *Journal of Democracy*, 29/2 (2018); Avery Goldstein, 'China's Grand Strategy under Xi Jinping', *International Security*, 45/1 (2020).

5. Joshua D. Kertzer and Dustin Tingley, 'Political Psychology in International Relations: Beyond the Paradigms', *Annual Review of Political Science*, 21 (2018), 319–39; Matthias Ecker-Ehrhardt, 'Cosmopolitan Politicization', *European Journal of International Relations*, 18/3 (2012), 481–508; Nicholas Ross Smith, 'The Re-emergence of a 'Mirror Image' in West-Russia Relations?', *International Politics*, 55 (2018), 575–94; Michael Clarke, 'French and British Security', *International Affairs*, 76/4 (2000), 725–39.
6. Susan L. Shirk, *Overreach* (New York: Oxford University Press, 2023).
7. Central Political and Legal Affairs Commission of the CCP, '陈一新：来一场刀刃向内、刮骨疗毒式的自我革命', *ah.jcy.gov.cn* (9 July 2020), accessed 12 December 2013.
8. See: '李君如：在"两个确立"中继往开来迎接党的二十大，航船要有舵手，航行要有指南。要问这10年来之不易的历史性成就和历史性变革是怎么获得的，最根本的原因，就是党有了新时代的舵手和思想指南，确立了习近平同志党中央的核心、全党的核心地位，确立了习近平新时代中国特色社会主义思想的指导地位。', *epaper.gmw.cn* (15 August 2022), accessed 23 May 2024.
9. See, e.g.: Michael Pillsbury, *The Hundred-Year Marathon* (New York: Henry Holt, 2015).

CHAPTER 2

1. See Adrian Chan as an example of academic work about the important systematic, albeit leftist, treatment of the interrelationship between ideology, politics, and policy since the party's earliest years. Adrian Chan, *Chinese Marxism* (New York: Continuum, 2003).
2. See different definitional approaches to the term 'ideology', e.g. Martin Seliger, *Ideology and Politics* (London: Routledge, 2019); John Petrov Plamenatz,

Ideology (London: Pall Mall, 1970); Jean Baechler, *Qu'est-ce que l'idéologie?* (Paris: Éditions Gallimard, 1976); Richard Cox (ed.), *Ideology, Politics, and Political Theory* (Belmont, CA: Wadsworth, 1969); Antoine-Louis-Claude Destutt de Tracy, *A Treatise on Political Economy* (Indianapolis, IN: Liberty Fund, 2011); François Joseph Picavet, *Les Idéologues* (New York: Arno Press, 1975); Emmet Kennedy, *A Philosophe in the Age of Revolution* (Philadelphia: American Philosophical Society, 1978); George Lichtheim, *The Concept of Ideology and Other Essays* (New York: Random House, 1967); Karl Marx and Friedrich Engels, *The German Ideology* (New York: International Publishers, 1972). Recent treatments of ideology in the Marxist tradition include: Alvin W. Gouldner, *The Dialectic of Ideology and Technology* (London: Macmillan Education UK, 1976); Jorge Larraín, *The Concept of Ideology* (Athens: University of Georgia Press, 1979), and *Marxism and Ideology* (London: Macmillan, 1983); Colin Sumner, *Reading Ideologies* (Cambridge: Academic Press, 1979); Joe McCarney, *The Real World of Ideology* (Atlantic Highlands, NJ: Humanities Press, 1980). More advanced students will find useful Walter Carlsnaes, *The Concept of Ideology and Political Analysis* (Westport, CT: Greenwood, 1981).

3. John Gerring, 'Ideology', *Political Research Quarterly*, 50/4 (1997).
4. Antoine-Louis-Claude Destutt de Tracy, *Élémens d'idéologie* (Paris: Courcier, 1804).
5. Napoléon Bonaparte, '8620—A.M. Cambacérès', in *Correspondance de Napoléon Ier*, Vol. 10 (Paris: H. Plon, J. Dumaine, 1862), 342.
6. Marx and Engels, *German Ideology*; Ron Eyerman, 'False Consciousness and Ideology in Marxist Theory', *Acta Sociologica*, 24/1–2 (1981).
7. 'Ideology—Sociology, Knowledge, Beliefs', *britannica.com*, accessed 13 October 2023.
8. Gerring, 'Ideology', 968.
9. Karl Marx, *A Contribution to the Critique of Political Economy* (Chicago: Charles H. Kerr, 1904), 12.
10. Gerring, 'Ideology', 966–979.
11. Gerring, 'Ideology', 980.
12. Gerring, 'Ideology', 983.
13. See, e.g.: Stuart R. Schram, *Mao Tse-Tung* (Baltimore: Penguin, 1967); Suisheng Zhao, *A Nation-State by Construction* (Stanford, CA: Stanford University Press, 2004); Daniel Bell, *The China Model* (Princeton, NJ: Princeton University Press, 2015); Peter Gue Zarrow, *After Empire* (Stanford, CA: Stanford University Press, 2012); Arif Dirlik, *Anarchism in the Chinese Revolution* (Berkeley: University of California Press, 1991); Elizabeth J. Perry, *Anyuan* (Berkeley: University of California Press, 2012).
14. Feng Chen, 'An Unfinished Battle in China', *China Quarterly*, no. 158 (1999).
15. Franz Schurmann, *Ideology and Organization in Communist China* (Berkeley: University of California Press, 1973).
16. Schurmann, *Ideology and Organization*, 18.

17. Schurmann, *Ideology and Organization*, 21.
18. Immanuel Kant, *Critique of Judgment*, trans. Werner S. Pluhar (Indianapolis, IN: Hackett, 1987).
19. Pluhar translates Weltanschauung as our 'intuition of the world': Kant, *Critique of Judgment*, 111–12.
20. Richard Rorty, 'The World Well Lost', in *Consequences of Pragmatism* (Minneapolis: University of Minnesota Press, 1982).
21. Karl Marx, *Thesen über Feuerbach* (Hamburg: Argument, 1998) 15.
22. John McMurtry, *Structure of Marx's World-View* (Princeton, NJ: Princeton University Press, 2016).
23. Schurmann, *Ideology and Organization*, 22–23.
24. See: Stuart R. Schram, *The Thought of Mao Tse-Tung* (Cambridge; Cambridge University Press, 1989); Maurice Meisner, *Marxism, Maoism, and Utopianism* (Madison: University of Wisconsin Press, 1982); Arif Dirlik, *The Origins of Chinese Communism* (Oxford: Oxford University Press, 1989); Conrad Brandt, Benjamin Schwartz, and John K. Fairbank, *A Documentary History of Chinese Communism* (London: Routledge & Kegan Paul, 1952); Alexander V. Pantsov and Steven I. Levine, *Mao: The Real Story* (New York: Simon & Schuster, 2012); Peter Van Ness, *Revolution and Chinese Foreign Policy* (Berkeley: University of California Press, 1970); Timothy Cheek, *Mao Zedong and China's Revolutions* (Boston: Bedford/St. Martin's, 2002); Bill Brugger and David Kelly, *Chinese Marxism in the Post-Mao Era* (Stanford, CA: Stanford University Press, 1990); Lucien Bianco, *Origins of the Chinese Revolution* (Stanford, CA: Stanford University Press, 1971); Jian Chen, 'The Myth of America's 'Lost Chance' in China', *Diplomatic History*, 21/1 (1997).
25. Schurmann, *Ideology and Organization*, 25.
26. Xi Jinping, 'Adapt Marxism to China's Realities and Keep It Up-to-Date', in *The Governance of China*, Vol. 4; '习近平：在新时代伟大实践中不断开辟马克思主义中国化时代化新境界', *qstheory.cn* (1 August 2022), accessed 29 January 2024.
27. See Shalom H. Schwartz, 'Universals in the Content and Structure of Values', *Advances in Experimental Social Psychology*, 25 (1992); Schurmann, *Ideology and Organization*, 18–36; A. James Gregor, *A Place in the Sun* (New York: Hachette, 2017).
28. Schurmann, *Ideology and Organization*, 27.
29. Schurmann, *Ideology and Organization*, 39.
30. Vladimir Ilyich Lenin, 'The State and Revolution', in *Essential Works of Lenin* (New York: Dover, 1987).
31. Schurmann, *Ideology and Organization*, 23.
32. Schurmann, *Ideology and Organization*, 23.
33. Schurmann, *Ideology and Organization*, 19–20. See also 49–50 on the processes of inner conversion.
34. Schurmann, *Ideology and Organization*, 20.

35. Norberto Bobbio, *Left and Right* (Chicago: University of Chicago Press, 1996), 33. See also: Frits Bienfait and Walter E. A. van Beek, 'Political Left and Right', *Journal of Social and Political Psychology*, 2/1 (2014).
36. Andrew J. Nathan and Tianjian Shi, 'Left and Right with Chinese Characteristics', in Arthur M. Melzer, Jerry Weinberger, and M. Richard Zinman (eds.), *Politics at the Turn of the Century* (Lanham, MD: Rowman & Littlefield, 2001).
37. Nathan and Shi, 'Left and Right', 300.
38. Seymour Martin Lipset and Stein Rokkan, *Party Systems and Voter Alignments* (New York: Free Press, 1967).
39. Nathan and Shi, 'Left and Right' 301.
40. For more about Marxism and fascism in China, see Gregor, *A Place in the Sun*.
41. Li Honglin, '"Right" and "Left" in Communist China', *Journal of Contemporary China*, no. 6 (1994), 1.
42. Li, '"Right" and "Left"', 1.
43. E.g.: Foreign Languages Press, *Selected Articles Criticizing Lin Piao and Confucius*, Vol. 2 (Peking: Foreign Languages Press, 1975).
44. Central Committee of the CCP, *Resolution on Certain Questions in the History of Our Party since the Founding of the People's Republic of China* (Second Historical Resolution), *digitalarchive.wilsoncenter.org* (27 June 1981), accessed 22 March 2024.
45. See: 中共中央宣传部编, '习近平新时代中国特色社会主义思想学习纲要', 学习出版社,人民出版社 , *theory.people.com.cn* (2019), accessed 23 May 2024.
46. Nathan and Shi, 'Left and Right'; Andrew J. Nathan and Tianjian Shi, 'Cultural Requisites for Democracy in China', *Daedalus*, 122/2 (1993).
47. Nathan and Shi, 'Left and Right', 309.
48. Jennifer Pan and Yiqing Xu, 'China's Ideological Spectrum', *Journal of Politics*, 80/1 (2018).
49. Andrew Chubb, 'Chinese Popular Nationalism and PRC Policy in the South China Sea', Doctoral Thesis, University of Western Australia (2016), 5.
50. Jessica Chen Weiss, *Powerful Patriots* (Oxford: Oxford University Press, 2014), 9.
51. Kai Quek and Alastair Iain Johnston, 'Can China Back Down?', *International Security*, 42/3 (2018), 30. See also: Alastair Iain Johnston, 'Is Chinese Nationalism Rising?', *International Security*, 41/3 (2016); Chen Dingding, Pu Xiaoyu, and Alastair Iain Johnston, 'Debating China's Assertiveness', *International Security*, 38/3 (2013).
52. Weiss, *Powerful Patriots*, 10.
53. Chubb, 'Chinese Popular Nationalism', 5.
54. Johnston, 'Is Chinese Nationalism Rising?', 9.
55. Johnston, 'Is Chinese Nationalism Rising?', 41.
56. Bill Bishop, 'Outbreaks; Water Security; Big Plans for Digital Economy; Yan Xuetong', *sinocism.com* (12 January 2022), accessed 2 February 2022.

57. Zhou Enlai, 'Our Foreign Policies and Our Tasks', in *Selected Works of Zhou Enlai*, Vol. 2 (Beijing: Foreign Languages Press, 1989).
58. See: Zhao Tingyang, *World System: An Introduction to Philosophy of the World System*, Chinese Edition (Nanjing: Jiangsu Education Publishing House, 2005); also William A. Callahan, 'Chinese Visions of World Order', *International Studies Review*, 10/4 (2008).
59. Nien-Chung Chang Liao, 'The Sources of China's Assertiveness', *International Affairs*, 92/4 (2016). See also: Kevin Narizny, *The Political Economy of Grand Strategy* (Ithaca, NY: Cornell University Press, 2007), 11; Peng Lu, 'Chinese IR Sino-centrism Tradition and Its Influence on the Chinese School Movement', *Pacific Review*, 32/2 (2018); Dapeng Tang and Shiping Qi, 'Sino-centrism and US-centrism in China's Foreign Policy Discourse', *World Economics and Politics*, 12 (2008).
60. Michael D. Swaine, 'Perceptions of an Assertive China', *China Leadership Monitor*, 32 (2010); Brantly Womack, 'Beyond Win-Win', *International Affairs*, 89 (2013); Thomas J. Christensen, 'The Advantages of an Assertive China', *Foreign Affairs*, 90/2 (2011); Liao, 'The Sources of China's Assertiveness'.
61. Thomas Aquinas, *The Summa Theologica* (London: Burns Oates & Washbourne, 1922), 52/1.

CHAPTER 3

1. Xi Jinping, '习近平双峰会"妙语集锦":孤举者难起 众行者易趋', *cpc.people.com.cn* (1 October 2015). See also: Xi Jinping, '习近平在第四届中国国际进口博览会开幕式上的主旨演讲', *gov.cn* (4 November 2021); Xi Jinping, '习近平在金砖国家领导人第五次会晤时的主旨讲话', *gov.cn* (27 March 2013), all accessed 15 December 2023.
2. John King Fairbank and Ta-tuan Ch'en, *The Chinese World Order* (Cambridge, MA: Harvard University Press, 1968), 6.
3. William Kirby, 'Traditions of Centrality, Authority and Management in Modern Chinese Foreign Policy', in *Chinese Foreign Policy: Theory and Practice* (New York: Clarendon Press: 1994), 20–21.
4. Fairbank and Ch'en, *Chinese World Order*, 3.
5. Fairbank and Ch'en, *Chinese World Order*, 21.
6. Fairbank and Ch'en, *Chinese World Order*, 3–7.
7. James Legge, *The Chinese Classics*, Vol. 5 (Hong Kong: Lane, Crawford & Co., 1872), 349.
8. Xi Jinping, '习近平在金砖国家领导人第五次会晤时的主旨讲话'. See also: Xi Jinping, 'China's Xi Jinping Talks of Deeper Australian Ties ahead of G20', *afr.com* (14 November 2014); Xi Jinping, 'Full Text of Chinese President's Signed Article in Ecuadorian Newspaper', *chinatoday.com.cn* (17 November 2016); Xinhua, 'Xi Delivers Video Speech to Colombian People as Chinese Vaccines Arrive', *gov.cn* (21 March 2021), all accessed 13 January 2024.

9. See: *The Seven Military Classics of Ancient China* (London: Arcturus, 2020).
10. See, e.g.: Mao Zedong, 'Discussions at the Central Work Symposium', in *Selected Works of Mao Tse-Tung*, Vol. 9 (Paris: Foreign Languages Press, 2021).
11. Mao Zedong, 'Speech at the Second Session of the Eighth Party Congress (1)', in *Selected Works of Mao Tse-Tung*, Vol. 8 (Paris: Foreign Languages Press, 2020).
12. Kuo Chien, 'The Novel "Battle of Xiang Jiang" Is Banned', *Daily Report China* (24 January 1991); see also: Qian Liqun, 'Mao Zedong and His Era', in *Voices from the Chinese Century* (New York: Columbia University Press, 2020).
13. In 1958, Mao was recorded condemning "the reactionary essence of attacks on Ch'in Shih-huang as attacks on revolutionary violence and the dictatorship of the proletariat": Schram, *Thought of Mao*, 180–81. In 1959, Mao accused critics of making the Qin "into a villain" and rejected rightist comparisons between his Great Wall and Mao's own construction near the Tiananmen during the Great Leap Forward: Mao Zedong, 'Critique of Stalin's Economic Problems of Socialism in the USSR' and 'Speech at the Lushan Conference', both in *Selected Works of Mao Tse-Tung,* Vol. 8.
14. Alastair Iain Johnson, *Cultural Realism* (Princeton, NJ: Princeton University Press, 1994).
15. Johnson, *Cultural Realism.*
16. Nick Knight, *Marxist Philosophy in China* (Dordrecht: Springer, 2010), 205.
17. Xi Jinping, '习近平双峰会"妙语集锦"：孤举者难起 众行者易趋' . See also: Xi Jinping, '习近平在第四届中国国际进口博览会开幕式上的主旨演讲'.
18. Fairbank and Ch'en, *Chinese World Order.* For dissenting views on the universality of Fairbank's Tributary State system, see: Gungwu Wang, 'Early Ming Relations with Southeast Asia', in *Chinese World Order*; Gungwu Wang, 'The Rhetoric of a Lesser Empire', in *China among Equals* (Berkeley: University of California Press, 1983); Zhang Feng, 'Rethinking the "Tribute System"', in *China and International Relations* (London: Routledge, 2010).
19. Fairbank and Ch'en, *Chinese World* Order, 10–11.
20. John E. Wills, *Embassies and Illusions* (Los Angeles: Figueroa, 2009).
21. David Kang, *East Asia before the West* (New York: Columbia University Press, 2010).
22. Kang, *East Asia before the West*, 1–17.
23. Kang, *East Asia before the West*, 1–4.
24. Kang, *East Asia before the West*, 2.
25. Kang, *East Asia before the West*, 4.
26. Quoted in Kang, *East Asia before the West*, 4.
27. Knight, *Marxist Philosophy*, 8.
28. Mao Zedong, 'Lecture Notes on Dialectical Materialism', in *Mao Zedong on Dialectical Materialism* (Armonk, NY: M. E. Sharp, 1990), 106.
29. Nick Knight, 'Soviet Marxism and the Development of Mao Zedong's Philosophical Thought', in *Mao Zedong on Dialectical Materialism*, 24.

30. Mao, 'The Law of the Unity of Contradictions', in *Mao Zedong on Dialectical Materialism*, 207.
31. Mao, 'On Contradiction', in *Five Essays on Philosophy* (Utrecht: Foreign Languages Press, 2018), 35
32. Knight, 'Soviet Marxism and Mao', 15-30.
33. Mao, 'On Practice', in *Five Essays on Philosophy*, 21.
34. Nick Knight, *Marxist Philosophy in China* (Dordrecht: Springer, 2006), 173.
35. Karl Marx, 'The Eighteenth Brumaire of Louis Bonaparte', in *Surveys from Exile* (London: Verso, 2010) 146.
36. Mao, 'The Unity of Contradictions', 185–86.
37. Mao, 'The Unity of Contradictions', 180.
38. Mao, 'The Unity of Contradictions', 180.
39. Michael Hunt, *The Genesis of Chinese Communist Foreign Policy* (New York: Columbia University Press, 1996), 4. See further: Michael Hunt and Odd Arne Westad, 'The Chinese Communist Party and International Affairs', *China Quarterly*, 122 (1990); Harry Harding, *China's Foreign Relations in the 1980s* (New Haven, CT: Yale University Press, 1984).
40. Hunt, *Genesis of Chinese Communist Foreign Policy*, 30.
41. Hunt, *Genesis of Chinese Communist Foreign Policy*, 28.
42. Hunt, *Genesis of Chinese Communist Foreign Policy*. See further: John Gittings, *The World and China* (Abingdon: Routledge, 2019); *Chinese Foreign Policy* (Oxford: Clarendon Press, 1994).
43. Steven Levine, 'Perception and Ideology in Chinese Foreign Policy', in *Chinese Foreign Policy*, 39.
44. Levine, 'Perception and Ideology', 55.
45. Levine, 'Perception and Ideology', 55.
46. Mao Zedong, 'Speeches at the 1957 "Moscow Conference"', *Journal of Communist Studies*, 2/2 (1986).
47. Gittings, *The World and China*, 205.
48. Deng Xiaoping, 'Teng Hsiao-Ping's Speech at UN Special Session', *Current Background*, 1016 (1974), 27–38.
49. Tracy B. Strong and Helene Keyssar, 'Anna Louise Strong: Three Interviews with Chairman Mao Zedong', *China Quarterly*, 103 (1985), 506; Mao Zedong, 'There Are Two Intermediate Zones', in *Mao Zedong on Diplomacy* (Beijing: Foreign Languages Press, 1988).
50. Deng, 'UN Special Session', 36.
51. Mao Zedong, 'On the People's Democratic Dictatorship', in *Selected Works of Mao Tse-Tung*, Vol. 4 (Paris: Foreign Languages Press, 2021).
52. 'Record of Conversation between Polish Delegation and PRC Leader Mao Zedong, Wuhan', *digitalarchive.wilsoncenter.org* (2 April 1958).
53. See: Mao Zedong, 'Directives on Cultural Revolution', in *Selected Works of Mao Tse-Tung*, Vol. 8 (Hyderabad: Sramikavarga Prachuranalu, 1994). In all other cases, references to this volume are the 2021 edition by Foreign Languages Press.

54. Deng Xiaoping, 'Uphold the Four Cardinal Principles', in *Selected Works of Deng Xiaoping*, Vol. 2 (Beijing: Foreign Languages Press, 1995).
55. Second Historical Resolution, 1981. See also: 'Remarks on Successive Drafts of the Resolution on Certain Questions on the History of Our Party since the Founding of the People's Republic of China', in *Selected Works of Deng Xiaoping*, Vol. 2.
56. Ryan Haass, *The Trajectory of Chinese Foreign Policy* (Washington, DC: Brookings Institution, 2017).
57. Shigeo Kobayashi, Jia Baobo, and Junya Sano, 'The "Three Reforms" in China', *RIM*, 45 (1999).
58. Sun Yan, *The Chinese Reassessment of Socialism* (Princeton, NJ: Princeton University Press, 2001), 8–13.
59. Mao Zedong, 'Opening Address at the Eighth National Congress of the Communist Party of China', in *Eighth National Congress of the Communist Party of China,* Vol. 1 (Peking: Foreign Languages Press, 1956), 7–11
60. Sun, *Chinese Reassessment of Socialism*, 46.
61. Deng, 'Four Cardinal Principles', 189.
62. Second Historical Resolution, 1981.
63. Sun, *Chinese Reassessment of Socialism*, 184–85.
64. 中共中央文献研究室：三中全会以来重要文献选编（下）(Beijing: People's Publishing House, 1982), 839. Analyses include: Xiaofeng Yan, '论新时代我国社会主要矛盾的变化', *theory.people.com.cn* (5 May 2019), accessed 2 April 2022.
65. Second Historical Resolution, 1981.
66. Sun, *Chinese Reassessment of Socialism*, 9–10
67. Sun, *Chinese Reassessment of Socialism*, 14.
68. Deng Xiaoping, 'China's Foreign Policy', in *Selected Works of Deng Xiaoping*, Vol. 2, 407–9.
69. Chen Jian, 'From Mao to Deng', *CWIHP Working Papers*, 92 (2019), 15.
70. Deng Xiaoping, 'Seize the Opportunity to Develop the Economy', in *Selected Works of Deng Xiaoping*, Vol. 3 (Beijing: Foreign Languages Press, 1994).
71. See 王缉思. "中国的国际定位问题与 "韬光养晦, 有所作为" 的战略思想." 国际问题研究 2 (2011). See also: Susan Shirk, 'Regional Views on Asia-Pacific Regional Cooperation', *NBR Analysis*, 5/5 (1994), 12; and Shirk, *Overreach*, 333.
72. Deng Xiaoping, 'Excerpts from Talks Given in Wuchang, Shenzhen, Zhuhai, and Shanghai', in *Selected Works of Deng Xiaoping,* Vol. 3 (Beijing: Foreign Languages Press, 2013).
73. Jiang Zemin, *Accelerating the Reform, the Opening to the Outside World and the Drive for Modernization, so as to Achieve Greater Successes in Building Socialism with Chinese Characteristics* (Report to the 14th Party Congress, 1992).
74. According to World Bank data, China's nominal per capita GDP quadrupled from RMB2,334 (USD423) to RMB9506 (USD1149) between 1992

and 2002; and China's gini coefficient, which measures income inequality on a scale of 0 to 100, rose from 34 to 42 between 1993 and 2002.

75. Zheng Wang, 'National Humiliation, History Education and the Politics of Historical Memory', *International Studies Quarterly*, 52/4 (2008).
76. Jiang, Report to the 14th Party Congress.
77. Jiang, Report to the 14th Party Congress.
78. Jiang, Report to the 14th Party Congress.
79. Jiang Zemin, *Hold High the Great Banner of Deng Xiaoping Theory for an All-round Advancement of the Cause of Building Socialism with Chinese Characteristics into the 21st Century* (Report to the 15th Party Congress, 1997).
80. Jiang Zemin, *Build a Well-off Society in an All-Round Way and Create a New Situation in Building Socialism with Chinese Characteristics* (Report to the 16th Party Congress, 2002).
81. Jiang, Report to the 16th Party Congress.
82. Jiang, Report to the 16th Party Congress.
83. 'Guidelines of the 11th Five-Year Plan for Economic and Social Development of the People's Republic of China' (11th Five-Year Plan), *policy.asiapacific-energy.org* (2006), accessed 22 March 2024.
84. National Congress of the CCP, 'Constitution of Communist Party of China', *china.org.cn* (14 November 2012), accessed 24 March 2024. See also: Gang Wu and Shuang Yan, 'Xi Jinping Pledges "Great Renewal of Chinese Nation"', *globaltimes.cn* (30 November 2012), accessed 6 February 2024.
85. Jiang, Report to the 16th Party Congress.
86. Ministry of Foreign Affairs (PRC), 'President Hu Urges Joint Efforts for New Int'l Order', *mu.china-embassy.gov.cn* (28 May 2003), accessed 6 February 2022.
87. Jiang, Report to the 16th Party Congress.
88. Jiang, Report to the 16th Party Congress.
89. Valérie Niquet, 'China and Central Asia', *China Perspectives*, no. 67 (2006).
90. Hu Jintao, *Hold High the Great Banner of Socialism with Chinese Characteristics and Strive for New Victories in Building a Moderately Prosperous Society in All Respects* (Report to the 17th Party Congress, 2007).
91. George Walker Bush, 'Address to a Joint Session of Congress and the American People', 21 September 2001.
92. Josef Gregory Mahoney and Xiuling Li, 'A Marxist Perspective on Chinese Reforms', *Science & Society*, 73/2 (2009), 177.
93. Hu, Report to the 17th Party Congress.
94. See: Xinhua, '胡锦涛主持政治局学习强调保证群众行使民主权利', *gov.cn* (1 December 2006), accessed 6 February 2024. See further: Cheng Li, '中式民主的启动', *brookings.edu* (18 January 2010), accessed 11 April 2022.
95. Hu, Report to the 17th Party Congress.
96. Hu Jintao, 'Build towards a Harmonious World of Lasting Peace and Common Prosperity', *un.org* (15 September 2005); State Council (PRC), 'White Paper on Peaceful Development Road Published', *china.org.cn* (December 2011); State Council Information Office (PRC), 'China's Peaceful Development', *gov.cn* (6 September 2011), all accessed 22 March 2024.

97. Xinhua, 'Hu Makes 4-Point Proposal for Building Harmonious World', *china.org.cn* (16 September 2005), accessed 22 March 2024
98. See: Zou Keyuan, 'Building a Harmonious World', *Copenhagen Journal of Asian Studies*, 30/2 (2013); Su Hao, 'Harmonious World', in *China's Shift: Global Strategy of the Rising Power*, NIDS Joint Research Series, no. 3 (Tokyo: National Institute for Defence Studies, 2009), 29–55.
99. See: Ross Munro, 'Awakening Dragon', *Policy Review*, 60 (1992); Jean-Marc Blanchard, 'Harmonious World and China's Foreign Economic Policy', *Journal of Chinese Political Science*, 22 April 2008.
100. Hu Jintao, *Firmly March on the Path of Socialism with Chinese Characteristics and Strive to Complete the Building of a Moderately Prosperous Society in All Respects* (Beijing: Report to the 18th Party Congress, 2012)
101. Hu, Report to the 18th Party Congress.
102. Hu, Report to the 18th Party Congress.

CHAPTER 4

1. Xi Jinping, 'Speech at the Ceremony Commemorating the Bicentenary of the Birth of Marx', *Qiushi English*, 3 (2018). See also: Xi Jinping, '习近平：在纪念马克思诞辰200周年大会上的讲话', *xinhuanet.com* (2018), accessed 22 March 2024. Xi has a higher usage of the terms 'Marxism' (more than 400 times), 'materialism' (more than 90 times), 'struggle' (more than 230 times) and 'contradiction' (more than 300 times), than Jiang Zemin and Hu Jintao. This is based on a comparative survey of Xi's domestic public speeches to the Central Party School and the Politburo Group Study Sessions, *Qiushi* articles, reports to the party congresses, and the selected works of the former general secretaries.
2. Xi Jinping, *Secure a Decisive Victory in Building a Moderately Prosperous Society in All Respects and Strive for the Great Success of Socialism with Chinese Characteristics for a New Era* (Report to the 19th Party Congress, 2017).
3. Xi, Report to the 19th Party Congress.
4. Xi, Report to the 19th Party Congress.
5. Xi, Report to the 19th Party Congress.
6. According to a comparison between Jiang Zemin, Hu Jintao, and Xi Jinping, the percentages of their Congress reports mentioning 'Marxism' are 38%, 26%, and 48% respectively; the percentages of works mentioning 'Historical Materialism' and 'Dialectical Materialism' are 9%, 6%, and 13%; the percentages of works mentioning 'struggle' and 'contradiction' were 43%, 35%, and 54%. Research based on reports to the CCP National Congresses by Jiang Zemin, Hu Jintao, and Xi Jinping.
7. Xi Jinping, 'Dialectical Materialism Is the Worldview and Methodology of Chinese Communists', *Qiushi English,* no. 1 (2019). See also: '不断开拓当代中国马克思主义政治经济学新境界', *Qiushi*, no. 16 (2020).
8. See Xi's 2013 Speech on Ideology and Propaganda: '网传习近平8•19讲话全文：言论方面要敢抓敢管敢于亮剑', *chinadigitaltimes.net*; and "Xi Jinping's

19 August Speech Revealed? (Translation)", *chinacopyrightandmedia.wordpress.com* (12 November 2013), both accessed 14 February 2020. See also: Xi Jinping, '坚持历史唯物主义不断开辟当代中国马克思主义发展新境界', *Qiushi*, no. 2 (2020); and Xi, 'Bicentenary of the Birth of Marx'. Similar addresses by Xi's predecessors are not as substantive on Marxist theory; see: Jiang Zemin, '科学对待马克思主义', in 江泽民文选(第三卷)(Beijing: People's Publishing House, 2006); Hu Jintao, '党的先进性建设是关系马克思主义政党生存发展的根本性问题', and '关于提高党的建设科学化水平和建设马克思主义学习型政党', in 胡锦涛文选(第三卷) (Beijing: People's Publishing House, 2016), 263–72 and 252–56.

9. Xi, Speech on Ideology and Propaganda.
10. Xi, Speech on Ideology and Propaganda.
11. Xi, Speech on Ideology and Propaganda.
12. Xi, Speech on Ideology and Propaganda.
13. See, e.g.: Deng Xiaoping, 'The Present Situation and the Tasks before Us', in *Selected Works of Deng Xiaoping*, Vol. 2; D. Ray Heisey, 'China's President Hu Jintao's Rhetoric of Socialization', *Intercultural Communication Studies* 8/3 (2004); Richard Bernstein, 'Jiang's Warning: No Forgiveness', *New York Times* (30 June 1989).
14. Xi, Speech on Ideology and Propaganda.
15. See, e.g.: Mao Zedong, 'Speech at the Tenth Plenum of the Eighth CPC Central Committee', in *Selected Works of Mao Tse-Tung*, Vol. 8, 437–44.
16. Xinhua, '斗争!习近平这篇讲话大有深意', *xinhuanet.com*, (4 September 2019), accessed 16 February 2020.
17. Unless otherwise noted, quotes in this section are from: Xi, Speech on Ideology and Propaganda.
18. General Office of the Central Committee of the CCP, 'Communiqué on the Current State of the Ideological Sphere (Document Number 9, 2013)', *digichina.standford.edu* (22 April 2013) and *chinafile.com* (8 November 2013), both accessed 22 March 2024.
19. Document Number 9, 2013.
20. Document Number 9, 2013.
21. Xi, 'Dialectical Materialism Is the Worldview'.
22. Unless otherwise noted, quotes in this section are from: Xi, 'Dialectical Materialism Is the Worldview'.
23. Mao Zedong. 'On Contradiction', 89-92.
24. Xi, '坚持历史唯物主义不断开辟当代中国马克思主义发展新境界'.
25. Joseph Torigian, 'Elite Politics and Foreign Policy in China from Mao to Xi', *brookings.edu* (22 January 2019), accessed 16 February 2020.
26. Xi, '坚持历史唯物主义不断开辟当代中国马克思主义发展新境界'.
27. Gao Hua, Stacy Mosher, and Guo Jian, *How the Red Sun Rose* (Hong Kong: Chinese University of Hong Kong Press, 2018). See also: Mao Zedong,

'Lecture Notes on Dialectical Materialism', in *Mao Zedong on Dialectical Materialism*, 84–131.

28. Gao, Mosher, and Guo, *How the Red Sun Rose*. See also: Mao Zedong, 'Rectify the Party's Style of Work', in *Selected Works of Mao Zedong*, Vol. 3 (Paris: Foreign Languages Press, 2021).
29. In November 2012, Xi Jinping said "many pressing problems within the party . . . need to be resolved, especially problems such as corruption and bribe-taking. . . . All comrades in the party [need] to be resolute in ensuring that the party supervises its own conduct [and] enforces strict discipline." See: BBC News, 'Full Text: China's New Party Chief Xi Jinping's Speech', *bbc.com* (15 November 2012), accessed 9 February 2024.
30. Unless otherwise noted, quotes in this section are from: Xi, '坚持历史唯物主义不断开辟当代中国马克思主义发展新境界'.
31. Unless otherwise noted, quotes in this section are from: Xi, Report to the 19th Party Congress.
32. See Deng Xiaoping, 'The Party's Urgent Tasks on the Organizational and Ideological Fronts', in *Selected Works of Deng Xiaoping*, Vol. 2.
33. Xi, Report to the 19th Party Congress.
34. Xi, Report to the 19th Party Congress.
35. See Yan Xiaofeng, '论新时代我国社会主要矛盾的变化', *theory.people.com.cn* (5 May 2019); Yan Xiaofeng, '我国社会主要矛盾变化的重大意义', *theory.people.com.cn* (4 January 2018), both accessed 15 December 2023.
36. Xi, Report to the 19th Party Congress.
37. Unless otherwise noted, quotes in this section are from: Xi, 'Bicentenary of the Birth of Marx'.
38. Xi, 'Bicentenary of the Birth of Marx'. See also: Marx and Engels, *The German Ideology*, 58.
39. Xi, 'Bicentenary of the Birth of Marx'.
40. Xi, Report to the 19th Party Congress.
41. Xi, Report to the 19th Party Congress.
42. See, e.g.: Deng Xiaoping, 'To Build Socialism We Must First Develop the Productive Forces', in *Selected Works of Deng Xiaoping*, Vol. 2; 'China Celebrates 30th Anniversary of Landmark Reform, Opening-up', *cctv.com* (18 December 2008), accessed 7 March 2024; and Jiang, Report to the 15th Party Congress.
43. Ministry of Foreign Affairs (PRC), 'The Central Conference on Work Relating to Foreign Affairs Was Held in Beijing (2014)', *fmprc.gov.cn* (29 November 2014), accessed 15 December 2023.

CHAPTER 5

1. Elizabeth Perry, 'Debating Maoism in Contemporary China', *Asia-Pacific Journal: Japan Focus*, 1 (2021), 265.

2. Kerry Brown and Una Aleksandra Bērziņa-Čerenkova, 'Ideology in the Era of Xi Jinping', *Journal of Chinese Political Science*, 24/3 (2018).
3. In their discussion of bands of meaning, Brown and Bērziņa-Čerenkova draw on Terry Eagleton's description of ideology including "the process of production of meanings, signs, and values in social life; a body of ideas characteristic of a particular social group or class; ideas which help to legitimize a dominant political power". See Terry Eagleton, *Ideology* (London: Verso, 2001), 1–2.
4. Perry, 'Debating Maoism in Contemporary China', 266.
5. See: Nis Grünberg and Katja Drinhausen, 'The Party Leads on Everything', *MERICS China Monitor* (2019). See further: Alice Miller, 'More Already on the Central Committee's Leading Small Groups', *China Leadership Monitor*, no. 44 (2013).
6. Grünberg and Drinhausen, 'The Party Leads on Everything'.
7. Alice Miller, 'Xi Jinping and the Party's "Guiding Ideology"', *China Leadership Monitor*, no. 54 (2017), 41.
8. Xinhua, 'Party Members Called On to Unite around CPC Central Committee with Xi as "core"', *xinhuanet.com* (27 October 2010), accessed 12 February 2024. See also: Ping Lin and Qiao Long, 'China's Ruling Party Endorses Xi as Core Leader after Meeting', *rfa.org* (27 October 2016), accessed 22 October 2021.
9. Deng Xiaoping, 'We Must Form a Promising Collective Leadership That Will Carry Out Reform', in *Selected Works of Deng Xiaoping*, Vol. 3.
10. Central Committee of the CCP, 'Work Regulations of the Central Committee of the Communist Party of China', *chinacopyrightandmedia.wordpress.com* (30 September 2020), accessed 12 February 2024.
11. Qiao Long, 'Chinese Leader Xi Jinping Inscribes Himself into Party Procedural Rules', *rfa.org* (29 September 2020), accessed 22 October 2021.
12. Xinhua, 'Senior Officials Urged to Uphold Leadership of CPC Central Committee', *xinhuanet.com* (27 October 2017), accessed 20 February 2024.
13. Central Committee of the CCP, 'Work Regulations of the Central Committee'.
14. James Mulvenon, 'The Cult of Xi and the Rise of the CMC Chairman Responsibility System', *China Leadership Monitor*, no. 55 (2018), 2.
15. Mulvenon, 'Cult of Xi'.
16. Mulvenon, 'Cult of Xi'.
17. Mulvenon, 'Cult of Xi'.
18. Alice Lyman Miller, 'Xi Jinping and the Evolution of Chinese Leadership Politics', in *Fateful Decisions*, 45.
19. China Daily, 'Support for Amendments Belies Naysayers' Prejudice', *chinadaily.com.cn* (11 March 2018), accessed 11 March 2021.
20. Xinhua, '中国共产党一百年大事记(1921年7月—2021年6月)', *xinhuanet.com* (27 June 2021), accessed 12 February 2024.

21. Jun Mai, 'Xi Jinping's Anti-Corruption Drive Brings Down More Generals than 20th Century Warfare', *scmp.com* (17 November 2017), accessed 22 October 2021.
22. Stephen McDonell, 'Ren Zhiqiang: Outspoken Ex-Real Estate Tycoon Gets 18 Years Jail', *bbc.com* (22 September 2020), accessed 22 October 2021.
23. John Sudworth, 'Why China's Ruling Party Is Bearing Down on "Cliques"', *BBC News* (5 January 2015), accessed 22 October 2021.
24. Xinhua, '中国共产党第十九届中央委员会第五次全体会议公报', *xinhuanet.com* (29 October 2020), accessed 21 October, 2021. See also: Qian Gang, 'A Brief History of the Helmsman', *chinamediaproject.org* (2 November 2020), accessed 12 February 2024.
25. Mao's successor in 1976, Hua Guofeng, was briefly referred to as the 'wise leader', but this title existed for a very short period; see: People's Daily, '两报一刊社论：乘胜前进', *huaguofeng.org* (1 January 1977), accessed 24 April 2021. Deng Xiaoping referred to himself briefly as 'core' but only in the context of conferring that title upon his successor, Jiang; see Deng Xiaoping, 'Urgent Tasks of China's Third Generation of Collective Leadership', in *Selected Works of Deng Xiaoping*, Vol. 3.
26. *Constitution of the CCP* (24 October 2017); *Constitution of the PRC* (11 March 2018).
27. E.g.: Jean-Pierre Cabestan, 'Is Xi Jinping the Reformist Leader China Needs?', *China Perspectives,* no. 3 (2012); Andrew Mertha, 'Fragmented Authoritarianism 2.0', *China Quarterly*, 200 (2009); Kenneth G. Lieberthal and David M. Lampton (eds.), *Bureaucracy, Politics, and Decision Making in Post-Mao China* (Berkeley: University of California Press, 2018); Sebastian Heilmann and Matthias Stepan (eds.), 'China's Core Executive' (Berlin: MERICS, 2016); Gang Chen, 'What Is New for China's Technocracy in Xi Jinping's Time?', *China: An International Journal*, 18/1 (2020); Stephan Ortmann and Mark Thompson, 'Introduction: The "Singapore Model" and China's Neo-Authoritarian Dream', *China Quarterly*, 236 (2018); François Bougon, *Inside the Mind of Xi Jinping* (London: Hurst & Co, 2018); Xiao Gongqin, 'China's Four Decades of Reforms', *Man and the Economy*, 6/1 (2019); Lu Yi, '回顾一场几乎被遗忘的论争—"新权威主义"之争述评', *21st Century (Online),* no. 83 (February 2009).
28. Xinhua, '中国共产党第十九次全国代表大会关于《中国共产党章程（修正案）》的决议', *gov.cn* (24 October 2017), accessed 14 February 2024. For comparison, see: People's Daily, 'The Party Exercises Overall Leadership', *mednexus.org* (1 July 1974), accessed 12 February 2024.
29. "Our leading organs at various levels have taken charge of many matters which they should not and cannot handle or cannot handle efficiently. These matters could have been easily handled by the enterprises, institutions, and communities at the grass-roots level, provided we had proper rules and regulations and they acted according to the principles of democratic centralism.

Difficulties have arisen from the custom of referring all these things to the leading organs and central departments of the Party and government. . . . Historically, we ourselves have repeatedly placed too much emphasis on ensuring centralism and unification by the Party, and on combating decentralism and any assertion of independence. And we have placed too little emphasis on ensuring the necessary degree of decentralization, delegating necessary decision-making power to the lower organizations, and opposing the over-concentration of power in the hands of individuals." From Deng Xiaoping, 'On Reform of the System of Party and State Leadership', in *Selected Works of Deng Xiaoping*, Vol. 2. See also: Hu Wei, '邓小平40年前的这篇讲话为什么极为重要？', *qzcdi.gov.cn* (22 September 2020), accessed 11 April 2022.

30. Kjeld Erik Brødsgaard, 'China's Political Order under Xi Jinping', *China: An Internal Journal*, 16/3 (2018).
31. Xi was an undergraduate student at the Chemical Engineering Department of Tsinghua University between 1975 and 1979.
32. The first article of the first chapter of the Constitution of the PRC reads: "The People's Republic of China is a socialist state governed by a people's democratic dictatorship that is led by the working class and based on an alliance of workers and peasants. The socialist system is the fundamental system of the People's Republic of China. Leadership by the Communist Party of China is the defining feature of socialism with Chinese characteristics."
33. Xinhua, 'Xi Focus: Xi Stresses Consolidating Achievements in Reform of Party, State Institutions', *xinhuanet.com* (5 July 2019), accessed 11 September 2019. See also: Xinhua, '中共中央关于深化党和国家机构改革的决定', *gov.cn* (4 March 2018), and Xinhua, '扬帆破浪再启航—以习近平同志为核心的党中央推进党和国家机构改革纪实', *gov.cn* (6 July 2019), both accessed 16 March 2022.
34. Xinhua, '中共中央印发《深化党和国家机构改革方案》', *gov.cn* (21 March 2018), accessed 14 February 2024.
35. Grünberg and Drinhausen, 'The Party Leads on Everything'.
36. Xinhua, 'CPC Releases Plan on Deepening Reform of Party and State Institutions', *en.people.cn* (22 March 2018), accessed 22 October 2021.
37. Central Committee of the CCP, '中国共产党党内监督条例(2016年10月27日中国共产党第十八届中央委员会第六次全体会议通过)', *12371.cn* (2 November 2016); Xinhua, '关于新形势下党内政治生活的若干准则(2016年10月27日中国共产党第十八届中央委员会第六次全体会议通过)', *12371.cn* (27 October 2016); Xinhua, '关于党内政治生活的若干准则（1980年2月29日中国共产党第十一届中央委员会第五次全体会议通过）', *news.12371.cn* (11 March 2015). For examples of 'party spirit' education in implementation, see: Peking University Party Committee, '北京大学党性教育读书班实施方案', *shehui.pku.edu.cn* (December 2014); Qin Caiping, '党性修养需要制度维护, *dangjian.people.com.cn* (5 December 2017), all accessed 22 October 2021.

38. Xi Jinping, '在中央和国家机关党的建设工作会议上的讲话', *Qiushi,* no. *21* (2019): "新形势下，中央和国家机关党的建设的使命任务是：以新时代中国特色社会主义思想为指导，增强"四个意识"，坚定"四个自信"，做到"两个维护"，以党的政治建设为统领，着力深化理论武装，着力夯实基层基础，着力推进正风肃纪，全面提高中央和国家机关党的建设质量，在深入学习贯彻新时代中国特色社会主义思想上作表率，在始终同党中央保持高度一致上作表率，在坚决贯彻落实党中央各项决策部署上作表率，建设让党中央放心、让人民群众满意的模范机关." See also: Xinhua, 'Xi Highlights Party Building in Central Party, State Institutions', *xinhuanet.com* (9 July 2019), accessed 16 December 2023.
39. For examples, see: Communist Party of China, '省储备局认真学习贯彻落实《关于当前意识形态领域情况的通报》', *hndj.gov.cn via archive.org* (16 May 2013), accessed 22 March 2024; State Commission Office of Public Sectors Reform, '学习贯彻习近平总书记重要讲话精神 巩固深化党和国家机构改革成果', *Qiushi*, no. *14* (2019). For Xi-era literature attacking constitutionalism see: Yang Xiaoqing, '宪政与人民民主制度之比较研究', *Hongqi Wengao*, no. *10* (2013); Xi Jinping, 'Provide Sound Legal Guarantees for Socialist Modernization', in *The Governance of China*, Vol. 4: "It must be noted that in the drive to advance law-based governance, under no circumstances should we try to duplicate the models and practices of other countries or adopt such Western models a 'constitutionalism', 'separation of powers', and 'judicial independence'."
40. Deng Jinting, 'The National Supervision Commission', *International Journal of Law, Crime and Justice*, 52 (2018) ; '杨亚澜, 为什么有了纪委，还要设立监委？', *politics.people.com.cn* (12 January 2019), accessed 22 October 2021.
41. Christopher Carothers, 'Xi's Anti-Corruption Campaign', *China Leadership Monitor*, no. *67* (2021).
42. Carothers, 'Xi's Anti-Corruption Campaign'.
43. These include new 'Rules of the CCP for Disciplinary Action', revised in July 2018; 'Regulations for CPC Accountability', revised in September 2019; and the 'Law on Governmental Sanctions for Public Employees', adopted in June 2020. See: Central Commission for Discipline Inspection and State Supervision Commission, '《中国共产党纪律处分条例》修订前后对照表', *xinhuanet.com* (27 August 2018); Central Committee of the CCP, '中国共产党问责条例', *xinhuanet.com* (4 September 2019); National People's Congress, '中华人民共和国公职人员政务处分法', *gov.cn* (20 June 2020), all accessed 20 March 2024.
44. See: Xi Jinping, 'China's New Party Chief Xi Jinping's Speech', *bbc.com* (15 November 2012), accessed 21 October 2021; Xi Jinping, 'Study, Disseminate and Implement the Guiding Principles of the 18th CPC National Congress', in *The Governance of China*, Vol. 1.
45. Carothers, 'Xi's Anti-Corruption Campaign'.
46. Carothers, 'Xi's Anti-Corruption Campaign'.

47. Chen Gang. 'Reinforcing Leninist Means of Corruption Control in China', *Copenhagen Journal of Asian Studies*, 35/2 (2017).
48. Carothers, 'Xi's Anti-Corruption Campaign'.
49. Carothers, 'Xi's Anti-Corruption Campaign'.
50. Indeed, there is a vast literature already on multiple frameworks of analyses for the anti-corruption campaigns; see, e.g.: Samson Yuen, 'Disciplining the Party', *China Perspectives*, no. *3* (2014); William H. Overholt, 'The Politics of China's Anti-Corruption Campaign', *East Asia Forum Quarterly*, 7/2 (2015); Xi Lu and Peter L. Lorentzen, 'Rescuing Autocracy from Itself', *SSRN Electronic Journal* (January 2016); John Griffin, Clark Liu, and Tao Shu, 'Is the Chinese Anti-Corruption Campaign Effective?', *SSRN Electronic Journal* (January 2016); Chen Gang, 'Reinforcing Leninist Means of Corruption Control in China', *Copenhagen Journal of Asian Studies*, 35/2 (2017); Tony Lee, 'Pernicious Custom?', *Crime, Law and Social Change*, 70/3 (2018); John Griffin, Clark Liu, and T. Shu, 'Is the Chinese Corporate Anti-Corruption Campaign Authentic?', Working Paper, Tsinghua University (2018); Christopher Carothers, 'Combating Corruption in Authoritarian Regimes', Doctoral Thesis, Harvard University (2019); Pan Xiaofei and Gary Gang Tian, 'Political Connections and Corporate Investments', *Journal of Banking & Finance*, 119 (2020).
51. See, e.g.: David Lague, Benjamin Kang Lim, and Charlie Zhu, *Fear and Retribution in Xi's Corruption Purge* (London: Reuters, 2014); L. L. Gore, 'Leninism for the 21st Century', *China: An International Journal*, 21/2 (2023)
52. Li Ling, 'New Political-Legal Rectification Campaign 2020–2021', *thechinacollection.org* (14 July 2020), accessed 21 October 2021.
53. Li, 'New Political-Legal Rectification'.
54. Li Ling, 'Politics of Anticorruption in China', *Journal of Contemporary China*, 28/115 (2019). These are also reflected in relevant studies by Barry Naughton and Tony Saich such as: Barry Naughton, 'The General Secretary's Extended Reach', *China Leadership Monitor*, 54 (2017); Tony Saich, 'What Does General Secretary Xi Jinping Dream About?' (Harvard: Ash Center for Democratic Governance and Innovation, 2017).
55. William Zheng, 'China's Top Law Enforcement Body Unveils Campaign to Purge "Corrupt Elements"', *scmp.com* (10 July 2020), accessed 15 February 2024.
56. Vanessa Cai, 'Chinese Communist Party's Top Corruption Watchdog Takes Aim at "Double Dealers" within Its Ranks', *scmp.com* (16 March 2023), accessed 15 February 2024.
57. Mao Zedong, 'Intra-Party Directive on Rectification', in *The Writings of Mao Zedong 1945–1976, Vol. 1* (1986).
58. William Zheng, 'Chinese Official Leading Security Purge "May Be on Fast Track to Promotion", Analysts Say', *scmp.com* (17 July 2020).
59. Bill Bishop, 'Rectification in the Politics and Legal Affairs System; Xi and Putin Talk; TikTok; Wang Wei 王維', *sinocism.com* (8 July 2020), accessed 19 February 2024.

60. Zhang Zhihao, 'Corruption Investigation into Official Begins', *global.chinadasily.com.cn* (4 October 2021), accessed 15 February 2024.
61. Wu Guoguang, 'Continuous Purges', *China Leadership Monitor*, 66 (2020).
62. Wu, 'Continuous Purges'.
63. Li, 'Politics of Anticorruption in China'.
64. Sheena Chestnut Greitens, 'Domestic Security in China under Xi Jinping', *China Leadership Monitor*, 59. See also People's Daily, '习近平:坚持总体国家安全观 走中国特色国家安全道路', *xinhuanet.com* (15 April 2014), accessed 20 March 2024.
65. Xinhua, 'CPC Issues Regulation on Democratic Life Meetings', *xinhuanet.com* (12 January 2017), accessed 16 February 2024. For previous regulations, see: Alice Miller, 'Leadership Presses Party Unity in Time of Economic Stress', *China Leadership Monitor*, 28 (2009).
66. John Dotson, 'The "Democratic Life Meetings" of the Chinese Communist Party Politburo', *China Brief*, 20/2 (2020).
67. Dotson, '"Democratic Life Meetings"'.
68. Xi, Speech on Ideology and Propaganda.
69. Xi Jinping, '习近平关于防范风险挑战、应对突发事件论述摘编' (Beijing: Central Party Literature Press, 2020). See also: Kevin Rudd, 'China Has Politics Too', *asiasociety.org* (9 December 2020), accessed 20 March 2024.
70. Xi Jinping, '习近平在第二届世界互联网大会开幕式上的讲话', *xinhuanet.com* (16 December 2015), accessed 20 March 2024.
71. Xinhua, '中共中央印发《中国共产党政法工作条例》', *gov.cn* (18 January 2019), accessed 16 December 2023.
72. Xinhua, 'Xi Focus: Xi Stresses Sticking to Socialist Rule of Law with Chinese Characteristics', *xinhuanet.com* (18 November 2020), accessed 16 February 2024.
73. Xinhua, 'Xi Jinping to Lead National Security Commission', *globaltimes.cn* (25 January 2014), accessed 29 November 2023.
74. China Law Translate, 'National Security Law', *chinalawtranslate.com* (2015) accessed 16 February 2024. See also: Xinhua, 'Hong Kong Holds Activities to Mark National Security Education Day', *english.news.cn* (16 April 2023), accessed 16 February 2024.
75. National People's Congress, 'National Intelligence Law of the People's Republic of China', *cs.brown.edu* (12 June 2018), accessed 16 February 2024.
76. Harry Haitao Liu, Yang Haiyan, Luo Chenchen, Pan Chenyu, and Li Ange, 'Amendments to PRC Counterespionage Law and Matters for Attention', *kwm.com* (18 May 2023), accessed 16 February 2024.
77. Liu Caiyu, Fan Anqi, and Lou Kang, 'China Adopts New Anti-Espionage Regulation, to Name Key Institutes Susceptible to Foreign Infiltration', *globaltimes.cn* (26 April 2021), accessed 22 October 2021
78. Liu, Fan, and Lou, 'China Adopts New Anti-Espionage Regulation'.
79. Tony Saich, *Governance and Politics of China* (London: Palgrave, 2015), 367.

80. Freedom House, 'China: Freedom on the Net 2017 Country Report', *freedomhouse.org* (2017), accessed 16 February 2024.
81. Cyberspace Administration of China (PRC), 'Provisions on the Governance of the Online Information Content Ecosystem', *wilmap.stanford.edu* (20 December 2019), accessed 16 February 2024.
82. Vincent Brussee, *Social Credit* (Singapore: Palgrave Macmillan, 2023). See also: China News Service, '发改委：7月份全国限制购买动车高铁票9万人次 防止失信"黑名单"认定泛化、扩大化', 环球网, *m.huanqiu.com* (2019), accessed 23 May 2024.
83. 'The 14th Five-Year Plan (2021–2025) for National Economic and Social Development and Vision 2035 of the People's Republic of China' (14th Five-Year Plan and Vision 2035), *cset.georgetown.edu* (9 August 2021).
84. The 14th Five-Year Plan and Vision 2035.
85. State-Owned Assets Supervision and Administration Commission (PRC), 'Economic Daily Published Economists' Interpretation of the 14th Five-Year Plan and the Outline of 2035 Long-Term Goals', *guojianjituan.com* (undated), accessed 19 February 2024.
86. Central Political and Legal Affairs Commission, '陈一新：学深悟透习近平法治思想， 做到"八个深刻把握"，达到"五个成效', *moj.gov.cn* (23 November 2020), accessed 16 December 2023.
87. Document Number 9, 2013.
88. Gwynn Guilford, 'In China, Being Retweeted 500 Times Can Get You Three Years in Prison', *qz.com* (9 September 2013), accessed 16 February 2024.
89. Associated Press, 'Xi Jinping Asks for "Absolute Loyalty" from Chinese State Media', *theguardian.com* (20 February 2016), accessed 16 February 2024.
90. Xu Beina and Eleanor Albert, 'Media Censorship in China', *cfr.org* (17 February 2017), accessed 21 October 2021.
91. William Zheng, 'Journalists in Chinese State Media to be Tested on Loyalty to President Xi Jinping', *scmp.com* (19 September 2019), accessed 16 February 2024.
92. Jane Tang, 'China's Shiny New Press Card Means Total State Control of Media: Journalists', *rfa.org* (11 November 2020), accessed 22 October 2021.
93. Hsiao-hwa Hsia and Man Jojo, 'China Forces Journalists to Take Exam to Demonstrate Loyalty, Political Correctness', *rfa.org* (12 January 2023), accessed 16 February 2024.
94. Xi Jinping, 'Speech at the Forum on Literature and Art', *chinacopyrightandmedia.wordpress.com* (15 October 2014), accessed 20 March 2024.
95. Xinhua, '中共中央关于繁荣发展社会主义文艺的意见', *gov.cn* (19 October 2015), accessed 16 February 2024.
96. Carl Minzner, 'Intelligentsia in the Crosshairs', *China Leadership Monitor*, 62 (2019).
97. See Lisa Movius, '"Walls Close In" on China's Art World as President Xi Jinping Lays Out Cultural Agenda', *The Art Newspaper* (15 November

2022); Vincent Ni and Helen Davidson, 'China's Cultural Crackdown', *The Guardian* (10 September 2021).

98. Minxin Pei, 'Ideological Indoctrination under Xi Jinping', *China Leadership Monitor,* no. *62* (2019).
99. Minzner, 'Intelligentsia in the Crosshairs', 2. See also: 'Opinions Concerning Further Strengthening and Improving Propaganda and Ideology Work in Higher Education under New Circumstances'. Originally published by *Xinhua,* translated by Rogier Creemers, *digichina.stanford.edu.* (2015), accessed 23 May 2024.
100. Xinhua, 'Opinions Concerning Further Strengthening in Higher Education'.
101. Xinhua, 'Opinions Concerning Further Strengthening in Higher Education'.
102. Xinhua, 'Opinions Concerning Further Strengthening in Higher Education'.
103. Xinhua, 'Opinions Concerning Further Strengthening in Higher Education'.
104. Julia Bowie and David Glitter, 'The CCP's Plan to "Sinicize" Religions', *thediplomat.com* (14 June 2018), accessed 16 February 2024.
105. National People's Congress (PRC), 'Law of the People's Republic of China on Administration of Activities of Overseas Nongovernmental Organizations in the Mainland of China', *chinafile.com* (28 April 2016); Mark Sidel, 'Securitizing Overseas Nonprofit Work in China', *USALI Perspectives*, 2/6 (2021); Isabella Jingwen Zhong, 'How Are Foreign NGOs Getting On in China after Four Years of Reform?', *chinadevelopmentbrief.org* (21 January 2021); ChinaFile, 'Fact Sheet on China's Foreign NGO Law', *chinafile.com* (1 November 2017), all accessed 16 February 2024.
106. Adrian Zenz, 'Thoroughly Reforming Them towards a Healthy Heart Attitude', *Central Asian Survey*, 38/1 (2019). See also: Office of the High Commissioner for Human Rights, 'OHCHR Assessment of Human Rights Concerns in the Xinjiang Uyghur Autonomous Region, People's Republic of China', *ohchr.org* (31 August 2022), accessed 16 February 2024.
107. State Council (PRC), 'Regulations on Religious Affairs', *sara.gov.cn* (14 June 2017), accessed 16 February 2024.
108. Benjamin Haas, 'China and Its War on Christianity', *theguardian.com* (28 September 2018); Steven Lee Myers, 'A Crackdown on Islam Is Spreading across China', *nytimes.com* (21 September 2019); Roderick MacFarquhar, 'China's Astounding Religious Revival', *chinafile.com* (8 June 2017), accessed 22 October 2021.
109. Central Political and Legal Affairs Commission, '陈一新：学深悟透习近平法治思想'.
110. Central Political and Legal Affairs Commission, '陈一新：学深悟透习近平法治思想'.
111. Central Political and Legal Affairs Commission, '陈一新：学深悟透习近平法治思想'.

112. Central Political and Legal Affairs Commission, '陈一新:学深悟透习近平法治思想'.
113. Central Political and Legal Affairs Commission, '陈一新:学深悟透习近平法治思想'.
114. See further: Law Society of England and Wales, 'Stakeholder Submission to the UN Human Rights Council's Universal Periodic Review—CHINA', *ohchr.org* (2024), accessed 19 February 2024.
115. Central Political and Legal Affairs Commission, '陈一新:学深悟透习近平法治思想'.
116. Congressional-Executive Committee on China (US), 'Five Years after 709 Crackdown, Lawyers Continue to Face Repression and Punishment', *cecc.gov* (2020), accessed 19 February 2024.
117. Central Political and Legal Affairs Commission, '陈一新:学深悟透习近平法治思想'.
118. The core socialist values are national prosperity, democracy, civility, and harmony (*fuqiang*, *minzhu*, *wenming*, and *hexie*); societal freedom, equality, justice, and rule of law (*ziyou*, *pingdeng*, *gongzheng*, and *fazhi*); and at the personal level: patriotism, dedication, integrity, and friendliness (*aiguo*, *jingye*, *chengxin*, and *youshan*). See: Xi Jinping, 'Foster and Practice Core Socialist Values from Childhood', in *The Governance of China*, Vol. 1.
119. Miao Ying, 'Romanticising the Past', *Journal of Current Chinese Affairs*, 49/2 (2021), accessed 22 October 2021.
120. BBC News, '"Xi Jinping Thought" Introduced into Curriculum', *bbc.com* (25 August 2021), accessed 22 October 2021.
121. Xinhua, '习近平:人民有信仰民族有希望国家有力量', *xinhuanet.com* (28 February 2015), accessed 19 February 2024.
122. Xinhua, '中共中央关于加强党的政治建设的意见', *gov.cn* (27 February 2019), accessed 22 October 2021.
123. Xinhua, '中共中央关于加强党的政治建设的意见'.
124. Wang Jikun and Lv Lujun, 'The Opportunity, Challenge and Strategy of MOOC Bringing to Ideological and Political Theory Course in College', *Advances in Economics, Business and Management*, 94 (2019).
125. Xinhua, 'Xi Focus: Showing the Way Forward to Convey China's Stories Globally', *xinhuanet.com* (2 July 2021), accessed 19 February 2024.
126. Xinhua, '习近平出席"不忘初心、牢记使命"主题教育工作会议并发表重要讲话', *gov.cn* (31 May 2019), accessed 19 February 2024.
127. Grünberg and Drinhausen, 'The Party Leads on Everything'.
128. Grünberg and Drinhausen, 'The Party Leads on Everything'.
129. Xi Jinping, 'Speech at a Review Meeting on the Campaign Themed "Staying True to Our Original Aspiration and Founding Mission"', *en.qstheory.cn* (9 November 2020), accessed 22 October 2021.
130. Xi, 'Speech at a Review Meeting on "Staying True to Our Original Aspiration"'.

131. Xi, 'Speech at a Review Meeting on "Staying True to Our Original Aspiration"'.
132. Xi, 'Speech at a Review Meeting on "Staying True to Our Original Aspiration"'.
133. Xi, 'Speech at a Review Meeting on "Staying True to Our Original Aspiration"'. See also: Deng, 'On the Reform of the System of Party and State Leadership'.
134. Xi, 'Speech at a Review Meeting on "Staying True to Our Original Aspiration"'.
135. Xinhua, '习近平在中央党校(国家行政学院)中青年干部培训班开班式上发表重要讲话强调', *xinhuanet.com* (2 March 2021), accessed 19 February 2024.
136. Xinhua, '习近平在中央党校(国家行政学院)中青年干部培训班开班式上发表重要讲话强调'.

CHAPTER 6

1. Central Committee of the CCP, 'Decision of the Central Committee of the Communist Party of China on Some Major Issues Concerning Comprehensively Deepening the Reform' ('The Decision'), *china.org.cn* (16 January 2014), accessed 22 March 2024.
2. People's Daily, '2020年中央经济工作会议(2020年12月16日-18日', *qizhiwang.org.cn* (12 April 2022), accessed 8 March 2024.
3. For analysis, see: Arthur R. Kroeber, *China's Economy* (Oxford: Oxford University Press, 2020); Nicholas R. Lardy, *The State Strikes Back* (Washington, DC: Peterson Institute for International Economics, 2019); Barry Naughton, *The Rise of China's Industrial Policy* (Ciudad Universitaria: Universidad Nacional Autónoma de México, 2021).
4. Xi Jinping, 'Understanding the New Development Stage, Applying the New Development Philosophy, and Creating a New Development Dynamic', *en.qstheory.cn* (8 July 2021), accessed 20 February 2024. Originally published as '把握新发展阶段,贯彻新发展理念,构建新发展格局', *Qiushi*, no. 9 (2021). See further: Xi Jinping, '深入学习坚决贯彻党的十九届五中全会精神 确保全面建设社会主义现代化国家开好局', *people.cn* (12 January 2021), accessed 22 March 2024.
5. See: Charles Redenius, 'Justifying Economic Reform in China', *Journal of Social, Political, and Economic Studies*, 13/3 (1988); Ian Wilson, 'Socialism with Chinese Characteristics', *Politics*, 24/1 (1989); Tao Wenzhao, '深刻把握新发展阶段', *xinhuanet.com* (25 January 2021), accessed 20 March 2022; Yi Li, '认识把握新发展阶段的几个问题', *qstheory.cn* (16 August 2021), accessed 20 March 2022.
6. Xi, 'Understanding the New Development Stage'.
7. Al L. Sargis, 'Ideological Tendencies and Reform Policy in China's Primary Stage of Socialism', *Nature, Society and Thought*, 11/4 (1998).

8. Mao Zedong, 'Reading Notes on the Soviet Text *Political Economy*', in *Selected Works of Mao Tse-Tung*, Vol. 8.
9. Xi, 'Understanding the New Development Stage'.
10. Deng, 'Excerpts from Talks Given in Wuchang, Shenzhen, Zhuhai and Shanghai'.
11. Examples of Zhao's, Jiang's, and Hu's language on the duration of the primary stage of socialism can be found in their reports to the 13th, 15th, and 17th Party's Congresses respectively.
12. Xinhua, 'CPC Q&A: What Are China's Two Centennial Goals and Why Do They Matter?', *xinhuanet.com* (17 October 2017), accessed 20 February 2024.
13. The 14th Five-Year Plan and Vision 2035.
14. Xi, 'Understanding the New Development Stage'.
15. Zhao Ziyang, *Advance along the Road of Socialism with Chinese Characteristics* (Report to the 13th Party Congress, 1987). See also: Stuart R. Schram, 'China after the 13th Congress', *China Quarterly*, 114 (1988).
16. Loren Brandt et al., 'Recent Productivity Trends in China: Evidence from Macro- and Firm-Level Data', *China: An International Journal*, 20/1 (2022). See also: World Bank, 'World Bank Country and Lending Groups', datahelpdesk.worldbank.org (27 June 2023), accessed 10 May 2024.
17. Zhao, Report to the 13th Party Congress.
18. Michael Schoenhals, *Doing Things with Words in Chinese Politics* (Berkeley: University of California Press, 1992).
19. Schoenhals, *Doing Things with Words*, 3.
20. Jiang, Reports to the 14th, 15th, and 16th Party Congresses; Hu, Reports to the 17th and 18th Party Congresses; Xi, Report to the 19th Party Congress; Xi Jinping, *Hold High the Great Banner of Socialism with Chinese Characteristics and Strive in Unity to Build a Modern Socialist Country in All Respects* (Report to the 20th Party Congress, 2022).
21. Matthias von Hein, 'Xi Jinping—China's Great Helmsman 2.0', *dw.com* (25 October 2017), accessed 20 February 2024.
22. Comparison of official readouts, which recount the core points of leaders' addresses, of Central Economic Work Conferences between 1994 and 2023, as published through Xinhua.
23. This tally includes usage of 'patriotic' as well as 'patriotism'.
24. Qian Gang, 'The Tea Leaves of Xi-Era Discourse', *chinamediaproject.org* (14 November 2017), accessed 24 October 2021.
25. Qian, 'The Tea Leaves'.
26. Qian, 'The Tea Leaves'.

CHAPTER 7

1. Central Committee of the CCP, 'The Decision'.

2. Xinhua, '中央经济工作会议在北京举行' (2014 CEWC Readout), *gov.cn* (11 December 2014), accessed 23 February 2024. See readouts of CEWCs 2012-2021, http://www.qizhiwang.org.cn/GB/422362/443602/443609/443710/, 2022, https://www.gov.cn/xinwen/2022-12/16/content_5732408.htm and 2023, http://www.news.cn/politics/leaders/2023-12/12/c_1130022917.htm, all accessed 23 May 2024.
3. Zhou Lin, 'Chinese Economy Embraces Supply-Side Reform', *chinatoday.com.cn* (1 June 2016), accessed 23 February 2024.
4. E.g.: Xinhua, 'Xi Stresses Development of Marxist Economic Philosophy', *china.org.cn* (24 November 2015), accessed 23 February 2024.
5. Xinhua, '中共中央政治局常务委员会召开会议 习近平主持', *xinhuanet.com* (14 May 2020), accessed 23 February 2024.
6. Xinhua, 'Xi Focus: Xi Says China to Further Promote Common Prosperity', *xinhuanet.com*, (3 November 2020). For pre-Xi formulations on 'common prosperity', see: David Bandurski, 'A History of Common Prosperity', *chinamediaproject.org* (27 August 2021), both accessed 20 March 2024.
7. As outlined in chapter 2, by 'left' I mean: greater ideological justification to intervene in the economy to correct 'imbalances' delivered by the era of reform and opening; greater powers of economic policy direction being relocated to party over the technical apparatus of the state; a greater role for state industrial policy in the allocation of resources as opposed to the market; an expanded role for state-owned enterprises and a diminished autonomy for the private sector; and a large-scale unfolding agenda on income distribution to deal with inequality.
8. Central Committee of the CCP, 'The Decision'.
9. Central Committee of the CCP, 'The Decision of the Chinese Communist Party Central Committee on Major Issues Concerning Upholding and Improving the System of Socialism with Chinese Characteristics and Advancing the Modernization of China's System and Capacity for Governance', *airuniversity.af.edu* (November 2019), accessed 22 March 2024.
10. Central Committee of the CCP, 'The Decision'.
11. Lardy, *The State Strikes Back*, 41.
12. Arthur R. Kroeber, 'Xi Jinping's Ambitious Agenda for Economic Reform in China', *brookings.edu* (17 November 2013), accessed 24 October 2021.
13. Kroeber, 'Xi Jinping's Ambitious Agenda'.
14. Xu Zhifeng, '句句是改革 字字有力度', *people.com.cn* (15 November 2013), 2.
15. Central Committee of the CCP, 'The Decision'.
16. Xu, '句句是改革 字字有力度'.
17. Central Committee of the CCP, 'The Decision'. See also: Yi Zhang, '混合所有制发展：从管企业到管资本', *people.com.cn* (15 November 2013), accessed 23 February 2024; Jude Blanchette, 'From "China Inc." to "CCP Inc."', *China Leadership Monitor*, 66 (2020).

18. Central Committee of the CCP, 'The Decision'.
19. Xinhua, '中央经济工作会议在北京举行' (2013 CEWC Readout), *gov.cn* (13 December 2013), accessed 23 February 2024.
20. Asia Society Policy Institute, 'The China Dashboard—Winter 2021', *chinadashboard.gist.asiasociety.org* (2021), accessed 24 October 2021. See also: Evan Feigenbaum, 'A Chinese Puzzle', *carnegieendowment.org* (26 February 2018), accessed 21 March 2024; Lardy, *The State Strikes Back*.
21. Asia Society Policy Institute, 'Decoding Chinese Politics', *asiasociety.org* (2024), accessed 23 February 2024.
22. The Leading Group on Comprehensively Deepening Reform was upgraded to a 'Commission' in March 2018. See: Nis Grünberg and Vincent Brussee, 'Xi's Control Room', *MERICS* (2022), accessed 23 February 2024.
23. Blanchette, 'From "China Inc." to "CCP Inc."'; Lardy, *The State Strikes Back*.
24. Xinhua, '中国共产党一百年大事记（1921年7月—2021年6月）: '. . . 十八届三中全会召开七年多来，各方面共推出2485个改革方案，十八届三中全会提出的改革目标任务总体如期完成。'
25. Xinhua, 'Highlights of China's Central Economic Work Conference', *People's Daily* (12 December 2014), accessed 23 February 2024.
26. Xinhua, 'China Should Adapt to New Norm of Growth: Xi', *China Daily* (11 May 2014), accessed 23 February 2024.
27. Xinhua, 'New Normal to Be Logic of China's Future Growth', *China Daily* (11 December 2014); Martin Feldstein, 'What Is China's "New Normal"?', *World Economic Forum* (27 March 2015), both accessed 23 February 2024.
28. Xi Jinping, 'Towards a Community of Common Destiny and a New Future for Asia', *china.org.cn* (28 March 2015), accessed 21 March 2024.
29. The Central Economic Work Conference in December 2014 noted that "in the past, China's consumption had the characteristic of imitation, and that that chapter has now closed. . . . It is important to adopt the right consumption policy and release consumption's potential to allow consumption to play a fundamental role in promoting economic development . . . the meeting to accurately grasp the 'New Normal' of economic development". See further: Xinhua, 2014 CEWC Readout (11 December 2014), accessed 24 October 2021.
30. Cai Fang (ed.), *China's Economic New Normal* (Singapore: Springer, 2020).
31. Cai, 'New Normal Brings New Opportunities', in *China's Economic New Normal*, 1–4.
32. Li Yang, 'Understanding and Adapting to the New Normal', in *China's Economic New Normal*, 5–12.
33. Huang Yiping, 'Positive Changes in China's Economic Structure', in *China's Economic New Normal*, 79–85.
34. Li, 'Understanding and Adapting to the New Normal'.
35. Xinhua, 2014 CEWC Readout.
36. Xinhua, '中国共产党一百年大事记 (1921年7月—2021年6月)'.

37. Xinhua, '中央经济工作会议举行' (2015 CEWC Readout), *gov.cn* (21 December 2015), accessed 24 October 2021.
38. Xinhua, 2015 CEWC Readout.
39. Xinhua, 2015 CEWC Readout.
40. Dwyer Gunn, 'Leverage, Fire Sales, and the 2015 Chinese Stock Market Crash', *The NBER Digest (*November 2018), 2–3.
41. Barry Naughton, 'Two Trains Running', *China Leadership Monitor* 50 (2016), 2.
42. E.g.: Roberto Bendini, *Exceptional Measures* (Brussels: European Parliament DG EXPO, 2015), 6.
43. Xinhua, '中央经济工作会议在北京举行' (2016 CEWC Readout), *gov.cn* (16 December 2016), accessed 24 October 2021.
44. Xinhua, 2016 CEWC Readout.
45. Xinhua, 2016 CEWC Readout. See also: Yanfei Wang and Ziman Yang, 'NDRC: Overcapacity Top Reform Priority for 2017', *chindaily.com.cn* (19 December 2016), accessed 23 February 2024.
46. Xinhua, '中央经济工作会议举行' (2017 CEWC Readout), *gov.cn* (20 December 2017), accessed 21 March 2024.
47. Xinhua, 2017 CEWC Readout.
48. Xinhua, '中央经济工作会议在北京举行' (2018 CEWC Readout), *gov.cn* (21 December 2018), accessed 24 October 2021. See also: Xiankun Jin, Liping Xu, Yu Xin, and Ajay Adhikari, 'Political Governance in China's State-Owned Enterprises', *China Journal of Accounting Research*, 15/2 (2022).
49. Xinhua, '中央经济工作会议在北京举行' (2019 CEWC Readout), *xinhuanet.com* (12 December 2019), accessed 23 February 2024.
50. Xi, 'Understanding the New Development Stage'. See also '深入学习坚决贯彻党的十九届五中全会精神 确保全面建设社会主义现代化国家开好局'.
51. Xinhua, 'Communiqué of 5th Plenary Session of 19th CPC Central Committee Released', *gov.cn* (30 October 2020), accessed 26 February 2024.
52. Xinhua, '中共十八届五中全会公报' (Communiqué of the Fifth Plenum of the 18th Central Committee), *Beijing Review* (2 December 2015), accessed 24 October 2021. See also: 'Communiqué of the Fifth Plenary Meeting of the 18th Central Committee of the Chinese Communist Party', *chinacopyrightandmedia.wordpress.com* (29 October 2015), accessed 8 March 2024.
53. Xinhua, '治國理政新實踐：不斷開拓治國理政新境界', *cpc.people.com.cn* (1 March 2016), accessed 26 February 2024.
54. Xinhua, 2016 CEWC Readout.
55. Xinhua, 'To Revive China, Xi Holds High Banner of Socialism with Chinese Characteristics', *gov.cn* (28 July 2017), accessed 21 March 2024.
56. Xi, Report to the 19th Party Congress.
57. Xinhua, 2017 CEWC Readout.
58. Unless otherwise noted, all quotes in this section are from: Xinhua, 2019 CEWC Readout.

59. Xi, '深入学习坚决贯彻党的十九届五中全会精神 确保全面建设社会主义现代化国家开好局', *gov.cn* (11 January 2021), accessed 21 March 2024.
60. Xinhua, 2019 CEWC Readout.
61. Xinhua, 2019 CEWC Readout.
62. Xinhua, 'Xi Focus: Xi Explains New Development Pattern', *xinhuanet.com* (3 November 2020), accessed 26 February 2024.
63. Xinhua, '习近平在中共中央政治局第二十七次集体学习时强调 完整准确全面贯彻新发展理念 确保'十四五'时期我国发展开好局起好步', *xinhuanet.com* (29 January 2021), accessed 31 October 2021.
64. Xinhua, '习近平在中共中央政治局第二十七次集体学习时强调'.
65. Qiushi, '习近平总书记谈新发展理念', *qstheory.cn* (22 January 2021), accessed 31 October 2021.
66. Unless otherwise noted, quotes in this section are from: Xi, 'Understanding the New Development Stage'.
67. Xi, 'Understanding the New Development Stage'. See also: Liu He, '刘鹤：加快构建以国内大循环为主体、国内国际双循环相互促进的新发展格局', *gov.cn* (25 November 2020), accessed 24 October 2021.
68. Xinhua, 'Xi Focus: How Will China Shape Its Development Strategy for New Stage?', *xinhuanet.com* (27 August 2020), accessed 26 February 2024.
69. Xinhua, 'How Will China Shape Its Development Strategy?'
70. Xinhua, 2020 CEWC Readout.
71. Xinhua, '习近平主持召开中央财经委员会第十次会议第十次会议强调 在高质量发展中促进共同富裕 统筹做好重大金融风险防范化解工作李克强汪洋王沪宁韩正出席' (2021 CFEAC Readout), *xinhuanet.com* (17 August 2021), accessed 24 October 2021.
72. Xinhua, 2021 CFEAC Readout.
73. Xinhua, 2021 CFEAC Readout.
74. Xi, 'Understanding the New Development Stage'.
75. Deng Xiaoping, 'Remarks during an Inspection Tour of Tianjin', in *Selected Works of Deng Xiaoping*, Vol. 3.
76. Xi Jinping, 'Solidly Promote Common Prosperity', *interpret.csis.org* (15 October 2021), accessed 26 February 2024.
77. Xi, 'Solidly Promote Common Prosperity'.
78. China Keywords, 'Scientific Outlook on Development', *keywords.china.org.cn* (13 July 2022), accessed 26 February 2024.
79. Xi, 'Understanding the New Development Stage'.
80. Xinhua, '中国共产党第十九届中央委员会第五次全体会议公报' (Communique of the Fifth Plenary Session of the 19th Central Committee), *guancha.cn* (29 October 2020), accessed 26 February 2024.
81. Xi, 'Understanding the New Development Stage'.
82. Xinhua, '习近平主持召开中央财经委员会第十次会议强调' (2021 CFEAC Readout), *xinhuanet.com* (17 August 2021), accessed 21 March 2024.
83. Xi, 'Solidly Promote Common Prosperity'.

84. Xi, 'Solidly Promote Common Prosperity'. See also: Wu Guoguang, *China's Common Prosperity Program* (New York: Asia Society Policy Institute, 2022).
85. Cai Fang, 'Right Time for China's "Common Prosperity" drive', *eastasiaforum.org* (19 September 2021), accessed 26 February 2024.
86. Xi, 'Solidly Promote Common Prosperity'.
87. Xinhua, 'China's Common Prosperity Boon to World', *xinhuanet.com* (21 December 2021), accessed 21 March 2024.
88. E.g.: Xi Jinping, '不断做强做优做大我国数字经济', *Qiushi*, no. *2* (2022); Xi Jinping, '努力成为世界主要科学中心和创新高地', *Qiushi*, no. *6* (2021).
89. Xi Jinping, *How to Deepen Reform Comprehensively* (Beijing: Foreign Languages Press, 2014), 79–81. See also: Xi Jinping, '在民营企业座谈会上的讲话', *xinhuanet.com* (1 November 2018); Xiao Yaqing, '深化国有企业改革', *gov.cn* (13 December 2017), both accessed 24 October 2021; Curtis J. Milhaupt and Zhen Wentong, 'Why Mixed-Ownership Reforms Cannot Fix China's State Sector', Paulson Policy Memorandum (Chicago: Paulson Institute, 2016); Ann Listerud, 'MOR Money MOR Problems', *New Perspectives in Foreign Policy*, 18 (2019).
90. Xi, 'Solidly Promote Common Prosperity'.
91. Xi, 'Solidly Promote Common Prosperity'.
92. Xi, 'Understanding the New Development Stage'.
93. Nicholas R. Lardy, 'China Has Been Overstating the Role of Private Investment in Its Economy', *piie.com* (5 March 2020), accessed 26 February 2024; Hanming Fang, 'Where's China's Economy Headed?', in *Building a More Resilient US Economy* (Washington, DC: Aspen Institute, 2023). See also: Edward White, 'China's Business Confidence Problem', *ft.com* (12 September 2023); World Bank Open Data, both accessed 26 February 2024.
94. The 14th Five-Year Plan and Vision 2035. See also: Xinhua, '国民经济和社会发展第十二个五年规划纲要 (The 12th Five Year-Plan)', *gov.cn* (16 March 2011); '中华人民共和国国民经济和社会发展第十三个五年规划纲要' (The 13th Five-Year Plan), *gov.cn* (17 March 2016).
95. The 14th Five-Year Plan and Vision 2035.
96. See: Abraham Maslow, *Motivation and Personality* (New York: Harper & Row, 1954) 80–106.
97. See: Chris Buckley, 'Vows of Change in China Belie Private Warning', *nytimes.com* (14 February 2013), accessed 27 February 2024.

CHAPTER 8

1. The 14th Five-Year Plan and Vision 2035.
2. The 14th Five-Year Plan and Vision 2035.
3. The 14th Five-Year Plan and Vision 2035.
4. Naughton, *The Rise of China's Industrial Policy*, 21.
5. Naughton, *The Rise of China's Industrial Policy*, 51–71.

6. The most notable example of Chinese industrial policy is Made in China 2025: State Council (PRC), '国务院关于印发《中国制造2025》的通知' (Made in China 2025), 14349/2015-00078 (19 May 2015). For analyses of MIC25, see: Max J. Zenglein and Anna Holzmann, 'Evolving Made in China 2025', *MERICS Papers on China*, no. *8* (2019); Bonnie S. Glaser, 'Made in China 2025 and the Future of American Industry', *csis.org* (27 February 2019), accessed 27 February 2024; Li Ling, 'China's Manufacturing Locus in 2025', *Technological Forecasting and Social Change*, 135 (2018), 66–74; Ma Huimin, Xiang Wu, Yan Li, Huang Han, Han Wu, Jie Xiong, and Zhang Jinlong, 'Strategic Plan of "Made in China 2025" and Its Implementation', in *Analyzing the Impacts of Industry 4.0 in Modern Business Environments* (Hershey, PA: IGI Global, 2018).
7. Naughton, *The Rise of China's Industrial Policy*, 71–84.
8. This compares with the 13th Plan's emphasis on the market: "We will make clear the functions and roles of different types of entities involved in innovation and establish an innovation network that integrates the efforts of government, enterprises, universities, research institutes, and end-users. We will strengthen the position of enterprises as principal entities for innovation as well as the leading role of enterprises in innovation, encourage them to conduct basic and frontier research, implement the 100 Most Innovative Enterprises initiative, develop innovative and internationally competitive enterprises, and support the growth of small and medium high-tech enterprises."
9. The 14th Five-Year Plan and Vision 2035.
10. Constitution of the CCP (2017).
11. Elsa B. Kania and Lorand Laskai, *Myths and Realities of China's Military-Civil Fusion Strategy* (Washington, DC: Center for a New American Security, 2021).
12. Naughton, *The Rise of China's Industrial Policy*, 101.
13. Doris Fischer, Hannes Gohli, and Sabrina Habich-Sobiegalla, 'Industrial Policies under Xi Jinping', *Issues & Studies*, 57/4 (2021).
14. Jost Wübbeke, Mirjam Meissner, Max J. Zenglein, Jaqueline Ives, and Björn Conrad, 'Made in China 2025: The Making of a High-Tech Superpower and Consequences for Industrial Countries', *MERICS Papers on China*, no. *2* (2016).
15. Huang Tianlei, 'Government-Guided Funds in China', *piie.com* (17 June 2019), accessed 24 October 2021.
16. Huang 'Government-Guided Funds in China'.
17. Zenglein and Holzmann, *Evolving Made in China 2025*.
18. Dic Lo and Wu Mei, 'The State and Industrial Policy in Chinese Economic Development', in *Transforming Economies* (Geneva: International Labour Office, 2014), 320.
19. In 2017, the state sector accounted for 24.6% of real estate and only 8.8% of hotels and catering. By contrast, the state's share of construction sector was 38.5%. See: Chunlin Zhang, 'How Much Do State-Owned Enterprises

Contribute to China's GDP and Employment?', *World Bank*, Working Paper 140361 (2019).

20. Xi Jinping, 习近平谈治国理政 (Beijing: Foreign Languages Press, 2014, 2017, 2020, and 2022).
21. Xinhua, '中国规划明年经济 "健增长"', *xinhuanet.com*, (16 December 2012). This was also emphasized at the CEWCs in 2015 ('会议强调，要坚持瞄准全面建成小康社会目标，牢牢抓住发展这个第一要务不放松，科学确定经济社会发展主要预期目标，把握好稳增长和调结构的平衡，稳定和完善宏观经济政策，加大对实体经济支持力度。') and 2016 ('着力振兴实体经济。') as well as the Second Session of the Fifth Plenum in October 2015: '我们的政策基点要放在企业特别是实体经济企业上，高度重视实体经济健康发展，增强实体经济赢利能力。' See: Xi Jinping, '在党的十八届五中全会第二次全体会议上的讲话', *cpc.people.com.cn* (29 October 2015), accessed 21 March 2024. More recent emphases are found in Xi's inspection tours of Guizhou in February 2021 ('创新发展是构建新发展格局的必然选择。要着眼于形成新发展格局，推动大数据和实体经济深度融合，培育壮大战略性新兴产业，加快发展现代产业体系。') and Guangxi in April 2021 ('制造业高质量发展是我国经济高质量发展的重中之重，建设社会主义现代化强国、发展壮大实体经济，都离不开制造业，要在推动产业优化升级上继续下功夫。') See: Party Building Online Micro Platform, '习近平：不断壮大实体经济', *dangjian.com* (11 August 2022); Guizhou Daily, '加快建设现代化产业体系', *gz.xinhuanet.com* (8 November 2023), both accessed 21 March 2024.
22. Xi Jinping, 'The New Normal', 2015, in *The Governance of China*, Vol. 2.
23. See People's Daily, '主动适应、把握、引领经济发展新常态，着力推进供给侧结构性改革—旗帜网', *qiziwang.org.cn* (26 November 2018), accessed 29 February 2024.
24. Yiming Guo, 'Economist: Property Tax to Stabilize Housing Prices, Curb Speculation', *china.org.cn* (3 March 2017); Summer Zhen, 'What President Xi's Congress Message Means for China's Housing Market', *scmp.com* (24 October 2017), both accessed 24 October 2021. This line appeared earlier in the communiqué of the 2016 CEWC; see Nan Yu and Nan Li, 'Keep the Graph Growing', *Beijing Review*, no. 52 (2016).
25. Karl Marx, *Capital* (Moscow: Progress Publishers, 1974), 400–13. See also: Yinxing Hong, 'Socialist Political Economy with Chinese Characteristics in a New Era', *China Political Economy*, 3/2 (2020); David Harvey, *The Limits to Capital* (Oxford: Basil Blackwell, 1982).
26. Marx, *Capital*, 515.
27. Marx, *Capital*, 469.
28. Liu He, '3 Critical Battles China Is Preparing to Fight', *weforum.org* (24 January 2018), accessed 28 February 2024.
29. Xinhua, '习近平在广东考察', *gov.cn* (25 October 2018), accessed 24 October 2021.

30. Zongyuan Zoe Liu, 'Does Evergrande's Collapse Threaten China's Economy?', *cfr.org* (13 February 2024), accessed 28 February 2024.
31. Xinhua, '习近平：深刻认识建设现代化经济体系重要性 推动我国经济发展焕发新活力迈上新台阶', *xinhuanet.com* (1 February 2018), accessed 19 December 2023.
32. People's Daily, '国有企业作用不可替代', *gov.cn* (29 November 2018), accessed 17 March 2022.
33. Chiang-Tai Hsieh and Zheng (Michael) Song, 'Grasp the Large, Let Go of the Small', *Brookings Papers on Economic Activity* (Spring 2015), 304.
34. Constitution of the PRC (2018).
35. Blanchette, 'From "China Inc" to "CCP Inc" '.
36. Central Committee of the CCP, 'The Decision'.
37. Asia Pacific Foundation of Canada, *State-Owned Enterprises at a Crossroads* (Vancouver: Asia Pacific Foundation of Canada, 2016).
38. This was documented in a series of party-issued 'guidelines' and 'opinions' between 2014 and 2017. See: ReformPedia, 'State Owned Enterprise', *macropolo.org*, accessed 28 February 2024.
39. State-Owned Assets Supervision and Administration Commission, Ministry of Finance and National Development and Reform Commission, '关于国有企业功能界定与分类的指导意见', *mof.gov.cn* (2015), accessed 28 February 2024.
40. Blanchette, 'From "China Inc" to "CCP Inc" '.
41. Office of the State Council, '结构调整与重组的指导意见', Notice 14349/2016–156 (26 July 2016).
42. Office of the State Council, '结构调整与重组的指导意见'.
43. Zhizong Ma, '充分发挥国有企业党委（党组）在新时代的领导作用', *dangjian.people.com.cn* (8 January 2018), accessed 28 February 2024.
44. Xinhua, '中共中央、国务院关于深化国有企业改革的指导意见', *gov.cn* (24 August 2015), accessed 28 February 2024.
45. Blanchette, 'From "China Inc" to "CCP Inc" '.
46. Office of the State Council, '国务院办公厅关于进一步完善国有企业法人治理结构的指导意见', Notice 14349/217-89 (24 April 2017).
47. Constitution of the CCP (2017).
48. Xi, Report to the 19th Party Congress.
49. Blanchette, 'From "China Inc" to "CCP Inc" '.
50. Central Committee of the CCP, 'The Decision'.
51. Liu He, '刘鹤：不支持民营企业发展的行为必须坚决予以纠正', *xinhuanet.com* (20 October 2018), accessed 24 October 2021.
52. Dorothy J. Solinger, *Chinese Business under Socialism* (Berkeley: University of California Press, 1984).
53. Yan Xiaojun and Huang Jie, 'Navigating Unknown Waters', *China Review*, 17/2 (2017), 45–46.

54. Central Committee of the CCP, '中国共产党支部工作条例（试行）', *politics.people.com.cn* (26 November 2018), accessed 28 February 2024.
55. Grünberg and Drinhausen, 'The Party Leads on Everything'.
56. Central Committee of the CCP, '关于加强新时代民营经济统战工作的意见', *xinhuanet.com* (15 September 2020), accessed 24 October 2021.
57. Central Committee of the CCP, '关于加强新时代民营经济统战工作的意见'.
58. Central Committee of the CCP, '关于加强新时代民营经济统战工作的意见'.
59. Central Committee of the CCP, '关于加强新时代民营经济统战工作的意见'.
60. Xinhua, 'Xi Stresses Unswerving Support for Development of Private Enterprises', *xinhuanet.com* (2 November 2018), accessed 24 October 2021.
61. Xinhua, 'Xi Stresses Unswerving Support'.
62. Liu He, '所谓"国进民退"的议论既是片面的也是错误的', *xinhuanet.com* (20 October 2018), accessed 23 May 2024.
63. Xi Jinping, '习近平：在企业家座谈会上的讲话', *xinhuanet.com* (21 July 2020), accessed 24 October 2021.
64. Central Committee of the CCP, 'Opinions on Strengthening the United Front Work of the Private Economy in the New Era', *interpret.csis.org* (15 September 2020).
65. The 14th Five-Year Plan and Vision 2035. See also National Bureau of Statistics, '对外经贸开启新征程 全面开放构建新格局—新中国成立70周年经济社会发展成就系列报告之二十二', *stats.gov.cn* (27 August 2019), accessed 29 February 2024.
66. Xi Jinping, '正确认识和把握中长期经济社会发展重大问题', *Qiushi*, no. 2 (2021), accessed 24 October 2021.
67. Xi, 'Understanding the New Development Stage'.
68. The 14th Five-Year Plan and Vision 2035.
69. Xi, 'Understanding the New Development Stage'.
70. Nicholas Lardy and Huang Tianlei, 'China's Financial Opening Accelerates', *PIIE Policy Brief*, no. 17 (2020).
71. US-China Economic and Security Review Commission, '2020 Annual Report to Congress' (Washington, DC: US Government Publishing Service, 2020), 248–49.
72. Bank of Finland Institute for Emerging Economies, 'China Now Has the World's Second Largest Bond Market after the US', *BOFIT Weekly Review*, no. 30 (2021); Juan J. Cortina, Maria Soledad Martinez Peria, Sergio L. Schmukler, and Jasmine Xiao, 'The Internationalization of China's Equity Markets', IMF Working Paper 23/26 (2023); Nicole Adams, David Jacobs, Stephen Kenny, Serena Russell, and Maxwell Sutton, 'China's Evolving Financial System and Its Global Importance', *Reserve Bank of Australia*

Bulletin (September 2021); Shanghai Stock Exchange, 'Overseas Investors Ownership Statistics', *sse.com.cn*, accessed 29 February 2024.

73. See Larry Diamond and Orville Schell, 'China's Influence and American Interests: Promoting Constructive Vigilance' (Stanford, CA: Hoover Institution Press, 2018).
74. Xiao Gang, '深剖中国资本市场五大变革，总结制度执行利弊得失', *wallstreetcn.com* (9 July 2020), accessed 29 February 2021.
75. E.g.: Jiang Zemin, 'The Present International Situation and Our Diplomatic Work', in *Selected Works of Jiang Zemin*, Vol. 2 (Beijing: Foreign Languages Press, 2012).

CHAPTER 9

1. Xi Jinping, '习近平:在庆祝中国共产党成立100周年大会上的讲话', *gov.cn* (1 July 2021), accessed 21 March 2024.
2. Xi Jinping, '习近平：在文艺工作座谈会上的讲话', *xinhuanet.com* (15 October 2015), accessed 2 February 2022. See further Xinhua, '习近平与文艺工作者畅谈"心里话"', *news.cn* (16 December 2021), accessed 16 December 2023.
3. Deng's 'diplomatic guidance' is described further in chapter 3.
4. Xi, Speech on Ideology and Propaganda.
5. Xi, Speech on Ideology and Propaganda.
6. Xi, Speech on Ideology and Propaganda.
7. Xi, Speech on Ideology and Propaganda.
8. Xi, Speech on Ideology and Propaganda.
9. Xinhua, '习近平: 承前启后 继往开来 继续朝着中华民族伟大复兴目标奋勇前进', *gov.cn* (29 November 2012), accessed 2 February 2022; Xinhua, '习近平在周边外交工作座谈会上发表重要讲话', *xinhuanet.com* (25 October 2013); Xinhua, 'Xi Eyes More Enabling Int'l Environment for China's Peaceful Development', *globaltimes.cn* (30 November 2014); Xinhua, 'Xi Urges Breaking New Ground in Major Country Diplomacy with Chinese Characteristics', *xinhuanet.com* (24 June 2018); Xi, Report to the 19th Party Congress; Xinhua, '中央国家安全委员会第一次会议召开 习近平发表重要讲话', *gov.cn* (15 April 2014); Central Committee of the CCP, *Resolution of the CPC Central Committee on the Major Achievements and Historical Experience of the Party over the Past Century* (Third Historical Resolution), *gov.cn* (16 November 2021), all accessed 29 February 2024.
10. Xi Jinping, 'Address at AIIB Inauguration Ceremony', *chinadaily.com.cn* (16 January 2016); Xi Jinping, 'Promote Friendship between Our People and Work Together to Build a Bright Future', *toronto.china-consulate.gov.cn* (7 September 2013); Ministry of Foreign Affairs (PRC), 'Xi Jinping Calls for the Building of New Type of International Relations with Win-Win Cooperation at the Core in a Speech at the Moscow State Institute of International Relations', *id.china-embassy.gov.cn* (27 March 2013); Xi Jinping,

'Work Together to Build a Community of Shared Future for Mankind', *xinhuanet.com* (18 January 2017); Xi Jinping, 'New Approach for Asian Security Cooperation', in *The Governance of China*, Vol. 1; Ministry of Foreign Affairs (PRC), 'Xi Addresses CICA Foreign Ministers' Meeting', *vienna.china-mission.gov.cn* (28 April 2016); Xi Jinping, 'Xi Jinping at the Opening Ceremony of the Fifth CICA Foreign Ministers' Meeting', *ccmg.gov.cn* (4 January 2017); Xinhua, 'Xi Urges Joint Efforts to Open Up New Prospects for Asian Security, Development', *xinhuanet.com* (15 June 2019); 'Full Text of Xi Jinping Keynote at the World Economic Forum', *america.cgtn.com* (17 January 2017), all accessed 21 March 2024.

11. Xinhua, '习近平: 承前启后 继往开来'.
12. Wang Jiayu, 'Representing Chinese Nationalism/Patriotism through President Xi Jinping's "Chinese Dream" Discourse', *Journal of Language and Politics*, 16/6 (2017).
13. Maria Adele Carrai, 'Chinese Political Nostalgia and Xi Jinping's Dream of Great Rejuvenation', *International Journal of Asian Studies*, 18/1 (2021). See also: Maurice Halbwachs, *On Collective Memory* (Chicago: University of Chicago Press, 1992).
14. Angus Maddison, *Chinese Economic Performance in the Long Run* (Paris: OECD Publishing, 2007), 44.
15. Rush Doshi, *The Long Game* (New York: Oxford University Press, 2021), 27–30. See also: Orville Schell and John Delury, *Wealth and Power* (New York: Random House, 2013).
16. Doshi, *The Long Game*. Doshi notes that Jiang's call for 'rejuvenation' was not the first at a Party Congress and credited Sun Yat-sen as the slogan's originator. See Jiang, Report to the 15th Party Congress.
17. Doshi, *Long Game*, 30.
18. See China Keywords, '"三步走"发展战略', *keywords.china.org.cn* (30 October 2018), accessed 2 February 2022.
19. Jiang Zemin, '80th Anniversary of Communist Party', *c-span.org* (1 July 2001), accessed 1 March 2024.
20. Xinhua, '修宪擎旗 领航时代—习近平新时代中国特色社会主义思想载入宪法的时代意义', *12371.cn* (25 March 2018), accessed 2 February 2022. Central Commission for Discipline Inspection, '党章修正案调整完善'两个一百年'奋斗目标的意义何在?', *ccdi.gov.cn* (11 February 2018), accessed 2 February 2022.
21. Xi, Report to the 19th Party Congress.
22. Xi, Report to the 19th Party Congress.
23. Xinhua, 'Xi Eyes More Enabling Int'l Environment'.
24. Document Number 9.
25. See also Camilla T. N. Sørensen, 'The Significance of Xi Jinping's "Chinese Dream" for Chinese Foreign Policy: From "Tao Guang Yang Hui" to "Fen Fa You Wei"', *Journal of China and International Relations*, 3/1 (2015).

26. Carrai, 'Chinese Political Nostalgia', 13.
27. Lu Zhouxiang, 'Introduction', in *Chinese National Identity in the Age of Globalisation* (Singapore: Palgrave Macmillan, 2020), 3.
28. Jiang Ning, 'Fostered Idols and Chinese Identity', in *Chinese National Identity in the Age of Globalisation*, 113–37.
29. Xi Jinping, Speech on Ideology and Propaganda.
30. Feng Pengzhi, '从"三个自信"到"四个自信"', *theory.people.com.cn* (7 July 2016), accessed 2 February 2022.
31. Hu, Report to the 18th Party Congress.
32. Xi, Report to the 19th Party Congress.
33. Xi, Report to the 19th Party Congress.
34. See also: Xi, Report to the 20th Party Congress.
35. See United States Office of International Religious Freedom, 'China (Includes Tibet, Xinjiang, Hong Kong, and Macau): 2021 International Religious Freedom Report', *state.gov* (2022), accessed 1 March 2024.
36. Qu Qingshan, '制度优势是党和国家的最大优势', *dangjian.people.com.cn* (17 August 2020), accessed 2 February 2022.
37. Yang Jiechi, '新形势下中国外交理论和实践创新', *gov.cn* (16 August 2013); '深入学习贯彻习近平总书记外交思想　不断谱写中国特色大国外交新篇章', *cpc.people.com.cn* (17 July 2017), both accessed 2 February 2022.
38. Liu Yoqiu, '评新编历史剧《当马克思遇见孔夫子》', *mzfxw.com* (19 October 2023), accessed 19 January 2023; Tao Zhang, 'When Marx Met Confucius', *theconversation.com* (10 November 2023), accessed 1 March 2024.
39. Xi, '习近平：在文艺工作座谈会上的讲话'; Xinhua, '在中央城市工作会议上的讲话', *planning.org.cn* (23 December 2015); Xi Jinping, '在哲学社会科学工作座谈会上的讲话', *politics.people.com.cn* (17 May 2016); Xi Jinping, '在庆祝中国共产党成立九十五周年大会上的讲话', *Qiushi*, no. *8* (2021); Xi Jinping, '在中国文联十大、中国作协九大开幕式上的讲话', *xinhuanet.com* (30 November 2016); Xi Jinping, '在中国共产党第十九次全国代表大会上的报告', *gov.cn* (18 October 2017); Ministry of Foreign Affairs (PRC), 'Xi Jinping Attends the CPC in Dialogue with World Political Parties High-Level Meeting and Delivers a Keynote Speech', *ag.china-embassy.gov.cn* (16 March 2023), all accessed 16 November 2023.
40. E.g.: Zhou Pingjian, 'Communist Party of China Turns 100 and Still Going Strong', *mfa.gov.cn* (accessed 1 March 2024).
41. Michael Pillsbury, *China Debates the Future Security Environment* (Washington, DC: National Defense University Press, 2000), 204.
42. 'Wuzi', in *The Seven Military Classics of Ancient China* (London: Arcturus, 2017). See also: Robin D. S. Yates, 'New Light on Ancient Chinese Military Texts', *T'oung Pao*, 74/4 (1988); Johnston, *Cultural Realism*; Michael J. Deane, *The Soviet Concept of the "Correlation of Forces"* (Arlington, VA: Stanford Research Institute, 1976).

43. Pillsbury, *China Debates the Future Security Environment*, 203–58. See also: Weihong Zhang, 'China's Cultural Future', *International Journal of Cultural Policy*, 16/4 (2010), 383–402.
44. Hu Angang and Men Honghua, 'The Rising of Modern China', originally published in *Strategy and Management*, 3/2 (2002).
45. Sean Golden, 'China's Perception of Risk and the Concept of Comprehensive National Power', *Copenhagen Journal of International Studies*, 29/2 (2011), 97–104.
46. Golden, 'China's Perception of Risk', 102.
47. Golden, 'China's Perception of Risk', 103–5.
48. Paul Nantulya, 'Strategic Application of the Tao 道 of Soft Power', *The African Review*, no. 47 (2020), 496.
49. People's Daily, '新时代中国特色社会主义的核心要义', *theory.people.com.cn* (2020), accessed 1 March 2024.
50. Doshi, *The Long Game*, 163.
51. Xi, Report to the 20th Party Congress, 2022
52. Xinhua, '习近平接见2017年度驻外使节工作会议与会使节并发表重要讲话', *xinhuanet.com* (28 December 2017), accessed 2 February 2022.
53. See: Xi, Report to the 19th Party Congress.
54. China Cadre Learning Network, '习近平首提'两个引导'有深意', *politics.people.com.cn* (21 February 2017), accessed 1 March 2024.
55. Xinhua, 'Xi Eyes More Enabling Int'l Environment'.
56. Xi, Report to the 19th Party Congress.
57. Xi, Report to the 19th Party Congress.
58. See: Mao Zedong, 'US Imperialism Is a Paper Tiger' and 'All Reactionaries Are Paper Tigers', both in *Selected Works of Mao Tse-Tung*, Vol. 5 (Paris: Foreign Languages Press, 2021).
59. See: Doshi, *The Long Game*, 163.
60. Jiang, Report to the 16th Party Congress.
61. See: Xi Jinping, 'China's Diplomacy Must Befit Its Major-Country Status', 'The Decisive Stage in Achieving the First Centenary Goal', 'Keep Hold of the Strategic Initiative on National Security', and 'Deeper Civil-Military Integration', in *The Governance of China*, Vol. 2.
62. Xinhua, '习近平接见2017年度驻外使节工作会议与会使节并发表重要讲话'.
63. Xi Jinping, 'Break New Ground in China's Major-Country Diplomacy', in *The Governance of China*, Vol. 3.
64. Xinhua, '习近平出席推进"一带一路"建设工作5周年座谈会并发表重要讲话', *gov.cn* (27 August 2018), accessed 2 February 2022. See also: CGTN, 'Belt & Road Initiative—5 Years On', *news.cgtn.com* (27 August 2018), accessed 21 March 2024.
65. Ministry of Foreign Affairs (PRC), '习近平会见美国前国务卿基辛格', *un.china-mission.gov.cn* (20 July 2023), accessed 21 March 2024.

66. Ministry of Foreign Affairs (PRC), 'Xi Jinping Meets with United Nations Secretary-General Guterres', *sanfrancisco.china-consulate.gov.cn* (26 April 2019), accessed 18 December 2023.
67. Ministry of Foreign Affairs (PRC), 'Xi Jinping Holds Talks with General Secretary of the Central Committee of the Lao People's Revolutionary Party (LPRP) and President Bounnhang Vorachith of Laos', *fmprc.gov.cn* (30 April 2014), accessed December 18 2023.
68. Xi Jinping, '习近平：在党史学习教育动员大会上的讲话', *xinhuanet.com* (20 February 2021), accessed 18 December 2023. See also: Xi Jinping, 'Talk Given at the Party History Learning and Education Mobilization Meeting', *interpret.csis.org* (20 February 2021), accessed 1 March 2024; and James Legge, *The Chinese Classics*, Vol. 2 (Hong Kong: Hong Kong University Press, 1960), 183.
69. Xi Jinping, '百年未有之大变局，总书记这些重要论述振聋发聩', *qstheory.cn* (27 August 2021). See also: People's Daily, '学习问答 | 8.世界正经历百年未有之大变局，变在何处？', *12371.cn* (4 August 2021); People's Daily, '人间正道开新篇（习近平新时代中国特色社会主义思想学习问答④）', *cpc.people.com.cn* (22 July 2021); Wang Derong, '理论前沿 | 新时代推进马克思主义中国化时代化基本经验研究', *qizhiwang.org.cn* (6 September 2023), all accessed 21 March 2024.
70. Xi Jinping, 'Make China a Global Center for Science and Innovation', in *The Governance of China*, Vol. 3.
71. Xi Jinping, '坚持、完善和发展中国特色社会主义国家制度与法律制度', *guoqing.china.com.cn* (2 December 2019), accessed 1 March 2024.
72. Xinhua, '习近平会见出席"2019从都国际论坛"外方嘉宾', *xinhuanet.com* (3 December 2019), accessed 2 February 2022.
73. Xi Jinping, '习近平在第二十三届圣彼得堡国际经济论坛全会上的致辞（全文）', *xinhuanet.com* (7 June 2019), accessed 2 February 2022.
74. This is a quote from Foreign Minister Wang Yi during Xi's visit to Myanmar in 2020. See: Ministry of Foreign Affairs (PRC), 'Do Not Say You Start Too Early; and You Have Close Friends Wherever You Go', *mm.china-embassy.gov.cn* (21 January 2020), accessed 1 March 2022.
75. Xi Jinping, '习近平在世界经济论坛"达沃斯议程"对话会上的特别致辞', *xinhuanet.com* (25 January 2021), accessed 1 March 2024.
76. Xi Jinping, '国家中长期经济社会发展战略若干重大问题', *Qiushi*, no. *21* (2020), accessed 2 February 2022.
77. Xinhua, '习近平在中央政治局第二十二次集体学习时强调 统一思想坚定信心鼓足干劲抓紧工作 奋力推进国防和军队现代化建设', *xinhuanet.com* (31 July 2020), accessed 2 February 2022.
78. Xi Jinping, '在经济社会领域专家座谈会上的讲话', *gov.cn* (24 August 2020), accessed 11 April 2022.
79. Xi Jinping, 'Statement at the General Debate of the 75th United Nations General Assembly', *fmprc.gov.cn* (23 September 2020), accessed 11 April 2022.

80. Xi Jinping, '在浦东开发开放30周年庆祝大会上的讲话', *gov.cn* (12 November 2020), accessed 18 December 2023.
81. Xi Jinping, 'Keynote Speech by Chinese President Xi Jinping at APEC CEO Dialogues', *xinhuanet.com* (19 November 2020), accessed 2 February 2022.
82. Xi, '百年未有之大变局，总书记这些重要论述振聋发聩'.
83. Xi, 'Focus on Our Tasks—Bear in Mind the National Goal and Changing Conditions', in *The Governance of China*, Vol. 3.
84. Xinhua, '习近平在中共中央政治局第二十七次集体学习时强调 完整准确全面贯彻新发展理念 确保"十四五"时期我国发展开好局起好步', *xinhuanet.com* (29 January 2021), accessed 10 April 2022.
85. Xi Jinping, '习近平:在庆祝中国共产党成立100周年大会上的讲话'.

CHAPTER 10

1. Communiqué of the Fifth Plenum of the 19th Central Committee.
2. The literature on this includes: Dingding Chen and Jianwei Wang, 'Lying Low No More?', *China: An International Journal*, 9/2 (2011); Yan Xuetong, 'From Keeping a Low Profile to Striving for Achievement', *Chinese Journal of International Politics*, 7/2 (2014); Camilla T. N. Sørensen, 'The Significance of Xi Jinping's "Chinese Dream" for Chinese Foreign Policy', *Journal of China and International Relations*, 3/1 (2015); Jisi Wang, '中国的国际定位问题与 "韬光养晦, 有所作为" 的战略思想', 国际问题研究, 2 (2011).
3. Doshi, *The Long Game*, 59.
4. Doshi, *The Long Game*, 60.
5. Doshi, *The Long Game*, 61.
6. Doshi, *The Long Game*, 61–62.
7. Yan, 'From Keeping a Low Profile to Striving for Achievement'. See also: People's Daily, '习近平在周边外交工作座谈会上发表重要讲话强调 ：为我国发展争取良好周边环境', *cpc.people.com.cn* (26 October 2013), accessed 19 December 2023. See also: Kong Xuanyou, '习近平外交思想和中国周边外交理论与实践创新', *Qiushi*, no. *8* (2019).
8. Yan, 'From Keeping a Low Profile to Striving for Achievement', 160–82.
9. Taylor Fravel, 'Revising Deng's Foreign Policy', *thediplomat.com* (17 January 2012), accessed 19 December 2023. For Hu's original words, see Hu Jintao, '统筹国内国际两个大局提高外交工作能力水平', in 胡锦涛文选 第三卷 (Beijing: People's Publishing House, 2016), 234–46.
10. Doshi, *The Long Game*, 177.
11. Doshi, *The Long Game*, 160.
12. Yan, 'From Keeping a Low Profile to Striving for Achievement'.
13. '习近平接见2017年度驻外使节工作会议与会使节并发表重要讲话'.
14. China Cadre Learning Network, '习近平首提'两个引导'有深意', *politics.people.com.cn* (20 February 2017), accessed 7 March 2024.

15. Ministry of Foreign Affairs (PRC), 'The Central Conference on Work Relating to Foreign Affairs Was Held in Beijing' (2014); Xinhua, '习近平出席中央外事工作会议并发表重要讲话' (2014 CFEAC Readout), *People's Daily* (29 November 2014); Xinhua, 'Xi Eyes More Enabling Int'l Environment for China's Peaceful Development', all accessed 5 March 2024.
16. Xi's 'new era' for China's domestic political economy is discussed further in chapter 8.
17. Yan Xuetong, '阎学通教授：从韬光养晦到奋发有为，中国崛起势不可挡', *sss.tsinghua.edu.cn* (25 November 2013), accessed 26 December 2023.
18. Pang Zhongying, 'From Tao Guang Yang Hui to Xin Xing', *Trends in Southeast Asia*, no. 7 (2020), 12.
19. Jiang Zemin, 'The Present International Situation and Our Diplomatic Work', in *Selected Works of Jiang Zemin*, Vol. 2.
20. Xinhua, 'Xi Jinping: China to Further Friendly Relations with Neighboring Countries', *lk.china-embassy.org.cn* (28 October 2013), accessed 5 March 2024. See also: Xinhua, '习近平：让命运共同体意识在周边国家落地生根', *xinhuanet.com* (25 October 2013), accessed 12 February 2022; Ministry of Foreign Affairs (PRC), 'Xi Jinping: Let the Sense of Community of Common Destiny Take Deep Root in Neighbouring Countries', *christchurch.china-consulate.gov.cn* (25 October 2013), accessed 4 March 2024; Xi Jinping, 'Diplomacy with Neighboring Countries Characterized by Friendship, Sincerity, Reciprocity, and Inclusiveness', in *The Governance of China*, Vol. 1.
21. Nanfang Daily, '中国周边外交：推进大战略', *theory.people.com.cn* (28 October 2013), accessed 16 December 2023.
22. Xinhua, 'Xi Jinping: China to Further Friendly Relations with Neighboring Countries'.
23. Xinhua, 'Xi Jinping: China to Further Friendly Relations with Neighboring Countries'.
24. Xinhua, 'Xi Jinping: China to Further Friendly Relations with Neighboring Countries'.
25. '对那些长期对华友好而自身发展任务艰巨的周边和发展中国家，要更多考虑对方利益': Wang Yi, '王毅：坚持正确义利观 积极发挥负责任大国作用', *theory.people.com.cn*, accessed 12 December 2022.
26. Xinhua, 'Xi Jinping: China to Further Friendly Relations with Neighboring Countries'.
27. Xinhua, 'Xi Jinping: China to Further Friendly Relations with Neighboring Countries'.
28. For analyses of South China Sea policy under Hu Jintao, see: Mingjiang Li, 'China's Non-Confrontational Assertiveness in the South China Sea', *eastasiaforum.org* (14 June 2012), accessed 5 March 2024; Rush Doshi, 'Hu's to Blame for China's Foreign Assertiveness?', in *Global China* (Washington, DC: Brookings Institution, 2021).

29. The Spratly Islands, in the southern South China Sea, are: claimed entirely by China, Taiwan and Vietnam; claimed in part by the Philippines, Malaysia, and Brunei; and occupied in part by all of these countries except Brunei. For more information see: Ronald O'Rourke, *US-China Strategic Competition in South and East China Seas* (Washington, DC: Congressional Research Service, 2024).
30. Xi Jinping, 'New Asian Security Concept for New Progress in Security Cooperation', *en.chinadiplomacy.org.cn* (21 May 2014), accessed 14 February 2022.
31. Xi Jinping, '在庆祝中国人民解放军建军90周年大会上的讲话', *Qiushi*, no. 15 (2022).
32. Xinhua, 'Xi Jinping: China to Further Friendly Relations with Neighboring Countries'.
33. Xinhua, 'Xi Jinping: China to Further Friendly Relations with Neighboring Countries'.
34. Doshi, *The Long Game*, 169, 179.
35. Xu Jin and Du Zheyuan, 'The Dominant Thinking Sets in Chinese Foreign Policy Research', *Chinese Journal of International Politics*, 8/3 (2015), 277.
36. Dai Bingguo, 'Remarks by H.E. Dai Bingguo State Councilor of the People's Republic of China at the Opening Session of the First Round of the China-US Strategic and Economic Dialogues', *tl.china-embassy.gov.cn* (28 July 2009), accessed 5 March 2024.
37. Hu Jintao, '胡锦涛在第四轮中美战略与经济对话开幕式上的致辞', *gov.cn* (3 May 2012), accessed 15 February 2022.
38. Hu, Report to 18th Party Congress.
39. Ministry of Foreign Affairs (PRC), 'Vice-President Xi Jinping Attends the Welcome Luncheon Hosted by the U.S. Friendly Groups and Delivers a Speech', *us.china-embassy.gov.cn* (16 February 2012), accessed 5 March 2024.
40. Wang Yi, 'Exploring the Path of Major-Country Diplomacy with Chinese Characteristics', *mfa.gov.cn* (27 June 2013), accessed 5 March 2024.
41. Wang, 'Exploring the Path of Major-Country Diplomacy'.
42. Wang Yi, 'Toward a New Model of Major-Country Relations between China and the United States', *brookings.edu* (20 September 2013), accessed 16 December 2023.
43. Yang Jiechi, 'Innovations in China's Diplomatic Theory and Practice under New Conditions', *Qiushi*, no. *16* (2013).
44. Yang, 'Innovations in China's Diplomatic Theory and Practice'.
45. Yang, 'Innovations in China's Diplomatic Theory and Practice'.
46. Yang, 'Innovations in China's Diplomatic Theory and Practice'.
47. Xinhua, 2014 CFEAC Readout.
48. Michael D. Swaine, 'Xi Jinping's Address to the Central Conference on Work Relating to Foreign Affairs', *China Leadership Monitor*, no. *46* (2015).
49. Xinhua, 2014 CFEAC Readout. For more remarks on this by Xi, see: Xinhua, '从"两个大局"把握重要战略机遇期新变化新特征', *xinhuanet.com*

(31 October 2020), accessed 14 February 2022; Haiqing Li, '我国发展仍然处于重要战略机遇期', *Red Flag*, no. 22 (2020).

50. Xinhua, 2014 CFEAC Readout.
51. Xinhua, 2014 CFEAC Readout.
52. Xinhua, 2014 CFEAC Readout.
53. Xinhua, 2014 CFEAC Readout.
54. Xinhua, 2014 CFEAC Readout.
55. Yang Jiechi, 'Deepen the Promotion of Foreign Affairs Work in the New Era Guided by Xi Jinping Thought on Diplomacy', *interpret.csis.org* (1 August 2018), accessed 5 March 2024.
56. Yang, 'Deepen the Promotion of Foreign Affairs Work'.
57. See: Stephen S. Roach, *Frayed Relations*, C.V. Starr and Co. Annual Lecture on China, Council on Foreign Relations (13 February 2023), accessed 5 March 2024.
58. Yan, 'From Keeping a Low Profile to Striving for Achievement', 168.
59. Yang Jiechi, 'Following the Guidance of Xi Jinping Thought on Diplomacy to Advance Diplomatic Work in the New Era (Excerpt)', *dm.china-embassy.gov.cn* (1 September 2018), accessed 5 March 2024.
60. Yang Jiechi, '在习近平外交思想指引下奋力推进中国特色大国外交', *cpc.people.com.cn* (2 September 2019), accessed 19 December 2023. See also: Ministry of Foreign Affairs (PRC), 'Advancing China's Major-Country Diplomacy under the Guidance of Xi Jinping Thought on Foreign Affairs', *vu.china-embassy.gov.cn* (3 September 2019), accessed 5 March 2024.
61. Yang, '在习近平外交思想指引下奋力推进中国特色大国外交'.
62. See, e.g.: Wei Du, '2014: A Year of Turbulence in Global Landscape and Adjustment in International System', *Foreign Affairs Journal*, no. 15 (2014).
63. Tony Louthan, 'State Media's Masterful Memes on the Alaska Summit', *chinatalk.media* (23 March 2021), accessed 5 March 2024.
64. Antony Blinken, Jake Sullivan, Wang Yi, and Yang Jiechi, 'How It Happened: Transcript of the US-China Opening Remarks in Alaska', *asia.nikkei.com* (19 March 2021), accessed 15 February 2022.
65. Blinken, Sullivan, Wang, and Yang, 'How It Happened: Transcript'.
66. See, e.g.: Niu Tanqin, '中美阿拉斯加对话，这十个细节非同寻常', *news.sina.cn* (20 March 2021); Huoxing Fang Zhen, '阿拉斯加会谈清楚地表明：中国对美国展开正式反击', *new.qq.com* (19 March 2021); Phoenix New Media, '凤凰记者亲历中美交锋现场，杨洁篪据理力争：美方为何怕记者在场?', *news.ifeng.com* (19 March 2021); '杨洁篪这段话，太硬气了！', *sohu.com* (19 March 2021); Xi'an Polytechnic University, '外交官的硬气依托的是祖国的实力——我校举办第42期共读一本书《李鸿章传》阅读交流会', *xpu.edu.cn* (29 March 2021), all accessed 15 February 2022.
67. Xinhua, 2014 CFEAC Readout.
68. Kevin Rudd, *US-China 21* (Cambridge: Belfer Center for Science and International Affairs, 2015), 23–24.

69. White House (US), *National Security Strategy of the United States of America*, trumpwhitehouse.archives.gov (December 2017), accessed 19 December 2023.
70. E.g., Deng said in 1989: "After years of struggle, the international situation is becoming more relaxed, and a world war can be avoided." See 'Maintain the Tradition of Hard Struggle', in *Selected Works of Deng Xiaoping*, Vol. 3.
71. Information Office of the State Council (PRC), 'China's Peaceful Development', *english.gov.cn* (6 September 2011), accessed 6 March 2024.
72. Doshi, *The Long Game*, 211.
73. '合作共赢，就是要倡导人类命运共同体意识，在追求本国利益时兼顾他国合理关切，在谋求本国发展中促进各国共同发展，建立更加平等均衡的新型全球发展伙伴关系，同舟共济，权责共担，增进人类共同利益'; Hu, Report to the 18th Party Congress.
74. Wang Yi, 'Speech by Foreign Minister Wang Yi at the Opening of Symposium on International Developments and China's Diplomacy in 2017', *fmprc.gov.cn* (10 December 2017), accessed 16 December 2023.
75. Ministry of Foreign Affairs (PRC), 'Xi Jinping Holds Discussion Meeting with Foreign Experts', *ag.china-embassy.gov.cn* (5 December 2012), accessed 6 March 2024; Xi Jinping, 'Follow the Trend of the Times and Promote Global Peace and Development', in *The Governance of China*, Vol. 1.
76. Xi Jinping, 'Towards a Community of Common Destiny and a New Future for Asia', *xinhuanet.com* (28 March 2015), accessed 17 February 2022.
77. Xi Jinping, 'Working Together to Create a New Mutually Beneficial Partnership and Community of Shared Future for Mankind', *en.chinadiplomacy.org.cn* (28 September 2015), accessed 12 April 2022.
78. Xi Jinping, 'Work Together to Build a Community of Shared Future for Mankind', *en.chinadiplomacy.org.cn* (18 January 2017), accessed 12 April 2022.
79. Xi, Report to the 19th Party Congress.
80. 'Amendment of National People's Congress of the People's Republic of China', National People's Congress (PRC), *en.npc.gov.cn* (11 March 2018); Xinhua, 'Full Text of Resolution on Amendment to CPC Constitution', *xinhuanet.com* (24 October 2017), both accessed 6 March 2024.
81. Xi's quotations on CCD are published in annual collations. See: Xi Jinping, '习近平论人类命运共同体', *cidca.gov.cn* (2012–2021), accessed 6 March 2024.
82. Xi, Report to the 19th Party Congress.
83. Han Zhenfeng, '中国梦是中华民族近代以来最伟大的梦想', *qstheory.cn* (undated), accessed 7 March 2024.
84. Xi Jinping, 'Towards a Community of Common Destiny and a New Future for Asia'.
85. Yang Jiechi, 'Firmly Uphold and Practice Multilateralism and Build a Community with a Shared Future for Mankind', *global.chinadaily.com.cn* (22 February 2021), accessed 6 March 2024.
86. Yang Jiechi, '杨洁篪在人民日报撰文谈构建人类命运共同体', *gov.cn* (19 November 2017), accessed 6 March 2024. Senior diplomats also began

using this formulation at the same time, tracing its origins to the 19th Party Congress. See also: Propaganda Department of the CCP, 《习近平新时代中国特色社会主义思想基本问题》, 36

87. People's Daily, '十七、推动构建人类命运共同体', *theory.people.com.cn* (14 August 2019), accessed 11 March 2024.
88. Zheng Yongnian, '塑造更加公正合理的国际新秩序', *xinhuanet.com* (4 May 2017), accessed 17 February 2022; Xi Jinping, 'Hand in Hand toward a Community of Shared Development', *english.news.cn* (2 August 2023), accessed 6 March 2024.
89. Chris Buckley, ' "Uncle Xi" to Exalted Ruler: China's Leader Embodies His Authoritarian Era', *nytimes.com* (14 October 2022), accessed 6 March 2024.
90. Fu Ying, 'The US World Order Is a Suit That No Longer Fits', *ft.com* (6 January 2016), accessed 17 February 2022.
91. Yang, '杨洁篪在人民日报撰文谈构建人类命运共同体'.
92. Xi, Report to the 19th Party Congress.
93. Xi, 'Work Together to Build a Community of Shared Future for Mankind'.
94. Xi, 'Towards a Community of Common Destiny and a New Future for Asia'.
95. Xi, 'Towards a Community of Common Destiny and a New Future for Asia'.
96. Xi, Report to the 19th Party Congress.
97. Xi Jinping, 'Forging a Strong Partnership to Enhance Prosperity of Asia', *fmprc.gov.cn* (7 November 2015), accessed 17 December 2023.
98. Xi Jinping, 'Working Together to Forge a New Partnership of Win-Win Cooperation and Create a Community of Shared Future for Mankind', *gadebate.un.org* (28 September 2015).
99. Xi Jinping, 'President Xi's New Year Address', *news.cgtn.com* (31 December 2017), accessed 22 March 2024; Ministry of Foreign Affairs (PRC), 'Yang Jiechi Meets Respectively with BRICS High Representatives for Security Issues of South Africa, Brazil, and India', *fmprc.gov.cn* (27 July 2017), both accessed 6 March 2024.
100. Blinken, Sullivan, Wang, and Yang, 'How It Happened: Transcript'.
101. Xinhua, 'Xi Calls for More Just, Equitable World Order at BRICS Forum', *english.news.cn* (23 August 2023), accessed 6 March 2024.
102. Xi Jinping, 'Openness for Greater Prosperity, Innovation for a Better Future', *us.china-embassy.gov.cn* (10 April 2018), accessed 6 March 2024.
103. Yang Jiechi, '杨洁篪在人民日报撰文谈构建人类命运共同体'.
104. Xun Qingshi, '理解人类命运共同体的三个重要层面', *theory.people.com.cn* (15 August 2017), accessed 17 February 2022.
105. China Institute of International Studies, '习近平外交思想研究中心成立仪式成功举行', *ciis.org.cn* (21 July 2020), accessed 19 December 2023.
106. See: Richard McGregor and Neil Thomas, 'China's Great Foreign Policy Shake-Up', *afr.com* (7 July 2022), accessed 6 March 2024.
107. See relevant secondary analyses: Nathan and Zhang, 'A Shared Future for Mankind'; Steve Tsang and Olivia Cheung, 'Uninterrupted Rise', *The Asan Forum*, 9/2 (2021); John Garnaut, 'Engineers of the Soul', *sinocism.*

com (17 January 2019), accessed 22 March 2024; Alice Miller, 'Xi Jinping and the Party's "Guiding Ideology"'; Willy Wo-Lap Lam, 'What Is Xi Jinping Thought?', *China Brief*, 17/12 (2017); Kjeld Erik Brødsgaard, 'China's Political Order under Xi Jinping', *China: An International Journal*, 16/3 (2018); Ondřej Klimeš and Maurizio Marinelli, 'Introduction', *Journal of Chinese Political Science*, 23 (2018); Andreas Møller Mulvad, 'Xiism as a Hegemonic Project in the Making', *Review of International Studies*, 45/3 (2019); Kalpana Misra, *Rethinking Marxism in Post-Mao China* (Ann Arbor: University of Michigan Press, 1992); Su Xiaobo, 'Revolution and Reform', *Journal of Contemporary China*, 20/69 (2011); Shanding Zhou, *Changes of the Chinese Communist Party's Ideology and Reform since 1978* (Brisbane: Griffith University, 2012); Brown and Bērziņa-Čerenkova, 'Ideology in the Era of Xi Jinping'; Chris Buckley, 'Xi Jinping Thought Explained', *nytimes.com* (26 February 2018), accessed 22 March 2024; The Economist, 'The Meaning of the Man behind China's Ideology', *economist.com* (2 November 2017), accessed 22 March 2024; Jessica Batke, 'The National People's Congress in 2017', *China Leadership Monitor*, 53 (2017); Yan Xuetong, 'Chinese Values vs Liberalism', *Chinese Journal of International Politics*, 11/1 (2018); Andrew J. Nathan, 'The New Ideology', *New Republic* (6 December 2012). See further references in Bibliography.

108. See, e.g.: Xi, 'Bicentenary of the Birth of Marx'.
109. Xi, Report to the 19th Party Congress.
110. Yang Jiechi:, '杨洁篪：推动构建人类命运共同体 共同建设更加美好的世界', *aisixiang.com* (18 January 2021), accessed 6 March 2024.
111. Yang Jiechi, '杨洁篪：推动构建人类命运共同体 共同建设更加美好的世界'.
112. E.g.: Xinhua, 'Chinese Landmark Concept Put into UN Resolution for First Time', *xinhuanet.com* (11 February 2017), accessed 7 March 2024.

CHAPTER 11

1. See: Alastair Iain Johnston, 'How New and Assertive Is China's New Assertiveness', *Quarterly Journal: International Security*, 37/4 (2013); Dingding Chen, Xiaoyu Pu, and Alastair Iain Johnston, 'Debating China's Assertiveness'; Michael Yahuda, 'China's New Assertiveness in the South China Sea', *Journal of Contemporary China*, 22/81 (2013); Kai He and Huiyun Feng, 'Xi Jinping's Operational Code Beliefs and China's Foreign Policy', *Chinese Journal of International Politics*, 6/3 (2013); Oriana Skylar Mastro, 'Why Chinese Assertiveness Is Here to Stay', *Washington Quarterly*, 37/4 (2014); Merriden Varrall, *Chinese Worldviews and China's Foreign Policy* (Sydney: Lowy Institute: 2015); Nien-Chung Chang Liao, 'The Sources of China's Assertiveness'; Peter Ferdinand, 'Westward Ho—The China Dream and "One Belt, One Road"', *International Affairs*, 92/4 (2016); Hoo Tiang Boon, 'Hardening the Hard, Softening the Soft', *Journal of*

Strategic Studies, 40/5 (2017); Stephen N. Smith, 'Community of Common Destiny', *International Journal*, 73/3 (2018); Pu Xiaoyu and Wang Chengli, 'Rethinking China's Rise', *International Affairs*, 94/5 (2018); Jaebeom Kwon, 'The Turn of the Tide', *International Relations*, 7/2 (2019); Andrew Chubb, 'Assessing Public Opinion's Influence on Foreign Policy', *Asian Security*, 15/2 (2019); Andrew Chubb, 'PRC Assertiveness in the South China Sea', *International Security*, 45/3 (2020); Liu Feng, 'The Recalibration of Chinese Assertiveness', *International Affairs*, 96, no. 1 (2020); Andrew Yeo, 'China's Rising Assertiveness and the Decline in the East Asian Regionalism Narrative', *International Relations of the Asia-Pacific*, 20/3 (2020); Avery Goldstein, 'China's Grand Strategy under Xi Jinping'. Camilla T. N. Sørensen, 'The Roots of China's Assertiveness in East Asia', *Copenhagen Journal of Asian Studies*, 39/2 (2021); Rush Doshi, *The Long Game*; Jessica Chen Weiss, 'China's Self-Defeating Nationalism—Brazen Diplomacy and Rhetorical Bluster Undercut Beijing's Influence', *foreignaffairs.com* (16 July 2020), accessed 17 December 2023; Peter Martin, 'Why China Is Alienating the World', *foreignaffairs.com* (6 October 2021), accessed 11 April 2022. See also a quite relevant joint report by joint task force of the Asia Society and UCSD co-chaired by Orville Schell and Susan Shirk, *China's New Direction* (La Jolla: UC San Diego School of Global Policy and Strategy, 2021).

2. Yuji Nitta, 'South Korea's Lotte Opens Hanoi Mall in Vietnam Investment Drive', *asia.nikkei.com* (22 September 2023), accessed 19 December 2023.
3. Ministry of National Defense (ROC), 'PLA Activities in the Waters and Airspace around Taiwan', mnd.gov.tw (various dates), accessed 15 March 2024. Figure for 2019 is approximate.
4. Data from Ministry of Defense (Japan), 'Statistics on Scrambles', mod.go.jp (various dates), accessed 15 March 2024.
5. Data from CSIS China Power, 'Are Maritime Law Enforcement Forces Destabilizing Asia?', *chinapower.csis.org* (4 March 2024); Japan Coast Guard, 'The Numbers of China Coast Guard and Other Vessels That Entered Japan's Contiguous Zone or Intruded into Territorial Sea Surrounding the Senkaku Islands', *kaiho.mlit.go.jp* (undated), both accessed 19 March 2024.
6. Data from CSIS China Power and Japan Coast Guard.
7. Military expenditure measured in US dollars (current). US treaty allies are: Australia, Japan, the Philippines, Thailand, and South Korea. Data from SIPRI, 'SIPRI Military Expenditure Database', *milex.sipri.org* (2024).
8. Rounded to nearest hundred. Data from Good Car Bad Car, 'Brand Sales (by Market)', *goodcarbadcar.net* (undated), accessed 15 March 2024.
9. Rounded to nearest hundred. Data from Good Car Bad Car, 'Brand Sales (by Market)'.
10. From interview with Ambassador A.
11. From interview with Ambassador A.
12. From interview with Ambassador A.

13. From interview with Ambassador A.
14. From interview with Ambassador B.
15. From interview with Ambassador D.
16. From interview with Ambassador D.
17. From interview with Ambassador D.
18. From interview with Ambassador E.
19. From interview with Ambassador E.
20. From interview with Ambassador E.
21. 'P5' is an abbreviation of the 'Permanent 5' members of the Security Council: China, France, Russia, the UK, and the United States.
22. From interview with Ambassador C.
23. From interview with Ambassador E.
24. From interview with Ambassador C.
25. Ted Piccone, 'China's Long Game on Human Rights at the United Nations' (New York: Brookings Institution, 2018).
26. From interview with Ambassador A.
27. From interview with Ambassador A.
28. The UN Charter reads at article 1, section 4: "All Members shall refrain in their international relations from the threat or use of force against the territorial integrity or political independence of any state, or in any other manner inconsistent with the Purposes of the United Nations." See United Nations, *Charter of the United Nations and Statute of the International Court of Justice* (San Francisco: United Nations, 1945).
29. From interview with Ambassador B.
30. From interview with Ambassador C.
31. From interview with Ambassador F.
32. From interview with Ambassador C.
33. From interview with Ambassador C.
34. From interview with Ambassador D.
35. From interview with Ambassador D.
36. From interview with Ambassador E.
37. From interview with Ambassador E.
38. From interview with Ambassador E.
39. China was the tenth-largest government donor to the UN system overall in 2015, but ranked thirty-third in donations to the UNHCR. Data from UN Transparency Portal, 'How Is the UN System Funded?', *open.un.org* (undated), accessed 22 March 2024.
40. From interview with Ambassador A.
41. From interview with Ambassador C.
42. Zeid Ra'ad al-Hussein, 'Opening Statement', *ohchr.org* (11 September 2017), accessed 22 March 2024.
43. From interview with Ambassador F.
44. From interview with Ambassador F.

45. From interview with Ambassador F.
46. From interview with Ambassador F.
47. From interview with Ambassador C.
48. From interview with Ambassador C.
49. Courtney J. Fung, 'China's Small Steps into UN Peacekeeping Are Adding Up', *theglobalobservatory.org* (24 May 2023), accessed 22 March 2024.
50. From interview with Ambassador A.
51. From interview with Ambassador A.
52. Xinhua, 'Chinese Outcome List of the Meeting between the Chinese and U.S. Presidents in Hangzhou', *china.org.cn* (4 September 2016), accessed 22 March 2024.
53. Xinhua: 'Chinese Outcome List'.
54. From interview with Ambassador A.
55. From interview with Ambassador B.
56. From interview with Ambassador C.
57. The International Conference on the Great Lakes Region is composed of Angola, Burundi, Central African Republic, Republic of Congo, Democratic Republic of Congo, Kenya, Uganda, Rwanda, South Sudan, Sudan, Tanzania, and Zambia.
58. From interview with Ambassador C.
59. From interview with Ambassador C.
60. At the UN General Assembly in 2015, Xi announced "China's decision to establish a ten-year, US$1 billion China-UN peace and development fund to support the UN's work, advance multilateral cooperation, and contribute more to world peace and development". See: Xi, 'Working Together to Forge a New Partnership'.
61. From interview with Ambassador C.
62. UNPDF's guidelines are published online: *https://un.org/unpdf.*
63. From interview with Ambassador D. In a 2018 interview, Hu Wongbo said: "All international civil servants have their nationalities, but it doesn't mean we neglect the interests of our countries. . . . I don't yield in the matters concerning Chinese national sovereignty and security interests and resolutely defend the interests of the motherland." See The Voice, '前联合国副秘书长吴红波：优秀的外交官要有强烈的爱国心和进取精神', *youtube.com* (23 December 2018), accessed 7 March 2024.
64. From interview with Ambassador D.
65. From interview with Ambassador D.
66. From interview with Ambassador E.
67. From interview with Ambassador E.
68. From interview with Ambassador B.
69. From interview with Ambassador B.
70. From interview with Ambassador D.
71. From interview with Ambassador D.

72. From interview with Ambassador D.
73. From interview with Ambassador D.
74. The five regional groups are: African, Asia-Pacific, Eastern European, Latin American and Caribbean, and Western European and Others.
75. Vladimir Putin and Xi Jinping, 'Joint Statement of the Russian Federation and the People's Republic of China on the International Relations Entering a New Era and the Global Sustainable Development', *en.kremlin.ru* (4 February 2022), accessed 7 March 2024.
76. Bailiang Chu, '「東升西降」:習近平的後疫情時代中國崛起藍圖', *cn.nytimes.com* (4 March 2021), accessed 7 March 2024.
77. Xinhua, 'Chinese Landmark Concept Put into UN Resolution for First Time'.
78. Devirupa Mitra, 'Explained: Why India Joined the West to Object to a Phrase in the Final UN75 Declaration', *thewire.in* (30 June 2020), accessed 7 March 2024.

CHAPTER 12

1. References in this chapter are to the 'Resolution of the CPC Central Committee on the Major Achievements and Historical Experience of the Party over the Past Century' (Third Historical Resolution).
2. National Congress of the CCP, 'Resolution of the 19th National Congress of the Communist Party of China on the Report of the 18th Central Committee', *xinhuanet.com* (24 October 2017), accessed 8 March 2024.
3. Qian Gang, 'China Discourse Report: What Was Hot-and-Not in 2018 Political Terminology', *hongkongfp.com* (4 January 2019), accessed 11 April 2022.
4. Qian, 'China Discourse Report'.
5. John Garrick and Yan Chang Bennett, 'Xi Jinping Thought', *China Perspectives*, no. 1–2 (2018), 99.
6. Also called the 'Four-Pronged Strategy', the 'Four Comprehensives' outlined in December 2014 were: comprehensively building a moderately well-off society; comprehensively deepening reform; comprehensively implementing the rule of law; and comprehensively strengthening party discipline. See Xinhua, '习总书记首谈'四个全面'意味着什么', *xinhuanet.com* (16 December 2014), accessed 17 December 2023.
7. Brown and Bērziņa-Čerenkova, 'Ideology in the Era of Xi Jinping'.
8. 'Resolution on Certain Questions in the History of Our Party' (First Historical Resolution, 1945), in *Selected Works of Mao Tse-Tung*, Vol. 3 (Paris: Foreign Languages Press, 2021).
9. Second Historical Resolution, 1981.
10. Stanley Kubrick, Terry Southern, and Peter George, 'Dr Strangelove', *indiegroundfilms.files.wordpress.com* (1963), 53–89, accessed 17 January 2024.
11. Barbara Demick, 'China's Xi More Maoist than Reformer Thus Far', *latimes.com* (8 June 2013), accessed 11 April 2022.

12. Brown and Bērziņa-Čerenkova, 'Ideology in the Era of Xi Jinping', 330
13. Qian, 'China Discourse Report'.
14. Manoranjan Mohanty, 'The New Ideological Banner', *China Report*, 34/1 (1998), 101.
15. The forty references to 'Marxism' include those to Marxism-Leninism.
16. Xi, Report to the 19th Party Congress.
17. E.g., the Third Historical Resolution's lengthy section on 'The CCP in the New Era' mentions 'reform and opening' only twice, stating in passing: "We should deepen reform and opening up across the board" and "will rise to the tests facing the party in . . . reform and opening up".
18. See Central Committee of the CCP, '中国共产党第十一届中央委员会第三次全体会议公报', *cpc.people.com.cn* (22 December 1978); Central Committee of the CCP, 'Communiqué of the Third Plenary Session of the 18th Central Committee of the Communist Party of China', *china.org.cn* (2013), accessed 10 March 2024.
19. Xi, Report to the 19th Party Congress.
20. Xi, Report to the 19th Party Congress. See further: National People's Congress, '全过程人民民主，习近平向世界讲述民主的"中国叙事"', *npc.gov.cn* (22 October 2021), accessed 10 March 2021.
21. For perspectives on 'intra-party democracy' see: Yuan Zaijun, *The Failure of China's Democratic Reforms* (Lanham, MD: Lexington Books, 2012), accessed 10 March 2024; Guo Dinping, 'The Growth of Intra-party Democracy and Its Implications for China's Democratic Future', *Fudan Journal of the Humanities and Social Sciences*, 7/1 (2014).
22. Xi, Report to the 19th Party Congress.
23. See Ji Fengyuan, *Linguistic Engineering* (Honolulu: University of Hawai'i Press, 2004) 178.
24. E.g., see: Deng Xiaoping, 'On the Reform of the System of Party and State Leadership'; Jiang, Report to the 16th Party Congress; Willy Wo-Lap Lam, 'Chinks in the Armour of the Hu Jintao Administration', *China Perspectives*, no. 3 (2007), 6.

CHAPTER 13

1. See: Angel Paternina-Caicedo et al., 'Effectiveness of CoronaVac and BNT162b2 COVID-19 Mass Vaccination in Colombia', *The Lancet Regional Health–Americas*, 12/100296 (2022).
2. Public opinion surveys showed China's standing substantially improved in several countries that received vaccines. E.g.: in Kenya, China's net favourability rose from 19% in 2021 to 66% in 2022; and, in Egypt, it rose from 10% to 31%. Data from YouGov Cambridge, 'Globalism 2022', *docs.cdn.yougov.com* (2022), accessed 10 March 2024.
3. See: Thomas Shattuck, 'One Year Later', *Global Taiwan Brief*, 8/18 (2023).

4. See: Jim Garamone, 'F-22 Safely Shoots Down Chinese Spy Balloon off South Carolina Coast', *defense.gov* (4 February 2023).
5. Third Historical Resolution, 1981.
6. National Congress of the CCP, 'Full Text of Resolution on Party Constitution Amendment', *gov.cn* (October 2022), accessed 10 March 2024.
7. Unless otherwise specified, references in this section are to: Xi Jinping, '更好把握和运用党的百年奋斗历史经验', *Qiushi,* no. 13 (2022). See also: Xi Jinping, 'Adapt Marxism to China's Realities and Keep It Up-to-Date', in *The Governance of China*, Vol. 4.
8. See, e.g.: Deng Xiaoping, 'Talks in Wuchang, Shenzhen, Shuhai, and Shanghai'.
9. Mao, 'On Contradiction', 77.
10. Second Historical Resolution, 1981.
11. See: Mao Zedong, 'Conclusion at the Seventh National Congress of the Chinese Communist Party', in *Mao's Road to Power*, Vol. 8 (New York: Routledge, 2015).
12. Xi Jinping, '全面从严治党探索出依靠党的自我革命跳出历史周期率的成功路径', *Qiushi*, no. 3 (2023), accessed 13 December 2023. See also: Xi Jinping, 'Make Further Progress in Party Self-Governance', in *The Governance of China*, Vol. 4.
13. Xi Jinping, '全面从严治党探索出依靠党的自我革命跳出历史周期率的成功路径'.
14. Xi Jinping, 'The Correct Understanding of Major Theoretical and Practical Problems of China's Development', *CSIS Interpret* (15 May 2022), accessed 10 March 2024.
15. Xi, 'The Correct Understanding of Major Theoretical and Practical Problems of China's Development'.
16. Xi, 'The Correct Understanding of Major Theoretical and Practical Problems of China's Development'.
17. Xi, 'The Correct Understanding of Major Theoretical and Practical Problems of China's Development'.
18. Xi Jinping, '坚定不移走中国人权发展道路，更好推动我国人权事业发展', *Qiushi*, no. 12 (2022). See also: Xi Jinping, 'Steadfastly Following the Chinese Path to Promote Further Progress in Human Rights', *en.qstheory.cn* (14 September 2022), accessed 10 March 2024.
19. Xi, '坚定不移走中国人权发展道路，更好推动我国人权事业发展'. See also: Karl Marx, *Critique of the Gotha Program* (Paris: Foreign Languages Press, 2021), 16; and Nikolai Ivanovich Bukharin, 'Marx's Teaching and Its Historical Importance', in *Marxism and Modern Thought* (New York: Harcourt, Brace, 1935), 14
20. Xi, '坚定不移走中国人权发展道路, 更好推动我国人权事业发展'.
21. Xi, '坚定不移走中国人权发展道路, 更好推动我国人权事业发展'.

22. E.g.: Ren Zhongping, 'Keeping Original Aspiration, CPC Creates Glorious Achievements', *en.people.cn* (30 September 2019); Jiang Jinquan, 'The Great Changes in the First Decade of the New Era', *en.qstheory.cn* (2 March 2023); Jiang Jianguo, 'Promoting and Practicing and Contemporary Chinese Perspective on Human Rights', *en.qstheory.cn* (5 January 2024), all accessed 22 March 2024.
23. Xinhua, 'Xi says Chinese Are People with Great Spirit of Struggle', *xinhuanet.com* (20 March 2018), accessed 10 March 2024.
24. Xi, Report to the 20th Party Congress.
25. Xi, Report to the 20th Party Congress.
26. National Congress of the CCP, 'Full Text of Resolution on Party Constitution Amendment'.
27. Xi, Report to the 20th Party Congress.
28. Xi, Report to the 20th Party Congress. According to the 19th Plenum of the 19th Central Committee, the CCP "has led the people in great endeavors and accumulated valuable historical experience over the past century. This covers the following ten aspects: upholding the Party's leadership, putting the people first, advancing theoretical innovation, staying independent, following the Chinese path, maintaining a global vision, breaking new ground, standing up for ourselves, promoting the united front, and remaining committed to self-reform. These ten points represent valuable practical experience gained over the long term and intellectual treasures created through the joint efforts of the Party and the people. All of us must cherish them, uphold them over the long term, and continue to enrich and develop them in practice in the new era." The '14 commitments' are to: "Ensure Party leadership over all work; commit to a people-centred approach; continue to comprehensively deepen reform; adopt a new vision for development; see that the people run the country; ensure every dimension of governance is law-based; uphold core socialist values; ensure and improve living standards through development; ensure harmony between human and nature; pursue a holistic approach to national security; uphold absolute Party leadership over the people's forces; uphold the principle of 'one country, two systems' and promote national reunification; promote the building of a community with a shared future for mankind; and exercise full and rigorous governance over the Party." The '13 areas of achievement' are: "upholding the Party's overall leadership; exercising full and rigorous self-governance; pursuing economic development; deepening reform and opening up; advancing political work; comprehensively advancing law-based governance; driving cultural advancement; promoting social advancement; spurring ecological advancement; strengthening national defense and the armed forces; safeguarding national security; upholding the One Country, Two Systems policy and promoting national reunification; and bolstering the diplomatic front". See: Han Zhengfen, '全面学习领会习近平新时代中国特色社会主义思想', *dangjian.com* (12 April 2023), accessed 10 March 2024.

29. Xi, Report to the 20th Party Congress.
30. See: Deng Xiaoping, 'A Letter to the Political Bureau of the Central Committee of the Communist Party of China', in *Selected Works of Deng Xiaoping*, Vol. 3.
31. E.g., see: Xi Jinping, '习近平：坚持自我革命，确保党不变质、不变色、不变味', *people.com.cn* (23 January 2022); Xinhua, '习近平在二十届中央纪委二次全会上发表重要讲话', *gov.cn* (2023); Anhui Theory, '习近平总书记强调的'红色基因, *ll.anhuinews.com* (6 May 2023); Xinhua, '习近平在中共中央政治局第九次集体学习时强调 铸牢中华民族共同体意识 推进新时代党的民族工作高质量发展', *people.com.cn* (28 October 2023), all accessed 11 March 2024.
32. Xi, Report to the 20th Party Congress.
33. China Central Television, '大型电视专题片《领航》', *tv.cctv.com* (25 June 2023), accessed 11 March 2024.
34. See: People's Daily, '引领—从党的二十大看中国共产党的成功密码之一', *dangjian.people.com.cn* (21 December 2022), accessed 11 March 2024. See also: Xinhua, '习近平：切实贯彻落实新时代党的组织路线 全党努力把党建设得更加坚强有力', *gov.cn* (4 July 2018), accessed 11 March 2024; Delia Lin and Susan Trevaskes, 'Law-Morality Ideology in the Xi Jinping Era', in *Law and the Party in China* (Cambridge: Cambridge University Press, 2020), 139.
35. BBC News, '习近平强调"定于一尊"是背离正统还是警告讯号', *bbc.com* (20 July 2018), accessed 11 March 2024.
36. David L. Bandurski and Yang Chu, 'China's Political Discourse September 2023', *sinocism.com* (30 November 2023), accessed 22 March 2024. See also: People's Daily, '人民日报评论部：坚持党的全面领导是坚持和发展中国特色社会主义的必由之路—更加坚定走'必由之路'的自信①', *12371.cn* (15 March 2022).
37. Xi Jinping, 'Keep Matters of National Significance to the Fore', in *The Governance of China*, Vol. 4.
38. Xi Jinping, 'Strengthen Commitment to the Four Consciousnesses, the Four-Sphere Confidence and the Two Upholds', 2017–2019, in *The Governance of China*, Vol. 3.
39. National Congress of the CCP, 'Full Text of Resolution on Party Constitution Amendment'.
40. E.g.: Xi Jinping, '二、坚持党的全面领导—心怀'国之大者'，切实把增强'四个意识'、坚定'四个自信'、做到'两个维护'落到行动上', *ndrc.gov.cn* (30 December 2022), accessed 11 March 2024.
41. Party Congress reports are published on the *People's Daily* website.
42. Zhong Zhengsheng, 'Plenty of Room for Policy Adjustment Going Forward', *chinadaily.com.cn* (12 December 2022), accessed 22 March 2024.
43. Xi, Report to the 20th Party Congress.
44. Xi, Report to the 20th Party Congress.
45. See: Maia Nikoladze and Mrugank Bhusari, 'Russia and China Have Been Teaming Up to Reduce Reliance on the Dollar. Here's How It's Going', *atlanticcouncil.org* (22 February 2023), accessed 11 March 2024.

46. Xi Jinping, '中国式现代化是强国建设、民族复兴的康庄大道', *Qiushi*, no. 16 (2023). See also: Edwin Ong, 'Politics Takes Precedence over Economy in Xi's Chinese-Style Modernization', *thinkchina.sg* (17 August 2023); Qin Gang, 'Chinese Modernization', *mfa.gov.cn* (21 April 2023), both accessed 11 March 2024.
47. See, e.g.: Xi Jinping, 'Major Issues in Economic Work', *en.qstheory.cn* (4 May 2023); Verna Yu, 'China Crackdown on Business Has Maoist Roots', *theguardian.com* (21 May 2023); Amy Hawkins, 'British Private Schools in China under Threat as New "Patriotic" Law Comes In', *theguardian.com* (31 December 2023), all accessed 11 March 2024.
48. See: Edward Luce and Chris Miller, 'The Risks of US-China Decoupling', *ft.com* (10 February 2024), accessed 11 March 2024
49. Xi Jinping, '十九大报告:决胜全面建成小康社会 夺取新时代中国特色社会主义伟大胜利——. 在中国共产党第十九次全国代表大会上的报告', *gov.cn* (18 October 2017), accessed 22 March 2024.
50. E.g., in 2017, Xi Jinping said: "China is still in an important period of strategic opportunity for development". In 2012, Hu Jintao said: "China remains in an important period of strategic opportunities".
51. Xi, Report to the 20th Party Congress. A 'grey rhino' is a "highly probable, high impact yet neglected threat . . . not random surprises, but [they] occur after a series of warnings and visible evidence": Kelsey Munro, 'China Cabinet: Black Swans, Grey Rhinos, an Elephant in the Room', *lowyinstitute.org* (24 January 2019), accessed 11 March 2024.
52. Xi, Report to the 20th Party Congress.
53. See Xi, Report to the 19th Party Congress; Chris Buckley, Keith Bradher, Vivian Wang, and Austin Ramzy, 'China's Leader Strikes a Defiant Note, Warning of "Stormy Seas"', *nytimes.com* (16 October 2022); Xinhua, '习近平在瞻仰延安革命纪念地时强调 弘扬伟大建党精神和延安精神 为实现党的二十大提出的目标任务而团结奋斗', *news.cn* (27 October 2022), both accessed 22 March 2024.
54. Xi, Report to the 20th Party Congress.
55. Xi, Report to the 20th Party Congress. See also: Chong Ja Ian, 'The Many "One Chinas'" Multiple Approaches to Taiwan and China', *carnegieendowment.org* (9 February 2023), accessed 11 March 2024.
56. Xi, Report to the 20th Party Congress.
57. Xi, Report to the 20th Party Congress.
58. See Yew Lun Tian, 'Shanghai COVID Crisis Puts Spotlight on Key Xi Ally', *reuters.com* (8 May 2022), accessed 11 March 2024.
59. Atsushi Okudera, 'Guangdong Chief Li Chosen to Head Anti-Corruption Drive in China', *asahi.com* (23 October 2022), accessed 11 March 2024.
60. Geremie R. Barmé, 'A Monkey King's Journey to the East', *chinaheritage.net* (1 January 2017), accessed January 18, 2024.

61. The Guardian, 'New Footage from China Congress Fuels Questions about Why Hu Jintao Was Hauled Out', *youtube.com* (26 October 2022), accessed 11 March 2024.
62. William Zheng, 'Why Former Chinese Leader Hu Jintao Was Highest Profile Absentee from Jiang Zemin's Funeral', *scmp.com* (6 December 2022), accessed 11 March 2024; 'Hu Jintao Escorted out of Party Congress', *reuters.com* (23 October 2022), accessed 14 May 2024.
63. Ministry of Foreign Affairs (PRC), 'Chinese President Hu Jintao Meets with Australian Prime Minister Kevin Rudd', *fmprc.gov.cn* (12 April 2008), accessed 11 March 2024; 'Vice Regal', *Canberra Times* (13 March 1986), 2.

CHAPTER 14

1. Third Historical Resolution, 1981.
2. Under the 'dynamic zero-COVID' policy: anyone infected with COVID-19 was isolated or hospitalized; their close contacts were also isolated; severe outbreaks would shut down entire cities (notably Shanghai and Chengdu); travel to China was restricted; inbound travellers were isolated for ten days, including one week in quarantine; contact-tracing apps were required for public spaces, and regular mandatory testing imposed; individuals were classified as 'green', 'yellow', or 'red' depending on their activities and contacts, requiring quarantine and extensive testing. See: Austin Ramzy, 'China's Zero-Covid Approach Explained', *nytimes.com* (8 September 2022), accessed 11 March 2024.
3. Fei Mingxin, 'Dynamic Aero-COVID: A Must Approach for China', *fmprc.gov.cn* (15 July 2022); Xi Jinping, 'Respond to COVID-19 with a Dedicated Effort', in *The Governance of China*, Vol. 4, both accessed 11 March 2024.
4. One study estimated with 95% credibility there were between 1.14 and 1.73 million COVID-19 deaths in China between 16 December 2022 and 19 January 2023: Du Zhanwei, Wang Yuchen, Bai Yuan, Wang Lin, Benjamin John Cowling, and Lauren Ancel Meyers, 'Estimate of COVID-19 Deaths, China, December 2022–February 2023', *Emerging Infectious Diseases*, 29/10 (2023). Another study estimated between approximately 50,000 and 700,000 COVID-19 deaths in mainland China between December 2022 and summer of 2023: John P. A. Ioannidis, Francesco Zonta, and Michael Levitt, 'Estimates of COVID-19 Deaths in Mainland China after Abandoning Zero COVID Policy', *European Journal of Clinical Investigation*, 53/ (2023). An unreviewed analysis of published obituaries estimated with 95% confidence that between 710,000 and 4.43 million all-cause excess deaths among over-30s in the two months after the policy was lifted: Hong Xiao, Wang Zhicheng, Fang Liu, and Joseph M. Unger, 'Excess All-Cause Mortality in China after Ending

the Zero COVID Policy', *JAMA Network Open*, 6/8 (2023). Chinese officials announced 59,938 deaths related to COVID-19 in medical institutions between 8 December 2022 and 12 January 2023, rising to 83,150 by February 9: Xinhua, 'Chinese Mainland Reports 59,938 COVID-Related Deaths in Past 30-plus Days', *gov.cn* (15 January 2023); James Glanz, Mara Hvistendahl, and Agnes Chang, 'How Deadly Was China's Covid Wave?', *nytimes.com* (15 February 2023), all accessed 11 March 2024.

5. International Monetary Fund, *World Economic Outlook* (Washington, DC: IMF, October 2022), 9; International Monetary Fund, *World Economic Outlook: Update* (Washington, DC: IMF, January 2023), 6. For analysis, see: Scott Kennedy, Logan Wright, John L. Holden, and Claire Reade, 'China's Economic Downturn', *Center for Strategic and International Studies, csis.org* (31 August 2023); Daniel H. Rosen, Logan Wright, Charlie Vest, and Rogan Quinn, 'Through the Looking Glass', *rhg.com* (29 December 2023), accessed 22 March 2024.
6. Laurie Chen and Albee Zhang, 'China Suspends Youth Jobless Data after Record High Readings', *reuters.com* (15 August 2023); Josh Zumbrun, 'How China Made a Youth Unemployment Crisis Disappear', *wsj.com* (8 December 2023), both accessed 11 March 2024.
7. International Monetary Fund, *People's Republic of China*, IMF Country Report No.24/38 (Washington, DC: IMF, 2024).
8. International Monetary Fund, *External Sector Report: External Rebalancing in Turbulent Times* (Washington, DC: IMF, 2023); UN Conference on Trade and Development, *Trade and Development Report 2023* (Washington, DC: IMF, 2023). See also: Marcin Szczepański, *China's Economic Coercion* (Brussels: European Parliamentary Research Service, 2022); Kristin Huang, 'China Must Mend Ties with Japan and Avoid US Conflict: Ex-PLA Instructor', *scmp.com* (8 January 2022); Frank Chen and Luna Sun, 'China-India Trade Tensions May Continue in 2024, but Beijing Doesn't Want to Rock the Boat', *scmp.com* (31 December 2023); Kana Inagaki, 'China Curtails "Dangerous" Fighter Jet Manoeuvres after Xi-Biden Summit', *Financial Times, ft.com* (18 December 2023); 'US Approves Direct Military Aid to Taiwan for the First Time', *lemonde.fr* (31 August 2023); Jeremy Mark and Dexter Tiff Roberts, *United States–China Semiconductor Standoff* (Washington, DC: Atlantic Council, 2023), all accessed 12 January 2024.
9. Robin Wigglesworth, 'The Implications of China's Middle-Income Trap', *ft.com* (27 February 2023), accessed 11 March 2024.
10. Most notable was *The Economist*'s 11 May cover story. See: The Economist, 'Is Chinese Power about to Peak?', *economist.com* (11 May 2023), accessed 12 January 2024. See also: Antara Ghosal Singh, 'Chinese Anxiety over "Peak China" and How It May Impact China-India Ties', *orfonline.org* (1 March 2024); China News, '中国智库发布首份批驳'中国崛起顶峰论'报告', *chinanews.com.cn* (20 May 2023); Wen Wang, 'Busting 6 "Peak China" Myths',

thediplomat.com (9 March 2024); Global Times, 'Prominent Economist Justin Lin Debunks "Peak China" Claims, Highlights China's Potential to Surpass US', *globatimes.cn* (8 March 2024), all accessed 11 March 2024.

11. White House, 'Readout of President Joe Biden's Meeting with President Xi Jinping of the People's Republic of China', *whitehouse.gov* (14 November 2022); Wang Yi, 'Wang Yi Briefs the Media on the Meeting between Chinese and U.S. Presidents and Answers Questions', *fmprc.gov.cn* (15 November 2022), accessed 11 March 2024.
12. Ning Mao, 'Foreign Ministry Spokesperson Mao Ning's Regular Press Conference on February 6, 2023', *mfa.gov.cn* (6 February 2023), accessed 11 March 2024.
13. US Embassy and Consulates in Japan, 'Trilateral Leaders' Summit of the United States, Japan, and the Republic of Korea', *jp.usembassy.gov* (19 August 2023), accessed 11 March 2024; Emma Chanlett-Avery, K. Alan Kronstadt, and Bruce Vaughn, *The "Quad": Cooperation among the United States, Japan, India, and Australia* (Washington, DC: Congressional Research Service, 2023); 'Agreement between the Government of Australia, the Government of the United Kingdom of Great Britain and Northern Ireland, and the Government of the United States of America for the Exchange of Naval Nuclear Propulsion Information', *UN Treaties Collection* 57347 (2022); 'The United States and the Republic of the Philippines Bilateral Defense Guidelines', *media.defense.gov* (3 May 2023); 'Readout of Virtual IPEF Ministerial Meeting Hosted by Ambassador Tai', *ustr.gov* (5 October 2023), all accessed 11 March 2024.
14. Yukon Huang, Isaac Kardon, and Matt Sheehan, 'Three Takeaways from the Biden-Xi Meeting', *carnegieendowment.org* (16 November 2023); White House, 'Readout of President Joe Biden's Meeting with President Xi Jinping of the People's Republic of China', *whitehouse.gov* (15 November 2023); Wang Yi, 'Wang Yi Speaks to the Press about the Summit Meeting between Chinese and U.S. Presidents in San Francisco', *mfa.gov.cn* (16 November 2023), all accessed 12 March 2024.
15. Xinhua, 'China Holds Central Economic Work Conference to Plan for 2023', *gov.cn* (17 December 2022); Xi Jinping, 'Speech at the First Session of the 14th NPC', *scio.gov.cn* (13 March 2023); Xinhua, 'China Holds Central Economic Work Conference to Plan for 2024', *gov.cn* (12 December 2023); Alexander Davey, 'The "Missing" Third Plenum Suggests Xi Is Sticking to His Plan', *merics.org* (5 March 2024). See also: Kevin Rudd, 'China's Competing Ideological and Economic Policy Objectives in 2023', *asiasociety.org* (15 February 2023), all accessed 11 March 2024.
16. See Laura Silver, Christine Huang, Laura Clancy, Nam Lam, Shannon Greenwood, John Carlo Mandapat, and Chris Baronavski, 'Comparing Views of the U.S. and China in 24 Countries', *pewresearch.org* (6 November 2023), accessed 22 March 2024.

17. Xi Jinping, '推进中国式现代化需要处理好若干重大关系', *gov.cn* (30 September 2023), accessed 11 March 2024. See also: Mao Zedong, 'On the Ten Major Relationships', in *Selected Works of Mao Tse-Tung*, Vol. 5.
18. Xi, '推进中国式现代化需要处理好若干重大关系'.
19. The Central Institute of Party History and Literature, '从党的百年奋斗历史经验中汲取智慧和力量', *Qiushi*, no. 13 (2022). See also the speech to which it refers, discussed in chapter 13 of this book: Xi, '更好把握和运用党的百年奋斗历史经验' or 'Adapt Marxism to China's Realities and Kept It Up-to-Date'.
20. Central Institute of Party History and Literature, '从党的百年奋斗历史经验中汲取智慧和力量'.
21. The post was abolished by the 12th Party Congress in 1982. In his report, the last Party Chairman Hu Yaobang said: "In light of our historical experience and lessons . . . the Party 'forbids all forms of personality cult'. . . . The Central Committee is to have no Chairman but only a General Secretary. . . . All these stipulations should help to reinforce the Party's collective leadership." See Hu Yaobang, 'Create a New Situation in All Fields of Socialist Modernization', *Beijing Review*, 25/37 (1982), 33.
22. Zhao Cheng, 'China Advocates Mutual Learning among Civilizations with Concrete Actions', *en.people.cn* (16 May 2019), accessed 11 March 2024.
23. See, e.g.: Xi Jinping, 'Be Prepared for the Great Struggle', in *The Governance of China*, Vol. 4.
24. E.g.: Xi Jinping, 'Study, Disseminate, and Implement the Guiding Principles of the 18th CPC National Congress', in *The Governance of China*, Vol. 1.
25. E.g.: Xi Jinping, 'Power Must Be "Caged" by the System', in *The Governance of China*, Vol. 1; 'Stronger Discipline Inspection Tours Make for Stricter Party Self-Governance' and 'Study Is the Prerequisite and Action Is the Key', in *The Governance of China*, Vol. 2; 'Stay True to the Party's Original Aspiration and Founding Mission and Carry Out Self-Reform', in *The Governance of China*, Vol. 3.
26. Xi Jinping, '继承和发扬党的优良革命传统和作风 弘扬延安精神', *Qiushi*, no. *24* (2022). See also: Xinhua, 'Xi Urges Efforts to Carry Forward Great Founding Spirit of CPC and Yan'an Spirit', *en.qstheory.cn* (31 October 2022), accessed 11 March 2024.
27. It has been estimated that more than 10,000 were killed during the Yan'an Rectification between 1941 and 1945. See Ja Ian Chong, 'Chinese Nationalism Reconsidered', in *Democratization in China, Korea and Southeast Asia?* (Oxford: Routledge, 2014), 221
28. Between 1968 and 1975, the fifteen-year-old Xi Jinping was famously sent to Liangjiahe for re-education while his father, Xi Zhongxun, was purged.
29. Xi, '继承和发扬党的优良革命传统和作风 弘扬延安精神'.
30. Xi, '继承和发扬党的优良革命传统和作风 弘扬延安精神'.

31. Xi Jinping, '健全全面从严治党体系 推动新时代党的建设新的伟大工程向纵深发展', *Qiushi*, no. *12* (2023). See also: Xinhua, 'Xi Stresses Need to Promote Full, Rigorous Party Self-Governance', *gov.cn* (9 January 2023), accessed 11 March 2024.
32. Xi, '健全全面从严治党体系'.
33. Commonly known as the 'two safeguards'.
34. Xi, '健全全面从严治党体系'.
35. Xi, '健全全面从严治党体系'.
36. Xi Jinping, '在中央党校建校90周年庆祝大会暨2023年春季学期开学典礼上的讲话', *Qiushi*, no. *7* (2023). See also: Wei Xu, 'General Secretary Sets Out New Vision for Party Schools', *chinadaily.com.cn* (2 March 2023), accessed 11 March 2024.
37. Xi, '在中央党校建校90周年庆祝大会'.
38. Xi, '在中央党校建校90周年庆祝大会'.
39. Xi, '在中央党校建校90周年庆祝大会'.
40. See, e.g.: Wang Jiawei and Xie Xueqin, 'Update on Anti-Monopoly Law in China', *roedl.com* (22 February 2023); European Chamber, *Position Paper 2019/20*, *swisscham.org* (July 2019), both accessed 14 March 2024.
41. For more detail on the anti-market policy measures adopted and expanded during 2022, see: Kevin Rudd, 'The Chinese Economy, the 20th Party Congress, and Implications for U.S.-China Relations', *asiasociety.org* (29 July 2022); Kevin Rudd, 'We Are Witnessing Profound Change, Kevin Rudd on Understanding How China Sees the World', *asiasociety.org* (2 June 2022), both accessed 12 March 2024.
42. Xinhua, '中共中央政治局召开会议分析研究2023年经济工作,研究部署党风廉政建设和反腐败工作, 习近平主持会议', *gov.cn* (7 December 2022), accessed 22 March 2024.
43. A detailed analysis of the 15 December 2022 Central Economic Work Conference is outlined in a policy paper by the Asia Society Policy Institute: Center for China Analysis, 'China's Political-Economy, Foreign and Security Policy: 2023', *asiasociety.org* (17 January 2023), accessed 13 March 2024.
44. Xinhua, '中央经济工作会议在北京举行' (2022 CEWC Readout), *news.cn* (16 December 2022), accessed 10 December 2023.
45. Xinhua, '中央经济工作会议在北京举行' (2023 CEWC Readout), *news.cn* (12 December 2023), accessed 10 December 2023.
46. Xinhua, 2023 CEWC Readout.
47. Xinhua, 2023 CEWC Readout.
48. Xinhua, 2023 CEWC Readout.
49. Xi Jinping, 'Chinese Modernization Is Socialist Modernization Led by the CPC', *en.qstheory.cn* (13 September 2023), accessed 12 March 2024; Xi Jinping, '中国式现代化是中国共产党领导的社会主义现代化', *Qiushi*, no. *11* (2023).

50. Xi Jinping, '中国式现代化是强国建设、民族复兴的康庄大道', *Qiushi*, no. *16* (2023). See also: Xi Jinping, 'Chinese Modernization Is a Sure Path to Building a Great Country and Rejuvenating the Nation', *Qiushi English*, no. *6* (2023).
51. Xi Jinping, '中国式现代化是强国建设、民族复兴的康庄大道'.
52. Xi Jinping, '推进中国式现代化需要处理好若干重大关系'.
53. Xinhua, 2023 CEWC Readout.
54. Xinhua, 2020 CEWC Readout. See further: Bill Bishop, 'Central Economic Work Conference; Progress vs Stability; PRC-Philippines Standoffs; Fentanyl', *sinocism.com* (12 December 2023), accessed 22 March 2024.
55. See Nargiza Salidjanova, Rachel Lietzow, and Daniel H. Rosen, 'China Pathfinder: H2 2022 Update', *Rhodium Group*, *rhg.com* (8 February 2023); Alexander Chipman Koty, 'Why People Don't Trust China's Official Statistics', *china-briefing.com* (30 March 2017); Michael T. Owyang and Hannah Shell, 'China's Economic Data', *stlouisfed.org* (25 July 2017); Scott Kennedy and Qin (Maya) Mei, 'Measurement Muddle', *bigdatachina.csis.org* (13 September 2023), all accessed 22 March 2024.
56. Michael Smith, 'US Companies Pull Out of China as Relations Sour', *afr.com* (19 September 2023), accessed 22 March 2024; Sun Yu, 'US Consultancy Gallup Withdraws from China', *ft.com* (4 November 2023); Helen Davidson, 'China Targets Foreign Consulting Companies in Anti-Spying Raids', *theguardian.com* (9 May 2023), all accessed 12 March 2024.
57. Xinhua, 'A Closer Look at Economic Potential behind China's Growth Target', *english.scio.gov.cn* (11 March 2024); Jack Stone Truitt, 'How Reliable Is China's GDP Data?', *asia.nikkei.com* (20 January 2024), both accessed 12 March 2024
58. Daniel H. Rosen, Charlie Vest, and Rogan Quinn, 'Now for the Hard Part', *rhg.com* (29 December 2022), Daniel H. Rosen, Logan Wright, Charlie Vest, and Rogan Quinn, 'Through the Looking Glass'. See also: Kevin Yao and Ellen Zhang, 'China's 2022 Economic Growth One of the Worst on Record, Post-pandemic Policy Faces Test', *reuters.com* (17 January 2023); Michael Pettis, 'What Will It Take for China's GDP to Grow at 4–5 Percent over the Next Decade?', *carnegieendowment.org* (4 December 2023), all accessed 22 March 2024.
59. The Economist, 'Is Chinese Power about to Peak?'; The Economist, 'A Dragon out of Puff', *economist.com* (15 June 2002); The Economist; 'How Soon and at What Height Will China's Economy Peak?', *economist.com* (11 May 2023); Michael Pettis, 'Can China's Long-Term Growth Rate Exceed 2–3 Percent?', *carnegieendowment.org* (6 April 2023), all accessed 12 March 2024.
60. Zhang Zhuoyuan, '十八大后十年经济走势', *theory.people.com.cn* (9 July 2014); '十年展望：中国的经济增长率会降至多少？[2]', *finance.people.com.cn* (31 October 2013); national accounts data from World Bank Open Data and OECD Statistics and Data Directorate, all accessed 11 January 2024.

61. See: Nathan Sheets, 'When Will China's GDP Surpass the US? And What Will It Mean?', *citigroup.com*, 19 January 2023; The Economist, 'When Will China's GDP Overtake America's?', *economist.com* (7 June 2023); Jasmine Ng, 'China Slowdown Means It May Never Overtake US Economy, Forecast Shows', *bloomberg.com* (5 September 2023), all accessed 12 March 2024.
62. See China Government, '政府工作报告重磅！加快发展新质生产力', *gov.cn* (5 March 2024), accessed 10 March 2024.
63. Kevin Rudd, 'The Chinese Economy, the 20th Party Congress, and Implications for U.S.-China Relations'.

CHAPTER 15

1. Xi, Report to the 19th Party Congress.
2. Xi Jinping, 'Xi Sends Letter to World Symposium for Marxist Political Parties', *xinhuanet.com* (27 May 2021). See also: Xi Jinping, '推动全党学习和掌握历史唯物主义,更好认识规律更加能动地推进工作', *cpc.people.com.cn* (5 December 2013), both accessed 22 March 2024.
3. George Washington, 'To Brigadier-General Nelson, Virginia', in *The Writings of George Washington*, Vol. 6 (Boston: Russell, Odiorne and Metcalf and Hillard Gray and Co., 1834); The Evening News, 'The Great White Fleet: Enters Port Jackson This Morning', *The Evening News* (20 August 1908), 8; John Winthrop, 'A Modell of Christian Charity', in *Collections of the Massachusetts Historical Society*, Vol. 8 (Boston: Charles C. Little & James Brown, 1838).
4. Xinhua, 'Xi Declares "Complete Victory" in Eradicating Absolute Poverty in China', *xinhuanet.com* (26 February 2021), accessed 13 March 2024.
5. Segments of this speech—delivered to a study session for new members and alternate members of the CPC Central Committee and principal officials at the provincial and ministerial level on 7 February 2023, are alternatively published as: Xi Jinping, '中国式现代化是强国建设、民族复兴的康庄大道'; Xi Jinping, 'Chinese Modernization Is Socialist Modernization Led by the CPC'; Xi Jinping, 'Chinese Modernization Is a Sure Path to Building a Great Country and Rejuvenating the Nation'; Xi Jinping, '推进中国式现代化需要处理好若干重大关系', *Qiushi*, no. 19 (2023); '中国式现代化是中国共产党领导的社会主义现代化', *Qiushi*, no. 11 (2023).
6. Xi, '中国式现代化是强国建设、民族复兴的康庄大道'.
7. Xi Jinping, 'Staying True to APEC Founding Mission and Enhancing Unity and Cooperation to Jointly Promote High-Quality Growth in the Asia-Pacific', *english.news.cn* (18 November 2023); Xi Jinping, 'Meeting Challenges with Unity of Purpose to Write a New Chapter for Asia-Pacific Cooperation', *english.news.cn* (17 November 2023); Xi Jinping, 'Galvanizing Our Peoples into a Strong Force for the Cause of China-U.S. Friendship', *english.news.cn* (16 November 2023), all accessed 13 March 2024.

8. Xi, 'Galvanizing Our Peoples into a Strong Force for the Cause of China-US Friendship'.
9. Swaine, 'Xi Jinping's Address to the Central Conference on Work Relating to Foreign Affairs'.
10. Ministry of Foreign Affairs (PRC), 'The Central Conference on Work Relating to Foreign Affairs Was Held in Beijing', *fmprc.gov.cn* (28 December 2023).
11. Xinhua, '习近平接见2023年度驻外使节工作会议与会使节并发表重要讲话', *news.cn* (29 December 2023), accessed 13 March 2024.
12. Wang Yi, '深入贯彻中央外事工作会议精神,不断开创中国特色大国外交新局面', *Qiushi*, no. 2 (2024). See also: Wang Yi, 'Implementing the Guiding Principles of the Central Conference on Work Relating to Foreign Affairs and Breaking New Ground in Major-Country Diplomacy with Chinese Characteristics', *us.china-embassy.gov.cn* (16 January 2024), accessed 22 March 2024.
13. Wang, '深入贯彻中央外事工作会议精神,不断开创中国特色大国外交新局面'.
14. Ministry of Foreign Affairs (PRC), 'The Central Conference on Work Relating to Foreign Affairs Was Held in Beijing (2023)'.
15. Wang, '深入贯彻中央外事工作会议精神,不断开创中国特色大国外交新局面'.
16. Ministry of Foreign Affairs (PRC), 'The Central Conference on Work Relating to Foreign Affairs Was Held in Beijing (2023)'.
17. Wang, '深入贯彻中央外事工作会议精神,不断开创中国特色大国外交新局面'.
18. Wang, '深入贯彻中央外事工作会议精神,不断开创中国特色大国外交新局面'.
19. Wang, '深入贯彻中央外事工作会议精神,不断开创中国特色大国外交新局面'.
20. Wang, '深入贯彻中央外事工作会议精神,不断开创中国特色大国外交新局面'.
21. Ministry of Foreign Affairs (PRC), 'The Central Conference on Work Relating to Foreign Affairs Was Held in Beijing (2023)'.
22. Ministry of Foreign Affairs (PRC), 'The Central Conference on Work Relating to Foreign Affairs Was Held in Beijing (2023)'.
23. Ministry of Foreign Affairs (PRC), 'The Central Conference on Work Relating to Foreign Affairs Was Held in Beijing (2023)'.
24. Ministry of Foreign Affairs (PRC), 'The Central Conference on Work Relating to Foreign Affairs Was Held in Beijing (2023)'.
25. Ministry of Foreign Affairs (PRC), 'The Central Conference on Work Relating to Foreign Affairs Was Held in Beijing (2023)'.
26. Wang, '深入贯彻中央外事工作会议精神,不断开创中国特色大国外交新局面'.

27. Wang, '深入贯彻中央外事工作会议精神,不断开创中国特色大国外交新局面'.
28. Wang, '深入贯彻中央外事工作会议精神,不断开创中国特色大国外交新局面'.
29. Ministry of Foreign Affairs (PRC), 'The Central Conference on Work Relating to Foreign Affairs Was Held in Beijing (2014)'.
30. Xi Jinping, 'Break New Ground in China's Major-Country Diplomacy', in *The Governance of China*, Vol. 3.
31. Ministry of Foreign Affairs (PRC), 'The Central Conference on Work Relating to Foreign Affairs Was Held in Beijing (2023)'.
32. Wang, '深入贯彻中央外事工作会议精神,不断开创中国特色大国外交新局面'.
33. Ministry of Foreign Affairs (PRC), 'The Central Conference on Work Relating to Foreign Affairs Was Held in Beijing (2023)'.
34. Ministry of Foreign Affairs (PRC), 'The Central Conference on Work Relating to Foreign Affairs Was Held in Beijing (2023)'.
35. Ministry of Foreign Affairs (PRC), 'The Central Conference on Work Relating to Foreign Affairs Was Held in Beijing (2023)'.
36. Xinhua, 'China Asks EU to Uphold Idea of Common Security', *en.people.cn* (13 March 2024); Chenglong Jiang, 'Mutual Trust Highlighted at Security Forum', *chinadaily.com.cn* (31 October 2023), both accessed 13 March 2024.
37. Augustine of Hippo, *City of God* (London: Penguin, 1984).
38. Wang, '深入贯彻中央外事工作会议精神,不断开创中国特色大国外交新局面'.
39. Wang, '深入贯彻中央外事工作会议精神,不断开创中国特色大国外交新局面'.
40. Wang, '深入贯彻中央外事工作会议精神,不断开创中国特色大国外交新局面'.
41. Ministry of Foreign Affairs (PRC), 'Xi Meets Chinese Diplomatic Envoys to Foreign Countries', *mfa.gov.cn* (29 December 2023), accessed 13 March 2024.
42. John Williamson, 'What Should the World Bank Think about the Washington Consensus?', *World Bank Research Observer*, 15/2 (2000); United Nations, 'Universal Declaration of Human Rights', *ohchr.org* (1948), accessed 15 May 2024; Ministry of Foreign Affairs (PRC), 'Global Security Initiative Concept Paper', *fmprc.gov.cn* (21 February 2023); Ministry of Foreign Affairs (PRC), 'Global Development Initiative Concept Paper', *mfa.gov.cn* (21 September 2021); Xinhua, 'Global Civilization Initiative Injects Fresh Energy into Human Development', *english.news.cn* (17 March 2023), accessed 15 May 2024.
43. Wang, '深入贯彻中央外事工作会议精神,不断开创中国特色大国外交新局面'.
44. Ministry of Foreign Affairs (PRC), 'Xi Meets Chinese Diplomatic Envoys to Foreign Countries'.

45. Dale Carnegie, *How to Win Friends and Influence People* (New York: Simon & Schuster, 1936).
46. Wang, '深入贯彻中央外事工作会议精神,不断开创中国特色大国外交新局面'.
47. Wang, '深入贯彻中央外事工作会议精神,不断开创中国特色大国外交新局面'. The United Front Work Department is a Party agency responsible for managing relationships with 'overseas Chinese' as well as ethnic and religious affairs.
48. Wang, '深入贯彻中央外事工作会议精神,不断开创中国特色大国外交新局面'.
49. Xinhua, '习近平接见2023年度驻外使节工作会议与会使节并发表重要讲话'.
50. Ministry of Foreign Affairs (PRC), 'The Central Conference on Work Relating to Foreign Affairs Was Held in Beijing (2023)'.
51. Ministry of Foreign Affairs (PRC), 'The Central Conference on Work Relating to Foreign Affairs Was Held in Beijing (2023)'.
52. Wang, '深入贯彻中央外事工作会议精神,不断开创中国特色大国外交新局面'.
53. Ministry of Foreign Affairs (PRC), 'Xi Meets Chinese Diplomatic Envoys to Foreign Countries'.
54. Wang, '深入贯彻中央外事工作会议精神,不断开创中国特色大国外交新局面'.
55. Xi Jinping, '新发展阶段贯彻新发展理念必然要求构建新发展格局', *Qiushi*, no. 17 (2022); Xinhua, '习近平主持召开二十届中央国家安全委员会第一次会议强调 加快推进国家安全体系和能力现代化 以新安全格局保障新发展格局', *news.cn* (30 May 2023); Xinhua, 'Xi Urges Accelerated Efforts to Modernize National Security System, Capacity', *english.news.cn* (2023), all accessed 13 March 2024.
56. 'Statement by Peking on Nuclear Test', *nytimes.com* (17 October 1964), accessed 13 March 2024.
57. Taiwan Affairs Office of the State Council (PRC), *The Taiwan Question and China's Reunification in the New Era*, *gm.china-embassy.gov.cn* (August 2022), accessed 13 March 2024.
58. Li-Hua Chung and Jonathan Chin, 'Poll Shows 48.9% Support Independence', *taipeitimes.com* (2 September 2023); Data from Election Study Center at National Chengchi University, both accessed 13 March 2024.
59. United States of America and Philippines, *Mutual Defense Treaty*, UN Treaties Collection 2315 (1951).
60. Ministry of Defense (Japan), 'Defense Buildup Program', *mod.go.jp* (16 December 2022), accessed 13 March 2024.
61. Chen Yawen, 'China's Growth Is Buried under Great Wall of Debt', *reuters.com* (12 September 2023), accessed 13 March 2024.

CHAPTER 16

1. Xi Jinping, '深刻认识马克思主义时代意义和现实意义,继续推进马克思主义中国化时代化大众化', *cpc.people. com.cn* (30 September 2017), accessed 12 March 2024. See also Xi Jinping, 'Develop and Popularize Marxism in the Modern Context', in *The Governance of China*, Vol. 2.
2. People's Daily, '习近平、蔡奇同志在学习贯彻习近平新时代中国特色社会主义思想主题教育工作会议上的讲话', *ztjy.people.cn* (3 April 2023). See also: Xinhua, 'Xi Urges Solid Implementation of Party Education Campaign to Enhance Cohesion, Pool Strengths', *news.cn* (3 April 2023), both accessed 12 March 2024.
3. Xi Jinping, '开辟马克思主义中国化时代化新境界', *Qiushi*, no. *20* (2023).
4. Xinhua, 'Xi Jinping Stressed Continuously Deepening the Principles-Based Understanding of the Party's Theoretical Innovation, and Obtaining More Fruitful Theoretical Innovation Accomplishments on the New Journey in the New Era at the 6th Collective Study Session of the CCP Central Committee Politburo', *interpret.csis.org* (30 June 2023), accessed 12 March 2024.
5. Xinhua, 'Xi Jinping Stressed Continuously Deepening the Principles-Based Understanding of the Party's Theoretical Innovation'. See also: Friedrich Engels, *Socialism: Utopian and Scientific* (Chicago: Charles H. Kerr, 1908); Vladimir Ilyich Lenin, 'The Recent Revolution in Natural Science and Philosophical Idealism', in *Lenin: Collected Works*, Vol. 14 (Moscow: Progress Publishers, 1977); Karl Marx, 'Marx to Engels, 31 July 1865', in *Marx and Engels: Collected Works*, Vol. 42 (London: Lawrence & Wishart, 2010), 173.
6. Xi Jinping, '在文化传承发展座谈会上的讲话', *Qiushi*, no. *17* (2023). See also: Xi Jinping, 'Speech at the Meeting on Cultural Inheritance and Development', *Qiushi English*, no. 5 (2023); Xi Jinping, 'Speech at a Ceremony Marking the Centenary of the Communist Party of China', *asia.nikkei.com* (1 July 2021), accessed 12 March 2024.
7. Qiu Ping, 'Profound Significance of the "Two Integrations"', *en.qstheory.cn* (20 December 2023); CPC Leadership Group of the Chinese Academy of Social Sciences, 'Understanding the Historical Significance and Contemporary Value of the Distinctive Features of Chinese Civilization', *Qiushi English*, no. *1* (2024); Chinese Academy of History, 'A Guiding Light for the Development of Modern Chinese Civilization', *Qiushi English*, no. 5 (2023); Qiushi Commentary, 'A New Cultural Mission: Developing a Modern Chinese Civilization', *Qiushi English*, no. *4* (2023); Miao Xiaojuan, 'President Xi's "Second Integration" Theory', *english.news.cn* (17 January 2024), all accessed 12 March 2024.
8. Xi Jinping, '在文化传承发展座谈会上的讲话'.
9. Xi Jinping, '在文化传承发展座谈会上的讲话'.
10. Xi Jinping, '在文化传承发展座谈会上的讲话'. See also: Ministry of Foreign Affairs (PRC), 'Wang Yi Envisions China's Diplomacy in 2024', *id.china-embassy.gov.cn* (7 March 2023), accessed 26 May 2024.

11. Tillman Durdin, 'China Transformed by Elimination of "Four Olds"', *nytimes.com* (19 May 1971), accessed 12 March 2024.
12. Pew Research Center, 'Religious Composition by Country, 2010–2050', *pewresearch.org* (21 December 2022), accessed 12 March 2024.
13. Unless otherwise noted, quotes from this section are from: He Yiting, '马克思主义中国化时代化新的飞跃', 2024, *paper.people.com.cn* (6 February 2024), accessed 10 March 2024.
14. Zhou Enlai proposed the 'four modernizations' in January 1963, prior to Cultural Revolution, and re-announced it in January 1975. Zhou died in January 1976, followed by Mao in September. See Zhou Enlai, 'The Key to Building a Powerful Socialist Country Is to Modernize Science and Technology', in *Selected Works of Zhou Enlai*, Vol. 2 (Beijing: Foreign Languages Press, 1989); Zhou Enlai, 'Report on the Work of the Government', *Peking Review* 18/4 (1975).
15. Li Qiang, 'Speech by Chinese Premier Li Qiang at the Opening Ceremony of the World Economic Forum Annual Meeting 2024', *mfa.gov.cn* (16 January 2024); Eduardo Baptista and Yew Lun Tian, 'China's New Premier Seeks to Reassure Private Sector as Parliament Wraps Up', *reuters.com* (13 March 2023), both accessed 13 March 2024.
16. Data from United Nations, *World Population Prospects 2022*, *population.un.org*, accessed 13 March 2024.
17. Katrin Kinzelbach, Staffan I. Lindberg, Lars Pelke, and Janika Spannagel, 'Academic Freedom Index—Update 2023', *academic-freedom-index.net* (March 2023), accessed 13 March 2024.
18. Data from Freedom House, *Freedom on the Net* 2023.
19. John Ross, '"Anti-Western" Recruitment "Could Turn Chinese off Foreign Study"', *timeshighereducation.com* (11 November 2023), accessed 13 March 2024.
20. Annabelle Liang, 'China Crackdown Pushes LGBT Groups into the Shadows', *bbc.com* (28 June 2023), accessed 13 March 2024.
21. Xinhua, 'China Introduces Supportive Policies to Aid Military Personnel in Child-Rearing', *english.news.cn* (7 September 2023), accessed 13 March 2024.
22. See Leta Hong Fincher, *Betraying Big Brother* (London: Verso, 2019).
23. US Commission on International Religious Freedom, 'Annual Report of the US Commission on International Religious Freedom', *uscirf.gov* (April 2023).
24. Wang Xiangwei, '"Great Leader Xi" or "Xi, the Great Leader": It's a Fine Line', *scmp.com* (26 November 2017), accessed 13 March 2024.
25. Kevin Yao and Ben Blanchard, 'Fearing Graft Probes, Chinese Officials Shun Spotlight, Seek Retirement', *reuters.com* (9 July 2014), accessed 13 March 2024.
26. Liu He, '刘鹤: 不支持民营企业发展的行为必须坚决予以纠正', *xinhuanet.com* (20 October 2018). See further: Liu He, 'Those Who Don't Support Development of Private Enterprises Must Be Corrected', *caixinglobal.com* (20 October 2018), both accessed 21 October 2021.

27. See Lulu Yilun Chen, 'China's Rich Entrust Total Strangers to Sneak Cash out of the Country', *bloomberg.com* (9 October 2023).
28. Neil Thomas, 'Xi Jinping's Succession Dilemma', *asiasociety.org* (14 February 2024), accessed 13 March 2024.
29. International Monetary Fund, *People's Republic of China.*
30. Jasmine Ng, 'China Slowdown Means It May Never Overtake US Economy, Forecast Shows'.
31. W. Raphael Lam and Marialuz Moreno-Badia, *Fiscal Policy and the Government Balance Sheet in China*, IMF Working Paper 23/154 (August 2023); Laura He, 'Chinese Cities Are So Broke, They're Cutting Medical Benefits for Seniors', *cnn.com* (31 March 2023), accessed 13 March 2024.
32. See, e.g.: Zongyuan Zoe Liu, 'China's Pensions System Is Buckling under an Aging Population', *foreignpolicy.com* (29 June 2023); Hu Dezhuang, Li Hongbin, Li Tang, Meng Lingsheng, and Binh Thai Nguyen, 'The Burden of Education Costs in China', *SSRN* (31 August 2023); Luna Sun, 'Chinese Students Have New Source of Stress as Universities Raise Tuition Fees', *scmp.com* (29 September 2023); Hu Hairong, Ding Feng, and Han Wei, 'China Aims to Ease Property Crunch via New Affordable Housing Push', *asia.nikkei.com* (30 December 2023); Mandy Zuo, 'China's Healthcare Costs Fuel Consumption in Ageing Society, but Alarms Are Blaring in the Medical Insurance Fund', *scmp.com* (16 August 2023), accessed 13 March 2024.
33. The Economist, 'China's Defeated Youth', *economist.com* (17 August 2023); Nicole Goldin, 'Youth Unemployment in China: New Metric, Same Mess', *atlanticcouncil.org* (16 February 2024).
34. Although China represents about one-quarter of global economic activity outside the United States, it accounts for only 2.8% of credit issued in US dollars to non-bank borrowers, according to the Bank for International Settlements.
35. Edward Cunningham, Tony Saich, and Jessica Turiel, *CCP Resilience* (Cambridge, MA: Ash Center, Harvard Kennedy School, 2020).
36. US Embassy and Consulates in Japan, 'Trilateral Leaders' Summit of the United States, Japan, and the Republic of Korea', *jp.usembassy.gov* (19 August 2023), accessed 11 March 2024; Emma Chanlett-Avery, K. Alan Kronstadt, and Bruce Vaughn, *The "Quad"* (Washington, DC: Congressional Research Service, 2023); 'Agreement between the Government of Australia, the Government of the United Kingdom of Great Britain and Northern Ireland, and the Government of the United States of America for the exchange of naval nuclear propulsion information', *UN Treaties Collection* 57347 (2022); 'The United States and the Republic of the Philippines Bilateral Defense Guidelines', media.defense.gov (3 May 2023); 'Readout of Virtual IPEF Ministerial Meeting Hosted by Ambassador Tai', ustr.gov (5 October 2023), all accessed 11 March 2024.

37. Putin and Xi, 'Joint Statement of the Russian Federation and the People's Republic of China on the International Relations Entering a New Era and the Global Sustainable Development'.
38. BBC News, 'Ukraine War: What Support Is China Giving Russia?', *bbc.com* (20 March 2023); Raf Casert and Samuel Petrequin, 'EU Lashes Out at China for Support of Russia in Ukraine War', *apnews.com* (5 April 2023).
39. E.g.: Viking Bohman, 'The Limits of Economic Coercion', *ui.se* (November 2021); Bryan Frederick and Howard J. Shatz, 'The Global Movement against China's Economic Coercion Is Accelerating', *rand.org* (9 June 2023), both accessed 13 March 2024.
40. See, e.g.: Matthew Reynolds and Matthew P. Goodman, 'China's Economic Coercion: Lessons from Lithuania', *csis.org* (6 May 2022); Richard McGregor, 'Chinese Coercion, Australian Resilience', *lowyinstitute.org* (20 October 2022).
41. E.g.: UN Human Rights Council, 'China Review—45th Session of Universal Periodic Review', *webtv.un.org* (23 January 2024), accessed 13 March 2024.
42. Nadia Clark, 'The Rise and Fall of the BRI', *cfr.org* (6 April 2023), accessed 22 March 2024.
43. David Stanway, 'China 2023 Coal Power Approvals Rose, Putting Climate Targets at Risk', *reuters.com* (22 February 2024), accessed 22 March 2024.
44. Joel Rogers de Waal, 'China's Reputation Declines While America's Gets a Boost', *yougov.co.uk* (24 October 2022), accessed 22 March 2024.
45. Yang Kai and Stephan Ortmann, 'From Sweden to Singapore: The Relevance of Foreign Models for China's Rise', *China Quarterly*, no. *236* (2018).
46. Tony Saich, 'Reforming the Political Structure', in *Reforming the Revolution* (London: Palgrave Macmillan, 1988).
47. See Andrew Nathan, 'Zhao Ziyang's Vision of Chinese Democracy', *China Perspectives*, no. *3* (2008); Hu Yaobang, 'Create a New Situation in All Fields of Socialist Modernization', *Beijing Review* 25/37.
48. Xi Jinping, '习近平：努力成长为对党和人民忠诚可靠、堪当时代重任的栋梁之才', *Qiushi*, no. *13* (2023); '习近平：在纪念五四运动100周年大会上的讲话', *xinhuanet.com* (30 April 2019), accessed 22 March 2024.
49. Kevin Rudd, *The Avoidable War* (New York: Public Affairs, 2022).

Bibliography

Part 1 of the bibliography lists English-language sources, both primary and secondary. Part 2 lists Chinese-language sources. For ease of reference, the categories of documents covered within Parts 1 and 2 are also listed immediately below, before proceeding to the bibliography proper. Some sources may be listed multiple times in the bibliography. For example, a speech excerpt may have been published originally in Chinese, then have been the subject of unofficial translation into English, before later being republished with an official English translation. The same speech may also have been summarized by state media in Chinese and English prior to the publication of a more complete text, or else republished with new detail not contained in previous iterations. Should you have difficulty finding a particular source, please consider emailing the author's office in Australia via kevinrudd.com.

Structure of Bibliography

Part 1: English-Language Sources

1.1 English-Language Primary Sources

Part 2: Chinese-Language Sources

2.1 Chinese-Language Primary Sources

Part 1: English-Language Sources

1.1. English-Language Primary Sources

1.1.1. Three Historical Resolutions by the CCP (1945, 1981, 2021)

'Resolution on Certain Questions in the History of Our Party', Adopted at the Seventh Plenary Session of the Sixth Central Committee of the Communist Party of China, April 1945, in Mao Zedong, *Selected Works of Mao Zedong*, Vol. 3 (Paris: Foreign Languages Press, 2021).

'Resolution on Certain Questions in the History of Our Party since the Founding of the People's Republic of China: Review of the History of the Twenty-Eight Years before the Founding of the People's Republic', Adopted at the Sixth Plenary Session of the Eleventh Central Committee of the Communist Party of China, Wilson Center, June 1981, https://digitalarchive.wilsoncenter.org/document/resolution-certain-questions-history-our-party-founding-peoples-republic-china.

'Resolution of the Central Committee of the Communist Party of China on the Major Achievements and Historical Experience of the Party over the Past Century', Adopted at the Sixth Plenary Session of the 19th Central Committee of the Communist Party of China on November 11, 2021, https://english.www.gov.cn/policies/latestreleases/202111/16/content_WS6193a935c6d0df57f98e50b0.html.

1.1.2. Reports to the National Congresses of the CCP (1992–2022)

Jiang Zemin, 'Accelerating the Reform, the Opening to the Outside World and the Drive for Modernization, so as to Achieve Greater Successes in Building Socialism with Chinese Characteristics (加快改革开放和现代化建设步伐,夺取有中国特色社会主义事业的更大胜利)', Report to the Fourteenth National Congress of the Communist Party of China on October 12, 1992, http://www.bjreview.com.cn/document/txt/2011-03/29/content_363504.htm, in Literature Research Office of the Chinese Communist Party Central Committee, *Selection of Important Documents since the 14th Party Congress*, Vol. 1 (Beijing: Central Party Literature Press, 1996).

Jiang Zemin, 'Hold High the Great Banner of Deng Xiaoping Theory for an All-Round Advancement of the Cause of Building Socialism with Chinese Characteristics to the 21st Century (高举邓小平理论伟大旗帜,把建设有中国特色社会主义事业全面推向二十一世纪)', Report to the Fifteenth National Congress of the Communist Party of China on September 12, 1997, http://www.bjreview.com.cn/document/txt/2011-03/25/content_363499.htm, in Literature Research Office of the Chinese Communist Party Central Committee, *Selection of Important Documents since the 15th Party Congress*, Vol. 1 (Beijing: Central Party Literature Press, 2000).

Jiang Zemin, 'Build a Well-off Society in an All-Round Way and Create a New Situation in Building Socialism with Chinese Characteristics (全面建设奔小康社会,开创中国特色社会主义事业新局面)', Report to the Sixteenth National Congress of the Communist Party of China on November 8, 2002, http://www.bjreview.com.cn/document/txt/2011-03/24/content_360557.htm, in Literature Research Office of the Chinese Communist Party Central Committee, *Selection of Important Documents since the 16th Party Congress*, Vol. 1 (Beijing: Central Party Literature Press, 2005).

Hu Jintao, 'Hold High the Great Banner of Socialism with Chinese Characteristics and Strive for New Victories in Building a Moderately Prosperous Society in All Respects 高举中国特色社会主义伟大旗帜,为夺取全面建设小康社会新胜利而奋斗)', Report to the Seventeenth National Congress of the Communist Party of China on October 15, 2007, http://www.bjrev

iew.com.cn/document/txt/2007-11/20/content_86325.htm, in Literature Research Office of the Chinese Communist Party Central Committee, *Selection of Important Documents since the 17th Party Congress*, Vol. 1 (Beijing: Central Party Literature Press, 2009).

Hu Jintao, 'Firmly March on the Path of Socialism with Chinese Characteristics and Strive to Complete the Building of a Moderately Prosperous Society in All Respects (坚定不移沿着中国特色社会主义道路前进,为全面建成小康社会而奋斗)', Report to the Eighteenth National Congress of the Communist Party of China on Nov 8, 2012, https://www.mfa.gov.cn/ce/cebel//eng/sghd/t990697.htm, in Literature Research Office of the Chinese Communist Party Central Committee, *Selection of Important Documents since the 18th Party Congress*, Vol. 1 (Beijing: Central Party Literature Press, 2014).

Xi Jinping, 'Secure a Decisive Victory in Building a Moderately Prosperous Society in All Respects and Strive for the Great Success of Socialism with Chinese Characteristics for a New Era (决战全面建成小康社会,夺取新时代中国特色社会主义伟大胜利)', Report to the 19th National Congress of the Communist Party of China on October 18, 2017, http://www.xinhuanet.com/english/download/Xi_Jinping's_report_at_19th_CPC_National_Congress.pdf.

Xi Jinping, 'Hold High the Great Banner of Socialism with Chinese Characteristics and Strive in Unity to Build a Modern Socialist Country in All Respects (高举中国特色社会主义伟大旗帜为全面建设社会主义现代化国家而团结奋斗)', Report to the 20th National Congress of the Communist Party of China on October 25, 2022, https://www.mfa.gov.cn/eng/zxxx_662805/202210/t20221025_10791908.html.

1.1.3. Communiqués/Readouts of the Plenary Sessions of the 18th–20th Central Committees of the CCP (2012–2024)

First Plenary Session of the 18th Central Committee, November 2012. http://www.chinadaily.com.cn/china/2014cpctps/2013-11/07/content_18760670.htm.

Second Plenary Session of the 18th Central Committee, February 2013. http://www.chinadaily.com.cn/china/2014cpctps/2013-11/07/content_18760669.htm.

Third Plenary Session of the 18th Central Committee, November 2013. http://www.china.org.cn/chinese/2014-01/16/content_31213800.htm.

Fourth Plenary Session of the 18th Central Committee, October 2014. https://www.en84.com/nonfiction/statements/201501/00015838.html.

Fifth Plenary Session of the 18th Central Committee, October 2015. https://chinacopyrightandmedia.wordpress.com/2015/10/29/communique-of-the-fifth-plenary-meeting-of-the-18th-central-committee-of-the-chinese-communist-party/.

Sixth Plenary Session of the 18th Central Committee, October 2016. http://www.bjreview.com/Beijing_Review_and_Kings_College_London_Joint_Translation_Project/2016/201707/t20170703_800099462.html.

Seventh Plenary Session of the 18th Central Committee, October 2017. https://english.www.gov.cn/news/top_news/2017/10/14/content_281475906814610.htm.

First Plenary Session of the 19th Central Committee, October 2017. http://english.scio.gov.cn/topnews/2017-10/25/content_41790157.htm.

Second Plenary Session of the 19th Central Committee, January 2018. http://www.xinhuanet.com/english/2018-01/19/c_136908984.htm.

Third Plenary Session of the 19th Central Committee, February 2018. http://www.scio.gov.cn/32618/Document/1624249/1624249.htm.

Fourth Plenary Session of the 19th Central Committee, October 2019. http://english.www.gov.cn/news/topnews/201910/31/content_WS5dbae8adc6d0bcf8c4c16202.html.

Fifth Plenary Session of the 19th Central Committee, October 2020. https://www.airuniversity.af.edu/CASI/Display/Article/2834176/itow-communiqu-of-the-fifth-plenary-session-of-the-19th-central-committee-of-th/.

Sixth Plenary Session of the 19th Central Committee, November 2021. http://www.npc.gov.cn/englishnpc/c23934/202111/c91cf9aa6aee453b8ce8160b00cc8ba8.shtml.

Seventh Plenary Session of the 19th Central Committee, October 2022. http://english.scio.gov.cn/topnews/2022-10/14/content_78465143.htm.

First Plenary Session of the 20th Central Committee, October 2022. http://english.scio.gov.cn/20thcpccongress/2022-10/24/content_78482624.html.

First Plenary Session of 20th Central Commission for Discipline Inspection, October 2022. http://english.scio.gov.cn/20thcpccongress/2022-10/23/content_78481743.html.

Second Plenary Session of the 20th Central Committee, February 2023. http://english.scio.gov.cn/topnews/2023-03/02/content_85137665.htm.

Second Plenary Session of the 20th Central Commission for Discipline Inspection, January 2023. https://news.cgtn.com/news/2023-01-10/CCDI-issues-communique-stressing-discipline-1gudyEASml2/index.html.

Third Plenary Session of the 20th Central Commission for Discipline Inspection, January 2024. https://news.cgtn.com/news/2024-01-10/CCDI-plenary-session-adopts-communique-1qfMsnVShYQ/p.html.

1.1.4. Resolutions of the Sessions of the 18th–20th Central Committee of the CCP (2012–2024)

'Plan for Institutional Reform and Functional Transformation of the State Council', Adopted at the Second Plenary Session of the 18th Central Committee of the Communist Party of China on February 28, 2013. https://www.lawinfochina.com/display.aspx?id=13772&lib=law.

'Decision of the Central Committee of the Communist Party of China on Some Major Issues concerning Comprehensively Deepening Reform', Adopted at the Third Plenary Session of the 18th Central Committee of the Communist Party of China on November 12, 2013. http://www.china.org.cn/chinese/2014-01/16/content_31215162.htm.

'Decision of the CPC Central Committee on Major Issues Pertaining to Comprehensively Promoting the Rule of Law', Adopted at the Fourth Plenary Session of the 18th Central Committee of the Communist Party of China on October 23, 2014. http://www.china.org.cn/china/third_plenary_session/2014-01/16/content_31212602.htm.

'Central Committee's Proposal for Formulating the 13th Five-Year Plan for National Economic and Social Development', Adopted at the Fifth Plenary Session of the 18th Central Committee of the Communist Party of China on October 29, 2015. https://en.ndrc.gov.cn/policies/202105/P020210527785800103339.pdf.

'Code of Conduct for Intraparty Political Life under New Circumstances: The Regulations of the Communist Party of China on Internal Oversight', Adopted at the Sixth Plenary Session of the 18th Central Committee of the Communist Party of China on October 27, 2016. https://www.en84.com/2077.html?viewall=true.

'Regulations on Religious Affairs', Revised and adopted at the 176th Executive Meeting of the State Council on June 14, 2017. https://www.sara.gov.cn/static/content/flfg/2018-10-08/1181540556363268098.html.

'Resolution of the 19th National Congress of the CPC on the Report of the 18th Central Committee', Adopted 24 October, 2017. http://www.xinhuanet.com/english/2017-10/24/c_136702625.htm.

'Suggestions of the CPC Central Committee on Amending Some Contents of the Constitution', Adopted at the Second Plenary Session of the 19th Central Committee of the Communist Party of China on January 19, 2018. https://npcobserver.com/2018/02/25/translation-communist-partys-proposals-for-amending-the-p-r-c-constitution-2018/.

'Decision of the CPC Central Committee on Deepening the Reform of the Party and State Institutions, Plan for Deepening the Institutional Reform of the Party and State', Adopted at the Third Plenary Session of the 19th Central Committee of the Communist Party of China on February 28, 2018. http://www.lawinfochina.com/display.aspx?id=27798&lib=law&EncodingName=big5.

'Decision of the Central Committee of the Communist Party of China on Major Issues concerning Upholding and Improving Socialism with Chinese Characteristics and Modernizing the State

Governance System and Capacity', Adopted at the Fourth Plenary Session of the 19th Central Committee of the CPC on October 31, 2019. https://www.airuniversity.af.edu/Portals/10/CASI/documents/Translations/2020-01-15%20Decision%20of%20the%20Central%20Committee%20of%20the%20Chinese%20Communist%20Party.pdf.

'Opinions on Strengthening the United Front Work of the Private Economy in the New Era', Published by the General Office of the CCP Central Committee on 15 September, 2020. https://interpret.csis.org/translations/the-general-office-of-the-ccp-central-committee-issued-the-opinion-on-strengthening-the-united-front-work-of-the-private-economy-in-the-new-era/.

'Outline of the People's Republic of China 14th Five-Year Plan for National Economic and Social Development and Long-Range Objectives for 2035 (Vision 2035)', Adopted at the Fifth Plenary Session of the 19th Central Committee of the Communist Party of China on October 29, 2020. https://cset.georgetown.edu/publication/china-14th-five-year-plan/.

1.1.5. Laws, Regulations, and Guidance

'Guidelines of the Eleventh Five-Year (2006–2010) Plan of the People's Republic of China for the National Economic and Social Development', 2006. https://policy.asiapacificenergy.org/sites/default/files/11th%20Five-Year%20Plan%20%282006-2010%29%20for%20National%20Economic%20and%20Social%20Development%20%28EN%29.pdf.

'National Security Law of the People's Republic of China', Passed at the 15th meeting of the Standing Committee of the 12th National People's Congress on July 1, 2015. https://govt.chinadaily.com.cn/s/201812/11/WS5c0f1b56498eefb3fe46e8c9/national-security-law-of-the-peoples-republic-of-china-2015-effective.html.

'Law of the People's Republic of China on Administration of Activities of Overseas Nongovernmental Organizations in the Mainland of China', Adopted by the National People's Congress Standing Committee on 28 April, 2016. https://www.chinafile.com/ngo/laws-regulations/law-of-peoples-republic-of-china-administration-of-activities-of-overseas.

'Full Text of Resolution on Amendment to CPC Constitution', Adopted at the 19th National Congress of the CPC on October 24, 2017. https://english.www.gov.cn/news/top_news/2017/10/24/content_281475919837140.htm.

'Constitution of the Communist Party of China, Revised and adopted at the 19th National Congress of the Communist Party of China on October 24, 2017. http://www.xinhuanet.com//english/download/Constitution_of_the_Communist_Party_of_China.pdf.

'National Intelligence Law of the People's Republic of China, Adopted at the 28th meeting of the Standing Committee of the 12th National People's Congress on June 27, 2017. https://cs.brown.edu/courses/csci1800/sources/2017_PRC_NationalIntelligenceLaw.pdf.

'Amendment to the Constitution of the People's Republic of China', Adopted at the First Session of the 13th National People's Congress on March 11, 2018. https://faolex.fao.org/docs/pdf/chn180555.pdf.

'Constitution of the People's Republic of China, Revised and adopted at the First Sesssion of the 13th National People's Congress on March 11, 2018. http://www.xinhuanet.com/politics/2018lh/2018-03/22/c_1122572202.htm.

'Provisions on the Governance of the Online Information Content Ecosystem', Adopted at the executive meeting of the Cyberspace Administration of China on 15 December, 2019. https://wilmap.stanford.edu/entries/provisions-governance-online-information-content-ecosystem.

'Opinions on Strengthening the United Front Work of the Private Economy in the New Era', Issued by the General Office of the CCP Central Committee on 15 September 2020. https://interpret.csis.org/translations/the-general-office-of-the-ccp-central-committee-issued-the-opinion-on-strengthening-the-united-front-work-of-the-private-economy-in-the-new-era/.

'Work Regulations of the Central Committee of the Communist Party of China', Deliberated and approved at the CCP Central Committee Politburo meeting of 28 September 2020, and issued on 30 September 2020 by the CCP Central Committee, 2020. https://chinacopyrightandme

dia.wordpress.com/2020/09/30/work-regulations-of-the-central-committee-of-the-communist-party-of-china/.

'Constitution of the Communist Party of China, Revised and adopted at the 20th National Congress of the Communist Party of China on October 22, 2022. https://language.chinadaily.com.cn/a/202210/26/WS635fc9a1a310fd2b29e7f835.html.

1.1.6. Collations of the Selected Works and Individual Speeches, Articles of Mao Zedong, Deng Xiaoping, Jiang Zemin, Hu Jintao, V. I. Lenin, Karl Marx, Zhao Ziyang, and Zhou Enlai

Deng Xiaoping. *Build Socialism with Chinese Characteristics*. Beijing: Foreign Languages Press, 1984.

Deng Xiaoping. *Selected Works of Deng Xiaoping*. Vol. 1. Beijing: Foreign Languages Press, 1995.

Deng Xiaoping. *Selected Works of Deng Xiaoping*. Vol. 2. Beijing: Foreign Languages Press, 1995.

Deng Xiaoping. *Selected Works of Deng Xiaoping*. Vol. 3. Beijing: Foreign Languages Press, 1994.

Jiang Zemin. *Selected Works of Jiang Zemin*. Vol. 1. Beijing: Foreign Languages Press, 2011

Jiang Zemin. *Selected Works of Jiang Zemin*. Vol. 2. Beijing: Foreign Languages Press, 2012

Jiang Zemin. *Selected Works of Jiang Zemin*. Vol. 3. Beijing: Foreign Languages Press, 2013

Lenin, Vladimir Ilyich. *Essential Works of Lenin*. New York: Dover, 1987

Lenin, Vladimir Ilyich. *Collected Works*. Vol. 14. Moscow: Progress Publishers, 1977

Mao Zedong. *Selected Works of Mao Tse-Tung*. Vol. 1. Paris: Foreign Languages Press, 2021.

Mao Zedong. *Selected Works of Mao Tse-Tung*. Vol. 2. Paris: Foreign Languages Press, 2021.

Mao Zedong. *Selected Works of Mao Tse-Tung*. Vol. 3. Paris: Foreign Languages Press, 2021.

Mao Zedong. *Selected Works of Mao Tse-Tung*. Vol. 4. Paris: Foreign Languages Press, 2021.

Mao Zedong. *Selected Works of Mao Tse-Tung*. Vol. 5. Paris: Foreign Languages Press, 2021.

Mao Zedong. *Selected Works of Mao Tse-Tung*. Vol. 6. Paris: Foreign Languages Press, 2021.

Mao Zedong. *Selected Works of Mao Tse-Tung*. Vol. 7. Paris: Foreign Languages Press, 2020.

Mao Zedong. *Selected Works of Mao Tse-Tung*. Vol. 8. Paris: Foreign Languages Press, 2020.

Mao Zedong. *Selected Works of Mao Tse-Tung*. Vol. 9. Paris: Foreign Languages Press, 2021.

Mao Zedong. *Selected Works of Mao Tse-Tung*. Vol. 9. Hyderabad: Sramikavarga Prachuranalu, 1994.

Mao Zedong. *Collected Works of Mao Tse-Tung (1917–1949)*. Springfield, VA: National Technical Information Service, 1978.

Mao Zedong. *Five Essays on Philosophy*. Utrecht: Foreign Languages Press, 2018.

Mao Zedong. *Mao's Road to Power: Revolutionary Writings*. Vol. 8. Stuart Schram, Timothy Cheek, and Nancy J. Hodes eds. New York: Routledge, 2015.

Mao Zedong. *Mao Zedong on Dialectical Materialism*. Nick Knight ed. Armonk, NY: M. E. Sharp, 1990.

Mao Zedong. *Mao Zedong on Diplomacy*. Beijing: Foreign Languages Press, 1988.

Mao Zedong. *The Secret Speeches of Chairman Mao: From the Hundred Flowers to the Great Leap Forward*. Roderick MacFarquhar, Timothy Cheek, and Eugene Wu eds. Harvard: Council on East Asian Studies, 1989.

Mao Zedong. 'Speeches at the 1957 "Moscow Conference"'. Michael Schoenhals trans. *Journal of Communist Studies*, 2/2 (1986): 109–126.

Mao Zedong. *The Writings of Mao Zedong 1945–1976*. Vol. 1. John K. Leung and Michael Y. M. Kau eds. New York: M. E. Sharpe, 1986.

Marx, Karl. *Collected Works*. Vol. 42. London: Lawrence & Wishart, 2020.

Marx, Karl. *Surveys from Exile*. London: Verso, 2010.

Marx, Karl. *Thesen über Feuerbach*. Edited by Georges Labica. Hamburg: Argument, 1998.

Marx, Karl, and Friedrich Engels. *The German Ideology*. Edited by C. J. Arthur. New York: International Publishers, 1972.

Zhou Enlai. *Selected Works of Zhou Enlai*. Vol. 1. Beijing: Foreign Languages Press, 1981.

Zhou Enlai. *Selected Works of Zhou Enlai*. Vol. 2. Beijing: Foreign Languages Press, 1989.

1.1.7. Collations of Selected Works of Xi Jinping

The Governance of China. Vol. 1. Beijing: Foreign Languages Press, 2014.

The Chinese Dream of the Great Rejuvenation of the Chinese Nation. Beijing: Foreign Languages Press, 2014.

How to Deepen Reform Comprehensively. Beijing: Foreign Languages Press, 2014.
The Governance of China. Vol. 2. Beijing: Foreign Languages Press, 2016.
Up and Out of Poverty. Beijing: Foreign Languages Press, 2016.
The Law-Based Governance of China. Beijing: Central Compilation & Translation Press, 2017.
On Building a Human Community with a Shared Future. Beijing: Central Compilation & Translation Press, 2019.
The Belt and Road Initiative. Beijing: Foreign Languages Press, 2019.
Xi Jinping Coordinating the COVID-19 Response with Economic and Social Development Selected Speeches and Statements. Beijing: Central Compilation & Translation Press, 2020.
The Governance of China. Vol. 3. Beijing: Foreign Languages Press, 2020.
The Governance of China. Vol. 4. Beijing: Foreign Languages Press, 2023.
Chinese Modernization (习近平关于中国式现代化论述摘编,英文版). Beijing: Central Compilation & Translation Press, 2023.
Chinese Modernization (习近平关于中国式现代化论述摘编,双语版). Beijing: Central Compilation & Translation Press, 2023.

1.1.8. Individual Speeches and Articles by Xi Jinping

'Cast the Net Wider When Bringing in New Personnel', 2003.
'Cultural Works Should Also Have "Box Office Value"', 2003.
'Do Good Things in the Right Way', 2003.
'Drought Relief Must Focus on the People', 2003.
'Environmental Protection Requires Voluntary and Conscious Action', 2003.
'Establish Five Noble Sentiments', 2003.
'Field Research Must Incorporate Depth, Pragmatism, Thoroughness, Accuracy, and Efficacy', 2003.
'Informal Remarks Reveal Whether the People Are Satisfied after an Official Leaves Office', 2003.
'It's Better to Walk on Two Legs', 2003.
'Officials Cannot Be Cultivated Like Greenhouse Plants', 2003.
'Officials Should Not Be Misled into Focusing Exclusively on Governance by Ballot', 2003.
'Orchestrate a Multitude of Voices into a Symphony', 2003.
'Perform a Well-Coordinated "Duet Dance"', 2003.
'Prioritize Support for People in Difficulties', 2003.
'Private Capital Has Great Potential', 2003.
'The Road Lies before Us', 2003.
'Seek a Clear Conscience before the People rather than Personal Power', 2003.
'Select the Worthy and Capable through Multiple Pairs of Eyes', 2003.
'Strengthen the Preservation of West Lake Cultural Heritage', 2003.
'Strengthen Unity', 2003.
'Strive to Create a "Creditworthy Zhejiang"', 2003.
'Theoretical Study Requires Three Perspectives', 2003.
'Think Boldly but Seek Evidence Carefully in Pilot Programs', 2003.
'Uphold Major Principles and Be Flexible in Minor Matters', 2003.
'We Need a Global Vision and Strategic Thinking', 2003.
'Abstract Work Must Be Done Concretely', 2004.
'Accelerate the Development of Underdeveloped Areas', 2004.
'Adopt an Overall View to Balance Urban and Rural Development', 2004.
'Adopt Both Preventive and Punitive Measures against Corruption', 2004.
'Anything That Benefits the People Must Be Done Well', 2004.
'Attainments of Thought Have Long-Term Significance', 2004.
'Attitude and Competence Are of the Utmost Importance in Governance', 2004.
'Balance Economic Development and Ecological Conservation', 2004.
'Balance Three Types of Relationship', 2004.
'The Better Things Are, the More Realistic and Pragmatic We Must Be', 2004.
'Build a Knowledge Structure in Keeping with the Times', 2004.
'Building an Environmentally Friendly Province Is a Long-Term, Strategic Mission', 2004.

'A Campaign That Involves the Interests of All Families', 2004.
'Cherish the Time in Office', 2004.
'Combine Innovation and Inheritance to Develop Tourism', 2004.
'Coordinated Material and Cultural Progress', 2004.
'Create Quality Tourist Attractions', 2004.
'Create Wealth through Hard Work Let Knowledge Become Strength', 2004.
'Cultural Progress Starts from Childhood', 2004.
'Develop the Art of Leadership', 2004.
'Development Poses Questions, Reform Offers Answers', 2004.
'Do Not Allow Systems to Become Paper Tigers', 2004.
'Endeavour to Make Officials Incorruptible', 2004.
'Enhance the Approach to Leadership Visits to the Grassroots', 2004.
'Ensure Sustainable Development of Tourism', 2004.
'Evaluate the All-Round Performance of Officials', 2004.
'GDP Must Be Considered, but Not Exclusively', 2004.
'Go Directly to the People', 2004.
'Grassroots Officials Play an Important Role', 2004.
'Guard against Arrogance and Haste, Especially in Good Times', 2004.
'Heighten Public Awareness of Ecological Conservation', 2004.
'Improve the Quality and Standard of News Reporting', 2004.
'Keep Our Feet Planted in the Present, Keep Our Eyes Fixed on the Future', 2004.
'A Lack of Pressure Undermines Effectiveness', 2004.
'Lay Groundwork for the Future', 2004.
'Leadership Visits to the Grassroots Must Be Effective', 2004.
'Leading Officials Must Pursue Integrity and Self-Discipline', 2004.
'Learn to Play the Piano with All Ten Fingers', 2004.
'Look at the Big Picture When Searching for Solutions to the Three Rural Issues', 2004.
'Maintain the Enthusiasm of Grassroots Officials', 2004.
'Nothing Can Be Accomplished unless We Take a Pragmatic Approach to Implementation', 2004.
'Officials Must Have a Positive Attitude', 2004.
'Officials Should Welcome Public Scrutiny', 2004.
'One Must Learn to Be Upright Before One Can Become Useful', 2004.
'Open up Potential to Achieve Greater Development', 2004.
'Opportunity Favours Those Who Dare to Compete', 2004.
'Optimize Our Province's Economic Configuration', 2004.
'The Path to Success Lies in Perseverance', 2004.
'Promoting Growth and Safeguarding Stability are Both Commendable Achievements', 2004.
'Pursue Green GDP', 2004.
'Resolve Grievances at the Grassroots', 2004.
'Scale Down Festival Celebrations', 2004.
'Seizing a Period of Strategic Opportunities Requires a Historic Sense of Urgency', 2004.
'Small Things Serve as Mirrors', 2004.
'The Solution Lies with the People', 2004.
'Stability, Not Mediocrity', 2004.
'Strengthen Prevention in Sectors That Are Prone to Corruption', 2004.
'Success Can Only Come through Implementation', 2004.
'Take a New Approach to Social Stability', 2004.
'Theory Steers Development', 2004.
'Tighten Land Use in the Long Run', 2004.
'To Be Realistic and Pragmatic Requires Concrete Action', 2004.
'To Be Worthy of Public Office We Must Have the Common People in Our Hearts', 2004.
'Treat Difficulties as Opportunities', 2004.

'The Ultimate Purpose of Political Achievement Is to Benefit the People', 2004.
'Understand the Real Essence, Don't Just Feign Compliance', 2004.
'The Value of Leadership Visits to the Grassroots', 2004.
'Work Resolutely for the People', 2004.
'Achieve Overall Success through Small Victories', 2005.
'Advance Reform and Opening Up to Promote Rural Development', 2005.
'Advance without Fear of Hardship', 2005.
'All Professions Are Equally Worthy', 2005.
'Balance Investment and Consumption', 2005.
'Become a Close Friend of the People', 2005.
'Build a Conservation-Based Society', 2005.
'Build Zhejiang into a Province of Major Brands', 2005.
'Carry on the Mission of Implementing the Scientific Outlook on Development', 2005.
'Clear Waters and Green Mountains Are as Valuable as Gold and Silver', 2005.
'Convert Pressure into Impetus', 2005.
'Coordinate Urban and Rural Planning to Promote Rural Development', 2005.
'Create an Eco-Friendly Society', 2005.
'Criticism and Self-Criticism Should Be Done in Earnest', 2005.
'Cultivate Charisma and Lead by Example', 2005.
'Culture Breeds Harmony', 2005.
'Culture Is the Soul', 2005.
'Develop High- Efficiency Eco-Agriculture', 2005.
'Development Must Not Take the Old Path', 2005.
'The Dialectics of Transforming the Economic Growth Model', 2005.
'Establish the Concept of a Harmonious Society', 2005.
'Every Party Member Should Stand Out as a Good Example', 2005.
'Favour Light or Heavy Industry as Appropriate', 2005.
'Give More Support to the Grassroots', 2005.
'Good Public Communication', 2005.
'Grow the Service Industry into an Economic Powerhouse', 2005.
'Ideals, Responsibility, and Values Must Be Put into Practice', 2005.
'The Importance of a Proactive Approach to Work', 2005.
'The Importance of Grassroots Officials in Governance', 2005.
'Improve the Mechanism of Social Mobilization', 2005.
'Improvement and Reinvention of the Private Sector from Within', 2005.
'Intangible and Tangible Achievements in Work', 2005.
'Invest More Effort in Work at the Grassroots', 2005.
'Investigative Research Is Like Gestation', 2005.
'Leading Officials Must Live Up to Their Responsibility', 2005.
'Leverage the Role of Imports', 2005.
'Lift the "Two Ends" for Balanced Regional Development', 2005.
'Look beyond Zhejiang for Further Development', 2005.
'Make the Three Rural Issues a Top Priority in Exercising Power for the People', 2005.
'Move from Passive Response to Proactive Reform', 2005.
'Our Advanced Nature Means Being in the Vanguard', 2005.
'Practice Self-Discipline through Self-Reflection', 2005.
'Preserve the Advanced Nature of Party Members', 2005.
'Pressure and Impetus Can Morph into One Another', 2005.
'Prioritize Efficiency and Safeguard Fairness', 2005.
'Promote a Realistic and Pragmatic Spirit', 2005.
'Promote the Spirit of Battling the Typhoons', 2005.
'Raise Awareness of Being in the Vanguard', 2005.

'Resolve the Three Rural Issues in a People-Centred Way', 2005.
'A Selective Approach to Attracting Investment', 2005.
'Stability and Harmony Are Integral to the Scientific Outlook on Development', 2005.
'Take a Realistic and Pragmatic Approach to the Three Rural Issues', 2005.
'Take Results-Oriented Actions in Developing a Circular Economy', 2005.
'Uphold a Scientific Outlook on Safeguarding Rights', 2005.
'Well-Rounded Education Is the Foundation of a Country of Innovators', 2005.
'Writing Style Embodies Work Style', 2005.
'Balanced and Sustainable Development Must First Be Safe Development', 2006.
'Be Adept at Identifying Role Models', 2006.
'Be Adept at Learning from Role Models', 2006.
'Be Bold in Taking on Responsibilities', 2006.
'Beautiful Rural Areas Depend on Development', 2006.
'Building a New Countryside Must Be Adapted to Local Conditions', 2006.
'Building a New Countryside Must Reflect Balanced and Sustainable Development', 2006.
'Champion the Rule of Law and the Rule of Virtue Equally', 2006.
'Connect Study to Practice', 2006.
'Consistency between Upward and Downward Accountability', 2006.
'Consolidate the Frontline Platform for Social Stability', 2006.
'Correctly Handle Problems among the People in the New Era', 2006.
'Cultivate Virtue and Good Governance through Extensive Reading', 2006.
'The Culture Economy Brightens Up Zhejiang's Economy', 2006.
'Dedication Shines in Hardships', 2006.
'Deeper Reform Is the Driving Force towards a Conservation-Based Society', 2006.
'Deepen Reform with "Two Hands"', 2006.
'The Dialectical Unity of the Four-Point Development Strategy', 2006.
'Eliminate Vice and Exalt Virtue', 2006.
'Energize Rural Areas through Reform', 2006.
'Examine the "Three Rural Issues" from Two Perspectives', 2006.
'Expand the Zhejiang Economy with the "Zhejiang People Economy"', 2006.
'Government Must Lead by Example in Establishing a Conservation-Based Society', 2006.
'Guard against Impetuousness in Character and Action', 2006.
'Happiness Lies in Unity among the People', 2006.
'A Harmonious Society Is Based on the Rule of Law', 2006.
'Implementation Is Like Hammering Nails', 2006.
'Investigative Research Must Link the Specific with the General', 2006.
'Leadership Transition Tests the Party Spirit of Leading Officials', 2006.
'Leveraging Local Strengths Starts with Planning', 2006.
'Market Economy Only Works under the Rule of Law', 2006.
'Master Correct Work Methods', 2006.
'Modernize Rural Areas through Education', 2006.
'New Requirements for Advancing the Rule of Law', 2006.
'Officials Are Better When Tempered in Difficult Environments', 2006.
'One Who Dedicates Himself to the People Wins Their Hearts', 2006.
'One Who Governs Needs to Study and Reflect', 2006.
'Our Business Culture Sustains Zhejiang Entrepreneurs', 2006.
'The Party's Leadership Assures the Rule of Law', 2006.
'Prevent Elements of Instability from Becoming a "Chronic Disease"', 2006.
'Promote Joint Prosperity of Urban and Rural Areas', 2006.
'Promote Stability in Rural Areas with the Rule of Law', 2006.
'The Questions Are the Mottoes of a Period', 2006.
'Reshuffling Leadership Tests Officials', 2006.

'Resolve Grassroots Problems through Grassroots Democracy', 2006.
'Restructure Industry with "Two Birds"', 2006.
'Save the Environment with "Two Types of Mountain"', 2006.
'Say No to Empty Words, Say Yes to Practical Deeds', 2006.
'Scale the Heights of Balanced and Sustainable Development', 2006.
'Social Development Is Key to a Harmonious Society', 2006.
'Solve the Paradox of Economic Development and Environmental Conservation', 2006.
'Strengthen Rural Areas through Development', 2006.
'Strengthening Regulation Is Necessary for Building a Conservation-Based Society', 2006.
'A Strong Party Leadership Team at the Village Level', 2006.
'Structural Adjustment Lays the Groundwork for a Conservation-Based Society', 2006.
'Technological Innovation Is the Key to a Conservation-Based Society', 2006.
'A Three-Pronged Approach to Bringing in Investment', 2006.
'The "Three Rural Issues" Are Our Top Priority', 2006.
'Uphold and Practice the Rule of Law', 2006.
'The Virtue of Dedication to and Pleasure in Work', 2006.
'Action Is Key to Solving Real Problems for the People', 2007.
'Be Down-to-Earth in Solving Real Problems for the People', 2007.
'Be Watchful over Oneself When Alone', 2007.
'Clean Governance Should Dominate Our Work', 2007.
'Correctly Understand Better and Faster Development', 2007.
'Enhance Corporate Social Responsibility', 2007.
'A Good Person and a Good Official', 2007.
'Harmony Precedes Unity', 2007.
'Improve Party Conduct Based on the People's Needs', 2007.
'Looking Backward and Forward, a Requirement for Newly Appointed Officials', 2007.
'Moral Progress through Charity', 2007.
'Officials Must Serve the People', 2007.
'Officials Must Take the Lead in Improving Party Conduct', 2007.
'Officials Should Avoid Putting on Airs', 2007.
'Pedants Are Not What We Need', 2007.
'Personal Lifestyle Is Not a Trivial Matter', 2007.
'Power Is Sacred', 2007.
'Practice and Theory Are Equally Important', 2007.
'Reduce Expenditures for a Stronger Foundation', 2007.
'Solve Real Problems for the People', 2007.
'Take Learning and Practice to New Levels', 2007.
'We Need Both Democracy and Centralism', 2007.
Note: There is no publicly available compendium of Xi's speeches between 2008-11.
'Achieving Rejuvenation Is the Dream of the Chinese People', 2012.
'Build Strong National Defense and Powerful Military Forces', 2012.
'Build Up Our National Defense and Armed Forces', 2012.
'China's New Party Chief Xi Jinping's Speech', 2012.
'Commemorate the 30th Anniversary of the Promulgation and Implementation of the Current Constitution', 2012.
'Economic Growth Must Be Genuine and Not Inflated', 2012.
'Eliminate Poverty and Accelerate Development in Impoverished Areas', 2012.
'Focussing on Six Aspects in Fully Implementing the Guiding Principles of the 18th National Congress of the CPC', 2012.
'The People's Wish for a Good Life Is Our Goal', 2012.
'Reform and Opening Up Is Always Ongoing and Will Never End', 2012.
'Study, Disseminate, and Implement the Guiding Principles of the 18th CPC National Congress', 2012.

'Accelerate the Development of Housing Security and Supply', 2013.
'Address to the First Session of the 12th National People's Congress', 2013.
'Align Our Thinking with the Guidelines of the Third Plenary Session of the 18th CPC Central Committee', 2013.
'Always Put People's Lives First', 2013.
'Be Trustworthy Friends and Sincere Partners Forever', 2013.
'Better and Fairer Education for the 1.3 Billion Chinese People', 2013.
'A Better Environment for a Beautiful China', 2013.
'A Better Future for Asia and the World', 2013.
'Build a New Model of Major-Country Relations between China and the United States', 2013.
'Build People's Armed Forces That Follow the Party's Commands, Are Able to Win Battles, and Have Fine Conduct', 2013.
'Carry Forward the "Shanghai Spirit" and Promote Common Development', 2013.
'Carry On the Enduring Spirit of Mao Zedong Thought', 2013.
'Central Economic Work Conference', 2013
'China to Further Friendly Relations with Neighbouring Countries', 2013.
'The Chinese Dream Will Benefit Not Only the People of China, but Also of Other Countries', 2013.
'The Correct Understanding of Major Theoretical and Practical Problems of China's Development', 2022
'Deepen Reform and Opening Up and Work Together for a Better Asia Pacific', 2013.
'Develop a Law-Based Country, Government, and Society', 2013.
'Diplomacy with Neighbouring Countries Characterized by Friendship, Sincerity, Reciprocity, and Inclusiveness', 2013.
'Encourage the Whole Party to Study and Master Historical Materialism, Better Grasp Marxist Laws, and Pursue Work More Proactively', 2013
'Enhance China's Cultural Soft Power', 2013.
'Enhance Publicity and Theoretical Work', 2013.
'Establish and Promote the Conduct of "Three Stricts and Three Earnests"', 2013.
'Explanatory Notes to the "Decision of the Central Committee of the Communist Party of China on Some Major Issues Concerning Comprehensively Deepening Reform"', 2013.
'Follow a Good Blueprint', 2013.
'Follow the Trend of the Times and Promote Global Peace and Development', 2013.
'Forge a Stronger Partnership between China and Latin America and the Caribbean', 2013.
'Give Full Play to the Leading Role of the Asia-Pacific Maintain and Advance an Open World Economy', 2013.
'Governing a Big Country Is as Delicate as Frying a Small Fish', 2013.
'The Guiding Thoughts and Goals for the Program of Mass Line Education and Practice', 2013.
'Handle Cross-Straits Relations in the Overall Interests of the Chinese Nations', 2013.
'Hard Work Makes Dreams Come True', 2013.
'Historical Wisdom Helps Us Combat Corruption and Uphold Integrity', 2013.
'Hong Kong, Macao, and the Chinese Mainland Are Closely Linked by Destiny', 2013.
'Implementing the Guiding Principles of the 18th National Congress of the CPC with a View to Upholding and Developing Socialism with Chinese Characteristics', 2013.
'Jointly Maintain and Develop an Open World Economy', 2013.
'Keep the Larger Picture in Mind, Grasp General Trends, Look towards Great Matters, Do Propaganda and Ideological Work Even Better', 2013.
'Leave to Our Future Generations Blue Skies, Green Fields, and Clean Water', 2013.
'Let the Sense of Community of Common Destiny Take Deep Root in Neighbouring Countries', 2013.
'The Mass Line: Fundamental to the CPC', 2013.
'New Approach for Asian Security Cooperation', 2013.
'Open Wider to the Outside World', 2013.
'Power Must Be "Caged" by the System', 2013.
'Promote Friendship between Our People and Work Together to Build a Bright Future', 2013.

'Realize Youthful Dreams', 2013.
'Right Time to Innovate and Make Dreams Come True', 2013.
'Strengthen the Foundation for Pursuing Peaceful Development', 2013.
'Strong Ethical Support for the Realization of the Chinese Dream', 2013.
'Study for a Brighter Future', 2013.
'Train and Select Good Officials', 2013.
'Uphold and Develop Socialism with Chinese Characteristics', 2013.
'Usher in a New Era of Ecological Progress', 2013.
'Work Hand in Hand for Common Development', 2013.
'Work Together for a Better Asia Pacific', 2013.
'Work Together to Build a 21st-Century Maritime Silk Road', 2013.
'Work Together to Build the Silk Road Economic Belt', 2013.
'Follow the Trend of the Times and Promote Peace and Development', 2013.
'Accelerating the Establishment of Socialist Rule of Law in China', 2014.
'Asia-Pacific Partnership of Mutual Trust, Inclusiveness, Cooperation, and Win-Win Progress', 2014.
'A Bright Future for Socialism with Chinese Characteristics', 2014.
'Broad, Multilevel, and Institutionalized Consultative Democracy', 2014.
'Build a Bridge of Friendship and Cooperation across the Eurasian Continent', 2014.
'Build China into a Cyberpower', 2014.
'Central Foreign Affairs Work Conference', 2014
'Central Economic Work Conference', 2014.
'China's Commitment to Peaceful Development', 2014.
'China's Diplomacy Must Befit Its Major-Country Status', 2014.
'China's Xi Jinping Talks of Deeper Australian Ties ahead of G20', 2014.
'Chinese President Proposes an Asia-Pacific Dream', 2014.
'Closing Remarks at the 22nd APEC Economic Leaders' Meeting', 2014.
'Confidence in the Political System of Chinese Socialism', 2014.
'Cultivate and Disseminate the Core Socialist Values', 2014.
'Economic Work Should Be Adapted to the New Normal', 2014.
'Exchanges and Mutual Learning Make Civilizations Richer and More Colourful', 2014.
'Follow a Sensible, Coordinated, and Balanced Approach to Nuclear Security', 2014.
'Foster and Practice Core Socialist Values from Childhood', 2014.
'A Holistic View of National Security', 2014.
'Implement the Free Trade Zone Strategy', 2014.
'Improve Governance Capacity through the Socialist System with Chinese Characteristics', 2014.
'Improve Party Conduct, Uphold Integrity, and Combat Corruption', 2014.
'The "Invisible Hand" and the "Visible Hand"', 2014.
'Make Solid Efforts to Advance Reform', 2014.
'New Approach for Asian Security Cooperation', 2014.
'New Asian Security Concept for New Progress in Security Cooperation', 2014
'Progress in Practicing "One Country, Two Systems" in Macao', 2014.
'Promote Social Fairness and Justice, Ensure a Happy Life for the People', 2014.
'Promote Socialist Rule of Law', 2014.
'Promote the Silk Road Spirit, Strengthen China-Arab Cooperation', 2014.
'Push Ahead with Reform despite More Difficulties', 2014.
'The Rejuvenation of the Chinese Nation Is a Dream Shared by All Chinese', 2014.
'Revolutionize Energy Production and Consumption', 2014.
'Safeguard National Security and Social Stability', 2014.
'Strengthen and Improve the Political Work of the Military', 2014.
'Take On the Task of Expanding Cross-Straits Relations and Achieving National Rejuvenation', 2014.
'Together Fulfil the Chinese Dream of National Rejuvenation', 2014.
'Transform and Boost Traditional Culture in a Creative Way', 2014.

'Transition to Innovation-Driven Growth', 2014.
'Young People Should Practice the Core Socialist Values', 2014.
'Address at the Commemoration of the 70th Anniversary of the Victory of the Chinese People's War of Resistance against Japanese Aggression and the World Anti-Fascist War', 2015.
'Be a Good County Party Secretary', 2015.
'Central Economic Work Conference', 2015.
'The Chinese Dream Is the People's Dream', 2015.
'The Decisive Stage in Achieving the First Centenary Goal', 2015.
'Dialectical Materialism Is the Worldview and Methodology of Chinese Communists', 2015.
'Forging a Strong Partnership to Enhance Prosperity of Asia', 2015.
'Guide Development with New Concepts', 2015.
'How to Resolve Major Difficulties in Realizing the First Centenary Goal', 2015.
'Improve the Work of the United Front', 2015.
'Join Hands to Consolidate Peace and Development in Cross-Straits Relations', 2015.
'Keep in Line with the CPC Central Committee', 2015.
'The Leading Role of the Asia-Pacific in Meeting Global Economic Challenge', 2015.
'A New Era of China-Africa Cooperation and Common Development', 2015.
'The New Normal: How to Respond and Adapt', 2015.
'Observe Discipline and Rules', 2015.
'Officials Must Set a Good Example in Observing the Law', 2015.
'Opening Up New Frontiers for Marxist Political Economy in Contemporary China', 2015.
'The Party's Work with Social Organizations', 2015.
'Promote Ecological Progress and Reform Environmental Management', 2015.
'Reform the Judicial System', 2015.
'Remember the Past and Our Martyrs, Cherish Peace, and Build a New Future', 2015.
'Speech at a Gathering to Celebrate the Spring Festival', 2015.
'Speech at a Medal Presentation Ceremony Marking the 70th Anniversary of the Chinese People's Victory in the War of Resistance against Japanese Aggression', 2015.
'Speech at an Event to Celebrate the "May 1st" International Labor Day', 2015.
'Speech at the 23rd Asia-Pacific Economic Cooperation (APEC) Economic Leaders' Meeting', 2015.
'Speech at the BRICS Summit in Ufa', 2015.
'Staying Committed to and Jointly Promoting Development to Bring Asia-Pacific Cooperation to New Heights', 2015.
'Strengthen the Armed Forces through Reform', 2015.
'Take Targeted Measures against Poverty', 2015.
'Towards a China-EU Partnership for Peace, Growth, Reform, and Civilization', 2015.
'Towards a Community of Common Destiny and a New Future for Asia', 2015.
'Towards a Mutually Beneficial Partnership for Sustainable Development', 2015.
'When the People Are Firm in Their Convictions, the Nation Will Flourish', 2015.
'Working Together to Forge a New Partnership of Win-Win Cooperation and Create a Community of Shared Future for Mankind', 2015.
'Address at Inauguration Ceremony of the Asian Infrastructure Investment Bank', 2016.
'The Belt and Road Initiative and Connectivity Are Mutually Reinforcing', 2016.
'The Belt and Road Initiative Benefits the People', 2016.
'A Brighter Future for China-Russia Relations', 2016.
'Build an Innovative, Invigorated, Interconnected, and Inclusive World Economy', 2016.
'Build China into a World Leader in Science and Technology', 2016.
'Central Economic Work Conference', 2016.
'China Renews Call for Building FTAAP as Economic Globalization Falters', 2016.
'Clear Waters and Green Mountains Are Invaluable Assets', 2016.
'Confidence in Chinese Culture', 2016.
'CPC Policies on Ethnic Affairs and Religion', 2016.

'A Deeper Understanding of the New Development Concepts', 2016.
'Develop Philosophy and Social Sciences with Chinese Feature', 2016.
'Eco-Environmental Protection Is an Integral Component of Development', 2016.
'Enhance Party Conduct, Uphold Clean Government, and Fight Corruption', 2016.
'Expanding the Middle-Income Group', 2016.
'Family Values, Family Education, and Family Tradition', 2016.
'The Four Consciousnesses and the Authority of the Central Committee', 2016.
'Chinese President's Signed Article in Ecuadorian Newspaper', 2016.
'Implement the New Development Concepts', 2016.
'Improve All Aspects of the Party's Media Leadership', 2016.
'Improve Our Ability to Participate in Global Governance', 2016.
'Improve the Wellbeing of the People', 2016.
'Increase Sino-Arab Dialogue and Expand Common Ground', 2016.
'Let a Healthy Internet Guide and Reflect Public Opinion', 2016.
'Make Targeted Efforts in Reform', 2016.
'A National Supervision System Covering State Organs and Public Servants', 2016.
'A New Starting Point for China's Development: A New Blueprint for Global Growth', 2016.
'Party Leadership Is the Unique Strength of SOEs', 2016.
'Promote a Healthy China', 2016.
'Promote Supply-Side Structural Reform', 2016.
'Promote the Belt and Road Initiative, Extend Reform and Development', 2016.
'Promote the Healthy Development of Diverse Forms of Ownership', 2016.
'Reinforce the Party's Internal Scrutiny', 2016.
'Forge Ahead into the Future for Progress and Prosperity in the Asia-Pacific', 2016.
'The Rule of Law and the Rule of Virtue', 2016.
'Secure the People's Basic Needs', 2016.
'Speech at a Ceremony Marking the 95th Anniversary of the Founding of the Communist Party of China', 2016.
'Speech at a Symposium on Cybersecurity and IT Application', 2016.
'Speech at the Fifth Plenary Session of the Eighteenth CPC Central Committee', 2016.
'Stay True to Our Original Aspiration and Continue Marching Forward', 2016.
'Stronger Discipline Inspection Tours Make for Stricter Party Self-Governance', 2016.
'Tighten Political Activities within Our Party', 2016.
'Today We Must Succeed in a New "Long March"', 2016.
'Towards World-Class Universities and Disciplines', 2016.
'Uphold and Consolidate the Party's Ideological Leadership', 2016.
'What Is the New Normal in China's Economic Development?', 2016.
'Jointly Create a Better Future of Peace and Prosperity for Asia through Dialogue and Consensus', 2016.
'Carry Forward the Spirit of Saihanba, a Model in Afforestation', 2017.
'Central Economic Work Conference', 2017.
'Complete a Moderately Prosperous Society and Realize the Chinese Dream', 2017.
'Continue to Strengthen Our Military', 2017.
'Deeper Civil-Military Integration', 2017.
'Develop and Popularize Marxism in the Modern Chinese Context', 2017.
'Eliminate Poverty in Severely Impoverished Areas', 2017.
'Seizing the Opportunity of a Global Economy in Transition and Accelerating Development of the Asia-Pacific', 2017.
'Promoting Openness and Inclusiveness to Achieve Interconnected Growth', 2017.
'Work Together to Build the Silk Road Economic Belt and the 21st Century Maritime Silk Road', 2017.
'Working Together for a New Chapter of Win-Win Cooperation in the Asia-Pacific', 2017.
'Further Reform Must Be Systematic, Integrated, and Coordinated', 2017.
'Green Development Model and Green Way of Life', 2017.

'Implement the New Development Concept to Build a Modern Economic System', 2017.

'Jointly Shoulder Responsibility of Our Times, Promote Global Growth', 2017.

'Keep Hold of the Strategic Initiative for Our National Security', 2017.

'Meet the Standards for Party Members', 2017.

'"One Country, Two Systems": Long-Term Prosperity and Stability for Hong Kong', 2017.

'Keep Abreast of the Trend of the Times to Shape a Bright Future', 2017

'Social Governance under Socialism with Chinese Characteristics', 2017.

'Sound, Circular, and Healthy Development of the Economy and Finance', 2017.

'Speech at the First Plenary Session of the 19th CPC Central Committee', 2017.

'Study Is the Prerequisite and Action Is the Key', 2017.

'There Are a Thousand Reasons to Make the China-US Relationship a Success', 2017.

'Three Initiatives for Balanced Regional Development', 2017.

'Towards a Community of Shared Future for Mankind', 2017

'Usher In the Second Golden Decade of BRICS Cooperation', 2017.

'Xi Jinping at the Opening Ceremony of the Fifth CICA Foreign Ministers Meeting', 2017.

'Central Economic Work Conference', 2018.

'Central Foreign Affairs Work Conference', 2018.

'Deeply Understand the Importance of Building a Modern Economic System, Push China's Economic Development to a New Level', 2018.

'Harnessing Opportunities of Our Times to Jointly Pursue Prosperity in the Asia-Pacific', 2018.

'Meeting Challenges with Unity of Purpose To Write a New Chapter for Asia-Pacific Cooperation', 2018.

'Speech at the Ceremony Commemorating the Bicentenary of the Birth of Marx', 2018.

'Speech at the Private Enterprise Symposium', 2018.

'Speech at a Symposium on the Targeted Poverty Alleviation Campaign', 2018.

'Address to Leaders' Roundtable of the Second Belt and Road Forum for International Cooperation', 2019.

'Address to the Fifth Summit of the Conference on Interaction and Confidence Building Measures, Development', 2019.

'Central Economic Work Conference', 2019.

'Deep Understanding of New Development Concepts', 2019.

'Focus on Our Tasks—Bear in Mind the National Goal and Changing Conditions', 2019.

'Strengthen Commitment to the Four Consciousnesses, the Four-Sphere Confidence, and the Two Upholds', 2019

'Strengthen the Party and Its Organizational Line in the New Era', 2018.

'Speech at the Opening Ceremony of the Training Class for Young and Middle-Aged Cadres at the Central Party School (National School of Administration)', 2019.

'Speech by President Xi Jinping in Celebration of the 70th Anniversary of the Founding of the People's Republic of China', 2019.

'Stay True to the Party's Original Aspiration and Founding Mission and Carry Out Self-Reform', 2019.

'Talks with General Secretary of the Central Committee of the Lao People's Revolutionary Party and President Bounnhang Vorachith of Laos', 2019.

'We Must Promote China's Manufacturing Industry', 2019.

'Working Together to Deliver a Brighter Future for Belt and Road Cooperation', 2019.

'Working Together to Realize Rejuvenation of the Chinese Nation and Advance China's Peaceful Reunification', 2019.

'Accelerate Educational Modernization and Prepare a New Generation for National Rejuvenation', 2020.

'Address Problems Related to Agriculture, Rural Areas, and Rural People in the New Development Stage', 2020.

'Adhere to the Marxist Historical Materialism and Continue to Open Up New Horizons for the Development of Marxism in Contemporary China', 2020.

'Always Put the People First', 2020.

'Be Prepared for the Great Struggle', 2020.

'Boost China-Arab Cooperation and Move Forward Together', 2020.

'Build a Better Cyberspace', 2020.
'Build a Strong Public Health System', 2020.
'Build an Eco-Civilization for Sustainable Development', 2020
'Building on Past Achievements and Launching a New Journey for Global Climate Actions', 2020.
'Carry Forward the Spirit of the War to Resist US Aggression and Aid Korea in the Great Historic Struggle', 2020.
'Carrying Forward the Shanghai Spirit and Deepening Solidarity and Collaboration for a Stronger Community with a Shared Future', 2020.
'Central Economic Work Conference', 2020.
'Certain Major Issues for Our National Medium- to Long-Term Economic and Social Development Strategy', 2020.
'Create a New Development Dynamic and Sharpen the Competitive Edge', 2020.
'Create New Prospects for Chinese Literature and Art', 2020.
'Defeating COVID-19 with Solidarity and Cooperation', 2020.
'Develop China on More Secure and Reliable Foundations', 2020.
'Focus All Reform Efforts on Creating a New Development Dynamic', 2020.
'Follow the Chinese Path to Modernization', 2020.
'Fostering a New Development Paradigm and Pursuing Mutual Benefit and Win-Win Cooperation', 2020.
'Give Greater Prominence to Cultural Development', 2020.
'A Great Advance towards National Rejuvenation', 2020.
'Greater Breakthroughs for Reform in the New Development Stage', 2020.
'Keeping Up the Momentum and Working Together for a New Chapter in China-CEEC Cooperation', 2020.
'Implement the Civil Code in Earnest', 2020.
'Keep Food Security in Our Own Hands', 2020.
'Keep Up the Fight to Achieve National Rejuvenation', 2020.
'Major Issues Concerning China's Strategies for Mid-to-Long-Term Economic and Social Development', 2020.
'Major Points on the Recommendations of the CPC Central Committee for Formulating the 14th Five-Year Plan for Economic and Social Development and Long-Range Objectives through the Year 2035', 2020.
'March towards the Second Centenary Goal', 2020.
'Optimize Social Governance Based on Collaboration, Participation, and Common Interests', 2020.
'The People's Support Is Our Top Political Priority', 2020.
'Priorities in Epidemic Prevention and Control', 2020.
'Promote Integrated, High-Quality Development of the Yangtze River Delta', 2020.
'Provide Sound Legal Guarantees for Socialist Modernization', 2020.
'Pursue a Holistic Approach to National Security', 2020.
'Raise Reform and Opening Up to a Higher Level', 2020.
'Reinforce CPC Central Leadership over the Epidemic Response', 2020.
'Remarks at the Global Trade in Services Summit of the 2020 China International Fair for Trade in Services', 2020.
'Remarks at the High-Level Meeting to Commemorate the 75th Anniversary of the United Nations', 2020.
'Remarks at the Leaders' Side Event on Safeguarding Planet of the G20 Riyadh Summit', 2020.
'Remarks at the Opening Ceremony of the Fifth Annual Meeting of the Asian Infrastructure Investment Bank', 2020.
'Remarks at the Opening Ceremony of the 17th China-ASEAN Expo and China-ASEAN Business and Investment Summit', 2020.
'Remarks on Novel Coronavirus Response', 2020.
'Remarks to Symposium of Scientists', 2020.
'Speech at a Forum of Experts in Economic and Social Fields', 2020.
'Speech at Opening Ceremony of 3rd China International Import Expo', 2020.

'Speech at a Review Meeting on the Campaign Themed "Staying True to Our Original Aspiration and Founding Mission" ', 2020.
'Speech at the Series of Celebrations for the 70th Anniversary of the Establishment of Diplomatic Relations between China and Myanmar and the Launching Ceremony for the China-Myanmar Cultural Tourism Year', 2020.
'Speech on 30th Anniversary of the Development and Opening-up of Pudong', 2020.
'Standing Together to Fight COVID-19', 2020.
'Statement at the General Debate of the 75th Session of the UN General Assembly', 2020.
'Statement at the High-Level Meeting on the Twenty-fifth Anniversary of the Fourth World Conference on Women', 2020.
'Statement at the United Nations Summit on Biodiversity', 2020.
'Strengthen COVID-19 Control and Promote Economic and Social Development', 2020.
'Strengthen Our Political Acumen, Understanding, and Capacity to Deliver', 2020.
'Together, Let Us Fight COVID-19 and Create a Better Future', 2020
'Turn the Fighting Spirit against COVID-19 into a Powerful Force for National Rejuvenation', 2020.
'2021 New Year Address', 2020.
'Unity and Cooperation are the International Community's Most Potent Weapon to Overcome the Pandemic', 2020.
'Work Together for Asia-Pacific Prosperity', 2020.
'Work Together to Boost Global Trade in Services', 2020.
'Work Together to Protect the Lives and Health of All', 2020.
'Working Together for an Asia-Pacific Community with a Shared Future', 2020.
'Working Together to Defeat the COVID-19 Outbreak', 2020.
'Yangtze River Economic Belt: A Showcase for Green Development', 2020.
'Achieve Modernization Based on Harmony Between Humanity and Nature', 2021.
'Apply the New Development Philosophy in Full', 2021.
'Build a Strong National Shield against Biosecurity Threats', 2021.
'Build a Talent-Strong Military in the New Era', 2021.
'Build on Macao's Success with the One Country, Two Systems Policy', 2021.
'The Centennial Events of the Communist Party of China (July 1921–June 2021)', 2021.
'Central Economic Work Conference', 2021.
'Correctly Understand and Grasp the Major Problems of Medium- and Long-Term Economic and Social Development', 2021.
'Develop Quality and Sustainable Social Security', 2021.
'Develop the System of Socialist Rule of Law with Chinese Characteristics', 2021.
'Earn and Keep the People's Support in Consolidating Party Leadership', 2021.
'Expand and Strengthen the Digital Economy', 2021.
'Explanation of the Resolution of the CPC Central Committee on the Major Achievements and Historical Experience of the Party over the Past Century', 2021.
'Explanation of the Resolution of the Central Committee of the Communist Party of China on the Major Achievements and Historical Experience of the Party over the Past Century', 2021.
'Fight for a Bright New Future', 2021.
'For Man and Nature: Building a Community of Life Together', 2021.
'Fully Understand the New Development Stage', 2021
'Heighten the Sense of National Identity and Improve the Party's Work on Ethnic Affairs in the New Era', 2021.
'Implementing the Guiding Principles of the Fifth Plenary Session of the 19th CCP Central Committee', 2021.
'In-Depth Study and Resolutely Carry Out the Spirit of the Fifth Plenary Session of the 19th Central Committee of the Communist Party of China to Ensure That the Overall Construction of a Socialist Modern Country Will Start a Good Start', 2021.
'Join Hands to Achieve Complete Reunification and National Rejuvenation', 2021.

'Keeping Up the Momentum and Working Together for a New Chapter in China-CEEC Cooperation', 2021.
'Key Issues in the New Development Stage', 2021.
'Let the Breeze of Openness Bring Warmth to the World', 2021.
'Let China's Openness Benefit the World', 2021.
'Let the Torch of Multilateralism Light Up Humanity's Way Forward', 2021.
'Letter to World Symposium for Marxist Political Parties', 2021.
'Make Solid Progress towards Common Prosperity', 2021,
'Meet the Centenary Goal of the Armed Forces', 2021.
'Move Faster to Create a New Development Dynamic', 2021.
'The People's Concerns Are My Concerns, and the People's Expectations Are My Goals', 2021.
'Present an Accurate, Multidimensional, and Panoramic Image of China', 2021.
'Promote Common Prosperity in High-Quality Development and Do a Good Job in Preventing and Resolving Major Financial Risks', 2021.
'Promote Traditional Culture and Increase Cultural Confidence', 2021.
'Pulling Together through Adversity and towards a Shared Future for All', 2021.
'Reinforce Our Party's Political Foundations for Unity and Solidarity', 2021.
'Religions in China Should Conform to China's Realities', 2021.
'Remarks during Visit to Tsinghua University', 2021.
'Remarks at Ceremony for "Complete Victory" in Eradicating Absolute Poverty', 2021.
'Working Together to Build a Global Community of Health for All', 2021.
'Speech at the Ceremony Marking the Centenary of the Communist Party of China', 2021.
'Speech at the National Conference to Review the Fight against Poverty and Commend Outstanding Individuals and Groups', 2021.
'Spread Traditional Chinese Culture from a Marxist Standpoint', 2021.
'Strengthen Overall CPC Leadership in Socialist Modernization', 2021.
'Strive for Greater Strength and Self-Reliance in Science and Technology', 2021
'Talk Given at the Party History Learning and Education Mobilization Meeting', 2021.
'Understanding the New Development Stage, Applying the New Development Philosophy, and Creating a New Development Dynamic', 2021.
'Uphold and Improve the People's Congress System', 2021.
'Uphold the Principle of Patriots Governing Hong Kong to Secure the Success of the One Country, Two Systems Policy', 2021.
'Video Speech to Colombian People', 2021.
'Whole-Process People's Democracy: The Most Extensive, Genuine, and Effective Socialist Democracy', 2021.
'Adapt Marxism to China's Realities and Keep It Up-to-Date', 2022.
'Carry Forward the Spirit of the Beijing Winter Olympics and Paralympics and Build China into a Strong Sporting Nation', 2022.
'Carrying Forward Our Millennia-Old Friendship and Jointly Creating a Better Future', 2022.
'Carrying Forward the Spirit of China-Arab Friendship and Jointly Building a China-Arab Community with a Shared Future in the New Era', 2022.
'Central Economic Work Conference', 2022
'Ensure Long-Term Multiparty Cooperation Led by the CPC', 2022.
'Forge Ahead with Confidence and Fortitude to Jointly Create a Better Post-COVID World', 2022.
'Follow the Chinese Path of Comprehensive Progress in Human Rights', 2022.
'Foster New Opportunities and Open Up New Horizons', 2022.
'Give of Your Best in National Rejuvenation', 2022.
'Guide and Regulate the Capital Market', 2022.
'Keep Matters of National Significance to the Fore', 2022.
'Let the Yellow River Serve the Nation', 2022.
'Make China a Global Center for Science and Innovation', 2022.

'Make Further Progress in Party Self-Governance', 2022.
'Our Party's Mission Is to Serve the People', 2022.
'Peak Carbon and Carbon Neutrality: An Extensive and Profound Transformation', 2022.
'Respond to COVID-19 with a Dedicated Effort', 2022.
'Run the Military in Accordance with the Law', 2022.
'Speech at Memorial Meeting for Comrade Jiang Zemin', 2022.
'Speech during Visit to Yan'an', 2022.
'Steadfastly Following the Chinese Path to Promote Further Progress in Human Rights', 2022.
'The Way Forward in the New Era', 2022.
'Building a China-Vietnam Community with a Shared Future That Carries Strategic Significance and Writing Together a New Chapter in Our Modernization Drive', 2023.
'Building an Open, Inclusive, and Interconnected World for Common Development', 2023.
'Central Economic Work Conference', 2023.
'Central Foreign Affairs Work Conference', 2023.
'Chinese Modernization Is a Sure Path to Building a Great Country and Rejuvenating the Nation', 2024.
'Chinese Modernization Is Socialist Modernization Led by the CPC', 2023.
'Comprehensively and Strictly Governing the Party: Exploring the Successful Path of Relying on the Party's Self-Revolution to Break Free from the Historical Cycle', 2023.
'Galvanizing Our Peoples into a Strong Force for the Cause of China-US Friendship', 2023.
'Forging Ahead to Open a New Chapter of China-Russia Friendship, Cooperation, and Common Development', 2023.
'Join Hands on the Path towards Modernization', 2023.
'Joining Hands to Advance Modernization and Create a Great Future for China and Africa', 2023.
'Letter to Representatives of Outstanding Teachers', 2023.
'Major Issues in Economic Work', 2023.
'Meeting Challenges with Unity of Purpose to Write a New Chapter for Asia-Pacific Cooperation', 2023.
'Meeting with Former US Secretary of State Henry Kissinger', 2023.
'Perfecting the System of Comprehensively and Strictly Governing the Party and Promoting the New Great Project of Party Building in the New Era', 2023.
'President's New Year Message', 2023.
'Renewing Traditional Friendship and Embarking on a New Journey to Build a China-Vietnam Community with a Shared Future', 2023.
'Sailing the Giant Ship of China-South Africa Friendship and Cooperation towards Greater Success', 2023.
'Staying True to APEC Founding Mission and Enhancing Unity and Cooperation to Jointly Promote High-Quality Growth in the Asia Pacific', 2023.
'Staying True to Our Founding Mission and Advancing Unity and Coordination to Realize Greater Development', 2023.
'Working towards a Ceasefire and Realizing Lasting Peace and Sustainable Security', 2023.
'Remarks to a Meeting on the Education Campaign about the Study and Implementation of Xi Jinping Thought on Socialism with Chinese Characteristics for a New Era', 2023.
'Remarks to the First Meeting of the National Security Commission under the 20th CPC Central Committee', 2023.
'Remarks to the Politburo's 9th Collective Study Session on Forging a Strong Sense of Community for the Chinese Nation', 2023.
'Speech at the First Session of the 14th National People's Congress', 2023.
'Speech at the Meeting on Cultural Inheritance and Development', 2023.
'Speech for the 90th Anniversary of the Central Party School and Opening of its Spring Semester', 2023.
'Speech to the Second Plenary Session of the 20th Central Commission for Discipline Inspection', 2023.
'Speech to the Third Plenary Session of the 20th Central Commission for Discipline Inspection', 2024.

1.1.9. Selected Speeches and Articles on Foreign Policy

Dai Bingguo. 'Opening Session of the First Round of the China-US Strategic and Economic Dialogues', July 2009. http://tl.china-embassy.gov.cn/eng/xwdt/200908/t20090807_1113076.htm.

Deng Xiaoping. 'Teng Hsiao-Ping's Speech at UN Special Session [The Three Worlds]'. *Current Background*, no. 1016 (1974).

Hu Yaobang. 'Create a New Situation in All Fields of Socialist Modernization'. *Beijing Review*, 25/37 (1982).

Hu Jintao. 'President Hu Urges Joint Efforts for New Int'l Order', 2003. http://mu.china-embassy.gov.cn/eng/sgxw/200305/t20030528_6480443.htm.

Hu Jintao. 'Full Text of Hu Jintao's Speech at BFA Annual Conference 2004 China's Development Is an Opportunity for Asia', 2004. http://www.china.org.cn/english/features/93897.htm.

Hu Jintao. 'Build towards a Harmonious World of Lasting Peace and Common Prosperity', 2005. https://www.un.org/webcast/summit2005/statements15/china050915eng.pdf.

Hu Jintao. 'Continuing Reform and Opening-Up and Advancing Win-Win Cooperation', 2008. https://www.bjreview.com/document/txt/2008-06/11/content_126555.htm.

Hu Jintao. 'Speech at a Meeting Commemorating the 90th Anniversary of the Founding of the Communist Party of China', 2011. http://www.china.org.cn/china/CPC_90_anniversary/2011-07/01/content_22901507.htm.

Jiang Zemin. '80th Anniversary of Communist Party', 2001. https://www.c-span.org/video/?165164-1/80th-anniversary-communist-party.

Li Qiang. 'Speech by Chinese Premier Li Qiang at the Opening of the World Economic Forum Annual Meeting', 2024. https://www.mfa.gov.cn/eng/zxxx_662805/202401/t20240117_11225446.html.

Mao Zedong. 'On the People's Democratic Dictatorship: In Commemoration of the Twenty-Eighth Anniversary of the Communist Party of China', 1949. https://digitalarchive.wilsoncenter.org/document/mao-zedong-peoples-democratic-dictatorship-commemoration-twenty-eighth-anniversary.

Mao Zedong. 'Record of Conversation between Polish Delegation and PRC Leader Mao Zedong, Wuhan', 1958. https://digitalarchive.wilsoncenter.org/document/record-conversation-between-polish-delegation-and-prc-leader-mao-zedong-wuhan.

Mao Zedong. 'There Are Two Intermediate Zones', 1963–1964. https://digitalarchive.wilsoncenter.org/document/mao-zedong-there-are-two-intermediate-zones.

Putin, Vladimir, and Xi Jinping, 'Joint Statement of the Russian Federation and the People's Republic of China on the International Relations Entering a New Era and the Global Sustainable Development', 2022. http://www.en.kremlin.ru/supplement/5770.

Wang Yi. 'As a Member of the Developing World China Will Always Speak Up for Developing Countries', 2013. https://www.fmprc.gov.cn/mfa_eng/wjb_663304/wjbz_663308/2461_663310/ t1081897.shtml.

Wang Yi. 'Exploring the Path of Major-Country Diplomacy with Chinese Characteristics', 2013. http://in.china-embassy.gov.cn/eng/xwfw/xxfb/201306/t20130630_2373756.htm.

Wang Yi. 'Sustainable Development—The Road to Achieve Chinese Dream and Human Progress', 2013. https://www.mfa.gov.cn/eng/wjb_663304/wjbz_663308/2461_663310/201309/t20130926_468441.html.

Wang Yi. 'Toward a New Model of Major-Country Relations between China and the United States'. 2013. https://www.brookings.edu/on-the-record/wang-yi-toward-a-new-model-of-major-country-relations-between-china-and-the-united-states/.

Wang Yi. 'Insist on Correct View of Righteousness and Benefits, Actively Play the Role of Responsible Great Powers: Deeply Comprehend the Spirit of Comrade Xi Jinping's Important Speech on Diplomatic Work'. 2013. http://opinion.people.com.cn/n/2013/0910/c1003- 22862978.html.

Wang Yi. 'Forge Ahead under the Guidance of General SecretaryXi Jinping's Thought on Diplomacy', 2017. https://www.fmprc.gov.cn/mfa_eng/wjdt_665385/zyjh_665391/201709/t20170901_678631.html.

Wang Yi. 'Speech by Foreign Minister Wang Yi at the Opening of Symposium on International Developments and China's Diplomacy in 2017', 2017. https://www.fmprc.gov.cn/mfa_eng/wjb_663304/wjbz_663308/2461_663310/201712/t20171210_468660.html.

Wang Yi. 'Build on Twenty Years of Proud Achievements and Open Up a New Chapter in China-Africa Relations', 2020. https://www.fmprc.gov.cn/mfa_eng/wjb_663304/wjbz_663308/2461_663310/ t1831815.shtml.

Wang Yi. 'Following Xi Jinping Thought on Diplomacy to Build a Community with a Shared Future for Mankind through International Cooperation against COVID-19', 2020. https://www.fmprc.gov.cn/mfa_eng/zxxx_662805/t1771257.shtml.

Wang Yi. 'Study and Implement Xi Jinping Thought on Diplomacy Conscientiously and Break New Ground in Major-Country Diplomacy with Chinese Characteristics', 2020. https://www.fmprc.gov.cn/mfa_eng/zxxx_662805/t1799305.shtml.

Wang Yi. 'A New Journey Ahead after Fifty Extraordinary Years—Keynote Address by State Councilor and Foreign Minister Wang Yi at the Lanting Forum on China and the UN: Cooperation in 50 Years and Beyond', 2021. https://www.fmprc.gov.cn/mfa_eng/wjdt_665385/zyjh_665391/202106/t20210625_9170552.html.

Wang Yi. 'A People-Centred Approach for Global Human Rights Progress', 2021. https://www.fmprc.gov.cn/mfa_eng/zxxx_662805/t1855685.shtml.

Wang Yi. 'Remarks by State Councilor and Foreign Minister Wang Yi at the United Nations Security Council High-Level Meeting on the Theme "Maintenance of International Peace and Security: Upholding Multilateralism and the United Nations–Centred International System"', 2021. https://www.fmprc.gov.cn/mfa_eng/wjdt_665385/zyjh_665391/202105/t20210508_9170544.html.

Wang Yi. 'Rise to the Challenges, Serve the Nation, and Embark on a New Journey for Major-Country Diplomacy with Chinese Characteristics', 2021. https://www.fmprc.gov.cn/mfa_eng/zxxx_662805/t1846769.shtml.

Wang Yi. 'State Councillor and Foreign Minister of the People's Republic of China at the United Nations Security Council Open Debate on "Peace and Security in Africa: Addressing Root Causes of Conflict in Post-Pandemic Recovery in Africa"', 2021. http://www.yingyushijie.com/exam/detail/id/8502/category/60.html.

Wang Yi. 'State Councillor and Foreign Minister of the People's Republic of China at the United Nations Security Council Open Debate on "The Situation in the Middle East, including the Palestinian Question"', 2021. http://chnun.chinamission.org.cn/eng/chinaandun/securitycouncil/202107/t20210729_9126853.htm.

Wang Yi. 'State Councillor and Foreign Minister of the People's Republic of China at the Conference on Disarmament in Geneva', 2021. https://www.mfa.gov.cn/ce/cegv/eng/tpxw/t1883331.htm.

Wang Yi. 'Wang Yi Speaks to the Press about the Summit Meeting between Chinese and U.S. Presidents in San Francisco', 2023. https://www.mfa.gov.cn/eng/topics_665678/xjpfmgjxzmyshwtscxapec/202311/t20231117_11182054.html.

Wang Yi. 'Implementing the Guiding Principles of the Central Conference on Work Relating to Foreign Affairs and Breaking New Ground in Major-Country Diplomacy with Chinese Characteristics', 2024. http://se.china-embassy.gov.cn/eng/zgxw_0/202401/t20240119_11229429.htm.

Yang Jiechi. 'Work Together to Achieve Common Security and Development', 2012. https://www.fmprc.gov.cn/mfa_eng/topics_665678/diaodao_665718/t975077.shtml.

Yang Jiechi. 'Innovations in China's Diplomatic Theory and Practice under New Conditions'. *Qiushi*, 2013. http://ie.china-embassy.gov.cn/eng/zt/diplomacy/201308/t20130820_2540459.htm.

Yang Jiechi. 'Full Text of Chinese State Councilor's Article on Xi Jinping's Diplomacy Thought', 2017. http://english.www.gov.cn/state_council/state_councilors/2017/07/19/content_281475739702802.htm.

Yang Jiechi. 'Yang Jiechi's Remarks on the Xi Jinping Thought on Diplomacy', 2018. https://www.mfa.gov.cn/ce/cedom/eng/zt/xi1/t1657090.htm.

Yang Jiechi. 'Deepen the Promotion of Foreign Affairs Work in the New Era Guided by Xi Jinping Thought on Diplomacy, 2018. https://interpret.csis.org/translations/deepen-the-promotion-of-foreign-affairs-work-in-the-new-era-guided-by-xi-jinping-thought-on-diplomacy/.

Yang Jiechi. 'Following the Guidance of Xi Jinping Thought on Diplomacy to Advance Diplomatic Work in the New Era', 2018. http://english.qstheory.cn/2018-12/21/c_1123801028.htm.

Yang Jiechi. 'Advancing China's Major-Country Diplomacy under the Guidance of Xi Jinping Thought on Foreign Affairs', *Qiushi*, 2019. http://vu.china-embassy.org/eng/zt/xjpwjsx/202007/t20200730_320215.htm.

Yang Jiechi. 'Yang Jiechi's Keynote Speech at the 55th Munich Security Conference', 2019. http://www.xinhuanet.com/english/2019-02/17/c_137827311.htm.

Yang Jiechi, 'Firmly Uphold and Practice Multilateralism and Build a Community with a Shared Future for Mankind'. 2021. https://www.chinadaily.com.cn/a/202102/22/WS60330e12a3102 4adobaaa225.html

Zhao Ziyang. 'Advance along the Road of Socialism with Chinese Characteristics'. *Beijing Review*, 30/45 (1987).

Zhou Enlai. 'Report on the Work of the Government'. *Peking Review*, 18/4 (1975).

1.1.10. Other English-Language Primary Sources (listed chronologically)

Antoine-Louis-Claude Destutt de Tracy. *Élémens d'idéologie*. Paris: Chez Courcier. 1804.

George Washington. *The Writings of George Washington*, Vol. 6. Boston: Russell, Odiorne and Metcalf and Hillard Gray and Co., 1834.

Collections of the Massachusetts Historical Society, Vol. 8. Boston: Charles C. Little & James Brown, 1838.

Napoléon Bonaparte. *Correspondance de Napoléon Ier*, Vol. 10. Paris: H. Plon, J. Dumaine, 1862.

Karl Marx. *Capital: A Critical Analysis of Capitalist Production*. New York: Humboldt, 1890.

Karl Marx. *A Contribution to the Critique of Political Economy*. Chicago: Charles H. Kerr, 1904.

Thomas Aquinas. *Summa Theologica*. London: Burns Oates & Washbourne, 1922.

United Nations. *Charter of the United Nations and Statute of the International Court of Justice*. San Francisco: United Nations, 1945.

United Nations. 'Universal Declaration of Human Rights'. 1948. https://www.ohchr.org/sites/default/files/UDHR/Documents/UDHR_Translations/eng.pdf

'United States of America and Philippines Mutual Defense Treaty', Signed at Washington on 30 August 1951. https://treaties.un.org/doc/Publication/UNTS/Volume%20177/volume-177-I-2315-English.pdf.

Eighth National Congress of the Communist Party of China, Vol. 1. Peking: Foreign Languages Press, 1956.

Stanley Kubrick, Terry Southern, and Peter George. '*Dr Strangelove or: How I Learned to Stop Worrying and Love the Bomb*'. Shepperton: Hawk Films Ltd., 1963. https://indiegroundfilms.wordpress.com/wp-content/uploads/2014/01/dr-strangelove-jan27-63-numbered-revised.pdf.

'Statement by Peking on Nuclear Test', *New York Times*, 1964. https://www.nytimes.com/1964/10/17/archives/statement-by-peking-on-nuclear-test.html.

Karl Marx and Friedrich Engels. *The German Ideology*. New York: International Publishers, 1972.

Selected Articles Criticizing Lin Piao and Confucius, Vol. 2. Beijing: Foreign Languages Press, 1975.

Karl Marx. *A Contribution to the Critique of Political Economy*. Moscow: Progress Publishers, 1977.

'The Resolution of the November 1978 Central Party Work Conference and Related Speeches', 1978. https://digitalarchive.wilsoncenter.org/collection/185/reform-and-opening-in-china-1978.

Central Intelligence Agency, National Foreign Assessment Center (US). 'Deng Xiaoping and the Taiwan Question', March 1981. https://digitalarchive.wilsoncenter.org/document/central-intelligence-agency-national-foreign-assessment-center-deng-xiaoping-and-taiwan.

Augustine of Hippo. *The City of God*. London: Penguin, 1984.

Vladimir Ilyich Lenin. *The State and Revolution*. London: Penguin, 1992.

Karl Marx. *Thesen über Feuerbach*. Hamburg: Argument, 1998.

George W. Bush. 'Address to a Joint Session of Congress and the American People', 21 September 2001. https://georgewbush-whitehouse.archives.gov/news/releases/2001/09/20010920-8.html

'Declaration on the Conduct of Parties in the South China Sea', Adopted in Phnom Penh, Cambodia, 2002. https://cil.nus.edu.sg/wp-content/uploads/2017/07/2002-Declaration-on-the-Conduct-of-Parties-in-the-South-China-Sea.pdf.

Information Office of the State Council (PRC). 'China's Peaceful Development', September 2011. http://english.gov.cn/archive/white_paper/2014/09/09/content_281474986284646.htm.

Antoine-Louis-Claude Destutt de Tracy. *A Treatise on Political Economy*. Indianapolis: Liberty Fund, 2011.

Ministry of Foreign Affairs (PRC). 'Xi Jinping Holds Discussion Meeting with Foreign Experts', 2012. http://ag.china-embassy.gov.cn/eng/zgxw/201212/t20121210_3471783.htm.

'A Communiqué on the Current State of the Ideological Sphere (Document Number 9)', April 2013. https://www.chinafile.com/document-9-chinafile-translation, https://digichina.stanford.edu/work/communique-on-the-current-state-of-the-ideological-sphere-document-no-9/.

Zeid Ra'ad Al-Hussein. 'Opening Statement'. *Human Rights Council*. 36th Session, September 2017. https://www.ohchr.org/en/statements/2017/09/darker-and-more-dangerous-high-commissioner-updates-human-rights-council-human.

Sun Tzu et al. *The Seven Military Classics of Ancient China*. London: Arcturus, 2017.

Ministry of Foreign Affairs (PRC). 'Yang Jiechi Meets Respectively with BRICS High Representatives for Security Issues of South Africa, Brazil and India', 2017. https://www.fmprc.gov.cn/eng/gjhdq_665435/3447_665449/3473_665008/3475_665012/201708/t20170801_594909.html.

Liu He. 'Three Critical Battles China Is Preparing to Fight'. *World Economic Forum*, 2018. https://www.weforum.org/agenda/2018/01/pursue-high-quality-development-work-together-for-global-economic-prosperity-and-stability/.

Ministry of Foreign Affairs (PRC). 'Do Not Say You Start Too Early; and You Have Close Friends Wherever You Go', 2020. http://mm.china-embassy.gov.cn/eng/sgjj/202001/t20200121_1380479.htm.

Congressional-Executive Committee on China (US). 'Five Years after 709 Crackdown, Lawyers Continue to Face Repression and Punishment', July 2020. https://www.cecc.gov/publications/commission-analysis/five-years-after-709-crackdown-lawyers-continue-to-face-repression.

US-China Economic and Security Review Commission. Annual Report to Congress, 2020. https://www.uscc.gov/annual-report/2020-annual-report-congress.

Friedrich Engels. *Socialism, Utopian and Scientific*. Paris: Foreign Languages Press, 2020.

Ministry of Foreign Affairs (PRC). 'Global Development Initiative Concept Paper'. 2021. https://www.mfa.gov.cn/eng/wjbxw/202302/t20230221_11028348.html.

Yang Jiechi, and Antony Blinken. 'How It Happened: Transcript of the US-China Opening Remarks in Alaska'. *Nikkei Asia*, March 2021. https://asia.nikkei.com/Politics/International-relations/US-China-tensions/How-it-happened-Transcript-of-the-US-China-opening-remarks-in-Alaska.

Cui, Tiankai. 'Ambassador Cui Tiankai Takes an Interview in Anchorage (English Translation of the Transcript)'. *Xinhua*, March 2021. http://www.xinhuanet.com/english/northamerica/2021-03/18/c_139819032.htm.

Zhou Pingjian. 'Communist Party of China Turns 100 and Still Going Strong', June 2021. https://www.mfa.gov.cn/eng/wjb_663304/zwjg_665342/zwbd_665378/202106/t20210622_9169743.html.

National Development and Reform Commission (PRC). 'Fully Implementing the New Development Philosophy and Accelerating Efforts to Foster a New Development Dynamic'. *Qiushi*, 2021. http://en.qstheory.cn/2021-07/08/c_640515.htm.

Karl Marx. *Critique of the Gotha Program*. Paris: Foreign Languages Press, 2021.

Department of State (US). 'China (Includes Tibet, Xinjiang, Hong Kong, and Macau)'. *Report on International Religious Freedom*, 2021. https://www.state.gov/reports/2021-report-on-international-religious-freedom/china/.

Taiwan Affairs Office of the State Council of the PRC. 'The Taiwan Question and China's Reunification in the New Era: The People's Republic of China', 2022. http://gm.china-embassy.gov.cn/eng/sgxw/202208/P020220810850182763063.pdf.

Fei Mingxin. 'Dynamic Zero-COVID: A MUST Approach for China', 2022. https://www.fmprc.gov.cn/mfa_eng/wjb_663304/zwjg_665342/zwbd_665378/202207/t20220715_10722.

Ministry of Defense (Japan). 'Defense Buildup Program', 2022. https://www.mod.go.jp/j/policy/agenda/guideline/plan/pdf/program_en.pdf.

AUKUS. 'Agreement between the Government of Australia, the Government of the United Kingdom of Great Britain and Northern Ireland, and the Government of the United States of America for the exchange of naval nuclear propulsion information', 2022. https://treaties.un.org/Pages/showDetails.aspx?objid=08000002805edc16.

IPEF. 'Leaders' Statement on Indo-Pacific Economic Framework for Prosperity', White House, 2023. https://www.whitehouse.gov/briefing-room/statements-releases/2023/11/16/leaders-statement-on-indo-pacific-economic-framework-for-prosperity/.

'The United States and the Republic of the Philippines Bilateral Defense Guidelines'. 2023. https://www.defense.gov/News/Releases/Release/Article/3383607/fact-sheet-us-philippines-bilateral-defense-guidelines.

'Trilateral Leaders' Summit of the United States, Japan, and the Republic of Korea', *US Department of State*, 2023. https://jp.usembassy.gov/trilateral-leaders-summit-us-japan-south-korea/.

White House (US). 'Readout of President Joe Biden's Meeting with President Xi Jinping of the People's Republic of China', 2023. https://www.whitehouse.gov/briefing-room/statements-releases/2023/11/15/readout-of-president-joe-bidens-meeting-with-president-xi-jinping-of-the-peoples-republic-of-china-2/.

Ministry of Foreign Affairs (PRC). 'Global Security Initiative Concept Paper'. 2023. https://www.mfa.gov.cn/eng/wjbxw/202302/t20230221_11028348.html.

Office of the US Trade Representative. 'Readout of Virtual IPEF Ministerial Meeting Hosted by Ambassador Tai', 2023. https://ustr.gov/about-us/policy-offices/press-office/press-releases/2023/october/readout-virtual-ipef-ministerial-meeting-hosted-ambassador-tai.

United Nations Environment Programme. 'Emissions Gap Report 2023'. Nairobi: UNEP, 2023.

United Nations Human Rights Council. 'China Review—45th Session of Universal Periodic Review', 2024. *UN Web TV,* https://webtv.un.org/en/asset/k1z/k1z43db5bt.

US Commission on International Religious Freedom. Annual Report, 2024. https://www.uscirf.gov/publication/2023-annual-report.

1.2. English-Language Secondary Sources (listed alphabetically by authors)

Acharya, Amitav. '"Theorising the International Relations of Asia: Necessity or Indulgence?" Some Reflections'. *Pacific Review*, 30/6 (November 2017), 816–28.

Adams, Nicole, David Jacobs, Stephen Kenny, Serena Russell, and Maxwell Sutton. 'China's Evolving Financial System and Its Global Importance'. *Reserve Bank of Australia Bulletin*, September 2021.

Agence France-Presse. 'China's Xi Jinping Calls for Greater State Control of AI to Counter "Dangerous Storms"'. *The Guardian*, June 2023.

Albers, Martin, and Zhong Zhong Chen. 'Socialism Capitalism and Sino-European Relations in the Deng Xiaoping Era, 1978–1992'. *Cold War History*, 17/2 (April 2017), 115–19.

Albert, Eleanor. 'Christianity in China'. *Council on Foreign Relations*, 2018. https://www.cfr.org/backgrounder/christianity-china.

Albert, Eleanor, Lindsay Maizland, and Xu Beina. 'The Chinese Communist Party'. *Council on Foreign Relations*, 2021. https://www.cfr.org/backgrounder/chinese-communist-party.

Alden, Chris, and Christopher R. Hughes. 'Harmony and Discord in China's Africa Strategy: Some Implications for Foreign Policy'. *China Quarterly*, 199 (September 2009), 563–84.

Allison, Graham. *Destined for War: Can America and China Escape Thucydides's Trap?* New York: Mariner Books, 2018.

Anderlini, Jamil, and Lucy Hornby. 'China Overtakes US as World's Largest Goods Trader'. *Financial Times*, January 2014. https://www.ft.com/content/7c2dbd70-79a6-11e3-b381-00144feabdc0.

Anderson, Benedict. *Imagined Communities: Reflections on the Origin and Spread of Nationalism*. London: Verso, 2006.

Andrésy, Agnès. *Xi Jinping: Red China, the Bext Generation*. Lanham, MD: University Press of America, 2015.

Ang, Yuen Yuen. 'How Resilient Is the CCP?'. *Journal of Democracy*, 33 (July 2022), 77–91.

Asia Maritime Transparency Initiative. 'A Survey of Marine Research Vessels in the Indo-Pacific'. *Center for Strategic and International Studies (CSIS)*, 2020. https://amti.csis.org/a-survey-of-marine-research-vessels-in-the-indo-pacific/.

Asia Pacific Foundation of Canada. *State Owned Enterprises at a Crossroads*. Vancouver: APFC, 2016.

Asia Society Policy Institute. 'The China Dashboard', 2021. https://chinadashboard.gist.asiasociety.org/winter-2021/page/overview.

Asia Society Policy Institute. *'Decoding Chinese Politics'*, 2024. https://asiasociety.org/policy-institute/decoding-chinese-politics.

Associated Press. 'Xi Jinping Asks for "Absolute Loyalty" from Chinese State Media'. *The Guardian*, 20 February 2016. https://www.theguardian.com/world/2016/feb/19/xi-jinping-tours-chinas-top-state-media-outlets-to-boost-loyalty.

Babones, Salvatore. 'Taking China Seriously: Relationality, Tianxia, and the "Chinese School" of International Relations'. In *Oxford Research Encyclopedia of Politics*. (Oxford University Press, 2017).

Babones, Salvatore. 'The Meaning of Xi Jinping Thought'. *Foreign Affairs*, November 2017. https://www.foreignaffairs.com/articles/china/2017-11-02/meaning-xi-jinping-thought.

Bader, Jeffrey A. 'How Xi Jinping Sees the World . . . and Why'. *Asia Working Group Paper. Foreign Policy at Brookings*, 2016. https://www.brookings.edu/wp-content/uploads/2016/07/xi_jinping_worldview_bader-1.pdf.

Baechler, Jean. *Qu'est-ce que l'idéologie?* Paris: Éditions Gallimard, 1976.

Bandurski, David. 'Claiming 21st Century Marxism'. *China Media Project*, June 2020. https://chinamediaproject.org/2020/06/18/claiming-21st-century-marxism/.

Bandurski, David. 'A Diplomatic Bow to Xi Jinping'. *China Media Project*, August 2020. https://chinamediaproject.org/2020/08/03/wang-yis-discourse-of-diplomacy/.

Bandurski, David. 'A History of Common Prosperity', *China Media Project*, 27 August 2021.

Bandurski, David. 'The Tea Leaves of Xi-Era Discourse'. *China Media Project*, November 2017. https://chinamediaproject.org/2017/11/14/the-tea-leaves-of-xi-era-discourse/.

Bandurski, David. 'Xi Gets Research Centers to Match His Thought'. *China Media Project*, December 2017. https://chinamediaproject.org/2017/12/18/xi-gets-research-centers-to-match-his-thought/.

Bandurski, David. 'Xi Jinping, Playing with Fire'. *China Media Project*, October 2013. https://chinamediaproject.org/2013/10/17/xi-jinping-playing-with-fire/.

Bank of Finland Institute for Emerging Economies. 'China Now Has the World's Second Largest Bond Market after the US'. *BOFIT*, 2021. https://www.bofit.fi/en/monitoring/weekly/2021/vw202130_2/.

Baptista, Eduardo, Yew Lun Tian, and Yew Lun Tian. 'China's New Premier Seeks to Reassure Private Sector as Parliament Wraps Up'. *Reuters*, March 2023. https://www.reuters.com/world/china/chinas-xi-stresses-security-calls-its-military-great-wall-steel-2023-03-13/.

Barmé, Geremie R. 'A Monkey King's Journey to the East'. *China Heritage [blog]*, January 2017. https://chinaheritage.net/journal/a-monkey-kings-journey-to-the-east/.

Barrington, Lowell W. '"Nation" and "Nationalism": The Misuse of Key Concepts in Political Science'. *PS: Political Science and Politics*, 30/4 (1997), 712–16.

Barwick, Panle Jia, Myrto Kalouptsidi, and Nahim Bin Zahur. 'China's Industrial Policy: An Empirical Evaluation'. *Working Paper Series. National Bureau of Economic Research*, July 2019.

Batke, Jessica. 'The National People's Congress in 2017: Security, Ideology, and Experimentation'. *China Leadership Monitor*, 2017. https://www.hoover.org/sites/default/files/research/docs/clm53jb.pdf.

Batke, Jessica. 'Party All the Time: Governance and Society in the New Era'. *China Leadership Monitor*, 2018. https://www.hoover.org/sites/default/files/research/docs/clm55-jb-final.pdf.

Baum, Richard. 'The Fifteenth National Party Congress: Jiang Takes Command?'. *China Quarterly*, no. 153 (1998), 141–56.

BBC News. 'China Schools: "Xi Jinping Thought" Introduced into Curriculum'. *BBC News*, August 2021. https://www.bbc.com/news/world-asia-58301575.

BBC News. 'Ukraine War: What Support Is China Giving Russia?'. *BBC News*, March 2022. https://www.bbc.com/news/60571253.

Bekkevold, Jo Inge, and Bobo Lo (eds.). *Sino-Russian Relations in the 21st Century*. Cham: Springer International Publishing, 2019.

Bell, Daniel. *The China Model: Political Meritocracy and the Limits of Democracy*. Princeton, NJ: Princeton University Press, 2015.

Bendini, Roberto. *Exceptional Measures*. Brussels: European Parliament DG EXPO, 2015.

Benedikter, Roland, and Verena Nowotny. *China's Road Ahead: Problems, Questions, Perspectives*. Springer Briefs in Political Science. New York: Springer, 2013.

Benewick, Robert, Marc Blecher, and Sarah Cook (eds.). *Asian Politics in Development*. London: Routledge, 2004.

Benewick, Robert, and Paul Wingrove (eds.). *Reforming the Revolution*. London: Macmillan Education UK, 1988.

Bernstein, Richard. 'Jiang's Warning: No Forgiveness'. *New York Times*, 30 June 1989.

Bhusari, Mrugank, and Maia Nikoladze. 'Russia and China Have Been Teaming Up to Reduce Reliance on the Dollar. Here's How It's Going'. *Atlantic Council*, February 2023. https://www.atlanticcouncil.org/blogs/new-atlanticist/russia-and-china-have-been-teaming-up-to-reduce-reliance-on-the-dollar-heres-how-its-going/.

Bianco, Lucien. *Origins of the Chinese Revolution: 1915–1949*. Stanford, CA: Stanford University Press, 1984.

Bishop, Bill. 'Central Economic Work Conference; Progress vs Stability; PRC-Philippines Standoffs; Fentanyl'. *Sinocism*, December 2023. https://sinocism.com/p/central-economic-work-conference-36c.

Bishop, Bill. 'China's Political Discourse September 2023: Struggling with Negotiation in the US-China Relationship'. *Sinocism*, 2023. https://sinocism.com/p/chinas-political-discourse-september23.

Bishop, Bill. 'Outbreaks; Water Security; Big Plans for Digital Economy; Yan Xuetong'. *Sinocism*, 12 January 2022. https://sinocism.com/p/outbreaks-water-security-big-plans.

Bishop, Bill. 'Rectification in the Politics and Legal Affairs System; Xi and Putin Talk; TikTok; Wang Wei 王維', *Sinocism*, 8 July 2020. https://sinocism.com/p/rectification-in-the-politics-and.

Bishop, Bill, Chu Yang, and David L. Bandurski. 'China's Political Discourse September 2023: Struggling with Negotiation in the US-China Relationship'. *Sinocism*, November 2023. https://sinocism.com/p/chinas-political-discourse-september23.

Blackwill, Robert D., and Kurt M. Campbell. *Xi Jinping on the Global Stage: Chinese Foreign Policy under a Powerful but Exposed Leader*. Council Special Report, no. 74. New York: Council on Foreign Relations, 2016.

Blanchard, Jean-Marc F. 'Harmonious World and China's Foreign Economic Policy: Features, Implications, and Challenges'. *Journal of Chinese Political Science*, 13/2 (August 2008), 165–92.

Blanchette, Jude. *China's New Red Guards: The Return of Radicalism and the Rebirth of Mao Zedong*. New York: Oxford University Press, 2019.

Blanchette, Jude. 'CLM Insights Interview with Jude Blanchette'. *China Leadership Monitor*, no. 62 (2019). https://www.prcleader.org/_files/ugd/10535f_6dcca1d54bfa404a94fa20aa35bfb420.pdf.

Blanchette, Jude. 'From "China Inc" to "CCP Inc": A New Paradigm for Chinese State Capitalism'. *Hinrich Foundation*, February 2021. https://www.hinrichfoundation.com/media/swapcczi/from-china-inc-to-ccp-inc-hinrich-foundation-february-2021.pdf.

Blanchette, Jude. 'Ideological Security as National Security'. *Center for Strategic and International Studies (CSIS)*, December 2020. https://www.csis.org/analysis/ideological-security-national-security.

Blanchette, Jude. 'Strengthening the CCP's "Ideological Work"'. *Center for Strategic and International Studies (CSIS)*, August 2020. https://www.csis.org/analysis/strengthening-ccps-ideological-work.

Blanchette, Jude, and Andrew Polk. 'Dual Circulation and China's New Hedged Integration Strategy'. *Center for Strategic and International Studies (CSIS)*, August 2020. https://www.csis.org/analysis/dual-circulation-and-chinas-new-hedged-integration-strategy.

Bo, Zhiyue. *China's Political Dynamics under Xi Jinping*. Hackensack, NJ: World Scientific, 2017.

Bo, Zhiyue. 'Hu Jintao and the CCP's Ideology: A Historical Perspective'. *Journal of Chinese Political Science*, 9/2 (September 2004), 27–45.

Bobbio, Norberto, and Allan Cameron. *Left and Right: The Significance of a Political Distinction*. Chicago: University of Chicago Press, 1996.

Bohman, Viking. 'The Limits of Economic Coercion: Why China's Red-Line Diplomacy Is Failing in Lithuania and the Wider European Union'. 2021. https://www.ui.se/english/research/swedish-national-china-centre/Publications/the-limits-of-economic-coercion/.

Boon, Hoo Tiang. 'Hardening the Hard, Softening the Soft: Assertiveness and China's Regional Strategy'. *Journal of Strategic Studies*, 40/(July 2017), 639–62.

Bougon, François. *China's Four Decades of Reforms*. London: Hurst & Co, 2018.

Bougon, François. *Inside the Mind of Xi Jinping*. Updated English edition. London: Hurst & Co, 2018.

Boulter, John. 'China's Supply-Side Structural Reform'. *Reserve Bank of Australia, December* 2018. https://www.rba.gov.au/publications/bulletin/2018/dec/chinas-supply-side-structural-reform.html.

Bowie, Julia and David Glitter. 'The CCP's Plan to "Sincize" Religions', *The Diplomat*, 14 June 2018. https://thediplomat.com/2018/06/the-ccps-plan-to-sinicize-religions/.

Brandt, Conrad, Benjamin I. Schwartz, and John King Fairbank. *A Documentary History of Chinese Communism*. Cambridge, MA: Harvard University Press, 1952.

Brandt, Loren, John Litwack, Mileva Elitz, Luhang Wang. 'Recent Productivity Trends in China: Evidence from Macro- and Firm-Level Data', *China: An International Journal*, 20/1 (2022)

Brødsgaard, Kjeld Erik. 'China's Political Order under Xi Jinping: Concepts and Perspectives'. *China: An International Journal*, 16/3 (2018), 1–17.

Brødsgaard, Kjeld Erik (ed.). *Critical Readings on the Chinese Communist Party*. Leiden: Brill, 2017.

Brødsgaard, Kjeld Erik, and Yongnian Zheng (eds.). *The Chinese Communist Party in Reform*. Routledge Studies on the Chinese Economy. New York: Routledge, 2006.

Brown, Chris. *Understanding International Relations*. 5th ed. London: Red Globe Press, 2019.

Brown, Kerry. 'The Anti-Corruption Struggle in Xi Jinping's China: An Alternative Political Narrative'. *Asian Affairs*, 49/1 (January 2018), 1–10.

Brown, Kerry. *Carnival China: China in the Era of Hu Jintao and Xi Jinping*. London: Imperial College Press, 2014.

Brown, Kerry. 'The CCP and the One Party State'. In Christopher Ogden (ed.), *Handbook of China's Governance and Domestic Politics*. London: Routledge, 2012.

Brown, Kerry, *CEO, China: The Rise of Xi Jinping*. London, New York: I. B. Tauris, 2016.

Brown, Kerry. *China's 19th Party Congress: Start of a New Era*. World Scientific Publishing UK, 2018.

Brown, Kerry. 'China's Foreign Policy since 2012: A Question of Communication and Clarity'. *China Quarterly of International Strategic Studies*, 3/3 (January 2017), 325–39.

Brown, Kerry (ed.). *China 2020: The Next Decade for the People's Republic of China*. Asian Studies Series. Oxford: Chandos Publishing, 2010.

Brown, Kerry. 'The Chinese Communist Party's Evolution'. In Czeslaw Tubilewicz (ed.), *Critical Issues in Contemporary China*. 2nd ed. New York: Routledge, 2016.

Brown, Kerry. 'The Communist Party of China and Ideology'. *China: An International Journal*, 10/2 (August 2012), 52–68.

Brown, Kerry. 'Foreign Policy Making under Xi Jinping: The Case of the South China Sea'. *Journal of Political Risk*, 4/2 (2016). https://www.jpolrisk.com/foreign-policy-making-under-xi-jinping-the-case-of-the-south-china-sea/.

Brown, Kerry. *Hu Jintao: China's Silent Ruler*. Hackensack, NJ: World Scientific, 2012.

Brown, Kerry. 'The Role of Leadership in Political and Economic Transition in China'. In Evan Berman and M. Shamsul Haque (eds.), *Asian Leadership in Policy and Governance*. Public Policy and Governance 24. Leeds: Emerald Publishing, 2015, 213–31.

Brown, Kerry. *The World According to Xi: Everything You Need to Know about the New China*. London: I. B. Tauris, 2018.

Brown, Kerry. *Xi: A Study in Power*. La Vergne, TN: Icon Books, 2022.

Brown, Kerry, and Simone van Nieuwenhuizen. *China and the New Maoists*. Asian Arguments. London: Zed Books, 2016.

Brown, Kerry, and Claude Zanardi. 'The Chinese Military: Its Political and Economic Function'. In Anna Stavrianakis and Jan Selby (eds.), *Militarism and International Relations: Political Economy, Security, Theory*. Cass Military Studies. New York: Routledge, 2012.

Brown, Kerry and Una Aleksandra Bērziņa-Čerenkova. 'Ideology in the Era of Xi Jinping'. *Journal of Chinese Political Science*, 24/3 (2018).

Brugger, Bill. 'From "Revisionism" to "Alienation," from Great Leaps to "Third Wave"'. *China Quarterly*, no. 108 (1986), 643–51.

Brugger, Bill, and David Kelly. *Chinese Marxism in the Post-Mao Era*. Stanford, CA: Stanford University Press, 1990.

Brussee, Vincent. *Social Credit: The Warring States of China's Emerging Data Empire*. Singapore: Palgrave Macmillan, 2023.

Buckley, Chris. '"Uncle Xi" to Exalted Ruler: China's Leader Embodies His Authoritarian Era'. *New York Times*, 14 October 2022. https://www.nytimes.com/2022/10/14/world/asia/china-xi-jinping-communist-party.html.

Buckley, Chris. 'Vows of Change in China Belie Private Warning'. *New York Times*, February 2013. https://www.nytimes.com/2013/02/15/world/asia/vowing-reform-chinas-leader-xi-jinping-airs-other-message-in-private.htm.

Buckley, Chris. 'Xi Jinping Thought Explained: A New Ideology for a New Era'. *New York Times*, February 2018. https://www.nytimes.com/2018/02/26/world/asia/xi-jinping-thought-explained-a-new-ideology-for-a-new-era.html.

Buckley, Chris, Keith Bradher, Vivian Wang, and Austin Ramzy. 'China's Leader Strikes a Defiant Note, Warning of "Stormy Seas"'. *New York Times*, 16 October 2022. https://www.nytimes.com/2022/10/16/world/asia/china-congress-xi-jinping.html.

Bukharin, N.I., A.M. Deborin, Y.M. Yuranovsky, S.I. Vavilov, V.L. Komarov, and A.I. Tiumeniev. *Marxism and Modern Thought*. New York: Harcourt, Brace and Co., 1935.

Buhi, Jason. 'Foreign Policy and the Chinese Constitutions during the Hu Jintao Administration'. *Boston College International and Comparative Law Review*, 37/2 (2014). https://lira.bc.edu/.

Burgh, Hugo de. 'The Re-Imagining of China under President Xi Jinping'. China Media Research, 2018. https://www.thefreelibrary.com/The+Re-imagining+of+China+under+President+Xi+Jinping.-a0526575437.

Cabestan, Jean-Pierre. 'China's Institutional Changes in the Foreign and Security Policy Realm under Xi Jinping: Power Concentration vs. Fragmentation without Institutionalization'. *East Asia*, 34/2 (June 2017), 113–31.

Cabestan, Jean-Pierre. 'Is Xi Jinping the Reformist Leader China Needs?'. *China Perspectives*, 2012/3 (October 2012), 69–76.

Cai, Fang (ed.). *China's Economic New Normal: Growth, Structure, and Momentum*. Research Series on the Chinese Dream and China's Development Path. Singapore: Springer, 2020.

Cai, Fang. 'Right Time for China's "Common Prosperity" drive'. *East Asia Forum*, 19 September 2021. https://eastasiaforum.org/2021/09/19/right-time-for-chinas-common-prosperity-drive/.

Cai, Vanessa. 'Chinese Communist Party's Top Corruption Watchdog Takes Aim at "Double Dealers" within Its Ranks', *South China Morning Post*. 16 March 2023. https://www.scmp.com/news/china/politics/article/3213780/chinese-communist-partys-top-corruption-watchdog-takes-aim-double-dealers-within-its-ranks.

Caixin Global. 'Those Who Don't Support Development of Private Enterprises Must Be Corrected: Liu He'. *Caixin Global*, 2018. https://www.caixinglobal.com/2018-10-20/those-who-do-not-support-the-development-of-private-enterprises-must-be-resolutely-corrected-liu-he-101337150.html.

Callahan, William A. 'Book Review: Rebranding China: Contested Status Signaling in the Changing Global Order'. *China Information*, 34/1 (March 2020), 144–46.

Callahan, William A. 'China 2035: From the China Dream to the World Dream'. *Global Affairs*, 2/3 (May 2016), 247–58.

Callahan, William A. *China Dreams: 20 Visions of the Future*. Oxford: Oxford University Press, 2013.

Callahan, William A. 'Chinese Visions of World Order: Post-Hegemonic or a New Hegemony?'. *International Studies Review*, 10/4 (December 2008), 749–61.

Callahan, William A. 'Dreaming as a Critical Discourse of National Belonging: China Dream, American Dream and World Dream'. *Nations and Nationalism*, 23/2 (April 2017), 248–70.

Callahan, William A. 'Great Walls: From Ideology to Experience'. *Journal of Narrative Politics*, 6/2 (May 2020). https://jnp.journals.yorku.ca/index.php/default/article/view/123.

Callahan, William A. 'History, Identity, and Security: Producing and Consuming Nationalism in China'. *Critical Asian Studies*, 38/2 (June 2006), 179–208.

Callahan, William A. 'National Insecurities: Humiliation, Salvation, and Chinese Nationalism'. *Alternatives* 29 (2004).

Callahan, William A. 'Nationalism, Civilization and Transnational Relations: The Discourse of Greater China'. *Journal of Contemporary China*, 14/43 (May 2005), 269–89.

Callahan, William A. 'Tianxia, Empire and the World: Soft Power and China's Foreign Policy Discourse in the 21st Century'. 2007. https://www.semanticscholar.org/paper/Tianxia%2C-Empire-and-the-World%3A-Soft-Power-and-in-Callahan/b1d49b4f0d3981 9ee49db87329e3412c17d474c9.

Callahan, William A. '"You Can See China from Here": The Evolution of a Border,' 2020. https://thediplomat.com/2020/04/you-can-see-china-from-here-the-evolution-of-a-border/.

Campbell, Kurt M., and Robert D. Blackwill. 'Xi Jinping on the Global Stage'. *Council on Foreign Relations*, 2016. https://www.cfr.org/report/xi-jinping-global-stage.

Campbell, Kurt M., and Rush Doshi. 'How America Can Shore Up Asian Order'. *Foreign Affairs*, January 2021. https://www.foreignaffairs.com/articles/united-states/2021-01-12/how-america-can-shore-asian-order.

Campbell, Kurt M., and Rush Doshi. 'The Coronavirus Could Reshape Global Order'. *Foreign Affairs*, March 2020. https://www.foreignaffairs.com/articles/china/2020-03-18/coronavirus-could-reshape-global-order.

Canberra Times. 'Vice Regal', *Canberra Times*, 13 March 1986. https://trove.nla.gov.au/newspaper/article/118106654/13025024.

Cao, Tian Yu, Xueping Zhong, and Liao Kebin (eds.). *Culture and Social Transformations in Reform Era China*. Leiden: Brill, 2010.

Carlsnaes, Walter. *The Concept of Ideology and Political Analysis: A Critical Examination of Its Usage by Marx, Lenin, and Mannheim*. Contributions in Philosophy, 17. Westport, CT: Greenwood, 1981.

Carnegie, Dale. *How to Win Friends and Influence People*. New York: Simon & Schuster, 1936.

Carothers, Christopher. 'Combating Corruption in Authoritarian Regimes'. May 2019. https://dash.harvard.edu/handle/1/42029832.

Carothers, Christopher. 'Xi's Anti-Corruption Campaign: An All-Purpose Governing Tool'. *China Leadership*, March 2021. https://www.prcleader.org/post/xi-s-anti-corruption-campaign-an-all-purpose-governing-tool.

Carrai, Maria Adele. 'Chinese Political Nostalgia and Xi Jinping's Dream of Great Rejuvenation'. *International Journal of Asian Studies*, 18/1 (January 2021), 7–25.

Casert, Raf, and Samuel Petrequin. 'EU Lashes Out at China for Support of Russia in Ukraine War'. *Associated Press*, 5 April 2023. https://apnews.com/article/eu-china-blinken-russia-ukraine-61c81520b6a97e0a90c97a2402cda5b3.

Center for China Analysis. 'China's Political-Economy, Foreign and Security Policy: 2023'. Asia Society Policy Institute, 2023. https://asiasociety.org/policy-institute/chinas-political-economy-foreign-and-security-policy-2023.

Center on US-China Relations. *China's Influence & American Interests: Promoting Constructive Vigilance: Report of the Working Group on Chinese Influence Activities in the United States*. Rev. ed. Stanford, CA: Hoover Institution Press, 2019.

Chai, Winberg. 'The Ideological Paradigm Shifts of China's World Views: From Marxism-Leninism-Maoism to the Pragmatism-Multilateralism of the Deng-Jiang-Hu Era'. *Asian Affairs*, 30/3 (2003), 163–75.

Chai, Winberg, and May-lee Chai. 'The Meaning of Xi Jinping's Chinese Dream'. *American Journal of Chinese Studies*, 20/2 (2013), 95–97.

Chan, Adrian. *Chinese Marxism*. London: Continuum, 2003.

Chan, Alfred L. *Xi Jinping: Political Career, Governance, and Leadership, 1953–2018*. New York: Oxford University Press, 2022.

Chance, Alek. 'American Perspectives on the Belt and Road Initiative: Sources of Concern, Possibilities for US-China Cooperation'. Washington, DC: Institute for China-American Studies, November 2016.

Chang-Liao, Nien-chung. 'China's New Foreign Policy under Xi Jinping'. *Asian Security*, 12/2 (May 2016), 82–91.

Chang-Liao, Nien-Chung. 'The Sources of China's Assertiveness: The System, Domestic Politics or Leadership Preferences?'. *International Affairs*, 92/4 (2016), 817–33.

Chanlett-Avery, Emma, K. Alan Kronstadt, and Bruce Vaughn. 'The "Quad": Cooperation among the United States, Japan, India, and Australia'. IF11678. Congressional Research Service, 2022.

Chase, Michael S., Cortez A. Cooper III, Keith Crane, Liisa Ecola, Scott W. Harold, Timothy R. Heath, Bonny Lin, Lyle J. Morris, and Andrew Scobell. 'China, Inside and Out: A Collection of Essays on Foreign and Domestic Policy in the Xi Jinping Era'. *RAND Corporation*, October 2015. https://www.rand.org/pubs/corporate_pubs/CP797.html.

Cheek, Timothy. *The Intellectual in Modern Chinese History*. Cambridge: Cambridge University Press, 2015.

Cheek, Timothy. *Living with Reform: China since 1989*. Global History of the Present. Nova Scotia: Fernwood, 2006.

Cheek, Timothy. *Mao Zedong and China's Revolutions: A Brief History with Documents*. The Bedford Series in History and Culture. Boston: Bedford/St. Martin's, 2002.

Cheek, Timothy, David Ownby, and Joshua A. Fogel (eds.). *Voices from the Chinese Century: Public Intellectual Debate from Contemporary China*. New York: Columbia University Press, 2019.

Chen, Chien-Kai. 'Comparing Jiang Zemin's Impatience with Hu Jintao's Patience Regarding the Taiwan Issue, 1989–2012'. *Journal of Contemporary China*, 21/78 (November 2012), 955–72.

Chen, Dingding, Xiaoyu Pu, and Alastair Iain Johnston. 'Debating China's Assertiveness'. *International Security*, 38/3 (2013), 176–83.

Chen, Dingding, and Jianwei Wang. 'Lying Low No More? China's New Thinking on the Tao Guang Yang Hui Strategy'. *China: An International Journal*, 9/2 (September 2011), 195–216.

Chen, Feng. 'An Unfinished Battle in China: The Leftist Criticism of the Reform and the Third Thought Emancipation'. *China Quarterly*, no. 158 (1999), 447–67.

Chen, Frank, and Luna Sun. 'China Doesn't Want to Rock the Boat, but India Trade Tensions May Continue'. *South China Morning Post*, December 2023. https://www.scmp.com/economy/global-economy/article/3246682/china-india-trade-tensions-may-continue-2024-beijing-I-want-rock-boat.

Chen, Gang. 'Reinforcing Leninist Means of Corruption Control in China: Centralization, Regulatory Changes and Party-State Integration'. *Copenhagen Journal of Asian Studies*, 35/2 (2017), 30–51.

Chen, Gang. 'What Is New for China's Technocracy in Xi Jinping's Time?' *China: An International Journal*, 18/1 (February 2020), 123–33.

Chen, Jian. 'From Mao to Deng: China's Changing Relations with the United States'. Wilson Center, 2019. https://www.wilsoncenter.org/publication/mao-to-deng-chinas-changing-relations-the-united-states.

Chen, Jian. *Mao's China and the Cold War*. The New Cold War History. Chapel Hill: University of North Carolina Press, 2001.

Chen, Jian. 'The Myth of America's "Lost Chance" in China: A Chinese Perspective in Light of New Evidence'. *Diplomatic History*, 21/1 (1997), 77–86.

Chen, Kuan-Wu, and Yu-Shan Wu. 'Power Position and Taiwan Policy: How Beijing Responds to Taipei's Stimuli during the Jiang Zemin and Hu Jintao Periods'. *Journal of Contemporary East Asia Studies*, 6/2 (July 2017), 132–52.

Chen, Laurie, Albee Zhang, and Laurie Chen. 'China Suspends Youth Jobless Data after Record High Readings'. *Reuters*, August 2023. https://www.reuters.com/world/china/china-stop-releasing-youth-jobless-rate-data-aug-says-stats-bureau-2023-08-15/.

Chen, Ling, and Barry Naughton. 'A Dynamic China Model: The Co-Evolution of Economics and Politics in China'. *Journal of Contemporary China*, 26/103 (2017), 18–34.

Chen, Lulu Yilun. 'China's Rich Entrust Total Strangers to Sneak Cash Out of the Country'. *Bloomberg.com*, October 2023. https://www.bloomberg.com/news/articles/2023-10-08/how-china-s-rich-are-using-underground-networks-to-move-their-money-abroad,

Chen, Yawen. 'China's Growth Is Buried under Great Wall of Debt'. *Reuters*, September 2023. https://www.reuters.com/breakingviews/chinas-growth-is-buried-under-great-wall-debt-2023-09-13/.

Chen, Zhimin. 'Nationalism, Internationalism and Chinese Foreign Policy'. *Journal of Contemporary China*, 14/42 (February 2005), 35–53.

Cheng, Joseph Yu-shek. 'The Policy Programme and Human Rights Position of the Xi Jinping Administration'. *Contemporary Chinese Political Economy and Strategic Relations*, 4/2 (August 2018), 319–47.

Cheng, Joseph Yu-Shek, and Franklin Wakung Zhan. 'Chinese Foreign Relation Strategies under Mao and Deng: A Systematic and Comparative'. *Kasalinlan Philippine Journal of Third World Studies*, 14/3 (1999). https://www.journals.upd.edu.ph/index.php/kasarinlan/article/view/1415.

Cheng, Ta-chen. 'Jiang Zemin's Military Thought and Legacy'. *International Relations of the Asia-Pacific*, 6/2 (2006), 227–47.

Cheng, Xiaohe. 'From Jiang Zemin to Hu Jintao: The Evolution of China's Policies toward the Korean Peninsula'. *Korea Observer*, no. 43 (2012), 675–99.

Cheng, Zhao. 'China Advocates Mutual Learning among Civilizations with Concrete Actions'. *People's Daily*, 2019. http://en.people.cn/n3/2019/0516/c90000-9578723.html.

Chenglong, Jiang. 'Mutual Trust Highlighted at Security Forum'. *China Daily*, 2023. https://www.chinadaily.com.cn/a/202310/31/WS653fd996a31090682a5eb856.html.

Cheung, Tai Ming. 'The Chinese National Security State Emerges from the Shadows to Center Stage'. *China Leadership Monitor*, no. 65 (2020). https://www.prcleader.org/post/the-chinese-national-security-state-emerges-from-the-shadows-to-center-stage.

Chhabra, Tarun, Rush Doshi, Ryan Hass, and Emilie Kimball (eds). *Global China: Assessing China's Growing Role in the World*. New York: Brookings Institution Press, 2021.

Chien, Kuo. 'The Novel "Battle of Xiang Jiang" Is Banned', *Daily Report China*, 24 January 1991.

China Daily. 'Support for Amendments Belies Naysayers' Prejudice: China Daily Comment'. *China Daily*, 2018. https://www.chinadaily.com.cn/a/201803/11/WS5aa5471da3106e7dcc140e7c.html.

ChinaFile. 'Fact Sheet on China's Foreign NGO Law'. ChinaFile, November 2017. https://www.chinafile.com/ngo/latest/fact-sheet-chinas-foreign-ngo-law.

ChinaFile. 'United Front Work Department's Austrian Chapter Registers as a Foreign NGO in China'. *The China NGO Project*, 2019. https://www.chinafile.com/ngo/latest/united-front-work-departments-austrian-chapter-registers-foreign-ngo-china.

China.org.cn. 'China Keywords', 2018. http://www.china.org.cn/english/china_key_words.

China Media Project. 'The CMP Dictionary'. *China Media Project*, n.d. https://chinamediaproject.org/CMP-Dictionary/.

Chinese Academy of History. 'A Guiding Light for the Development of Modern Chinese Civilization'. *Qiushi*, 2023. http://en.qstheory.cn/2023-11/14/c_938422.htm.

Christensen, Thomas J. 'The Advantages of an Assertive China'. *Foreign Affairs*, 90/2 (February 2011). https://www.foreignaffairs.com/articles/east-asia/2011-02-21/advantages-assertive-china.

Christensen, Thomas J. 'Chinese Realpolitik'. *Foreign Affairs*, 75/5 (1996), 37–52.

Chubb, Andrew. 'Assessing Public Opinion's Influence on Foreign Policy: The Case of China's Assertive Maritime Behavior'. *Asian Security*, 15/2 (May 2019), 159–79.

Chubb, Andrew. 'Chinese Popular Nationalism and PRC Policy in the South China Sea'. Doctoral Thesis, University of Western Australia, 2016. https://research-repository.uwa.edu.au/en/publications/chinese-popular-nationalism-and-prc-policy-in-the-south-china-sea.

Chubb, Andrew. 'PRC Assertiveness in the South China Sea: Measuring Continuity and Change, 1970–2015'. *International Security*, 45/3 (January 2021), 79–121.

Chung, Li-Hua, and Chin Jonathan. 'Poll Shows 48.9% Support Independence'. *Taipei Times*, September 2023. https://www.taipeitimes.com/News/taiwan/archives/2023/09/02/2003805648.

Chung, Yousun. 'Manifestation of Authoritarian Resilience? Evolution of Property Management in Beijing'. *Journal of International and Area Studies*, 24/1 (2017), 85–103.

Civil Service College. *A Changing China: Emerging Governance, Economic and Social Trends*. Singapore: Civil Service College, 2012.

Clark, Nadia. 'The Rise and Fall of the BRI'. *Council on Foreign Relations*, 2023. https://www.cfr.org/blog/rise-and-fall-bri.

Clarke, Michael. 'French and British Security: Mirror Images in a Globalized World'. *International Affairs*, 76/4 (October 2000), 725–39.

Cliff, Roger. *China's Military Power: Assessing Current and Future Capabilities.* New York: Cambridge University Press, 2015.

Cook, Sarah. 'The Battle for China's Spirit'. *Special Report. Freedom House*, 2017. https://freedomhouse.org/report/special-report/2017/battle-chinas-spirit.

Cortina, Juan. *The Internationalization of China's Equity Markets.* Washington, DC: International Monetary Fund, 2023.

CPC Leadership Group of the Chinese Academy of Social Sciences. 'Understanding the Historical Significance and Contemporary Value of the Distinctive Features of Chinese Civilization'. *Qiushi*, 2024. http://en.qstheory.cn/2024-03/11/c_969196.htm.

Creemers, Rogier. 'Why Marx Still Matters: The Ideological Drivers of Chinese Politics'. *ChinaFile*, December 2014. https://www.chinafile.com/reporting-opinion/viewpoint/why-marx-still-matters-ideological-drivers-chinese-politics.

Creemers, Rogier J. E. H., and Susan Trevaskes (eds.). *Law and the Party in China: Ideology and Organisation.* Cambridge: Cambridge University Press, 2020.

Cunningham, Fiona S. and M. Taylor Fravel. 'Dangerous Confidence? Chinese Views on Nuclear Escalation'. *Belfer Center for Science and International Affairs*, 2019. https://www.belfercenter.org/publication/dangerous-confidence-chinese-views-nuclear-escalation.

Cunningham, Edward, Tony Saich, and Jessie Turiel. 'Understanding CCP Resilience: Surveying Chinese Public Opinion through Time'. Cambridge, MA: Ash Center, Harvard Kennedy School, 2020.

Dallmayr, Fred, and Zhao Tingyang (eds.). *Contemporary Chinese Political Thought: Debates and Perspectives.* Lexington: University Press of Kentucky, 2012. https://www.jstor.org/stable/j.ctt2jcsvm.

Daly, Kevin, and Tadas Gedminas. 'The Path to 2075—Slower Global Growth, but Convergence Remains Intact'. Global Economics Paper. Goldman Sachs Research, December 2022. https://www.goldmansachs.com/intelligence/pages/gs-research/the-path-to-2075-slower-global-growth-but-convergence-remains-intact/report.pdf.

Dassù, Marta, and Tony Saich (eds.). *The Reform Decade in China: From Hope to Dismay.* Abingdon: Routledge, 2019.

Davey, Alexander. 'The "missing" Third Plenum Suggests Xi Is Sticking to His Plan'. *MERICS*, 5 March 2024. https://merics.org/en/comment/missing-third-plenum-suggests-xi-sticking-his-plan.

Davidson, Helen. 'China Targets Foreign Consulting Companies in Anti-Spying Raids'. *The Guardian*, May 2023. https://www.theguardian.com/world/2023/may/09/china-targets-foreign-consulting-companies-in-anti-spying-raids.

Deane, Michael. 'The Soviet Concept of the "Correlation of Forces"'. Arlington, VA: Stanford Research Institute, 1976. https://apps.dtic.mil/sti/citations/ADA027223.

deLisle, Jacques, and Avery Goldstein (eds.). *To Get Rich Is Glorious: Challenges Facing China's Economic Reform and Opening at Forty.* Washington, DC: Brookings Institution Press, 2019. https://www.jstor.org/stable/10.7864/j.ctvbd8m70.

Dellios, Rosita, and R. James Ferguson. *China's Quest for Global Order: From Peaceful Rise to Harmonious World.* Lanham, MD: Lexington Books, 2013.

Demick, Barbara. 'China's Xi More Maoist than Reformer Thus Far'. *Los Angeles Times*, June 2013. https://www.latimes.com/archives/la-xpm-2013-jun-08-la-fg-china-xi-20130608-story.html.

Deng, Jinting. 'The National Supervision Commission: A New Anti-Corruption Model in China'. *International Journal of Law, Crime and Justice*, 52 (March 2018), 58–73.

Deng, Zhenglai, Sujian Guo, and Guo Sujian, eds. Reviving Legitimacy: Lessons for and from China. Challenges Facing Chinese Political Development. Lanham, MD: Lexington Books, 2011.

Denyer, Simon. 'Chinese Universities Scramble to Open Centers to Study President Xi Jinping Thought'. *Washington Post*, April 2023. https://www.washingtonpost.com/world/chinese-universities-scramble-to-open-centers-to-study-president-xi-jinping-thought/2017/11/01/a845e664-bed8-11e7-af84-d3e2ee4b2af1_story.html.

Dickson, Bruce J. *The Dictator's Dilemma: The Chinese Communist Party's Strategy for Survival*. New York: Oxford University Press, 2016.

Dimitrov, Martin. 'The Resilient Authoritarians'. *Current History*, 107/705 (January 2008), 24–29.

Ding, Arthur S., and Jagannath P. Panda (eds.). *Chinese Politics and Foreign Policy under Xi Jinping: The Future Political Trajectory*. Routledge Studies on Think Asia. London: Routledge, 2021.

Dirlik, Arif. *Anarchism in the Chinese Revolution*. Berkeley: University of California Press, 1991.

Dirlik, Arif. 'The Idea of a "Chinese Model": A Critical Discussion'. *China Information*, 26/3 (November 2012), 277–302.

Dirlik, Arif. 'Mao Zedong in Contemporary Chinese Official Discourse and History'. *China Perspectives* 2012/2 (June 2012), 1727.

Dirlik, Arif. *Marxism in the Chinese Revolution*. State and Society in East Asia Series. Lanham, MD: Rowman & Littlefield, 2005.

Dirlik, Arif. *The Origins of Chinese Communism*. New York: Oxford University Press, 1989.

Dirlik, Arif. 'Postsocialism? Reflections on "Socialism with Chinese Characteristics"'. *Bulletin of Concerned Asian Scholars*, 21, no. 1 (March 1989), 33–44.

Dirlik, Arif. 'The Predicament of Marxist Revolutionary Consciousness: Mao Zedong, Antonio Gramsci, and the Reformulation of Marxist Revolutionary Theory'. *Modern China*, 9/2 (1983), 182–211.

Dittmer, Lowell. 'China's New Leadership and Global Role'. In *Asian Leadership in Policy and Governance*, 21–43. Public Policy and Governance, 24. Leeds: Emerald Group, 2015.

Dittmer, Lowell, and Guoli Liu (eds.). *China's Deep Reform: Domestic Politics in Transition*. Lanham, MD: Rowman & Littlefield, 2006.

Dollar, David, Yiping Huang, and Yang Yao. 'Opinion: What China Needs to Do If It Wants to Achieve Its Ambitious Economic Goals by 2049'. *CNN*, June 2021. https://www.cnn.com/2021/06/21/perspectives/imf-china-economy/index.html.

Dollar, David, and Aart Kraay. 'Neither a Borrower nor a Lender: Does China's Zero Net Foreign Asset Position Make Economic Sense?'. *Journal of Monetary Economics* 53/5 (July 2006), 943–71.

Doshi, Rush. 'Hu's to Blame for China's Foreign Assertiveness?'. *Brookings*, 2019. https://www.brookings.edu/articles/hus-to-blame-for-chinas-foreign-assertiveness/.

Doshi, Rush. *The Long Game: China's Grand Strategy to Displace American Order. Bridging the Gap*. New York: Oxford University Press, 2021.

Doshi, Rush. 'The United States, China, and the Contest for the Fourth Industrial Revolution'. *Brookings*, 2020. https://www.brookings.edu/articles/the-united-states-china-and-the-contest-for-the-fourth-industrial-revolution/.

Doshi, R., A. Dale-Huang, and G. Zhang. 'Northern Expedition: China's Arctic Activities and Ambitions'. *Brookings*, 2021. https://www.brookings.edu/articles/northern-expedition-chinas-arctic-activities-and-ambitions/.

Dotson, John. 'The "Democratic Life Meetings" of the Chinese Communist Party Politburo'. *China Brief*, 20/2 (2020). https://jamestown.org/program/the-democratic-life-meetings-of-the-chinese-communist-party-politburo/.

Dotson, John. 'Xi Jinping's Summer Foreign Policy Tour Displays "Great Power Diplomacy with Chinese Characteristics"'. *China Brief*, 19/3 (2019). https://jamestown.org/program/xi-jinpings-summer-foreign-policy-tour-displays-great-power-diplomacy-with-chinese-characteristics/.

Downs, Erica Strecker, and Phillip C. Saunders. 'Legitimacy and the Limits of Nationalism: China and the Diaoyu Islands'. *International Security*, 23/3 (1998), 114–46.

Du, Wei. '2014: A Year of Turbulence in Global Landscape and Adjustment in International System'. *Foreign Affairs Journal*, no. 15 (2014).

Du, Zhanwei, Yuchen Wang, Yuan Bai, Lin Wang, Benjamin John Cowling, and Lauren Ancel Meyers. 'Estimate of COVID-19 Deaths, China, December 2022–February 2023'. *Emerging Infectious Diseases*, 29/10 (October 2023).

Dunne, Timothy, Milja Kurki, and Steve Smith (eds.). *International Relations Theories: Discipline and Diversity*. 3rd ed. Oxford: Oxford University Press, 2013.

Durdin, Tillman. 'China Transformed by Elimination of "Four Olds"'. *New York Times*, May 1971. https://www.nytimes.com/1971/05/19/archives/china-transformed-by-elimination-of-four-olds.html.

Durham, Meenakshi Gigi, and Douglas Kellner (eds.). *Media and Cultural Studies: Keyworks*. 2nd ed. Malden, MA: Wiley-Blackwell, 2012.

Ecker-Ehrhardt, Matthias. 'Cosmopolitan Politicization: How Perceptions of Interdependence Foster Citizens' Expectations in International Institutions'. *European Journal of International Relations*, 18/3 (September 2012), 481–508.

The Economist. 'China's Defeated Youth'. *The Economist*, 2023. https://www.economist.com/briefing/2023/08/17/chinas-defeated-youth.

The Economist. 'A Dragon out of Puff'. *The Economist*, 2002. https://www.economist.com/special-report/2002/06/15/a-dragon-out-of-puff.

The Economist. 'Is Chinese Power about to Peak?'. *The Economist*, 2023. https://www.economist.com/leaders/2023/05/11/is-chinese-power-about-to-peak.

The Economist. 'The Meaning of the Man behind China's Ideology'. The Economist, 2017. https://www.economist.com/china/2017/11/02/the-meaning-of-the-man-behind-chinas-ideology.

The Economist. 'When Will China's GDP Overtake America's?'. *The Economist*, 2023. https://www.economist.com/graphic-detail/2023/06/07/when-will-chinas-gdp-overtake-americas.

Economy, Elizabeth. '30 Years after Tiananmen: Dissent Is Not Dead'. *Journal of Democracy*, 30/2 (2019), 57–63. https://www.journalofdemocracy.org/articles/30-years-after-tiananmen-dissent-is-not-dead/.

Economy, Elizabeth. 'China's Neo-Maoist Moment'. *Foreign Affairs*, October 2019. https://www.foreignaffairs.com/articles/china/2019-10-01/chinas-neo-maoist-moment.

Economy, Elizabeth. *The Third Revolution: Xi Jinping and the New Chinese State*. New York: Oxford University Press, 2019.

Esteban, Mario. 'The Foreign Policy of Xi Jinping after the 19th Congress: China Strives for a Central Role on the World Stage'. *Elcano Royal Institute*, 2017. https://www.realinstitutoelcano.org/en/analyses/the-foreign-policy-of-xi-jinping-after-the-19th-congress-china-strives-for-a-central-role-on-the-world-stage/.

European Union Chamber of Commerce in China. 'Competitive Neutrality: Reining In China's Industrial Hegemons'. *European Chamber of Commerce in China*, 2019. http://www.swisscham.org/wp-content/uploads/sites/2/2018/04/Executive_Position_Paper_2019_2020.pdf.

European Chamber of Commerce in China. 'Overcapacity in China'. *European Chamber of Commerce in China*, 2016. https://www.europeanchamber.com.cn/en/publications-overcapacity-in-china.

Evans, Alfred B. *Soviet Marxism-Leninism: The Decline of an Ideology*. Westport, CT: Praeger, 1993.

Eyerman, Ron. 'False Consciousness and Ideology in Marxist Theory'. *Acta Sociologica*, 24/1–2 (January 1981), 43–56.

Fairbank, John King (ed). *The Chinese World Order: Traditional China's Foreign Relations*. Repr. Harvard East Asian Series 32. Cambridge, MA: Harvard University Press, 1974.

Feigenbaum, Evan A. 'A Chinese Puzzle: Why Economic "Reform" in Xi's China Has More Meanings than Market Liberalization'. *Carnegie Endowment for International Peace [blog]*, 2018. https://carnegieendowment.org/2018/02/26/chinese-puzzle-why-economic-reform-in-xi-s-china-has-more-meanings-than-market-liberalization-pub-75668.

Feldstein, Martin. 'What Is China's "New Normal"?'. World Economic Forum. 27 March 2015. https://www.weforum.org/agenda/2015/03/what-is-chinas-new-normal/.

Feng, Zhang. 'The Tianxia System: World Order in a Chinese Utopia'. *Global Asia*, 2009. https://www.globalasia.org/v4no4/book/the-tianxia-system-world-order-in-a-chinese-utopia_zhang-feng.

Ferdinand, Peter. 'Westward Ho—The China Dream and "One Belt, One Road": Chinese Foreign Policy under Xi Jinping'. *International Affairs*, 92/4 (July 2016), 941–57.

Fewsmith, Joseph. 'The 19th Party Congress: Ringing in Xi Jinping's New Age'. *China Leadership Monitor*, 55 (2018). https://www.hoover.org/research/19th-party-congress-ringing-xi-jinpings-new-age.

Fewsmith, Joseph. 'Balances, Norms and Institutions: Why Elite Politics in the CCP Have Not Institutionalized'. *China Quarterly*, 248/S1 (November 2021), 265–82.

Fewsmith, Joseph. *China since Tiananmen: From Deng Xiaoping to Hu Jintao*. New York: Cambridge University Press, 2008.

Fewsmith, Joseph. *China since Tiananmen: From Deng Xiaoping to Hu Jintao*. 2nd ed. Cambridge Modern China Series. Cambridge: Cambridge University Press, 2008.

Fewsmith, Joseph. *The Logic and Limits of Political Reform in China*. Cambridge: Cambridge University Press, 2013.

Fewsmith, Joseph. 'Promoting the Scientific Development Concept'. *China Leadership Monitor*, no. 11 (2004). https://www.hoover.org/sites/default/files/uploads/documents/clm11_jf.pdf.

Fewsmith, Joseph (ed.). *China Today, China Tomorrow: Domestic Politics, Economy, and Society*. Lanham, MD: Rowman & Littlefield, 2010.

Fewsmith, Joseph, and Andrew J. Nathan. 'Authoritarian Resilience Revisited: Joseph Fewsmith with Response from Andrew J. Nathan'. *Journal of Contemporary China*, 28/116 (March 2019), 167–79.

Fiddler, Connor. 'Xi Jinping's Two Year Plan'. *RealClearWorld*, November 2020. https://www.realclearworld.com/articles/2020/11/17/xi_jinpings_two_year_plan_650092.html.

Fingar, Thomas, and Jean C. Oi (eds.). *Fateful Decisions: Choices That Will Shape China's Future*. Stanford, CA: Stanford University Press, 2020.

Fischer, Doris, Hannes Gohli, and Sabrina Habich-Sobiegalla. 'Industrial Policies under Xi Jinping: A Steering Theory Perspective'. *Issues & Studies*, 57/4 (December 2021), 2150016.

Foot, Rosemary. '"Doing Some Things" in the Xi Jinping Era: The United Nations as China's Venue of Choice'. *International Affairs*, 90/5 (2014), 1085–1100.

Fox, Ralph (ed.). *Marxism and Modern Thought*. New York: Brace & Co., 1935.

Francis, Michael J. 'For the Study of Ideology—Richard H. Cox, Editor: *Ideology, Politics, and Political Theory* [Review]'. *Review of Politics*, 33/4 (October 1971), 601–2.

Fravel, M. Taylor. *Active Defense: China's Military Strategy since 1949*. Princeton Studies in International History and Politics. Princeton, NJ: Princeton University Press, 2019.

Fravel, M. Taylor. 'China's "World-Class Military" Ambitions: Origins and Implications'. *Washington Quarterly*, 43/1 (January 2020), 85–99.

Fravel, M. Taylor. 'International Relations Theory and China's Rise: Assessing China's Potential for Territorial Expansion'. *International Studies Review*, 12/4 (December 2010), 505–32.

Fravel, M. Taylor. 'Revising Deng's Foreign Policy'. *The Diplomat*, January 2012. https://web.archive.org/web/20120117091253/http://the-diplomat.com/china-power/2012/01/17/revising-deng%E2%80%99s-foreign-policy/.

Fravel, M. Taylor. 'Shifts in Warfare and Party Unity: Explaining China's Changes in Military Strategy'. *International Security*, 42/3 (January 2018), 37–83. https://dspace.mit.edu/handle/1721.1/118865.

Frederick, Bryan, and Howard J. Shatz. 'The Global Movement against China's Economic Coercion Is Accelerating'. *The Hill*, June 2023. https://www.rand.org/pubs/commentary/2023/06/the-global-movement-against-chinas-economic-coercion.html.

Freeden, Michael, and Marc Stears (eds.). *The Oxford Handbook of Political Ideologies*. Vol. 1. Oxford: Oxford University Press, 2013.

Freitas, Marcus Vinicius de. 'Reform and Opening-up: Chinese Lessons to the World'. May 2019. https://www.policycenter.ma/publications/reform-and-opening-chinese-lessons-world.

Fu, Ying. 'The US World Order Is a Suit That No Longer Fits'. *Financial Times*, January 2016. https://www.ft.com/content/c09cbcb6-b3cb-11e5-b147-e5e5bba42e51.

Fung, Courtney J. 'China's Small Steps into UN Peacekeeping Are Adding Up'. *IPI Global Observatory*, 24 May 2023. https://theglobalobservatory.org/2023/05/chinas-small-steps-into-un-peacekeeping-are-adding-up/

Gallagher, Mary E., and Jonathan K. Hanson. 'Power Tool or Dull Blade? Selectorate Theory for Autocracies'. *Annual Review of Political Science*, 18/1 (May 2015), 367–85.

Gan, Yong, and David Ownby. '"Unifying the Three Traditions" in the New Era: The Merging of Three Chinese Traditions'. *Reading the China Dream*, May 2005. https://www.readingthechinadream.com/gan-yang-tongsantong-chapter-1.html.

Gang, Qian. 'China Discourse Report: What Was Hot-and-Not in 2018 Political Terminology'. *Hong Kong Free Press*, January 2019. http://hongkongfp.com/2019/01/04/china-discourse-report-hot-not-2018-political-terminology/.

Gang, Qian. 'A Brief History of the Helmsman', *China Media Project*, 2 November 2020. https://chinamediaproject.org/2020/11/02/a-brief-history-of-the-helmsman/

Gang, Wu and Shuang Yan. 'Xi Jinping Pledges "Great Renewal of Chinese Nation"', *Global Times*, 30 November 2012, https://www.globaltimes.cn/content/747443.shtml.

Gao, Charlotte. 'Amid Tensions with US, China Holds an Unusually High-Level Meeting on Diplomacy'. *The Diplomat*, 2018. https://thediplomat.com/2018/06/amid-tensions-with-us-china-holds-an-unusually-high-level-meeting-on-diplomacy/.

Gao, Hua, Stacy Mosher, and Jian Guo. *How the Red Sun Rose: The Origins and Development of the Yan'an Rectification Movement, 1930–1945*. Hong Kong: Chinese University Press, 2018.

Gao, Mobo Changfan. 'The Rise of Neo-Nationalism and the New Left: A Postcolonial and Postmodern Perspective'. In Leong H. Liew and Shaoguang Wang (eds.), *Nationalism, Democracy and National Integration in China*. London: Routledge, 2003.

Garamone, Jim. 'F-22 Safely Shoots Down Chinese Spy Balloon off South Carolina Coast'. US Department of Defense, 2023. https://www.defense.gov/News/News-Stories/Article/Article/3288543/f-22-safely-shoots-down-chinese-spy-balloon-off-south-carolina-coast/.

Garnaut, John. 'Engineers of the Soul: Ideology in Xi Jinping's China by John Garnaut'. *Sinocism*, January 2019. https://sinocism.com/p/engineers-of-the-soul-ideology-in.

Garnaut, John. 'John Garnaut Takes a Deep Look at What Drives China and "What Australia Needs to Know about Ideology in Xi Jinping's China"'. *Interest.co.nz*, January 2019. https://www.interest.co.nz/opinion/97675/john-garnaut-takes-deep-look-what-drives-china-and-what-australia-needs-know-about.

Garrick, John, and Yan Chang Bennett. '"Xi Jinping Thought"'. *China Perspectives*, 2018/1–2 (June 2018), 99–105.

Garrick, John, and Yan Chang Bennett (eds.). *China's Socialist Rule of Law Reforms under Xi Jinping*. London: Routledge, 2016.

Garver, John W. *China's Quest: The History of the Foreign Relations of the People's Republic of China*. New York: Oxford University Press, 2016.

Geddes, Barbara, Joseph Wright, and Erica Frantz. *How Dictatorships Work: Power, Personalization, and Collapse*. Cambridge: Cambridge University Press, 2018.

Geis, John P., and Blaine Holt. '"Harmonious Society": Rise of the New China'. *Strategic Studies Quarterly*, 3/4 (2009), 75–94.

Gellner, Ernest. *Nations and Nationalism*. New Perspectives on the Past. Ithaca, NY: Cornell University Press, 1983.

Gerring, John. 'Ideology: A Definitional Analysis'. *Political Research Quarterly*, 50/4 (1997), 957–94.

Gewirtz, Julian. 'Xi Jinping Thought Is Facing a Harsh Reality Check'. *Foreign Policy*, March 2024. https://foreignpolicy.com/2018/08/15/xi-jinping-thought-is-facing-a-harsh-reality-check/.

Giannakos, Symeon. 'Chinese Nationalism: Myths, Reality, and Security Implications'. *Nationalities Papers*, 47/1 (January 2019), 149–61.

Gill, Bates. 'China's Future under Xi Jinping: Challenges Ahead'. *Political Science*, 69/1 (January 2017), 1–15.

Gill, Indermit S., and Homi Kharas. 'The Middle-Income Trap Turns Ten'. *Policy Research Working Paper 7403. World Bank Group,* August 2015. https://documents1.worldbank.org/curated/en/291521468179640202/pdf/WPS7403.pdf.

Gilley, Bruce. 'China's Changing Role of Guard: The Limits of Authoritarian Resilience'. *Journal of Democracy*, 14/1 (January 2003), 18–26. https://www.journalofdemocracy.org/articles/chinas-changing-of-the-guard-the-limits-of-authoritarian-resilience/.

Gittings, John. *The World and China, 1922–1972*. The China Library. London: Eyre Methuen, 1974.

Glanz, James, Mara Hvistendahl, and Agnes Chang. 'How Deadly Was China's Covid Wave?'. *New York Times*, February 2023. https://www.nytimes.com/interactive/2023/02/15/world/asia/china-covid-death-estimates.html.

Glaser, Bonnie S. 'Made in China 2025 and the Future of American Industry'. *CSIS*, February 2019. https://www.csis.org/analysis/made-china-2025-and-future-american-industry.

Glaser, Bonnie S., and Evan S. Medeiros. 'The Changing Ecology of Foreign Policy-Making in China: The Ascension and Demise of the Theory of "Peaceful Rise"'. *China Quarterly*, 190 (June 2007), 291–310.

Global Times. 'Prominent Economist Justin Lin Debunks "Peak China" Claims, Highlights China's Potential to Surpass US'. *Global Times*, 2024. https://www.globaltimes.cn/page/202403/1308456.shtml.

Global Times. 'China Releases Key Publication on the CPC's Mission and Contributions'. *Global Times*. August 2021. https://www.globaltimes.cn/page/202108/1232505.shtml.

Goh, Evelyn. 'In Response: Alliance Dynamics, Variables, and the English School for East Asia'. *International Politics*, 57/2 (April 2020), 278–84.

Golden, Sean. 'China's Perception of Risk and the Concept of Comprehensive National Power'. *Copenhagen Journal of Asian Studies*, 29/2 (2011), 79–109.

Goldin, Nicole. 'Youth Unemployment in China: New Metric, Same Mess'. *Atlantic Council*, February 2024. https://www.atlanticcouncil.org/blogs/econographics/youth-unemployment-in-china-new-metric-same-mess/.

Goldman, Merle, Timothy Cheek, and Carol Lee Hamrin (eds.). *China's Intellectuals and the State: In Search of a New Relationship*. Harvard Contemporary China Series. Cambridge, MA: Harvard University Press, 1987.

Goldstein, Avery. 'China's Grand Strategy under Xi Jinping: Reassurance, Reform, and Resistance'. *International Security*, 45/1 (2020), 164–201.

Goldstein, Avery, and Edward D. Mansfield (eds.). *The Nexus of Economics, Security, and International Relations in East Asia*. Stanford Security Studies. Stanford, CA: Stanford University Press, 2012.

Gong Qing, Xiao. 'China's Four Decades of Reforms: A View from Neo-Authoritarianism'. *Man and the Economy*, 6/1 (July 2019), 20190003.

Gore, Lance L. P. 'Elevating Xi Jinping to the "Core" of Chinese Leadership'. *East Asian Policy*, 8/4 (October 2016), 5–13.

Gore, Lance L. P. 'Leninism for the 21st Century: Xi Jinping's Ideological Party-Building'. *China: An International Journal*, 21/2 (May 2023), 8–25.

Gouldner, Alvin W. *The Dialectic of Ideology and Technology*. London: Macmillan Education UK, 1976.

The Evening News. 'The Great White Fleet'. *The Evening News*, 20 August 1908. http://nla.gov.au/nla.news-article114757661.

Greer, Tanner. 'Xi Jinping in Translation: China's Guiding Ideology'. *Palladium*, May 2019. https://www.palladiummag.com/2019/05/31/xi-jinping-in-translation-chinas-guiding-ideology/.

Gregor, A. James. *A Place in the Sun: Marxism and Fascism in China's Long Revolution*. Boulder, CO: Westview, 2000.

Greiteins, Sheena Chestnut. 'Domestic Security in China under Xi Jinping'. *China Leadership Monitor*, March 2019. https://web.archive.org/web/20200527121118/https://www.prcleader.org/greitens.

Greitens, Sheena Chestnut. 'The Saohei Campaign, Protection Umbrellas, and China's Changing Political-Legal Apparatus'. *China Leadership Monitor*, September 2020. https://www.prcleader.org/post/the-saohei-campaign-protection-umbrellas-and-china-s-changing-political-legal-apparatus.

Griffin, John M., Clark Liu, and Tao Shu. 'Is the Chinese Anti-Corruption Campaign Effective?', *SSRN Electronic Journal*, January 2016.

Griffin, John M., Clark Liu, and Tao Shu. 'Is the Chinese Anti-Corruption Campaign Authentic?', Working Paper, Tsinghua University, 2018.

Griffin, John M., Clark Liu, and Tao Shu. 'Is the Chinese Anti-Corruption Campaign Authentic? Evidence from Corporate Investigations'. 29th Annual Conference on Financial Economics & Accounting 2018, Finance Down Under 2019 Building on the Best from the Cellars of Finance, Paris December 2018 Finance Meeting EUROFIDAI—AFFI, PBCSF-NIFR Research Paper. April 2021.

Grünberg, Nis, and Katja Drinhausen. 'The Party Leads on Everything'. *MERICS*, September 2019. https://merics.org/en/report/party-leads-everything.

Grünberg, Nis, Katja Drinhausen, Mikko Huotari, John Lee, and Helena Legarda. 'The CCP's Next Century: Expanding Economic Control, Digital Governance and National Security'.

MERICS, June 2021. https://merics.org/en/report/ccps-next-century-expanding-economic-control-digital-governance-and-national-security.

Grünberg, Nis, and Vincent Brussee. 'Xi's Control Room'. *MERICS*, 2022. https://merics.org/en/comment/xis-control-room-commission-comprehensively-deepening-reform.

The Guardian. 'New Footage from China Congress Fuels Questions about Why Hu Jintao Was Hauled Out'. *YouTube*, 2022. https://www.youtube.com/watch?v=HzPoIXXbiO8.

Guilford, Gwynn. 'In China, Being Retweeted 500 Times Can Get You Three Years in Prison', *Quartz*, 9 September 2013. https://qz.com/122450/in-china-500-retweets-of-a-libelous-statement-can-get-you-three-years-in-prison.

Gunn, Dwyer. 'Leverage, Fire Sales, and the 2015 Chinese Stock Market Crash', *The NBER Digest*, November 2018.

Guo, Dingping. 'The Growth of Intra-Party Democracy and Its Implications for China's Democratic Future'. *Fudan Journal of the Humanities and Social Sciences*, 7/1 (March 2014), 1–19.

Guo, Sujian. *Chinese Politics and Government: Power, Ideology and Organization*. New York: Routledge, 2012.

Guo, Sujian. *Post-Mao China: From Totalitarianism to Authoritarianism?* Westport, CT: Praeger, 2000.

Guo, Sujian (ed.). *Political Science and Chinese Political Studies: The State of the Field*. Berlin: Springer, 2013.

Guo, Sujian, and Baogang Guo (eds.). *Challenges Facing Chinese Political Development*. Lanham, MD: Lexington Books, 2007.

Guo, Sujian, and Tianyu Jiang. 'China's "New Normal": From Social Control to Social Governance'. *Journal of Chinese Political Science*, 22/3 (September 2017), 327–40.

Guo, Yiming. 'Economist: Property Tax to Stabilize Housing Prices, Curb Speculation'. *China.org.cn*, 2017. http://www.china.org.cn/china/NPC_CPPCC_2017/2017-03/03/content_40401452.htm.

Guo, Yingjie. *Cultural Nationalism in Contemporary China: The Search for National Identity under Reform*. RoutledgeCurzon Studies on China in Transition. London: Routledge, 2004.

Haas, Benjamin. 'We Are Scared, but We Have Jesus: China and Its War on Christianity'. *The Guardian*, 28 September 2018. https://www.theguardian.com/world/2018/sep/28/we-are-scared-but-we-have-jesus-china-and-its-war-on-christianity.

Haas, Ernst B. '*What Is Nationalism and Why Should We Study It?* Edited by Benedict Anderson, Ernest Gellner, Dudley Seers, and Anthony D. Smith [review]'. *International Organization*, 40/3 (1986), 707–44.

Haass, Ryan. 'The Trajectory of Chinese Foreign Policy: From Reactive Assertiveness to Opportunistic Activism'. *Brookings*, 2017. https://www.brookings.edu/articles/the-trajectory-of-chinese-foreign-policy-from-reactive-assertiveness-to-opportunistic-activism/.

Halbwachs, Maurice, and Lewis A. Coser. *On Collective Memory*. The Heritage of Sociology. Chicago: University of Chicago Press, 1992.

Hall, Todd H. *Emotional Diplomacy: Official Emotion on the International Stage*. Ithaca, NY: Cornell University Press, 2019.

Hall, Todd H. '"I'll Tell You Something about China": Thoughts on the Specialist Study of the International Relations of the People's Republic of China'. *St Antony's International Review*, 16/1 (August 2020), 184–90.

Hall, Todd. 'The Long Game: China's Grand Strategy to Displace American Order'. *International Affairs*, 97/6 (November 2021), 2023–25.

Hall, Todd. 'An Unclear Attraction: A Critical Examination of Soft Power as an Analytical Category'. *Chinese Journal of International Politics*, 3/2 (2010), 189–211.

Harding, Harry (ed.). *China's Foreign Relations in the 1980s*. New Haven, CT: Yale University Press, 1984.

Harvey, David. *The Limits to Capital*. Oxford: Basil Blackwell, 1984.

Hawkins, Amy. 'British Private Schools in China under Threat as New "Patriotic" Law Comes In'. *The Observer*, December 2023. https://www.theguardian.com/world/2023/dec/31/british-private-schools-in-china-under-threat-as-new-patriotic-law-comes-in.

He, K., and H. Feng. 'Xi Jinping's Operational Code Beliefs and China's Foreign Policy'. *Chinese Journal of International Politics*, 6/3 (September 2013), 209–31.

He, Laura. 'Chinese Cities Are So Broke, They're Cutting Medical Benefits for Seniors'. *CNN*, March 2023. https://www.cnn.com/2023/03/31/economy/china-pension-protests-aging-society-intl-hnk/index.html.

Heath, Timothy R. *China's New Governing Party Paradigm*. London: Routledge, 2016.

Heath, Timothy R. 'China's Pursuit of Overseas Security'. Santa Monica, CA: RAND Corporation, 2018.

Heath, Timothy R. 'China's Strengthening of Communist Party Rule Is Not Just a Power Grab'. *World Politics Review*, April 2018. https://www.worldpoliticsreview.com/china-s-strengthening-of-communist-party-rule-is-not-just-a-power-grab/.

Heath, Timothy R., Derek Grossman, and Asha Clark. 'China's Quest for Global Primacy: An Analysis of Chinese International and Defense Strategies to Outcompete the United States'. Santa Monica, CA: RAND Corporation, 2021. https://www.rand.org/pubs/research_reports/RRA447-1.html.

Heilmann, Sebastian (ed.). *China's Political System*. Lanham, MD: Rowman & Littlefield, 2017.

Heilmann, Sebastian, and Elizabeth J. Perry (eds.). *Mao's Invisible Hand: The Political Foundations of Adaptive Governance in China*. Harvard Contemporary China Series. Cambridge, MA: Harvard University Press, 2011.

Heisey, D. Ray. 'China's President Hu Jinato's Rhetoric of Socialization'. *Intercultural Communication Studies*, 8/3 (2004).

Hickey, Dennis Van Vranken. 'The Taiwan Strait Crisis of 1996: Implications for US Security Policy'. *Journal of Contemporary China*, 7/19 (November 1998), 405–19.

Holbig, Heike. 'China after Reform: The Ideological, Constitutional, and Organisational Makings of a New Era'. *Journal of Current Chinese Affairs*, 47/3 (December 2018), 187–207.

Holbig, Heike. 'Remaking the CCP's Ideology: Determinants, Progress, and Limits under Hu Jintao'. *Journal of Current Chinese Affairs*, 38/3 (September 2009), 35–61.

Hong, Yinxing. 'Socialist Political Economy with Chinese Characteristics in a New Era'. *China Political Economy*, 3/2 (December 2020), 259–77.

Hong Fincher, Leta. *Betraying Big Brother: The Feminist Awakening in China*. London: Verso, 2018.

Honglin, Li. '"Right" and "Left" in Communist China: A Self-Account by a Theoretician in the Chinese Communist Party'. *Journal of Contemporary China*, 3/6 (June 1994), 1–38.

Hornby, Lucy, and Jamil Anderlini. 'Fresh Corporate Default Tests China's Resolve'. *Financial Times*, March 2014. https://www.ft.com/content/27f9f4aa-aa82-11e3-9fd6-00144feab7de.

Houghton, David Patrick. 'Reinvigorating the Study of Foreign Policy Decision Making: Toward a Constructivist Approach'. *Foreign Policy Analysis*, 3/1 (2007), 24–45.

Hsia, Hsiao-hwa, and Man Jojo. 'China Forces Journalists to Take Exam to Demonstrate Loyalty, Political Correctness'. *Radio Free Asia*, 12 January 2023. https://www.rfa.org/english/news/china/china-journalist-exam-01122023163055.html.

Hsieh, Chang-Tai, and Zheng (Michael) Song. 'Grasp the Large, Let Go of the Small: The Transformation of the State Sector in China'. *SSRN Electronic Journal*, 2015.

Hsiung, James C. 'China's Omni-Directional Diplomacy: Realignment to Cope with Monopolar U.S. Power'. *Asian Survey*, 35/6 (June 1995), 573–86.

Hsiung, James C., Hong Liu, Ying Chen, Xingwang Zhou, and Huoshen Tan (eds.). *The Xi Jinping Era: His Comprehensive Strategy toward the China Dream*. New York: CN Times Books, 2015.

Hu, Angang, and Honghua Men. 'The Rising of Modern China: Comprehensive National Power and Grand Strategy'. *Strategy and Management*, 3, no. 2 (2002). https://catalog.ihsn.org/index.php/citations/62782.

Hu, Angang, Yilong Yan, and Xiao Tang. *Xi Jinping's New Development Philosophy*. Singapore: Springer Singapore, 2018.

Hu, Dezhuang, Hongbin Li, Tang Li, Lingsheng Meng, and Binh Thai Nguyen. 'The Burden of Education Costs in China: A Struggle for All, but Heavier for Lower-Income Families'. *SSRN Electronic Journal*, 2023.

Hu, Weixing. 'Xi Jinping's "Big Power Diplomacy" and China's Central National Security Commission (CNSC)'. *Journal of Contemporary China*, 25, no. 98 (March 2016), 163–77.

Hu, Weixing. 'Xi Jinping's "Major Country Diplomacy": The Role of Leadership in Foreign Policy Transformation'. *Journal of Contemporary China*, 28/115 (January 2019), 1–14.

Huang, Jing. *Factionalism in Chinese Communist Politics.* Cambridge: Cambridge University Press, 2000.

Huang, Kristin. 'China Must Mend Ties with Japan and Avoid US Conflict: Ex-PLA Instructor'. *South China Morning Post*, January 2022. https://www.scmp.com/news/china/diplomacy/article/3162603/china-urged-push-better-ties-japan-and-seek-three-way-talks-us.

Huang, Tianlei. 'Government-Guided Funds in China: Financing Vehicles for State Industrial Policy'. *China Economic Watch*, June 2019. https://www.piie.com/blogs/china-economic-watch/2019/government-guided-funds-china-financing-vehicles-state-industrial.

Huang, Yasheng. 'China Has a Big Economic Problem, and It Isn't the Trade War'. *New York Times*, January 2020. https://www.nytimes.com/2020/01/17/opinion/china-economy.html.

Huang, Yasheng. 'China's Use of Big Data Might Actually Make It Less Big Brother-Ish'. *MIT Technology Review*, August 2018. https://www.technologyreview.com/2018/08/22/140655/chinas-use-of-big-data-might-actually-make-it-less-big-brother-ish/.

Huang, Yasheng. 'Jack Ma Is Retiring. Is China's Economy Losing Steam?'. *New York Times*, September 2018. https://www.nytimes.com/2018/09/28/opinion/jack-ma-alibaba-china-economy.html.

Huang, Yasheng. 'Just How Capitalist Is China?' *SSRN Electronic Journal*, April 2008.

Huang, Yasheng, and Heiwai Tang. 'Are Foreign Firms Favored in China? Firm-Level Evidence on the Collection of Value-Added Taxes'. *Journal of International Business Policy*, 1, no. 1–2 (June 2018), 71–91.

Huang, Yukon, Isaac Kardon, and Matt Sheehan. 'Three Takeaways from the Biden-Xi Meeting'. *Carnegie Endowment for International Peace*, November 2023. https://carnegieendowment.org/2023/11/16/three-takeaways-from-biden-xi-meeting-pub-91042.

Hückel, Bettina. 'Theory of International Relations with Chinese Characteristics: The Tian-Xia System from a Metatheoretical Perspective'. *Diskurs*, 8/2 (2013). https://web.archive.org/web/20151123060712/https://diskurs-zeitschrift.de/wp-content/uploads/2013/01/hueckel.pdf.

Hudson, Valerie M. 'Foreign Policy Analysis: Actor-Specific Theory and the Ground of International Relations'. *Foreign Policy Analysis*, 1/1 (February 2005), 1–30.

Hunt, Michael H. *The Genesis of Chinese Communist Foreign Policy.* New York: Columbia University Press, 1996.

Hunt, Michael H. *Ideology and U.S. Foreign Policy.* New Haven, CT: Yale University Press, 1987. https://www.jstor.org/stable/j.ctt5vktc7.

Hunt, Michael H., and Odd Arne Westad. 'The Chinese Communist Party and International Affairs: A Field Report on New Historical Sources and Old Research Problems'. *China Quarterly*, no. 122 (1990), 258–72.

Huotari, Mikko, Jan Weidenfeld, Thomas S. Eder, Helena Legarda, and Sabine Mokry. 'China's Emergence as a Global Security Actor'. *MERICS*, June 2017. https://merics.org/en/report/chinas-emergence-global-security-actor.

Hurrell, Andrew. *On Global Order: Power, Values, and the Constitution of International Society.* Oxford: Oxford University Press, 2007.

Hsia, Hsiao-hwa, and Man Jojo. 'China Forces Journalists to Take Exam to Demonstrate Loyalty, Political Correctness'. *Radio Free Asia*, 12 January 2023. https://www.rfitigronglish/news/china/china-journalist-exam-01122023163055.html

Ian, Chong Ja. 'The Many "One Chinas": Multiple Approaches to Taiwan and China'. *Carnegie Endowment for International Peace*, 2023. https://carnegieendowment.org/2023/02/09/many-one-chinas-multiple-approaches-to-taiwan-and-china-pub-89003.

'Ideology—Sociology, Knowledge, Beliefs'. *Britannica*, n.d. https://www.britannica.com/topic/ideology-society/The-sociology-of-knowledge.

Iida, Masafumi. 'Xi Jinping's Diplomacy and the Rise of His Political Authority'. *Journal of Contemporary East Asia Studies*, 9/2 (July 2020), 127–43.

Iida, Masafumi (ed.). *China's Shift: Global Strategy of the Rising Power.* Tokyo: National Institute for Defense Studies, 2009.

Ikenberry, G. John (ed.). *Power, Order, and Change in World Politics.* Cambridge: Cambridge University Press, 2014.

Ikenberry, G. John, and Darren Lim. 'China's Emerging Institutional Statecraft: The Asian Infrastructure Investment Bank and the Prospects for Counter-Hegemony'. *Brookings Institution Press*, 2017. https://openresearch-repository.anu.edu.au/handle/1885/217906.

Ikenberry, G. John, Jisi Wang, and Feng Zhu (eds.). *America, China, and the Struggle for World Order: Ideas, Traditions, Historical Legacies, and Global Visions*. Asia Today. New York: Palgrave Macmillan, 2015.

Inagaki, Kana. 'China Curtails "Dangerous" Fighter Jet Manoeuvres after Xi-Biden Summit'. *Financial Times*, December 2023. https://www.ft.com/content/c141df36-dc64-44ae-bcf5-fa9eb1683d1c.

International Monetary Fund. 'External Rebalancing in Turbulent Times'. *External Sector Report*, 2023. https://www.imf.org/en/Publications/ESR/Issues/2023/07/19/2023-external-sector-report.

International Monetary Fund. 'Inflation Peaking amid Low Growth'. January 2023. https://www.imf.org/en/Publications/WEO/Issues/2023/01/31/world-economic-outlook-update-january-2023.

International Monetary Fund. 'Countering the Cost-of-Living Crisis'. *World Economic Outlook*, October 2022. https://www.imf.org/en/Publications/WEO/Issues/2022/10/11/world-economic-outlook-october-2022.

International Monetary Fund. 'People's Republic of China'. *IMF Country Report*, 2024. https://www.imf.org/-/media/Files/Publications/CR/2024/English/1CHNEA2024001.ashx.

Ioannidis, John P. A., Francesco Zonta, and Michael Levitt. 'Estimates of COVID-19 Deaths in Mainland China after Abandoning Zero COVID Policy'. *European Journal of Clinical Investigation*, 53/4 (April 2023), e13956.

Ip, Hung-Yok. 'The Origins of Chinese Communism: A New Interpretation'. *Modern China*, 20/1 (1994), 34–63.

Jan, Hung-yi. 'Deng Xiaoping's Line of Four Modernizations and Opening Up and Chinese Foreign Policy: An Analysis of China's Policies in the GATT/WTO, Nonproliferation and Human Rights Regimes'. *PhD thesis, University of South Carolina*, 1998. https://babel.hathitrust.org/cgi/pt?id=uc1.31822027831718.

Jenco, Leigh. *Changing Referents: Learning across Space and Time in China and the West*. New York: Oxford University Press, 2015.

Jenco, Leigh. 'Chinese Political Thought'. In Terence Ball et al. (eds.), *Cambridge Dictionary of Political Thought*. Cambridge: Cambridge University Press, n.d.

Jenco, Leigh. '*Contemporary Chinese Political Thought: Debates and Perspectives*, Edited by Fred Dallmayr and Zhao Tingyang [review]'. *China Journal*, 70 (July 2013), 249–51.

Jenco, Leigh. 'Modern Chinese Political Thought'. In *Chinese Studies* [online]. Oxford University Press, 2014.

Jenco, Leigh K. (ed.). *Chinese Thought as Global Theory: Diversifying Knowledge Production in the Social Sciences and Humanities*. SUNY Series in Chinese Philosophy and Culture. Albany: State University of New York Press, 2016.

Jett, Jennifer, and Cheng Cheng. 'Nearly 2 Million Excess Deaths after China Ended "Zero-Covid": Study'. *NBC News*, August 2023. https://www.nbcnews.com/news/world/china-excess-deaths-zero-covid-study-rcna101746.

Ji, Fengyuan. *Linguistic Engineering: Language and Politics in Mao's China*. Honolulu: University of Hawai'i Press, 2020.

Ji, You. 'China's National Security Commission: Theory, Evolution and Operations'. *Journal of Contemporary China*, 25/98 (March 2016), 178–96.

Jiang, Chenglong. 'Mutual Trust Highlighted at Security Forum'. *China Daily*, 2023. https://www.chinadaily.com.cn/a/202310/31/WS653fd996a31090682a5eb856.html.

Jiang, Jianguo. 'Promoting and Practicing a Contemporary Chinese Perspective on Human Rights'. *Qiushi Journal*, 19 (2023).

Jiang, Jinquan. 'The Great Changes in the First Decade of the New Era'. *Qiushi Journal*, 22 (2022). http://en.qstheory.cn/2023-03/02/c_931426.htm.

Jikun, Wang and Lv Lujun. 'The Opportunity, Challenge and Strategy of MOOC Bringing to Ideological and Political Theory Course in College'. *Advances in Economics, Business and Management*, 94. 2019.

Jin, Keyu. *The New China Playbook: Beyond Socialism and Capitalism.* New York: Viking, 2023.

Jin, Xianun, Liping Xu, Yu Xin, and Ajay Adhikari. 'Political Governance in China's State-Owned Enterprises', *China's Journal of Accounting Research*, 15/2 (2002)

Jin, Xu, and Du Zheyuan. 'The Dominant Thinking Sets in Chinese Foreign Policy Research: A Criticism'. *Chinese Journal of International Politics*, 8/3 (2015), 251–79.

Jing, Jing. 'Chinese and Western Interpretations of China's "Peaceful Development" Discourse: A Rule-Oriented Constructivist Perspective'. *Journal of China and International Relations*, 2/1 (May 2014).

Johnson, Christopher K. 'Thoughts from the Chairman: Xi Jinping Unveils His Foreign Policy Vision'. *CSIS*, December 2014. https://www.csis.org/analysis/thoughts-chairman-xi-jinping-unveils-his-foreign-policy-vision.

Johnson, Christopher K., and Scott Kennedy. 'Xi Jinping Opens 19th Party Congress Proclaiming a New Era—His'. *CSIS*, October 2017. https://www.csis.org/analysis/xi-jinping-opens-19th-party-congress-proclaiming-new-era-his.

Johnston, Alastair Iain. 'China in a World of Orders: Rethinking Compliance and Challenge in Beijing's International Relations'. *International Security*, 44/2 (October 2019), 9–60.

Johnston, Alastair I. *Cultural Realism: Strategic Culture and Grand Strategy in Chinese History.* Princeton Studies in International History and Politics. Princeton, NJ: Princeton University Press, 1998.

Johnston, Alastair Iain. 'The Failures of the "Failure of Engagement" with China'. *Washington Quarterly*, 42/2 (April 2019), 99–114.

Johnston, Alastair Iain. 'How New and Assertive Is China's New Assertiveness?'. *International Security*, 37/4 (April 2013), 7–48.

Johnston, Alastair Iain. 'Is Chinese Nationalism Rising? Evidence from Beijing'. *International Security*, 41/3 (January 2017), 7–43.

Johnston, Alastair Iain. 'What (If Anything) Does East Asia Tell Us about International Relations Theory?'. *Annual Review of Political Science*, 15/1 (June 2012), 53–78.

Joseph, William A. *China Briefing, 1992.* New York: Routledge, 1993.

Joseph, William A. (ed.). *Politics in China: An Introduction.* 3rd ed. New York: Oxford University Press, 2019.

Jun, Zhang. 'Has China's Economy Peaked?'. *Project Syndicate*, January 2024. https://www.project-syndicate.org/commentary/china-economy-has-not-peaked-structural-reforms-will-spur-recovery-by-zhang-jun-2024-01.

Kaczmarski, Marcin. 'Silk Globalisation'. *Point of View*, 60 (2016).

Kalathil, Shanthi. 'Redefining Development'. *Journal of Democracy*, 29/2 (2018), 52–58.

Kallio, Jyrki. 'Xi Jinping Thought and China's Future Foreign Policy'. Briefing Paper. Helsinki: FIIA, August 2018.

Kang, David C. *East Asia before the West: Five Centuries of Trade and Tribute.* New York: Columbia University Press, 2010. https://www.jstor.org/stable/10.7312/kang15318.

Kania, Elsa B., and Lorand Laskai (eds.). 'Front Matter'. In *Myths and Realities of China's Military-Civil Fusion Strategy.* Washington, DC: Center for a New American Security, 2021. https://www.jstor.org/stable/resrep28654.1.

Kant, Immanuel. *Critique of Judgment.* Translated by Werner S. Pluhar. Indianapolis: Hackett, 1987.

Kearney, Melissa S., Justin Schardin, and Luke Pardue (eds). *Building a More Resilient US Economy.* Washington: The Aspen Institute, 2023.

Keith, Ronald C. 'China's Modernization and the Policy of "Self-Reliance"'. *China Report*, 19/2 (March 1983), 19–34.

Keith, Ronald C. 'Chinese Politics and the New Theory of "Rule of Law"'. *China Quarterly*, no. 125 (1991), 109–18.

Kennedy, Emmet. *A Philosophe in the Age of Revolution, Destutt de Tracy and the Origins of 'Ideology'.* Memoirs of the American Philosophical Society, Vol. 129. Philadelphia: American Philosophical Society, 1978.

Keohane, Robert O. *After Hegemony: Cooperation and Discord in the World Political Economy.* Princeton, NJ: Princeton University Press, 2005.

Kertzer, Joshua D., and Dustin Tingley. 'Political Psychology in International Relations: Beyond the Paradigms'. *Annual Review of Political Science*, 21/1 (May 2018), 319–39.

Khan, Sulmaan Wasif. *Haunted by Chaos: China's Grand Strategy from Mao Zedong to Xi Jinping, with a New Afterword*. Cambridge, MA: Harvard University Press, 2022.

Kim, Suk-kyoon. 'Illegal Chinese Fishing in the Yellow Sea: A Korean Officer's Perspective'. *Journal of East Asia and International Law*, 5/2 (November 2012), 455–77.

Kinzelbach, Katrin, Staffan I. Lindberg, Lars Pelke, and Janika Spannagel. 'Academic Freedom Index—2023 Update'. *FAU Erlangen-Nürnberg and V-Dem Institute*, 2023.

Klimeš, Ondřej, and Maurizio Marinelli. 'Introduction: Ideology, Propaganda, and Political Discourse in the Xi Jinping Era'. *Journal of Chinese Political Science*, 23/3 (September 2018), 313–22.

Klinkner, Kenneth Karl. 'Crafting Socialism with Chinese Characteristics: Modernization and Ideology in Post-Mao China'. *University of Illinois at Urbana-Champaign*, 1994. https://hdl.handle.net/2142/22580.

Knight, Nick. *Marxist Philosophy in China: From Qu Qiubai to Mao Zedong, 1923–1945*. Dordrecht: Springer, 2005.

Kobayashi, Shigeo, Jia Baobo, and Junya Sano. 'The "Three Reforms" in China: Progress and Outlook'. *RIM*, no. 45 (1999), 1.

Kornai, János, Yingyi Qian, and International Economic Association (eds.). *Market and Socialism: In the Light of the Experiences of China and Vietnam*. IEA Conference Vol. 146. Houndmills: Palgrave Macmillan, 2009.

Koty, Alexander Chipman. 'Why People Don't Trust China's Official Statistics'. *China Briefing*, March 2017. https://www.china-briefing.com/news/peopleIt-trust-chinas-official-statistics/.

Krasner, Stephen D. (ed.). *International Regimes*. Cornell Studies in Political Economy. Ithaca, NY: Cornell University Press, 2004.

Kristin, Shi-Kupfer, Simon Lang, and Bertram Lang. 'Ideas and Ideologies Competing for China's Political Future'. *MERICS*, October 2017. https://merics.org/en/report/ideas-and-ideologies-competing-chinas-political-future.

Kroeber, Arthur R. *China's Economy: What Everyone Needs to Know*. 2nd ed. New York: Oxford University Press, 2020.

Kroeber, Arthur R. 'Xi Jinping's Ambitious Agenda for Economic Reform in China'. *Brookings*, 2013. https://www.brookings.edu/articles/xi-jinpings-ambitious-agenda-for-economic-reform-in-china/.

Kuang, Yingqiu. 'Contemporary China Series: State-Owned Enterprises at a Cross Roads: Key Features of China's New SOE Reform'. *Asia Pacific Foundation of Canada*, 2016. https://www.asiapacific.ca/research-report/contemporary-china-series-state-owned-enterprises-cross.

Kubat, Aleksandra. 'Morality as Legitimacy under Xi Jinping: The Political Functionality of Traditional Culture for the Chinese Communist Party'. *Journal of Current Chinese Affairs*, 47/3 (December 2018), 47–86.

Kuhn, Robert Lawrence. *How China's Leaders Think: The Inside Story of China's Past, Current, and Future Leaders*. Rev. ed. Singapore: John Wiley & Sons, 2011.

Kwon, Jaebeom. 'The Turn of the Tide: Explaining China's Growing Assertiveness in the South China Sea'. *International Relations and Diplomacy*, 7/2 (February 2019).

Lague, David, Benjamin Kang Lim, and Charlie Zhu, *Fear and Retribution in Xi's Corruption Purge*. London: Reuters, 2014.

Lam, Waikei R., and Marialuz Moreno Badia. 'Fiscal Policy and the Government Balance Sheet in China'. *IMF Working Papers 2023*, no. 154 (August 2023), 1.

Lam, Willy. 'Chinks in the Armour of the Hu Jintao Administration'. *China Perspectives*, no. 3 (2007)

Lam, Willy. *Chinese Politics in the Era of Xi Jinping*. New York: Routledge, 2015.

Lam, Willy. 'Early Warning Brief: Xi Jinping Issues Tough Warnings to Enemies within the Party'. *China Brief*, 21/15 (2021). https://jamestown.org/program/early-warning-brief-xi-jinping-issues-tough-warnings-to-enemies-within-the-party/.

Lam, Willy. 'The Maoist Revival and the Conservative Turn in Chinese Politics'. *China Perspectives*, 2012/2 (June 2012), 515.

Lam, Willy. *Routledge Handbook of the Chinese Communist Party*. London: Routledge, 2018.

Lam, Willy. 'What Is Xi Jinping Thought?'. *China Brief*, 17/12 (2017). https://jamestown.org/program/what-is-xi-jinping-thought/.

Lam, Willy. *Xi Jinping: The Hidden Agendas of China's Ruler for Life*. London: Routledge, 2023.

Lam, Willy. 'Xi Jinping Boosts the Party's Control and His Own Authority'. *China Brief*, 21/1 (2021). https://jamestown.org/program/xi-jinping-boosts-the-partys-control-and-his-own-authority/.

Lampton, David M. *Following the Leader: Ruling China, from Deng Xiaoping to Xi Jinping*. Berkeley: University of California Press, 2014.

Lampton, David M. 'Xi Jinping and the National Security Commission: Policy Coordination and Political Power'. *Journal of Contemporary China*, 24/95 (September 2015), 759–77.

Lampton, David M. (ed.). *The Making of Chinese Foreign and Security Policy in the Era of Reform, 1978–2000*. Stanford, CA: Stanford University Press, 2001.

Lams, Lutgard. 'Examining Strategic Narratives in Chinese Official Discourse under Xi Jinping'. *Journal of Chinese Political Science*, 23/3 (September 2018), 387–411.

Lanteigne, Marc. 'Water Dragon? China, Power Shifts and Soft Balancing in the South Pacific'. *Political Science*, 64/1 (June 2012), 21–38.

Lapid, Yosef. 'The Third Debate: On the Prospects of International Theory in a Post-Positivist Era'. *International Studies Quarterly*, 33/3 (1989), 235–54.

Lardy, Nicholas R. 'China Has Been Overstating the Role of Private Investment in Its Economy', PIIE China Economic Watch, 5 March 2020. https://www.piie.com/blogs/china-economic-watch/china-has-been-overstating-role-private-investment-its-economy.

Lardy, Nicholas R. *The State Strikes Back: The End of Economic Reform in China?* Washington, DC: Peterson Institute for International Economics, 2019.

Lardy, Nicholas R., and Tianlei Huang. 'China's Financial Opening Accelerates'. *Policy Brief. Peterson Institute for International Economics*, 2020. https://www.piie.com/publications/policy-briefs/chinas-financial-opening-accelerates.

Larraín, Jorge. *The Concept of Ideology*. Athens: University of Georgia Press, 1979.

Larraín, Jorge. *Marxism and Ideology*. Contemporary Social Theory. London: Macmillan, 1983.

Law Society of England and Wales. 'Stakeholder Submission to the UN Human Rights Council's Universal Periodic Review—CHINA'. 2024. https://uprdoc.ohchr.org/uprweb/downloadfile.aspx?filename=12472&file=EnglishTranslation.

Lee, John. 'Understanding Authoritarian Resilience and Countering Autocracy Promotion in Asia'. *Asia Policy*, 13/4 (2018), 99–122.

Lee, Tony C. 'Can Xi Jinping Be the Next Mao Zedong? Using the Big Five Model to Study Political Leadership'. *Journal of Chinese Political Science*, 23/4 (December 2018), 473–97

Lee, Tony C. 'Pernicious Custom? Corruption, Culture, and the Efficacy of Anti-Corruption Campaigning in China'. *Crime, Law and Social Change*, 70/3 (October 2018), 349–61.

Legge, James. *The Chinese Classics*, Vol. 2. Hong Kong: Hong Kong University Press, 1960.

Legge, James. *The Chinese Classics*, Vol. 5. Hong Kong: Lane Crawford and Co., 1872.

Le Monde with Agence France-Presse. 'US Approves Direct Military Aid to Taiwan for the First Time'. *LeMonde.fr*, August 2023. https://www.lemonde.fr/en/united-states/article/2023/08/31/us-approves-direct-military-aid-to-taiwan-for-the-first-time_6117085_133.html.

Leng, Tse-Kang, and Rumi Aoyama (eds.). *Decoding the Rise of China*. Singapore: Springer, 2018.

Lensing, Dexter. 'From Mao to Xi: Chinese Political Leadership and the Craft of Consolidating Power'. *McNair Scholars Research Journal*, May 2016. https://www.semanticscholar.org/paper/From-Mao-to-Xi%3A-Chinese-Political-Leadership-and-of-Lensing/6b2b315ab44391a8e288b202b6417ccc2de1f754.

Leys, Simon. *The Chairman's New Clothes: Mao and the Cultural Revolution*. London: Allison & Busby, 1981.

Li, Cheng. *China's Leaders: The New Generation*. Lanham, MD: Rowman & Littlefield, 2001.

Li, Cheng. 'The Chinese Communist Party: Recruiting and Controlling the New Elites'. In *Critical Readings on the Communist Party of China*, 930–47. Leiden: Brill, 2017.

Li, Cheng. *Chinese Politics in the Xi Jinping Era: Reassessing Collective Leadership*. Washington, DC: Brookings Institution Press, 2016. https://www.jstor.org/stable/10.7864/j.ctt15hvr7t.

Li, Cheng. 'The End of the CCP's Resilient Authoritarianism? A Tripartite Assessment of Shifting Power in China'. *China Quarterly*, no. 211 (2012), 595–623.

Li, Cheng. 'Leadership Transition in the CPC: Promising Progress and Potential Problems'. *China: An International Journal*, 10/2 (August 2012), 23–33.

Li, Cheng. 'The New Political Elite and the New Trend in Factional Politics'. Edited by François Godement. *Les Cahiers d'Asie*, no. 3 (2003).

Li, Cheng (ed.). *China's Changing Political Landscape: Prospects for Democracy*. Washington, DC: Brookings Institution Press, 2008.

Li, Cheng, and David Bachman. 'Localism, Elitism, and Immobilism: Elite Formation and Social Change in Post-Mao China'. *World Politics*, 42/1 (1989), 64–94.

Li, Cheng. 'Jiang Zemin's Successors: The Rise of the Fourth Generation of Leaders in the PRC'. *China Quarterly* 161, (March 2000), 1–40.

Li, Cheng, and Lynn White. 'The Army in the Succession to Deng Xiaoping: Familiar Fealties and Technocratic Trends'. *Asian Survey*, 33/8 (1993), 757–86.

Li, Haiqing, and Han Shanshan. 'Further Promoting Sinicization of Marxism'. *China Daily*, November 2021. https://www.chinadaily.com.cn/a/202111/22/WS619ace61a310cdd39bc76943.html.

Li, He. *Political Thought and China's Transformation*. Houndmills: Palgrave Macmillan, 2015.

Li, Honglin. '"Right" and "Left" in Communist China: A Self-Cccount by a Theoretician in the Chinese Communist Party'. *Journal of Contemporary China*, 3/6 (June 1994), 1–38.

Li, Ling. 'China's Manufacturing Locus in 2025: With a Comparison of "Made-in-China 2025" and "Industry 4.0"'. *Technological Forecasting and Social Change*, 135 (October 2018), 66–74.

Li, Ling. 'New Political-Legal Rectification Campaign 2020–2021'. *The China Collection*, July 2020. https://thechinacollection.org/new-political-legal-rectification-campaign-2020-2021/.

Li, Ling. 'Politics of Anticorruption in China: Paradigm Change of the Party's Disciplinary Regime 2012–2017'. *Journal of Contemporary China*, 28/115 (January 2019), 47–63.

Li, Ling. 'Xi's 2021 Political-Legal Rectification Campaign'. *The China Story*, August 2020. https://www.thechinastory.org/xis-2021-political-legal-rectification-campaign/.

Li, Mingjiang. 'China's Non-Confrontational Assertiveness in the South China Sea'. *East Asia Forum*, June 2012. https://eastasiaforum.org/2012/06/14/china-s-non-confrontational-assertiveness-in-the-south-china-sea/.

Li, Mingjiang. 'Hainan Province in China's South China Sea Policy: What Role Does the Local Government Play?'. *Asian Politics & Policy*, 11/4 (October 2019), 623–42.

Li, Rex. 'The Taiwan Strait Crisis and the Future of China—Taiwan Relations'. *Security Dialogue*, 27/4 (December 1996), 449–58.

Liang, Annabell. 'China Crackdown Pushes LGBT Groups into the Shadows'. *BBC News*, June 2023. https://www.bbc.com/news/business-65806846.

Liang, Zhiping. 'Tianxia and Ideology'. *Reading the China Dream*, 2018. https://www.readingthechinadream.com/liang-zhiping-tianxia-and-ideology.html.

Lichtheim, George. *The Concept of Ideology and Other Essays*. New York: Random House, 1967.

Lieberthal, Kenneth, and David M. Lampton (eds.). *Bureaucracy, Politics, and Decision Making in Post-Mao China*. Studies on China 14. Berkeley: University of California Press, 1992.

Liew, Leong H., and Shaoguang Wang (eds.), *Nationalism, Democracy and National Integration in China*. London: Routledge, 2003.

Lipset, Seymour Martin, and Stein Rokkan. *Party Systems and Voter Alignments*. New York: Free Press, 1967.

Listerud, Ann. 'MOR Money MOR Problems', *New Perspectives in Foreign Policy*, 18 (2019).

Liu, Caiyu, Anqi Fan, and Kang Lou. 'China Adopts New Anti-Espionage Regulation, to Name Key Institutes Susceptible to Foreign Infiltration'. *Globaltimes.cn*, April 2011. https://www.globaltimes.cn/page/202104/1222185.shtml.

Liu, Feng. 'The Recalibration of Chinese Assertiveness: China's Responses to the Indo-Pacific Challenge'. *International Affairs*, 96/1 (January 2020), 9–27.

Liu, Guoli. 'Domestic Sources of China's Emerging Grand Strategy'. *Journal of Asian and African Studies*, 43/5 (October 2008), 543–61.

Liu, Harry Haitao, Yang Haiyan, Luo Chenchen, Pen Chenyu, and Li Ange. 'Amendments to PRC Counterespionage Law and Matters for Attention'. *King and Wood Mallesons*. May 2023. https://www.kwm.com/cn/en/insights/latest-thinking/amendments-to-the-prc-counterespionage-lawand-matters-enterprises-should-be-aware-of-in-operation.html.

Liu, Zongyuan Zoe. 'China's Pensions System Is Buckling under an Aging Population'. *Foreign Policy*, March 2024. https://foreignpolicy.com/2023/06/29/china-pensions-aging-demographics-economy/.

Liu, Zongyuan Zoe. 'Does Evergrande's Collapse Threaten China's Economy?'. *Council on Foreign Relations*, 2024. https://www.cfr.org/in-brief/does-evergrandes-collapse-threaten-chinas-economy.

Livingston, Scott. 'The Chinese Communist Party Targets the Private Sector'. *CSIS*, October 2020. https://www.csis.org/analysis/chinese-communist-party-targets-private-sector.

Loh, Dylan M. H. 'Diplomatic Control, Foreign Policy, and Change under Xi Jinping: A Field-Theoretic Account'. *Journal of Current Chinese Affairs*, 47/3 (December 2018), 111–45.

Long, Qiao. 'Chinese Leader Xi Jinping Inscribes Himself into Party Procedural Rules'. *Radio Free Asia*, 2020. https://www.rfa.org/english/news/china/xi-jinping-09292020120632.html.

Louthan, Tony. 'State Media's Masterful Memes on the Alaska Summit'. *ChinaTalk*, 23 March 2021. https://www.chinatalk.media/p/the-chinese-internets-take-on-the

Lu, Xi, and Peter L. Lorentzen. 'Rescuing Autocracy from Itself: China's Anti-Corruption Campaign'. *SSRN Electronic Journal*, 2016.

Lu, Zhouxiang (ed.). *Chinese National Identity in the Age of Globalisation*. Singapore: Springer, 2020.

Luce, Edward, and Chris Miller. 'The Risks of US-China Decoupling'. *Financial Times*, 2024. https://www.ft.com/content/6072fef7-f32d-491a-84b8-c1c25c1f828a.

Lührmann, Anna, and Staffan I. Lindberg. 'A Third Wave of Autocratization Is Here: What Is New about It?'. *Democratization*, 26/7 (October 2019), 1095–1113.

Lynch, Daniel. 'Chinese Thinking on the Future of International Relations: Realism as the Ti, Rationalism as the Yong?'. *China Quarterly*, 197 (March 2009), 87–107.

Ma, Guonan. 'China's High and Rising Corporate Debt'. *MERICS*, August 2019. https://merics.org/en/report/chinas-high-and-rising-corporate-debt.

Ma, Lian. 'Thinking of China's Grand Strategy: Chinese Perspectives'. *International Relations of the Asia-Pacific*, 13/1 (January 2013), 155–68.

MacFarquhar, Roderick. 'China's Astounding Religious Revival'. *ChinaFile*, June 2017. https://www.chinafile.com/library/nyrb-china-archive/chinas-astounding-religious-revival.

MacFarquhar, Roderick. *The Origins of the Cultural Revolution*. Vol. 3: *The Coming of the Cataclysm, 1961–1966*. Studies of the East Asian Institute. Oxford: Oxford University Press, 1997.

MacFarquhar, Roderick (ed). *The Politics of China: The Eras of Mao and Deng*. 2nd ed. Cambridge: Cambridge University Press, 1997.

Macpherson, Kerrie. 'Renewal: The Chinese State and the New Global History by Wang Gungwu'. *South China Morning Post*, September 2013. https://www.scmp.com/lifestyle/books/article/1304765/renewal-chinese-state-and-new-global-history-wang-gungwu.

Maddison, Angus. *Chinese Economic Performance in the Long Run*. Development Centre Studies. Paris: OECD, 1998.

Maerz, Seraphine F. 'The Many Faces of Authoritarian Persistence: A Set-Theory Perspective on the Survival Strategies of Authoritarian Regimes'. *Government and Opposition*, 55/1 (January 2020), 64–87.

Magnus, George. *Red Flags: Why Xi's China Is in Jeopardy*. New Haven, CT: Yale University Press, 2018.

Mahoney, Josef Gregory. 'Ideology, Telos, and the "Communist Vanguard" from Mao Zedong to Hu Jintao'. *Journal of Chinese Political Science*, 2/14 (2009), 135–66.

Mai, Jun. 'Xi Jinping's Anti-Corruption Drive Brings Down More Generals than 20th Century Warfare'. *South China Morning Post*, November 2017. https://www.scmp.com/news/china/policies-politics/article/2120430/xi-jinpings-anti-corruption-drive-brings-down-more.

Mannheim, Karl, and Louis Wirth. *Ideology and Utopia: An Introduction to the Sociology of Knowledge*. Mansfield Centre, CT: Martino Publishing, 2015.

Mao Zedong. *Mao Zedong on Dialectical Materialism: Writings on Philosophy, 1937*. Edited by Nick Knight. Chinese Studies on China. Armonk, NY: M. E. Sharpe, 1990.

Mao Zedong. 'Talks at the Yanan Forum on Literature and Art'. In *Selected Works of Mao Tse-Tung*, Vol. 3.

Marinelli, Maurizio. 'Jiang Zemin's Discourse on Intellectuals: The Political Use of Formalised Language and the Conundrum of Stability'. *Journal of Current Chinese Affairs*, 42/2 (June 2013), 111–40.

Mark, Chi-Kwan. *China and the World since 1945: An International History. The Making of the Contemporary World*. London: Routledge, 2012.

Mark, Jeremy. 'China's Fourteenth Five-Year Plan: The Technologies That Shall Not Be Named'. *New Atlanticist*, November 2020. https://www.atlanticcouncil.org/blogs/new-atlanticist/chinas-fourteenth-five-year-plan-the-technologies-that-shall-not-be-named/.

Mark, Jeremy, and Dexter Tiff Roberts. 'United States–China Semiconductor Standoff: A Supply Chain under Stress'. *Atlantic Council, February* 2023. https://www.atlanticcouncil.org/in-depth-research-reports/issue-brief/united-states-china-semiconductor-standoff-a-supply-chain-under-stress/.

Martin, Peter. 'Why China Is Alienating the World'. *Foreign Affairs*, October 2021. https://www.foreignaffairs.com/articles/china/2021-10-06/why-china-alienating-world.

Martinez, Felipe, and Richard Brunet-Thornton (eds.). *Analyzing the Impacts of Industry 4.0 in Modern Business Environments*. Hershey, PA: IGI Global, 2018.

Maslow, Abraham, *Motivation and Personality*. New York: Harper & Row, 1954.

Mastro, Oriana Skylar. 'The Stealth Superpower'. *Foreign Affairs*, 98/1 (December 2018). https://www.foreignaffairs.com/articles/china/china-plan-rule-asia.

Mastro, Oriana Skylar. 'Why Chinese Assertiveness Is Here to Stay'. *Washington Quarterly*, 37/4 (October 2014), 151–70.

McBride, James, and Andrew Chatzky. 'Is "Made in China 2025" a Threat to Global Trade?' *Council on Foreign Relations*, 2019. https://www.cfr.org/backgrounder/made-china-2025-threat-global-trade.

McCarney, Joe. *The Real World of Ideology*. Atlantic Highlands, NJ: Humanities Press, 1980.

McDonnell, Stephen. 'Ren Zhiqiang: Outspoken Ex-Real Estate Tycoon Gets 18 Years Jail'. *BBC News*, September 2020. https://www.bbc.com/news/world-asia-china-54245327.

McGregor, Richard. 'Chinese Coercion, Australian Resilience'. *Lowy Institute*, 2022. https://www.lowyinstitute.org/publications/chinese-coercion-australian-resilience.

McGregor, Richard. 'Echoes of Mao as Xi Jinping Ends Term Limits'. *The Interpreter*, 2018. https://www.lowyinstitute.org/the-interpreter/echoes-mao-xi-jinping-ends-term-limits.

McGregor, Richard. 'Has China's Leader Xi Jinping Now Passed His Peak?' *Lowy Institute*, 2018. https://www.lowyinstitute.org/publications/has-china-leader-xi-jinping-now-passed-his-peak.

McGregor, Richard. 'Party Man: Xi Jinping's Quest to Dominate China'. *Lowy Institute*, 2019. https://www.lowyinstitute.org/publications/party-man-xi-jinping-s-quest-dominate-china.

McGregor, Richard. *The Party: The Secret World of China's Communist Rulers*. New York: Harper, 2010.

McGregor, Richard. 'Why Xi Will Shelter behind the Great Wall of Secrecy'. Lowy Institute, 2020. https://www.lowyinstitute.org/publications/why-xi-will-shelter-behind-great-wall-secrecy.

McGregor, Richard. *Xi Jinping: The Backlash*. Lowy Institute Paper. Docklands, VIC: Penguin Random House Australia, 2019.

McGregor, Richard. 'Xi Jinping and the Grip of the Party'. *The Interpreter*, 2018. https://www.lowyinstitute.org/the-interpreter/xi-jinping-grip-party.

McGregor, Richard. 'Xi Jinping's Ideological Ambitions'. Lowy Institute, 2018. https://www.lowyinstitute.org/publications/xi-jinping-s-ideological-ambitions.

McGregor, Richard. 'Xi Jinping's Moment'. Lowy Institute, 2017. https://www.lowyinstitute.org/publications/xi-jinping-moment.

McGregor, Richard, and Jude Blanchette. 'After Xi: Future Scenarios for Leadership Succession in Post-Xi Jinping Era'. *CSIS*, April 2021. https://www.csis.org/analysis/after-xi-future-scenarios-leadership-succession-post-xi-jinping-era.

McGregor, Richard, and Neil Thomas. 'China's Great Foreign Policy Shake-Up', *Australian Financial Review*, 7 July 2022. https://www.afr.com/world/asia/changing-of-the-guard-china-s-great-foreign-policy-shake-up-20220705-p5azd9.

McMurtry, John. *Structure of Marx's World-View*. Princeton Legacy Library. Princeton, NJ: Princeton University Press April 2016.

Mearsheimer, John J. 'Can China Rise Peacefully?'. *National Interest*, October 2014. https://nationalinterest.org/commentary/can-china-rise-peacefully-10204.

Mearsheimer, John J. 'The Gathering Storm: China's Challenge to US Power in Asia'. *Chinese Journal of International Polit¾¾*, 3/4 (2010), 381–96.

Mearsheimer, John J. *The Tragedy of Great Power Politics*. The Norton Series in World Politics. New York: W. W. Norton, 2014.

Mei, Qin (Maya), and Kennedy Scott. 'Measurement Muddle: China's GDP Growth Data and Potential Proxies'. *Big Data China*, September 2023. https://bigdatachina.csis.org/measurement-muddle-chinas-gdp-growth-data-and-potential-proxies/.

Meisner, Maurice J. *Marxism, Maoism, and Utopianism: Eight Essays*. Madison: University of Wisconsin Press, 1982.

Melzer, Arthur M., Jerry Weinberger, and M. Richard Zinman (eds.), *Politics at the Turn of the Century*. Lanham: Rowman and & Littlefield, 2001.

Mertha, Andrew. '"Fragmented Authoritarianism 2.0": Political Pluralization in the Chinese Policy Process'. *China Quarterly*, 200 (December 2009), 995–1012.

Miao, Xiaojuan. 'President Xi's "Second Integration" Theory'. *Xinhua*, 2024. https://english.news.cn/20240117/5c15e5497d4444e3b1f08bcef4a15725/c.html.

Miao, Ying. 'Romanticising the Past: Core Socialist Values and the China Dream as Legitimisation Strategy'. *Journal of Current Chinese Affairs*, 49/2 (August 2020), 162–84.

Milhaupt, Curtis J., and Wentong Zheng. 'Why Mixed-Ownership Reforms Cannot Fix China's State Sector'. *Paulson Policy Memorandum*. Paulson Institute, January 2016. https://www.paulsoninstitute.org/wp-content/uploads/2017/01/PPM_SOE-Ownership_Milhaupt-and-Zheng_English_R.pdf.

Miller, Alice. 'China's New Party Leadership'. *China Leadership Monitor*, no. 23 (2008). https://www.hoover.org/sites/default/files/uploads/documents/CLM23AM.pdf.

Miller, Alice. '"Core" Leaders, "Authoritative Persons", and Reform Pushback'. *China Leadership Monitor*, no. 50 (2016). https://hoover.org/sites/default/files/research/docs/clm50am.pdf.

Miller, Alice. 'How Strong Is Xi Jinping?'. *China Leadership Monitor*, no. 43 (2014). https://www.hoover.org/sites/default/files/research/docs/clm43am.pdf.

Miller, Alice. 'Leadership Presses Party Unity in Time of Economic Stress'. *China Leadership Monitor*, no. 28 (2009)

Miller, Alice. 'More Already on the Central Committee's Leading Small Groups'. *China Leadership Monitor*, no. 44 (2013). https://www.hoover.org/research/more-already-central-committees-leading-small-groups.

Miller, Alice. 'Only Socialism Can Save China; Only Xi Jinping Can Save Socialism'. *China Leadership Monitor*, no. 56 (2018). https://www.hoover.org/sites/default/files/research/docs/clm56am.pdf.

Miller, Alice. 'Politburo Processes under Xi Jinping'. *China Leadership Monitor*, no. 47 (2015). https://www.hoover.org/sites/default/files/research/docs/clm47am.pdf.

Miller, Alice. 'The Politburo Standing Committee under Hu Jintao'. *China Leadership Monitor*, no. 35 (2011). http://media.hoover.org/sites/default/files/documents/CLM35AM.pdf.

Miller, Alice. 'Valedictory: Analyzing the Chinese Leadership in an Era of Sex, Money, and Power'. *China Leadership Monitor*, no. 57 (2018). https://www.hoover.org/sites/default/files/research/docs/clm57-am-final.pdf.

Miller, Alice. 'What Would Deng Do?'. *China Leadership Monitor*, no. 52 (2017). https://www.hoover.org/sites/default/files/research/docs/calm52am.pdf.

Miller, Alice. 'Xi Jinping and the Party's "Guiding Ideology"'. *China Leadership Monitor*, no. 54 (2017). https://www.hoover.org/sites/default/files/research/docs/clm54am.pdf.

Miller, Tom. *China's Asian Dream: Empire Building along the New Silk Road*. London: Zed Books, 2017.

Minzner, Carl. *End of an Era: How China's Authoritarian Revival Is Undermining Its Rise*. New York: Oxford University Press, 2018.

Minzner, Carl. 'Intelligentsia in the Crosshairs: Xi Jinping's Ideological Rectification of Higher Education in China'. *China Leadership Monitor*, no. 62 (2019). https://www.prcleader.org/_files/ugd/10535f_f8bcb6f9c65c4a4da55f04c196ca14a9.pdf.

Misra, Kalpana. 'Rethinking Marxism in Post-Mao China: The Erosion of Official Ideology, 1978–1984'. 1992. http://deepblue.lib.umich.edu/handle/2027.42/103275.

Mitra, Devirupa. 'Explained: Why India Joined the West to Object to a Phrase in the Final UN75 Declaration'. *The Wire*, June 2020. https://thewire.in/world/explained-un75-declaration-xi-jinping-phrase-india-object.

Mitter, Rana. 'Presentism and China's Changing Wartime Past'. *Past & Present*, 234/1 (February 2017), 263–74.

Modongal, Shameer. 'Development of Nationalism in China'. Edited by Zhouxiang Lu. *Cogent Social Sciences* 2/1 (December 2016), 1235749.

Mohanty, Manoranjan. '"Harmonious Society": Hu Jintao's Vision and the Chinese Party Congress'. *Economic and Political Weekly*, 47/50 (2012), 12–16.

Mohanty, Manoranjan. *Ideology Matters: China from Mao Zedong to Xi Jinping*. Delhi: Aakar Books, 2014.

Mohanty, Manoranjan. 'The New Ideological Banner', *China Report*, 34/1 (1998).

Mohanty, Manoranjan, Rong Ma, Richard Baum, and George Mathew (eds.). *Grass-Roots Democracy in India and China: The Right to Participate*. New Delhi: Sage Publications, 2007.

Mollet, Frederico. 'China's Grand Industrial Strategy and What It Means for Europe'. European Policy Centre, 2021. https://www.epc.eu/en/Publications/Chinas-grand-industrial-strategy-and-what-it-means-for-Europe~3ded84.

Movius, Lisa. '"Walls Close In" on China's Art World as President Xi Jinping Lays Out Cultural Agenda', *The Art Newspaper*, 15 November 2022. https://www.theartnewspaper.com/2022/11/15/walls-close-in-on-chinas-art-world-as-president-xi-jinping-lays-out-cultural-agenda

Mouvement Bonapartiste. 'Des idées napolóniennes'. Mouvement Bonapartiste, October 2019. https://mouvementbonapartiste.wordpress.com/2019/10/15/des-idees-napoleoniennes-chapitres-on-napoleonic-ideas-chapters/.

Mulvad, Andreas Møller. 'China's Ideological Spectrum: A Two-Dimensional Model of Elite Intellectuals' Visions'. *Theory and Society*, 47/5 (October 2018), 635–61.

Mulvad, Andreas. 'From Deng to the Demos? Han Dongfang's Laborism, Wen Tiejun's Peasantism, and the Future of Capitalism and Democracy in China'. *Capital & Class*, 41/1 (February 2017), 23–49.

Mulvad, Andreas Møller. 'Xiism as a Hegemonic Project in the Making: Sino-Communist Ideology and the Political Economy of China's Rise'. *Review of International Studies*, 4 /3 (July 2019), 449–70.

Mulvenon, James C. 'And Then There Were Seven: The New, Slimmed-Down Central Military Commission'. *China Leadership Monitor*, 2018. https://www.hoover.org/research/and-then-there-were-seven-new-slimmed-down-central-military-commission.

Mulvenon, James. 'The Cult of Xi and the Rise of the CMC Chairman Responsibility System'. *China Leadership Monitor*, no. 55 (January 2018). https://www.hoover.org/research/cult-xi-and-rise-cmc-chairman-responsibility-system.

Mulvenon, James. 'Oh Fang, Where Art Thou? Xi Jinping and the PLA's 90th Anniversary'. *China Leadership Monitor*, no. 54 (2017). https://www.hoover.org/sites/default/files/research/docs/clm54jm.pdf.

Mulvenon, James. 'Xi Jinping Has a Cool New Nickname: "Commander-in-Chief"'. *China Leadership Monitor*, no. 51 (2016). https://www.hoover.org/research/xi-jinping-has-cool-new-nickname-commander-chief.

Mulvenon, James C., and Andrew N. D. Yang. 'The People's Liberation Army as Organization'. *RAND Corporation*, January 2002. https://www.rand.org/pubs/conf_proceedings/CF182.html.

Mulvenon, James C., and Andrew N. D. Yang. 'Seeking Truth from Facts: A Retrospective on Chinese Military Studies in the Post-Mao Era'. *RAND Corporation*, January 2001. https://www.rand.org/pubs/conf_proceedings/CF160.html.

Munro, Kelsey. 'China Cabinet: Black Swans, Grey Rhinos, an Elephant in the Room'. Lowy Institute, n.d. https://www.lowyinstitute.org/the-interpreter/china-cabinet-black-swans-grey-rhinos-elephant-room.

Munro, Ross H. 'Awakening Dragon: The Real Danger in Asia Is Coming from China'. *Policy Review*, September 1992. https://www.semanticscholar.org/paper/Awakening-Dragon%3A-The-Real-Danger-in-Asia-Is-Coming-Munro/b400304da9be2e96110ad07a3f5544d206449d3b.

Murray, Charles. 'From "Lying Low" to "Harmonious World": Changes in Chinese Foreign Policy from the 1970s to the 2000s'. Dissertations, Theses, and Masters Projects, January 2014. https://dx.doi.org/doi:10.21220/s2-rmk7-k278.

Myer, Marshall W. 'China's Mixed-Ownership Enterprise Model: Can the State Let Go?'. *Knowledge at Wharton*, 2014. https://knowledge.wharton.upenn.edu/article/will-chinas-mixed-ownership-enterprise-model-work/.

Myers, Steven Lee. 'A Crackdown on Islam Is Spreading across China'. *New York Times*, 21 September 2019. https://www.nytimes.com/2019/09/21/world/asia/china-islam-crackdown.html.

Nan, Yu and Nan Li. 'Keep the Graph Growing'. *Beijing Review*, no.52 (2016).

Nantulya, Paul. 'Strategic Application of the Tao 道 of Soft Power: The Key to Understanding China's Expanding Influence in Africa'. *African Review: A Journal of African Politics, Development and International Affairs*, 47/2 (2020), 481–529.

Narayanan, Raviprasad. 'Stability with Chinese Characteristics: Hu Jintao's Taiwan Policy'. *China Report*, 49/4 (November 2013), 413–24.

Narizny, Kevin. *The Political Economy of Grand Strategy*. Cornell Studies in Security Affairs. Ithaca, NY: Cornell University Press, 2007.

Nathan, Andrew J. 'China: Back to the Future'. *New York Review of Books*, 65/8 (May 2018). https://www.nybooks.com/articles/2018/05/10/china-back-to-the-future/.

Nathan, Andrew J. 'China's Changing of the Guard: Authoritarian Resilience'. *Journal of Democracy*, 14/1 (2003), 6–17.

Nathan, Andrew J. 'The New Ideology', *New Republic*, 6 December 2012.

Nathan, Andrew J. 'Zhao Ziyang's Vision of Chinese Democracy', *China Perspectives*, no. 3 (2008)

Nathan, Andrew J., and Bruce Gilley. *China's New Rulers: The Secret Files*. New York: New York Review of Books, 2002.

Nathan, Andrew J., and Tianjian Shi. 'Cultural Requisites for Democracy in China: Findings from a Survey'. *Daedalus*, 122/2 (1993), 95–123.

Nathan, Andrew J., Tianjian Shi, and Helena V. S. Ho. *China's Transition*. A Study of the East Asian Institute. New York: Columbia University Press, 1997.

Nathan, Andrew J., and Boshu Zhang. '"A Shared Future for Mankind": Rhetoric and Reality in Chinese Foreign Policy under Xi Jinping'. *Journal of Contemporary China*, 31/133 (January 2022), 57–71.

Nau, Henry R., and Deepa Mary Ollapally. *Worldviews of Aspiring Powers: Domestic Foreign Policy Debates in China, India, Iran, Japan and Russia*. New York: Oxford University Press, 2012.

Naughton, Barry. 'China's Economic Think Tanks: Their Changing Role in the 1990s'. *China Quarterly*, no. 171 (2002), 625–35.

Naughton, Barry. 'China's Economy: Complacency, Crisis & the Challenge of Reform'. *Daedalus*, 143/2 (April 2014), 14–25.

Naughton, Barry. 'China's Macroeconomy in Transition'. *China Quarterly*, 144 (December 1995), 1083–1104.

Naughton, Barry. 'China's Plans for the Future'. Berkeley Law, April 2021. https://www.law.berkeley.edu/wp-content/uploads/2021/04/Naughton.pdf.

Naughton, Barry. 'Chinese Industrial Policy and the Digital Silk Road: The Case of Alibaba in Malaysia'. *Asia Policy*, 15/1 (January 2020), 23–39.

Naughton, Barry. 'Implications of the State Monopoly over Industry and Its Relaxation'. *Modern China*, 18/1 (1992), 14–41.

Naughton, Barry. 'In China's Economy, the State's Hand Grows Heavier'. *Current History*, 108/719 (September 2009), 277–83.

Naughton, Barry. 'Inside and Outside: The Modernized Hierarchy That Runs China'. *Journal of Comparative Economics*, 44/2 (May 2016), 404–15.

Naughton, Barry. 'Is China Socialist?'. *Journal of Economic Perspectives* 31/1 (February 2017), 3–24.

Naughton, Barry. *The Chinese Economy: Transitions and Growth*. Cambridge, MA: MIT Press, 2007.

Naughton, Barry. 'The General Secretary's Extended Reach'. *China Leadership Monitor*, no. 54 (2017). https://www.hoover.org/sites/default/files/research/docs/clm54bn.pdf.

Naughton, Barry. 'The Impact of the Tiananmen Crisis on China's Economic Transition'. *China Perspectives*, 2009/2 (June 2009), 63–78.

Naughton, Barry. 'The Return of Planning in China: Comment on Heilmann-Melton and Hu Angang'. *Modern China*, 39/6 (2013), 640–52.

Naughton, Barry. *The Rise of China's Industrial Policy, 1978 to 2020*. México: Universidad Nacional Autónoma de México, Facultad de Economía, 2021.

Naughton, Barry. 'The Third Front: Defence Industrialization in the Chinese Interior'. *China Quarterly*, no. 115 (1988), 351–86.

Naughton, Barry. 'Two Trains Running'. *China Leadership Monitor*, no. 50 (2016). https://www.hoover.org/sites/default/files/research/docs/clm50bn.pdf.

Naughton, Barry, and Kellee S. Tsai (eds.). *State Capitalism, Institutional Adaptation, and the Chinese Miracle*. Comparative Perspectives in Business History. New York: Cambridge University Press, 2015.

Naughton, Barry, and Dali L. Yang (eds.). *Holding China Together: Diversity and National Integration in the Post-Deng Era*. New York: Cambridge University Press, 2004.

Neil, Thomas. 'Xi Jinping's Succession Dilemma'. Asia Society Policy Institute, 2024. https://asiasociety.org/policy-institute/xi-jinpings-succession-dilemma.

Ng, Jasmine. 'China Slowdown Means It May Never Overtake US Economy, Forecast Shows'. *Bloomberg.com*, September 2023. https://www.bloomberg.com/news/articles/2023-09-05/china-slowdown-means-it-may-never-overtake-us-economy-be-says.

Ni, Vincent, and Helen Davidson. 'China's Cultural Crackdown: Few Areas Untouched as Xi Reshapes Society'. *The Guardian*, 10 September 2021. https://www.theguardian.com/world/2021/sep/10/chinas-cultural-crackdown-few-areas-untouched-as-xi-reshapes-society.

Niquet, Valérie. 'China and Central Asia'. *China Perspectives*, 2006/5 (October 2006).

Noakes, Stephen. 'The Role of Political Science in China: Intellectuals and Authoritarian Resilience'. *Political Science Quarterly*, 129/2 (2014), 239–60.

O'Brien, Barbara. 'How Buddhism Came to China: A History of the First Thousand Years'. Learn Religions, 2019. https://www.learnreligions.com/buddhism-in-china-the-first-thousand-years-450147.

O'Brien, Conor Cruise. 'The Wrath of Ages'. *Foreign Affairs*, 72/5 (December 1993). https://www.foreignaffairs.com/reviews/review-essay/1993-12-01/wrath-ages.

Okudera, Atsushi. 'Guangdong Chief Li Chosen to Head Anti-Corruption Drive in China'. *Asahi Shimbun*, 2022. https://www.asahi.com/ajw/articles/14750084.

Ong, Edwin. 'Politics Takes Precedence over Economy in Xi's Chinese-Style Modernisation'. ThinkChina, August 2023. https://www.thinkchina.sg.

Ooi, Kee Beng. 'Wang Gungwu 王赓武 on Living Chinese History'. *The China Story*, 2015. https://archive.thechinastory.org/2015/11/wang-gungwu-%E7%8E%8B%E8%B5%93%E6%AD%A6-on-living-chinese-history/.

O'Rourke, Ronald. 'U.S.-China Strategic Competition in South and East China Seas: Background and Issues for Congress'. *Congressional Research Service*, 2024. https://sgp.fas.org/crs/row/R42784.pdf.

Orr, Bernard. 'Nearly 2 Million Excess Deaths Followed China's Sudden End of COVID Curbs, Study Says'. *Reuters*, August 2023. https://www.reuters.com/world/china/nearly-2-million-excess-deaths-followed-chinas-sudden-end-covid-curbs-study-2023-08-25/.

Ortmann, Stephan, and Mark R. Thompson. 'Introduction: The "Singapore Model" and China's Neo-Authoritarian Dream'. *China Quarterly*, 236 (December 2018), 930–45.

Ou, Xinyi. 'The Successful Integration of Buddhism with Chinese Culture: A Summary'. *Grand Valley Journal of History*, 1/2 (April 2012). https://scholarworks.gvsu.edu/gvjh/vol1/iss2/3.

Overholt, William. 'The Politics of China's Anti-Corruption Campaign'. *East Asia Forum Quarterly*, 7/2 (2015).

Ownby, David. *Falun Gong and the Future of China*. Oxford: Oxford University Press, 2008.

Owyang, Michael T., and Hannah Shell. 'China's Official Economic Data: Is It Accurate?'. Regional Economist, 2017. https://www.stlouisfed.org/publications/regional-economist/second-quarter-2017/chinas-economic-data-an-accurate-reflection-or-just-smoke-and-mirrors.

Pan, Jennifer, and Yiqing Xu. 'China's Ideological Spectrum'. *Journal of Politics*, 80/1 (January 2018), 254–73.

Pan, Xiaofei, and Gary Gang Tian. 'Political Connections and Corporate Investments: Evidence from the Recent Anti-Corruption Campaign in China'. *Journal of Banking & Finance*, 119 (October 2020), 105108.

Pang, Zhongying. *From Tao Guang Yang Hui to Xin Xing: China's Complex Foreign Policy Transformation and Southeast Asia*. Trends in Southeast Asia. Singapore: ISEAS–Yusof Ishak Institute, 2020.

Pantsov, Alexander, and Steven I. Levine. *Mao: The Real Story*. New York: Simon & Schuster, 2013.

Paternina-Caicedo, Angel, et al. 'Effectiveness of CoronaVac and BNT162b2 COVID-19 Mass Vaccination in Colombia'. *The Lancet Regional Health–Americas*, 12/100296 (2022).

Paus, Eva, Penelope B. Prime, and Jon W. Western (eds.). *Global Giant: Is China Changing the Rules of the Game?* New York: Palgrave Macmillan, 2009.

Pei, Minxin. 'Beijing's New Economic Strategy from the Resolution of the CCP Central committees 5th Plenum'. *China Leadership Monitor*, December 2020. https://www.prcleader.org/post/beijing-s-new-economic-strategy-from-the-resolution-of-the-ccp-central-committee-s-5th-plenum.

Pei, Minxin. 'Bureaucratic Strategies of Coping with Strongman Rule: How Local Officials Survive in President Xi Jinping's New Order'. *China Leadership Monitor*, no. 61 (2019). https://www.prcleader.org/_files/ugd/10535f_f5d4602bd23445c1975b0822d72007a1.pdf.

Pei, Minxin. 'China: From Tiananmen to Neo-Stalinism'. *Journal of Democracy*, 31/1 (2020), 148–57.

Pei, Minxin. 'China in 2017'. *Asian Survey*, 58/1 (February 2018), 21–32.

Pei, Minxin. 'China's Coming Upheaval'. *Foreign Affairs*, 99/3 (April 2020). https://www.foreignaffairs.com/articles/united-states/2020-04-03/chinas-coming-upheaval.

Pei, Minxin. *China's Crony Capitalism: The Dynamics of Regime Decay*. Cambridge, MA: Harvard University Press, 2016.

Pei, Minxin. 'China's Fateful Year by Minxin Pei'. Project Syndicate, January 2021. https://www.project-syndicate.org/magazine/covid19-hong-kong-damage-china-relations-with-the-west-by-minxin-pei-2021-01.

Pei, Minxin. 'China's Governance Crisis'. *Foreign Affairs*, 81/5 (2002), 96.

Pei, Minxin. *China's Trapped Transition: The Limits of Developmental Autocracy*. Cambridge, MA: Harvard University Press, 2008.

Pei, Minxin. 'How Has the Coronavirus Crisis Affected Xi's Power: A Preliminary Assessment'. *China Leadership Monitor*, no. 64 (June 2020). https://www.prcleader.org/post/how-has-the-coronavirus-crisis-affected-xi-s-power-a-preliminary-assessment.

Pei, Minxin. 'How Not to Fight Corruption: Lessons from China'. *Daedalus*, 147/3 (2018), 216–30.

Pei, Minxin. 'Ideological Indoctrination Under Xi Jinping'. *China Leadership Monitor*, no. 62 (2019). https://www.prcleader.org/_files/ugd/10535f_973ed89773a94a03abad4e70fd5a1612.pdf.

Pei, Minxin. 'Is China Democratizing?'. *Foreign Affairs*, 77/1 (January 1998). https://www.foreignaffairs.com/articles/asia/1998-01-01/china-democratizing.

Pei, Minxin. 'A Play for Global Leadership'. *Journal of Democracy*, 29/2 (2018), 37–51.

Pei, Minxin. 'Playing Hard to Get: Why Has China Been Reluctant To Help Europe?'. *Georgetown Journal of International Affairs*, 13/2 (2012), 151–54.

Pei, Minxin. 'Rewriting the Rules of the Chinese Party-State: Xi's Progress in Reinvigorating the CCP'. *China Leadership Monitor*, no. 60 (2019). https://www.prcleader.org/_files/ugd/10535f_c22e9e10b681444c93167478999e548c.pdf.

Pei, Minxin. 'Small Change'. *South China Morning Post*, May 2011. https://www.scmp.com/article/966854/small-change.

Pei, Minxin. 'Squaring the Circle: Rule According to Law in a One-Party State'. *New Perspectives Quarterly*, 32/1 (January 2015), 31–33.

Pei, Minxin. 'A Tale of Three Speeches: How Xi Jinping's 40th Anniversary Speech Marks a Departure'. *China Leadership Monitor*, no. 59 (2019). https://www.prcleader.org/_files/ugd/10535f_cfbad8bda8c9461f89a9ceda78a9a12c.pdf.

Pei, Minxin. 'Threading the Needle: Balancing Security and Development in the 14th Five-Year Plan'. *China Leadership Monitor*, no. 68 (June 2021). https://www.prcleader.org/post/threading-the-needle-balancing-security-and-development-in-the-14th-five-year-plan.

Pei, Minxin. 'Xi Jinping's Dilemma: Back Down or Double Down?'. *China Leadership Monitor*, no. 58 (2018). https://www.prcleader.org/_files/ugd/10535f_98fb257ede9c4cbab367084232063cd4.pdf.

Peng, Lu. 'Chinese IR Sino-Centrism Tradition and Its Influence on the Chinese School Movement'. *Pacific Review*, 32/2 (March 2019), 150–67.

Peng, Xiujan. 'China's Population Shrinks Again and Is Set to More than Halve'. Victoria University, 2024. https://www.vu.edu.au/about-vu/news-events/news/chinas-population-shrinks-again-and-is-set-to-more-than-halve.

People's Daily. 'The Party Exercises Overall Leadership', *Chinese Medical Journal*, no. 8 (1974). https://mednexus.org/doi/pdf/10.5555/cmj.0366-6999.87.08.p129.01.

Perez Garcia, Manuel, and Lucio De Sousa (eds.). *Global History and New Polycentric Approaches: Europe, Asia and the Americas in a World Network System*. Singapore: Springer Singapore, 2018.

Perry, Elizabeth J. *Anyuan: Mining China's Revolutionary Tradition*. Asia: Local Studies/Global Themes 24. Berkeley: University of California Press, 2012.

Perry, Elizabeth J. 'Debating Maoism in Contemporary China: Reflections on Benjamin I. Schwartz, Chinese Communism and the Rise of Mao'. *Asia-Pacific Journal*, 19/1 (2021), 1–11.

Perry, Elizabeth J . 'The Illiberal Challenge of Authoritarian China'. *Taiwan Journal of Democracy*, 8/2 (2012), 3–15.

Perry, Elizabeth J. 'Making Communism Work: Sinicizing a Soviet Governance Practice'. *Comparative Studies in Society and History*, 61/3 (July 2019), 535–62.

Perry, Elizabeth J . 'The Populist Dream of Chinese Democracy'. *Journal of Asian Studies*, 74/4 (November 2015), 903–15.

Perry, Elizabeth J. 'The Promise of PRC History'. *Journal of Modern Chinese History*, 10/1 (January 2016), 113–17.

Perry, Elizabeth J., and Richard Haass. 'Centennial Speaker Series Session 7: Will the 21st Century Be China's?'. *Council on Foreign Relations*, 2021. https://www.cfr.org/event/centennial-speaker-series-session-7-will-21st-century-be-chinas.

Peters, Michael A. 'The Chinese Dream: Xi Jinping Thought on Socialism with Chinese Characteristics for a New Era'. *Educational Philosophy and Theory*, 49/14 (December 2017), 1299–1304.

Peterson, E. Wesley F. 'The Unintended Consequences of China's One-Child Policy'. *Cornhusker Economics*, 2023. https://agecon.unl.edu/unintended-consequences-china%E2%80%99s-one-child-policy.

Petri, Peter A. 'Peak China: Why Do China's Growth Projections Differ So Much?'. *Brookings*, 2023. https://www.brookings.edu/articles/peak-china-why-do-chinas-growth-projections-differ-so-much/.

Pettis, Michael. *Avoiding the Fall: China's Economic Restructuring*. Washington, DC: Carnegie Endowment for International Peace, 2013. https://muse.jhu.edu/pub/451/monograph/book/30611.

Pettis, Michael. 'Can China's Long-Term Growth Rate Exceed 2–3 Percent?'. *Carnegie Endowment for International Peace [blog]*, 2023. https://carnegieendowment.org/chinafinancialmarkets/89466.

Pettis, Michael. 'China's Economy Is Headed for a Slowdown'. *Wall Street Journal*, August 2011. https://www.wsj.com/articles/SB10001424053111904140604576498353661884930.

Pettis, Michael. 'China's Great Demand Challenge'. *Far Eastern Economic Review*, 172/1 (2009).

Pettis, Michael. 'China's Growth Miracle Has Run Out of Steam'. *Financial Times*, November 2017. https://www.ft.com/content/cb6bbf84-cb8e-11e7-ab18-7a9fb7d6163e.

Pettis, Michael. 'China's Many Economies'. *Stanford Social Innovation Review*, 15 (2016), 71.

Pettis, Michael. 'Chinese Inflation: It's Money, Not Pork'. *Far Eastern Economic Review*, 171/3 (2008). https://www.botlc.or.th/item/article/02000002433.

Pettis, Michael. 'The Coming China Meltdown'. *Newsweek*, 153/10 (2009).

Pettis, Michael. 'Distortions in the Balance Sheet Matter to China's Growth'. *Asia Policy*, 20/1 (2015), 148–52.

Pettis, Michael. *The Great Rebalancing: Trade, Conflict, and the Perilous Road Ahead for the World Economy*. Princeton, NJ.: Princeton University Press, 2014.

Pettis, Michael. 'Slowdown in China Isn't Bad News'. Carnegie Endowment for International Peace, 2013. https://carnegieendowment.org/2013/08/13/slowdown-in-china-isn-t-bad-news-pub-52663.

Pettis, Michael. 'What China Can Learn from 1929'. *Newsweek*, 152/25 (2008).

Pettis, Michael. 'What Does Evergrande Meltdown Mean for China?'. Carnegie Endowment for International Peace, 2021. https://carnegieendowment.org/chinafinancialmarkets/85391.

Pettis, Michael. 'What Will It Take for China's GDP to Grow at 4–5 Percent over the Next Decade?'. *Carnegie Endowment for International Peace*, December 2023. https://carnegieendowment.org/chinafinancialmarkets/91161.

Pettis, Michael. 'Why Beijing Should Dump Its Debt'. *Carnegie Endowment for International Peace*, 2018. https://carnegieendowment.org/2018/01/16/why-beijing-should-dump-its-debt-pub-75290.

Pettis, Michael. 'Will China's Economy Crash?'. *CNN*, July 2013. https://www.cnn.com/2013/07/29/opinion/pettis-china-economy/index.html.

Pettis, Michael. 'Winners and Losers in China's Next Decade'. McKinsey, 2013. https://www.mckinsey.com/featured-insights/asia-pacific/winners-and-losers-in-chinas-next-decade#/.

Phillips, Tom. '"A Huge Deal" for China as the Era of Xi Jinping Thought Begins'. *The Guardian*, October 2017. https://www.theguardian.com/world/2017/oct/19/huge-deal-china-era-of-xi-jinping-thought-politics.

Picavet, François Joseph. *Les Idéologues*. European Sociology. New York: Arno Press, 1975.

Piccone, Ted. 'China's Long Game on Human Rights at the United Nations'. Brookings, September 2018. https://www.brookings.edu/articles/chinas-long-game-on-human-rights-at-the-united-nations/.

Pieke, Frank N. *The Good Communist: Elite Training and State Building in Today's China*. Cambridge: Cambridge University Press, 2009.

Pieke, Frank N., and Bert Hofman (eds.). *CPC Futures: The New Era of Socialism with Chinese Characteristics*. Singapore: NUS Press, 2022.

Pillsbury, Michael. *China Debates the Future Security Environment*. Washington, DC: National Defense University Press, 2000.

Pillsbury, Michael. *The Hundred-Year Marathon: China's Secret Strategy to Replace America as the Global Superpower*. New York: Henry Holt, 2015.

Ping, Lin, and Qiao Long. 'China's Ruling Party Endorses Xi as "Core Leader" after Meeting'. Radio Free Asia, 2016. https://www.rfa.org/english/news/china/xi-core-10272016104629.html.

Plamenatz, John Petrov. *Ideology*. Key Concepts in Political Science. London: Pall Mall, 1970.

Poh, Angela, and Mingjiang Li. 'A China in Transition: The Rhetoric and Substance of Chinese Foreign Policy under Xi Jinping'. *Asian Security*, 13/2 (May 2017), 84–97.

Poole, Richard E. 'China's "Harmonious World" in the Era of the Rising East'. *Inquiries Journal*, 6/10 (2014). http://www.inquiriesjournal.com/articles/932/chinas-harmonious-world-in-the-era-of-the-rising-east.

Porch, Douglas. 'The Taiwan Strait Crisis of 1996: Strategic Implications for the United States Navy'. *Naval War College Review*, 52/3 (1999), 15–48.

Pu, Xiaoyu. *Rebranding China: Contested Status Signaling in the Changing Global Order*. Studies in Asian Security. Stanford, CA: Stanford University Press, 2019.

Pu, Xiaoyu, and Chengli Wang. 'Rethinking China's Rise: Chinese Scholars Debate Strategic Overstretch'. *International Affairs*, 94/5 (September 2018), 1019–35.

Pye, Lucian W. 'Jiang Zemin's Style of Rule: Go for Stability, Monopolize Power and Settle for Limited Effectiveness'. *China Journal*, no. 45 (2001), 45–51.

Qi, Rui, Chenchen Shi, and Mark Wang. 'The Over-Cascading System of Cadre Evaluation and China's Authoritarian Resilience'. *China Information*, 35/1 (March 2021), 67–88.

Qian, Jing. 'Decoding Xi's "Tone-Changing" U.S.-China Speech in San Francisco'. *Asia Society Policy Institute*, November 2023. https://asiasociety.org/policy-institute/decoding-xis-tone-changing-us-china-speech-san-francisco.

Qian, Jing. 'What to Watch during the Two Sessions'. *Asia Society Policy Institute*, March 2023. https://asiasociety.org/policy-institute/what-watch-during-two-sessions.

Qian, Licheng, Bin Xu, and Dingding Chen. 'Does History Education Promote Nationalism in China? A "Limited Effect" Explanation'. *Journal of Contemporary China*, 26/104 (March 2017), 199–212.

Qimao, Chen. 'The Taiwan Strait Crisis: Its Crux and Solutions'. *Asian Survey*, 36/11 (November 1996), 1055–66.

Qin, Yaqing. 'Development of International Relations Theory in China: Progress through Debates'. *International Relations of the Asia-Pacific*, 11/2 (May 2011), 231–57.

Qingguo, Jia. 'Disrespect and Distrust: The External Origins of Contemporary Chinese Nationalism'. *Journal of Contemporary China*, 14/42 (February 2005), 11–21.

Qiu, Ping. 'Profound Significance of the "Two Integrations"'. *Qiushi*, 2023. http://en.qstheory.cn/2023-11/202023-11.

Qiushi Commentary. 'A New Cultural Mission: Developing a Modern Chinese Civilization'. *Qiushi*, 2023. http://en.qstheory.cn/2023-09/13/c_918752.htm.

Qiushi Commentary. 'Consolidate the Guiding Position of Marxism in the Ideological Area'. *China Copyright and Media*, October 2013. https://chinacopyrightandmedia.wordpress.com/2013/10/04/seeking-truth-consolidate-the-guiding-position-of-marxism-in-the-ideological-area/.

Quek, Kai, and Alastair Iain Johnston. 'Can China Back Down? Crisis De-Escalation in the Shadow of Popular Opposition'. *International Security*, 42/3 (January 2018), 7–36.

Ramo, Joshua Cooper. *The Beijing Consensus*. London: The Foreign Policy Centre, 2004.

Ramzy, Austin. 'China's Zero-Covid Approach Explained'. *New York Times*, September 2022. https://www.nytimes.com/2022/09/08/world/asia/china-zero-covid-explainer.html.

Ray, Dennis. '"Red and Expert" and China's Cultural Revolution'. *Pacific Affairs*, 43/1 (1970), 22–33.

Redenius, Charles M. 'Justifying Economic Reform in China: The Theory of the Primary Stage of Socialism'. *Journal of Social, Political, and Economic Studies*, 13/3 (1988).

ReformPedia. 'State Owned Enterprise'. Macro Polo. Undated. https://macropolo.org/policy_library/soe/

Ren, Zhongpin. 'Keeping Original Aspiration, CPC Creates Glorious Achievements'. *People's Daily*, September 2019. http://en.people.cn/n3/2019/0930/c90000-9619725.html.

Reynolds, Matthew, and Matthew P. Goodman. 'China's Economic Coercion: Lessons from Lithuania'. *CSIS*, May 2022. https://www.csis.org/analysis/chinas-economic-coercion-lessons-lithuania.

Ringen, Stein. *The Perfect Dictatorship: China in the 21st Century*. Hong Kong: Hong Kong University Press, 2016. https://www.jstor.org/stable/j.ctt1d4tz8w.

Roach, Stephen S. *Frayed Relations*. Council on Foreign Relations. 13 February 2023. https://www.cfr.org/event/cv-starr-co-annual-lecture-china-frayed-relations-united-states-and-china

Roberts, Dexter Tiff. 'Xi Jinping's Politics in Command Economy'. Atlantic Council, July 2021. https://www.atlanticcouncil.org/in-depth-research-reports/issue-brief/issue-brief-xi-jinpings-politics-in-command-economy/.

Robinson, Thomas W., and David L. Shambaugh (eds.). *Chinese Foreign Policy: Theory and Practice*. Studies on Contemporary China. Oxford: Oxford University Press, 1994.

Rolland, Nadège. *China's Eurasian Century? Political and Strategic Implications of the Belt and Road Initiative*. Seattle, WA: National Bureau of Asian Research, 2017.

Rorty, Richard. *Consequences of Pragmatism: Essays, 1972–1980*. Minneapolis: University of Minnesota Press, 1982.

Rosen, Daniel H. 'China and the Subprime Scorpion'. *Far Eastern Economic Review*, 170/7 (2007), 18–22.

Rosen, Daniel H. 'China's Economic Reckoning'. *Foreign Affairs*, 100/4 (June 2021). https://www.foreignaffairs.com/articles/china/2021-06-22/chinas-economic-reckoning.

Rosen, Daniel H., and Thilo Hanemann. 'The Changing US-China Investment Relationship'. *China Economic Journal*, 7/1 (January 2014), 84–102.

Rosen, Daniel H., and Thilo Hanemann. 'The Rise in Chinese Overseas Investment and What It Means for American Businesses'. *China Business Review*, July 2012. https://www.chinabusinessreview.com/the-rise-in-chinese-overseas-investment-and-what-it-means-for-american-businesses/.

Rosen, Daniel, and Kevin Rudd. 'China's Economic Crossroads'. *Project Syndicate*, June 2020. https://www.project-syndicate.org/commentary/china-2020-economic-reform-agenda-real-or-just-rhetoric-by-kevin-rudd-and-daniel-rosen-2020-06.

Rosen, Daniel H., Logan Wright, Charlie Vest, and Rogan Quinn. 'Through the Looking Glass: China's 2023 GDP and the Year Ahead'. Rhodium Group, 2023. https://rhg.com/research/through-the-looking-glass-chinas-2023-gdp-and-the-year-ahead/.

Ross, John. '"Anti-Western" Recruitment "Could Turn Chinese off Foreign Study"'. *Times Higher Education*, November 2023. https://www.timeshighereducation.com/news/anti-western-recruitment-could-turn-chinese-foreign-study.

Ross, John. 'Why China Is a Socialist Country—China's Theory Is in Line with Marx (but Not the Post-1929 Soviet Union)'. *Learning from China*, August 2017. https://learningfromchina.net/why-china-is-a-socialist-country-chinas-theory-is-in-line-with-marx-but-not-stalin/.

Ross, Robert S. 'The 1996 Taiwan Strait Crisis: Lessons for the United States, China, and Taiwan'. *Security Dialogue*, 27/4 (1996), 463–70.

Ross, Robert S., and Jo Inge Bekkevold (eds.). *China in the Era of Xi Jinping: Domestic and Foreign Policy Challenges*. Washington, DC: Georgetown University Press, 2016.

Rossabi, Morris (ed.). *China among Equals: The Middle Kingdom and Its Neighbors, 10th–14th Centuries*. Berkeley: University of California Press, 1983.

Roy, Denny. 'China's Reaction to American Predominance'. *Global Politics and Strategy*, 14/3 (2003), 57–78.

Roy, Denny. '"Xi Jinping Thought on Diplomacy" Fails to Impress—or Reassure'. *The Diplomat*, April 2020. https://thediplomat.com/2020/04/xi-jinping-thought-on-diplomacy-fails-to-impress-or-reassure/.

Rozman, Gilbert. *Chinese Strategic Thought toward Asia*. Basingstoke: Palgrave Macmillan, 2010.

Rudd, Kevin. 'America and China Are Rivals with a Common Cause'. *Financial Times*, 2015. https://www.ft.com/content/3055b448-e426-11e4-9039-00144feab7de.

Rudd, Kevin. 'ASEAN Must Respond Boldly to Growing US-China Competition'. *Nikkei Asia*, 2018. https://asia.nikkei.com/Opinion/ASEAN-must-respond-boldly-to-growing-US-China-competition.

Rudd, Kevin. *The Avoidable War: The Dangers of a Catastrophic Conflict between the US and Xi Jinping's China*. New York: PublicAffairs, 2022.

Rudd, Kevin. 'Beijing's Early Reactions to the Biden Administration: Strategic Continuity and Tactical Change'. *Asia Society Policy Institute*, March 2021. https://asiasociety.org/policy-institute/beijings-early-reactions-biden-administration-strategic-continuity-and-tactical-change.

Rudd, Kevin. 'Beware the Guns of August—in Asia'. *Foreign Affairs*, August 2020. https://www.foreignaffairs.com/articles/united-states/2020-08-03/beware-guns-august-asia.

Rudd, Kevin. 'The Biden Administration's Approach to China'. *Asia Society*, May 2022. https://asiasociety.org/policy-institute/opening-remarks-biden-administrations-approach-china.

Rudd, Kevin. 'Biden Should Prioritize Reversing Trump's Blanket Ban on Chinese and Other Foreign Students'. *South China Morning Post*, July 2021. https://www.scmp.com/comment/opinion/article/3119247/biden-should-prioritise-reversing-trumps-blanket-ban-chinese-and.

Rudd, Kevin. 'Can China and the United States Avoid War?'. *Proceedings*, 144/12 (December 2018). https://www.usni.org/magazines/proceedings/2018/december/can-china-and-united-states-avoid-war.

Rudd, Kevin. 'Can the US and China Make a Deal?'. *Project Syndicate*, October 2019. https://www.project-syndicate.org/commentary/us-china-deal-to-end-trade-war-by-kevin-rudd-2019-10.

Rudd, Kevin. 'The Case for Managed Strategic Competition'. *Major Speeches in 2019*. Asia Society Policy Institute, January 2020. https://asiasociety.org/policy-institute/avoidable-war-case-managed-strategic-competition.

Rudd, Kevin. 'The Challenge for Small States in Navigating Turbulent Geopolitical Times'. Asia Society, 2023. https://asiasociety.org/policy-institute/challenge-small-states-navigating-turbulent-geopolitical-times.

Rudd, Kevin. 'China: An Economic and Political Outlook for 2022'. *Asia Society Policy Institute*, January 2022. https://asiasociety.org/sites/default/files/2022-01/ASPI_ChinaEconPolitOutlk2022.pdf.

Rudd, Kevin. 'China and the US Need to See Eye to Eye Again. It's in Both Their Interests'. *The Guardian*, September 2015. https://www.theguardian.com/commentisfree/2015/sep/23/china-us-chinese-xi-jinping.

Rudd, Kevin. 'China Has Politics Too'. *Asia Society Policy Institute*, December 2020. https://asiasociety.org/policy-institute/china-has-politics-too.

Rudd, Kevin. 'China's Brutally Pragmatic Response to a Shifting World Order'. *Financial Times*, 2016. https://www.ft.com/content/00e4e1b2-adb9-11e6-ba7d-76378e4fef24.

Rudd, Kevin. 'China's Competing Ideological and Economic Policy Objectives in 2023'. Asia Society, February 2023. https://asiasociety.org/policy-institute/chinas-competing-ideological-and-economic-policy-objectives-2023.

Rudd, Kevin. 'China's Economic Downturn Gives Rise to a Winter of Discontent'. *Wall Street Journal*, January 2022. https://www.wsj.com/articles/chinas-economic-woes-give-rise-to-a-winter-of-discontent-president-xi-jinping-cewc-common-prosperity-11642777025.

Rudd, Kevin. 'China's Economic Reforms Cannot, Should Not Stop'. *Caixin Global*, 2018. https://www.caixinglobal.com/2018-11-12/kevin-rudd-chinas-economic-reforms-cannot-should-not-stop-101345665.html.

Rudd, Kevin. 'China's Great Policy Correction: Can It Get Reform Back on Track?'. *South China Morning Post*, December 2018. https://www.scmp.com/comment/insight-opinion/united-states/article/2178351/chinas-great-policy-correction-opening-economy.

Rudd, Kevin. 'China's Political Economy into 2020'. Asia Society, 2019. https://asiasociety.org/policy-institute/chinas-political-economy-2020.

Rudd, Kevin. 'The Chinese Economy, the 20th Party Congress, and Implications for U.S.-China Relations'. *Asia Society*, July 2022. https://asiasociety.org/policy-institute/chinese-economy-20th-party-congress-and-implications-us-china-relations.

Rudd, Kevin. 'COVID-19 and Financial Contagions Demand a Joint Response from the World'. *South China Morning Post*, March 2020. https://www.scmp.com/comment/opinion/article/3075354/coronavirus-and-financial-contagions-demand-joint-response-can.

Rudd, Kevin. 'The Dangers of a Catastrophic Conflict between the U.S. and Xi Jinping's China'. Asia Society, March 2022. https://www.theguardian.com/commentisfree/2018/dec/05/donald-trump-xi-jinping-trade-buenos-aires.

Rudd, Kevin. 'The Decade of Living Dangerously'. *Major Speeches in 2020. Asia Society Policy Institute*, February 2021. https://asiasociety.org/policy-institute/avoidable-war-decade-living-dangerously.

Rudd, Kevin. 'Donald Trump and Xi Jinping Have Brokered Peace. It Will Be Sorely Tested'. *The Guardian*, December 2018. https://www.theguardian.com/commentisfree/2018/dec/05/donald-trump-xi-jinping-trade-buenos-aires.

Rudd, Kevin. 'Ending the Trade War'. *Asia Society Policy Institute*, 2019. https://asiasociety.org/policy-institute/ending-trade-war.

Rudd, Kevin. 'Even a Deal on Trade Won't Paper Over the Widening Gap between Washington and Beijing'. *Washington Post*, April 2019. https://www.washingtonpost.com/opinions/2019/04/24/even-deal-trade-wont-paper-over-widening-gap-between-washington-beijing/.

Rudd, Kevin. 'Fasten Your Seatbelts, China Has Drawn Its Red Lines against Trump'. *The Sydney Morning Herald*, June 2019. https://www.smh.com.au/national/fasten-your-seatbelts-china-has-drawn-its-red-lines-against-trump-20190612-p51wy4.html.

Rudd, Kevin. 'Has the "Great Decoupling" Gone Viral?'. *Project Syndicate*, February 2020. https://www.project-syndicate.org/onpoint/has-the-great-decoupling-gone-viral-by-kevin-rudd-2020-02.

Rudd, Kevin. 'How to Avoid an Avoidable War'. *Foreign Affairs*, October 2018. https://www.foreignaffairs.com/articles/china/2018-10-22/how-avoid-avoidable-war.

Rudd, Kevin. 'How Xi Jinping Views the World'. *Foreign Affairs*, May 2018. https://www.foreignaffairs.com/articles/china/2018-05-10/how-xi-jinping-views-world.

Rudd, Kevin. 'Jiang Zemin, Steward of China's Rise'. Lowy Institute, 2022. https://www.lowyinstitute.org/the-interpreter/kevin-rudd-jiang-zemin-steward-china-s-rise.

Rudd, Kevin. 'Managed Strategic Competition'. *Asia Society*, February 2021. https://asiasociety.org/policy-institute/managed-strategic-competition.

Rudd, Kevin. 'Preventing a US-China Nuclear Arms Race'. *Project Syndicate*, December 2021. https://www.project-syndicate.org/magazine/us-china-nuclear-arms-control-by-kevin-rudd-2021-12.

Rudd, Kevin. 'Prospects for US-China Relations in 2019'. *Project Syndicate*, December 2018. https://www.project-syndicate.org/commentary/united-states-china-relations-in-2019-by-kevin-rudd-2018-12.

Rudd, Kevin. 'Questions in US-China Relations'. *Asia Society*, September 2022. https://asiasociety.org/policy-institute/opening-remarks-chinese-foreign-minister-wang-yis-address-asia-society.

Rudd, Kevin. 'Reflections on U.S.-China Relations and the End of Strategic Engagement'. Major Speeches in 2018. Asia Society Policy Institute, January 2019. https://asiasociety.org/sites/default/files/2019-01/The%20Avoidable%20War%20-%20Full%20Report.pdf.

Rudd, Kevin. 'The Return of Red China'. *Foreign Affairs*, November 2022. https://www.foreignaffairs.com/china/return-red-china.

Rudd, Kevin. 'Rivals within Reason?'. *Foreign Affairs*, July 2022. https://www.foreignaffairs.com/china/rivals-within-reason.

Rudd, Kevin. 'Security, Not Growth, Is Xi's Focus'. *Wall Street Journal*, October 2022. https://www.wsj.com/articles/security-not-growth-xi-jinping-ccp-13th-party-congress-report-economy-military-supply-chain-2030-taiwan-11665591402.

Rudd, Kevin. 'Short of War'. *Foreign Affairs*, 100/2 (February 2021). https://www.foreignaffairs.com/articles/united-states/2021-02-05/kevin-rudd-usa-chinese-confrontation-short-of-war.

Rudd, Kevin. 'This Is a New and Dangerous Phase'. Australian Financial Review, January 2019. https://www.afr.com/policy/kevin-rudd-on-uschina-relations-this-is-a-new-and-dangerous-phase-20190122-h1acu6.

Rudd, Kevin. 'To Deal, or Not to Deal: The U.S.-China Trade War Enters the End-Game'. *Asia Society*, September 2019. https://asiasociety.org/policy-institute/to-deal-or-not-to-deal.

Rudd, Kevin. 'To Decouple or Not to Decouple?'. *Asia Society*, November 2019. https://asiasociety.org/policy-institute/decouple-or-not-decouple.

Rudd, Kevin. 'The Top 10 Questions about China Ahead of Xi's U.S. Visit'. *Huffington Post*, September 2015. https://www.huffpost.com/entry/china-questions-xi-jinping-us-visit_b_8169352.

Rudd, Kevin. 'Trump Hands China an Easy Win in the Trade War'. *New York Times*, May 2019. https://www.nytimes.com/2019/05/29/opinion/trump-china-trade-war.html.

Rudd, Kevin. 'UN 2030: Rebuilding Order in a Fragmenting World'. Chair's Report. International Peace Institute, 2016. https://www.ipinst.org/wp-content/uploads/2016/08/IPI-ICM-UN-2030-Chairs-Report2FINAL.pdf.

Rudd, Kevin. 'Understanding China's Rise under Xi Jinping'. Asia Society, 2018. https://asiasociety.org/policy-institute/understanding-chinas-rise-under-xi-jinping.

Rudd, Kevin. 'Understanding the Anxieties behind Chinese Aggression towards India'. *Indian Express*, August 2021. https://indianexpress.com/article/opinion/columns/former-australian-prime-minister-kevin-rudd-writes-understanding-the-anxieties-behind-chinese-aggression-towards-india-7449486/.

Rudd, Kevin. 'U.S.-China 21: The Future of U.S.-China Relations under Xi Jinping—Toward a New Framework of Constructive Realism for a Common Purpose'. Summary Report. Cambridge, MA: Harvard Kennedy School Belfer Center for Science and International Affairs, April 2015. https://www.belfercenter.org/sites/default/files/legacy/files/Summary%20Report%20US-China%2021.pdf.

Rudd, Kevin. 'US-China Decoupling Is More Rhetoric than Fact—for Now'. *Nikkei Asia*, 2019. https://asia.nikkei.com/Opinion/US-China-decoupling-is-more-rhetoric-than-fact-for-now.

Rudd, Kevin. 'We Are Witnessing Profound Change'. *Asia Society Switzerland*, 2022. https://asiasociety.org/switzerland/we-are-witnessing-profound-change.

Rudd, Kevin. 'What Biden and Xi Can Agree On'. *The Atlantic*, November 2022. https://www.theatlantic.com/ideas/archive/2022/11/g20-summit-2022-bali-biden-xi-jinping-china/672103/.

Rudd, Kevin. 'What Explains Xi's Pivot to the State?'. *Wall Street Journal*, September 2021. https://www.wsj.com/articles/xi-jinping-term-tencent-alibaba-crackdown-communist-party-ideology-authoritarian-11632079586?mod=opinion_lead_pos5.

Rudd, Kevin. 'What the West Doesn't Get about Xi Jinping'. *New York Times*, March 2018. https://www.nytimes.com/2018/03/20/opinion/xi-jinping-china-west.html.

Rudd, Kevin. 'Where Will It End? The US-China Trade War and the Threat to the Global Economy'. *Nikkei Asia*, 2019. https://asia.nikkei.com/Opinion/Where-will-it-end-The-US-China-trade-war-and-the-threat-to-the-global-economy.

Rudd, Kevin. 'Why the Quad Alarms China'. *Foreign Affairs*, August 2021. https://www.foreignaffairs.com/articles/united-states/2021-08-06/why-quad-alarms-china.

Rudd, Kevin. 'The World According to Xi Jinping'. *Foreign Affairs*, 101/6 (October 2022). https://www.foreignaffairs.com/china/world-according-xi-jinping-china-ideologue-kevin-rudd.

Rudd, Kevin. 'Xi Jinping, China and the Global Order'. 2018. https://asiasociety.org/policy-institute/kevin-rudd-xi-jinping-china-and-global-order.

Rudd, Kevin. 'Xi Jinping Is China's Most Audacious Leader for Decades'. *The Economist*, October 2022. https://www.economist.com/by-invitation/2022/10/25/xi-jinping-is-chinas-most-audacious-leader-for-decades-argues-kevin-rudd.

Rudd, Kevin . 'Xi Jinping Offers a Long-Term View of China's Ambition'. *Financial Times*, 2017. https://www.ft.com/content/24eeae8a-b5a1-11e7-8007-554f9eaa90ba.

Rudd, Kevin. '"Xi Jinping Thought" Makes China a Tougher Adversary'. *Wall Street Journal*, November 2021. https://www.wsj.com/articles/xi-jinping-thought-makes-china-a-tougher-adversary-ccp-rise-marxist-reappointment-11636750676.

Rudd, Kevin. 'Xi Jinping's Pivot to the State'. *Asia Society*, September 2021. https://asiasociety.org/policy-institute/understanding-evergrande.

Rudd, Kevin. 'Xi Jinping's Vision for Global Governance'. *Project Syndicate*, July 2018. https://www.project-syndicate.org/commentary/xi-jinping-has-a-coherent-global-vision-by-kevin-rudd-2018-07.

Rudd, Kevin. 'Xi Jinping's Year of Instability'. *Asia Society Policy Institute*, May 2022. https://asiasociety.org/policy-institute/xi-jinpings-year-instability-4.

Rudd, Kevin. 'Xi's Congress Report Lays Bare an Aggressive and Statist Worldview'. *Financial Times*, 2022. https://www.ft.com/content/8576916d-2cf5-483f-bfe4-2238080a5c70.

Rudd, Kevin. 'Xi's Third Term May Offer a Limited Window to Stabilize EU-China Relations'. *Le Monde*, October 2022. https://www.lemonde.fr/en/opinion/article/2022/10/12/former-australian-pm-kevin-rudd-xi-s-third-term-may-offer-a-limited-window-to-stabilize-eu-china-relations_6000070_23.html.

Rudd, Kevin, Helen Clark, and Carl Bildt. 'The Trade War Threatens the World's Economy'. *New York Times*, October 2019. https://www.nytimes.com/2019/10/11/opinion/china-trade.html.

Rudd, Kevin, and Alistair Ritchie. 'China's National ETS Needs High-Level Political Support to Succeed'. *China Dialogue*, May 2021. https://chinadialogue.net/en/climate/chinas-national-ets-needs-high-level-political-support-to-succeed/.

Rudd, Kevin, and Daniel Rosen. 'China Backslides on Economic Reform'. *Wall Street Journal*, September 2020. https://www.wsj.com/articles/china-backslides-on-economic-reform-11600813771.

Rudolph, Jennifer M., and Michael Szonyi (eds.) *The China Questions: Critical Insights into a Rising Power.* Cambridge, MA: Harvard University Press, 2018.

Ryan, Manuel. 'Twists in the Belt and Road'. *China Leadership Monitor*, no. 61 (2019). https://www.wita.org/atp-research/twists-in-the-belt-and-road/.

Saba, Paul (ed.). *China's Foreign Policy: A Leninist Policy.* San Francisco: The Revolutionary Union, 1972. https://www.marxists.org/history/erol/ncm-1/china-foreign.htm.

Saich, Tony. 'China in 2005: Hu's in Charge'. *Asian Survey*, 46/1 (February 2006), 37–48.

Saich, Tony. 'The Chinese Communist Party and the Future'. *China Information*, 4/4 (March 1990), 15–30.

Saich, Tony. 'The Chinese Communist Party at the Thirteenth Party Congress'. *Issues and Studies*, 25/1 (1989).

Saich, Tony. 'Controlling Political Communication and Civil Society under Xi Jinping'. *MERICS Papers on China*, 1 (2016). https://www.hks.harvard.edu/publications/controlling-political-communication-and-civil-society-under-xi-jinping.

Saich, Tony. 'The Fourteenth Party Congress: A Programme for Authoritarian Rule'. *China Quarterly*, no. 132 (1992), 1136–60.

Saich, Tony. *Governance and Politics of China*. 4th ed. New York: St Martin's Press, 2015.

Saich, Tony. 'How China's Citizens View the Quality of Governance under Xi Jinping'. *Journal of Chinese Governance*, 1/1 (January 2016), 1–20.

Saich, Tony. 'Party and State Reforms in the People's Republic of China'. *Third World Quarterly*, 5/3 (July 1983), 627–39.

Saich, Tony. 'Party Building since Mao—a Question of Style?'. *World Development*, 11/8 (August 1983): 747–65.

Saich, Tony. 'Party Consolidation and Spiritual Pollution in the People's Republic of China'. *Communist Affairs Documents and Analysis*, 3/3 (1984).

Saich, Tony. 'The Party since the "Gang of Four"'. BACS Annual, 1981.

Saich, Tony. 'What Does General Secretary Xi Jinping Dream About?'. Ash Center Occasional Papers, August 2017. https://dash.harvard.edu/handle/1/42367427.

Saint-Pulgent, Maryvonne de, Pierre-Jean Benghozi, and Thomas Paris. *Mondialisation et diversité culturelle*. Réactions et réponses à la mondialisation 6. Paris: Institut français des relations internationales, 2003.

Salazar Xirinachs, José Manuel, Irmgard Nübler, and Richard Kozul-Wright (eds.). *Transforming Economies: Making Industrial Policy Work for Growth, Jobs and Development*. Geneva: International Labour Organization, 2014.

Salidjanova, Nargiza, Rachel Lietzow, and Daniel H. Rosen. 'China Pathfinder: H2 2022 Update'. Rhodium Group, February 2023. https://rhg.com/research/china-pathfinder-h2-2022-update/.

Sargis, Al L. 'Ideological Tendencies and Reform Policy in China's "Primary Stage of Socialism"'. *Nature, Society, and Thought: A Journal of Dialectical and Historical Materialism*, 11/4 (1998). https://hdl.handle.net/11299/149986.

Saunders, Phillip C., Arthur S. Ding, Andrew Scobell, Andrew N. D. Yang, and Joel Wuthnow (eds.). *Chairman Xi Remakes the PLA: Assessing Chinese Military Reforms*. Washington, DC: National Defense University Press, 2019.

Schell, Orville. 'On Kissinger, China and the "End of Engagement"'. *The Wire China*, December 3, 2023. https://www.thewirechina.com/2023/12/03/reflections-on-kissinger-china-and-the-end-of-engagement/.

Schell, Orville. 'The Wolf of Beijing Will Be the Downfall of China: So-Called "Warrior" Diplomacy Has Left Xi Jinping Isolated'. *The Telegraph*, September 5, 2023, https://www.telegraph.co.uk/news/2023/09/05/china-economy-slowdown-xi-jinping-taiwan-south-china-sea/.

Schell, Orville, and Delury, John. *Wealth and Power: China's Long March to the Twenty-First Century*. New York: Random House, 2013.

Schell, Orville, and Delury, John. 'Chairman of the Board: How Mao Unintentionally Created China's Capitalist Revolution'. *Foreign Policy*, July 12, 2013, https://foreignpolicy.com/2013/07/12/chairman-of-the-board/.

Schell, Orville, and Diamond, Larry. *China's Influence and American Interests: Promoting Constructive Vigilance*. Stanford, CA: Hoover Institution Press, 2019.

Schell, Orville, and Shambaugh, David (eds.). *The China Reader: The Reform Era*. New York: Vintage, 1999.

Schell, Orville, Shirk, Susan, and Panda, Ankit. 'Reassessing U.S.-China Relations'. *Carnegie.org*, July 31, 2019. https://www.carnegie.org/our-work/article/competition-confrontation-or-collision-course-reassessing-us-china-relations/.

Schoenhals, Michael. *Doing Things with Words in Chinese Politics: Five Studies*. China Research Monograph 41. Berkeley: Center for Chinese Studies, Institute of East Asian Studies, University of California, 1992.

Schoenhals, Michael. 'Mao Zedong: Speeches at the 1957 "Moscow Conference"'. *Journal of Communist Studies*, 2/2 (June 1986), 109–26.

Schram, Stuart R. 'Chinese and Leninist Components in the Personality of Mao Tse-Tung'. *Asian Survey*, 3/6 (1963), 259–73.

Schram, Stuart R. *Mao Tse-Tung: With 29 Plates*. Political Leaders of the Twentieth Century 840. Harmondsworth: Penguin, 1967.

Schram, Stuart R. 'A Review Article: *Mao Tse-Tung as Marxist Dialectician*. Edited by Arthur A. Cohen [review]. *China Quarterly*, no. 29 (1967), 155–65.

Schram, Stuart R. 'China after the 13th Congress', *China Quarterly*, 114 (1988).

Schram, Stuart R. *The Thought of Mao Tse-Tung*. Contemporary China Institute Publications. Cambridge: Cambridge University Press, 1989.

Schram, Stuart R. 'To Utopia and Back: A Cycle in the History of the Chinese Communist Party'. *China Quarterly*, 87 (September 1981), 407–39.

Schurmann, Franz. *Ideology and Organization in Communist China*. 2nd ed. Berkeley: University of California Press, 1973.

Schwarck, Edward. 'Intelligence and Informatization: The Rise of the Ministry of Public Security in Intelligence Work in China'. *China Journal*, 80 (July 2018), 1–23.

Schwartz, Benjamin Isadore. *Communism and China: Ideology in Flux*. Cambridge, MA: Harvard University Press, 1970.

Schwartz, Shalom H. 'Universals in the Content and Structure of Values: Theoretical Advances and Empirical Tests in 20 Countries'. *Advances in Experimental Social Psychology*, 25 (1992), 1–65

Schweller, Randall. 'Opposite but Compatible Nationalisms: A Neoclassical Realist Approach to the Future of US-China Relations'. *Chinese Journal of International Politics*, 11/1 (March 2018), 23–48.

Scobell, Andrew. 'Show of Force: Chinese Soldiers, Statesmen, and the 1995–1996 Taiwan Strait Crisis'. *Political Science Quarterly*, 115/2 (2000), 227–46.

Scoggins, Suzanne E. 'Rethinking Authoritarian Resilience and the Coercive Apparatus'. *Comparative Politics*, 53/2 (January 2021), 309–30.

Scott, David. 'China's Public Diplomacy Rhetoric, 1990–2012: Pragmatic Image-Crafting'. *Diplomacy & Statecraft*, 26/2 (April 2015), 249–65.

Seliger, Martin. *Ideology and Politics*. London: Routledge, 2019.

Shambaugh, David. *China and the World*. New York: Oxford University Press, 2020.

Shambaugh, David, *China Goes Global: The Partial Power*. New York: Oxford University Press, 2013.

Shambaugh, David. *The China Reader: Rising Power*. New York: Oxford University Press, 2016.

Shambaugh, David. *China's Future*. Cambridge: Polity, 2016.

Shambaugh, David. 'China's Propaganda System: Institutions, Processes and Efficacy'. In Kjeld Erik Brødsgaard (ed.), *Critical Readings on the Communist Party of China*, 25–58. Leiden: Brill, 2017.

Shambaugh, David. *Modernizing China's Military: Progress, Problems, and Prospects*. Berkeley: University of California Press, 2003.

Shambaugh, David. *Where Great Powers Meet: America & China in Southeast Asia*. New York: Oxford University Press, 2020.

Shambaugh, David, and Joseph Brinley. *China's Communist Party: Atrophy and Adaptation*. Berkeley: University of California Press, 2008.

Shan, Wei, Yongxin Gu, and Juan Chen. 'Layering Ideologies from Deng Xiaoping to Xi Jinping: Tracing Ideological Changes of the Communist Party of China Using Text Analysis'. *China: An International Journal*, 212 (May 2023), 26–50.

Shao, Binhong (ed.). *China under Xi Jinping: Its Economic Challenges and Foreign Policy Initiatives*. Leiden: Brill, 2015.

Sharp, Jonathan (ed.). *The China Renaissance: The Rise of Xi Jinping and the 18th Communist Party Congress*. Singapore: World Scientific, 2013.

Shattuck, Thomas. 'One Year Later: How Has China's Military Pressure on Taiwan Changes since Nancy Pelosi's Visit?'. *Global Taiwan Brief*, 8/18 (September 2023). https://globaltaiwan.org/wp-content/uploads/2023/09/GTB-8.18-PDF-Final.pdf.

Sheets, Nathan. 'When Will China's GDP Surpass the US? And What Will It Mean?'. *Citi Research*, January 2023. https://www.citigroup.com/global/insights/when-will-china-s-gdp-surpass-the-us-and-what-will-it-mean-.

Shei, Chris, and Weixiao Wei (eds.). *The Routledge Handbook of Chinese Studies*. Abingdon: Routledge, 2021.

Shih, Chih-yu, and Chiung-chiu Huang. 'China's Quest for Grand Strategy: Power, National Interest, or Relational Security?'. *Chinese Journal of International Politics*, 8/1 (March 2015), 1–26.

Shih, Gerry. 'Xi Urges Chinese Communist Party to Embrace Marxist Roots'. *AP News*, July 2016. https://apnews.com/general-news-7b0d70e02e044dcfb9f741484eadddf6.

Shirk, Susan. 'Regional Views on Asia-Pacific Regional Cooperation", *NBR Analysis*, no.5, 1994.

Shirk, Susan. *China: Fragile Superpower*. New York: Oxford University Press, 2008.

Shirk, Susan L. 'China in Xi's "New Era"'. *Journal of Democracy*, 29/2 (2018), 20–21.

Shirk, Susan L. *Overreach: How China Derailed Its Peaceful Rise*. New York: Oxford University Press, 2023.

Shirk, Susan L. 'The Return to Personalistic Rule'. *Journal of Democracy*, 29/2 (2018), 22–36.

Shue, Vivienne, and Patricia M. Thornton (eds.). *To Govern China: Evolving Practices of Power*. Cambridge: Cambridge University Press, 2017.

Sidel, Mark. 'Securitizing Overseas Nonprofit Work in China', *USALI Perspectives*, 2/6 (2021).

Silver, Laura, Christine Huang, Laura Clancy, Nam Lam, Shannon Greenwood, John Carlo Mandapat, and Chris Baronavski. 'Comparing Views of the U.S. and China in 24 Countries'. Pew Research Center's Global Attitudes Project, November 2023. https://www.pewresearch.org/global/2023/11/06/comparing-views-of-the-us-and-china-in-24-countries/.

Singh, Antara Ghosal. 'Chinese Anxiety over "Peak China" and How It May Impact China-India Ties'. Observer Research Foundation, March 2024.

Singh, Teshu. 'Contemporary Foreign Policy of China: Legacy of Deng Xiaoping'. Institute of Peace and Conflict Studies, September 2014. https://www.ipcs.org/comm_select.php?articleNo=4653.

Slater, Adam. 'Chinese Catch-up Prospects Recede as the US Outperforms'. Research Briefing. Oxford Economics, December 2023. https://www.oxfordeconomics.com/wp-content/uploads/2023/12/20231518-RB-ChinaUS.pdf.

Smith, Anthony D. *Nationalism*. 2nd ed. Polity Key Concepts in the Social Sciences Series. Oxford: Wiley, 2013.

Smith, Michael. 'US Companies Pull Out of China as Relations Sour'. *Australian Financial Review*, September 2023. https://www.afr.com/world/asia/us-companies-pull-out-of-china-as-relations-sour-20230918-p5e5n8.

Smith, Nicholas Ross. 'The Re-Emergence of a "Mirror Image" in West-Russia Relations?'. *International Politics*, 55/5 (September 2018), 575–94.

Smith, Stephen N. 'Community of Common Destiny: China's "New Assertiveness" and the Changing Asian Order'. *International Journal*, 73/3 (2018), 449–63.

Solinger, Dorothy J. *Chinese Business under Socialism: The Politics of Domestic Commerce, 1949–1980*. Berkeley: University of California Press, 1984.

Sørensen, Camilla T. N. 'The Roots of China's Assertiveness in East Asia'. *Copenhagen Journal of Asian Studies*, 39/2 (December 2021), 10–32.

Sørensen, Camilla T. N. 'The Significance of Xi Jinping's "Chinese Dream" for Chinese Foreign Policy: From "Tao Guang Yang Hui" to "Fen Fa You Wei"'. *Journal of China and International Relations*, 3/1 (May 2015).

Stahl, Rune Møller, and Andreas Christian Møller Mulvad. 'Under the Banner of Democracy: Left Parties in a New Age of Oligarchy,' October 2014. https://research.cbs.dk/en/publications/under-the-banner-of-democracy-left-parties-in-a-new-age-of-oligar.

Stanway, David. 'China 2023 Coal Power Approvals Rose, Putting Climate Targets at Risk'. *Reuters*, February 2024. https://www.reuters.com/sustainability/climate-energy/china-2023-coal-power-approvals-rose-putt'ng-c'limate-targets-risk-2024-02-22/.

State-Owned Assets Supervision and Administration Commission (PRC). 'Economic Daily Published Economists' Interpretation of the 14th Five-Year Plan and the Outline of 2035 Long-Term Goals'. Undated. http://www.guojianjituan.com/en/index.php/Index/News_details/981.html

Stepan, Matthias, and Sebastian Heilmann (eds.). 'China's Core Executive: Leadership Styles, Structures, and Processes under Xi Jinping'. *MERICS*, 2016. https://www.researchgate.net/publication/304348339.

Stoffey, J. David. 'Lessons from History: The Han-Xiongnu War and Modern China'. *Small Wars Journal*, 2017. https://smallwarsjournal.com/jrnl/art/lessons-from-history-the-han-xiongnu-war-and-modern-china.

Stoner, Kathryn, and Michael McFaul (eds.). *Transitions to Democracy: A Comparative Perspective*. Baltimore: Johns Hopkins University Press, 2013.

Strauss, Julia C. 'Framing and Claiming: Contemporary Globalization and "Going Out" in China's Rhetoric towards Latin America'. *China Quarterly*, 209 (March 2012), 134–56.

Strong, Tracy B., and Helene Keyssar. 'Anna Louise Strong: Three Interviews with Chairman Mao Zedong', *The China Quarterly*, 103, 1985.

Su, Xiaobo. 'Revolution and Reform: The Role of Ideology and Hegemony in Chinese Politics'. *Journal of Contemporary China*, 20/69 (March 2011), 307–26.

Sudworth, John. 'Why China's Ruling Party Is Bearing Down on "Cliques"'. *BBC News*, January 2015. https://www.bbc.com/news/blogs-china-blog-30685782.

Sumner, Colin. *Reading Ideologies: An Investigation into the Marxist Theory of Ideology and Law*. Law, State, and Society Series. London: Academic Press, 1979.

Sun, Luna. 'Chinese Students Have New Source of Stress as Universities Raise Tuition Fees'. *South China Morning Post*, September 2023. https://www.scmp.com/economy/china-economy/article/3235868/chinese-universities-squeeze-new-students-tuition-increases.

Sun Tzu, Qi Wu, Lao Wei, Rangju Sima, and Ziya Jiang. *The Seven Military Classics of Ancient China*. London: Arcturus, 2017.

Sun, Yan. *The Chinese Reassessment of Socialism 1976–1992*. Princeton, NJ: Princeton University Press, 1995.

Sun, Yu, and Ryan McMorrow. 'US Consultancy Gallup Withdraws from China'. *Financial Times*, November 2023. https://www.ft.com/content/dff10673-f3e3-4117-8a71-cb57a9cc4ccb.

Sutter, Robert G. *Foreign Relations of the PRC: The Legacies and Constraints of China's International Politics since 1949*. 2nd ed. Lanham, MD: Rowman & Littlefield, 2019.

Swaine, Michael D. 'Perceptions of an Assertive China'. *China Leadership Monitor*, no. 32 (2010). https://www.hoover.org/research/perceptions-assertive-china.

Swaine, Michael D. 'Xi Jinping on Chinese Foreign Relations: The Governance of China and Chinese Commentary'. Hoover Institution, 2015. https://www.hoover.org/research/xi-jinping-chinese-foreign-relations-governance-china-and-chinese-commentary.

Swaine, Michael D. 'Xi Jinping's Address to the Central Conference on Work Relating to Foreign Affairs: Assessing and Advancing Major Power Diplomacy with Chinese Characteristics'. *Hoover Institution*, 2015. https://www.hoover.org/research/xi-jinpings-address-central-conference-work-relating-foreign-affairs-assessing-and.

Szczepański. Marcin. 'China's Economic Coercion: Evolution, Characteristics and Countermeasures'. European Parliamentary Research Service, 2022. https://www.europarl.europa.eu/thinktank/en/document/EPRS_BRI(2022)738219.

Takeuchi, Hiroki. 'Domestic Politics of Chinese Foreign Policy: Where Will Xi Jinping Bring China?'. *Asian Security*, 15/2 (May 2019), 205–13.

Tan, Andrew T. H. (ed.). *Security and Conflict in East Asia*. London: Routledge, 2015.

Tang, Dapeng and Shiping Qi. 'Sino-centrism and US-centrism in China's Foreign Policy Discourse', *World Economics and Politics*, no. 12, 2008.

Tang, Jane. 'China's Shiny New Press Card Means Total State Control of Media: Journalists'. Translated by Luisetta Mudie. Radio Free Asia, November 2020. https://www.rfa.org/english/news/china/press-11112020092314.html.

Tang, Wenfang. *Populist Authoritarianism: Chinese Political Culture and Regime Sustainability*. New York: Oxford University Press, 2016.

Tang, Wenfang. 'The "Surprise" of Authoritarian Resilience in China'. *American Affairs Journal*, February 2018. https://americanaffairsjournal.org/2018/02/surprise-authoritarian-resilience-china/.

Tao, Xie. 'Chinese Foreign Policy with Xi Jinping Characteristics'. Carnegie Endowment for International Peace, 2017. https://carnegieendowment.org/2017/11/20/chinese-foreign-policy-with-xi-jinping-characteristics-pub-74765.

Task Force on U.S.-China Policy and UC San Diego. 'Asia Society–University of California San Diego Joint Report on China's New Direction: Challenges and Opportunities for U.S.'. Asia Society Centre on US-China Relations, 2021. https://china.ucsd.edu/_files/2021-china-new-direction-report.pdf.

Tatlow, Didi Kirsten. 'China's Cosmological Communism: A Challenge to Liberal Democracies'. *MERICS*, July 2018. https://merics.org/en/report/chinas-cosmological-communism-challenge-liberal-democracies.

Teon, Aris. 'The Deterioration of China's Media Freedom in the Xi Jinping Era'. *Greater China Journal*, February 2019. https://china-journal.org/2019/02/20/the-deterioration-of-chinas-media-freedom-in-the-xi-jinping-era/.

Tepperman, Jonathan. 'China's Great Leap Backward'. *Foreign Policy*, March 2024. https://foreignpolicy.com/2018/10/15/chinas-great-leap-backward-xi-jinping/.

Thomas, Neil. 'Chinese Foreign Policy under Xi Jinping'. *East Asia Forum*, 2018. https://www.eastasiaforum.org/2018/10/21/chinese-foreign-policy-under-xi-jinping/.

Tian, Gang, and Wen-Hsuan Tsai. 'Ideological Education and Practical Training at a County Party School: Shaping Local Governance in Contemporary China'. *China Journal*, 85 (January 2021), 1–25.

Tian, Yan Jing. '1.4 Billion People and Shrinking—China's Population Problem Visually Explained'. *South China Morning Post*, 2023. https://bit.ly/3X7Kbtn.

Tian, Yew Lun. 'Shanghai COVID Crisis Puts Political Spotlight on Key Xi Ally'. *Reuters*, May 2022. https://www.reuters.com/world/china/shanghai-covid-crisis-puts-political-spotlight-key-xi-ally-2022-05-08/.

Tobin, Daniel. 'How Xi Jinping's "New Era" Should Have Ended U.S. Debate on Beijing's Ambitions'. *CSIS*, May 2020. https://www.csis.org/analysis/how-xi-jinpings-new-era-should-have-ended-us-debate-beijings-ambitions.

Torigian, Joseph. 'Elite Politics and Foreign Policy in China from Mao to Xi'. *Brookings*, 2019. https://www.brookings.edu/articles/elite-politics-and-foreign-policy-in-china-from-mao-to-xi/.

Torigian, Joseph. 'Historical Legacies and Leaders' Worldviews: Communist Party History and Xi's Learned (and Unlearned) Lessons'. *China Perspectives*, 2018/1–2 (June 2018), 7–15.

Torigian, Joseph. 'Prestige, Manipulation, and Coercion: Elite Power Struggles and the Fate of Three Revolutions'. Thesis, Massachusetts Institute of Technology, 2016. https://dspace.mit.edu/handle/1721.1/107535.

Torigian, Joseph. *Prestige, Manipulation, and Coercion: Elite Power Struggles in the Soviet Union and China after Stalin and Mao*. New Haven, CT: Yale University Press, 2022.

Torigian, Joseph. 'The Shadow of Deng Xiaoping on Chinese Elite Politics'. *War on the Rocks*, January 2017. https://warontherocks.com/2017/01/the-shadow-of-deng-xiaoping-on-chinese-elite-politics/.

Torigian, Joseph. 'What Xi Jinping Learned—And Didn't Learn—From His Father about Xinjiang'. *The Diplomat*, 2019. https://thediplomat.com/2019/11/what-xi-jinping-learned-and-didnt-learn-from-his-father-about-xinjiang/.

Trevaskes, Susan. 'Rationalising Stability Preservation through Mao's Not So Invisible Hand'. *Journal of Current Chinese Affairs*, 42/2 (June 2013), 51–77.

Truitt, Jack Stone. 'How Reliable Is China's GDP Data?'. *Nikkei Asia*, 2024. https://asia.nikkei.com/Economy/How-reliable-is-China-s-GDP-data-2024-in-focus-after-debatable-2023.

Tsang, Steve. *China in the Xi Jinping Era*. The Nottingham China Policy Institute Series 14423. New York: Springer Science+Business Media, 2016.

Tsang, Steve. 'Consultative Leninism: China's New Political Framework'. *Journal of Contemporary China*, 1,/62 (November 2009), 865–80.

Tsang, Steve. 'From Japanese Colony to Sacred Chinese Territory: Taiwan's Geostrategic Significance to China'. *Twentieth-Century China*, 45/3 (2020), 351–68.

Tsang, Steve. 'Modern Hong Kong'. In *Oxford Research Encyclopedia of Asian History*. Oxford University Press, 2017.

Tsang, Steve. 'Party-State Realism: A Framework for Understanding China's Approach to Foreign Policy'. *Journal of Contemporary China*, 29/122 (March 2020), 304–18.

Tsang, Steve. 'The U.S. Military and American Commitment to Taiwan's Security'. *Asian Survey*, 52/4 (August 2012), 777–97.

Tsang, Steve. 'Xi Jinping's Brave New World'. *New Perspectives Quarterly*, 35/1 (January 2018), 19–21.

Tsang, Steve, and Olivia Cheung. 'Has Xi Jinping Made China's Political System More Resilient and Enduring?'. *Third World Quarterly*, 43/1 (January 2022), 225–43.

Tsang, Steve, and Olivia Cheung. 'Uninterrupted Rise: China's Global Strategy According to Xi Jinping Thought'. *The Asan Forum*, March 2021. https://theasanforum.org/uninterrupted-rise-chinas-global-strategy-according-to-xi-jinping-thought/.

Tsang, Steve Yui-Sang, and Olivia Cheung. *The Political Thought of Xi Jinping*. New York: Oxford University Press, 2024.

Tubilewicz, Czeslaw (ed.). 'The Chinese Communist Party's Evolution'. In *Critical Issues in Contemporary China: Unity, Stability and Development*. 2nd ed. London: Routledge, 2017.

United Nations. 'Universal Declaration of Human Rights'. *ohchr.org*, 1948. https://www.ohchr.org/en/human-rights/universal-declaration/translations/english.

United Nations Conference on Trade and Development. 'Chapter II: International Markets: Trade, Capital Flows, Commodities'. *UNCTAD*, October 2023. https://unctad.org/system/files/official-document/tdr2023ch2_en.pdf.

Van Ness, Peter. 'Hegemony, Not Anarchy: Why China and Japan Are Not Balancing US Unipolar Power'. *International Relations of the Asia-Pacific*, 2/1 (2002), 131–50.

Van Ness, Peter. *Revolution and Chinese Foreign Policy: Peking's Support for Wars of National Liberation*. Berkeley: University of California Press, 1973.

Von Hein, Matthias. 'Xi Jinping—China's Great Helmsman 2.0'. *DW*, 25 October 2017. https://www.dw.com/en/opinion-xi-jinping-chinas-great-helmsman-20/a-41096801

Vickers, Edward. 'Smothering Diversity: Patriotism in China's School Curriculum under Xi Jinping'. *Journal of Genocide Research*, 24/2 (April 2022), 158–70.

Vogel, Ezra. 'China under Deng Xiaoping's Leadership'. *East Asia Forum*, September 2011. https://eastasiaforum.org/2011/09/27/china-under-deng-xiaopings-leadership/.

Vogel, Ezra F. *Deng Xiaoping and the Transformation of China*. Cambridge, MA: Belknap Press of Harvard University Press, 2011.

Waal, Joel Rogers de. 'China's Reputation Declines While America's Gets a Boost'. YouGov, 2022. https://yougov.co.uk/international/articles/44996-chinas-reputation-declines-while-americas-gets-boo.

Waltz, Kenneth N. 'The Emerging Structure of International Politics'. *International Security*, 18/2 (1993), 44.

Wang, Gungwu. 'Ancient Past, Modern Ambitions: Wang Gungwu on China's Delicate Balance'. *South China Morning Post*, September 2019. https://www.scmp.com/week-asia/politics/article/3026041/ancient-past-modern-ambitions-historian-wang-gungwus-new-book.

Wang, Gungwu. *Nationalism and Confucianism*. Wu Teh Yao Memorial Lectures. Singapore: UniPress, Centre for the Arts, National University of Singapore, 1996.

Wang, Gungwu. *The Revival of Chinese Nationalism*. Lecture Series 6. Leiden: International Institute for Asian Studies, 1996.

Wang, Gungwu. 'Wang Gungwu 王赓武 on Tianxia 天下'. *The China Story [blog]*, August 2013. https://archive.thechinastory.org/2013/08/wang-gungwu-%E7%8E%8B%E5%BA%9A%E6%AD%A6-on-tianxia-%E5%A4%A9%E4%B8%8B/.

Wang, Gungwu, and Yongnian Zheng (eds.). *China: Development and Governance*. Hackensack, NJ: World Scientific, 2013.

Wang, Jianwei. 'Xi Jinping's "Major Country Diplomacy": A Paradigm Shift?'. *Journal of Contemporary China*, 28/115 (January 2019), 15–30.

Wang, Jiawei, and Xueqin Xie. 'Update on Anti-Monopoly Law in China'. 2023. Rödl & Partner, https://www.roedl.com/insights/antitrust-law/china-anti-monopoly-law-update.

Wang, Jiayu. 'Representing Chinese Nationalism/Patriotism through President Xi Jinping's "Chinese Dream" Discourse'. *Journal of Language and Politics*, 16/6 (January 2017), 830–48.

Wang, Q. Edward. 'Review of "Renewal: The Chinese State and the New Global History"'. *Journal of Chinese Studies*, no. 58 (2014).

Wang, Ray. 'Authoritarian Resilience versus Everyday Resistance: The Unexpected Strength of Religious Advocacy in Promoting Transnational Activism in China'. *Journal for the Scientific Study of Religion*, 56/3 (September 2017), 558–76.

Wang, Te-Yu (ed.). *China after the Sixteenth Party Congress: Prospects and Challenges*. International Studies in Social Science 7. Whitby, ON: de Sitter, 2005.

Wang, Wen. 'Busting 6 "Peak China" Myths'. *The Diplomat [blog]*, 2024. https://thediplomat.com/2024/03/busting-6-peak-china-myths/.

Wang, Xiangwei. '"Great Leader Xi" or "Xi, the Great Leader": It's a Fine Line'. *South China Morning Post*, November 2017. https://www.scmp.com/week-asia/opinion/article/2121473/china-fine-line-between-great-leader-xi-and-xi-great-leader.

Wang, Yanfei, and Yang Ziman. 'NDRC: Overcapacity Top Reform Priority for 2017'. *China Daily*, 19 December 2016. https://www.chinadaily.com.cn/cndy/2016-12/19/content_27704347.htm.

Wang, Yuan-kang. 'China's Response to the Unipolar World: The Strategic Logic of Peaceful Development'. *Journal of Asian and African Studies*, 45/5 (October 2010), 554–67.

Wang, Yuan-kang. 'Managing Regional Hegemony in Historical Asia: The Case of Early Ming China'. *Chinese Journal of International Politics*, 5/2 (June 2012), 129–53.

Wang, Yuhua, and Carl Minzner. 'The Rise of the Chinese Security State'. *China Quarterly*, 222 (June 2015), 339–59.

Wang, Zheng. 'National Humiliation, History Education and the Politics of Historical Memory', *International Studies Quarterly*, 52/4

Wang, Zhengxu, and Jinghan Zeng. 'Xi Jinping: The Game Changer of Chinese Elite Politics?'. *Contemporary Politics*, 22/4 (October 2016), 469–86.

Ware, Robert. 'Reflections on Chinese Marxism'. *Socialism and Democracy*, 27/1 (March 2013), 136–60.

Weatherford, M. Stephen. 'Measuring Political Legitimacy'. *American Political Science Review*, 86/1 (1992), 149–66.

Wei, Ling. 'Striving for Achievement in a New Era: China Debates Its Global Role'. *Pacific Review*, 33/3–4 (July 2020), 413–37.

Weiss, Jessica Chen. 'Authoritarian Signaling, Mass Audiences, and Nationalist Protest in China'. *International Organization*, 67/1 (2013), 1–35.

Weiss, Jessica Chen. 'China's Self-Defeating Nationalism'. *Foreign Affairs*, July 2020. https://www.foreignaffairs.com/articles/china/2020-07-16/chinas-self-defeating-nationalism.

Weiss, Jessica Chen. 'How Hawkish Is the Chinese Public? Another Look at "Rising Nationalism" and Chinese Foreign Policy'. *Journal of Contemporary China*, 28/119 (September 2019), 679–95.

Weiss, Jessica Chen. *Powerful Patriots: Nationalist Protest in China's Foreign Relations*. New York: Oxford University Press, 2014.

Weiss, Jessica Chen. 'A World Safe for Autocracy?'. *Foreign Affairs*, 98 /4 (June 2019). https://www.foreignaffairs.com/articles/china/2019-06-11/world-safe-autocracy.

Weiss, Jessica Chen, and Allan Dafoe. 'Authoritarian Audiences, Rhetoric, and Propaganda in International Crises: Evidence from China'. *International Studies Quarterly*, 63/4 (December 2019), 963–73.

Wendt, Alexander. 'Anarchy Is What States Make of It: The Social Construction of Power Politics'. *International Organization*, 46/2 (1992), 391–425.

Wendt, Alexander. *Social Theory of International Politics*. Cambridge Studies in International Relations. Cambridge: Cambridge University Press, 1999.

Westad, Odd Arne. *Decisive Encounters: The Chinese Civil War, 1946–1950*. Stanford, CA: Stanford University Press, 2003.

Westad, Odd Arne. *The Global Cold War: Third World Interventions and the Making of Our Times*. Cambridge: Cambridge University Press, 2005.

Westad, Odd Arne. 'The Sources of Chinese Conduct'. *Foreign Affairs*, 98/5 (August 2019). https://www.foreignaffairs.com/articles/china/2019-08-12/sources-chinese-conduct

White, Edward. 'China's Business Confidence Problem'. *Financial Times*. 11 September 2023. https://www.ft.com/content/fb73774a-a130-4769-80a5-6115555b22a1.

Whiting, Allen S. 'Assertive Nationalism in Chinese Foreign Policy'. *Asian Survey*, 23/8 (1983), 913–33.

Wigglesworth, Robin. 'The Implications of China's Middle-Income Trap'. *Financial Times*, February 2023. https://www.ft.com/content/a998c1bc-7632-47c1-baba-6ccd6aaef96e.

Williamson, John. 'What Should the World Bank Think about the Washington Consensus?'. *World Bank Research Observer*, 15/2 (2000).

Wills, John E. *Embassies and Illusions: Dutch and Portuguese Envoys to K'ang-Hsi, 1666–1687*. Harvard East Asian Monographs 113. Cambridge, MA: Council on East Asian Studies, Harvard University, 1984.

Wilson, Ian. 'Socialism with Chinese Characteristics: China and the Theory of the Initial Stage of Socialism'. *Politics*, 24/1 (May 1989), 77–84.

Wimmer, Andreas. *Waves of War: Nationalism, State Formation, and Ethnic Exclusion in the Modern World*. Cambridge: Cambridge University Press, 2013.

Womack, Brantly. 'Asymmetry and China's Tributary System'. *Chinese Journal of International Politics*, 5/1 (2012), 37–54.

Womack, Brantly. 'Beyond Win-Win: Rethinking China's International Relationships in an Era of Economic Uncertainty'. *International Affairs*, 89/4 (July 2013), 911–28.

Womack, Brantly (ed.). *China's Rise in Historical Perspective*. Lanham, MD: Rowman & Littlefield, 2010.

Wong, Christine. 'The Fiscal Stimulus Programme and Public Governance Issues in China'. *OECD Journal on Budgeting*, 11/3 (October 2011), 1–22.

Wong, Chun Han. *Party of One: The Rise of Xi Jinping and China's Superpower Future*. New York: Avid Reader Press, 2023.

Wong, John, and Lai Hongyi. *China into the Hu-Wen Era: Policy Initiatives and Challenges*. Series on Contemporary China 5. Singapore: World Scientific, 2006.

Wong, John, and Yongnian Zheng (eds.). *The Nanxun Legacy and China's Development in the Post-Deng Era*. Singapore: World Scientific, 2001.

Wright, Logan, John L. Holden, and Claire Reade. 'China's Economic Downturn: Structural, Cyclical, or Both?'. *CSIS*, August 2023. https://www.csis.org/analysis/chinas-economic-downturn-structural-cyclical-or-both-0.

Wu, Guanjun. *The Great Dragon Fantasy: A Lacanian Analysis of Contemporary Chinese Thought*. Singapore: World Scientific, 2014.

Wu, Guoguang. *The Anatomy of Political Power in China*. Politics & International Relations. Singapore: Marshall Cavendish Academic, 2005.

Wu, Guoguang, *China's Common Prosperity Program*. New York: Asia Society Policy Institute, 2022.

Wu, Guoguang. *China's Party Congress: Power, Legitimacy, and Institutional Manipulation*. Cambridge: Cambridge University Press, 2015.

Wu, Guoguang. 'Continuous Purges: Xi's Public Security Apparatus and the Changing Dynamics of CCP Elite Politics'. *China Leadership Monitor*, no. 66 (December 2020). https://www.prcleader.org/post/continuous-purges-xi-s-public-security-apparatus-and-the-changing-dynamics-of-ccp-elite-politics.

Wu, Guoguang. 'From Post-Imperial to Late Communist Nationalism: Historical Change in Chinese Nationalism from May Fourth to the 1990s'. *Third World Quarterly*, 29/3 (2008), 467–82.

Wu, Guoguang. 'From the CCP Dilemma to the Xi Jinping Dilemma: The Chinese Regime's Capacity for Governance'. *China Leadership Monitor*, March 2020. https://www.prcleader.org/post/from-the-ccp-dilemma-to-the-xi-jinping-dilemma-the-chinese-regime-s-capacity-for-governance.

Wu, Guogang. 'The King's Men and Others: Emerging Political Elites under Xi Jinping'. *China Leadership Monitor*, no. 60 (2019). https://www.prcleader.org/issue-60.

Wu, Guogang. 'A Setback or Boost for Xi Jinping's Concentration of Power? Domination versus Resistance within the CCP Elite'. *China Leadership Monitor*, no. 58 (2018). https://www.prcleader.org/issue-58.

Wu, Guoguang, and Helen Lansdowne (eds.). *China's Transition from Communism: New Perspectives*. China Policy Series. London: Routledge, 2016.

Wu, Ming. *China's Future: A Biography of Xi Jinping*. Hong Kong: CNHK Publications, 2012.

Wübbeke, Jost, Mirjam Meissne, Max J. Zenglein, Jaqueline Ives, and Björn Conrad. 'Made in China 2025: The Making of a High-Tech Superpower and Consequences for Industrial Countries'. *MERICS*, August 2016. https://merics.org/en/report/made-china-2025.

Wuthnow, Joel C., and Phillip C. Saunders. 'Chinese Military Reform in the Age of Xi Jinping: Drivers, Challenges, and Implications'. *Center for the Study of Chinese Military Affairs, Institute for National Strategic Studies*, National Defense University, 2017. https://apps.dtic.mil/sti/citations/AD1030342.

Xiao, Hong, Zhicheng Wang, Fang Liu, and Joseph M. Unger. 'Excess All-Cause Mortality in China after Ending the Zero COVID Policy'. *JAMA Network Open*, 6/8 (August 2023), e2330877.

Xiao, Ren, and Liu Ming. 'Chinese Perspectives on International Relations in the Xi Jinping Era'. NBR Special Report. Seattle, WA: The National Bureau of Asian Research, June 2020.

Xiaolin, Duan. 'Unanswered Questions: Why We May Be Wrong about Chinese Nationalism and Its Foreign Policy Implications'. *Journal of Contemporary China*, 26/108 (November 2017), 886–900.

Xing, Guoxin. 'Hu Jintao's Political Thinking and Legitimacy Building: A Post-Marxist Perspective'. *Asian Affairs: An American Review*, 36/4 (November 2009), 213–26.

Xinhua. 'China Asks EU to Uphold Idea of Common Security'. *People's Daily*, March 2024. http://en.people.cn/n3/2024/0313/c90000-20144532.html.

Xinhua. 'China Celebrates 30th Anniversary of Landmark Reform, Opening-Up'. *CCTV*, 18 December 2008. https://www.cctv.com/english/20081218/104942.shtml.

Xinhua. 'China Focus: CPC "Democratic Life" Meeting Highlights Xi's Core Status'. *Xinhua*, 2017. http://www.xinhuanet.com/english/2017-12/27/c_136855573.htm.

Xinhua. 'China Introduces Supportive Policies to Aid Military Personnel in Child-Rearing'. *Xinhua*, 2023. https://english.news.cn/20230907/a7eebe551c434fcf9d3bb06cf148bdee/c.html.

Xinhua. 'China Should Adapt to New Norm of Growth: Xi'. *China Daily*, 11 May 2014. https://www.chinadaily.com.cn/china/2014-05/11/content_17498743.htm.

Xinhua. 'China to Rectify Problems in Political, Legal Organs'. *Xinhua*, 2020. http://www.xinhuanet.com/english/2020-07/09/c_139200533.htm.

Xinhua. 'China's Common Prosperity Boon to World'. *Xinhua*, 2021. http://www.news.cn/english/2021-12/21/c_1310386179.htm.

Xinhua. 'Chinese Landmark Concept Put into UN Resolution for First Time'. *Xinhua*, 2017. http://www.xinhuanet.com/english/2017-02/11/c_136049319.htm.

Xinhua. 'Chinese Mainland Reports 59,938 COVID-Related Deaths in Past 30-plus Days'. *Xinhua*, 2023. https://english.www.gov.cn/statecouncil/ministries/202301/15/content_WS63c34c70c6d0a757729e579d.html.

Xinhua. 'CPC Constitution Enshrines Xi's Thought as Part of Action Guide'. State Council, 2017. http://english.www.gov.cn/news/top_news/2017/10/24/content_281475919751341.htm.

Xinhua. 'CPC Creates Xi Jinping Thought on Socialism with Chinese Characteristics for a New Era'. *Chinadaily.com.cn*, 2017. https://www.chinadaily.com.cn/china/19thcpcnationalcongress/2017-10/19/content_33438132.htm.

Xinhua. 'CPC Issues Regulation on Democratic Life Meetings'. *Xinhua*, 12 January 2017. http://www.xinhuanet.com/english/2017-01/12/c_135977827.htm.

Xinhua. 'CPC Q&A: What Are China's Two Centennial Goals and Why Do They Matter?'. *Xinhua*, 17 October 2017. http://www.xinhuanet.com/english/2017-10/17/c_136686770.htm.

Xinhua. 'CPC Releases Plan on Deepening Reform of Party and State Institutions'. *People's Daily*, 2018. http://en.people.cn/n3/2018/0322/c90000-9440252.html.

Xinhua. 'Economic Watch: A Closer Look at Economic Potential behind China's Growth Target'. *China.org.cn*, 2024. http://www.china.org.cn/china/Off_the_Wire/2024-03/10/content_117051430.htm.

Xinhua. 'Global Civilization Initiative Injects Fresh Energy into Human Development'. *Xinhua*, 17 March 2023. https://english.news.cn/20230317/61e4529fd37744618a015db754c11f2f/c.html.

Xinhua. 'Highlights of China's Central Economic Work Conference'. *China Daily*, 12 December 2014. https://www.chinadaily.com.cn/bizchina/2014-12/12/content_19071364.htm.

Xinhua. 'Hong Kong Holds Activities to Mark National Security Education Day'. *Xinhua*, 16 April 2023. https://english.news.cn/20230416/66e18e3321274483a259af5fbab629cd/c.html.

Xinhua. 'Hu Makes 4-Point Proposal for Building Harmonious World'. *China.org.cn*, 2005. http://www.china.org.cn/english/features/UN/142408.htm.

Xinhua. 'New Normal to Be Logic of China's Future Growth'. *China Daily*, 11 December 2014. https://www.chinadaily.com.cn/business/2014-12/11/content_19068433.htm.

Xinhua. 'Party Members Called On to Unite around CPC Central Committee with Xi as "core"'. *Xinhua*, 27 October 2010. http://news.xinhuanet.com/english/2016-10/27/c_135785387.htm.

Xinhua. 'Senior Officials Urged to Uphold Leadership of CPC Central Committee'. *Xinhua*, 2017. http://www.xinhuanet.com/english/2017-10/27/c_136710693.htm.

Xinhua. 'To Revive China, Xi Holds High Banner of Socialism with Chinese Characteristics'. State Council (PRC), 28 September 2017. http://english.www.gov.cn/news/top_news/2017/09/28/content_281475890831923.htm.

Xinhua. 'Top Political Advisor Stresses Enduring Stability in Xinjiang'. *Xinhua*, 2021. http://www.xinhuanet.com/english/2021-03/17/c_139817479.htm.

Xinhua. 'Xi Calls for More Just, Equitable World Order at BRICS Forum'. *Xinhua*, 23 August 2023. https://english.news.cn/20230823/d3f806618f8249d49e00882004ab5e02/c.html.

Xinhua. 'Xi Eyes More Enabling Int'l Environment for China's Peaceful Development'. *Global Times*, 30 November 2014. https://www.globaltimes.cn/content/894240.shtml.

Xinhua. 'Xi Focus: How Will China Shape Its Development Strategy for New Stage?'. *Xinhua*, 27 August 2020. http://www.xinhuanet.com/english/2020-08/27/c_139320229.htm.

Xinhua. 'Xi Focus: Showing the Way Forward to Convey China's Stories Globally'. *Xinhua*, 2 July 2021. http://www.xinhuanet.com/english/2021-06/02/c_139985436.htm.

Xinhua. 'Xi Focus: Xi Announces China Aims to Achieve Carbon Neutrality before 2060'. *Xinhua*, September 2020. http://www.xinhuanet.com/english/2020-09/23/c_139388764.htm.

Xinhua. 'Xi Focus: Xi Explains New Development Pattern'. *Xinhua*, 3 November 2020. http://www.xinhuanet.com/english/2020-11/03/c_139488445.htm.

Xinhua. 'Xi Focus: Xi Jinping Thought on Diplomacy Guides China's Actions as Responsible Country amid Pandemic'. *Xinhua*, December 2020. http://www.xinhuanet.com/english/2020-12/19/c_139602993.htm.

Xinhua. 'Xi Focus: Xi Says China to Further Promote Common Prosperity'. *Xinhua*, 3 November 2020. http://www.xinhuanet.com/english/2020-11/03/c_139488141.htm.

Xinhua. 'Xi Focus: Xi Stresses Consolidating Achievements in Reform of Party, State Institutions'. *Xinhua*, 2019. http://www.xinhuanet.com/english/2019-07/05/c_138202514_2.htm.

Xinhua. 'Xi Focus: Xi Stresses Sticking to Socialist Rule of Law with Chinese Characteristics'. *Xinhua*, 18 November 2020. http://www.xinhuanet.com/english/2020-11/18/c_139523201.htm.

Xinhua. 'Xi Highlights Party Building in Central Party, State Institutions'. *Xinhua*, 9 July 2019. http://www.xinhuanet.com/english/2019-07/09/c_138212488_2.htm.

Xinhua. 'Xi Jinping Stressed Continuously Deepening the Principles-Based Understanding of the Party's Theoretical Innovation, and Obtaining More Fruitful Theoretical Innovation Accomplishments on the New Journey in the New Era at the Sixth Collective Study Session of the CCP Central Committee Politburo'. CSIS Interpret, June 2023. https://interpret.csis.org/translations/xi-jinping-stressed-continuously-deepening-the-principles-based-understanding-of-the-partys-theoretical-innovation-and-obtaining-more-fruitful-theoretical-innovation-accomplishments-on-the-n/.

Xinhua. 'Xi Jinping to Lead National Security Commission'. *Global Times*, January 2014. https://www.globaltimes.cn/content/839220.shtml.

Xinhua. 'Xi Meets Chinese Diplomatic Envoys to Foreign Countries'. *Xinhua*, December 2023. https://english.news.cn/20231230/f480edc53ce548dbb52bea9e242c9a64/c.html.

Xinhua. 'Xi Stresses Development of Marxist Economic Philosophy'. *China.org.cn*, 24 November 2015. http://www.china.org.cn/china/2015-11/24/content_37153593.htm.

Xinhua. 'Xi Urges Breaking New Ground in Major Country Diplomacy with Chinese Characteristics'. *Xinhua*, 2018. http://www.xinhuanet.com/english/2018-06/24/c_137276269.htm.

Xinning, Song. 'International Relations Theory-Building in China'. *Political Science*, 49/1 (July 1997), 40–61.

Xu, Beina, and Eleanor Albert. 'Media Censorship in China'. Council on Foreign Relations, 2017. https://www.cfr.org/backgrounder/media-censorship-china.

Xu, Jilin. 'The New Tianxia'. Reading the China Dream, 2015. https://www.readingthechinadream.com/xu-jilin-the-new-tianxia.html.

Yahuda, Michael. 'China's New Assertiveness in the South China Sea'. *Journal of Contemporary China*, 22/81 (May 2013), 446–59.

Yan, Xiaojun, and Jie Huang. 'Navigating Unknown Waters: The Chinese Communist Party's New Presence in the Private Sector'. *China Review*, 17/2 (2017), 37–63.

Yan, Xuetong. 'From Keeping a Low Profile to Striving for Achievement'. *Chinese Journal of International Politics*, 7/2 (June 2014), 153–84.

Yan, Xuetong. 'The Age of Uneasy Peace'. *Foreign Affairs*, 98/1 (December 2018). https://www.foreignaffairs.com/china/age-uneasy-peace.

Yan, Xuetong. 'Xunzi's and Kautilya's Thoughts on Inter-State Politics'. *Strategic Analysis*, 44/4 (July 2020), 299–311.

Yan, Xuetong. 'Chinese Values vs. Liberalism: What Ideology Will Shape the International Normative Order?'. *Chinese Journal of International Politics*, 11/1 (March 2018), 1–22.

Yan, Xuetong. 'Political Leadership and Power Redistribution'. *Chinese Journal of International Politics*, 9/1 (March 2016), 1–26.

Yan, Xuetong. 'Young Chinese College Students Often Condescending towards Foreign Countries'. Translated by David Cowhig. David Cowhig's Translation Blog, December 2022. https://gaodawei.wordpress.com/2022/01/12/yan-xuetong-young-chinese-college-students-often-down-on-other-countries/.

Yan, Xuetong, Daniel Bell, Zhe Sun, and Edmund Ryden. *Ancient Chinese Thought, Modern Chinese Power*. The Princeton-China Series. Princeton, NJ: Princeton University Press, 2013.

Yang, Jiemian. *China's Diplomacy: Theory and Practice*. Hackensack, NJ: World Century, 2014.

Yang, Jiemian. 'China's Foreign Policy under President Xi Jinping'. *Monde Chinois*, 49/1 (September 2017), 54–59.

Yang, Kai, and Stephan Ortmann. 'From Sweden to Singapore: The Relevance of Foreign Models for China's Rise'. *China Quarterly*, 236 (December 2018), 946–67.

Yang, Lijun, and Chee Kia Lim. 'Three Waves of Nationalism in Contemporary China: Sources, Themes, Presentations and Consequences'. EAI Working Paper 155. Singapore: East Asian Institute, 2010.

Yang, Xiangfeng. 'Domestic Contestation, International Backlash, and Authoritarian Resilience: How Did the Chinese Party-State Weather the COVID-19 Crisis?'. *Journal of Contemporary China*, 30/132 (November 2021), 915–29.

Yang, Yuan. 'Inside China's Crackdown on Young Marxists'. *Financial Times*, February 2019. https://www.ft.com/content/fd087484-2f23-11e9-8744-e7016697f225.

Yao, Kevin, and Ben Blanchard. 'Fearing Graft Probes, Chinese Officials Shun Spotlight, Seek Retirement'. *Reuters*, July 2014. https://www.reuters.com/article/idUSKBN0FD2GV/.

Yao, Kevin, and Ellen Zhang. 'China's 2022 Economic Growth One of the Worst on Record, Post-Pandemic Policy Faces Test'. *Reuters*, January 2023. https://www.reuters.com/world/china/chinas-economy-slows-sharply-q4-2022-growth-one-worst-record-2023-01-17/.

Yao, Yang. 'Beijing Consensus or Washington Consensus: What Explains China's Economic Success?'. *Development Outreach*, 13/1 (April 2011), 26–31.

Yates, Robin D. S. 'New Light on Ancient Chinese Military Texts: Notes on Their Nature and Evolution, and the Development of Military Specialization in Warring States China'. *T'oung Pao*, 74/4 (1988): 211–48.

Ye, Zicheng, Steven I. Levine, and Guoli Liu. *Inside China's Grand Strategy: The Perspective from the People's Republic*. Asia in the New Millennium. Lexington: University Press of Kentucky, 2011.

Yeo, Andrew. 'China's Rising Assertiveness and the Decline in the East Asian Regionalism Narrative'. *International Relations of the Asia-Pacific*, 20/3 (September 2020), 445–75.

Yi, Jiexiong, Josef Gregory Mahoney, and Xiuling Li. 'A Marxist Perspective on Chinese Reforms: Interview with Jiexiong Yi'. *Science & Society*, 73/2 (2009), 177–92.

Yu, Hairong. 'China Aims to Ease Property Crunch via New Affordable Housing Push'. *Nikkei Asia*, 2023. https://asia.nikkei.com/Spotlight/Caixin/China-aims-to-ease-property-crunch-via-new-affordable-housing-push.

Yu, Jie (ed.). 'From Deng to Xi: Economic Reform, the Silk Road, and the Return of the Middle Kingdom'. London: London School of Economics, 2017. https://www.lse.ac.uk/ideas/Assets/Documents/reports/LSE-IDEAS-From-Deng-to-Xi.pdf.

Yu, Verna. '"We in the West Were Blinded": China Crackdown on Business Has Maoist Roots'. *The Guardian*, May 2023. https://www.theguardian.com/world/2023/may/21/china-expert-chris-marquis-tech-crackdown-xi-maoism.

Yuan, Zaijun. *The Failure of China's Democratic Reforms*. Challenges Facing Chinese Political Development. Lanham, MD: Lexington Books, 2012.

Yuen, Samson. 'Disciplining the Party: Xi Jinping's Anti-Corruption Campaign and Its Limits'. *China Perspectives*, 2014/3 (September 2014), 41–47.

Yuji, Nitta. 'South Korea's Lotte Opens Hanoi Mall in Vietnam Investment Drive'. *Nikkei Asia*, September 2023. https://asia.nikkei.com/Business/Retail/South-Korea-s-Lotte-opens-Hanoi-mall-in-Vietnam-investment-drive.

Zarrow, Peter Gue. *After Empire: The Conceptual Transformation of the Chinese State, 1885–1924*. Stanford, CA: Stanford University Press, 2012.

Zembilci, Eilish, Adrien Chorn, Victoria DeSimone, Caleb Diamond, Claire Felten, Jonas Heering, Ann Listerud, et al. 'New Perspectives in Foreign Policy Issue 18'. *CSIS*, October 2019. https://www.csis.org/analysis/new-perspectives-foreign-policy-issue-18.

Zenglein, Max J., and Anna Holzmann. 'Evolving Made in China 2025'. *MERICS*, 2019. https://merics.org/en/report/evolving-made-china-2025.

Zenz, Adrian. 'Thoroughly Reforming Them towards a Healthy Heart Attitude'. *Central Asian Survey*, 38/1 (2019)

Zhang, Changdong. 'A Fiscal Sociological Theory of Authoritarian Resilience: Developing Theory through China Case Studies'. *Sociological Theory*, 35/1 (2017): 39–63.

Zhang, Chunlin. 'How Much Do State-Owned Enterprises Contribute to China's GDP and Employment?'. Washington, DC: World Bank, 2019.

Zhang, Feng. 'Rethinking China's Grand Strategy: Beijing's Evolving National Interests and Strategic Ideas in the Reform Era'. *International Politics*, 49/3 (May 2012), 318–45.

Zhang, Feng. 'Striving for Power: Chinese Foreign Policy in Xi Jinping's "New Era"'. *The Strategist*, November 2017. https://www.aspistrategist.org.au/striving-for-power-chinese-foreign-policy-in-xi-jinpings-new-era/.

Zhang, Fenzhi. *Xi Jinping: How to Read Confucius and Other Chinese Classical Thinkers*. New York: CN Times Books, 2015.

Zhang, Tao. 'When Marx Met Confucius: Xi Jinping's Attempt to Influence China's Intellectual Loyalties Has Met with a Mixed Reception at Home and Abroad'. *The Conversation*, 10

November 2023. https://theconversation.com/when-marx-met-confucius-xi-jinpings-attempt-to-influence-chinas-intellectual-loyalties-has-met-with-a-mixed-reception-at-home-and-abroad-216568

Zhang, Qingmin. 'Towards an Integrated Theory of Chinese Foreign Policy: Bringing Leadership Personality Back In'. *Journal of Contemporary China*, 23/89 (September 2014), 902–22.

Zhang, Weihong. 'China's Cultural Future: From Soft Power to Comprehensive National Power'. *International Journal of Cultural Policy*, 16/4 (November 2010), 383–402.

Zhang, Yongjin. 'Introduction: Dynamism and Contention: Understanding Chinese Foreign Policy under Xi Jinping'. *International Affairs*, 92/4 (July 2016), 769–72.

Zhang, Zhihao. 'Corruption Investigation into Official Begins'. *China Daily*. 4 October 2021. https://www.chinadailyhk.com/hk/article/241390

Zhao, Quansheng. 'Chinese Foreign Policy in the Post–Cold War Era'. *World Affairs*, 159/ 3 (1997), 114–29.

Zhao, Suisheng. *A Nation-State by Construction: Dynamics of Modern Chinese Nationalism*. Stanford, CA: Stanford University Press, 2004.

Zhao, Suisheng. 'China's Pragmatic Nationalism: Is It Manageable?'. *Washington Quarterly*, 29/1 (2005), 131–44.

Zhao, Suisheng. 'Chinese Nationalism and Its International Orientations'. *Political Science Quarterly*, 115/1 (March 2000), 1–33.

Zhao, Suisheng. 'Chinese Foreign Policy under Hu Jintao: The Struggle between Low-Profile Policy and Diplomatic Activism'. *The Hague Journal of Diplomacy*, 5/4 (2010), 357–78.

Zhao, Suisheng. 'Foreign Policy Implications of Chinese Nationalism Revisited: The Strident Turn'. *Journal of Contemporary China*, 22/82 (July 2013), 535–53.

Zhao, Suisheng. 'Hu Jintao's Foreign Policy Legacy'. *E-International Relations*, December 2012. https://www.e-ir.info/pdf/30673.

Zhao, Suisheng. 'The Ideological Campaign in Xi's China'. *Asian Survey*, 56/6 (December 2016), 1168–93.

Zhao, Suisheng. 'A State-Led Nationalism: The Patriotic Education Campaign in Post-Tiananmen China'. *Communist and Post-Communist Studies*, 31/3 (September 1998), 287–302.

Zhao, Suisheng. 'Xi Jinping's Maoist Revival'. *Journal of Democracy*, 27/3 (2016). https://www.journalofdemocracy.org/articles/xi-jinpings-maoist-revival/.

Zhao, Tingyang. *World System: An Introduction to Philosophy of the World System (Chinese Edition)*'. Nanjing: Jiangsu Education Publishing House, 2011.

Zhao, Tingyang. 'Can This Ancient Chinese Philosophy Save Us from Global Chaos?'. *Washington Post*, October 2021. https://www.washingtonpost.com/news/theworldpost/wp/2018/02/07/tianxia/.

Zhen, Summer. 'What Xi's Congress Message Means for China's Housing Market'. *South China Morning Post*, October 2017. https://www.scmp.com/business/article/2116621/what-president-xis-congress-message-means-chinas-housing-market.

Zheng, Bijian. 'China's "Peaceful Rise" to Great-Power Status'. *Foreign Affairs*, 84/5 (September 2005).

Zheng, William. 'China's Top Law Enforcement Body Unveils Campaign to Purge "Corrupt Elements"', *South China Morning Post*. 10 July 2020. https://www.scmp.com/news/china/politics/article/3092559/chinas-top-law-enforcement-body-unveils-campaign-purge-corrupt

Zheng, William. 'Chinese Official Leading Security Purge "May Be on Fast Track to Promotion", Analysts Say', *South China Morning Post*. 17 July 2020. https://www.scmp.com/news/china/politics/article/3093711/chinese-official-leading-security-purge-may-be-fast-track.

Zheng, William. 'Journalists in Chinese State Media to Be Tested on Loyalty to President Xi Jinping'. *South China Morning Post*. 19 September 2019. https://www.scmp.com/news/china/politics/article/3028152/journalists-chinese-state-media-be-tested-loyalty-president-xi

Zheng, William. 'Why Former Chinese Leader Hu Jintao Was Highest Profile Absentee from Jiang Zemin's Funeral'. *South China Morning Post*, December 2022. https://www.scmp.com/news/china/politics/article/3202287/why-former-chinese-leader-hu-jintao-was-highest-profile-absentee-jiang-zemins-funeral.

Zheng, Yongnian. *The Chinese Communist Party as Organizational Emperor: Culture, Reproduction and Transformation*. China Policy Series. London: Routledge, 2010.

Zheng, Yongnian, and Lance Gore (eds.). *China Entering the Xi Jinping Era*. China Policy Series. London: Routledge, 2015.

Zheng, Yongnian, (ed.). *China and International Relations*. London: Routledge, 2010.

Zhong, Isabella Jingwen. 'How Are Foreign NGOs Getting On in China after Four Years of Reform?', *China Development Brief*. 21 January 2021. https://chinadevelopmentbrief.org/reports/how-are-foreign-ngos-getting-on-in-china-after-four-years-of-reform

Zhong, Yang, and Wonjae Hwang. 'Why Do Chinese Democrats Tend to Be More Nationalistic? Explaining Popular Nationalism in Urban China'. *Journal of Contemporary China*, 29/121 (January 2020), 61–74.

Zhou, Kate Xiao, Shelley Rigger, and Lynn T. White (eds.). *Democratization in China, Korea and Southeast Asia? Local and National Perspectives*. Politics in Asia. London: Routledge, 2017.

Zhou, Lin. 'Chinese Economy Embraces Supply-Side Reform', *China Today*, 1 June 2016. http://www.china.org.cn/business/2016-06/01/content_38580732_2.htm

Zhou, Pingjian. 'Communist Party of China Turns 100 and Still Going Strong'. Ministry of Foreign Affairs (PRC), June 2021. https://www.mfa.gov.cn/eng/wjb_663304/zwjg_665342/zwbd_665378/202106/t20210622_9169743.html.

Zhou, Shanding. *Changes of the Chinese Communist Party's Ideology and Reform since 1978*. Brisbane: Griffith University, 2012.

Zhou, Xueguang. *The Logic of Governance in China: An Organizational Approach*. Cambridge: Cambridge University Press, 2022.

Zhou, Xueguang. 'Partial Reform and the Chinese Bureaucracy in the Post-Mao Era.' *Comparative Political Studies* 28, no. 3 (October 1995), 440–68.

Zhou, Xueguang. 'The Separation of Officials from Local Staff: The Logic of the Empire and Personnel Management in the Chinese Bureaucracy'. *Chinese Journal of Sociology*, 2/2 (April 2016), 259–99.

Zou, Keyuan. 'Building a "Harmonious World": A Mission Impossible?'. *Copenhagen Journal of Asian Studies*, 30/2 (February 2014), 74–99.

Zumbrun, Josh. 'How China Made a Youth Unemployment Crisis Disappear'. *Wall Street Journal*, December 2023. https://www.wsj.com/world/china/how-china-made-a-youth-unemployment-crisis-disappear-32afa255.

1.3. Data

CSIS China Power project: https://chinapower.csis.org/maritime-forces-destabilizing-asia/.

Election Study Center at National Chengchi University. *Taiwanese Public Opinion Polling on Independence and Reunification with the Mainland*: https://esc.nccu.edu.tw/PageDoc/Detail?fid=7801&id=6963.

Freedom on the Net, Freedom House: https://freedomhouse.org/sites/default/files/2023-10/FOTN%202011-2023%20Score%20Data.xlsx.

Good Car Bad Car. 'Brand Sales (by Market)': https://www.goodcarbadcar.net/category/report-types/brand-sales/.

Ministry of Defense Joint Staff (Japan). 'Statistics on Scrambles': https://www.mod.go.jp/j/result.html?q="Statistics+on+scrambles"

Japan Coast Guard. 'The Numbers of China Coast Guard and Other Vessels That Entered Japan's Contiguous Zone or Intruded into Territorial Sea Surrounding the Senkaku Islands': https://www.kaiho.mlit.go.jp/mission/senkaku/senkaku.html.

Ministry of National Defense (ROC). 'PLA Activities in the Waters and Airspace around Taiwan': https://air.mnd.gov.tw/EN/News/News_List.aspx?CID=214.

OECD data: https://data.oecd.org/.

Pew Research Center. 'Religious Composition by Country, 2010–2050': https://www.pewresearch.org/religion/interactives/religious-composition-by-country-2010-2050.

Pew Research Center. 'Comparing Views of the U.S. and China in 24 Countries': https://www.pewresearch.org/global/2023/11/06/comparing-views-of-the-us-and-china-in-24-countries/.

Shanghai Stock Exchange. 'Overseas Investors Ownership Statistics': http://english.sse.com.cn/access/statistics/.
Stockholm International Peace Research Institute. 'SIPRI Military Expenditure Database': https://milex.sipri.org/.
United Nations Department of Economic and Social Affairs. 'World Population Prospects': https://population.un.org/wpp/Download/Standard/Population/.
United Nations revenue: https://open.un.org/un-systems-financials/revenue.
World Bank economic data: https://data.worldbank.org.
World Bank Country and Lending Groups: https://datahelpdesk.worldbank.org/knowledgebase/articles/906519-world-bank-country-and-lending-groups
World Data Lab. 'World Emissions Clock': https://worldemissions.io/.
YouGov Cambridge. Globalism 2022 Survey: https://d3nkl3psvxxpe9.cloudfront.net/documents/Globalism_2022_-_China_and_country_reputation_-_Annual_comparison.pdf.

Part 2: Chinese-Language Sources

2.1. Chinese-Language Primary Sources

三个历史决议（1945, 1981, 2021）以及相关历史文件
《关于若干历史问题的决议（一九四五年四月二十日中国共产党第六届中央委员会扩大的第七次全体会议通过）》, https://www.12371.cn/2021/11/09/ARTI1636455732201149.shtml.
《中国共产党第十一届中央委员会第三次全体会议公报》, 1978,
http://cpc.people.com.cn/GB/64162/64168/64563/65371/4441902.html.
《关于建国以来党的若干历史问题的决议（一九八一年六月二十七日中国共产党第十一届中央委员会第六次全体会议一致通过）》, https://www.gov.cn/test/2008-06/23/content_1024934.htm.
《中共中央关于党的百年奋斗重大成就和历史经验的决议（2021年11月11日中国共产党第十九届中央委员会第六次全体会议通过）》, http://www.gov.cn/zhengce/2021-11/16/content_5651269.htm.
中共中央文献研究室：《三中全会以来重要文献选编（上）》,北京：人民出版社1982年版。
中共中央文献研究室：《三中全会以来重要文献选编（下）》,北京：人民出版社1982年版。
邓小平：《在武昌、深圳、珠海、上海等地的谈话要点（一九九二年一月十八日——二月二十一日）》, http://www.reformdata.org/1992/0118/1801.shtml.

十四大至二十大党代会报告（1992-2022）

十四大报告：《加快改革开放和现代化建设步伐,夺取有中国特色社会主义事业的更大胜利——. 在中国共产党第十四次全国代表大会上的报告（1992年10月12日）》, http://cpc.people.com.cn/GB/64162/64168/64567/65446/4526308.html.
十五大报告：《高举邓小平理论伟大旗帜,把建设有中国特色社会主义事业全面推向二十一世纪——. 在中国共产党第十五次全国代表大会上的报告（1997年9月12日）》, http://cpc.people.com.cn/GB/64162/64168/64568/65445/4526285.html.
十六大报告：《全面建设小康社会,开创中国特色社会主义事业新局面——. 在中国共产党第十六次全国代表大会上的报告（2002年11月8日）》, http://www.gov.cn/test/2008-08/01/content_1061490.htm.
十七大报告：《高举中国特色社会主义伟大旗帜 为夺取全面建设小康社会新胜利而奋斗——. 在中国共产党第十七次全国代表大会上的报告（2007年10月15日）》, http://www.lswz.gov.cn/html/zhuanti/17da/20071026l-1.html.
十八大报告：《坚定不移沿着中国特色社会主义道路前进 为全面建成小康社会而奋斗——. 在中国共产党第十八次全国代表大会上的报告（2012年11月8日）》, http://www.gov.cn/ldhd/2012-11/17/content_2268826.htm.
十九大报告：《决胜全面建成小康社会 夺取新时代中国特色社会主义伟大胜利——. 在中国共产党第十九次全国代表大会上的报告（2017年10月18日）》, http://www.gov.cn/zhuanti/2017-10/27/content_5234876.htm.

二十大报告:《高举中国特色社会主义伟大旗帜　为全面建设社会主义现代化国家而团结奋斗——在中国共产党第二十次全国代表大会上的报告(2017年10月18日)》, https://www.gov.cn/xinwen/2022-10/25/content_5721685.htm.
各届党代会报告(一大至二十大), http://cpc.people.com.cn/GB/64162/64168/index.html.
'历次党代会专题网站', http://www.12371.cn/special/lcddh/.

十八-二十届中央全会历次公报(2012–2024)

十八届一中全会:《中国共产党第十八届中央委员会第一次全体会议公报(2012年11月15日中国共产党第十八届中央委员会第一次全体会议通过)》, http://www.xinhuanet.com//18cpcnc/2012-11/15/c_113697156.htm.
十八届二中全会:《中国共产党第十八届中央委员会第二次全体会议公报(2013年2月28日中国共产党第十八届中央委员会第二次全体会议通过)》, http://www.gov.cn/ldhd/2013-02/28/content_2342267.htm.
十八届三中全会:《中国共产党第十八届中央委员会第三次全体会议公报(2013年11月12日中国共产党第十八届中央委员会第三次全体会议通过)》, https://www.gov.cn/hudong/2015-06/09/content_2875841.htm.
十八届四中全会:《中国共产党第十八届中央委员会第四次全体会议公报(2014年10月23日中国共产党第十八届中央委员会第四次全体会议通过)》, http://news.12371.cn/2014/10/23/ARTI1414063058032813.shtml.
十八届五中全会:《中国共产党第十八届中央委员会第五次全体会议公报(2015年10月29日中国共产党第十八届中央委员会第五次全体会议通过)》, https://news.12371.cn/2015/10/29/ARTI1446118588896178.shtml.
十八届六中全会:《中国共产党第十八届中央委员会第六次全体会议公报(2016年10月27日中国共产党第十八届中央委员会第六次全体会议通过)》, https://www.gov.cn/xinwen/2016-10/27/content_5125093.htm.
十八届七中全会:《中国共产党第十八届中央委员会第七次全体会议公报(2017年10月14日中国共产党第十八届中央委员会第七次全体会议通过)》, http://www.gov.cn/zhuanti/2017-10/14/content_5231758.htm.
十九届一中全会:《中国共产党第十九届中央委员会第一次全体会议公报(2017年10月25日中国共产党第十九届中央委员会第一次全体会议通过)》, http://www.gov.cn/zhuanti/2017-10/25/content_5234340.htm#1.
十九届二中全会:《中国共产党第十九届中央委员会第二次全体会议公报(2018年1月19日中国共产党第十九届中央委员会第二次全体会议通过)》, http://www.gov.cn/xinwen/2018-01/19/content_5258601.htm.
十九届三中全会:《中国共产党第十九届中央委员会第三次全体会议公报(2018年2月28日中国共产党第十九届中央委员会第三次全体会议通过)》, http://www.gov.cn/xinwen/2018-02/28/content_5269534.htm.
十九届四中全会:《中国共产党第十九届中央委员会第四次全体会议公报(2019年10月31日中国共产党第十九届中央委员会第四次全体会议通过)》, http://www.xinhuanet.com/english/2019-10/31/c_138518832.htm.
十九届五中全会:《中国共产党第十九届中央委员会第五次全体会议公报(2020年10月29日中国共产党第十九届中央委员会第五次全体会议通过)》, http://www.xinhuanet.com/politics/2020-10/29/c_1126674147.htm.
十九届六中全会:《中国共产党第十九届中央委员会第六次全体会议公报(2021年11月11日中国共产党第十九届中央委员会第六次全体会议通过)》, http://www.news.cn/politics/2021-11/11/c_1128055386.htm.
十九届七中全会:《中国共产党第十九届中央委员会第七次全体会议公报(2022年10月12日中国共产党第十九届中央委员会第六次全体会议通过)》, https://www.gov.cn/xinwen/2022-10/12/content_5717943.htm.
二十届一中全会:《中国共产党第二十届中央委员会第一次全体会议公报(2022年10月23日中国共产党第二十届中央委员会第一次全体会议通过)》, https://www.gov.cn/gongbao/content/2022/content_5722379.htm.

二十届二中全会：中国共产党第二十届中央委员会第二次全体会议公报（2023年2月28日中国共产党第二十届中央委员会第二次全体会议通过），https://www.gov.cn/xinwen/2023-02/28/content_5743717.htm.

十八-二十届中央全会重要决议（2012–2024）

《国务院机构改革和职能转变方案》,十八届二中全会通过，2013年3月，http://www.gov.cn/2013lh/content_2354443.htm.
《中共中央关于全面深化改革若干重大问题的决定》,十八届三中全会通过，2013年11月，http://www.gov.cn/jrzg/2013-11/15/content_2528179.htm.
《中共中央关于全面推进依法治国若干重大问题的决定》,十八届四中全会通过，2014年10月，http://www.gov.cn/zhengce/2014-10/28/content_2771946.htm.
《中共中央关于制定国民经济和社会发展第十二个五年规划的建议》,十七届五中全会通过，2010年10月, https://www.gov.cn/jrzg/2010-10/27/content_1731694_2.htm.
'国民经济和社会发展第十二个五年规划纲要(全文)', 2011, https://www.gov.cn/2011lh/content_1825838.htm.
《中共中央关于制定国民经济和社会发展第十三个五年规划的建议》,十八届五中全会通过，2015年10月, http://www.gov.cn/xinwen/2015-11/03/content_2959432.htm.
《中华人民共和国国民经济和社会发展第十三个五年规划纲要》，2016年3月，https://www.gov.cn/xinwen/2016-03/17/content_5054992.htm.
《关于新形势下党内政治生活的若干准则》、《中国共产党党内监督条例》,十八届六中全会通过，2016年10月，https://news.12371.cn/2016/11/02/ARTI1478091665764299.shtml, https://news.12371.cn/2016/11/02/ARTI1478087905680175.shtml.
《中共中央关于修改宪法部分内容的建议》,十九届二中全会通过，2018年1月，http://www.gov.cn/xinwen/2018-02/25/content_5268679.htm.
《中共中央关于深化党和国家机构改革的决定》、《深化党和国家机构改革方案》,十九届三中全会通过，2018年2月，http://www.gov.cn/zhengce/2018-03/04/content_5270704.htm, http://www.gov.cn/zhengce/2018-03/21/content_5276191.htm#1.
《中共中央关于坚持和完善中国特色社会主义制度、推进国家治理体系和治理能力现代化若干重大问题的决定》,十九届四中全会通过，2019年10月，http://www.gov.cn/zhengce/2019-11/05/content_5449023.htm.
《中共中央关于制定国民经济和社会发展第十四个五年规划和二〇三五年远景目标的建议》,十九届五中全会通过, 2020年10月, http://www.gov.cn/zhengce/2020-11/03/content_5556991.htm.
《关于<中共中央关于制定国民经济和社会发展第十四个五年规划和二〇三五年远景目标的建议>的说明》, 2020年11月, http://www.xinhuanet.com/politics/2020-11/03/c_1126693341.htm.
《中华人民共和国国民经济和社会发展第十四个五年规划和2035年远景目标纲要》，2021年3月，http://www.gov.cn/xinwen/2021-03/13/content_5592681.htm.
《党和国家机构改革方案》, 中共二十届二中全会通过, 2022年10月, 2023年3月印发, http://www.news.cn/politics/2022-10/22/c_1129075493.htm.

中央经济会议官方通告文（1994–2024）

《1994年中央经济工作会议》，1994, http://www.ce.cn/zhuanti/caijing/hgjj/zygzhy/pages/1994zhongyang.htm.
《1995年中央经济工作会议》, 1995, https://www.gov.cn/test/2008-12/05/content_1168802.htm.
《1996年中央经济工作会议》, 1996, https://www.gov.cn/test/2008-12/05/content_1168803.htm.
《1997年中央经济工作会议》, 1997, https://www.gov.cn/test/2008-12/05/content_1168840.htm.
《1998年中央经济工作会议》, 1998, https://www.gov.cn/test/2008-12/05/content_1168856.htm.
《1999年中央经济工作会议》, 1999, https://www.gov.cn/test/2008-12/05/content_1168875.htm.
《2000中央经济工作会议》, 2000, http://www.71.cn/2015/1218/791768.shtml.
《2001中央经济工作会议》, 2001, http://www.71.cn/2015/1218/791769.shtml.
《2002年中央经济工作会议》, 2002, http://www.ce.cn/zhuanti/caijing/hgjj/zygzhy/pages/2002zhongyang.htm.

《中央经济工作会议在北京举行》, 2003, https://www.gov.cn/test/2005-07/04/content_11782.htm.
《中央经济工作会议召开,胡锦涛温家宝作重要讲话》, 2004, https://finance.sina.com.cn/g/20041205/19501203082.shtml.
《2005中央经济工作会议》, 2005, https://www.gov.cn/test/2008-12/05/content_1168954.htm.
《中央经济工作会议12月5日至12月7日在北京召开》, 2006, https://news.sina.com.cn/c/2006-12-08/090510714433s.shtml.
《中央经济工作会议在北京召开, 胡锦涛温家宝作重要讲话, 吴邦国贾庆林李长春习近平李克强贺国强周永康出席会议》, 2007, http://www.npc.gov.cn/zgrdw/npc/xinwen/syxw/2007-12/06/content_1382121.htm.
《中央经济工作会议在北京召开, 胡锦涛温家宝作重要讲话, 吴邦国贾庆林李长春习近平李克强贺国强周永康出席会议》, 2008, http://www.npc.gov.cn/zgrdw/npc/wbgwyz/content_1615813.htm.
《中央经济工作会议举行, 胡锦涛、温家宝作重要讲话》, 2009, http://www.lswz.gov.cn/html/zhuanti/n16/n3615/n3631/4425878.html.
《中央经济工作会议在京举行》, 2010, http://niigata.china-consulate.gov.cn/gdxw/201012/t20101215_5533342.htm.
《中央经济工作会议在北京举行, 胡锦涛吴邦国等出席》, 2011, http://www.npc.gov.cn/zgrdw/npc/xinwen/syxw/2011-12/15/content_1682023.htm.
《2012年中央经济工作会议(2012年12月15日-16日)》, 2012, http://www.qizhiwang.org.cn/n1/2022/0411/c443710-32396360.html.
《2013年中央经济工作会议(2013年12月10日-13日)》, 2013, http://www.qizhiwang.org.cn/n1/2022/0411/c443710-32396384.html.
《2014年中央经济工作会议(2014年12月9日-11日)》, 2014, http://www.qizhiwang.org.cn/n1/2022/0411/c443710-32396406.html.
《2015年中央经济工作会议(2015年12月18日-21日)》, 2015, http://www.qizhiwang.org.cn/n1/2022/0412/c443710-32396753.html.
《2016年中央经济工作会议(2016年12月14日-16日)》, 2016, http://www.qizhiwang.org.cn/n1/2022/0412/c443710-32396875.html.
《2017年中央经济工作会议(2017年12月18日-20日)》, 2017, http://www.qizhiwang.org.cn/n1/2022/0412/c443710-32396899.html.
《2018年中央经济工作会议(2018年12月19日-21日)》, 2018, http://www.qizhiwang.org.cn/n1/2022/0412/c443710-32396947.html.
《2019年中央经济工作会议(2019年12月10日-12日)》, 2019, http://www.qizhiwang.org.cn/n1/2022/0412/c443710-32396974.html.
《2020年中央经济工作会议(2020年12月16日-18日)》, 2020, http://www.qizhiwang.org.cn/n1/2022/0412/c443710-32396984.html.
《2021年中央经济工作会议(2021年12月8日-10日)》, 2021, http://www.qizhiwang.org.cn/n1/2022/0412/c443710-32397010.html.
《中央经济工作会议举行, 习近平李克强李强作重要讲话》, 2022, https://www.gov.cn/xinwen/2022-12/16/content_5732408.htm.
《中央经济工作会议在北京举行, 习近平发表重要讲话》, 2023, http://www.news.cn/politics/leaders/2023-12/12/c_1130022917.htm.

其它政策文件/法律法规/党纪党规

《关于党内政治生活的若干准则(1980年2月29日中国共产党第十一届中央委员会第五次全体会议通过)》, 1980, https://news.12371.cn/2015/03/11/ARTI1426059362559711.shtml.
《中共九号文件:关于当前意识形态领域情况的通报》, 2013.
'习近平"近平""3讲话精神传达提纲全文'话精神传达提纲全文'意识形态领域情况的通报2015/03/11/ARTI1426059362559711.shtmlnet, 2013, https://chinadigitaltimes.net/space/%E4%B9%A0%E8%BF%91%E5%B9%B3%228%C2%B719%22%E8%AE%B2%E8%AF%9D%E7%B2%BE%E7%A5%9E%E4%BC%A0%E8%BE%BE%E6%8F%90%E7%BA%B2%E5%85%A8%E6%96%87.

《中共中央关于全面深化改革若干重大问题的决定》, 2013, http://www.gov.cn/jrzg/2013-11/15/content_2528179.htm.

《中办发〔2013〕9号关于当前意识形态领域情况的通报 》, *hndj.gov.cn*, 16 May 2013, https://web.archive.org/web/20130615122048/http://www.hndj.gov.cn/html/jgdj/gzkx/2013/5168269.htm.（ See also:《学习贯彻习近平总书记重要讲话精神,巩固深化党和国家机构改革成果》, 求是, 2019, http://www.qstheory.cn/dukan/qs/2019-07/16/c_1124750268.htm）.

《国务院关于印发《中国制造2025》的通知' (Made in China 2025)》, 2015年5月, https://www.gov.cn/zhengce/content/2015-05/19/content_9784.htm.

'中共中央关于繁荣发展社会主义文艺的意见', 中国政府网, 2015, https://www.gov.cn/xinwen/2015-10/19/content_2950086.htm.

《中共中央国务院关于深化国有企业改革的指导意见》, 2015, http://www.gov.cn/zhengce/2015-09/13/content_2930440.htm.

《关于国有企业功能界定与分类的指导意见(国资发研究[2015]170号)》, 2015, http://www.sasac.gov.cn/n2588035/n2588320/n2588335/c4258285/content.html.

《国务院办公厅关于推动中央企业结构调整与重组的指导意见, 国办发 》, 2016, https://www.gov.cn/zhengce/content/2016-07/26/content_5095050.htm.

《中国共产党党内监督条例(2016年10月27日中国共产党第十八届中央委员会第六次全体会议通过)》, https://news.12371.cn/2016/11/02/ARTI1478087905680175.shtml.

《关于新形势下党内政治生活的若干准则(2016年10月27日中国共产党第十八届中央委员会第六次全体会议通过)》, https://news.12371.cn/2016/11/02/ARTI1478091665764299.shtml.

《国务院办公厅关于进一步完善国有企业法人治理结构的指导意见》, 2017, https://www.gov.cn/zhengce/content/2017-05/03/content_5190599.htm.

《中国共产党第十九次全国代表大会关于《中国共产党章程（修正案）》的决议（2017年10月24日中国共产党第十九次全国代表大会通过） 》, http://www.xinhuanet.com/politics/2017-10/24/c_1121850042.htm.

《中国共产党纪律处分条例》修订前后对照表, 2018, http://www.xinhuanet.com/politics/2018-08/27/c_1123332297.htm.

《中国共产党支部工作条例（试行）》, 2018, http://politics.people.com.cn/n1/2018/1126/c1001-30420219.html.

《中共中央关于深化党和国家机构改革的决定》, 2018, http://www.xinhuanet.com/politics/2018-03/04/c_1122485476.htm.

《中华人民共和国宪法》, 2018,
http://www.xinhuanet.com/politics/2018lh/2018-03/22/c_1122572202.htm.

《中华人民共和国宪法修正案》, 2018, http://www.npc.gov.cn/zgrdw/npc/xinwen/2018-03/12/content_2049190.htm.

《中国共产党问责条例》, 2019, http://www.xinhuanet.com/politics/2019-09/04/c_1124961071.htm.

《中共中央印发<中国共产党政法工作条例>》, 2019, https://www.gov.cn/zhengce/2019-01/18/content_5359135.htm.

《中共中央关于加强党的政治建设的意见》, 2019, http://www.gov.cn/zhengce/2019-02/27/content_5369070.htm.

《中华人民共和国公职人员政务处分法》, 2020, http://www.npc.gov.cn/npc/c30834/202006/2ce1931bad6d479192a00072ee67b9da9.shtml.

中共中央办公厅印发《关于加强新时代民营经济统战工作的意见》, *Xinhua*, September 2020, http://www.xinhuanet.com/politics/2020-09/15/c_1126497384.htm.

《中国共产党第二十次全国代表大会关于<中国共产党章程（修正案）>的决议》, 中国共产党第二十次全国代表大会通过, 2022年10月, http://www.news.cn/politics/2022-10/22/c_1129075493.htm.

《中华人民共和国国务院组织法》, 2024年3月11日修订通过, http://www.npc.gov.cn/rdxwzx/xwzx2024/xwzx2024014/202403/t20240312_435968.htm.

领导人文选与讲话（毛泽东、邓小平、江泽民、胡锦涛）

毛泽东：《毛泽东选集》（第一卷）,北京：人民出版社1991年版。

毛泽东：《毛泽东选集》（第二卷），北京：人民出版社1991年版。
毛泽东：《毛泽东选集》（第三卷），北京：人民出版社1991年版。
毛泽东：《毛泽东选集》（第四卷），北京：人民出版社1991年版。
毛泽东：《毛泽东选集》（第七卷），北京：人民出版社1991年版。
邓小平：《邓小平文选》（第一卷），北京：人民出版社1994年版。
邓小平：《邓小平文选》（第二卷），北京：人民出版社1994年版。
邓小平：《邓小平文选》（第三卷），北京：人民出版社1993年版。
邓小平：'邓小平在联大第六届特别会议上的发言', *12371.cn*, https://news.12371.cn/2015/09/28/ARTI1443384874163974.shtml?ticket=.
江泽民：《江泽民文选》（第一卷），北京：人民出版社2006年版。
江泽民：《江泽民文选》（第二卷），北京：人民出版社2006年版。
江泽民：《江泽民文选》（第三卷），北京：人民出版社2006年版。
胡锦涛：《胡锦涛文选》（第一卷），北京：人民出版社2016年版。
胡锦涛：《胡锦涛文选》（第二卷），北京：人民出版社2016年版。
胡锦涛：《胡锦涛文选》（第三卷），北京：人民出版社2016年版。
胡锦涛：'胡锦涛主持政治局学习强调保证群众行使民主权利', 2006, http://big5.www.gov.cn/gate/big5/www.gov.cn/govweb/ldhd/2006-12/01/content_459661.htm.
胡锦涛：'胡锦涛勉励中国企业坚决走出去', http://www.chinanews.com/gn/news/2009/02-12/1559609.shtml.
胡锦涛：'胡锦涛在第四轮中美战略与经济对话开幕式上的致辞', 2013, http://www.gov.cn/ldhd/2012-05/03/content_2129121.htm.
胡锦涛：'胡锦涛在中央党校发表重要讲话', http://www.xinhuanet.com//18CCPnc/2012-11/08/c_113636061.htm.

领导人文选（习近平）

习近平：《习近平谈治国理政》（第一卷），北京：外文出版社2014年版。
习近平：《习近平谈治国理政》（第二卷），北京：外文出版社2017年版。
习近平：《习近平谈治国理政》（第三卷），北京：外文出版社2020年版。
习近平：《习近平谈治国理政》（第四卷），北京：外文出版社2023年版。
《习近平关于党的群众路线教育实践活动论述摘编》，北京：党建读物出版社、中央文献出版社2014年版。
《习近平关于全面深化改革论述摘编》，北京：中央文献出版社2014年版。
《习近平关于党风廉政建设和反腐败斗争论述摘编》，北京：中央文献出版社2015年版。
《习近平关于全面依法治国论述摘编》，北京：中央文献出版社2015年版。
《习近平关于协调推进'四个全面'战略布局论述摘编》，北京：中央文献出版社2015年版。
《习近平关于严明党的纪律和规矩论述摘编》，北京：中央文献出版社、中国方正出版社2016年版。
《习近平关于科技创新论述摘编》，北京：中央文献出版社2016年版。
《习近平关于全面建成小康社会论述摘编》，北京：中央文献出版社2016年版。
《习近平关于全面从严治党论述摘编》，北京：中央文献出版社2016年版。
《习近平关于社会主义经济建设论述摘编》，北京：中央文献出版社2017年版。
《习近平关于社会主义政治建设论述摘编》，北京：中央文献出版社2017年版。
《习近平关于青少年和共青团工作论述摘编》，北京：中央文献出版社2017年版。
《习近平关于社会主义生态文明建设论述摘编》，北京：中央文献出版社2017年版。
《习近平关于社会主义文化建设论述摘编》，北京：中央文献出版社2017年版。
《习近平关于社会主义社会建设论述摘编》，北京：中央文献出版社2017年版。
《习近平关于总体国家安全观论述摘编》，北京：中央文献出版社2018年版。
《习近平扶贫论述摘编》，北京：中央文献出版社2018年版。
《习近平关于'不忘初心、牢记使命'论述摘编》，北京：中央文献出版社、党建读物出版社2019年版。
《习近平关于'三农'工作论述摘编》，北京：中央文献出版社2019年版。
《习近平关于实现中华民族伟大复兴的中国梦论述摘编》，北京：中央文献出版社2019年版。
《习近平关于中国特色大国外交论述摘编》，北京：中央文献出版社2020年版。
《习近平关于统筹疫情防控和经济社会发展重要论述选编》，北京：中央文献出版社2020年版。
《习近平关于力戒形式主义官僚主义重要论述选编》，北京：中央文献出版社2020年版。

《习近平关于防范风险挑战、应对突发事件论述摘编》,北京：中央文献出版社2020年版。
《习近平新时代中国特色社会主义思想学习论丛 （第一辑至第五辑）》,北京：中央文献出版社2020年版。
《习近平关于注重家庭家教家风建设论述摘编》,北京：中央文献出版社2021年版。
《习近平关于网络强国论述摘编》,北京：中央文献出版社2021年版。
《习近平关于尊重和保障人权论述摘编》,北京：中央文献出版社2021年版。
《习近平关于全面从严治党论述摘编（2021年版）》,北京：中央文献出版社2021年版。
《习近平关于坚持和完善党和国家监督体系论述摘编》,北京：中央文献出版社、中国方正出版社2022年版。
《习近平谈'一带一路'（2023年版）》, 北京：中央文献出版社2023年版。
《习近平关于中国现代化论述摘编》,北京：中央文献出版社2023年版。
《习近平关于金融工作论述摘编》,北京：中央文献出版社2024年版。

习近平著作集

习近平：《干在实处走在前列——. 推进浙江新发展的思考与实践》,北京：中共中央党校出版社2006年版。
习近平：《之江新语》,杭州：浙江人民出版社2007年版。习近平,之江新语,浙江人民出版社, 2007.
习近平：《摆脱贫困》,福州：福建人民出版社2014年版。
习近平：《知之深 爱之切》,石家庄：河北人民出版社2015年版。
习近平：《做焦裕禄式的县委书记》,北京：中央文献出版社2015年版。
习近平：《论坚持推动构建人类命运共同体》,北京：中央文献出版社2018年版。
习近平：《习近平谈'一带一路'》,北京：中央文献出版社2018年版。
习近平：《论坚持全面深化改革》,北京：中央文献出版社2018年版。
习近平：《论坚持党对一切工作的领导》,北京：中央文献出版社2019年版。
习近平：《论坚持全面依法治国》,北京：中央文献出版社2020年版。
习近平：《论党的宣传思想工作》,北京：中央文献出版社2020年版。
习近平：《论中国共产党历史》,北京：中央文献出版社2021年版。
习近平：《论把握新发展阶段、贯彻新发展理念、构建新发展格局》,北京：中央文献出版社2021年版。
习近平：《论坚持人民当家作主》,北京：中央文献出版社2021年版。
习近平：《论坚持人与自然和谐共生》,北京：中央文献出版社2022年版。
习近平：《习近平书信选集》（第一卷）,北京：中央文献出版社2022年版。
习近平：《习近平谈'一带一路'（2023年版）》, 北京：中央文献出版社2023年版。
习近平：《习近平著作选读（第二卷）》, 北京：人民出版社2023版。
习近平：《习近平著作选读（第二卷）》, 北京：人民出版社2023版。
习近平执政时期其他资料 (arranged chronologically)

2012

习近平, '习近平在首都各界纪念现行宪法公布施行30周年大会上的讲话',人民网, 2012, http://jhsjk.people.cn/article/19793598.
习近平, '认真学习党章 严格遵守党章',人民网, 2012, http://jhsjk.people.cn/article/19629551.
习近平, '紧紧围绕坚持和发展中国特色社会主义 学习宣传贯彻党的十八大精神',人民网, 2012, http://jhsjk.people.cn/article/19615998.
习近平, '习近平: 承前启后 继往开来 继续朝着中华民族伟大复兴目标奋勇前进',中国政府网, 2012, http://www.gov.cn/ldhd/2012-11/29/content_2278733.htm.
'国家副主席习近平同美国副总统拜登在白宫会谈', 新华网, 2012, http://www.gov.cn/ldhd/2012-02/15/content_2066913.htm.

2013

'中央经济工作会议举行 习近平、李克强作重要讲话', *Xinhua*, 新华网, 2013, http://www.gov.cn/ldhd/2013-12/13/content_2547546.htm.
习近平, '更好统筹国内国际两个大局,夯实走和平发展道路的基础',人民网, 2013, http://cpc.people.com.cn/xuexi/n/2015/0721/c397563-27337509.html.

'习近平：推动全党学习和掌握历史唯物主义 更好认识规律更加能动地推进工作', 2013, http://www.dangjian.com/shouye/tuijianqu/xuexiguance/zhongyaojianghua/202008/t20200818_5754969.shtml.

习近平, '顺应时代前进潮流 促进世界和平发展——. 习近平在莫斯科国际关系学院的演讲',人民网, 2013, http://theory.people.com.cn/n/2013/0325/c40531-20902911.html.

习近平, '永远做可靠朋友和真诚伙伴',人民网, 2013, http://cpc.people.com.cn/n/2013/0326/c64094-20911841.html.

习近平, '携手合作,共同发展',人民网, 2013, http://cpc.people.com.cn/xuexi/n/2015/0721/c397563-27338274.html.

习近平, '共同创造亚洲和世界的美好未来',求是, 2013, http://www.qstheory.cn/2019-07/01/c_1124694776.htm.

习近平, '构建中美新型大国关系',人民网, 2013, http://cpc.people.com.cn/xuexi/n/2015/0721/c397563-27337996.html.

'习近平在金砖国家领导人第五次会晤时的主旨讲话', 中国政府网, 2013, https://www.gov.cn/ldhd/2013-03/27/content_2364182.htm.

习近平, '共同维护和发展开放型世界经济',人民网, 2013, http://cpc.people.com.cn/xuexi/n/2015/0721/c397563-27338279.html.

习近平, '共同建设'丝绸之路经济带'',人民网, 2013, http://cpc.people.com.cn/xuexi/n/2015/0721/c397563-27338105.html.

习近平, '弘扬"上海精神",促进共同发展',人民网, 2013, http://cpc.people.com.cn/xuexi/n/2015/0721/c397563-27338283.html.

习近平, '共同建设二十一世纪"海上丝绸之路"',人民网, 2013, http://cpc.people.com.cn/xuexi/n/2015/0721/c397563-27338109.html.

习近平, '发挥亚太引领作用,维护和发展开放型世界经济',人民网, 2013, http://cpc.people.com.cn/n/2013/1008/c64094-23117724.html.

习近平, '坚持亲、诚、惠、容的周边外交理念',人民网, 2013, http://cpc.people.com.cn/xuexi/n/2015/0721/c397563-27338114.html.

习近平, '坚持理性、协调、并进的核安全观',人民网, 2013, http://cpc.people.com.cn/xuexi/n/2015/0721/c397563-27337514.html.

习近平, '在纪念毛泽东同志诞辰120周年座谈会上的讲话', 2013, http://www.gov.cn/ldhd/2013-12/26/content_2554937.htm.

习近平, '习近平致2013年全球创业周中国站活动组委会的贺信',人民网, 2013, http://jhsjk.people.cn/article/23485246.

习近平, '习近平致第十二届世界华商大会的贺信',人民网, 2013, http://jhsjk.people.cn/article/23039167.

习近平, '2013中国—阿拉伯国家博览会开幕 习近平致信祝贺',人民网, 2013, http://jhsjk.people.cn/article/22929726.

习近平, '习近平在第十二届全国人民代表大会第一次会议上的讲话',人民网, 2013, http://jhsjk.people.cn/article/20819130.

习近平, '全面贯彻落实党的十八大精神要突出抓好六个方面工作',人民网, 2013, http://jhsjk.people.cn/article/20083095.

习近平, '习近平在全国政协新年茶话会上的讲话',人民网, 2013, http://jhsjk.people.cn/article/23995316.

习近平, '关于《中共中央关于全面深化改革若干重大问题的决定》的说明',人民网, 2013, http://jhsjk.people.cn/article/23561783.

习近平, '习近平在中央党校建校80周年庆祝大会暨2013年春季学期开学典礼上的讲话',人民网, 2013, http://jhsjk.people.cn/article/20656845.

习近平, '习近平在全国政协新年茶话会上的讲话',人民网, 2013, http://jhsjk.people.cn/article/20070711.

习近平, '习近平给华中农业大学"本禹志愿服务队"回信',人民网, 2013, http://jhsjk.people.cn/article/23760920.

习近平, '习近平致"鲁本斯、凡·戴克与佛兰德斯画派——. 列支敦士登王室珍藏展"开展的贺信',人民网, 2013, http://jhsjk.people.cn/article/23446423.

习近平, ‘习近平在欧美同学会成立100周年庆祝大会上的讲话’,人民网, 2013, http://jhsjk.people.cn/article/23281641.
习近平, ‘习近平致第十届中国艺术节的贺信’,人民网, 2013, http://jhsjk.people.cn/article/23172358.
习近平, ‘习近平给全校学生回信表示祝贺’,人民网, 2013, http://jhsjk.people.cn/article/23113006.
习近平, ‘习近平主席在联合国“教育第一”全球倡议行动一周年纪念活动上发表视频贺词’,人民网, 2013, http://jhsjk.people.cn/article/23052930.
习近平, ‘习近平向全国广大教师致慰问信’,人民网, 2013, http://jhsjk.people.cn/article/22864548.
习近平, ‘习近平：南极仲冬节慰问电’,人民网, 2013, http://jhsjk.people.cn/article/21931271.
习近平, ‘习近平同各界优秀青年代表座谈时的讲话’,人民网, 2013, http://jhsjk.people.cn/article/21931271.
习近平, ‘习近平致生态文明贵阳国际论坛2013年年会的贺信’,人民网, 2013, http://jhsjk.people.cn/article/22266285.
习近平, ‘习近平主席接受印度尼西亚和马来西亚媒体联合采访’,人民网, 2013, http://jhsjk.people.cn/article/23099538.
习近平, ‘习近平接受拉美三国媒体联合书面采访’,人民网, 2013, http://jhsjk.people.cn/article/21697871.
习近平, ‘习近平致第一次上海合作组织成员国司法部长会议的贺信’,人民网, 2013, http://jhsjk.people.cn/article/22826449.
习近平, ‘习近平在周边外交工作座谈会上发表重要讲话强调 ：为我国发展争取良好周边环境,中国共产党新闻网, 2013, http://cpc.people.com.cn/n/2013/1026/c64094-23333683.html.
‘习近平：让命运共同体意识在周边国家落地生根’, 新华网, 2013, http://www.xinhuanet.com//politics/2013-10/25/c_117878944.htm.
‘中央经济工作会议在北京举行’, 共产党员网, 2013, http://news.12371.cn/2013/12/14/ARTI1386968513713965.shtml.

2014

‘中央国家安全委员会第一次会议召开 习近平发表重要讲话’,中国政府网 , 2014, https://www.gov.cn/xinwen/2014-04/15/content_2659641.htm.
习近平, ‘坚持总体国家安全观 走中国特色国家安全道路’ 新华网, 2014, http://www.xinhuanet.com//politics/2014-04/15/c_1110253910.htm.
习近平, ‘习近平：中国必须有自己特色的大国外交’,人民网, 2014, http://theory.people.com.cn/n1/2018/0104/c416126-29745990.html.
习近平, ‘人民日报：论贯彻落实中央外事工作会议精神’,人民日报, 2014, http://m.haiwainet.cn/middle/3542938/2018/0626/content_31341183_1.html.
习近平, ‘在联合国教科文组织总部的演讲’,人民网, 2014, http://cpc.people.com.cn/n/2014/0328/c64094-24759342.html.
习近平, ‘中国梦是追求和平幸福与奉献世界的梦’,人民网, 2014, http://theory.people.com.cn/n/2014/0605/c49150-25106528.html.
习近平, ‘在德国科尔伯基金会的演讲’,人民网, 2014, http://politics.people.com.cn/n/2014/0329/c1024-24772018.html.
习近平, ‘在布鲁日欧洲学院的演讲’,人民网, 2014, http://politics.people.com.cn/n/2014/0401/c1024-24798043.html.
习近平, ‘中国人民不接受“国强必霸”的逻辑’,人民网, 2014, http://cpc.people.com.cn/n1/2018/0104/c64094-29744185.html.
习近平, ‘积极树立亚洲安全观,共创安全合作新局面’,人民网, 2014, http://cpc.people.com.cn/xuexi/n/2015/0721/c397563-27338292.html.
习近平, ‘弘扬和平共处五项原则,建设合作共赢美好世界’,人民网, 2014, http://cpc.people.com.cn/n/2014/0629/c64094-25214109.html.
习近平, ‘深化合作,体现包容,传递信心’,人民网, 2014, http://world.people.com.cn/n/2014/0715/c1002-25284999.html.
习近平, ‘新起点,新愿景,新动力’,人民网, 2014, http://opinion.people.com.cn/n/2014/0717/c1003-25295508.html.

习近平, '努力构建携手共进的命运共同体',人民网, 2014, http://cpc.people.com.cn/n/2014/0719/c64094-25301723.html.
习近平, '欢迎大家搭乘中国发展的列车',人民网, 2014, http://military.people.com.cn/n/2014/0823/c172467-25523031.html.
习近平, '以"一带一路"为双翼 同南亚国家一道实现腾飞',形势政策网, 2014, http://www.xingshizhengce.com/ztch/ydyl/xjpyydyl/201704/t20170424_4200692.shtml.
习近平, '从延续民族文化血脉中开拓前进 推进各种文明交流交融互学互鉴',人民网, 2014, http://military.people.com.cn/n/2014/0925/c172467-25729279.html.
习近平, '联通引领发展伙伴聚焦合作',人民网, 2014, http://politics.people.com.cn/n/2014/1109/c1024-25997464.html.
习近平, '谋求持久发展 共筑亚太梦想',人民网, 2014, http://finance.people.com.cn/n/2014/1110/c1004-26000555.html.
习近平, '共建面向未来的亚太伙伴关系',人民网, 2014, http://cpc.people.com.cn/n/2014/1112/c64094-26008447.html.
习近平, '推动创新发展 实现联动增长',人民网, 2014, http://cpc.people.com.cn/n/2014/1116/c64094-26032955.html.
习近平, '永远做太平洋岛国人民的真诚朋友',人民网, 2014, http://politics.people.com.cn/n/2014/1122/c1024-26071913.html.
习近平, '中国必须有自己特色的大国外交',人民网, 2014, http://theory.people.com.cn/n1/2018/0104/c416126-29745990.html.
习近平, '在庆祝中华人民共和国成立65周年招待会上的讲话',人民网, 2014, http://jhsjk.people.cn/article/25770391.
习近平, '在中国科学院第十七次院士大会、中国工程院第十二次院士大会上的讲话',人民网, 2014, http://jhsjk.people.cn/article/25125594.
习近平, '切实把思想统一到党的十八届三中全会精神上来',人民网, 2014, http://jhsjk.people.cn/article/23995311.
习近平, '第四批全国干部学习培训教材《序言》',人民网, 2014, http://jhsjk.people.cn/article/26609371.
习近平, '习近平在澳门特别行政区政府欢迎晚宴上的致辞',人民网, 2014, http://jhsjk.people.cn/article/26244450.
习近平, '关于《中共中央关于全面推进依法治国若干重大问题的决定》的说明',人民网, 2014, http://jhsjk.people.cn/article/25926150.
习近平, '习近平在党的群众路线教育实践活动总结大会上的讲话',人民网, 2014, http://jhsjk.people.cn/article/25792940.
习近平, '在庆祝中国人民政治协商会议成立65周年大会上的讲话',人民网, 2014, http://jhsjk.people.cn/article/25704157.
习近平, '在庆祝全国人民代表大会成立60周年大会上的讲话',人民网, 2014, http://jhsjk.people.cn/article/25615123.
习近平, '在纪念中国人民抗日战争暨世界反法西斯战争胜利69周年座谈会上的讲话',人民网, 2014, http://jhsjk.people.cn/article/25599907.
习近平, '习近平在纪念邓小平同志诞辰110周年座谈会上的讲话',人民网, 2014, http://jhsjk.people.cn/article/25507193.
习近平, '习近平在纪念全民族抗战爆发七十七周年仪式上的讲话',人民网, 2014, http://jhsjk.people.cn/article/25250527.
习近平, '共圆中华民族伟大复兴的中国梦',人民网, 2014, http://jhsjk.people.cn/article/24399558.
习近平, '习近平在文艺工作座谈会上的讲话',人民网, 2014, http://jhsjk.people.cn/article/27699249.
习近平, '做党和人民满意的好老师',人民网, 2014, http://jhsjk.people.cn/article/25629946.
习近平, '青年要自觉践行社会主义核心价值观',人民网, 2014, http://jhsjk.people.cn/article/24973220.
习近平, '习近平给大学生村官张广秀复信：对全国大学生村官提出殷切期望',人民网, 2014, http://jhsjk.people.cn/article/24355763.

习近平, '习近平给全体在德留学人员回信',人民网, 2014, http://jhsjk.people.cn/article/24156687.
习近平, '习近平在纪念毛泽东同志诞辰120周年座谈会上的讲话',人民网, 2014, http://jhsjk.people.cn/article/23954163.
习近平, '习近平在纪念孔子诞辰2565周年国际学术研讨会暨国际儒学联合会第五届会员大会开幕会上的讲话',人民网, 2014, http://jhsjk.people.cn/article/25729647.
习近平, '习近平在庆祝澳门回归祖国15周年大会暨澳门特别行政区第四届政府就职典礼上的讲话',人民网, 2014, http://jhsjk.people.cn/article/26246398.
习近平, '习近平在南京大屠杀死难者国家公祭仪式上的讲话',人民网, 2014, http://jhsjk.people.cn/article/26203368.
习近平, '习近平致全军先进干休所先进离退休干部先进老干部工作者的贺信',人民网, 2014, http://jhsjk.people.cn/article/25843853.
习近平, '让工程科技造福人类、创造未来',人民网, 2014, http://jhsjk.people.cn/article/25099536.
习近平, '习近平在北京市海淀区民族小学主持召开座谈会时的讲话',人民网, 2014, http://jhsjk.people.cn/article/25088947.
习近平, '积极树立亚洲安全观 共创安全合作新局面',人民网, 2014, http://jhsjk.people.cn/article/25048467.
习近平, '习近平在中国国际友好大会暨中国人民对外友好协会成立60周年纪念活动上的讲话',人民网, 2014, http://jhsjk.people.cn/article/25024391.
习近平, '习近平致信祝贺中国残疾人福利基金会成立30周年',人民网, 2014, http://jhsjk.people.cn/article/24706324.
习近平, '习近平总书记给"郭明义爱心团队"的回信',人民网, 2014, http://jhsjk.people.cn/article/24529102.
习近平, '习近平致中国南极泰山站的贺信',人民网, 2014, http://jhsjk.people.cn/article/24303751.
习近平, '习近平在巴西国会的演讲:弘扬传统友好 共谱合作新篇',人民网, 2014, http://jhsjk.people.cn/article/25296593.
习近平, '习近平接受拉美四国媒体联合采访',人民网, 2014, http://jhsjk.people.cn/article/25280743.
习近平, '弘扬丝路精神 深化中阿合作',人民网, 2014, http://jhsjk.people.cn/article/25110795.
习近平, '中华人民共和国主席习近平致第三届中非民间论坛的贺信',人民网, 2014, http://jhsjk.people.cn/article/25008109.
习近平, '习近平在德国科尔伯基金会的演讲(全文)',人民网, 2014, http://jhsjk.people.cn/article/24773108.
习近平, '习近平在比利时《晚报》发表署名文章',人民网, 2014, http://jhsjk.people.cn/article/24773109.
习近平, '习近平在德国《法兰克福汇报》发表署名文章',人民网, 2014, http://jhsjk.people.cn/article/24770827.
习近平, '习近平在法国《费加罗报》发表署名文章',人民网, 2014 , http://jhsjk.people.cn/article/24736453.
'习近平出席中央外事工作会议并发表重要讲话', 2014, http://www.xinhuanet.com/politics/2014-11/29/c_1113457723.htm.

2015

习近平, '在中央城市工作会议上的讲话', 中国城市规划网 , 2015 , https://m.planning.org.cn/zx_news/3482.htm.
习近平, '在文艺工作座谈会上的讲话', 新华网, 2015, http://www.xinhuanet.com/politics/2015-10/14/c_1116825558.htm.
习近平, '习近平:人民有信仰民族有希望国家有力量', 新华网, 2015, http://www.xinhuanet.com//politics/2015-02/28/c_1114474084.htm.
习近平, '迈向命运共同体 开创亚洲新未来',新华网, 2015, http://www.xinhuanet.com/politics/2015-03/28/c_1114794507.htm.
习近平, '做大共同利益蛋糕,走向共同繁荣',新华网, 2015, http://www.xinhuanet.com/world/2015-04/21/c_127716691.htm?isappinstalled=0.

习近平, '弘扬万隆精神 推进合作共赢',人民网, 2015, http://theory.people.com.cn/n/2015/0423/c40531-26890650.html.

习近平, '携手打造金砖国家利益共同体',新民晚报, 2015, http://xmwb.xinmin.cn/xmwbusa/html/2015-07/09/content_2_2.htm.

习近平, '在纪念中国人民抗日战争暨世界反法西斯战争胜利70周年大会上的讲话',求是, 2015, http://www.qstheory.cn/2019-07/01/c_1124694846.htm.

习近平, '在华盛顿州当地政府和美国友好团体联合欢迎宴会上的演讲',新华网, 2015, http://www.xinhuanet.com//world/2015-09/23/c_1116656143.htm.

习近平, '在白宫南草坪欢迎仪式上的致辞',人民网, 2015, http://politics.people.com.cn/n/2015/0926/c1024-27636480.html.

习近平, '谋共同永续发展 做合作共赢伙伴',人民网, 2015, http://cpc.people.com.cn/n/2015/0927/c64094-27638798.html.

习近平, '携手构建合作共赢新伙伴, 同心打造人类命运共同体',人民网, 2015, http://theory.people.com.cn/n1/2018/0104/c416126-29746010.html.

习近平, '弘扬共商共建共享的全球治理理念',中国社会科学网, 2015, http://www.cssn.cn/zzx/zzxzt_zzx/zgqqzl/xjp/201511/t20151113_2590932.shtml.

习近平, '携手消除贫困 促进共同发展',求是, 2015, http://www.qstheory.cn/2019-07/01/c_1124695207.htm.

习近平, '中国是一个负责任大国',人民网, 2015, http://jhsjk.people.cn/article/27730625.

习近平, '中国始终将周边置于外交全局的首要位置',人民网, 2015, http://politics.people.com.cn/n/2015/1107/c1024-27788813.html.

习近平, '发挥亚太引领作用 应对世界经济挑战',人民网, 2015, http://politics.people.com.cn/n/2015/1119/c1024-27830907.html.

习近平, '携手构建合作共赢、公平合理的气候变化治理机制 ',求是, 2015, http://www.qstheory.cn/2019-07/01/c_1124695328.htm.

习近平, '开启中非合作共赢、共同发展的新时代',人民网, 2015, http://theory.people.com.cn/n1/2018/0104/c416126-29745996.html.

习近平, '在第二届世界互联网大会开幕式上的讲话',新华网, 2015, http://www.xinhuanet.com/politics/2015-12/16/c_1117481089.htm.

习近平, '在党的十八届五中全会第二次全体会议上的讲话(节选)',人民网, 2015, http://jhsjk.people.cn/article/28002398.

习近平, '致2015世界机器人大会贺信',人民网, 2015, http://jhsjk.people.cn/article/27847383.

习近平, '关于《中共中央关于制定国民经济和社会发展第十三个五年规划的建议》的说明',人民网, 2015, http://jhsjk.people.cn/article/27773638.

习近平, '习近平在全国政协新年茶话会上的讲话',人民网, 2015, http://jhsjk.people.cn/article/28002288.

习近平, '在纪念胡耀邦同志诞辰100周年座谈会上的讲话',人民网, 2015, http://jhsjk.people.cn/article/27839734.

习近平, '在会见全国优秀县委书记时的讲话',人民网, 2015, http://jhsjk.people.cn/article/27537307.

习近平, '习近平致全国青联十二届全委会和全国学联二十六大的贺信',人民网, 2015, http://jhsjk.people.cn/article/27358938.

习近平, '习近平总书记给国测一大队老队员老党员的回信',人民网, 2015, http://jhsjk.people.cn/article/27240745.

习近平, '习近平在纪念陈云同志诞辰110周年座谈会上的讲话',人民网, 2015, http://jhsjk.people.cn/article/27149072.

习近平, '习近平致中国中医科学院成立60周年贺信',人民网, 2015, http://jhsjk.people.cn/article/27963702.

习近平, '习近平致第二十二届国际历史科学大会的贺信',人民网, 2015, http://jhsjk.people.cn/article/27504654.

习近平, '习近平致申办冬奥会代表团的贺信',人民网, 2015, http://jhsjk.people.cn/article/27395214.

习近平, '习近平致信国际奥委会主席巴赫',人民网, 2015, http://jhsjk.people.cn/article/27395215.

习近平, '习近平致"2015·北京人权论坛"的贺信',人民网, 2015, http://jhsjk.people.cn/article/27596096.

习近平, ‘携手消除贫困 促进共同发展’,人民网, 2015, http://jhsjk.people.cn/article/27709112.

习近平, ‘习近平给“国培计划(二〇一四)”北师大贵州研修班参训教师回信’,人民网, 2015, http://jhsjk.people.cn/article/27565060.

习近平, ‘习近平致国际教育信息化大会的贺信’,人民网, 2015, http://jhsjk.people.cn/article/27050043.

习近平, ‘习近平在庆祝“五一”国际劳动节暨表彰全国劳动模范和先进工作者大会上的讲话’,人民网, 2015, http://jhsjk.people.cn/article/26921006.

习近平, ‘习近平在2015年春节团拜会上的讲话’,人民网, 2015, http://jhsjk.people.cn/article/26581566.

习近平, ‘在颁发“中国人民抗日战争胜利70周年”纪念章仪式上的讲话’,人民网, 2015, http://jhsjk.people.cn/article/27542879.

习近平, ‘习近平给内蒙古军区边防某团一连官兵回信 勉励官兵为筑牢祖国安全稳定屏障再立新功’,人民网, 2015, http://jhsjk.people.cn/article/26581563.

习近平, ‘致2015中非媒体领袖峰会的贺信’,中华人民共和国外交部, 2015, http://www.fmprc.gov.cn/web/ziliao_674904/zyjh_674906/t1320443.shtml.

习近平, ‘致2015中非媒体领袖峰会的贺信’,中华人民共和国外交部, 2015, http://www.fmprc.gov.cn/web/ziliao_674904/zyjh_674906/t1320443.shtml.

2016

习近平, ‘在哲学社会科学工作座谈会上的讲话’,新华网, 2016, http://www.xinhuanet.com//politics/2016-05/18/c_1118891128.htm.

习近平, ‘在庆祝中国共产党成立九十五周年大会上的讲话’, 求是, 2016, http://www.qstheory.cn/dukan/qs/2021-04/15/c_1127330615.htm.

习近平, ‘向全世界讲好“中国故事”’,人民网, 2016, http://theory.people.com.cn/n1/2018/0626/c409499-30087307.html.

习近平, ‘在亚洲基础设施投资银行开业仪式上的致辞’,人民网, 2016, http://cpc.people.com.cn/n1/2017/0105/c64094-29000774.html.

习近平, ‘共同开创中阿关系的美好未来’,人民网, 2016, http://cpc.people.com.cn/n1/2016/0122/c64094-28075098.html.

习近平, ‘加强国际核安全体系推进全球核安全治理’,人民网, 2016, http://politics.people.com.cn/n1/2016/0403/c1024-28246845.html.

习近平, ‘凝聚共识 促进对话 共创亚洲和平与繁荣的美好未来’,中华人民共和国中央人民政府, 2016, http://www.gov.cn/xinwen/2016-04/28/content_5068771.htm.

习近平, ‘推进“一带一路”建设,努力拓展改革发展新空间’,人民.网, 2016, http://theory.people.com.cn/n1/2018/0129/c40531-29791669.html.

习近平, ‘为构建中美新型大国关系而不懈努力’,人民网, 2016, http://cpc.people.com.cn/n1/2016/0607/c64094-28416143.html.

习近平, ‘共同推进中国——. 中亚——. 西亚经济走廊建设’,人民网, 2016.

习近平, ‘共创中俄关系更加美好的明天’,人民网, 2016, http://theory.people.com.cn/n1/2018/0104/c416126-29746000.html.

习近平, ‘让“一带一路”建设造福沿线各国人民’,新华网, 2016, http://www.xinhuanet.com/world/2016-08/17/c_1119408654.htm.

习近平, ‘中国发展新起点全球增长新蓝图’,人民网, 2016, http://cpc.people.com.cn/n1/2016/0905/c64094-28690521.html.

习近平, ‘从巴黎到杭州,应对气候变化在行动’,习近平二十国集团领导人杭州峰会讲话选编, 2016, http://paper.people.com.cn/zgcsb/html/2016-09/12/content_1712544.htm.

习近平, ‘构建创新、活力、联动、包容的世界经济’,人民网, 2016, http://theory.people.com.cn/n1/2018/0104/c416126-29746001.html.

习近平, ‘提高我国参与全球治理的能力’,人民网, 2016, http://world.people.com.cn/n1/2018/1210/c1002-30452972.html.

习近平, ‘坚定信心,共谋发展’,人民网, 2016, http://www.scgb.gov.cn/website/contents/63/439.html.

习近平, ‘深化伙伴关系,增强发展动力’,人民网, 2016, http://m.people.cn/n4/2016/1121/c2464-7940898.html.

习近平, '集思广益增进共识加强合作 让互联网更好造福人类',人民网, 2016, http://jhsjk.people.cn/article/28874030.

习近平, '习近平致信祝贺第一百二十届中国进出口商品交易会开幕',人民网, 2016, http://jhsjk.people.cn/article/28781379.

习近平, '在第十八届中央纪律检查委员会第六次全体会议上的讲话',人民网, 2016, http://jhsjk.people.cn/article/29000964.

习近平, '在全国政协新年茶话会上的讲话',人民网, 2016, http://jhsjk.people.cn/article/28990896.

习近平, '习近平在纪念万里同志诞辰100周年座谈会上的讲话',人民网, 2016, http://jhsjk.people.cn/article/28926864.

习近平, '习近平在纪念朱德同志诞辰130周年座谈会上的讲话',人民网, 2016, http://jhsjk.people.cn/article/28911124.

习近平, '习近平在纪念孙中山先生诞辰150周年大会上的讲话',人民网, 2016, http://jhsjk.people.cn/article/28855099.

习近平, '关于《关于新形势下党内政治生活的若干准则》和《中国共产党党内监督条例》的说明',人民网, 2016, http://jhsjk.people.cn/article/28830231.

习近平, '习近平在纪念红军长征胜利80周年大会上的讲话',人民网, 2016, http://jhsjk.people.cn/article/28798737.

习近平, '习近平致信祝贺中央社会主义学院建院六十周年',人民网, 2016, http://jhsjk.people.cn/article/28780605.

习近平, '习近平在学习《胡锦涛文选》报告会上的讲话',人民网, 2016, http://jhsjk.people.cn/article/28751570.

习近平, '习近平在纪念刘华清同志诞辰100周年座谈会上的讲话',人民网, 2016, http://jhsjk.people.cn/article/28748266.

习近平, '习近平在庆祝中国共产党成立95周年大会上的讲话',人民网, 2016, http://jhsjk.people.cn/article/28517655.

习近平, '习近平在省部级主要领导干部学习贯彻党的十八届五中全会精神专题研讨班上的讲话',人民网, 2016, http://jhsjk.people.cn/article/28337020.

习近平, '毫不动摇坚持我国基本经济制度 推动各种所有制经济健康发展',人民网, 2016, http://jhsjk.people.cn/article/28183110.

习近平, '习近平致信祝贺《大辞海》出版暨《辞海》第一版面世80周年',人民网, 2016, http://jhsjk.people.cn/article/28987898.

习近平, '习近平回信勉励北京市八一学校科普小卫星研制团队学生',人民网, 2016, http://jhsjk.people.cn/article/28984532.

习近平, '习近平在中国文联十大、中国作协九大开幕式上的讲话',人民网, 2016, http://jhsjk.people.cn/article/28915769.

习近平, '神舟十一号载人飞船发射成功 习近平致电表示热烈祝贺',人民网, 2016, http://jhsjk.people.cn/article/28785969.

习近平, '习近平致信祝贺我国五百米口径球面射电望远镜落成启用',人民网, 2016, http://jhsjk.people.cn/article/28739235.

习近平, '习近平向首届丝绸之路国际文化博览会致贺信',人民网, 2016, http://jhsjk.people.cn/article/28728403.

习近平, '习近平致首届清华大学苏世民书院开学典礼的贺信',人民网, 2016, http://jhsjk.people.cn/article/28706479.

习近平, '为建设世界科技强国而奋斗',人民网, 2016, http://jhsjk.people.cn/article/28400179.

习近平, '习近平在哲学社会科学工作座谈会上的讲话',人民网, 2016, http://jhsjk.people.cn/article/28361550.

习近平, '在知识分子、劳动模范、青年代表座谈会上的讲话',人民网, 2016, http://jhsjk.people.cn/article/28316364.

习近平, '在会见第一届全国文明家庭代表时的讲话',人民网, 2016, http://jhsjk.people.cn/article/28953602.

习近平, '习近平致信祝贺新华社建社85周年',人民网, 2016, http://jhsjk.people.cn/article/28837989.

习近平, '习近平致信祝贺中国医学科学院成立六十周年',人民网, 2016, http://jhsjk.people.cn/article/28817424.

习近平, '习近平致信祝贺第19届国际麻风大会开幕',人民网, 2016, http://jhsjk.people.cn/article/28725361.
习近平, '在网络安全和信息化工作座谈会上的讲话',人民网, 2016, http://jhsjk.people.cn/article/28303771.
习近平, '习近平致信祝贺"纪念《发展权利宣言》通过三十周年国际研讨会"开幕',人民网, 2016, http://jhsjk.people.cn/article/28923937.
习近平, '第三十九届国际标准化组织大会召开 习近平致贺信',人民网, 2016, http://jhsjk.people.cn/article/28710957.
习近平, '2016"一带一路"媒体合作论坛召开 习近平致贺信',人民网, 2016, http://jhsjk.people.cn/article/28587219.
习近平, '习近平在波兰媒体发表署名文章：推动中波友谊航船全速前进',人民网, 2016, http://jhsjk.people.cn/article/28454886.
习近平, '习近平在伊朗媒体发表署名文章 共创中伊关系美好明天',人民网, 2016, http://jhsjk.people.cn/article/28075085.
' 习近平：理直气壮做强做优做大国有企业', 新华网, 2016, http://www.xinhuanet.com/politics/2016-07/04/c_1119162333.htm.
' 习近平在中共中央政治局第三十次集体学习时强调 准确把握和抓好我国发展战略重点 扎实把"十三五"发展蓝图变为现实', 2016, https://news.12371.cn/2016/01/30/ARTI1454141920834363.shtml.

2017

习近平, '共担时代责任,共促全球发展',中共中央党校, 2017, https://www.ccps.gov.cn/xxsxk/zyls/202012/t20201215_145630.shtml.
习近平, '共同构建人类命运共同体',人民网, 2017, http://jhsjk.people.cn/article/31986596.
习近平, '有一千条理由把中美关系搞好',人民网, 2017, http://jhsjk.people.cn/article/29196117.
习近平, '开辟合作新起点,谋求发展新动力',人民网, 2017, http://politics.people.com.cn/n1/2017/0516/c1001-29277113.html.
习近平, '团结协作,开放包容,建设安全稳定、发展繁荣的共同家园',新华网, 2017, http://www.xinhuanet.com/mrdx/2017-06/10/c_136354781.htm.
习近平, '接受俄罗斯媒体采访时的答问',新华网, 2017, http://www.xinhuanet.com/world/2017-07/03/c_1121255558.htm.
习近平, '共同开创金砖合作第二个"金色十年"',人民网, 2017, http://cpc.people.com.cn/n1/2017/0904/c64094-29512050.html.
习近平, '深化金砖伙伴关系,开辟更加光明未来',人民网, 2017, http://cpc.people.com.cn/n1/2017/0905/c64094-29514692.html.
习近平, '坚持合作创新法治共赢,携手开展全球安全治理',人民网, 2017, http://politics.people.com.cn/n1/2017/0927/c1001-29561019.html.
习近平, '坚持和平发展道路,推动构建人类命运共同体',人民网, 2017, http://dangjian.people.com.cn/n1/2017/1108/c414210-29635042.html.
习近平, '中美合作是唯一正确选择, 共赢才能通向更好的未来',人民网, 2017, https://zzwb.zznews.gov.cn/content/c1412734.html.
习近平, '抓住世界经济转型机遇,谋求亚太更大发展',人民网, 2017, http://cpc.people.com.cn/n1/2017/1111/c64094-29639925.html.
习近平, '携手建设更加美好的世界',人民网, 2017, http://cpc.people.com.cn/n1/2017/1203/c415498-29682301.html.
习近平, '共担时代责任,共促全球发展',人民网, 2017, http://jhsjk.people.cn/article/31967487.
习近平, '习近平在庆祝香港回归祖国二十周年大会暨香港特别行政区第五届政府就职典礼上的讲话',人民网, 2017, http://jhsjk.people.cn/article/29376805.
习近平, '习近平致信祝贺全国台湾同胞投资企业联谊会成立十周年',人民网, 2017, http://jhsjk.people.cn/article/29298072.
习近平, '习近平在庆祝香港回归祖国二十周年大会暨香港特别行政区第五届政府就职典礼上的讲话',人民网, 2017, http://jhsjk.people.cn/article/29376805.

习近平, '习近平在香港特别行政区政府欢迎晚宴上的致辞', 人民网, 2017, http://jhsjk.people.cn/article/29376124.

习近平, '习近平致信祝贺中国农业科学院建院六十周年', 人民网, 2017, http://jhsjk.people.cn/article/29303371.

习近平, '习近平致信祝贺中国社会科学院建院四十周年', 人民网, 2017, http://jhsjk.people.cn/article/29282853.

习近平, '习近平在二〇一七年春节团拜会上的讲话', 人民网, 2017, http://jhsjk.people.cn/article/29051558.

习近平, '在深度贫困地区脱贫攻坚座谈会上的讲话', 人民网, 2017, http://jhsjk.people.cn/article/29508162.

习近平, '习近平致信祝贺第十九届国际植物学大会开幕', 人民网, 2017, http://jhsjk.people.cn/article/29425574.

习近平, '习近平致信祝贺金砖国家卫生部长会暨传统医药高级别会议召开', 人民网, 2017, http://jhsjk.people.cn/article/29388864.

习近平, '习近平致信祝贺中华职业教育社成立一百周年', 人民网, 2017, http://jhsjk.people.cn/article/29257879.

习近平, '习近平总书记给中国工合国际委员会、北京培黎职业学院的回信', 人民网, 2017, http://jhsjk.people.cn/article/29228508.

习近平, '习近平回信勉励库尔班大叔的后人', 人民网, 2017, http://jhsjk.people.cn/article/29022965.

习近平, '习近平致信祝贺《联合国防治荒漠化公约》第十三次缔约方大会高级别会议召开', 人民网, 2017, http://jhsjk.people.cn/article/29528976.

习近平, '习近平致信祝贺第二次青藏高原综合科学考察研究启动', 人民网, 2017, http://jhsjk.people.cn/article/29481439.

习近平, '习近平致信祝贺第十九届国际植物学大会开幕', 人民网, 2017, http://jhsjk.people.cn/article/29425574.

习近平, '习近平致信祝贺第十九届国际植物学大会开幕', 人民网, 2017, http://jhsjk.people.cn/article/29425574.

习近平, '习近平致第八届清洁能源部长级会议和第二届创新使命部长级会议的贺信', 人民网, 2017, http://jhsjk.people.cn/article/29325188.

习近平, '习近平在庆祝中国人民解放军建军90周年大会上的讲话', 人民网, 2017, http://jhsjk.people.cn/article/29443168.

习近平, '习近平致信祝贺金砖国家卫生部长会暨传统医药高级别会议召开', 人民网, 2017, http://jhsjk.people.cn/article/29388864.

习近平, '习近平向联合国世界旅游组织第22届全体大会致贺词', 新华网, 2017, http://www.xinhuanet.com//politics/2017-09/13/c_1121655327.htm.

习近平, '习近平论人类命运共同体(2017)', 国家国际发展合作署, 2017, http://www.cidca.gov.cn/2021-07/13/c_1211238623.htm.

习近平, '习近平关于国企改革的系列论述和讲话精神', 2017, http://gzw.wuhan.gov.cn/bmdt/gzjg/202004/t20200402_987604.html.

'习近平接见2017年度驻外使节工作会议与会使节并发表重要讲话', 新华网, 2017, http://www.xinhuanet.com/politics/leaders/2017-12/28/c_1122181743.htm.

习近平: '深刻认识马克思主义时代意义和现实意义,继续推进马克思主义中国化时代化大众化', 人民网, 2017, http://cpc.people.com.cn/n1/2017/0930/c64094-29568977.html.

2018

习近平, '习近平在中共中央政治局第九次集体学习时强调 铸牢中华民族共同体意识 推进新时代党的民族工作高质量发展', 中国共产党网, 2018, https://www.12371.cn/2023/10/28/ARTI1698472294693206.shtml.

习近平, '切实贯彻落实新时代党的组织路线 全党努力把党建设得更加坚强有力', 2018, https://www.gov.cn/xinwen/2018-07/04/content_5303550.htm.

'习近平在广东考察'近平中国政府网, 2018,
https://www.gov.cn/xinwen/2018-10/25/content_5334458.htm.

习近平, '习近平在中央外事工作会议上强调 坚持以新时代中国特色社会主义外交思想为指导努力开创中国特色大国外交新局面', 新华社, 2018, https://baijiahao.baidu.com/s?id=1604060074048442582&wfr=spider&for=pc.

习近平, '以习近平外交思想为指导 新时代对外工作这么干',新华社, 2018, https://baijiahao.baidu.com/s?id=1604212857767468480&wfr=spider&for=pc.

习近平, '为人类共同发展和繁荣提供中国方案',人民网, 2018, http://cpc.people.com.cn/big5/n1/2018/0625/c419242-30081419.html.

习近平, '推动全球治理体系朝着更加公正合理的方向发展',光明网, 2018, https://m.gmw.cn/baijia/2021-02/15/34618802.html.

习近平, '谱写中国特色大国外交新篇章',人民网, 2018, http://theory.people.com.cn/n1/2019/0801/c40531-31268388.html.

习近平, '共创人类美好未来的'中国方案'',人民网, 2018, http://theory.people.com.cn/n1/2018/0625/c40531-30081904.html.

'习近平:加强领导做好规划明确任务夯实基础 推动我国新一代人工智能健康发展', 中国共产党新闻网, 2018, http://cpc.people.com.cn/n1/2018/1101/c64094-30374958.html.

习近平, '习近平外交思想是新时代中国特色大国外交的根本遵循和行动指南',新华网, 2018, https://baijiahao.baidu.com/s?id=1604073196136970438&wfr=spider&for=pc.

习近平, '准确把握当前和今后一个时期的国际形势',人民日报, 2018, https://baijiahao.baidu.com/s?id=1604155308090517027&wfr=spider&for=pc.

习近平, '从新时代中国特色大国外交成就中汲取智慧和力量',新华网, 2018, https://baijiahao.baidu.com/s?id=1604257222177343277&wfr=spider&for=pc.

'习近平:深刻认识建设现代化经济体系重要性 推动我国经济发展焕发新活力迈上新台阶'动我新华网, 2018, http://www.xinhuanet.com/politics/leaders/2018-01/31/c_1122349103.htm.

习近平, '开放共创繁荣,创新引领未来',中共中央党校, 2018, https://www.ccps.gov.cn/xxsxk/zyls/201812/t20181216_125691_1.shtml.

习近平, '加强党中央对外事工作的集中统一领导,努力开创中国特色大国外交新局面',中国日报网, 2018, https://baijiahao.baidu.com/s?id=1600574800155887169&wfr=spider&for=pc.

习近平, '弘扬"上海精神",构建命运共同体",人民网, 2018, http://cpc.people.com.cn/n1/2019/0612/c164113-31133386.html.

习近平, '坚持以新时代中国特色社会主义外交思想为指导,努力开创中国特色大国外交新局面',旗帜, 2018, https://baijiahao.baidu.com/s?id=1604229635698644659&wfr=spider&for=pc.

习近平, '在纪念马克思诞辰200周年大会上的讲话', 新华网, 2018, http://www.xinhuanet.com/politics/2018-05/04/c_1122783997.htm.

'习近平出席推进"一带一路"建设工作5周年座谈会并发表重要讲话', 新华网, 2018, http://www.gov.cn/xinwen/2018-08/27/content_5316913.htm.

习近平, '在民营企业座谈会上的讲话'民营新华网, 2018, http://www.xinhuanet.com/politics/2018-11/01/c_1123649488.htm.

2019

'《求是》杂志发表习近平总书记重要文章《坚持、完善和发展中国特色社会主义国家制度与法律制度》', 中国网, 2019, http://guoqing.china.com.cn/2019zgxg/2019-12/02/content_75467651.html.'习近平出席"不忘初心、牢记使命"主题教育工作会议并发表重要讲话', 新华网, 2019, http://www.gov.cn/xinwen/2019-05/31/content_5396490.htm.

习近平, '习近平会见联合国秘书长古特雷斯',中华人民共和国外交部, 2019, https://www.fmprc.gov.cn/web/zyxw/t1658470.shtml.

习近平, '高质量共建'一带一路',第二届'一带一路'国际合作高峰论坛圆桌峰会上的开幕辞', 人民网, 2019, http://jhsjk.people.cn/article/31053841.

习近平, '在中法全球治理论坛闭幕式上的讲话',新华网, 2019, http://www.xinhuanet.com/politics/leaders/2019-03/26/c_1124286585.htm.

习近平, '和而不同 美美与共——习近平主席联合国教科文组织总部演讲5周年',央视网, 2019, http://m.news.cctv.com/2019/03/27/ARTIg5Sd2i3SES23WcJ7BnXx190327.shtml.

习近平, '在亚洲文明对话大会开幕式上的主旨演讲',新华网, 2019, http://www.xinhuanet.com/politics/leaders/2019-05/15/c_1124497022.htm.

习近平, '携手努力共谱合作新篇章——在金砖国家领导人巴西利亚会晤公开会议上的讲话 ',人民网, 2019, http://jhsjk.people.cn/article/31456481.

'习近平主持中央政治局第十七次集体学习并讲话', 中国政府网, 2019, http://www.gov.cn/xinwen/2019-09/24/content_5432784.htm.

'习近平会见出席"2019从都国际论坛"外方嘉宾', 新华网, 2019, http://www.xinhuanet.com/politics/leaders/2019-12/03/c_1125304297.htm.

'习近平在第二十三届圣彼得堡国际经济论坛全会上的致辞(全文)', 新华网, 2019, http://www.xinhuanet.com/world/2019-06/08/c_1124596100.htm.

'习近平:在中央和国家机关党的建设工作会议上的讲话',新华网, 2019, http://www.xinhuanet.com/politics/2019-11/01/c_1125180360.htm.

习近平, '坚定文化自信,建设社会主义文化强国', 求是, 2019, http://www.qstheory.cn/dukan/qs/2019-06/15/c_1124626824.htm?spm=zm5062-001.0.0.1.FuAYId.

习近平, '在纪念五四运动100周年大会上的讲话',新华网, 2019, http://www.xinhuanet.com/politics/2019-04/30/c_1124440193.htm.

2020

习近平, '习近平在联合国成立75周年纪念峰会上发表重要讲话',新华网, 2020, https://www.fmprc.gov.cn/web/zyxw/t1816765.shtml.

习近平, '习近平在第七十五届联合国大会一般性辩论上的讲话',新华网, 2020, http://www.xinhuanet.com/world/2020-09/22/c_1126527652.htm.

习近平, '习近平在联合国生物多样性峰会上的讲话',中华人民共和国外交部, 2020, https://www.fmprc.gov.cn/web/zyxw/t1820838.shtml.

习近平, '习近平在气候雄心峰会上发表重要讲话',新华网, 2020, http://www.xinhuanet.com/politics/leaders/2020-12/12/c_1126853600.htm.

习近平, '习近平在企业家座谈会上的讲话', 新华网, 2020, http://www.xinhuanet.com/politics/2020-07/21/c_1126267575.htm.

'习近平在中央全面依法治国工作会议上强调 坚定不移走中国特色社会主义法治道路 为全面建设社会主义现代化国家提供有力法治保障', 新华网, 2020, http://www.xinhuanet.com/politics/leaders/2020-11/17/c_1126751678.htm.

习近平, '习近平在联合国大会纪念北京世界妇女大会25周年高级别会议上的讲话',中华人民共和国外交部, 2020, https://www.fmprc.gov.cn/web/zyxw/t1821377.shtml.

习近平, '习近平在二十国集团领导人利雅得峰会"守护地球"主题边会上的致辞',中华人民共和国外交部, 2020, https://www.fmprc.gov.cn/web/ziliao_674904/zyjh_674906/t1834441.shtml.

习近平, '坚持和完善中国特色社会主义制度推进国家治理体系和治理能力现代化',求是, 2020, http://www.qstheory.cn/dukan/qs/2020-01/01/c_1125402833.htm.

习近平, '坚持历史唯物主义不断开辟当代中国马克思主义发展新境界',求是, 2020, http://www.qstheory.cn/dukan/qs/2020-01/15/c_1125459115.htm.

习近平, '在敦煌研究院座谈时的讲话',求是, 2020, http://www.qstheory.cn/dukan/qs/2020-01/31/c_1125497461.htm.

习近平, '在中央政治局常委会会议研究应对新型冠状病毒肺炎疫情工作时的讲话',求是, 2020, http://www.qstheory.cn/dukan/qs/2020-02/15/c_1125572832.htm.

习近平, '全面提高依法防控依法治理能力 健全国家公共卫生应急管理体系',求是, 2020, http://www.qstheory.cn/dukan/qs/2020-02/29/c_1125641632.htm.

习近平, '为打赢疫情防控阻击战提供强大科技支撑',求是, 2020, http://www.qstheory.cn/dukan/qs/2020-03/15/c_1125710612.htm.

习近平, '在湖北省考察新冠肺炎疫情防控工作时的讲话',求是, 2020, http://www.qstheory.cn/dukan/qs/2020-03/31/c_1125791549.htm.

习近平, '团结合作是国际社会战胜疫情最有力武器',求是, 2020, http://www.qstheory.cn/dukan/qs/2020-04/15/c_1125857091.htm.

习近平, '在打好精准脱贫攻坚战座谈会上的讲话',求是, 2020, http://www.qstheory.cn/dukan/qs/2020-04/30/c_1125923810.htm.

习近平, '在第十三届全国人民代表大会第一次会议上的讲话',求是, 2020, http://www.qstheory.cn/dukan/qs/2020-05/15/c_1125987668.htm.

习近平, '关于全面建成小康社会补短板问题',求是, 2020, http://www.qstheory.cn/dukan/qs/2020-05/31/c_1126055020.htm.

习近平, '充分认识颁布实施民法典重大意义 依法更好保障人民合法权益',求是, 2020, http://www.qstheory.cn/dukan/qs/2020-06/15/c_1126112148.htm.

习近平, ‘在“不忘初心、牢记使命”主题教育总结大会上的讲话’,求是, 2020, http://www.qstheory.cn/dukan/qs/2020-06/30/c_1126171670.htm.

习近平, ‘中国共产党领导是中国特色社会主义最本质的特征’,求是, 2020, http://www.qstheory.cn/dukan/qs/2020-07/15/c_1126234524.htm.

习近平, ‘贯彻落实新时代党的组织路线 不断把党建设得更加坚强有力’,求是, 2020, http://www.qstheory.cn/dukan/qs/2020-07/31/c_1126305988.htm.

习近平, ‘不断开拓当代中国马克思主义政治经济学新境界’,求是, 2020, http://www.qstheory.cn/dukan/qs/2020-08/15/c_1126365995.htm.

习近平, ‘思政课是落实立德树人根本任务的关键课程’,求是, 2020, http://www.qstheory.cn/dukan/qs/2020-08/31/c_1126430247.htm.

习近平, ‘构建起强大的公共卫生体系 为维护人民健康提供有力保障’,求是, 2020, http://www.gov.cn/xinwen/2020-09/15/content_5543609.htm.

习近平, ‘在庆祝中华人民共和国成立 70 周年大会上的讲话’,求是, 2020, http://www.xinhuanet.com/politics/leaders/2020-09/30/c_1126563213.htm.

习近平, ‘在庆祝中华人民共和国成立 70 周年招待会上的讲话’,求是, 2020, http://www.xinhuanet.com/politics/leaders/2020-09/30/c_1126563213.htm.

习近平, ‘在国家勋章和国家荣誉称号颁授仪式上的讲话’,求是, 2020, http://www.wenming.cn/ldhd/xjp/xjpjh/202009/t20200930_5807157.shtml.

习近平, ‘在全国抗击新冠肺炎疫情表彰大会上的讲话’,求是, 2020, http://www.qstheory.cn/dukan/qs/2020-10/15/c_1126613052.htm.

习近平, ‘国家中长期经济社会发展战略若干重大问题’,求是, 2020, http://www.qstheory.cn/dukan/qs/2020-10/31/c_1126680390.htm.

习近平, ‘推进全面依法治国,发挥法治在国家治理体系和治理能力现代化中的积极作用’,求是, 2020, http://www.qstheory.cn/dukan/qs/2020-11/15/c_1126739089.htm.

习近平, ‘建设中国特色中国风格中国气派的考古学 更好认识源远流长博大精深的中华文明’,求是, 2020, http://www.qstheory.cn/dukan/qs/2020-11/30/c_1126799145.htm.

习近平, “在经济社会领域专家座谈会上的讲话”, 中国政府网, 2020, https://www.gov.cn/gongbao/content/2020/content_5541470.htm.

习近平, “在浦东开发开放30周年庆祝大会上的讲话”, 中国政府网, 2020, https://www.gov.cn/gongbao/content/2020/content_5565805.htm.

‘习近平外交思想研究中心成立仪式成功举行’近平中国国际问题研究院, 2020, https://www.ciis.org.cn/xwdt/202009/t20200918_7390.html.

‘习近平总书记这篇重要讲话首提“新发展格局”’展格求是, 2020, http://www.qstheory.cn/zhuanqu/2020-10/31/c_1126682290.htm.

习近平, ‘共担时代责任,共促全球发展’,求是, 2020, http://www.qstheory.cn/dukan/qs/2020-12/15/c_1126857192.htm.

‘习近平在中央政治局第二十二次集体学习时强调 统一思想坚定信心鼓足干劲抓紧工作 奋力推进国防和军队现代化建设’, 新华网, 2020, http://www.xinhuanet.com/politics/leaders/2020-07/31/c_1126310486.htm.

习近平, ‘推动更深层次改革实行更高水平开放为构建新发展格局提供强大动力’, 新华网, 2020, http://www.xinhuanet.com/politics/leaders/2020-09/01/c_1126440786.htm.

习近平, ‘从‘两个大局’把握重要战略机遇期新变化新特征’, 新华网, 2020, http://www.xinhuanet.com/politics/2020-10/30/c_1126675607.htm.

2021

习近平, ‘习近平在世界经济论坛“达沃斯议程”对话会上的特别致辞’,新华网 , 2021 http://www.xinhuanet.com/world/2021-01/25/c_1127023884.htm.

‘习近平主持召开二十届中央财经委员会第一次会议强调 加快建设以实体经济为支撑的现代化产业体系 以人口高质量发展支撑中国式现代化’, 新华网, 2021, http://www.news.cn/politics/leaders/2023-05/05/c_1129592754.htm.

习近平, ‘习近平在中央党校(国家行政学院)中青年干部培训班开班式上发表重要讲话’,新华网, 2021, http://www.xinhuanet.com/politics/leaders/2021-03/01/c_1127154621.htm.

习近平, '习近平：凝心聚力,继往开来 携手共谱合作新篇章 —— 在中国—中东欧国家领导人峰会上的主旨讲话',人民网, 2021, http://jhsjk.people.cn/article/32027987.

习近平, '习近平出席世界经济论坛"达沃斯议程"对话会并发表特别致辞',新华网, 2021, http://www.xinhuanet.com/english/2021-02/09/c_139733388.htm.

习近平, '正确认识和把握中长期经济社会发展重大问题',求是, 2021, http://www.qstheory.cn/dukan/qs/2021-01/15/c_1126984966.htm.

习近平, '全面加强知识产权保护工作 激发创新活力推动构建新发展格局',求是, 2021, http://www.qstheory.cn/dukan/qs/2021-01/31/c_1127044345.htm.

习近平, '坚定不移走中国特色社会主义法治道路 为全面建设社会主义现代化国家提供有力法治保障',求是, 2021, http://www.qstheory.cn/dukan/qs/2021-02/28/c_1127146541.htm.

习近平, '努力成为世界主要科学中心和创新高地',求是, 2021, http://www.qstheory.cn/dukan/qs/2021-03/15/c_1127209130.htm.

习近平, '在党史学习教育动员大会上的讲话',求是, 2021, http://www.qstheory.cn/dukan/qs/2021-03/31/c_1127274518.htm.

习近平, '把握新发展阶段,贯彻新发展理念,构建新发展格局',求是, 2021, http://www.qstheory.cn/dukan/qs/2021-04/30/c_1127390013.htm.

习近平, '用好红色资源,传承好红色基因 把红色江山世世代代传下去',求是, 2021, http://www.qstheory.cn/dukan/qs/2021-05/15/c_1127446859.htm.

习近平, '学好"四史",永葆初心、永担使命',求是, 2021, http://www.qstheory.cn/dukan/qs/2021-05/31/c_1127509112.htm.

习近平, '以史为镜、以史明志 知史爱党、知史爱国',求是, 2021, http://www.qstheory.cn/dukan/qs/2021-06/15/c_1127561026.htm.

习近平, '学史明理 学史增信 学史崇德 学史力行',求是, 2021, http://www.qstheory.cn/dukan/qs/2021-07/02/c_1127617254.htm.

习近平, '在庆祝中国共产党成立100周年大会上的讲话',求是, 2021, http://www.qstheory.cn/dukan/qs/2021-07/15/c_1127656422.htm.

习近平, '加强党史军史和光荣传统教育 确保官兵永远听党话、跟党走',求是, 2021, http://www.qstheory.cn/dukan/qs/2021-07/31/c_1127715309.htm.

习近平, '总结党的历史经验 加强党的政治建设',求是, 2021, http://www.qstheory.cn/dukan/qs/2021-08/15/c_1127760220.htm.

习近平, '党的伟大精神永远是党和国家的宝贵精神财富',求是, 2021, http://www.qstheory.cn/dukan/qs/2021-08/31/c_1127810333.htm.

'习近平与文艺工作者畅谈心里话'近平党建网, 2021, http://www.dangjian.com/shouye/sixianglilun/xuexiyuandi/202112/t20211217_6270245.shtml.

习近平, '毫不动摇坚持和加强党的全面领导',求是, 2021, http://www.qstheory.cn/dukan/qs/2021-09/15/c_1127862367.htm.

习近平, '用好红色资源 赓续红色血脉 努力创造无愧于历史和人民的新业绩',求是, 2021, http://www.qstheory.cn/dukan/qs/2021-09/30/c_1127915721.htm.

习近平, '扎实推动共同富裕',求是, 2021, http://www.qstheory.cn/dukan/qs/2021-10/15/c_1127959365.htm.

习近平, '坚定理想信念 补足精神之钙',求是, 2021, http://www.qstheory.cn/dukan/qs/2021-10/31/c_1128014255.htm.

'习近平在第四届中国国际进口博览会开幕式上的主旨演讲', 中国政府网, 2021, https://www.gov.cn/xinwen/2021-11/04/content_5648892.htm.

习近平, '坚持用马克思主义及其中国化创新理论武装全党',求是, 2021, http://www.qstheory.cn/dukan/qs/2021-11/15/c_1128063854.htm.

习近平, '关于《中共中央关于党的百年奋斗重大成就和历史经验的决议》的说明',求是, 2021, http://www.qstheory.cn/dukan/qs/2021-11/30/c_1128110981.htm.

习近平, '深入实施新时代人才强国战略 加快建设世界重要人才中心和创新高地',求是, 2021, http://www.qstheory.cn/dukan/qs/2021-12/15/c_1128161060.htm.

'习近平在中共中央政治局第二十七次集体学习时强调 完整准确全面贯彻新发展理念 确保"十四五"时期我国发展开好局起好步', 2021, http://www.xinhuanet.com/politics/leaders/2021-01/29/c_1127042572.htm.

'深入学习坚决贯彻党的十九届五中全会精神 确保全面建设社会主义现代化国家开好局', 2021, http://chuxin.people.cn/n1/2021/0112/c428144-31996602.html.
'习近平主持召开中央财经委员会第十次会议第十次会议强调 在高质量发展中促进共同富裕 统筹做好重大金融风险防范化解工作 李克强汪洋王沪宁韩正出席', 新华网, 2021, http://www.xinhuanet.com/politics/2021-08/17/c_1127770343.htm

2022

'习近平：不断壮大实体经济', 上海机关党建，2022，https://www.shjgdj.gov.cn/node27/detail/1660201655085.html.
'习近平在瞻仰延安革命纪念地时强调 弘扬伟大建党精神和延安精神 为实现党的二十大提出的目标任务而团结奋斗', 2022, http://www.news.cn/politics/2022-10/27/c_1129084028.htm.
习近平, '以史为鉴、开创未来 埋头苦干、勇毅前行', 求是, 2022, http://www.qstheory.cn/dukan/qs/2022-01/01/c_1128219233.htm.
习近平, '不断做强做优做大我国数字经济', 求是, 2022, http://www.qstheory.cn/dukan/qs/2022-01/15/c_1128261632.htm.
习近平, '努力成为可堪大用能担重任的栋梁之才', 求是, 2022, http://www.qstheory.cn/dukan/qs/2022-01/31/c_1128312658.htm.
习近平, '坚持走中国特色社会主义法治道路 更好推进中国特色社会主义法治体系建设', 求是, 2022, http://www.qstheory.cn/dukan/qs/2022-02/15/c_1128367893.htm.
习近平, '在中央人大工作会议上的讲话（2021年10月13日）', 求是, 2022, http://www.qstheory.cn/dukan/qs/2022-02/28/c_1128420137.htm.
习近平, '在中央政协工作会议暨庆祝中国人民政治协商会议成立70周年大会上的讲话',求是, 2022, http://www.qstheory.cn/dukan/qs/2022-03/15/c_1128467849.htm.
习近平, '坚持把解决好'三农'问题作为全党工作重中之重 举全党全社会之力推动乡村振兴',求是, 2022, http://www.qstheory.cn/dukan/qs/2022-03/31/c_1128515304.htm.
习近平, '在北京冬奥会冬残奥会总结表彰大会上的讲话',人民网, 2022, http://politics.people.com.cn/n1/2022/0408/c1001-32394448.html.
习近平, '更好把握和运用党的百年奋斗历史经验', 求是, 2022, http://www.qstheory.cn/dukan/qs/2022-06/30/c_1128786667.htm.
习近平, '正确认识和把握我国发展重大理论和实践问题', 求是, 2022, http://www.qstheory.cn/dukan/qs/2022-05/15/c_1128649331.htm.
习近平, '坚定不移走中国人权发展道路, 更好推动我国人权事业发展',求是, 2022, http://dangjian.people.com.cn/n1/2022/0616/c117092-32447729.html.
习近平, '继承和发扬党的优良革命传统和作风 弘扬延安精神',求是, 2022, http://www.qstheory.cn/dukan/qs/2022-12/15/c_1129210015.htm.
'中共中央政治局召开会议分析研究2023年经济工作,研究部署党风廉政建设和反腐败工作, 习近平主持会议', 新华社, 2022, https://www.gov.cn/xinwen/2022-12/07/content_5730396.htm.
习近平, '新发展阶段贯彻新发展理念必然要求构建新发展格局', 求是, 2022, http://www.qstheory.cn/dukan/qs/2022-08/31/c_1128960034.htm.
习近平, '把中国文明历史研究引向深入 增强历史自觉坚定文化自信',求是, 2022，http://www.qstheory.cn/dukan/qs/2022-07/15/c_1128830256.htm.

2023

'习近平：坚持自我革命，确保党不变质、不变色、不变味', 人民网, 2023, http://politics.people.com.cn/n1/2022/0123/c1001-32337511.html.
'习近平在二十届中央纪委二次全会上发表重要讲话', 新华网, 2023, https://www.gov.cn/xinwen/2023-01/09/content_5735913.htm.
'习近平总书记强调的'红色基因', 安徽理论网, 2023, http://ll.anhuinews.com/llqy/202306/t20230605_6897773.shtml.
'习近平主持召开二十届中央国家安全委员会第一次会议强调 加快推进国家安全体系和能力现代化 以新安全格局保障新发展格局', 新华网, 2023, http://www.news.cn/politics/leaders/2023-05/30/c_1129657348.htm.

‘习近平会见美国前国务卿基辛格’，中华人民共和国驻联合国代表团，2023，http://un.china-mission.gov.cn/zgyw/202307/t20230720_11115775.htm.
习近平，‘全面从严治党探索出依靠党的自我革命跳出历史周期率的成功路径’,求是，2023，http://www.qstheory.cn/dukan/qs/2023-01/31/c_1129323988.htm.
习近平，‘坚持自我革命,确保党不变质、不变色、不变味’,人民网，2023，http://politics.people.com.cn/n1/2022/0123/c1001-32337511.html.
习近平，‘推进中国式现代化需要处理好若干重大关系’,求是，2023，https://www.gov.cn/yaowen/liebiao/202309/content_6907173.htm.
习近平，‘健全全面从严治党体系 推动新时代党的建设新的伟大工程向纵深发展’，求是，2023，http://www.qstheory.cn/dukan/qs/2023-06/15/c_1129694554.htm.
习近平，‘在中央党校建校90周年庆祝大会暨2023年春季学期开学典礼上的讲话’，求是，2023，http://www.qstheory.cn/dukan/qs/2023-03/31/c_1129478074.htm.
‘中央经济工作会议在北京举行 习近平发表重要讲话’，新华网，http://www.news.cn/politics/leaders/2023-12/12/c_1130022917.htm.
习近平，‘中国式现代化是中国共产党领导的社会主义现代化’，求是，2023，http://www.news.cn/politics/leaders/2023-05/31/c_1129659348.htm.
‘习近平接见2023年度驻外使节工作会议与会使节并发表重要讲话’度新华网，2023，http://www.news.cn/politics/leaders/20231229/3d7b7cf2e1854d078fc526ef67589e08/c.html.
习近平，‘中国式现代化是强国建设、民族复兴的康庄大道’，求是，2023，https://www.gov.cn/yaowen/liebiao/202308/content_6898422.htm.
‘习近平、蔡奇同志在学习贯彻习近平新时代中国特色社会主义思想主题教育工作会议上的讲话’，学习贯彻习近平主席新时代中国特色社会主义思想主题教育官网，2023年，http://ztjy.people.cn/n1/2023/0508/c457340-32681153.html.
‘习近平：开辟马克思主义中国化时代化新境界’，求是，2023，http://www.qstheory.cn/dukan/qs/2023-10/15/c_1129916904.htm.
习近平，‘在文化传承发展座谈会上的讲话’，求是，2023，http://www.qstheory.cn/dukan/qs/2023-08/31/c_1129834700.htm.
习近平，‘努力成长为对党和人民忠诚可靠、堪当时代重任的栋梁之才’,求是，2023，http://www.qstheory.cn/dukan/qs/2023-06/30/c_1129723161.htm.
习近平，‘在学习贯彻习近平新时代中国特色社会主义思想主题教育工作会议上的讲话’，求是，2023, http://www.qstheory.cn/dukan/qs/2023-04/30/c_1129581895.htm.

2024

习近平，‘国家主席习近平发表二〇二四年新年贺词’,人民网，2024，http://jhsjk.people.cn/article/40150459.
习近平，‘完整、准确、全面贯彻落实关于做好新时代党的统一战线工作的重要思想’，求是，2024，http://www.qstheory.cn/dukan/qs/2024-01/15/c_1130059591.htm.
习近平，‘铸牢中华民族共同体意识 推进新时代党的民族工作高质量发展’，求是，2024，http://www.qstheory.cn/dukan/qs/2024-01/15/c_1130059591.htm.
习近平，‘以美丽中国建设全面推进人与自然和谐共生的现代化’，求是，2024, http://www.qstheory.cn/dukan/qs/2023-12/31/c_1130048939.htm.
习近平，‘时刻保持解决大党独有难题的清醒和坚定，把党的伟大自我革命进行到底’,人民网，2024, http://jhsjk.people.cn/article/40196644.
习近平，‘坚定不移走中国特色金融发展之路 推动我国金融高质量发展’，人民网，2024，http://jhsjk.people.cn/article/40160565.
‘习近平就俄罗斯发生严重恐怖袭击事件向俄罗斯总统普京致慰问电’，人民网，2024，http://jhsjk.people.cn/article/40201871.

领导人综合文选

《毛泽东、邓小平、江泽民论世界观人生观价值观》,北京：人民出版社1997年版。毛泽东、邓小平、江泽民论世界观人生观价值观,人民出版社，1997.
《毛泽东 邓小平 江泽民 胡锦涛关于中国共产党历史论述摘编》,北京：中央文献出版社2021年版。

其他前领导人资料

刘少奇,《论党的建设》, 中央文献出版社1991年版。

刘云山, '刘云山：深入学习贯彻习近平新时代中国特色社会主义思想', 中国共产党新闻网, 2017, http://cpc.people.com.cn/n1/2017/1106/c64094-29628985.html.

温家宝. '关于社会主义初级阶段的历史任务和我国对外政策的几个问题.' 中华人民共和国国务院公报 10 (2007).

外交领域文选

王毅, '可持续发展是实现中国梦和人类进步的必由之路',中华人民共和国常驻联合国日内瓦办事处和瑞士其他国际组织代表团, 2013, http://www.china-un.ch/eng/bjzl/t1081555.htm.

王毅, '中国始终是发展中国家一员 始终为发展中国家仗义执言',中华人民共和国常驻联合国代表团, 2013, http://chnun.chinamission.org.cn/chn/zt/wangyi1/t1082069.htm.

王毅, '王毅部长在第二届世界和平论坛午餐会上的演讲', 中华人民共和国外交部, 2013, https://www.mfa.gov.cn/web/wjbz_673089/zyjh_673099/201306/t20130627_7588692.shtml.

王毅：'坚持正确义利观 积极发挥负责任大国作用——深刻领会习近平同志关于外交工作的重要讲话精神', 2013, http://theory.people.com.cn/n/2013/0910/c40531-22864489.html.

王毅, '王毅阐述安理会决议的重要意义',中华人民共和国常驻联合国代表团, 2013, http://chnun.chinamission.org.cn/chn/zt/wangyi1/t1082550.htm.

王毅, '"一带一路"建设在新起点上扬帆远航',求是, 2017, http://cpc.people.com.cn/n1/2017/0601/c64102-29310365.html.

王毅, '金砖合作扬帆未来 中国外交阔步前行',求是, 2017, http://www.qstheory.cn/dukan/qs/2017-09/15/c_1121647597.htm.

王毅, '开辟新时代中国特色大国外交新境界',求是, 2017, https://www.chinanews.com.cn/gn/2018/01-02/8414291.shtml.

王毅, '深入学习贯彻习近平总书记外交思想 不断谱写中国特色大国外交新篇章',求是, 2017, http://www.qstheory.cn/dukan/qs/2020-08/01/c_1126305967.htm.

王毅, '青岛峰会开启上海合作组织新征程',求是, 2018, http://www.qstheory.cn/dukan/qs/2018-06/29/c_1123054525.htm.

王毅, '携手构建更加紧密的中非命运共同体',求是, 2018, http://www.gov.cn/guowuyuan/2018-09/16/content_5322390.htm.

王毅, '王毅会见联合国秘书长古特雷斯',中华人民共和国外交部, 2019, https://www.fmprc.gov.cn/web/wjbzhd/t1658414.shtml.

王毅, '不忘初心 接续奋斗 全力开拓中国特色大国外交新局面',求是, 2020, http://www.gov.cn/guowuyuan/2020-01/01/content_5465723.htm.

王毅, '坚决打赢抗击疫情阻击战 推动构建人类命运共同体',求是, 2020, http://www.gov.cn/guowuyuan/2020-03/01/content_5485253.htm.

王毅, '以习近平外交思想为指引 在全球抗疫合作中推动构建人类命运共同体',求是, 2020, http://www.gov.cn/guowuyuan/2020-04/15/content_5502818.htm.

王毅, '谱写中国特色大国外交时代华章',中华人民共和国中央人民政府, 2018, http://www.gov.cn/guowuyuan/2019-09/23/content_5432243.htm.

王毅, '以习近平外交思想为引领 不断开创中国特色大国外交新局面',求是, 2019, http://www.gov.cn/guowuyuan/2019-01/01/content_5353914.htm.

王毅, '开启'一带一路'高质量发展新征程',求是, 2019, http://www.gov.cn/guowuyuan/2019-05/01/content_5388150.htm.

王毅, '深入学习贯彻习近平外交思想,不断开创中国特色大国外交新局面',求是网, 2020, http://www.qstheory.cn/dukan/qs/2020-08/01/c_1126305967.htm.

王毅, '不忘初心 接续奋斗 全力开拓中国特色大国外交新局面',人民网, 2020, http://cpc.people.com.cn/n1/2020/0102/c64094-31532532.html.

王毅, '坚决打赢抗击疫情阻击战 推动构建人类命运共同体',人民网, 2020, http://world.people.com.cn/n1/2020/0303/c1002-31613843.html.

王毅, '以习近平外交思想为指引 在全球抗疫合作中推动构建人类命运共同体',人民网, 2020, http://theory.people.com.cn/n1/2020/0512/c40531-31705940.html?ivk_sa=1023197a.

王毅, '王毅 百年变局与世纪疫情下的中国外交:为国家担当 对世界尽责——. 在2020年国际形势与中国外交研讨会上的演讲',中华人民共和国外交部, 2020, https://www.fmprc.gov.cn/web/ziliao_674904/zyjh_674906/t1839713.shtml.

王毅, '波澜壮阔二十年 奋楫破浪创新篇——. 王毅国务委员兼外长在中非合作论坛成立20周年纪念招待会上的讲话',中华人民共和国外交部, 2020, https://www.fmprc.gov.cn/web/ziliao_674904/zyjh_674906/t1831808.shtml.

王毅, '迎难而上 为国担当 奋力开启中国特色大国外交新征程',求是, 2021, http://www.qstheory.cn/dukan/qs/2021-01/16/c_1126985877.htm.

王毅, '坚持以人民为中心 推进全球人权进步, 王毅国务委员兼外长在联合国人权理事会第46届会议高级别会议上的讲话',中华人民共和国外交部, 2021, https://www.fmprc.gov.cn/web/wjbz_673089/zyjh_673099/202102/t20210222_9889221.shtml.

王毅, '王毅谈恢复联合国合法席位50周年',新华网, 2021, http://www.xinhuanet.com/2021-03/07/c_1127180087.htm.

王毅, '王毅出席联合国安理会新冠疫苗问题部长级公开会',中华人民共和国驻加拿大大使馆, 2021, http://ca.china-embassy.org/chn/zgxw/t1854956.htm.

王毅, '高举人类命运共同体旗帜阔步前行',求是, 2022, http://www.qstheory.cn/dukan/qs/2022-01/01/c_1128220367.htm.

王毅,'落实全球安全倡议,守护世界和平安宁',中华人民共和国外交部, 2022, https://www.mfa.gov.cn/web/wjbz_673089/zyjh_673099/202204/t20220424_10672812.shtml.

王毅,'筑牢金砖团结 携手共向未来——国务委员兼外长王毅在金砖国家外长视频会晤上的讲话',中华人民共和国外交部, 2022, https://www.mfa.gov.cn/web/wjbz_673089/zyjh_673099/202205/t20220520_10690218.shtml.

王毅, '中美新时代正确相处之道——王毅国务委员兼外长在美国亚洲协会的演讲', 中华人民共和国外交部, 2023, https://www.mfa.gov.cn/web/wjbz_673089/zyjh_673099/202209/t20220923_10770193.shtml.

王毅, '为中美关系把舵,为亚太合作领航——中共中央政治局委员、外交部长王毅谈习近平主席赴美国举行中美元首会晤同时出席亚太经合组织第三十次领导人非正式会议', 中华人民共和国外交部, 2023, https://www.mfa.gov.cn/web/wjbz_673089/zyjh_673099/202311/t20231118_11182995.shtml.

王毅, '王毅就中美元首旧金山会晤向媒体介绍情况并答问', 中华人民共和国外交部, 2023, https://www.mfa.gov.cn/web/wjbz_673089/zyjh_673099/202311/t20231116_11181420.shtml.

王毅, '全力消弥战火 共促中东和平——王毅在安理会巴以问题高级别会议上的讲话', 中华人民共和国外交部, 2023, https://www.mfa.gov.cn/web/wjbz_673089/zyjh_673099/202311/t20231130_11190296.shtml.

王毅, '自信自立、开放包容、公道正义、合作共赢——在2023年国际形势与中国外交研讨会上的演讲',中华人民共和国外交部, 2024, https://www.mfa.gov.cn/web/wjbz_673089/zyjh_673099/202401/t20240109_11220573.shtml.

王毅,'深入贯彻中央外事工作会议精神 不断开创中国特色大国外交新局面》',求是, 2024, http://www.qstheory.cn/dukan/qs/2024-01/16/c_1130059607.htm.

王毅, '坚定做动荡世界中的稳定力量——王毅在第60届慕尼黑安全会议'中国专场'上的主旨讲话', 中华人民共和国外交部, 2024, https://www.mfa.gov.cn/web/wjbz_673089/zyjh_673099/202402/t20240217_11246036.shtml.

王毅, '凝聚共识,团结合作,共同推动世界人权事业健康发展——在联合国人权理事会第55届会议高级别会议上的讲话', 中华人民共和国外交部, 2024, https://www.mfa.gov.cn/web/wjbz_673089/zyjh_673099/202402/t20240226_11250269.shtml.

杨洁篪, '杨洁篪在联合国大会第67届会议一般性辩论上的发言',联合国大会, 2012, https://www.un.org/zh/ga/67/meetings/china_ga67.shtml.

杨洁篪, '新形势下中国外交理论和实践创新', 中国政府网, 2013, http://www.gov.cn/ldhd/2013-08/16/content_2467887.htm.

杨洁篪, '杨洁篪谈习近平主席与奥巴马安纳伯格庄园会晤成果', 2013, http://www.gov.cn/ldhd/2013-06/09/content_2423489.htm.

杨洁篪,'当好贴心人 成为实干家 凝聚侨心侨力同圆共享中国梦—— 深入学习贯彻习近平总书记关于侨务工作的重要指示',求是, 2017, http://cpc.people.com.cn/n1/2017/0516/c64094-29278581.html.

杨洁篪, '深入学习贯彻习近平总书记外交思想 不断谱写中国特色大国外交新篇章',求是, 2017, http://www.gov.cn/guowuyuan/2017-07/16/content_5210812.htm.

杨洁篪,'当好贴心人 成为实干家 凝聚侨心侨力同圆共享中国梦—— 深入学习贯彻习近平总书记关于侨务工作的重要指示'人民网, 2017, http://cpc.people.com.cn/n1/2017/0516/c64094-29278581.html.

杨洁篪,'深入学习贯彻党的十九大精神 奋力开拓新时代中国特色大国外交新局面',中华人民共和国中央人民政府, 2017, http://www.gov.cn/xinwen/2017-12/01/content_5243638.htm.

杨洁篪, '杨洁篪在人民日报撰文谈构建人类命运共同体', 中华人民共和国中央人民政府, 2017, http://www.gov.cn/zhuanti/2017-11/19/content_5240782.htm.

杨洁篪, '以习近平外交思想为指导 深入推进新时代对外工作',人民网, 2018, http://cpc.people.com.cn/n1/2018/0802/c64094-30191578.html.

杨洁篪, '在习近平外交思想指引下奋力推进中国特色大国外交',人民网, 2019, http://cpc.people.com.cn/n1/2019/0902/c64094-31331718.html.

杨洁篪, '杨洁篪在第55届慕尼黑安全会议上的主旨演讲',中华人民共和国驻牙买加大使馆, 2019, http://jm.chineseembassy.org/chn/zgywnew/t1638506.htm.

杨洁篪, '杨洁篪会见第73届联合国大会主席埃斯皮诺萨',新华网, 2019, http://www.xinhuanet.com/world/2019-06/18/c_1124639638.htm.

杨洁篪,'在习近平外交思想指引下奋力推进中国特色大国外交', 求是, 2019/17, http://cpc.people.com.cn/n1/2019/0902/c64094-31331718.html.

杨洁篪,'深刻认识和用好国际法 坚定捍卫国家利益 共同维护世界和平与发展',求是, 2020, http://www.qstheory.cn/dukan/qs/2020-10/16/c_1126613584.htm.

杨洁篪, '推动构建人类命运共同体 共同建设更加美好的世界',求是, 2021, http://www.qstheory.cn/dukan/qs/2021-01/01/c_1126935807.htm.

杨洁篪, '中国共产党建党百年来外事工作的光辉历程和远大前景', 求是2021/10, http://www.qstheory.cn/dukan/qs/2021-05/16/c_1127447088.htm.

杨洁篪,'杨洁篪视频会见第75届联大安理会改革政府间谈判机制共同主席',中华人民共和国驻突尼斯共和国大使馆, 2021, http://tn.china-embassy.org/chn/zgyw/t1849543.htm.

杨洁篪, '推动构建人类命运共同体(学习贯彻党的十九届六中全会精神)', 2021, http://politics.people.com.cn/n1/2021/1126/c1001-32292253.html.

其他官员对习近平思想解读(Alphabetical order by authors' names/ article titles, chronological order of the same author)

蔡奇,《认真学习<习近平著作选读>, 持续把习近平新时代中国特色社会主义思想学习宣传贯彻引向深入》,人民网, 2023/05, http://cpc.people.com.cn/n1/2023/0523/c64094-32692599.html.

蔡奇, '在学习贯彻习近平新时代中国特色社会主义思想主题教育第一批总结暨第二批部署会议上的讲话', 共产党员网, 2023/09, https://www.12371.cn/2023/11/03/ARTI1698996385845632.shtml.

陈宝生, '培养又红又专的中国特色社会主义接班人',环球网, 2017, https://china.huanqiu.com/article/9CaKrnK2CnG.

陈一新, '学深悟透习近平法治思想,做到'八个深刻把握',达到'五个成效',中华人民共和国司法部, 2021, https://www.moj.gov.cn/pub/sfbgw/zwgkztzl/xxxcgcxjpfzsx/fzsxgczs/202102/t20210204_172814.html.

陈一新, '在新时代把党的自我革命推向深入(深入学习贯彻习近平新时代中国特色社会主义思想)',《 人民日报 》(2022年02月24日 第 09 版).

何立峰, '从百年党史中汲取力量 全力做好发展改革工作', 中华人民共和国发展和改革委员会, 2022, https://www.ndrc.gov.cn/fzggw/wld/hlf/lddt/202201/t20220106_1311522.html?code=&state=123.

何毅亭, '马克思主义中国化时代化新的飞跃(深入学习贯彻习近平新时代中国特色社会主义思想)', 《 人民日报 》, 2024, http://ztjy.people.cn/n1/2024/0206/c457340-40174021.html.

黄坤明, '习近平新时代中国特色社会主义思想实现了马克思主义中国化新的飞跃', 求是, http://www.qstheory.cn/qshyjx/2021-11/22/c_1128087180.htm.
栗战书, '习近平法治思想是全面依法治国的根本遵循和行动指南',求是2021/02, http://www.qstheory.cn/dukan/qs/2021-01/16/c_1126985734.htm.
刘鹤, '所谓'国进民退'的议论既是片面的也是错误的',新华网, 2018, http://m.xinhuanet.com/2018-10/20/c_129976064.htm.
刘鹤, t不支持民营企业发展的行为必须坚决予以纠正'支持新华网, 2018, http://www.xinhuanet.com/2018-10/20/c_129976060.htm.
刘鹤, '加快构建以国内大循环为主体、国内国际双循环相互促进的新发展格局', 2020, http://cpc.people.com.cn/n1/2020/1125/c64094-31944011.html.
曲青山, '深入领会新时代的历史性成就和历史性变革', 求是, 2022/01, http://www.qstheory.cn/dukan/qs/2022-01/01/c_1128220281.htm.
曲青山, '制度优势是党和国家的最大优势',求是, 2020, http://theory.people.com.cn/n1/2020/0817/c40531-31824208.html.
曲青山, '向毛泽东同志学习辩证法',求是, 2024/01, http://www.qstheory.cn/dukan/qs/2024-01/01/c_1130048921.htm.
王晨, '坚持以习近平法治思想为指导 谱写新时代全面依法治国新篇章',求是2021, http://www.qstheory.cn/dukan/qs/2021-02/01/c_1127044307.htm.
王沪宁, '王沪宁在统一战线专题研讨班上强调 用习近平新时代中国特色社会主义思想统一思想统一行动 汇聚推进中国式现代化建设强大合力',新华网, 2023, http://www.news.cn/politics/2023-04/17/c_1129531424.htm.
王沪宁, '当前最重要的政治任务,王沪宁提到 7 个讲清楚',人民网, 2017, http://m.people.cn/n4/2017/1102/c203-10057155.html.
肖亚庆, '国资委主任:深化国有企业改革', 中国政府网, 2017/12, https://www.gov.cn/zhuanti/2017-12/13/content_5246401.htm.
张又侠, '在党的旗帜引领下建设强大人民军队',求是, 2021/15, http://www.qstheory.cn/dukan/qs/2021-08/01/c_1127715927.htm.
张又侠, '坚持走中国特色强军之路',人民日报, http://www.qstheory.cn/qshyjx/2021-11/30/c_1128115594.htm.
赵乐际, '坚定不移全面从严治党',《人民日报》, 2022年11月, http://www.dangjian.com/shouye/zhuanti/zhuantiku/xuexiguancheershida/quanweijieduershida/202211/t20221111_6510253.shtml.
'赵乐际在深入学习贯彻习近平总书记关于坚持和完善人民代表大会制度的重要思想交流会上强调 全面贯彻落实党的二十大精神和中央人大工作会议精神 围绕推进中国式现代化履职尽责担当作为',新华社, 2023/12, http://www.news.cn/politics/leaders/20231224/9fcafe69609a4eadb763e34010f0008c/c.html.

2.2 Chinese-Language Secondary Sources (Alphabetical order by authors' names/ article title, chronological order of the same author)

'阿拉斯加会谈清楚地表明:中国对美国展开正式反击', 腾讯新闻, 2021, https://new.qq.com/omn/20210319/20210319V0D5FI00.html.
"北京大学党性教育读书班实施方案', 北京大学, 2014, http://www.shehui.pku.edu.cn/second/index.aspx?nodeid=237&page=ContentPage&contentid=148.
大型电视专题片'领航', 中央电视台, 2022, https://tv.cctv.com/2022/10/08/VIDAr1g6BOpGIk47TMzvHyZ6221008.shtm.
'党性修养需要制度维护', 党建网, 2017, http://dangjian.people.com.cn/n1/2017/1205/c117092-29686276.html.
'党章修正案调整完善"两个一百年"奋斗目标的意义何在?', 中央纪委监察网站, 2018, https://www.ccdi.gov.cn/special/zmsjd/zm19da_zm19da/201802/t20180209_163794.html.
丁俊萍, '中国共产党百年党性教育的历史经验', 人民网, 2021, http://dangshi.people.com.cn/n1/2021/0630/c436975-32144659.html.

'"东升西降"：习近平的后疫情时代中国崛起蓝图', 纽约时报, 2021, https://cn.nytimes.com/china/20210304/xi-china-congress/zh-hant/.
'斗争！习近平这篇讲话大有深意!', 新华网, 2019, http://www.xinhuanet.com/politics/xxjxs/2019-09/04/c_1124960210.htm.
'发改委：防止失信"黑名单"认定泛化、扩大化', 环球网, 2019, https://m.huanqiu.com/article/9CaKrnKmeUi.
'凤凰记者亲历中美交锋现场,杨洁篪据理力争：美方为何怕记者在场?', 凤凰新闻, 2021, https://news.ifeng.com/c/84jjzeoProb.
冯俊, "中国共产党在不断总结历史经验中前进, 《红旗文稿》, 2021/23, https://theory.gmw.cn/2021-12/11/content_35374285.htm.
冯鹏志, 从"三个自信"到"四个自信"——论习近平总书记对中国特色社会主义的文化建构', 人民网, 2016,http://theory.people.com.cn/n1/2016/0707/c49150-28532466.html.
甘阳,《古今中西之争》,北京,生活.读书.新知三联书店, 2012年版.
高毅, '分析：邓小平的外交政策的得与失', BBC News, 中文, 2014, https://www.bbc.com/zhongwen/simp/china/2014/08/140820_deng_foreign_policy_gains_losses.
'构建"人类命运共同体"入宪的时代意义', 人民网, 2018, http://theory.people.com.cn/n1/2018/0322/c40531-29882972.html.
国家统计局, '对外经贸开启新征程　全面开放构建新格局——新中国成立70周年经济社会发展成就系列报告之二十二', 中国政府网, 2019, https://www.gov.cn/xinwen/2019-08/27/content_5424966.htm.
'国家卫健委: 12月8日至1月12日,累计在院新冠病毒感染相关死亡病例59938例", 中新网, 2023, https://www.chinanews.com.cn/sh/2023/01-14/9935288.shtml.
'国有企业作用不可替代',中国政府网, 2018, http://www.gov.cn/xinwen/2018-11/29/content_5344296.htm.
古琳晖, '"党性教育"相关概念辨析', 党建网, 2017, http://dangjian.people.com.cn/n1/2017/0904/c117092-29512960.html.
'混合所有制发展：从管企业到管资本', 新华网, 2013, http://finance.people.com.cn/n/2013/1115/c1004-23559860.html.
蒋建国, '弘扬和践行当代中国人权观', 求是, 2023/19, http://www.qstheory.cn/dukan/qs/2023-10/01/c_1129890474.htm.
韩洁, '中国官方印发意见告诫党员不要相信鬼神', Radio Free Asia, 2019, https://www.rfa.org/mandarin/Xinwen/6-02272019140910.html.
韩振峰, '习近平新时代中国特色社会主义思想的内在逻辑', 人民网, 2017, http://theory.people.com.cn/n1/2017/1219/c40531-29715166.html.
韩振峰, '全面学习领会习近平新时代中国特色社会主义思想', 党建网, 2023, http://www.dangjian.com/shouye/sixianglilun/lilunqiangdang/202304/t20230412_6588885.shtml.
洪银兴, 刘伟, 高培勇, 金碚, 闫坤, 高世楫, 李佐军, '"习近平新时代中国特色社会主义经济思想"笔谈',中国社会科学, 9 (2018): 4–73. http://ztzx.ruc.edu.cn/docs/2020-04/ab264b5eefe74d019e7d8252cb45ca6e.pdf.
霍小光、张晓松、罗争光、姜琳,　小扬帆破浪再启航——以习近平同志为核心的党中央推进党和国家机构改革纪实', 新华社, 2019, http://www.gov.cn/xinwen/2019-07/06/content_5406818.htm.
胡伟, '邓小平40年前的这篇讲话为什么极为重要？', 中共泉州市纪律监察委员会, 2020, http://www.qzcdi.gov.cn/content/2020-09/22/content_6091808.htm.
'加快建设现代化产业体系', 新华网贵州频道, 2023, http://www.gz.xinhuanet.com/20231108/8da0bf2d3ae3427a8e7be63bdd31da67/c.html.
'坚持党的全面领导——心怀"国之大者", 切实把增强"四个意识"、坚定"四个自信"、做到"两个维护"落到行动上', 国家发展和改革委员会, 2022, https://www.ndrc.gov.cn/fggz/fgjh/djzc/202212/t20221230_1344916.html.
教育部中国特色社会主义理论体系研究中心,　'中国梦是中华民族近代以来最伟大的梦想—学习领会习近平总书记关于中国梦的重要论述', 人民网, 2017, http://theory.people.com.cn/n1/2017/1201/c40531-29679404.html.

经济日报课题组, ‘习近平经济思想研究评述’, 新华网, 2021, http://www.news.cn/politics/2021-11/29/c_1128112219.htm.

‘句句是改革　字字有力度（权威访谈•学习贯彻十八届三中全会精神）’, 人民网, 2013, https://web.archive.org/web/20131118092401/http://paper.people.com.cn/rmrb/html/2013-11/15/nw.D110000renmrb_20131115_1-02.htm.

孔铉佑, ‘习近平外交思想和中国周边外交理论与实践创新’, 求是, 2019, http://www.qstheory.cn/dukan/qs/2019-04/16/c_1124364176.htm.

‘两报一刊社论：乘胜前进’, 华国锋纪念网, 1977, http://www.huaguofeng.org/newsshow.php?cid=24&id=1786.

梁柱, ‘邓小平新时期对防止和平演变思想的坚持和发展’, 红色文化网, 2014, https://m.hswh.org.cn/wzzx/llyd/ls/2014-06-30/26497.html.

李成, ‘中式民主的启动’, 布鲁金斯学会, 2010, https://www.brookings.edu/zh-cn/opinions/中式民主的启动/.

李海青, ‘我国发展仍然处于重要战略机遇期’,求是, 2020, http://www.qstheory.cn/dukan/hqwg/2020-11/27/c_1126792478.htm.

李君如, ‘党对社会主义初级阶段主要矛盾认识的深化’ 中国党政干部论坛, 11 (1997): 6-8.

李君如：‘在“两个确立”中继往开来迎接党的二十大’,光明日报, 2022, https://epaper.gmw.cn/gmrb/html/2022-08/14/nw.D110000gmrb_20220814_2-02.htm.

刘国光, ‘关于社会主义初级阶段基本经济制度若干问题的思考’, 《经济学动态》, 7 (2011): 14–19, http://www.nopss.gov.cn/n1/2022/0815/c219544-32502627.html.

刘溜球 , ‘评新编历史剧《当马克思遇见孔夫子》’, 复兴网 , 2023 , https://www.mzfxw.com/e/action/ShowInfo.php?classid=12&id=179480.

刘元春, ‘认识把握我国发展的重要战略机遇期’,人民网, 2019,http://theory.people.com.cn/n1/2019/0522/c40531-31096799.html.

李毅, 把认识把握新发展阶段的几个问题’, 求是网, 2021, http://www.qstheory.cn/qshyjx/2021-08/16/c_1127763994.htm.

卢毅, ‘回顾一场几乎被遗忘的论争——“新权威主义”之争述评’, 2009, http://ww2.usc.cuhk.edu.hk/PaperCollection/Details.aspx?id=7061.

马智宏, ‘充分发挥国有企业党委（党组）在新时代的领导作用’, 人民网, 2018, http://dangjian.people.com.cn/n1/2018/0108/c117092-29751779.html.

南方日报, “中国周边外交：推进大战略”, 人民网, 2013, http://theory.people.com.cn/n/2013/1028/c136457-23344720.html.

欧阳雪梅, ‘毛泽东“又红又专”思想的提出及影响’, 毛泽东研究, 4 (2015): 45-51. https://47.95.242.172/thesis/detail/2175413.

‘前联合国副秘书长吴红波：优秀的外交官要有强烈的爱国心和进取精神’, The Voice, YouTube, 2018, https://www.youtube.com/watch?v=pmrI2n6d6VU&t=1496s.

秋石, ‘治国理政新实践：不断开拓治国理政新境界’, 中国共产党新闻网, 2016, http://cpc.people.com.cn/xuexi/BIG5/n1/2016/0302/c385474-28164895.html.

秋石, ‘习近平新时代中国特色社会主义经济思想的原创性贡献’, 求是, 2018, http://www.qstheory.cn/dukan/qs/2018-07/16/c_1123114982.htm.

求是网评论员：‘坚决做到“两个维护”’, 求是, 2018, http://opinion.people.com.cn/n1/2021/0821/c1003-32202449.html.

求是网评论员, ‘双循环新发展格局：历史大变局下的战略选择’, 求是, 2020, http://www.qstheory.cn/wp/2020-07/28/c_1126291938.html.

求是网评论员, ‘思想统一是政治统一、行动统一的基础’, 求是, 2023, http://www.qstheory.cn/wp/2023-12/24/c_1130043602.htm.

《求是》杂志编辑部, ‘全面学习、全面把握、全面落实党的二十大精神’, 求是, 2023/02, http://www.qstheory.cn/dukan/qs/2023-01/15/c_1129283148.htm.

《求是》杂志评论员, ‘中国特色大国外交必将更有作为’, 求是, 2024, http://www.qstheory.cn/dukan/qs/2024-01/16/c_1130059619.htm.

曲星, ‘坚持“韬光养晦, 有所作为”的外交战略’,中国人民大学学报, 5 (2001): 13–17.

'人民日报评论部：坚持党的全面领导是坚持和发展中国特色社会主义的必由之路——更加坚定走"必由之路"的自信①', 共产党员网, 2022/03, https://www.12371.cn/2022/03/15/ARTI1647300817268592.shtml.
人民网-理论频道，'新时代中国特色社会主义的核心要义', 人民网, 2020, http://theory.people.com.cn/n1/2020/1216/c40531-31968954.html.
人民网-理论频道，'主动适应、把握、引领经济发展新常态，着力推进供给侧结构性改革', 旗帜网, 2018, http://www.qizhiwang.org.cn/n1/2020/0628/c433104-31761625.html.
人民网-人民日报, "人间正道开新篇（习近平新时代中国特色社会主义思想学习问答④）", 旗帜网, 2021, http://www.qizhiwang.org.cn/n1/2021/0722/c422351-32166197.html.
'如身使臂,如臂使指（详解版）——习近平谈治国理政中的传统文化智慧', 共产党员网, 2021, https://www.12371.cn/2021/04/07/VIDE1617798960380755.shtml.
'"三步走"发展战略', 中国关键词 (原载当代中国与世界研究院), 2018, http://keywords.china.org.cn/2022-07/11/content_78317156.html.
'省储备局认真学习贯彻落实《关于当前意识形态领域情况的通报》'',湖南机关党建, 2013, https://web.archive.org/web/20130615122048/http://www.hndj.gov.cn/html/jgdj/gzkx/2013/5168269.html.
'十年展望：中国的经济增长率会降至多少？[2]',人民网, 2013, http://finance.people.com.cn/n/2013/1031/c348883-23383550-2.html.
是说新语, '新时代党的统战工作取得历史性成就"', 求是, 2024, http://www.qstheory.cn/laigao/ycjx/2024-01/22/c_1130064482.htm.
陶文昭, '深刻把握新发展阶段', 新华网，2021, http://www.xinhuanet.com/politics/2021-01/25/c_1127021068.htm.
田培炎, '新时代中国特色社会主义的历史贡献', 中共中央纪律检查委员会，中华人民共和国国家监察委员会, 2022, https://www.ccdi.gov.cn/lswhn/lilun/202201/t20220104_162092.html.
外交部党委理论学习中心组, '努力推动构建人类命运共同体——深入学习贯彻习近平新时代中国特色社会主义外交思想', 求是, 2018, http://www.qstheory.cn/dukan/qs/2018-09/30/c_1123498381.htm.
'外交官的硬气依托的是祖国的实力——我校举办第42期共读一本书《李鸿章传》阅读交流会', 西安工程大学, 2021, https://www.xpu.edu.cn/info/1134/17905.htm.
王晨, '习近平法治思想是马克思主义法治理论中国化的新发展新飞跃', 人民网, 2021, http://theory.people.com.cn/n1/2021/0420/c40531-32083076.html.
'网传习近平讲话全文:言论方面要敢抓敢管敢于亮剑'中国数字时代, 2013, https://chinadigitaltimes.net/chinese/321001.html.
王德蓉, '理论前沿 | 新时代推进马克思主义中国化时代化基本经验研究', 旗帜网，2023，http://www.qizhiwang.org.cn/n1/2023/0906/c448292-40071684.html.
王京清, '习近平党建思想略论', 共产党员网, 2018, https://news.12371.cn/2018/04/04/ARTI1522804993143482.shtml.
王缉思, '中国的国际定位问题与 '韬光养晦, 有所作为' 的战略思想', 《国际问题研究 》2, 2011, https://www.aisixiang.com/data/44303.html.
王伟光, "勇于自我革命: 中国共产党区别于其他政党的显著标志', 求是网, 2022, http://www.qstheory.cn/dukan/qs/2022-01/01/c_1128220246.htm.
魏玉坤、周圆, '2022年我国GDP突破120万亿元 增长3%', 新华网, 2023, https://www.gov.cn/xinwen/2023-01/17/content_5737514.htm.
肖钢, '深剖中国资本市场五大变革，总结制度执行利弊得失', 华尔街见闻，2020, https://wallstreetcn.com/articles/3598203.
谢长泰, 宋铮, '抓大放小：中国国有部门的转型', Brookings Papers on Economic Activity, 2016, https://www.brookings.edu/wp-content/uploads/2016/07/BPEA_ChineseTranslation2.pdf
'习近平强调"定于一尊"是背离正统还是警告讯号', BBC News, 中文, 2018, https://www.bbc.com/zhongwen/simp/chinese-news-44891034.
习近平强军思想研究中心, '马克思主义军事理论中国化时代化的新飞跃——全面深入学习领会习近平强军思想', 求是, 2019, http://www.qstheory.cn/dukan/hqwg/2019-08/22/c_1124901937.htm.

习近平生态文明思想研究中心, '"2021年深入学习贯彻习近平生态文明思想研讨会"发言摘登',求是, 2022, http://www.qstheory.cn/dukan/qs/2022-01/16/c_1128262079.htm.
'习近平双峰会""妙语集锦"":孤举者难起 众行者易趋"', 中国共产党网, 2015, http://cpc.people.com.cn/xuexi/n/2015/1120/c385474-27837131.html.
'修宪擎旗 领航时代——习近平新时代中国特色社会主义思想载入宪法的时代意义', 共产党员网, 2018, https://news.12371.cn/2018/03/25/ARTI1521935970071269.shtml.
'习总书记首谈"四个全面"意味着什么', 新华网, 2014, http://www.xinhuanet.com//politics/2014-12/16/c_1113661816.htm.
学而实习, '百年未有之大变局,总书记这些重要论述振聋发聩',求是, 2021, http://www.qstheory.cn/zhuanqu/2021-08/27/c_1127801606.htm.
学而时习, '习近平:在新时代伟大实践中不断开辟马克思主义中国化时代化新境界', 求是, 2022, http://www.qstheory.cn/zhuanqu/2022-08/01/c_1128880491.htm.
"学习贯彻习近平总书记重要讲话精神,巩固深化党和国家机构改革成果", 求是, 2019, http://www.qstheory.cn/dukan/qs/2019-07/16/c_1124750268.htm.
学习中国, '习近平首提"两个引导"有深意', 人民网, 2017, http://politics.people.com.cn/n1/2017/0220/c1001-29094518.html.
徐艳玲, '深刻把握习近平新时代中国特色社会主义思想的世界观和方法论', 求是, 2023/04, http://www.qstheory.cn/dukan/qs/2023-02/16/c_1129363213.htm.
'学习问答 | 8.世界正经历百年未有之大变局,变在何处?', 共产党员网, 2021, https://www.12371.cn/2021/08/04/ARTI1628057666635370.shtml.
徐元宫, '习近平总书记关于苏共亡党苏联解体原因的重要论述及其现实意义', 毛泽东邓小平理论研究 9 (2019): 7–14.
'杨洁篪这段话,太硬气了!' 搜狐网, 2021, https://www.sohu.com/a/456380154_161795.
杨晓青, '宪政与人民民主制度之比较研究', 红旗文稿, 2013, https://web.archive.org/web/20171117080219/http://www.qstheory.cn/hqwg/2013/201310/201305/t20130521_232618.htm.
颜晓峰, '进入新时代 踏上新征程, 我国社会主要矛盾变化的重大意义', 人民网, 2018, http://theory.people.com.cn/n1/2018/0104/c40531-29744175.html.
颜晓峰, '论新时代我国社会主要矛盾的变化', 人民网, 2019. http://theory.people.com.cn/n1/2019/0505/c40531-31063498.html.
'阎学通教授:从韬光养晦到奋发有为,中国崛起势不可挡', 清华大学社会科学学院, 2013, https://www.sss.tsinghua.edu.cn/info/1074/1902.htm.
姚茜, 杨亚澜, '为什么有了纪委,还要设立监委?', 人民网, 2019, http://politics.people.com.cn/n1/2019/1112/c429373-31450715.html.
易杰雄, '中国认识, 处理中西文化及其相互关系的历史与逻辑', 学术界, 1 (2007): 29–38.
易杰雄, '从"实践标准"到 "构建和谐社会"——改革开放过程中党的发展理念的哲学透视', 理论前沿, 17 (2008): 13–16.
'1958年毛主席大笑:骂我们是秦始皇,我们一概承认', 自由微信, 2020, https://freewechat.com/a/Mzg3NzAzNzg2Mg==/2247483689/8.
'引领——从党的二十大看中国共产党的成功密码之一', 党建网, 2022, http://dangjian.people.com.cn/n1/2022/1221/c117092-32590714.html.
郇庆治, '理解人类命运共同体的三个重要层面', 人民网, 2017, http://theory.people.com.cn/n1/2017/0815/c40531-29470252.html.
张雄, '当代中国马克思主义政治经济学的哲学智慧', 中国社会科学 (2021): 136–146, https://www.cssn.cn/dkzgxp/zgxp_zgshkx/2021nd6q/202208/t20220822_5479861.shtml.
张 铮, 孙明, '让世界更好读懂中国式现代化', 求是, 2024, http://www.qstheory.cn/yaowen/2024-01/26/c_1130067432.htm.
张志明, '习近平党建思想的创新与意义', 求是, 2018, http://www.qstheory.cn/dukan/qs/2018-06/29/c_1123054355.htm.
张卓元, '十八大后十年经济走势', 人民网, 2014, http://theory.people.com.cn/n/2014/0709/c40531-25260425.html.

赵汀阳：《天下体系：世界制度哲学导论》,南京：江苏教育出版社2005年版.

'政府工作报告重磅！加快发展新质生产力', 中国政府网, 2024, https://www.gov.cn/zhengce/jiedu/tujie/202403/content_6936388.htm.

郑永年, '塑造更加公正合理的国际新秩序 (原标题：'国际秩序面临新的拐点')', 新华网, 2017, http://www.xinhuanet.com/world/2017-05/04/c_129588261.htm.

中共国家发展和改革委员会党组, '深入学习贯彻中央经济工作会议精神 狠抓落实推动高质量发展 ', 求是, 2024, http://www.qstheory.cn/dukan/qs/2024-01/01/c_1130048917.htm.

中共中央党史和文献研究院 , '从党的百年奋斗历史经验中汲取智慧和力量', 求是, 2022, http://www.qstheory.cn/dukan/qs/2022-07/01/c_1128786581.htm.

中共中央宣传部编, '习近平新时代中国特色社会主义思想学习纲要', 学习出版社,人民出版社 , 2019, http://theory.people.com.cn/GB/68294/428935/index.html.

'中共中央政治局常务委员会召开会议 习近平主持', 新华网, 2020, http://www.xinhuanet.com/politics/leaders/2020-05/14/c_1125986000.htm.

'中国共产党一百年大事记（1921年7月—2021年6月）'新华网, 2021, http://www.xinhuanet.com/2021-06/28/c_1127603399.htm.

'中国规划明年经济"健增长" ', 新华网, 2021, http://www.xinhuanet.com//politics/2012-12/16/c_124102949.htm.

'ttp://www.xinhuanet.co, 中新网 , 2023 , https://www.chinanews.com.cn/gn/2023/05-20/10010863.shtml

'中美阿拉斯加对话,这十个细节非同寻常', 新浪网, 2021, https://news.sina.cn/gn/2021-03-20/detail-ikkntiam5740879.d.html.

'中美新型大国关系的由来', 新华网, 2013, http://news.xinhuanet.com/world/2013-06/06/c_116064614.htm.

钟三屏, '全过程人民民主,习近平向世界讲述民主的"中国叙事" ', 中国新闻网, 2021, https://www.chinanews.com/gn/2021/10-15/9587491.shtml.

中央政法委长安剑, '陈一新：来一场刀刃向内、刮骨疗毒式的自我革命', 安徽省人民检察院, 2020, http://www.ah.jcy.gov.cn/jctt/202007/t20200709_2872910.shtml.

中央组织部党建研究所, '坚持党的全面领导不动摇'', 求是, 2021,http://www.qstheory.cn/dukan/qs/2021-12/01/c_1128110859.htm. _

周维现, '树立"四个意识"就要坚定不移地维护党中央权威', 求是, 2017, http://www.qstheory.cn/dukan/hqwg/2017-02/23/c_1120519494.htm.

'作为党员 你得多少分——有关党性分析的探索', 山西日报, 2014, http://cpc.people.com.cn/n/2014/0225/c64387-24454873.html.

Index

For the benefit of digital users, indexed terms that span two pages (e.g., 52–53) may, on occasion, appear on only one of those pages.

Tables are indicated by *t* following the page number